AN ADVENTURE IN
STATISTICS

D0085869

Sara Miller McCune founded SAGE Publishing in 1965 to support the dissemination of usable knowledge and educate a global community. SAGE publishes more than 1000 journals and over 800 new books each year, spanning a wide range of subject areas. Our growing selection of library products includes archives, data, case studies and video. SAGE remains majority owned by our founder and after her lifetime will become owned by a charitable trust that secures the company's continued independence.

Los Angeles | London | New Delhi | Singapore | Washington DC | Melbourne

SECOND EDITION

AN ADVENTURE IN
STATISTICS
THE REALITY ENIGMA
ANDY FIELD

Los Angeles | London | New Delhi
Singapore | Washington DC | Melbourne

Los Angeles | London | New Delhi
Singapore | Washington DC | Melbourne

SAGE Publications Ltd
1 Oliver's Yard
55 City Road
London EC1Y 1SP

SAGE Publications Inc.
2455 Teller Road
Thousand Oaks, California 91320

SAGE Publications India Pvt Ltd
B 1/I 1 Mohan Cooperative Industrial Area
Mathura Road
New Delhi 110 044

SAGE Publications Asia-Pacific Pte Ltd
3 Church Street
#10-04 Samsung Hub
Singapore 049483

Editor: Jai Seaman
Development editor: Martha Cunneen
Assistant editor: Hannah Cavender-Deere
Production editor: Ian Antcliff
Marketing manager: Ben Griffin-Sherwood
Cover design: Wendy Scott
Typeset by: C&M Digitals (P) Ltd, Chennai, India
Printed in the UK

© Andy Field 2022

First edition published 2016. This second edition published 2022

Apart from any fair dealing for the purposes of research or private study, or criticism or review, as permitted under the Copyright, Designs and Patents Act, 1988, this publication may be reproduced, stored or transmitted in any form, or by any means, only with the prior permission in writing of the publishers, or in the case of reprographic reproduction, in accordance with the terms of licences issued by the Copyright Licensing Agency. Enquiries concerning reproduction outside those terms should be sent to the publishers.

Library of Congress Control Number: 2021949780

British Library Cataloguing in Publication data

A catalogue record for this book is available from the British Library

ISBN 978-1-5297-9714-5
ISBN 978-1-5297-9713-8 (pbk)

At SAGE we take sustainability seriously. We print most of our products in the UK. These are produced using responsibly sourced papers and boards. We undertake an annual audit on materials used to ensure that we monitor our sustainability in what we are doing. When we print overseas, we ensure that sustainable papers are used, as measured by the PREPS grading system.

Sara Miller McCune founded SAGE Publishing in 1965 to support the dissemination of usable knowledge and educate a global community. SAGE publishes more than 1000 journals and over 800 new books each year, spanning a wide range of subject areas. Our growing selection of library products includes archives, data, case studies and video. SAGE remains majority owned by our founder and after her lifetime will become owned by a charitable trust that secures the company's continued independence.

Los Angeles | London | New Delhi | Singapore | Washington DC | Melbourne

AN ADVENTURE IN
STATISTICS

D0085869

Contents

What's this Book About?

Statistics is the nerdy student in the classroom of disciplines: it cheerfully minds its own business helping all of the other kids to do their homework and yet no one seems to like it. It doesn't get invited to birthday parties, and it's always the last to be picked for the sports team. But where would the hipsters of psychology, medicine, business studies and biology be without statistics? They'd be setting fire to their own pants at a party: happier, perhaps, but directionless and in danger of getting burned. Statistics feels uncomfortable in social situations so it can seem aloof, unapproachable and difficult to fathom out. However, like most introverts, if you take the time to get to know us, you'll find a loyal friend. So don't run away or fear statistics. Strike up a conversation with it, be patient and kind and see what happens. That applies to other introverts too.

A while back I started a mission to make statistics a bit more pleasant to learn. As a student I got fed up with how relentlessly dull my textbooks were, and how incapable the authors were of remembering what it was like not to understand the stuff in their books. Being a lot less intelligent than these authors I figured that I was perfectly placed to empathize with any students who felt confused and out of their depth. 'Confused' and 'out of my depth' are my middle names. I wrote Discovering Statistics Using IBM SPSS Statistics and learnt quite a bit about statistics (and SPSS) in the process. My strategy for trying to avoid being relentlessly dull was to inject personal anecdotes, bizarre stories and crass examples. Some people think I'm odd and don't like the book, but others send me nice emails. My adaptation of this book for R has gone down fairly well too. All of which has encouraged me to do more of this textbook writing.

Does the world need another statistics textbook? Of course it doesn't: no one needs another statistics textbook. However, my other books race through a lot of the introductory material. It's like trying to build a house on foundations that were thrown down during a five-minute tea break: I fear that everyone's knowledge will come tumbling down. I could've just expanded my existing books, but they are already so long and heavy that people have to hire mechanical devices to carry them about. So instead, I thought I'd write a gentler introduction to statistics. I was tempted to fill this new introductory book with more of the debased filth that permeates my other books, but then I remembered an idea I had when I was writing the third edition of the SPSS book: 'what if I embed the statistical content within a fictional story?' The idea had nagged me for five years and writing a new book was an opportunity to have a crack at it. Naively, I thought it would be completely innovative to embed a statistics textbook within a fictional story, and to include graphic novel elements to drive the story along. Since starting writing though, people have pointed me towards the Manga Guide to Statistics and The Number Devil, and of course once I Googled them I found a million other books that do similar things and crush any belief I once had that I was attempting a new and interesting take on a statistics book. Still, I bet those other books don't have a bridge of death in them, and what's more exciting than a bridge of death? Nothing, that's what.

You might reasonably ask whether I have any experience of writing fiction. The answer is no. I do, however, have a lot of experience of writing statistics books, so you might just have bought (or be thinking of buying) a reasonably competent statistics textbook surrounded by a lot of tedious prose in which you're not interested because you just want to know about statistics. That doesn't work as a sales pitch, does it? Did I mention the bridge of death? Bridges of death are sick ...

The trouble with having written a fairly successful book is that you start to get ideas above your station. It's like rock bands that, after two or three successful albums, suddenly decide to do a double concept album, or a rock opera or something. This book is my The Lamb Lies Down on Broadway:[1] I hope that some people think it's the best thing I've ever done, but I suspect it's indulgent folly that will break up the band. Read it and decide. I hope that the story provides a bit of light relief from the statistics and makes this book more interesting to read, which in turn makes you want to engage with the statistics. That's the plan. If not, well, it's only seven years of my life wasted. I really hope that someone, somewhere finds it useful, but I especially hope that you are that person. If you do buy this book, thank you for your faith that it will be worth reading and apologies if you think it's batticks.

Andy Confused Out-of-My-Depth Field

---

[1] I realize that for anyone who doesn't share my obsession with rock music of the 1970s, which to be honest will be nearly everyone reading this sentence, this reference will be meaningless.

How to Use this Book

The whole 'embedding the statistics in a fictional story' thing makes this book a bit unusual compared to a lot of statistics textbooks. I realize that a lot of students and tutors don't like 'unusual', so here are some questions that I think some people might want to ask.

WHO IS THE BOOK AIMED AT?

The book is aimed at anyone interested in learning statistical methods. It assumes no prior knowledge at all.

HOW DO I TEACH WITH A BOOK THAT HAS A FICTIONAL NARRATIVE?

Fundamentally, I'd teach with it the same way as with any other book. Most of the chapters have a very similar structure: section of story, section of statistics, section of story, section of statistics, section of story. So, in most chapters there are two large sections of statistics that are book-ended by story, and there's a bit of story in the middle to offer some light relief. As such, it's fairly easy to ignore the story if you want to. The sections of statistics are all written as conversations between the main character and various people he meets. The academic content is what you'd expect to find but presented as a conversation between a student (the main character) and a teacher (the particular character in the story who is teaching him). This sort of Socratic style is a good tool for teaching because the main character (hopefully) asks the same sorts of questions that students often want to ask. Of course, you should feel free to embrace the story if that suits your teaching style, and I could imagine giving lectures that begin by setting the scene of the story, or which end with the chapter cliff-hangers. I'd *love* to hear of people doing that, but ultimately you have to do what works for your teaching style.

CAN I DIP INTO THE BOOK?

Having a story running through the book means that it works best if you read it from cover to cover. The idea is that once you get into the story it acts as a motivator to read the book, and therefore the statistics parts. One of the major problems in teaching statistics, I think, is that people tend to dip into it without laying the foundations in the correct order. In a sense, the intentions of this book are to encourage you to learn things in a sensible order and build up your knowledge; in doing so you will (hopefully) understand the material better. However, I think you can dip in if you really want to because the chapters are structured in a fairly standard way (see my answer to *How do I teach with a book that has a fictional narrative?*) so you can read the sections relating to statistics without necessarily having to know what's going on in the story. In my ideal world, though, you would start at the beginning and read until the end.

WHAT ONLINE RESOURCES ARE THERE?

This book is supported by a range of additional resources to support students and lecturers alike. Visit **https://study.sagepub.com/fieldaais2e**

For students

- **Multiple choice quizzes** let you test yourself and prepare for exams.
- **Data files** and *R* scripts for each chapter allow you to work through the Check your Brain problems and end of chapter puzzles.
- **Answers** to **end of chapter JIG:SAW's Puzzles** at **https://statisticsadventure.com/** for you to check your work.
- Links to a videos relevant to this book (as well as others) are available on my YouTube channel, at **www.youtube.com/user/ProfAndyField**
- For more support and news for this and my other books visit **http://www.discoveringstatistics.com/** or **https://www.facebook.com/ProfAndyField** or follow me **@ProfAndyField**
- Join the conversation: visit **https://www.facebook.com/DiscoveringStatisticsWithAndyField/**
- There is an R package that teaches R alongside the book at **https://www.statisticsadventure.com/adventr/**

For lecturers

- A **teaching guide** provides further support when using the book and provides ideas for how to use it's unique features in class.
- A **testbank** of multiple-choice question to help test students' knowledge and understanding of the material.
- **Editable PowerPoints** to allow easy integration of each chapter into lessons and to provide access to figures and tables from the book.
- All resources have been designed and formatted to **upload into your LMS** or **VLE**.

Guide for Students

- **Reality Check** Explains new concepts in an easy-to-understand, unintimidating way.
- **Zach's Facts** Recaps of key concepts in each chapter, and another opportunity to review what you've learnt.
- **Milton's Meowsings** Think critically about what you're learning via humorous letters from Professor Milton Grey. These notes give more insight into how you could approach solving difficult statistical questions and how those approaches affect the outcome.
- **Check Your Brain** Apply what you've learnt and practice critical thinking and problem-solving skills via these short exercises running throughout each chapter.
- **Key Terms** A handy reference list at the end of each chapter to help you go over important, newly learned concepts and terms.
- **JIG:SAW's Puzzles** A chance for you to further test your understanding of statistical concepts and to work through a range of problems at your own pace.

This book is dedicated to the four loves of my life: Zoë, Zach, Arlo, and Milton the spaniel. I wish memoryBank existed so I could have stored how I felt when my children were asleep in my arms and re-experience it now they are too big to sleep in my arms. As for my amazing wife Zoë, if she ever mysteriously disappears I will, without hesitation, cross a probability bridge to find her.

Prologue:
The Dying Stars

Zach Slade: the most inspirational, talented, creative musician in **Elpis**, the city of hope. His band, The Reality Enigma, has done virtual tours of the world to their fanatic followers, but only the people in our hometown, Elpis, get to see them in the flesh. Despite what the 'Chippers' will tell you, nothing beats the transcendental experience of a live band, and I have never missed one of their gigs. On stage, this intense, spellbinding man exorcises the souls of his audience with every note he plays, word he sings, and stare from his brooding eyes. Every gig I see a thousand people falling in love with him, but none of them knows the kind, gentle, and self-doubting man with whom I share my life. I can only dream of affecting people with my research like Zach does with his music. Although he barely registers it, Zach has changed thousands of people's lives, but none as much as mine when he first spoke to me in our college library ten years ago. He took a shy, lonely girl – estranged from the social world – and connected her; but since we met everything has changed.

Zach and I are children of the Reality Revolution: the first generation born after society collapsed. Before then, everyone believed that they were special, talented, and destined for fame. People blamed reality TV, but perhaps we all need to hope for a bright future to keep us sane. Whatever the reason, values of hard work and collective good were eroded and replaced with self-interest and entitlement. History blames Professor Milton Grey for the revolution because it was his invention – the reality prism – that started everything. The reality prism – a transparent pyramid worn on the head – split reality into the part that is objectively true and the part that is subjective experience. The prism went from an expensive prototype to a cheap mass-produced piece of technology almost overnight, and millions bought them.

The reality prism brought honesty to the world: propaganda and media influence became impossible in a world where people could bisect the objective truth from the subjective spin. Religions collapsed, not because the prism proved them wrong but because it exposed the organizations that profited from them. Everyone could know the truth about anything that they could look at, but the gift of the reality prism was also its curse. Inevitably people looked at themselves in mirrors through the prism. Imagine seeing yourself stripped of the small, harmless tricks that our minds play to make ourselves feel better about who we are. The prism let people see how intelligent, funny, attractive, and talented they really were, and for most people the truth didn't live up to their beliefs. Most of us are ordinary, and there's nothing wrong with that, unless society tells you that ordinary isn't good enough.

People became depressed and purposeless. They lost interest in everything because the media lost their power to hype anything: bands couldn't pretend that their latest album was their best, you couldn't be fooled into thinking the latest Proteus is much better than the previous one, no one

believed that a sports event was more important than a game that would be repeated every subsequent season with very little bearing on anything, and everyone knew that cosmetics could not perform the miracles that they claimed. Advertising failed, businesses collapsed, and political parties ceased to function in a world where they couldn't lie. The revolution itself was over in 5 years, but society has taken decades to rebuild. My parents describe the revolution as killing culture: without self-belief there is no creativity, and without creativity there cannot be musicians, artists, or writers. People abandoned these pursuits because the reality prisms made them believe that they had nothing of value to offer. Instead people looked back to the old world: the musicians and bands from the pre-revolution period of the 1970s to 2040s became revered because nobody believed they had the talent to emulate them. Our parents, who lived through the revolution, lost faith, but to Zach and me it was a story from before we were born, we'd never looked through a reality prism so we'd never seen our limitations. Zach absorbed the music of the past but believed he could use it to inspire something new: songs for our world, not a world of the past. He was brilliant at it.

The history I was taught as a child told me that the revolution sent us back to darker times, but I believe it saved us. To me, Milton Grey is a hero, not a villain. In the wake of the revolution, people across the world united in the common goal of rebuilding. Some believed that we should start from where we left off and embrace the technological advances of the pre-revolution, whereas others yearned to return to what they believed were simpler and happier times. As they delved into our cultural past, they fell back in love with the physical experience of books, art and vinyl LPs, all of which were thought obsolete before the revolution. These people were also driven by a desire to reconnect to the Earth through eco-friendly retro-technology: they embraced the pre-21st century culture of clockwork and steam technology. Over time these technologies merged with those of our own generation: clockwork and steam fusion were born.

The World Governance Agency (**WGA**) emerged from the ashes of the revolution: a humanitarian organization that built a new society on foundations of truth. The WGA worked to create order in a fragmented society; their primary goal was to promote community and well-being. It was largely due to their efforts that the different views on the new world were seamlessly merged: under their guidance, scientists developed steam and clockwork technologies to power both retro and modern devices, they built vast repositories to house collections of physical media and provided the space for people to enjoy them. The world became both brave and innovative, but sentimental to its past; it is a strange but beautiful mix of the modern and the antique. Unlike any political party before it, the WGA achieved the impossible: everyone was happy.

That was the utopian world that Zach and I grew up in, it is the backdrop of our early years, but is also an uncomfortable reminder of how things have changed since we met. First, the WGA started to 'chip' people. Small microchips had been implanted in family pets for more than a century, but with technological advancements it became possible to implant WiFi-enabled chips into humans, enabling them to record what they saw, thought and heard in real time. Those who embraced technology raced to be the first to have chips implanted, queuing at the chipping stations to have their minds tagged. We called them 'Chippers' and they labelled those refusing the chips as 'Clocktorians', a derogatory term to imply that we were backward-looking people stuck in a 'clockwork, Victorian' society. Perhaps they were right, but at least we didn't have chips in our brains.

Next *memoryBank* was launched: a virtual mind where Chippers broadcast their lives to each other as real-time, high-definition streams. With only a thought, Chippers could flag single moments in the video stream as highly significant events ('highsies'). These events were broadcast directly to the brains of other Chippers in the same network and their emotional reaction to it, their 'emo', was automatically recorded and tagged in real time. There was no hiding your feelings on *memoryBank*. Our lives were stored virtually; the pre-revolution idea of the cloud had been taken to a logical conclusion and everyone had a 'star': a limitless space to store their digital world. Friends and family could network their stars in constellations; *memoryBank* was the next step – a galaxy of Chippers' stars.

Clocktorians were ostracized from much of this online world: we had stars, but connected using technology instead of our minds; we retreated into retro-culture. Society was becoming fragmented again, and it felt like a metaphor for Zach and me. As I became more successful in my scientific career I became more reliant on evidence for my beliefs, and understood less his blind acceptance of his gut feelings. The more advanced my work became, the less he understood or even tried to understand it. The more science drives me towards technology the less I understand why he clings to an old-fashioned world that died more than a century ago. I know that I cannot love anyone as much as I love him so these feelings scare me, but not as much as what's happened in the last few weeks, and that's why I have to leave him. Worse than that, I can't tell him why. I hope he forgets me, and one day forgives me, but never sees how heartbroken I'm about to become.

Dr Alice Nightingale
The Beimeni Centre of Genetics
Elpis

IN THE NEXT CHAPTER, ZACH DISCOVERS ...

The scientific process
How to make a scientific statement
The various research methods

Why we need science
That Alice is acting weird

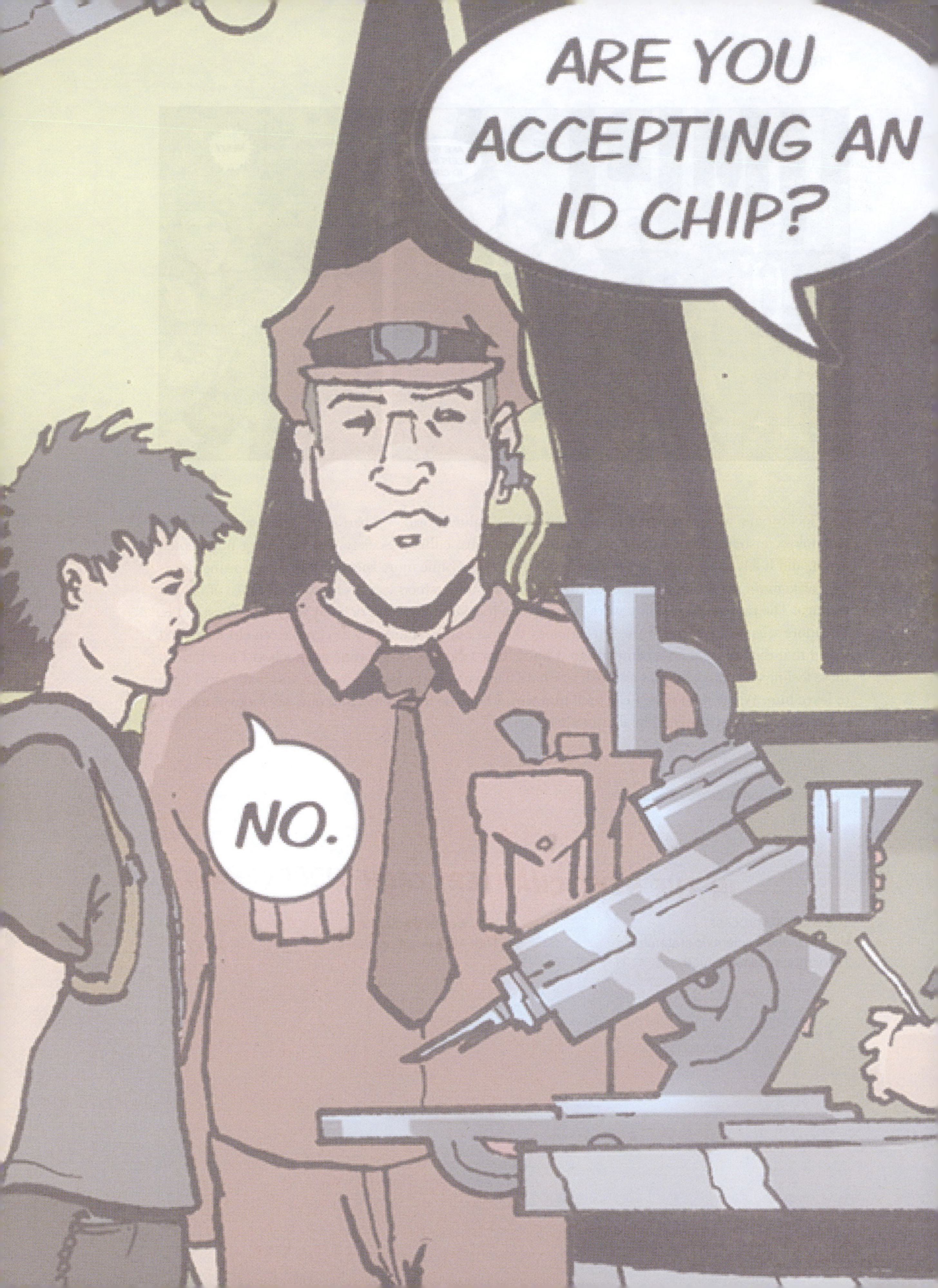
ARE YOU ACCEPTING AN ID CHIP?
NO.

1

Why You Need Science
The Beginning and the End

Alice had been acting strangely all night. I had returned from band practice to make dinner before she got in from work, but she was already home. Alice never left work early. She was on edge, and had been for weeks, as though she was hiding something. She was playing music too. Nothing strange about that, you might think, and, sure, when we first hooked up music was our shared passion, but Alice had lost interest. She would come to my gigs, but otherwise she seemed to live and work in silence. I worried sometimes that there was too much silence in her life – that she was too disconnected. Tonight, though, our apartment was full of the sound of an album we used to listen to back in the day, an album that transported me back to a time of staying up with her all night talking and avoiding sleep because it meant being apart. The riffs hit me as soon as I opened the door. It was strange not to return to an empty, silent apartment – it made me a little uneasy. I smiled when I registered that Alice was home and recognized the album she was playing: perhaps her world wasn't as silent as I feared, and maybe these songs still meant something to her? These hopes faded as I saw her nervous and distant expression. She barely registered that I was back, and I felt stupid for thinking that the music might be anything other than a random decision. Alice was a scientist, and that seemed to rule out being sentimental. I cooked, we ate, and Alice spoke only to snap at me. This was normal in recent weeks: things between us had become strained; I wasn't sure how we'd got to this place, or how to leave it.

Alice and I are Clocktorians, but I cling to the pre-revolution more than she does. I wish I had lived through those times; the turn of the 21st century sat in the middle of a golden era for music. People would gather in their thousands at events called 'festivals' to watch bands perform, not in virtual reality but in the flesh. Bands travelled the world, had a real, physical connection to their fans. Of course, my band plays gigs too, but only in our home city. For the rest of the world we are an image in an oculus riff: a multisensory headset for experiencing virtual gigs. For me, the world did so much right a century ago, I couldn't understand how it went so wrong, but people like me were doing our bit to bring back the old ways.

Before the ID chips came in everybody had a Proteus – a device made from programmable matter,[1] which means that it can transform shape and function. In the pre-revolution people had iWatches, iPods, iPhones and the like. The Proteus replaced them all with a single device: it could transform into a touch screen to type text messages, become an earpiece for streamed music, and would happily become a visual screen or project a 3-D image for a video. A Proteus could become whatever you wanted it to be: the owner had only to think of what they wanted it to look like and it would become that thought. You could wear it as a ring, a bracelet, or any design in your imagination. I mainly kept mine in the shape of a slim tombstone, across the top of which was inscribed 'In loving memory of your memory'. I called it my diePad. It was a joke to myself because I think everyone relies so much on technology that our memories have died. Of course Chippers not only don't need a memory, they don't need a Proteus: the chips in their heads relay their thoughts to others via *memoryBank*. This connectivity has made Clocktorians like us outsiders: it's difficult for us to connect to Chippers and they have to resort to a Proteus to get hold of a Clocktorian. It's a pain.

Alice had been on her Proteus most of the evening. She liked to wear hers as an earpiece with a small microphone to pick up her voice and a monocle to see the caller. This meant that I couldn't see who she was talking to or hear the conversation, but I could tell that something wasn't right. I wanted to help, but Alice didn't seem in the mood to talk to me. Fed up with her spiky mood, I put on my headphones to listen back to our rehearsal recordings and picked up my diePad to look at the news. Wearing headphones said a lot about me: Chippers had music transmitted directly to their brains, and even most Clocktorians used their Proteus for listening, but I liked the space and warmth created by dedicated headphones.

1.1   WILL YOU LOVE ME NOW?

As I listened, I found myself distracted by a news story about the Proteus. It claimed that some of the technology in the Proteus had its roots in pre-revolution mobile phones: primitive, inflexible blocks that people used to communicate before the first Proteus, they couldn't change shape or function. They were basically useless. The news story looked at some data from before the revolution that claimed that these old phones caused brain tumours. The journalist argued that the same was likely to be true of the Proteus. Alice spent a lot of time with her Proteus stuck in her ear, and this article worried me: what if she was harming herself? She'd been talking for ages while I'd been engrossed in the story. Now she was pacing around like she was looking for somewhere to offload the weight on her shoulders. I couldn't bear it any more; I took my headphones off and asked her if everything was level. She looked at the floor and reassured me that everything was fine. She always looked at the floor when she was lying.

'Maybe I can help?' I offered.

Alice sighed. It was one of those sighs that made her seem as though she'd become suddenly aware of how little of her lung capacity she normally used. In the Venn diagram of Alice and me there was a beautiful ellipse containing music, films, literature and a general belief in the goodness of humanity, but outside of it we were poles apart. At times like this Alice made me think the ellipse was shrinking. Her facial expression was a window into our growing differences.

She looked at me as though I'd said something ridiculous. 'It's work stuff, you wouldn't understand,' she said dismissively.

Alice did this a lot since she started working at the Beimeni Centre of Genetics: she assumes I'm stupid and uninterested in her research. She has a point. I don't understand maths and science and I never have. Science is dull, unemotional, uninspiring. It can't break your heart like a good resolution in a song. The mistake she makes is assuming that because I'm not interested in science, I am not interested in *her*. She couldn't be more wrong: I'm in awe of her ability to analyse and evaluate situations. She is the most intelligent person I know, and even other scientists think that she is brilliant: she won the World Science Federation's prestigious Einstein medal when she was 21 for her genetics research. She is a genius, of that I'm certain. I know exactly how brilliant she is, and every day I see a passion for knowledge burning in her every bit as strong as the one I have for music.

For real, the vibe was spooks tonight; I didn't know why, but I felt sure that Alice needed someone, and I wanted that person to be me. She had always taken an interest in my music, perhaps it was time I took an interest in science; it might be enough for her to let me in on whatever was going on.

'Maybe I *could* understand,' I said. 'Try me.'

Alice gave an exasperated sigh. 'It's too late for that, Zach; you can't just make everything better by suddenly showing an interest in me.'

Her directness hurt me, but it also seemed at odds with her vibe. The same album was still playing in the background, as though it comforted her to hear the songs that once were the glue that bonded us. Her eyes too; I couldn't explain, but in her eyes was *something*, the tiniest glint of something, that said 'It's *not* too late Zach, please help me.' Maybe it was nothing, but there was only one way to find out.

'I've been reading this,' I said passing my diePad to her. 'This guy believes that the Proteus might cause brain tumours – for real. It's based on pre-revolution science. He quotes newspaper headlines from last century: the *Daily Express* says "Just a few minutes a day on a mobile phone 'raises cancer risk'";[2] the *Daily Mail*, "Mobile phones may cause cancer, warn world health chiefs";[3] and *US News and World Report*, "Cellphone Use and Cancer: New Study Suggests a Link".[4] Even the BBC and CBS News report "Mobiles 'may cause brain cancer".[5, 6] Seems scary to me. You're a scientist, tell me how *you* would know if the cancer thing was true.'

Alice eyed me suspiciously. 'The headlines are there to grab your attention. I'd look at the *evidence*,' she said curtly.

Alice was trying to shut down the conversation, but I wasn't going to give in. I pulled a silver hunter-cased pocket watch from my jacket. On the silver cover was etched 'Be still, and know'. I pressed the winding mechanism to spring open the cover. Laying the watch flat on my palm, we looked at the familiar clockwork mechanism: a beautiful configuration of cogs, hairsprings, and red, yellow and blue jewels positioned equidistant inside the circular edge. The cogs accelerated into a blur of motion, and at the point of critical velocity the three jewels projected each of their colours upwards into a central mist that quickly settled into the shape of an opaque human head. Clockwork fusion never ceased to impress me: how could self-winding springs create the kind of power needed to generate a fully functional artificially intelligent head? The device was a 'reality checker' and the head within was linked to everything. Of course, you could find things out using a Proteus, or even an ID chip if you had one, but the reality checkers added something that none of these devices could: a brain much better than your own. A reality checker would assimilate data from everywhere, evaluate it, and give you the best answer it could to any question. Gone were the days of believing any nonsense that you uncovered on the internet; a reality checker would filter it all for you. Every head had a personality: for a price you could customize it, or choose one modelled on a favourite celebrity, but at the cheaper end the personalities were randomly generated. If you were as skint as me you bought one of the factory rejects, the ones with such quirky personalities that the manufacturers assumed nobody would want them. Mine was a nice dude, but he certainly was quirky. He refused to respond to any name except for 'The Head', as though he was the definitive model, and he kind of answered questions if he felt like it, and liked to wind me up with false information. Not what you want in a reality checker, but mine was more like an electronic friend. I didn't care about how straight his facts were, I just liked the banter and his beaming smile and deep, hearty laugh. He was pretty handsome too, with a chiselled face, dark skin, and shades. As vapour-based dudes went, the guy was sick.

'What you got for me, Z?' he said in his cheerful, lispy, North Carolina accent. He was the only person in the world I'd allow to call me *Zee*.

'I was discussing with Alice whether the Proteus causes brain tumours. She told me to look at the evidence. Can you help me out?'

'Hmm, does the Proteus create brain tumours? Let me see ... .' The corner of The Head's mouth curled up in a knowing smile. He span around as he checked his database. 'They do ... ' he smiled before spinning some more, 'or maybe they don't.' There was more spinning. 'Wait up ... looks like they do ... or don't ... or they *might* ... or not ... but possibly.' He span some more, and when he returned to a static state he had an overly arched, furrowed brow as though he was about to relay some terrible news. 'Bad news, *Z*. The evidence is contradictory,' he said. He pouted at me to convey the severity of the matter.

'OK ... and the answer is?' I raised my tone expectantly to let him know that his answer didn't fulfil his duty as a reality checker.

'Hmm,' he sulked. 'I *could* assimilate this contradictory evidence for you, but you don't like science, so I'll tell you a story instead. That's more your level.' Like I said, he answered questions when he felt like it. (*REALITY CHECK 1.1*)

'Way back in the day,' The Head began, 'before the revolution, in October 2012, Italy's highest civil court supported Innocente Marcolini's claim that a brain tumour he had developed was caused by long-term use of his mobile phone. Marcolini was a commerce manager and he spent up to 6 hours a day on his mobile phone over a 12-year period. The guy developed a non-cancerous tumour of the trigeminal ganglion – that's in his head. They removed it, but he was in pain. So, he asked INAIL – that's an agency that insures work-related health risks – for money. They rejected the claim and Marcolini went to the Appeal Court. Do you know what happens at an appeal court? It's where people appeal things. The judge agreed that phone use had caused his cancer. This story went around the world:

- Italian court rules man's tumour caused by mobile phone (CBS News, USA)
- Mobiles can give you a tumour, court rules (*Sun*, UK)
- Mobile phones *can* cause brain tumours, court rules in landmark case (*Daily Mail*, UK)
- Mobile phones can cause brain tumours, court rules (*Telegraph*, UK)
- Cell phones can cause brain tumours, Italy's top court rules in landmark case (*National Post*, Canada)
  - L'Italie reconnaît le lien entre mobile et tumeur crânienne (*Le Monde*, France)

In an interview with a UK newspaper, the *Sun*, Marcolini said: "This is significant for very many people. I wanted this problem to become public because many people still do not know the risks ... I wanted it recognised that there was a link between my illness and the use of mobile and cordless phones. Parents need to know their children are at risk of this illness."

Reality Check 1.1   A case study of subjective beliefs becoming 'facts'

This was typical of The Head, it was rarely clear if he was being helpful, so I closed his lid. I paused to take in Marcolini's story. Was this evidence the kind that Alice meant? Alice had been flitting nervously around the room, but I suspected she'd heard the story too, so I asked whether Marcolini's story showed that phones gave you cancer. She sat next to me. This *was* a small breakthrough.

'Even if we put aside how old this story is, Zach, it tells us nothing. I feel for Mr Marcolini, but his experience could be unique; in itself, it doesn't prove anything. There could have been a thousand other people back then who used their phones just as often as Mr Marcolini and *didn't* get cancer.'

'But the judge agreed, and judges know what they're talking about.'

'Perhaps, but they are not scientists. Science isn't perfect, and it's not the only way to view the world, but it does give us a system for trying to find answers to questions. You asked me to explain science to you, and I've tried, lots of times, but the trouble is that you're scared of it and you refuse to engage with it.'

I felt the breakthrough slipping away. We'd been here many times before, and she was right, I was scared that if she explained her world to me it would reveal to her how stupid I am. When I couldn't understand maths and science at school, it made me feel inferior and frustrated, like I wanted to throw my desk out of the window. I was the rad kid with the guitar, so I couldn't ask for help; I just kept telling myself that music was my thing, and you don't need maths and science to do music. She *had* tried to explain it before, and I *had* refused to engage. Tonight was different, though. Alice looked desperate, and maybe the soundtrack in the background was making me too emotionally charged, but I sensed that, for some reason, she needed me to understand her life, to understand why science was important. I reached for her hand, fixed her gaze and promised that if she tried one more time then I would listen.

1.2 HOW SCIENCE WORKS

1.2.1 The research process

Alice looked sceptical, but her relief was obvious. He eyes darted as she tried to think of a way to capitalize on my interest. Suddenly her expression changed, and I saw the first smile of the evening. 'I've got it!' she said, looking pleased with herself. 'Do you remember at your last Reality Enigma gig, you gave away a free wristband with every T-shirt? After the show you told me that you'd sold more shirts than the previous gig and you thought it was because of the free wristband. How do you *know* that it was because of the wristbands?' she asked.

I shrugged. 'I don't, it was just a hunch.'

'Exactly – and this is a question that science can answer for you,' she said. 'Do you always sell exactly the same number of T-shirts at concerts?'

'No – it's different at each gig.'

'Which means it could have been the wristband offer that made the difference, or perhaps it was just one of those nights where you happen to sell a lot of T-shirts?' She had a point. 'That's why it's useful to have a system, like science, for trying to find out the true answer to questions.'

Alice took her Proteus and stretched it into a large flat screen. Then she sketched a diagram on it. **(FIGURE 1.1)** 'This diagram shows the process of science,' she said. 'Scientists begin with an observation in the real world that they want to understand, and this observation could be based on data, like when you notice more T-shirts sold when you give away a free wristband, or it could be anecdotal, such as Mr Marcolini believing that his tumour was caused by phone use. These "data" could be an isolated observation such as noticing that one person was persuaded into buying a shirt when you offered them a wristband, or based on several, such as you noticing that nine out of ten people who you offered a wristband ended up buying a shirt. From these initial observations, you can generate a research question, such as "Do free gifts help to sell T-shirts?" or "Can a Proteus give you brain cancer?" Having a research question implies that you are trying to generate a **theory**, which is a well-established principle or set of general principles to explain a broad range of observations. For example, you observed more T-shirt sales at one gig compared to another, and your theory might be that people buy things when they believe that they are getting value for money. This theory explains general consumer behaviour. Although you might care only what happens with your band, The Reality Enigma, normally scientists are interested in theories that apply very generally – they want their theories to apply to an entire group of entities or situations. An entire set of entities is known as a **population**. A population can be quite diverse (for example, you might want to draw conclusions about the T-shirt sales of every band on the planet) but can also be more specific (you might be interested in drawing conclusions only about bands who play a certain style of music, like heavy metal). Different types of scientists might focus on different populations. I work in genetics, so I want my theories to generalize to the population of humans, and this population would also be interesting to psychologists, and epidemiologists too. However, an economist might be interested in the population of "small businesses" or "workers" or "managers", and biologists might be interested in the population of "cells". We want theories to be general and apply to the entire population rather than applying only to a specific case within that population; using the T-shirt example, it's more interesting to be able to say that free gifts, in general, will help any band (the population) to sell T-shirts than it is to conclude that free gifts are effective at increasing T-shirt sales if you happen to be in the band called The Reality Enigma, fronted by Zach Slade.'

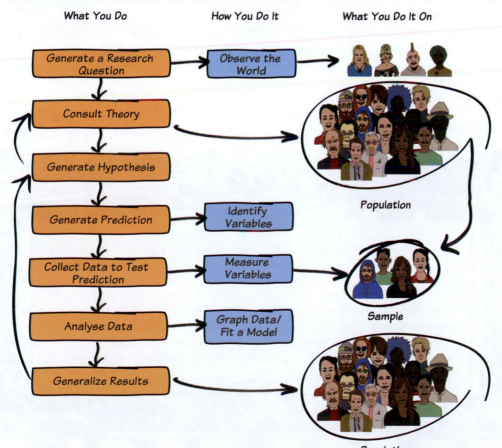

Figure 1.1   The research process

Alice smiled affectionately at me, and I loved seeing her relax a little. 'You can use existing theory, to generate a **hypothesis**, which is a proposed explanation of the specific observation that interests you. Based on consumer theory you might hypothesize "T-shirt sales increase because a free gift improves the value for money". A hypothesis can be tested by operationalizing it as a prediction about what will happen. In this case, we might predict from our hypothesis that "if a band offers a free gift, they will sell more T-shirts". **(FIGURE 1.1)** A prediction should be a scientific statement: a statement that can be verified (or not) using data. That means that you can break the statement down into things that you can measure, known as **variables**. Just now you told me that the number of T-shirts you sold varied from one concert to the next, so "T-shirt sales" is a variable.'

'You mean that I can count how many T-shirts we sell? I suppose I could also note down whether or not we gave away a free gift with the T-shirt at that gig?'

'Yes. You can test the hypothesis about free gifts with two variables: how many shirts were sold, and whether or not a free gift was offered with the T-shirt. You will often come across non-scientific statements, though, and these are statements that cannot be verified, often because they refer to things that can't be measured. For example, "Alice is the best girlfriend in the world"' – she threw me a cheeky smile – 'is not a scientific statement because you probably couldn't get anyone to agree on a definition of "best": different people will value different facets of people (some value looks highly, some intelligence, and others kindness or sociability – who's to say what is "best"?). However, you could turn it into a scientific statement by changing "best" to something that could be measured, such as intelligence. So, "Alice is the cleverest girlfriend" is a scientific statement because we could, in theory, get all of the girlfriends on the planet and measure their intelligence to evaluate this statement.'

'Right, so "The Reality Enigma are the most influential band in Elpis" would be non-scientific because it would be impossible to measure "influence" but "The Reality Enigma are the most popular band in Elpis" would be scientific because we could measure popularity by, for example, measuring how many nodes on *memoryBank* each band in Elpis has?'

'Exactly.'

- *Scientific statements* are ones that can be verified with reference to evidence. For example, 'Alice and I will stay together longer than the average couple' is testable: we can measure the average length of time a couple stays together, and we can (eventually) measure the amount of time that Alice and I stay together (it will be forever!).
- *Non-scientific statements* are ones that cannot be tested empirically. For example, 'Alice and I are the perfect couple' would be non-scientific because it is probably impossible to define what a 'perfect couple' is, so we couldn't measure it.

Zach's Facts 1.1 *Scientific statements*

I unrolled my diePad, touched the screen to activate it and, as Alice continued, I typed what I thought were the important bits. **(ZACH'S FACTS 1.1)**

Alice looked impressed that I made notes. 'The next step of the process is to collect some data. **(FIGURE 1.1)** The problem here is that you want to draw conclusions about the entire population, but it's usually impractical to collect data from every entity in the population. It would be quite difficult to get T-shirt sales and information about free gifts from all of the bands in our city, so instead we use a **sample**, which is a smaller set of entities from our population. We want the entities that we choose for our sample to be representative of the wider population, and we can do that by selecting them randomly. In doing so, we should get a group of bands that is not systematically different from all of the bands in the city. We can use the data in the sample to compute **statistics**, which are values that describe the sample. So, the average number of T-shirts sold in our sample is a statistic. However, we can use this value to estimate what the value would have been if we had collected data from the entire population. The value in the population is known as a **parameter**.'

'So, the average number of T-shirts in the sample is called a statistic, but the average number in the population is called a parameter? That's really confusing, why not call them the same thing – they're both the average?'

'The different names remind us that statistics can be computed directly from the actual data we collect, whereas the equivalent "statistic" in the population is something that we can only estimate based on the sample data.'

Alice sensed that I was still confused, and changed tack.

'It boils down to two things that you might want to do with data. The first is to describe what happened in the sample that you collected. You might draw a graph of the data, or calculate some summary information such as the average T-shirt sales. This is known as **descriptive statistics**. However, because scientists usually want to generalize their findings beyond the data they collected to the entire population, they use the sample data to estimate what the likely values are in the population. This is known as **inferential statistics**. Inferential statistics help us to make generalizations about what is going on in the real world, based on a sample of data that we have collected.'

Something clicked in me. 'Sweet, so you see whether offering free gifts increases T-shirt sales for, like, 20 bands and then, based on that, you can say whether it will work for every band. That's sick. *How* can you do that?'

'Let's imagine we could get together the whole population of rock bands.' Alice grabbed my diePad and began to draw. 'I'll draw the population as an ellipse and we'll put some band names in there. Obviously there's your band, The Reality Enigma, and you play with Chamber of the Damned and Zombie Wrath all the time.'

'Yeah, those guys are sick! There's also Hollow, Brain of Morbius, Forest of Trees …'

'… and that band with the amazing woman singing,' Alice added, struggling to think of their name.

'Ten Plagues,' I said.

'Of course … oh, and Kings of Archea,' Alice said, getting into the swing of the game.

Before long we'd listed all the bands we could think of. It was great to see Alice dropping her guard a little.

'Let's pretend that's all the bands that exist. That's our population. **(FIGURE 1.2)** Let's also say that on average across all of those bands, you expect to sell 35 T-shirts at a show. That's the magic number that we'd like to find out – the population parameter – but we can't ordinarily find it out directly because we don't have information from the entire population. However, we can estimate it by taking samples. Imagine we took a sample of three bands: Zombie Wrath, The Reality Enigma and Scansion. We work out the average number of T-shirts sold across those three bands and it's 37. This is the sample statistic. This value is slightly different from the population parameter: it is 2 T-shirts bigger. This difference is known as **sampling error**, which is the difference between what the population parameter actually is, and the value estimated from the sample.

Imagine we put these bands back into the population and took a different sample; this time we get Odin's Law, Forest of Trees and Habit of Hate. For these bands the average T-shirt sales are 42, which is not only different from the population parameter, but also different from the previous sample. The sampling error is bigger than for the first sample (the sample average is 7 T-shirts more than the population average in the second sample, but it was only 2 T-shirts more for the first). Finally, again pretend we put these bands back and randomly select another three to make up a third sample. In this sample the average T-shirt sales are 28, which underestimates the population value and is again different from the other sample values. This illustrates two important things: (1) statistics vary across different samples, which is known as **sampling variation**; and (2) the sampling error differs across samples.' **(FIGURE 1.2)**

Amazingly, this made sense to me. You can't get data from everyone, so you take a random sample instead, and use the data in the sample to estimate the value in the population, but the estimate might be wrong because samples will be different from one another, and might be slightly different from the population too. I was feeling pleased with myself. Normally Alice talking about science is a cue for my brain to start thinking about a song I was working on; today, though, she needed me, and I'd listened, and although I did get momentarily side-tracked by remembering that I hadn't seen the guys in Zombie Wrath for ages, I more or less understood. **(ZACH'S FACTS 1.2)** I was still missing something, though. How did this help us to find out whether a free wristband sells T-shirts?

Alice looked pleased at my question. 'That's the next step. We have to look at how descriptive and inferential statistics work together.' Alice drew me another picture **(FIGURE 1.3)**, and I was reminded of how she'd looked when I used to admire her in our college library. She had that same intensity and purpose right now. 'Imagine we take two samples of bands from the population of

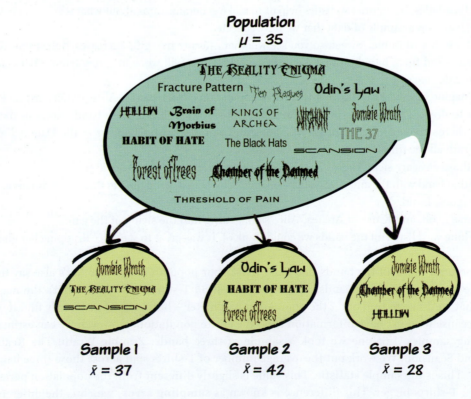

Figure 1.2 Sampling variation

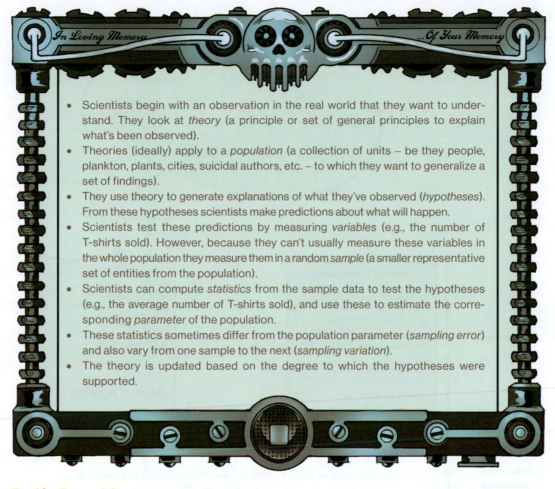

- Scientists begin with an observation in the real world that they want to under-stand. They look at *theory* (a principle or set of general principles to explain what's been observed).
- Theories (ideally) apply to a *population* (a collection of units – be they people, plankton, plants, cities, suicidal authors, etc. – to which they want to generalize a set of findings).
- They use theory to generate explanations of what they've observed (*hypotheses*). From these hypotheses scientists make predictions about what will happen.
- Scientists test these predictions by measuring *variables* (e.g., the number of T-shirts sold). However, because they can't usually measure these variables in the whole population they measure them in a random *sample* (a smaller representative set of entities from the population).
- Scientists can compute *statistics* from the sample data to test the hypotheses (e.g., the average number of T-shirts sold), and use these to estimate the corre-sponding *parameter* of the population.
- These statistics sometimes differ from the population parameter (*sampling error*) and also vary from one sample to the next (*sampling variation*).
- The theory is updated based on the degree to which the hypotheses were supported.

Zach's Facts 1.2 *The scientific process*

bands in Elpis. The bands in one sample we tell to offer a free wristband with every T-shirt, but the other sample of bands we tell not to. After the concert, we count how many T-shirts each band sold. We can then use descriptive statistics to quantify what has happened in each sample. For example, we could calculate the average T-shirts sales. Perhaps we find that the average sales are 37 for those bands that offered a free wristband, and 35 for those that did not. We know that two random samples will differ anyway because of sampling variation, so the question is whether our sample averages differ because of sampling variation, or because one sample offered a free wristband with every T-shirt. Inferential statistics helps us to distinguish which explanation is most likely.'

'Right, so to use the scientific process **(FIGURE 1.1)** to find out whether wristbands help T-shirts sales, you start with a theory of why free gifts improve sales. From that you generate a hypothesis that free gifts increase people's perception of value for money, and that leads to a prediction that when you offer a free wristband more T-shirts will sell than when you don't. You test that prediction by collecting data – you measured T-shirt sales and whether free gifts were offered in the two samples – then using statistics to compare the samples, you can see whether offering a free wristband, in general, will help to sell band T-shirts.' For the first time, I understood the use of science. I was impressed, but not as much as Alice was that I'd paid attention.

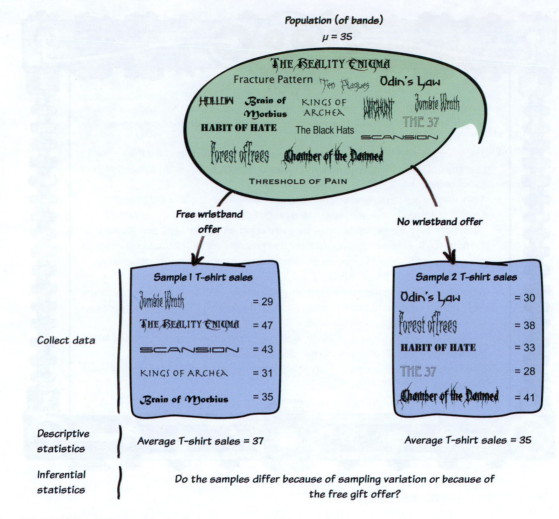

Figure 1.3   Using statistics to answer empirical questions

1.2.2 Science as a life skill

All this talk of T-shirts had got us away from my original question, which was how a scientist would know whether the Proteus device caused cancer. Remembering the article I felt panicky at the possibility that something bad could happen to Alice. I'd say that the thought of life without her was unthinkable, but that would be a lie because I constantly thought about it and it felt like imagining my last breath. I reminded her of our original purpose.

'You can apply everything I have just told you to addressing the question of whether using a Proteus increases your risk of a brain tumour. Rather than rely on the subjective opinion of Mr Marcolini about his phone, or believing a newspaper headline, or what a politician tells you, you can evaluate the objective evidence. Good science should attempt to be principled and by agreeing a system of discovery like the one I described, we establish standards that promote that. However, scientists are humans and you can never fully get away from some subjectivity. There will always be subjectivity in how data are interpreted, for example. This is why understanding the system of science empowers you, because it enables you to make your own judgements about the evidence. You don't have to believe everything you read in the paper, or what a scientist tells you.

18

You can look at the science for yourself. In this case, you could look at the studies before the revolution that investigated links between mobile phone use and brain tumours, then look at studies that address the same question about the Proteus (if they existed), and make your own judgement about the risk. You won't be relying on a journalist, who might want to spin the data to make a good story, or a politician, who might want to spin the data to make him or herself look better, or a Proteus salesman, who it might suit to play down the risks. You will be using your knowledge and skills to make an informed decision.'

'Wow, so, like, if I was ill and my doctor gave me some pills, rather than just take them I could find out how likely they are to help me first?'

'Yes.'

'Sick. So, how *would* a scientist know if a Proteus causes brain tumours?'

1.3   RESEARCH METHODS

Alice seemed conflicted. Her furrowed brow suggested that she desperately wished that I'd decided to ask her about science at a different time and place, but she also had softness in her face that hadn't been there earlier in the evening. Perhaps I *had* seen something in her that wanted me to help, or perhaps she knew this was a chance to shrink the space that had been growing between us. All that mattered was that she was talking to me rather than shutting me out.

'There are different ways to collect data,' she said, 'and different types of data that we can collect. Broadly speaking, we can test a hypothesis in one of two ways: by observing what naturally happens, or by manipulating some aspect of the environment and observing the effect it has on the variable that interests us.'

'So, just observing what happens to T-shirt sales when bands decided to give away wristbands, or actually making some bands give away wristbands, and preventing others from doing it.'

1.3.1 Correlational research methods

Alice nodded. 'When you observe what naturally happens in the world without directly interfering with it, it is known as **correlational research**. There are different ways to do this: we could take a snapshot of many variables at a single point in time (a **cross-sectional study**), or measure variables repeatedly at different time points (a **longitudinal study**). To look at the Proteus and cancer, we could measure how often a cross-section of people use the Proteus and how many of them have brain tumours, or we could take a sample of people, follow them over a long period of time and measure their Proteus use and whether they develop tumours over that period. Correlational research gives us a very natural view of the question we're researching because we're not influencing what happens and the measures of the variables should not be biased by the researcher being there. This makes it more likely that the study will have **ecological validity**, which means that the results of the study can be applied to real-life situations. There is a price to pay, which is that correlational research tells us nothing about whether one variable causes another. For example, even if we find an association between Proteus use and brain tumours, we cannot conclude that Proteus use causes brain tumours. This is particularly true of cross-sectional research because the variables are measured at the same point in time, so it would be equally valid to conclude that brain tumours cause Proteus use.'

'Get real! How can a brain tumour cause more Proteus use?'

'Well, perhaps having a tumour means that you call people more because you need social support, but you're right that sometimes explaining associations between variables does make more sense one way around than the other. For example, imagine that you discovered that popular people tend to be more attractive.[7] Although it makes more sense to assume that there's something about being attractive that makes you popular than it does to conclude that popularity changes your physical appearance, statistically both interpretations are equally valid. With longitudinal research you can make a slightly stronger statement about cause and effect if one variable predicts the other in the future, but not vice versa; for example, if attractiveness predicted your popularity in two years' time, but your popularity did not predict your attractiveness in two years' time. Even here though, you cannot be sure of cause and effect.'

'Why not?'

Alice sighed – a long, drawn-out sigh that was punctuated by her Proteus ringing. She jumped at the noise and was transported back into a state of tension. She felt inside my pocket and emerged with my reality checker. Her finger pressed gently on the winder to release the front cover and again the crystals glowed, the cogs whirred and the mist appeared.

'Doc Nightingale,' The Head said with a chuckle, 'this is the most pleasant surprise. We should spend more time together ... two geniuses, just hanging out, talking about genetics.' He turned to me and feigned surprise. 'Oh, you're still on the scene?' he asked cheekily.

'I need to take this call, so I need you to give Zach the lowdown on cause and effect please.' She kissed the top of The Head and he span. Alice's Proteus fizzed into a vaporous cloud and emerged looking like a strange alien brain. She twisted it into her ear and headed into the next room.

'Anything for you,' The Head shouted after her.

'Cause and effect, eh? That's gonna *cause* me to delve into my database and hope to have an *effect* on your brain.' The Head chuckled a deep, throaty laugh. (REALITY CHECK 1.2)

I was distracted by the conversation in the next room. I couldn't make out what Alice was saying over the voice of the jabbering Head, but she was becoming more animated and stressed. As The Head was finishing his jibber-jabber, Alice cut the call, and returned looking worried and distracted. I asked if she was level.

'I'm not sure ... well, it'll all be fine.'

She wasn't making any sense and I wasn't used to seeing her so indecisive – it made my guts churn.

'Tell me what's up.'

'It's work stuff. ... I've got a big decision to make – it's hard to explain. Don't worry.'

I held her hands in mine. 'I'd do anything for you, Alice. Look, it's a Friday night and I'm talking to you about science. I'm *trying* really hard to understand. Give me a chance.'

Alice was looking right through me as though I was missing the point, but she squeezed my hands. 'Maybe you're right, maybe it might help you one day to understand this stuff.'

What an odd thing to say: I couldn't imagine any situation between now and my death when I would need to know about statistics, but this was the first time in weeks that Alice was letting me into whatever was going on with her, and I wasn't going to blow the opportunity. She still looked distracted, so I reminded her what we'd been talking about.

'Of course ... yes ... the problem with correlational research ... cross-sectional research tells us nothing about the contiguity between different variables: we might find from a questionnaire study that attractive people are also popular, but we wouldn't know whether the popularity or attractiveness came first. Longitudinal research addresses this issue to some extent, but there is still the problem that other variables that you haven't measured, called **confounding variables**, might be influencing both variables. For example, perhaps personality affects both how physically attractive a person is perceived to be and also their popularity. People with a nice personality have more friends (because they are nice) but they are also perceived to be more attractive. In this example, a person's personality would be known as a third variable, or **tertium quid**, which is a variable that explains the apparent relationship between two other variables.'

'That's what The Head was talking about: using correlational research we can't know that attractiveness causes popularity because we aren't able to compare the popularity over time of someone who is and isn't attractive (the hypothesized cause).' Alice broke into a smile that came across as hiding sadness, and I continued with my epiphany. 'When we were talking about whether a free wristband

Having finished his chuckle, The Head explained: 'Most scientific questions imply a causal link between variables. The causal link can be obvious, such as "being physically attractive makes you more popular", but it can be, you know, subtle, like "physically attractive people are more popular", which implies that being attractive causes you to be more popular. It doesn't matter, though: regardless of whether the question mentions cause, most scientific questions break down into a proposed cause (in this case attractiveness) and a proposed outcome (popularity).

'The cause and the outcome are both variables: they vary. For the cause, some people will be more physically attractive than others. For the outcome, some people will have more friends than others. You answer the research question by uncovering the relationship between the proposed cause and the proposed outcome: are the more attractive people the more popular ones?

'Let's get philosophical. Hume[8, 9] said that to know about cause and effect: (1) cause and effect must happen at a similar time (which is called contiguity); (2) the cause should happen before the effect; and (3) cause and effect should always co-occur. Let me put it like this: causality can be inferred through *corroborating evidence*. To know that physical attractiveness caused you to be more popular, you would have to show that popularity and physical attractiveness co-occur and that the physical attractiveness emerged before the popularity.

'Sounds rad. But it isn't rad enough, because what happens if we find people who are attractive but also unpopular? This finding doesn't violate Hume's rules because he doesn't say anything about if you can have a cause without the expected effect. We need something else, and Mill[10] gave it to us: all other explanations of the cause–effect relationship must be ruled out. To do this, an effect should be present when the cause is present and absent when the cause is absent. The only way to show causality is to compare two controlled situations: one in which the cause is present and one in which the cause is absent.'

Reality Check 1.2   *Cause and effect*

would help to sell T-shirts, you used an example of comparing a sample that had been allowed to offer a free wristband with one that had not. Wouldn't this be comparing when the cause is there (the free gift) and when it is not (no free gift)?'. *(FIGURE 1.3)*

1.3.2 Experimental research methods

Alice's smile transformed into a more genuine one. 'Zach, that is perfect – *you* are perfect.' Alice fixed her watery gaze onto my eyes. I wasn't sure whether it was the call that had made her so emotional, or that I had set the baseline of my ability so low that any vaguely intelligent thing that I said was cause for her to break down. 'See, you can understand this stuff when you try. I don't know why you always underestimate yourself.'

'Come on, we all know who the brains in this relationship is, and it's not the guy with spiky hair.'

'True enough,' said The Head.

Alice ignored him. 'Look, just because I've made some of the most important genetic discoveries of the past 100 years doesn't mean I don't struggle with things. Remember what happened when you tried to teach me the guitar?'

That reminded me, I needed to pick my guitar up from the repair shop.

'I would never have dated you if I didn't think you were a clever guy.' Her use of the past tense unnerved me. 'The trouble is that you play the fool because you're scared that you will fail; but you're spot on with this. Comparing two conditions in a controlled way is at the heart of **experimental methods**: they provide a comparison of situations (usually called *treatments* or *conditions*) in which the proposed cause is present or absent, while controlling for all other variables that might influence the effect in which we're interested. This scenario is an **experiment**. The T-shirt sales example is a good one. Imagine we randomly select some bands, and half of them we asked to give away free gifts with every T-shirt, and the other half gave away nothing. The thing that we have manipulated is the incentive to buy a shirt (the free gift or no gift). This is known as an **independent variable** because it is not affected by the other variables in the experiment. More generally, it is known as a **predictor variable**, because it can be used to predict **scores** of another variable (i.e., we predict T-shirt sales based on whether or not a gift was offered). In this situation it is said to have two *levels*, because it has been manipulated in two ways (i.e., free gift or no free gift). The outcome in which we are interested is T-shirt sales. This variable is called the **dependent variable** because we assume that its value will depend upon whether or not a free gift was offered (the independent variable). More generally, we can refer to it as an **outcome variable**, because it is the variable that we're trying to predict the values of (i.e., we want to know how many T-shirt sales there are). The critical thing is the inclusion of the no-gift group because this is a group in which our proposed cause (an incentive to buy) is absent, and we can compare the outcome in this group against the situation in which the proposed cause is present (a free gift was offered). If the T-shirt sales are different when the free gift is offered (cause is present) compared to when it is not (cause is absent) then this difference can be attributed to the free gift. In other words, the free gift caused a difference in T-shirt sales.'

1.3.2.1 Two methods of data collection

'OK, that makes sense. So, you can infer cause only in experiments where you manipulate the thing that you think is the cause, and not in experiments where you just measure variables cross-sectionally.'

'Sort of, but be careful with your terminology. You can only call something an *experiment* if you have manipulated one variable and looked at the effect it has on another. If you measure variables without manipulating any of them then it is not an experiment, it is a correlational study. Lots of people make that mistake, but it's worth getting it right.'

'What would happen if the same sample of bands wanted to look at their T-shirt sales from one gig to the next when sometimes they use free gifts and sometimes not? Could that tell you anything about cause?'

'Actually it can: we can manipulate variables in experiments in two ways. The first is to manipulate the independent variable using different entities. This is the method we've been discussing – we allocate different bands, or entities, to two different groups – and it's known as a **between-groups, between-subjects,** or **independent design.**'

'Seriously? Three terms for the same thing? No wonder this stuff is confusing. Whose stupid idea was it to give the same idea three different names?'

'According to one ancient statistics text,[11] it was a character called Confusius who invented a confusion machine, but that story has never been verified. In any case, the second method is to manipulate the independent variable using the *same* entities. This would be similar to what you were suggesting: we tell a group of bands to give out a free gift with every T-shirt sold at one of their concerts and ask them not to use the free gift at the next concert (or vice versa). This is known as a **within-subject**, **related** or **repeated-measures design**.'

'Does everything in science have three different names?' I quipped.

1.3.2.2 Two types of variation

The conversation was going better than I had expected. I found myself becoming really interested in how I could sell more T-shirts. Our T-shirt designs were totally sick, some would say better than our music. I liked seeing people in them because it made me feel like I was doing some good in the world. After the Reality Revolution real music died out, and instead everyone looked to the great bands of the pre-revolution. Bands like mine were trying to recreate that old-school vibe, where music brought people together. There wasn't a soundtrack to the post-revolution, but my generation were trying to create one. When I listen to those old bands it's how I imagine it was for our parents when they wore a reality prism: it brings home how ordinary you are. Maybe you don't need a reality prism to be a victim of reality.

My mind was wandering, and Alice had noticed and stopped talking. She shot me the look that she gives me when I'm ignoring her and tersely suggested that it might be time to stop. I didn't want to stop, because I'd seen glimpses of the old Alice this evening. There had been cracks in her emotional armour that gave me hope that the past few weeks were an aberration. The key was to stay interested and keep her talking. I apologized and tried to reopen the conversation.

'I get that manipulating whether or not bands give away free gifts tells us about cause and effect, but if we do that experiment, and the T-shirt sales are more for the group that gave away gifts than for the group that didn't, then how do we know that is because of the free gift? I mean, earlier on you said that if you took different samples and measured their T-shirt sales they would be slightly different … erm, look, it's in my notes … sampling variation … so how do we know that the difference in the groups' T-shirt sales isn't just because of that?'. *(ZACH'S FACTS 1.2)*

'That's a brilliant question,' she said, and she was hooked in again. 'The answer is that you compare different types of variation in scores or T-shirt sales. Let's take a step back and think what would happen if we did *not* introduce an experimental manipulation. Imagine we have a sample of bands and we measure their T-shirt sales at two gigs (i.e., they never give away free gifts). If there is no experimental manipulation then we expect T-shirt sales to be similar in both conditions. In other words, their sales at the first gig should be similar to those at the second. We expect this because external factors such as the T-shirt designs, the price, the music played by the bands, and characteristics of the people at the gigs and what T-shirt designs appeal to them will be the same for both conditions (The Reality Enigma won't play heavy metal one week and break into some improvised jazz the next). A band's T-shirt sales at one concert should be very highly related to their sales at the other. Bands who sell a lot of T-shirts at one concert are likely to sell a lot at the next, and those that have low sales at the first concert are likely to have low sales at the next. However, sales won't be *identical*; there will be small differences in sales created by unmeasured or unknown factors. This variation is known as **unsystematic variation**. If we introduce an experimental manipulation (i.e., provide a free gift at one of the concerts), then we do something different to participants in one condition compared to what we do to them in the other. The *only* difference between the conditions (or concerts) is the manipulation that the experimenter has made (in this case that fans at one concert get a free gift if they buy a T-shirt). Therefore, any difference between the average of the two conditions is probably due to the experimental manipulation. If T-shirt sales are higher at one concert compared to the other then this *has* to be due to the fact that a free gift was offered with every T-shirt at one concert but not the other. Differences in performance created by a specific experimental manipulation are known as **systematic variation**.'

'But what if you had used different bands in the two samples?'

'In an independent design there are still two conditions, but different bands participate in each condition. Imagine again that we didn't have an experimental manipulation. If we did nothing to the groups, then we would still find some variation in sales between the groups because they contain different bands that will vary the shirt designs that they have on offer, their prices and other things that might affect sales. The factors that were held constant in the repeated-measures design are free to vary in the independent design. So, the unsystematic variation will be bigger than for a repeated-measures design. As before, if we introduce a manipulation (i.e., a free gift) then we would hope to see additional variation created by this manipulation. As such, in both the repeated-measures design and the independent design there is always systematic and unsystematic variance, it's just that, other things being equal, the unsystematic variance will be greater in independent designs. We can use statistical models to compare the size of the systematic variance to the unsystematic variance. In effect, we're looking at the effect of our experimental manipulation against a background of "noise" caused by random, uncontrollable differences between our conditions. In a repeated-measures design this "noise" is kept to a minimum and so the effect of the experiment is more likely to show up. This means that, other things being equal, repeated-measures designs have more power to detect effects than independent designs.'

1.3.3 Practice, order and randomization

'You said that if we didn't include an experimental manipulation then we'd expect the two samples to have similar T-shirt sales, but if we were using a, what was it called, you know, the same bands but tested twice ...'

'A repeated-measures design,' Alice replied.

'Yeah, if you were using a repeated-measures design, you might expect fewer T-shirts to be sold at the second gig because if people had bought a shirt at the first gig and then also come to the next one, they won't buy another shirt.'

'That's true, and in reality you would counterbalance the order in which the samples complete each condition. For our example that means that half of the bands would give away a free gift at the first concert and not at the second, but the others would give away the free gift at the second concert but not the first. **Counterbalancing** is a technique used to eliminate sources of systematic variation. One source of systematic variance is **practice effects**. Let's imagine that you wanted to see whether you could help people to overcome their fear of statistics by getting them to pretend to be someone else.[12] You give participants two comparable statistics tests. One of them they complete as themselves, but the other they complete while pretending to be someone who is really good at statistics. When the same entities participate in more than one experimental condition they are naive during the first experimental condition, but they come to the second experimental condition with prior experience of what is expected of them. For example, when they take the second statistics test they have had some practice at the types of questions that might be asked, they're familiar with the format of the test and so on. A second source of systematic variation is **boredom effects**, that is, when participants take part in several experimental conditions they are likely to become fatigued. Imagine we asked people to take statistics tests while pretending to be themselves, a student good at statistics, a statistics professor, someone who had never done statistics, and as a watermelon (as a control). They would have to complete five statistics tests. By the fifth test they'd be quite bored ...'

'Or by the first ...'

Alice gave me a disapproving look. 'The point is, the more tests they do, the more their attention is likely to wander as they get bored with the task. If every participant does the tests in the same order then we introduce a systematic bias because by the time they do the test as a watermelon, they are more bored and more practised than when they did it as themselves. So, we can

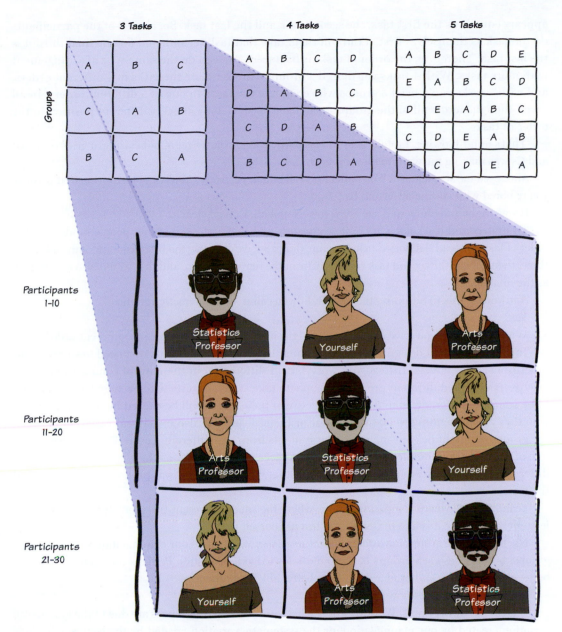

Figure 1.4 Latin square counterbalancing orders

combat these effects by counterbalancing the order in which people complete the tasks, or by having them complete the tasks in a random order. Sometimes people use a **Latin square** counterbalancing method. This is easy to visualize with a drawing.' Alice started to sketch. **(FIGURE 1.4)** 'Imagine we just had three conditions to our experiment: we asked 30 people to complete the statistics test as a statistics professor (A), as themselves (B), and as an arts professor (C). In a Latin square design with three conditions we'd split the 30 people into three equal groups. The first group would complete the tasks in order A, B, C (i.e., as the statistics professor, as themselves, then as the arts professor). However, the second group would complete it in order C, A, B (i.e., as the arts professor, as the statistics professor, then as themselves). The final group would complete the tasks in order B, C, A (i.e., as themselves, then as the arts professor, and finally as the statistics professor). The important thing is that across the participants each task or condition appears equally as the first task, the second task and the last task. So, a third of the participants do the task as themselves first, a third of them take that task second, and for the final third it is the last task. Therefore, the order of tasks is balanced. You can do the same type of arrangement with more tasks. With 4 tasks you'd need 4 groups who complete the tasks in 4 different orders, and with 5 tasks you'd need 5 groups who complete the tasks in one of 5 different orders. In all cases, though, across all of the groups a particular task is done at every different position in the order of tasks.'

'That's mind-blowing. I totally get it.' I was partly lying: I didn't get it, but staring at grids of As, Bs and Cs was making me want to blow up my mind.

Alice eyed me suspiciously. 'You understood all of that perfectly? You're not just saying that because you're bored with staring at As and Bs?'

It was frightening how well she knew me. 'Not at all. Crystal clear.'

'I'd understand if it's not – it's quite confusing, and that's why sometimes people randomize the order of tasks instead – it does much the same thing. So, we'd choose the first task randomly out of the three, then choose the second task randomly from the remaining two, and that would also leave a task as the final one.'

'And you do this to minimize the – what did you call it – unsystematic variance?'

'Yes.'

'What happens if you have one of those designs in which *different* people do different tasks?'

'In an independent design you follow a similar logic, it's just that you don't need to worry about practice or order effects. Instead you worry about differences in the natural composition of the groups. If we asked different groups of people to take statistics tests with each group pretending to be someone different, then differences between their scores will be caused by us manipulating who they are pretending to be (a professor or themselves) but also by natural variation between the groups. It might be convenient to take students from two different lecturers' stats classes, and one of these groups completes the test as themselves, and the other as their lecturer. If we find a difference between the groups can we conclude that who the student was pretending to be affected the test?'

'Yeah, because you're comparing groups where the cause is present (pretending to be a statistics lecturer) and where it is absent (taking the test as yourself).'

'No, because the groups have different lecturers, so not only does our manipulation vary across the groups, but so does each group's background knowledge in statistics. Perhaps one lecturer is much better than the other and produces students better able to do the test?'

'Maybe, but we don't know that for sure.'

'That's exactly my point. We don't know whether the group differences are due to the systematic variation created by our manipulation, or the systematic variation created by the lecturers in their teaching. This is why **randomization** is absolutely crucial in experimental research. If we randomize participants to different conditions, then, providing the randomization works, we should start the study with two groups who are comparable in age, sex and, most important in this example, statistical ability. If the randomization does its job then we can be confident that any differences between groups can only have been created by the manipulation that we carried out. Without randomization we can't be sure from where any group differences come. Sometimes though you can't randomize; for example, imagine we wanted to look at the effect of horror movies on children. It wouldn't be ethical to randomize some children into a group that watches a horror movie and others into a group that does not, because some of the children might be very disturbed by the movie. Instead, we would have to compare children who naturally decide to watch horror movies to those who do not. When you don't randomize participants into different groups it is known as a **quasi-experimental design**.'

CHECK YOUR BRAIN: Why is randomization important?

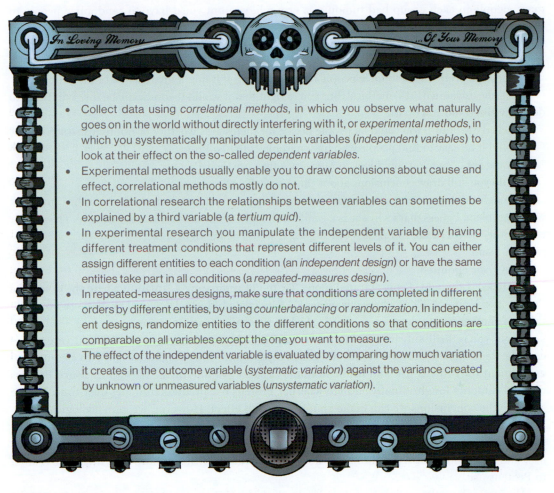

- Collect data using *correlational methods*, in which you observe what naturally goes on in the world without directly interfering with it, or *experimental methods*, in which you systematically manipulate certain variables (*independent variables*) to look at their effect on the so-called *dependent variables*.
- Experimental methods usually enable you to draw conclusions about cause and effect, correlational methods mostly do not.
- In correlational research the relationships between variables can sometimes be explained by a third variable (a *tertium quid*).
- In experimental research you manipulate the independent variable by having different treatment conditions that represent different levels of it. You can either assign different entities to each condition (an *independent design*) or have the same entities take part in all conditions (a *repeated-measures design*).
- In repeated-measures designs, make sure that conditions are completed in different orders by different entities, by using *counterbalancing* or *randomization*. In independent designs, randomize entities to the different conditions so that conditions are comparable on all variables except the one you want to measure.
- The effect of the independent variable is evaluated by comparing how much variation it creates in the outcome variable (*systematic variation*) against the variance created by unknown or unmeasured variables (*unsystematic variation*).

Zach's Facts 1.3   *Research methods*

1.3.4 Piecing it all together

'That's more or less all there is to know about how science works,' Alice said. 'Now you know it, how *would* you use science to discover whether Proteus use causes brain tumours?'

CHECK YOUR BRAIN: What are the different ways you could test Alice's hypothesis? What are the pros and cons?

I felt a wave of nausea. I thought I'd been paying attention, I really did, but now that Alice had put me on the spot I could feel my mind emptying. I stuttered, I ummed and ahed, and I caught the growing disappointment in Alice's eyes. She swayed her head from side to side, moving almost imperceptibly as though questioning why she'd believed I was capable of understanding what she'd said. I'd found hope of reaching the old Alice, but that hope drained as I fumbled around in my mind. I needed to get a grip, to find a hook to get me started. I remembered the T-shirts – I'd been interested in the T-shirts. Then the answer hit me.

'You'd want to compare the people who had used a Proteus to those who hadn't and see how many people in each group had tumours … erm, oh, yes, but you'd have to randomize people to the groups.'

Alice looked pleased, but she wasn't going to let me off easily. 'What's the problem with doing that?' she asked.

'I guess it's pretty mean to force people to use a Proteus if it might give them a brain tumour.'

'Yes!' she exclaimed. 'It's unethical, but you're right that it would theoretically be the right thing to do. How else could you do it?'

I racked my brain. 'You could let people decide for themselves whether or not they use a Proteus.'

'Would it be easy to find people who have never ever used a Proteus?'

'I guess not … but you could look at *how much* they use their Proteus.'

'Could you still draw conclusions about cause and effect?'

I thought Alice was being a bit negative. I was trying my best, but every suggestion she came back with a problem. I guess that's why she is a genius. I thought about the problem some more. The answer could either be yes or no, so I picked one hoping it would be the right choice.

'No,' I said.

'Why?' she enquired.

'Batticks!' I thought. I concentrated more. 'We're not comparing a situation where the cause, the Proteus use, is absent to one where it is present.' I felt deflated; she had defeated me because I couldn't think of another way to do it. I was surprised when she smiled warmly at me.

'Zach, you're brilliant. Everything you've said is right, but I want you to see that research is complicated: there are always trade-offs and compromises. You're right, we can't do a controlled experiment on Proteus use and brain tumours because it's unethical. We can measure Proteus use and tumours longitudinally and see whether Proteus use predicts tumours over time, but we sacrifice the conclusions we can make about cause and effect. However, we gain ecological valid-ity. So, what some scientists who have researched this have done is to look at cohorts of people, that is, people born at the same time, and followed them over time, making notes of their Proteus use, and using hospital records to see whether they end up with tumours that might be related to Proteus use.'

Alice opened up the reality checker and unleashed The Head.

'Twice in one day, Doc? I am honoured, let me take you on the information highway to knowledge paradise.'

'Sorry, I already booked my ticket for that particular trip, and I'm not allowed to take pets,' she said, cruelly. 'Get me the summary statistics of all the studies that were done on phone use and brain tumours before the revolution. I want point estimates and intervals around the effect sizes.'

'Now you're talking my language', said The Head with a chuckle.

She certainly wasn't talking *my* language, all I had heard was 'Get me the blah, blah, blah'. Alice and The Head had a weird dynamic where he would flirt with her and then she would put him in his place. My relationship with him was different: he liked to insult me. I think he just enjoyed any banter he could provoke from people and with me it was pretending to think I was an idiot. I wasn't sure Alice liked The Head at all, but despite his goading I did: he liked to talk nonsense, and I liked to fill up hours trying to think up questions that he couldn't answer. I never succeeded. The Head was spewing numbers and names at Alice; she made notes and then started sketching. **(FIGURE 1.5)**

'Zach, here are 23 studies from the pre-revolution that looked at whether mobile phone use is related to brain tumours.[13] There are no studies that have looked at the Proteus, so this is all we have to go on. I've listed the studies down the side of the picture. For each study, the scientists computed a statistic in the sample that represents the size of the effect that phone use had on brain tumours. This statistic is represented by the dots. Remember that we're interested in the effect of phone use on tumours in the whole population, not just in that particular sample. We could use this statistic as the estimate of the effect in the population. If we do this we are using a **point estimate** because we're using a single value, or point, to estimate the effect in the population. However, we know that there will be sampling error.'

'You mean that the value in the sample won't always be the same as the value in the population?'

'Yes, exactly, so we can instead compute an **interval estimate,** which is a range of values between which we think the population value is likely to fall, based on the amount of sampling error we expect for that sample. Notice for each study that there is a point estimate of the effect of phone use on brain tumours, but I have also drawn a horizontal line sticking out of each side of the point. These are limits: for each study we are estimating the limits between which we think the population value falls.'

'Every study has different limits, so is every study giving us a different answer?'

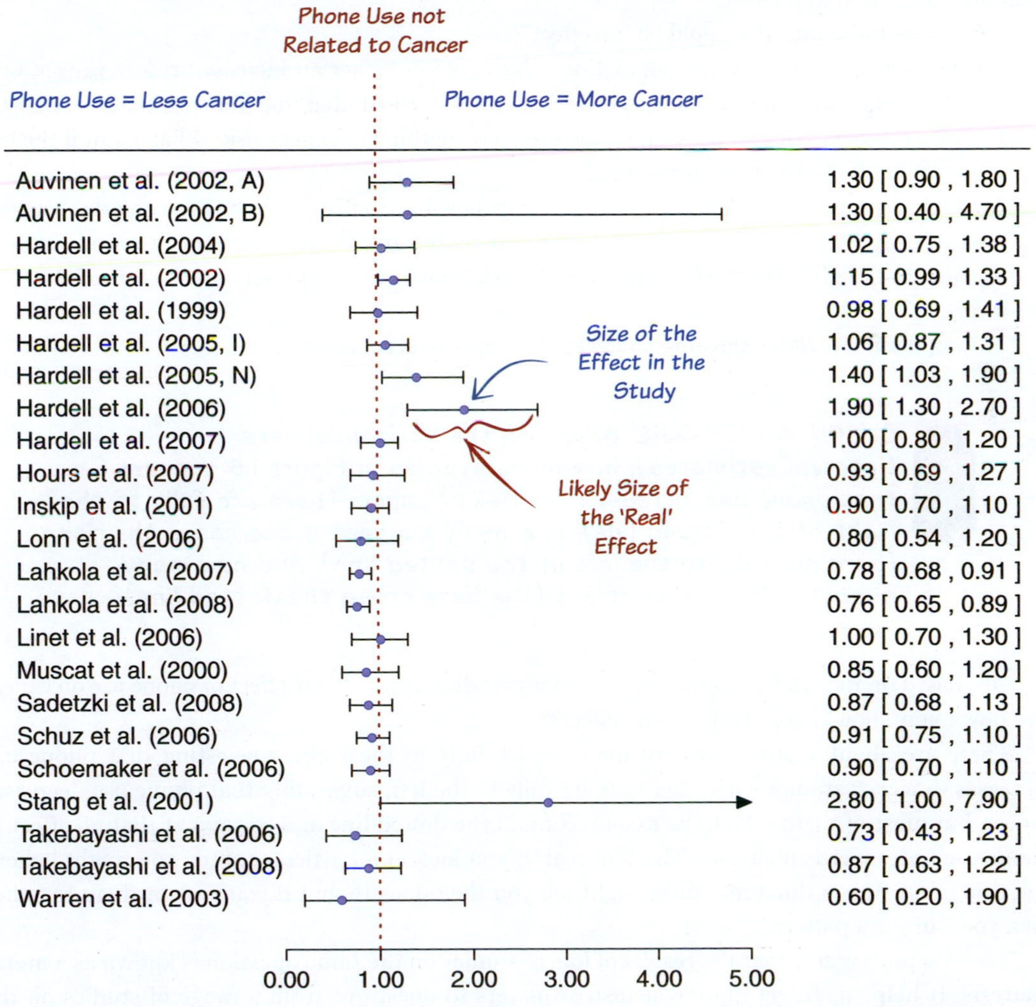

Figure 1.5   *Does your mobile phone cause cancer?*

'Yes, because of sampling variation. The important thing is that when you have lots of studies that have looked at the same question you can look for consistency in the pattern of results. For example, I have drawn a red dotted line at the value that represents "no effect". If the population value is the same as the red line then phone use had no effect whatsoever on brain tumours. Anything to the left of the dotted line means that phone use *decreased* brain tumours, and anything to the right means that phone use *increased* brain tumours. What do you notice about the dots?'

CHECK YOUR BRAIN: Based on the dots (point estimates), how many studies in Figure 1.5 suggest that phone use increases the risk of cancer, and how many suggest it decreases the risk?

I quickly counted the dots on each side of the line. 'About 11 dots are above the dotted line, which means phone use increases cancer, and 12 are below the line suggesting it decreases the risk. That's like half of the studies say one thing and half say the other, and actually a lot of the dots are close to the dotted line that shows no effect.'

'Let's look at the interval estimates,' Alice said. 'The horizontal bars estimate a range of values that the population value could be, based on the data in each study. If this bar crosses the dotted line, then what do you think that means?'

'That the population value could be "no effect"?'

'Exactly. It also means that the population value could be either an increased risk of cancer, or a decreased risk of cancer. In other words, if the bar contains the dotted line it means that there isn't a lot of evidence one way or another that phone use does anything to cancer risk. What about if the bar is completely on the right of the dotted line?'

'Would that mean the population value is definitely showing an effect of phone use increasing cancer?'

'We can't say "definitely", because these are estimates and there is a chance they are wrong, but we can say "likely". What about if the horizontal bars are completely on the left of the dotted line?'

'The population is *likely* showing an effect of phone use decreasing cancer.'

CHECK YOUR BRAIN: Based on the horizontal bars (interval estimates), how many studies in Figure 1.5 suggest that phone use increases the risk of cancer (bars are fully to the right of the dotted line), how many suggest it decreases the risk (bars are fully to the left of the dotted line), and how many suggest there is no effect (the bars cross the dotted line)?

'Yes. Based on the interval estimates, how many studies show a likely effect of phone use on cancer and how many show that it likely has no effect?'

'There are about 4 studies where the bars are fully to the right, suggesting that phone use increases cancer, 2 studies where the bars are fully to the left, suggesting that phone use decreases cancer, but most of them – 17, to be exact – contain the dotted line and so suggest that no effect of phone use on cancer is plausible. That's unreal: if you look at a particular study you might believe one thing, but then a different study might tell you the opposite, but if you look at them together then you can see a pattern.'

'Yes, and pulling together the results of lots of studies on the same question is known as a **meta-analysis**. It helps us to get more conclusive answers to questions from a range of studies on the same topic.'

'Basically, I should ignore the headlines and stop worrying about you getting a brain tumour from using your Proteus,' I said.

Alice pressed her palm to my cheek and smiled a sad smile.

1.4   WHY WE NEED SCIENCE

As our conversation ended I was struck by why Alice was so 'scientific'. It gave her power. She was always interested in the news and she always questioned what she read and saw. The news and politics made me feel helpless and depressed, but it made Alice want to change things. We are constantly bombarded with 'facts and figures' from politicians, journalists, and advertisements. Alice would say that throughout history the media would try to sell us remedies for which there's no evidence, or advise us not to protect our children from diseases based on flawed science.[14] When she heard these claims she would dispute them and find out more, whereas I accepted it all. The media could tell me I'm an intergalactic space frog and I'd probably believe it, but not Alice. It made sense, Alice understood the rules of science, she knew the system for evaluating evidence, and sometimes the jerks in power didn't play by the rules: they twist the evidence to suit their own needs, or line their own pockets. Science gave Alice the power to see through it all; in a way, she held her own reality prism to the truth.

I was reminded of when we first dated, so I told Alice how when we first got together I really admired her passion for the truth, her humanity, and the way that she always wanted to do the right thing. I told her how I now understand that science is a part of that; it's a system to help us to know what 'the right thing' is. It made total sense to me now.

Alice sucked the air out of the room before releasing it in an almighty sigh. Her breath wavered and she trembled as she exhaled. 'Thank you', she finally said, '... for listening, and for understanding. It makes everything easier.'

What did she mean by everything? Before I could ask she smiled beneath her distracted eyes, announced that she was going to bed, and headed towards the bathroom. That was my cue that the conversation was over.

'You said you had a big decision to make. ... Can I help?' I shouted after her.

'You already have,' came her reply.

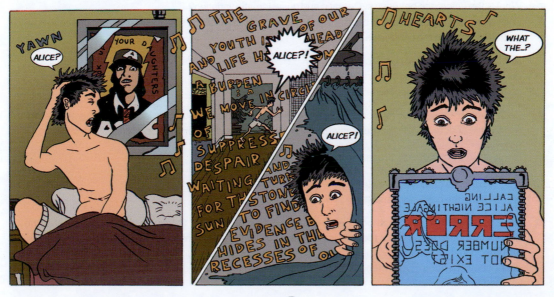

KEY TERMS

Between-groups design
Between-subjects design
Boredom effect
Confounding variables
Correlational research
Counterbalancing
Cross-sectional study
Dependent variable
Descriptive statistics
Ecological validity
Experiment (research)
Experimental methods
Hypothesis (hypotheses)
Independent design

Independent variable
Inferential statistics
Interval estimate
Latin square design
Longitudinal study
Meta-analysis
Outcome variable
Parameter
Point estimate
Population
Practice effect
Predictor variable
Quasi-experimental design
Randomization

Related design
Repeated-measures design
Sample
Sampling error
Sampling variation
Scores
Statistics
Systematic variation
Tertium quid
Theory
Unsystematic variation
Variable
Within-subject design

JIG:SAW'S PUZZLES

1   Zach wanted to impress Alice, so he asked The Head to find him some famous scientific theories. For each one, can you help him to try to generate a hypothesis that might arise from the theory.

    a   Galton[15] suggested that intelligence is hereditary (runs in families).
    b   Bandura[16] suggested that people learn their behaviours from watching others (observational learning).
    c   Paivio[17] suggested that things are easier to remember if you visualize them (dual-coding theory).
    d   Piaget[18] suggested that children develop logical thinking skills as they grow older.

2   What is the difference between descriptive and inferential statistics?
3   What is the difference between a statistic and a parameter?
4   What is the difference between sampling variation and sampling error?
5   What is the difference between a point and an interval estimate?
6   What is the difference between correlational and experimental research?
7   What is the difference between systematic and unsystematic variation?
8   Zach takes a group of fans of his band and gets them to rate each of five successive gigs according to how good they thought the band were.

    a   What kind of design has Zach used?
    b   What is the independent variable?
    c   What is the dependent variable?

9   Zach wants to know which musical instrument makes you the most popular. He looks at the *memoryBank* pages of a random selection of guitarists, drummers, bassists and singers and counts how many 'Hails' they have.

    a   What kind of design is this?
    b   What is the outcome variable?
    c   What is the predictor variable?

10   Alice wanted to see what methods were best for getting your partner to take an interest in your life. She got her friends to try different techniques on their partners giving them affection whenever they showed an interest in their lives, giving them chocolate when they showed an interest, or rebuking them when they did not pay attention. Every friend tried each method for one week and counted how often their partner listened to them.

a   How would you implement a Latin square counterbalancing for this study?

b   What is the outcome variable?

c   What is the independent variable?

d   What is the predictor variable?

e   What is the dependent variable?

IN THE NEXT CHAPTER, ZACH DISCOVERS ...

That his girlfriend doesn't exist

How to report research

Statistical notation

The mysteries of BODMAS

Levels of measurement

Measurement error

Validity and reliability

Never to corner a man who is clutching his sausage

2 Reporting Research, Variables and Measurement

Breaking the Law

I woke with a knot in my gut: something wasn't right and my sleeping body sensed it before my waking brain. Alice wasn't in the bed. During the week she was up and out before me, but today was Saturday and she never got up early on the weekend. Perhaps she couldn't sleep and had decided to get up, but the bedroom was a tip: and Alice, even if half asleep, moved within our apartment like a ghost unable to disrupt the objects around her. Alice wouldn't leave the room in this kind of state. I jumped out of bed and rushed around the apartment. It confirmed what I already felt: Alice was gone and something wasn't right. Her clothes were gone, her possessions were gone, and every photo of Alice and me that we beamed from our stars onto the walls of our apartment was gone. Our home had been stripped of everything that made it our home.

I went to call her Proteus, but she wasn't in my contacts and neither were her family or any of her friends. Their details weren't in my history and of course I had no idea what their numbers were: like everything else, I had them stored on my star, never thinking to store them in my own memory. 'In loving memory of my memory indeed,' I thought as I tried in vain to make my diePad take me somewhere where I could find her number. I found the number for the Beimeni Centre of Genetics, where she worked, but they told me that no one by the name of Alice Nightingale had ever worked there. Alice had been wiped from the planet.

As I was losing hope, I realized that her contact details would be in a document somewhere: something from her bank, or her work: you can't do anything official without putting down your number. I logged into our constellation but her star was gone. I checked my own and there amongst the digital flotsam and jetsam of our life was a glimmer of hope: our rental agreement for the apartment. My hands shook with nervous hope as I opened the file. It was there, in digital black and white: her Proteus number. I quickly dialled the number, fantasizing about her answering, her exasperated tone as she explained that she'd gone to get us breakfast, and her confusion at why I was fussing about her not being there. The fantasy came to an abrupt halt as my screen told me that the number had never existed.

The Head would know what to do: he knew everything. I opened my pocket watch, and expectantly awaited The Head's colourful entrance. As his face solidified, he yawned, 'Hey, Z, early doors?' He span through a slow circle, frowning, as though trying to get his bearings. 'This place is Caspered.'

He was right, the apartment felt eerie. I didn't feel the lump in my throat until I tried to talk to him. 'Where's Alice?' I croaked.

The Head whizzed around as he always did when he was checking whatever information sources it was that he checked. The spinning stopped suddenly and he looked serious. 'I don't know.' The hours I'd wasted trying to think up a question that The Head couldn't answer and I'd finally found one.

'Have you checked the street cameras? Police records? Tracked her Proteus? Looked at security camera footage? In the movies, they can find people.'

'Let me say something that might shock you. Prepare yourself, because, I fear this is the piece of knowledge that pushes you over some kind of mental edge. The ... movies ... are ... not ... real.' His eyes bulged as he said real, as though he was carefully inspecting my sanity.

What the frip? 'I ... am ... not ... an ... idiot,' I replied, emulating his bulging eyes. We stayed locked in a bulgy-eyed stare until The Head snapped out of it with a beaming grin.

'I'm glad, because for a moment there, Z, I thought you had forgotten that since the ID chips, we don't have street cameras, that the police don't keep track of every person's movements each day, that security cameras are, like, you know, secure, so any old Head can't just go looking at them, and that if someone doesn't activate their Proteus tracking then I stand more chance of tracking a fish on the other side of the Earth than I do of tracking them.'

Perhaps I was an idiot after all, but there must be something he could do – he must have access to something? The Head must have sensed my deflation. 'Look, I Sherlocked her good and proper. I searched more than 25 billion sources and your Alice Nightingale does not exist, so that woman doesn't want to be found, someone doesn't want her to be found, or she never existed.'

'Of course she exists – I was with her last night, you saw her last night?'

'I did, but every piece of information I examined tells me that I couldn't have.'

This was spooks; too frippin' spooks. The Head's words made me doubt myself. I felt alone and I wished my parents were still here. Alice is all I have, or had, and perhaps I never even had her? I was proud of being a Clocktorian, but right now it sucked. Half the world was instantly connected through these stupid chips in their heads and I couldn't access any of them.

I called Nick, the drummer in my band and my oldest friend. Nick and I met on my first day of school at the age of 4 and we've grown up together. Apart from the band, we hang out down at the Elpis Repository, sharing music and talking batticks. The Repositories were built by the WGA after the Reality Revolution to house vast underground physical collections of art, literature, music and film. They became the social hub of the city: people rediscovered the joy of experiencing music and films together, the debate that followed and the social connection that was lost by experiencing everything in a virtual world. Since the chipping began, though, *memoryBank* has offered a seemingly irresistible urge to catalogue life instead of living it; the Repositories have fallen silent. Many Clocktorians enjoy the solitude that the Repositories now offer, but I enjoy being there with a friend. For years that friend was Alice, but her interests lie elsewhere now and Nick is my regular companion.

Right now I needed Nick not just as a friend but because he was a Chipper – he had volunteered to have the chip so that we could promote the band using *memoryBank*. Nick is our connection to the Chipper's world; our lifeline beyond Elpis. I told Nick everything that had happened; he put the word out to our fans on *memoryBank*, with the tag #NightingaleFlyHome. He'd known Alice as long as I had, and he reassured me that if she didn't exist then he'd been imagining her too for the past 10 years.

When I got home and told The Head what Nick had said he adopted a look of pity, 'You're missing the obvious and you're not going to like it ... She's left you, and she doesn't want to be found.'

As my mind spiralled I was drawn to the song that had been playing on repeat in the apartment since I had got up. It was 'Faith in Others', the final song from the album that Alice had been playing last night. It instinctively made me think of Alice, of our youth, of our evenings in the Repository years ago. As the song repeated, the lyrics came into my mind; they were words I had once known by heart:

> The grave of our youth is up ahead
> And life has become a burden
> We move in circles of suppressed despair
> Waiting for the sun
> And turning stones to find evidence
> But it hides in the recesses of our hearts[19]

Were these words a message from Alice? As I thought about them I feared the worst. Was 'The grave of our youth is up ahead' suggesting that we had grown up – that our youth was dying? Did 'And life has become a burden' mean that she felt that our relationship had become a treadmill, never progressing? Was 'We move in circles of suppressed despair, Waiting for the sun' telling me that she felt we were clinging on to a false hope that our love, the sun of our lives, would shine again? Did 'And turning stones to find evidence, But it hides in the recesses of our hearts' mean that she looked for signs of our love, but couldn't find them because they were too deeply hidden?

The words painted a black picture and the realization of her message was a stranglehold around my neck. Perhaps The Head was right, this song did seem like a farewell message. It made perfect sense: we *had* been drifting apart. A song on repeat was a kind of weird way to end a relationship, though, not to mention removing all traces of your existence. It seemed a bit extreme. Surely there was more to it than that? This belief drove me to find the memory stone, and I stared at three files that Alice, presumably, had wanted me to find. I remembered the second of the three possibilities that The Head had said earlier: perhaps *someone else* doesn't want her to be found.

2.1 WRITING UP RESEARCH

I opened the file with the name that told me to read it. It was neither a bittersweet farewell note nor a clue to her abduction, instead it was a tedious report. *(LAB NOTES 2.1)* It meant nothing to me. Why would Alice want me to read that? Surely she would know that my brain would disengage by the second sentence. The other files were more of the same.

As I read I became agitated. 'I don't understand any of this; it makes no sense to me. It's stupid, stupid words, stupid symbols and even more stupid pictures. Why can't she just write something in English?' My eyes welled up in frustration. 'It's one of those articles that Alice reads for work, and that she writes sometimes. Why would she leave me that?'

'Show me,' said The Head in his soothing, unflappable tone. I held up my diePad screen. 'You're right, Z, that's a research paper for sure. One of hers, I imagine. Maybe she left it for a reason? Maybe she wants you to know what it's saying? Or maybe she forgot to take that stone with her when she left you.' He chuckled.

'Or when she was taken,' I added, wanting to retain the hope that she hadn't left me because she wanted to.

The Head became serious. 'What would happen if I spoke to you in another language ... which, by the way, I can?' he asked.

'I wouldn't understand you.'

'No, you wouldn't. This report is written in the language of science; understanding it is about understanding the language. You just need to learn the language. I can help you. Scientists use a standard format to communicate their research to each other. They want to tell others four things: the reason why they did the research, how they did it, what they found, and what it means.'

'Why? How? What? Who cares?'

'You got it. If every scientist wrote whatever they liked it would be confusing, so they write reports or research papers that follow a format that helps them to think about those four questions:

- *Abstract*: This is a summary of the whole study. It's slick. Scientists are busy people, they need to know "do I need to read this stuff?" That's what the abstract tells them. It has a sentence or two describing why the study was done, how it was done, what was found and what it means. It gives the reader a feel for whether the research is interesting or relevant enough to warrant reading the detailed paper.

- *Introduction*: This is the why. The history lesson. They talk about past research that others have done that has led to their own hypothesis. They might describe how other findings are inconsistent or ambiguous and then describe how their research will clarify the situation. The intro normally moves from the general to the specific: they start with the general background of the research and then describe specific studies. They usually finish by saying what their hypotheses are.

- *Method*: This is where they tell others how they did their research. There is enough detail that someone else could repeat the research, but not so much detail that they die of boredom reading it. It's common to split this section up into who took part (*participants*), what tasks were used (*measures/materials*), special equipment that was used (*apparatus*), the type of research design that was used (*design*), a description of what happened (*procedure*), and how the measures were scored (*scoring*). It's unusual not to see participants and procedure, but the other sections may or may not be there.

- *Results*: This is the money shot. This is where the mystery is revealed: what did they find? Remember Alice told you about descriptive and inferential statistics? (CHAPTER 1) Scientists normally start with some descriptive statistics about their sample, then they deal the killer blow of the inferential statistics. Those inferential stats are like a sergeant major, putting those hypotheses through their paces, seeing whether they come out strong or drop down dead. Only the strong hypotheses survive.

- *Discussion*: This section is deep; so deep you need a subwoofer. They summarize what they found in case you didn't understand the results, but also how it changes the world, and what still needs to be done. They start by summarizing the results. BOOM! Then they lay down what it means for their theory. BOOM! They tell you what it means for the real world. SUBSONIC BOOM! They tell you the limitations and what still needs to be done. When that's done, you're like "Whoa, get me a depth gauge so I can measure how deep that was."

- *References*: You can't write stuff in science without justifying it, you've got to let people know the science that supports what you're saying. Alice, in her intro (LAB NOTES 2.1), cites research papers when she makes a point. She writes the names of the authors and the year that the research was published. So, you need to collect that wisdom into a reference list so others can read it for themselves. Alice has one of those lists and all the names and dates she has cited appear in this list.'

This was a lot to take in, but it made sense of what I'd read. He was right, Alice's report had all of those sections: an abstract, introduction, method, results, references, but no discussion. As though thinking the same thought, The Head said, 'Looks to me like she hadn't finished the report: the abstract has no ending and it looks like she was scared to write the discussion.'

'Scared of what?' I asked.

'Read her words, it sounds like her results were gonna blow the world a new ass ...'

'I get the picture, but what *were* the implications?'

'That is a question I can't answer. I will admit to a staggering capacity to gather and assimilate information, but I'm no scientist. You're as on your own as a statistics professor on a dance floor.' Wow, two questions The Head couldn't answer in a day – usually that would have made me feel very smug.

Abstract

Recent advances suggest that a combination of programmable cells and synthetic genes (C-10XFMG) can be a successful way to heal damaged tissue. However, the results of early trials suggest only partial success. This study combined this technology with the implementation of a genetic toggle switch. Participants with facial injuries were administered the programmable cell/C-10XFMG therapy, but half were also implanted with a genetic toggle switch. All participants were then asked to heal their injuries by studying photos of themselves before the injury, or a same-sex stranger (controls). The results showed that ...

Introduction

Matter that can change from one physical form to another (so-called 'programmable matter') has long been used to construct versatile objects and buildings (Knaian, 2013). Cars that turn into boats and planes have become the mainstay of our transport system, and adaptive buildings that can change their room configuration within seconds are part of everyday life. Similar principles have been applied to living tissue. In the 21st century scientists began to develop 'programmable cells' (Kobayashi et al., 2004), hoping to create living tissue that can change form based on biochemical instructions. Such cells would have enormous clinical value, for example, in healing damaged tissue by instructing the cells to revert to their non-damaged state. Mice with programmable cells have been shown to be able to heal external injuries by issuing such instructions to those cells (Araya, Hanneman, King, & Lombardo, 2103). There have been two major challenges in realizing the true potential of this technology: (1) how to convert ordinary human cells into programmable ones; and (2) how to empower humans to control these cells. The first challenge has recently been solved: Nightingale developed the BLISS serum, which has been shown to fully convert normal human cells into ones which can be instructed to change their structure (Nightingale, 2110). In addition, significant steps towards the second aim have been made through synthesizing the genes of species that can change aspects of their physical appearance using hormones or neurotransmitters. One notable success is the so-called 'chameleon gene'. The chameleon lizard controls its external appearance by relocating particles of pigment in special cells called chromatophores; synthesis of the chameleon gene with human genes appears to enable humans to similarly control programmable cells within their body. A breakthrough study showed that humans with burn injuries could partially heal their skin by first converting their cells to programmable ones, then introducing the chameleon gene into their genetic structure, and then training the participants to focus on healing their wounds (Nightingale, 2112). This so-called C-gene therapy offers the exciting possibility of self-healing of many injuries and cancers; however, to date the therapy has been only partially successful.

Theoretically, control of programmable cells through the chameleon gene would be improved by the use of a genetic toggle switch (Deans, Cantor, & Collins, 2007) that can turn specific genes on and off. The logic is that introducing such a genetic switch would provide the individual with more precise access to both their existing gene structures and also the chameleon gene itself. This study aims to see whether the combined use of a genetic toggle switch with the chameleon gene will result in better self-healing in people with facial injury. We predict that the C-gene therapy combined with a genetic toggle switch will enable better healing than C-gene therapy alone.

Method

Participants

Participants were 17 males and 15 females aged 13 to 61 ($M = 35.84$, $SD = 12.53$) who had facial burns, recruited from Elpis City Hospital. All participants consented to the study after full disclosure of the safety of the procedures to be used.

Genetic Procedures

Two weeks prior to the study all participants were injected with the BLISS serum (Nightingale, 2110). Two days pre-test, cell samples were taken to confirm that the serum had converted cells to a programmable state. All participants responded as expected to the BLISS serum with no side effects. One week pre-test, the chameleon gene, C-10XFMG, was introduced into all participants, followed by 3 hours of adaptation during which participants were monitored. The quantity of C-gene for each person was synthesized using the standard equation (Nightingale, 2112):

$$y_i = \frac{\sum_1^n x_{\text{chameleon}}}{\left(\sum_1^n x_{\text{human}}\right)^2}$$

For the next 5 days participants underwent the attentional training used by Nightingale (2112), during which they were trained to mentally attune to the new gene. This training has been shown to help people to gain conscious control over the C-gene (Nightingale, 2112). Two days prior to test, the genetic toggle switch was introduced into half of the participants.

Tasks

Half of the participants were asked to look at a photograph of themselves from before their injury and to imagine the cells in their faces changing to become like the photo. The remainder acted as a control and were asked to look at a picture of a same-sex stranger and to try to change their face to become the person in the picture.

All participants looked at the picture for 6 sessions of 20 minutes each. At the end of the sessions their faces were scanned into a computer and compared to the face in the photograph. Facial recognition software produced a precise resemblance measure as a percentage (100% = the participant's face is exactly like the face in the photograph, 0% = the person in the photo bears no resemblance at all to the participant).

Design

The design was a 2 (Gene: chameleon gene, chameleon gene + genetic toggle switch) × 2 (Picture: self, same-sex stranger) independent design. The outcome was the facial resemblance (%) between the participant and the photo.

Results

There was a significant main effect of whether the participant had the chameleon gene alone or in combination with the genetic toggle switch, $F_{(1, 28)} = 440.83$, $p < 0.001$. There was also a significant main effect of whether the participant tried to resemble a photo of themselves pre-injury or the photo of a same-sex stranger,

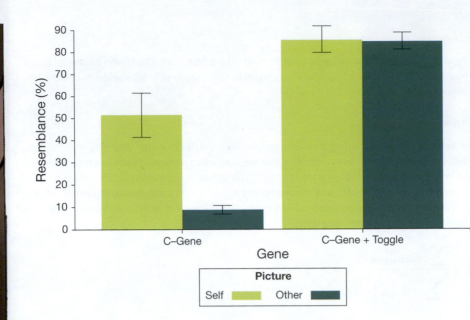

$F(1, 28) = 68.17$, $p < .001$. Finally, there was a significant interaction between the gene combination and the type of picture that the participants tried to copy, $F(1, 28) = 62.83$, $p < .001$.

Discussion

The implications are frightening ... I'm not sure I should make them public ...

References

Araya, T., Hanneman, J., King, K., & Lombardo, D. (2103). Feeding on the screams of the mutants we are creating. *Journal of Utterly Fabricated Nonsense, 666,* 1–25.

Deans, T. L., Cantor, C. R., & Collins, J. J. (2007). A tuneable genetic switch based on RNAi and repressor proteins for regulating gene expression in mammalian cells. *Cell*, 130(2), 363–372. doi: 10.1016/j.cell.2007.05.045

Knaian, A. N. (2013). Programmable matter. *Physics Today*, 66(6), 64–65.

Kobayashi, H., Kaern, M., Araki, M., Chung, K., Gardner, T. S., Cantor, C. R., et al. (2004). Programmable cells: Interfacing natural and engineered gene networks. *Proceedings of the National Academy of Sciences of the United States of America, 101*(22), 8414–8419. doi: 10.1073/pnas.0402940101

Nightingale, A. (2110). The BLISS serum. Anyone would think it was some made up sci-fi nonsense. *Proceedings of the World Academy of Very Important Scientists Who Like To Think That They Are Very Important, 12,* 1984–1985.

Nightingale, A. (2112). The chameleon gene: It won't give you a really long tongue and bug eyes. *Journal of Fairly Unethical Genetic Manipulation Studies, 13,* 812–833.

Alice's Lab Notes 2.1   Alice's research

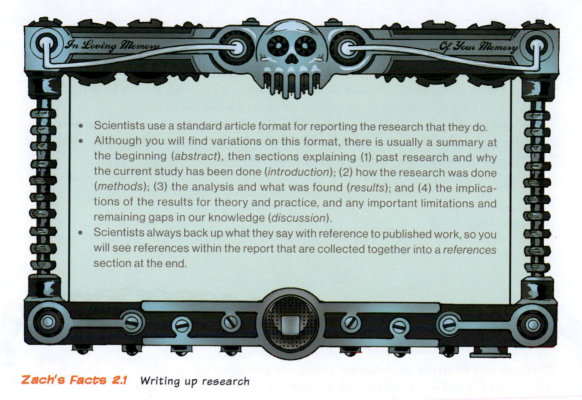

- Scientists use a standard article format for reporting the research that they do.
- Although you will find variations on this format, there is usually a summary at the beginning (*abstract*), then sections explaining (1) past research and why the current study has been done (*introduction*); (2) how the research was done (*methods*); (3) the analysis and what was found (*results*); and (4) the implications of the results for theory and practice, and any important limitations and remaining gaps in our knowledge (*discussion*).
- Scientists always back up what they say with reference to published work, so you will see references within the report that are collected together into a *references* section at the end.

Zach's Facts 2.1   **Writing up research**

2.2 MATHS AND STATISTICAL NOTATION

Somehow I needed to fathom out what Alice had found. I felt sure that she wanted me to read this report, and perhaps she trusted me to do something sensible with it. I couldn't understand why, though. She knew better than anyone that I was hopeless at this stuff; she operated on a higher mental plane than me. It just didn't make sense that she would trust this report to me – why not tell the professor she worked with, or some other colleague? Why give a report to someone who you know won't understand it? Maybe she wanted to give it to someone who she knew couldn't possibly understand it? The question rattled around in my empty head. What would Alice tell me to do? She would say I should evaluate the evidence, and this report was evidence.

'If you can't help with the science, what *can* you help with?' I asked The Head.

'The maths. I was the best man at Maths' wedding to Mrs Maths, I'm godfather to baby Maths, I look after goldfish Maths when the Maths family are on holiday. Maths is my sibs. What about you?'

'I walked past Maths on a crowded street once.'

'That's real bad. Let's start real simple. What is the result of $1 + 2 \times 3^2$?' The Head asked.

'That's easy, it's 27.'

The Head shook, 'No, it's 19.'

'Don't be ridiculous, 1 plus 2 is 3, multiply that by 3^2, which is 9, and you get 3 times 9, which is 27.'

'You're breaking Mr Maths' heart,' The Head said in an overly sad voice. 'You're forgetting BODMAS.' *(REALITY CHECK 2.1)*

'BODMAS? Who was he?'

'Father BODMAS was an old guy with a white beard who used to give children equations for Christmas.' The Head waited for a reaction, but continued when he got none, 'I'm yanking your chain. BODMAS tells us the order to do things in an equation. If you use BODMAS then you'll see that because there are no brackets the first thing to deal with is the order term: 3^2 is 9, so the equation becomes $1 + 2 \times 9$. There's no division, so we move on to multiplication: 2×9, which gives us 18. BODMAS tells us to deal with addition next: $1 + 18$, which gives us 19. If I'd asked you to solve $(1 + 2) \times 3^2$, then the answer would have been 27 'cos we deal with the brackets first: $(1 + 2) = 3$, so the equation becomes 3×3^2. We then deal with the order term, so the equation becomes $3 \times 9 = 27$'. Let's try a tricky one. What's the answer to this?' The Head projected an equation onto the wall.

$$10 + \frac{2(3+1)^2}{8} - 5$$

'BODMAS and PEMDAS are acronyms to help you remember which order to do things in when carrying out calculations or working out the result of an equation,' The Head explained. 'They are different versions of the same acronym so use whichever one you find easiest to remember. The acronyms stand for:

- **Brackets/Parentheses**: This means that anything within brackets is calculated first.
- **Order/Exponents**: "Order" is the old fashioned way of saying "to the power of". So, 3^2 is three to the order of 2. These are also called exponents. So, anything with an exponent should be calculated next.
  - **Division/Multiplication**: the acronyms place division and multiplication different ways around, but it doesn't matter because they should happen next, and the order in which they happen depends on where they are in the equation. The rule is you go left to right, so scanning from the left to the right, if you come across a multiplication first then do it and then carry on scanning to the right.
  - **Addition/Subtraction**: although addition is ordered before subtraction in both acronyms, they again happen at the same time, so the order is determined by doing any additions or subtractions as you come to them when you scan from the left of the equation to the right.'

Reality Check 2.1   BODMAS/PEMDAS

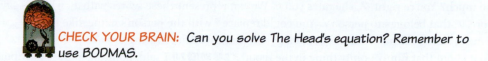

CHECK YOUR BRAIN: Can you solve The Head's equation? Remember to use BODMAS.

I got my diePad and started to draw to help me; **(FIGURE 2.1)** in retrospect it would have made more sense to have used the calculator app. 'Let me see, first I deal with the brackets, so that is $3 + 1 = 4$. So I change $(3+1)$ to 4.'

'Great,' said The Head.

'Next I do the orders or exponents. So, I take the 4^2 and change that to 16. Then I need to look for any multiplication or division. There is one of each: there's a 2×16 and also a divide by 8. As they are part of the same thing I guess it makes sense to do the 2×16 first because that's what gets divided by 8?'

'You know it makes sense,' The Head grinned.

'Sweet, so I replace the 2×16 with 32, and next I divide this value by 8, which gives me 4. Finally I deal with any addition and subtraction, and I do this from left to right, so that gives me $10 + 4$, which is 14, and then subtract 5 from it. So, the answer is 9?'

The Head nodded in appreciation 'You said you walked past Mr Maths on a crowded street? Well, you just ran back and invited the dude for a coffee!'

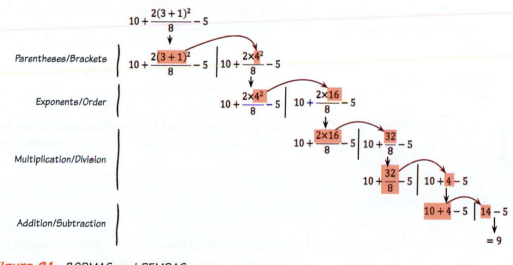

Figure 2.1 BODMAS and PEMDAS

There were other symbols that I didn't understand in Alice's report **(LAB NOTES 2.1)**, like the little i, and the x and y, so I asked The Head about those.

'y represents the outcome. That's the variable that you're predicting. When Alice talked about measuring T-shirt sales **(SECTION 1.2)**, that variable was an outcome, so we might represent T-shirt sales with the letter y. The letter x is a different letter altogether, and represents a predictor or independent variable. It is also used to denote scores. The i tells you to what or who the score belongs. If you and Alice rated how much you love each other out of 10, what number would you give Alice?'

'10.'

'Smooth, and I'm thinking she gives you a 7.'

'*What?*'

'Too much? You're right, Z, she rates you 6. We can represent these scores with x_i, which is saying 'the score, x, that belongs to person i'. You could replace i with the person's name, like this: $x_{Zach} = 10$ would mean Zach's rating of Alice is 10, or $x_{Alice} = 6$ meaning Alice's rating of Zach is 6.'

'What about that funny pointy thing in the report?' **(LAB NOTES 2.1)** I said, pointing at the funny pointy symbol.

'The sigma?' The Head projected a Σ out in front of him from the pocket watch, 'That means "add shit up".'

'Why does it have a 1 and an n by it?'

'Because you start adding at item 1, and you "add shit up" until you reach the last item; because the equation doesn't know how many things you have, it can't use a number to represent the last item so it uses the letter n, which you can think of as being short for '*number* of things you need to add up' or '*no* more numbers left to add up'. Imagine we wanted to add up your and Alice's ratings of love for each other. We can represent that like this'. The Head again projected some symbols. **(EQUATION 2.1)**

$$\sum_{i=1}^{n} x_i \tag{2.1}$$

'The $i = 1$ in the expression means that you should start with person 1's score; if it was $i = 2$ then it means you should start with person 2's score. The n symbol at the top means that you should keep adding scores until you reach the last score. So, with $i = 1$ this equation means that you take person 1's score ($i = 1$) score, then add it to person 2's score ($i = 2$), then add person 3's score ($i = 3$) to the previous scores, and carry on doing this up to and including the last person's score ($i = n$). With scores from just you and Alice we would have this.' The Head projected another equation **(2.2)**.

$$\sum_{i=1}^{n} x_i = 10 + 6 = 16 \tag{2.2}$$

The Head stepped things up. 'Of course, you can use the BODMAS principles with this symbol too. What do you think you would get for you and Alice's ratings from this expression?' **(EQUATION 2.3)** he asked.

$$\sum_{i=1}^{n} x_i^2 \tag{2.3}$$

I felt like The Head was torturing me. I was finding it hard to concentrate. Alice was missing, I needed answers and he was babbling on about maths. I thought back to BODMAS. There were no brackets in The Head's equation, so move onto powers. There was a squared symbol. 'Do we square each value and then add them?'

'Yes you do', The Head beamed, as he projected the full equation **(2.4)**.

$$\sum_{i=1}^{n} x_i^2 = 10^2 + 6^2 = 100 + 36 = 136 \tag{2.4}$$

'What about this expression?' **(2.5)** continued The Head, projecting yet another equation in front of me.

$$\left(\sum_{i=1}^{n} x_i\right)^2 \tag{2.5}$$

I thought back to BODMAS. The weird spiky symbol was in the brackets, and we have to deal with the brackets first, so that means we'd sum the scores first. Having done that we'd look for an exponent or power symbol. There was one: a squared outside of the brackets, so that must mean we square what is inside the brackets. 'We add the scores and then square the total, so it would be 16 squared,' I replied to The Head, who looked pleased and projected the answer for me. **(EQUATION 2.6)**

$$\left(\sum_{i=1}^{n} x_i \right)^2 = (10+6)^2 = 16^2 = 256 \tag{2.6}$$

'You're doing great,' The Head reassured me. 'The final hurdle is the equation in Alice's report' (Alice's Lab Notes 2.1). The Head projected the equation **(2.7)** on the wall to remind me.

$$y_i = \frac{\sum_{1}^{n} x_{\text{chameleon}}}{\left(\sum_{1}^{n} x_{\text{human}} \right)^2} \tag{2.7}$$

It looked complicated. I started to panic slightly. It felt too hard, and my mind was still racing about Alice. The Head told me to break it down into little bits. 'What's y_i?' he asked.

'Is it the outcome for person i?'

'Yeah, that's what they are trying to calculate: the quantity of C-gene to give to each person. Now, the xs represent values that either come from a chameleon lizard or the human themselves. Imagine we have 5 scores from a chameleon and 5 from the human.' The Head projected a table of numbers onto the wall. **(TABLE 2.1)**

Table 2.1   The data that The Head used to torment Zach

Chameleon	Human
3	2
1	3
2	5
4	7
2	3

 CHECK YOUR BRAIN: Using the scores in Table 2.1, can you work out the quantity of C-gene needed?

'Based on these scores, what quantity of C-gene is needed?' The Head asked.

I thought again of BODMAS. 'Brackets first, and there are brackets in the bottom part of the equation so I need to deal with those first. The adding symbol is inside the brackets, which means that I need to add up the human scores first; that will be 2 + 3 + 5 + 7 + 3, which is 20. Next is order terms, and there is an exponent in the lower part of the fraction, which tells me to square the 20, which will be ...' I paused.

'400,' said The Head as he projected the equation **(2.8)** on the wall as I worked through it.

$$y_i = \frac{\sum_1^n x_{\text{chameleon}}}{\left(\sum_1^n x_{\text{human}}\right)^2} = \frac{\sum_1^n x_{\text{chameleon}}}{(2+3+5+7+3)^2} = \frac{\sum_1^n x_{\text{chameleon}}}{20^2}$$

$$(2.8)$$

$$y_i = \frac{\sum_1^n x_{\text{chameleon}}}{\left(\sum_1^n x_{\text{human}}\right)^2} = \frac{\sum_1^n x_{\text{chameleon}}}{400}$$

'The next part of BODMAS is division, so I need to do that next, but to do it I have to sort out the top half of the fraction. The symbol on the top means I need to add the chameleon scores, so that will be $3 + 1 + 2 + 4 + 2$, which is 12. So, the final value would be 12 divided by 400.'

'Which is?' said The Head with a teasing look on his face.

'C'mon, you know I have no idea.'

'Yeah, I know, but I'm havin' fun. **(EQUATION 2.9)** It's 0.03'.

$$y_i = \frac{12}{400} = 0.03$$

$$(2.9)$$

- Do calculations and solve equations using BODMAS/PEMDAS, which stands for Brackets/Parentheses, Order/Exponents (in other words 'to the power of'), Multiplication and Division, then Addition and Subtraction.
- y usually denotes an outcome variable (a dependent variable), and x a predictor variable (which can be an independent variable). However, x is also used to denote the scores you have collected.
- $\sum$ means 'add everything up after the symbol'.

Zach's Facts 2.2 *Statistical notation*

Despite a small amount of pride at having followed what The Head told me, I was agitated. This lesson wasn't getting me any nearer to Alice. It felt like a waste of time: it would take me weeks to fully understand this report, and I needed to know what was going on *now*. I didn't want to believe that Alice had left me, but it was plausible, and if she hadn't then the implications were even worse:

someone had taken her and tried to erase her from the world. Alice would have told me to collect evidence, real evidence, not ambiguous evidence buried in a report or a song. Her friends and family may have been wiped from my contacts, but I knew she had been seeing a counsellor, and I knew his name: Dr Murali Genari. She spoke about their sessions, and to whom do you tell your secrets if not your counsellor? A counsellor's address should be easy enough to look up, and it was.

2.3 VARIABLES AND MEASUREMENT

2.3.1 The conspiracy unfolds

The voice startled me. I turned, my heart racing. Before me was a white-haired, short, plump man holding a massive sausage. I should have run – I could have easily pushed past him, back down the hallway, and been gone before he could react, but there was something about the sausage that disarmed me.

'I said, *what are you doing*!? Answer me!' shouted the man. He was quivering with rage. In my enthusiasm to find out why Alice had gone, I hadn't factored in being caught in the act of stealing a confidential file. This situation was a bit awkward. The man facing me, I assumed, was Dr Genari. He certainly looked the part: he was an old man, had a white beard, and dressed even more old-fashioned than Alice's parents. He posed no real threat to me, I could take the file and run, but what if he tried to challenge me? I didn't want to hurt the guy; I just wanted the file. I stared at him, both of us trying to get the measure of each other. Suddenly I realized that he wasn't shaking with rage, it was fear: he was afraid of me. What was I doing breaking into an office and terrifying some old guy? I had acted with my heart but my head, long overdue, kicked in. I had gone about this all wrong. I had assumed that a counsellor wouldn't give me the time of day, but the guy's job is to help people, why wouldn't he help me? I needed to diffuse the situation, to reassure him that I wouldn't hurt him, to get him on my side. I let go of Alice's files and turned to fully face him with my arms held up as though he was pointing a gun at me.

'I'm sorry, I don't want any trouble. Please ... Put. Your. Sausage. Away.' I smiled and tried to look unthreatening.

His head turned to face the sausage, which he observed with a lop-headed confusion. 'Damn this programmable matter.' He walked towards me as though instantly pacified. 'I can't get the hang of it at all. No, really I can't. One minute I'm thinking it to become a sword, because there's a degenerate in my office and a sword is a useful thing to have. A second later I notice that I am hungry and would like to eat a sausage and here I am standing in a doorway with a massive sausage in my hand. It completely undermines the sense of threat I was trying to create.'

He babbled to himself while circling the room tapping his forehead with the sausage. I could have left without him even noticing, but instead I picked up Alice's file, brought it to his desk and sat at his chair.

'It doesn't make any sense,' he continued.

'Yes it does. Programmable matter responds to your thoughts, so when you imagined it was a sword it became a sword but when you thought of a sausage ...'

'No, not the sausage ... you! *You* make no sense. Why would you take a crowbar, destroy my front door, enter my office and rifle through my files? You want to find something out about a client, that is obvious, but why did you break in?'

'Because I want to find something out about a client ...'

He interrupted and rolled his eyes, 'Yes, yes, but it's midday, why not ring the doorbell?'

Dr Genari didn't seem scared or angry any more. He had switched into some kind of detective or counsellor mode where all he could think about was trying to get to the bottom of my motives for being there. He paced around asking himself questions. His accent suggested he had grown up or spent a lot of time in India; he also had a lovely disjointed way of talking to himself – changing thought in mid-sentence as though hundreds of ideas were fighting for the attention of his voice. I wondered what his story was, how he had come to be in Elpis. Had he always been a counsellor? As he paced, and thought out loud, one thing was clear. He was a kind man: I had broken into his office, I had invaded his space, and yet he could only wonder why I needed help. I felt embarrassed that by breaking in I had not reciprocated his levels of consideration for me. I interrupted him.

'My girlfriend is your client. She's gone and I can't contact her, I'm worried, I figured maybe she'd told you something.'

'Something like how she doesn't like dating delinquents who break into offices?' His quip made me blush with shame. 'Let me guess, woman leaves, doesn't answer calls, boyfriend who has been too busy watching sport or playing guitar to pay her any attention wonders why she has suddenly left him? Tell me about your relationship.' Dr Genari sat in the very comfortable looking chair that I assumed was reserved for his clients. I could see why he was a counsellor – he was good.

I told Genari how I felt Alice and I were drifting apart, how I didn't understand her world and how the deeper she got into that world, the less she seemed interested in mine. I told him how we had shared a passion for music, but that nowadays she wasn't interested. As I spoke, the blob of programmable matter on his hand was involved in an ever-changing theatre of his internal thoughts. As I described Alice it rose up into a female figurine, only to shift, as I told him our history, into a small guitar, a miniature Beimeni Centre of Genetics, the Elpis Repository, and a Proteus. When it became a hat, a billiard cue, a penguin and a pizza, I wondered whether his attention was wandering.

'Very interesting,' he said. 'I lie, of course, none of that is remotely interesting, it is the story of every relationship: girl meets boy, girl and boy have lots in common, girl and boy grow up, life takes over, they drift apart. It is unremarkable, unlike your belief that she left you. You could be correct, but it's unlikely. I will explain. You say that the last evening you spent with her, you discussed her great passion, science? You also say that she has longed for you to take an interest in this passion, but you never do. Except last night, after years of refusing to engage with her world of science, you listen to her. Last night she got what she has longed for from you. It is a strange time to leave you.'

He had a point. He also looked bored by the conversation, as though he had had similar ones a thousand times before. It was also a conversation that wasn't getting me any closer to finding out what this man knew about Alice. I remembered that The Head had suggested other reasons why Alice might not be contactable and decided to throw one out at Dr Genari.

'Alice leaving me is one explanation, but there are others.' Genari's eyes lit up at the prospect. 'My reality checker said that maybe she doesn't want to be found or maybe *someone* else doesn't want her to be found.'

'Abduction?' Genari asked. He sat up to attention, looking very excited. 'Are you telling me that your girlfriend, my client, is in danger?'

Of course I didn't think that Alice was in danger, I just wanted to get to the bottom of all the weirdness, find out where she was and try to convince her to give me another chance. Why would anyone want Alice to disappear? I explained that she wasn't in danger. Genari looked deflated.

'Apart from the breaking and entering, you seem like a nice boy, but I cannot discuss confidential client matters, unless of course that client is in danger and it is better for them that I break my oath of confidentiality.' He raised his eyebrows expectantly. 'Are you *sure* she is not in danger?'

I could see the game he was playing. I lied and told him I believed that she could have been abducted.

He smiled and became very excited and animated. He leapt out of the chair and came around his desk to stand next to me. He clasped his hands together and wiggled his fingers before slowly and overly dramatically opening the file on the desk. 'Let's see who this girlfriend is,' he muttered to himself. The first page of the file showed a picture of Alice and some details about her. I looked up at Genari's face; it was pale, lifeless apart from the tears in his eyes.

2.3.2 Qualitative and quantitative data

Genari's expression panicked me: what did it mean? Was he worried about Alice's mental state? Did he know something about her that I didn't? Did he know a reason why she might actually be in danger? I was flustered. I spread the pages of the file across the table, searching for answers, but everything I saw was confusing: there were notes, questionnaires, sheets with numbers on, and photographs **(FIGURE 2.2)** – a mass of bewildering information.

Genari composed himself. 'As you say, many hypotheses are possible. We need to look at the evidence for each one,' he whispered more to reassure himself than me.

'You think Alice is in danger, don't you? Tell me what you know,' I demanded. I was impatient to find out where Alice was, and I hated feeling like I was missing something important.

Genari put his hand on my shoulder and smiled a reassuring smile. 'Please, I don't know anything more than what is in this file. I am sure she is not in danger; you know I had to play that game with you to give myself permission to show you the file.' He was lying; I had seen his face when he opened the file. But I had no choice but to go along with the lie if I wanted his help. I asked him how we would use the file to test our hypotheses about Alice.

'To test hypotheses you need to measure variables,' he began.

I didn't want to sit through another lecture about testing hypotheses, so I told him what Alice had taught me last night about the scientific process, and how you generate hypotheses and then work out what variables you need to measure.

'Good. Did she explain that there are different types of variables that you can collect and that they have different properties?' Alice hadn't told me that. 'For example, how might we tell whether Alice wants to leave you?'

'If she were here we could ask her, but she isn't.' I looked at the papers in front of me. 'It looks like she has answered some questions about our relationship by circling numbers on this Relationship Assessment Scale' (RAS).[20] **(FIGURE 2.2)**

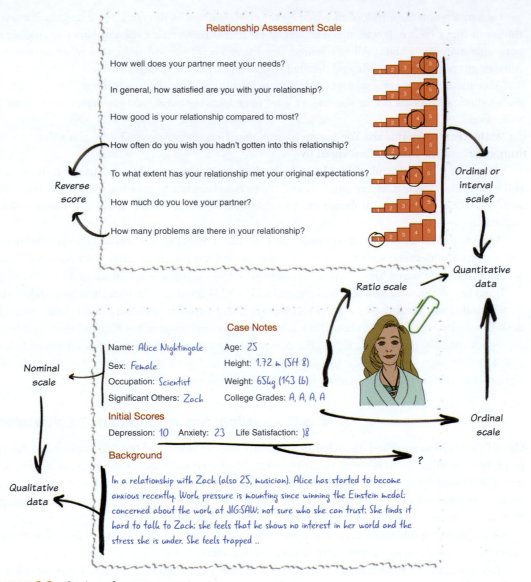

Figure 2.2 Scales of measurement

'How do these measures differ?'

'If we ask her then we have what she says, her words; but if we look at this questionnaire then we have the numbers that she circled.'

'For a man daft enough to break into an office during opening hours, you are quite smart.' The doctor smiled. 'You have highlighted two different approaches to testing hypotheses. The first is to gain support for a theory from what people say or write (**qualitative research**). One popular method for doing this is **discourse analysis**, which operates on the basic assumption that by studying what people say (and how they interact) you access real processes (whether they are psychological, societal, anthropological, and so on). For example, suppose Alice said during our sessions "I want to leave Zach". Her expression of intention is not based on only her internal experience, because the idea of leaving your partner is socially constructed; she has used that phrase because she has observed how others use that phrase. As such, her statement is taken within the context of social environment. People declare that they want to leave their partner but still very much love them and don't leave them, and perhaps Alice used that phrase within that context: it is an expression of discontentment but not an intention to leave. To do a discourse analysis you start with an individual interview (which has the advantage of control) or a group discussion (which has the advantage that you can look at natural interactions). These discussions would be transcribed. Not all of the material will be analysed, but instead, topics or themes are identified, often through reading the material and looking for reoccurring features of conversation, or intuition about important parts of the dialogue. You would then begin to index the transcripts according to the themes identified. You should reread the material to try to find counter-examples of things you've identified (this is especially important if you're working on intuitions). The analysis itself is based on writing an account of the themes you've identified or the intuitions you're following, and extracting data from the transcripts to back up (or contradict) your ideas. The analysis should be iterative: you should reassess your analysis and redraft it as readings of the transcripts throw up new ideas and examples.[21] The whole process can be theory- or data-driven. In theory-driven analysis you analyse discourse or interactions with respect to existing theory. In data-driven analysis you collect data with no particular theory in mind and let the analysis inform the development of a theory (sometimes called **grounded theory**).'

'So, to do a qualitative analysis I would need to read and transcribe all of these notes you've made from your interviews with Alice and try to pick out themes to support my hypothesis?' I didn't have time for that.

'Yes, my boy, that is what you do!' Genari said, breaking into a laugh.

'That seems like a lot of work.'

Genari's laugh escalated 'It is, my boy, it is! The alternative is to measure variables using numbers and then to use statistical methods to analyse these numbers to test your theory (**quantitative research**). You might, for example, look at Alice's scores on the Relationship Assessment Scale.'

I looked at the sheet with this scale on. The scores seemed quite positive. 'She has circled the highest score for me meeting her needs, her satisfaction, and given a low score to us having problems. **(FIGURE 2.2)** How would I know overall how she feels, though?'

'Simple, add the scores up. Notice that some questions are phrased differently than others: some ask how satisfied she is, and so if she circles a large number then it means that the relationship is good; whereas others ask what problems are in the relationship, so if she circles a large number it means the relationship is bad. First you have to reverse-score these questions that are phrased differently, then you can add all of her responses up to find out how she feels.'

CHECK YOUR BRAIN: Figure 2.2 shows Alice's responses to the seven questions on the Relationship Assessment Scale.

a. Reverse-score the two items that are reverse-phrased.

b. If i represents items on the questionnaire, what does $\sum_{i=1}^{n} x_i$ mean?

c. Do the calculation in (b) using Figure 2.2. What does the resulting score represent?

d. What is the maximum that anyone could score on the Relationship Assessment Scale?

e. Is Alice satisfied with her relationship with Zach?

I felt my diePad vibrate in my pocket. I unrolled it and noticed a message from someone called Milton. I made my apologies to the doctor and read the message. **(MEOWSINGS 2.1)** It was freaks: it addressed me as dear human, it talked about cats, but the biggest weirds was that it told me about reverse scoring: exactly what the doctor had just been explaining. I felt uneasy. Who was Milton, and how did he know my number, where I was, and what I was talking about? I scanned the room quickly; definitely only Genari and I were in here. Out of the corner of my eye I noticed a ginger cat jump down from the window ledge outside.

2.3.3 Levels of measurement

I passed the message off to Dr Genari as something about my band, and we added up Alice's scores on the Relationship Assessment Scale. It was 32 out of a maximum of 35, which made it look as though she was positive about our relationship. I was curious about what I could do with this total.

'To answer that question,' the doctor replied, 'you need to first answer the question of what type of variable you have and where it lies on the scale of measurement.'

Table 2.2 *Scoring the CAT questionnaire*

Question	Reverse phrasing?	Response given (out of 10)	Reverse score (10 – score)	Response used
How often do you wash by licking yourself?	N	9		9
How often do you scratch wood, carpets, furniture, your owner's treasured anatomical features?	N	7		7
How much do you *dislike* fish for dinner?	Y	1	9	9
How often do you sit on a fence eyeing anything that passes by with cold, suspicious indifference?	N	6		6
How much do you *dislike* sleeping?	Y	2	8	9

'The scale of what?'
'Measurement. Let me explain. Look at Alice's notes. **(FIGURE 2.2)** What variables can you identify?'

CHECK YOUR BRAIN: **List all of the variables (things that can vary) in Figure 2.2.**

'Err, variables are just things that can vary, or have different values, so her height, weight, age?'
'Very good, but there are others. The variables you mention are ones that can be directly observed: you can see her height and with a ruler measure it directly. Her occupation is also a variable, and that too can be measured directly. However, some variables you cannot measure directly, for example her depression, her anxiety, her life satisfaction, and her relationship satisfaction. In each case we can

Dear Human,

If you wanted to measure how cat-like people were, you could ask them 'How much do you like fish for dinner?', 'How much do you like to sleep?' and 'How often do you wash by licking yourself?' and get them to respond from 0 (not at all) to 10 (a lot). In each case if you are cat-like you give a higher rating than if you are not. In other words, each question is phrased so that a larger number represents more of the construct that you want to measure. However, one problem with having all of the questions phrased that way is that cat-like people might notice that all they have to do is write a '10' for every question, and because they are cat-like and, therefore, have better things to do like sleeping, and they hope that their reward for doing the survey might be a nice fish, they write '10' for every question without thinking. Likewise, the non-cat-like people might respond '0' to everything, regardless of the question. This is a form of **response bias**. To try to make people read and think about the questions on surveys it is common to use **reverse phrasing** on some questions. Normally questions are phrased so that a larger response represents more of the construct being measured; a reverse-phrased question is one where a larger response represents *less* of the construct being measured. For example, a reverse-phrased version of the question 'How much do you like fish for dinner?', would be 'How much do you *dislike* fish for dinner?'. If you were a fish lover you would give a high response to the first question, but you would give a low response to the second.

When reverse phrasing has been used for items on a questionnaire, then these items need to be **reverse-scored**, which is done by subtracting the score given from the sum of the maximum and minimum possible responses. Let us imagine we had a questionnaire to measure how cat-like someone was as described above, but with five items. Table 2.2 shows the questions. Two of them are reverse-phrased. The third column shows a person's responses on the questionnaire. For the normal questions they have given fairly large responses (9, 7, and 6 out of 10) indicating that they are quite cat-like. For the reverse-phrased items they have given lower responses (1 and 2) but, because the items are reverse-phrased, these low responses also indicate that they are quite cat-like. To make these scores comparable to the normal questions we must reverse-score them. This is done by subtracting the score on a reverse-phrased item from the maximum plus the minimum score for that item. Imagine an item where 5 responses are possible (1, 2, 3, 4, 5). The maximum plus minimum score is $5 + 1 = 6$. Reversing the scores is achieved by subtracting each score from 6, so 1 becomes 5 ($6 - 1 = 5$), 2 becomes 4 ($6 - 2 = 4$), 3 stays as 3 ($6 - 3 = 3$), 4 becomes 2 ($6 - 4 = 2$), and 5 becomes 1 ($6 - 5 = 1$). For our cat questionnaire, the largest possible response is 10, and the lowest 0, so if we add these together we get $10 + 0 = 10$. To reverse-score the items we therefore subtract them from 10: the 1 response for 'how much do you dislike fish for dinner?' becomes $10 - 1 = 9$, and the 2 response for 'how much do you dislike sleeping?' becomes $10 - 2 = 8$. As such, the low scores given by the responder on the reverse-phrased questions are converted to the corresponding high score that they would have given had the question been phrased normally.

Best fishes,
Milton

Milton's Meowsings 2.1 *Reverse scoring*

observe behaviours or responses that indicate the variable. For example, although we cannot directly measure her relationship satisfaction, if she is satisfied this will be indicated by her cognition (she will say she is satisfied), her behaviour (she will be affectionate towards you), and her physiology[22] (her pupils will dilate when she sees you). Something that cannot be directly measured is known as a **construct**. To measure these constructs you need an **operational definition** of the construct, which is a procedure (or set of procedures) for quantifying it; for example, the operational definition of "relationship satisfaction" might be "responses given to questions on the Relationship Assessment Scale".'

I was really starting to worry that this was just wasting time that I could be using to track Alice down. The doctor continued, though. 'Once you have measured a variable then what you can do with it depends on where it lies on the scale of measurement. The relationship between what is being measured and the numbers that represent what is being measured is known as the **level of measurement** (also known as the **scale of measurement**). The simplest scale of measurement is the **nominal scale**. A nominal scale is where the same names are attached to things that are the same, and different names distinguish things that are not the same. For example, I might label you "burglar" to distinguish you from me, who I might label as "civilized member of society". The doctor chuckled at his own joke. 'Similarly, we can label people according to their jobs: "musician", "scientist", "counsellor" and so on. Variables on the nominal scale are **categorical variables**, which are variables made up of categories. You will be aware already of the categorical variable of which of the natural kingdoms something belongs to: animals, fungi, plants, chromista, protozoa, or bacteria. We are both animals, and you can't be a bit of an 'animal' and a bit of a 'fungus', because otherwise you'd be an an-us and no one wants to be that.' Obviously a man who enjoyed his own jokes, he burst into a loud, wheezing laugh. 'Really, let me tell you, *no one* wants that,' he repeated slowly and laughed even harder. 'You know,' he eventually continued, 'some categorical variables contain only two categories, for example, being alive or dead, and responding "yes" or "no" to a question. A categorical variable consisting of only two categories is known as a **binary variable** or **dichotomous variable**.'

'If you're just naming things then what can you do with them?'

'You can count them. Imagine we took each thing that Alice said about your relationship in my notes and we categorized it as either "positive about Zach" or "negative about Zach". We could count how many times she is positive about you and compare it to how many times she is negative.'

'So you would be taking qualitative data – the things she said – and turning them into something quantitative?'

'Yes! Now you are getting things ... now you are getting things! Sometimes, numbers are used to denote categories. This is known as **coding**. For example, you told me that you are a musician, and I am a counsellor and Alice is a scientist. We could take the categories "musician", "scientist", and "counsellor" and assign them numbers 1, 2 and 3. Those numbers don't mean anything more than the names of the categories, but it can be helpful to use numbers to denote different categories. You can see this in real life: look at the numbers worn on the shirts of players in the Elpis soccer team; historically these numbers denote specific field positions, so the number 1 is worn by the goalkeeper and the number 9 by the centre forward. These numbers tell us nothing other than what position the player plays. We could equally have shirts with GK and CF instead of 1 and 9. A centre forward (number 9) is not necessarily better than a goalkeeper (number 1) just because she has a higher number – you wouldn't want to see your centre forward in goal! If the variable is made up of names you cannot do arithmetic on them.'

'Why not?'

'Isn't it obvious? Imagine you were managing a soccer team, your centre forward – the number 9 – is injured, do you send 9 goalkeepers (number 1s) onto the field of play in their place?' He laughed and I shook my head. 'No, and if you had categories of "drummer" and "guitarist" can you multiply them and get dru-gs?'

'Knowing most guitarists and drummers, probably ...'

'No, of course you can't', Genari interrupted, 'it is sillier than me trying to apprehend you with a sausage. The only way that nominal data can be used is to consider frequencies. We could, for example, count how often a number 9 scores a goal in a soccer game compared to a number 1.'

Dr Genari paused and took a white tissue from his trouser pocket. He wiped his glasses and looked at me, squinting his eyes. 'You have kind eyes. Caring eyes. Not burglar eyes.' He said. What an odd thing for him to say, I thought, but perhaps it was his way of explaining why he was helping me. In any case, it made me feel as though I should listen more if I wanted to know what was going on with Alice.

He placed his glasses back on and started asking me about my band. I explained that we were called The Reality Enigma. 'Oh goodness, what a grand name,' exclaimed the doctor, 'imagine your band entered one of those battle of the bands competitions, and the three winners were The Reality Enigma, Scansion and The Black Hats.' I was impressed that he knew of Scansion and The Black Hats. 'The names of the winners (a nominal variable) don't give us any information about where each band came in the contest; but if you label them according to their performance – first, second and third – then you do have this information. These categories are *ordered*. In using ordered categories we now know that the band that won was better than the bands that came second and third, but we still know nothing about the differences between categories. We do not, for example, know how much better the winner was than the runners-up: The Reality Enigma might have been easy victors, getting many more votes than Scansion and The Black Hats, or it might have been a very close contest that they won by only a single vote. When you have categories that have order, like this, you have an **ordinal scale** of measurement.'

'Is that what these ratings are that Alice gave about our relationship (FIGURE 2.2), because, you know, a 5 is a better rating than a 1 – the order matters?'

'Very good; ordinal data tell us more than nominal data (they tell us the order in which things happened) but they still do not tell us about the differences between points on a scale. To do this we need an **interval scale** or a **ratio scale**. Both of these scales of measurement have ordered categories, but also require that intervals between categories are equal. Let's think about Alice's ratings again. The Relationship Assessment Scale has a response scale with five ordered outcomes. To the question "how much do you love your partner?" Alice can answer 1, 2, 3, 4 or 5. For these values to form an interval scale it must be the case that the difference between ratings of 1 and 2 is the same as the difference between say 3 and 4, or 4 and 5. Similarly, the difference in ratings of 1 and 3 should be identical to the difference between ratings of 3 and 5. A ratio scale must also have a meaningful zero point.'

This idea confused me, and pre-empting my difficulty the doctor elaborated, 'All that means is that the zero point indicates a complete absence of the thing you are measuring. In Alice's case notes, her height and weight are both measured on ratio scales. They are ratio scales because not only are intervals consistent along the whole measure of weight and height (e.g., the difference between 100 cm and 150 cm is the same as the difference between 0 cm and 50 cm) but they have meaningful zero points: we can talk about weighing 0 kg, which means the complete absence of weight, or being 0 cm tall, which would mean the complete absence of height. Having a meaningful zero means that ratios (as well as intervals) are maintained along the measurement scale; for example, 20 kg is twice as heavy as 10 kg, and 5 kg is half the weight of 10 kg.'

Just as I wondered how you could ever be sure that a rating scale, like the one Alice completed, produced interval or ratio data, my diePad vibrated. It was another message from the mysterious Milton that was every bit as odd as the last one. (MEOWSINGS 2.2)

'Do you know someone called Milton?' I asked.

The doctor eyed me suspiciously. 'Not personally, but there are some very famous Miltons.'

I couldn't think of any. Genari asked why I was interested in people called Milton, so I showed him the message. He guessed that my earlier message had also been from this Milton and that I had lied. He really could read me very well.

Dear Human,

A lot of self-report data are probably ordinal. Imagine you and Alice both answer the question 'how much do you love your partner?' (Figure 2.2). If Alice and you both respond with a 4, can we be sure that you love each other equally? If you respond with a 5 and Alice responds with a 4, does this mean that you love Alice more than she loves you? If Alice responds with a 2 and you with a 4, do you love Alice twice as much as she loves you? Probably not: your ratings will depend on your subjective feelings about what constitutes love, and how you map them to the points on the response scale. When we ask people to rate something subjective we should probably regard these data as ordinal, although many scientists assume that people respond as though the response scale is interval. For example, we could reasonably assume that Alice's scores for her depression, anxiety and life satisfaction (Figure 2.2) are measured on an ordinal scale (Alice's score of 23 on anxiety probably means that she is more anxious than someone who scored 10), but are they interval or ratio scales? Is it meaningful to talk about 0 as signifying no anxiety at all? Can we be sure that two people who score 10 and 5 are as different in their anxiety as two people who score 12 and 17? Many scientists would treat this scale as interval, but hopefully you can see that this assumption is controversial.

Best fishes,
Milton

Milton's Meowsings 2.2   *Self-report data*

'All of the Miltons I can think of are either too famous or too dead to be messaging you,' he chuckled to himself again. 'I want to help you, but we need to move on.'

I was starting to get bored. Genari was a nice man, with an endearing, excitable manner, but I had come here to find answers about Alice and this wasn't giving them to me. It did at least take my mind off thinking about what might have happened. At least while we were talking we hadn't found evidence for a hypothesis that I wouldn't like.

The doctor interrupted my thoughts. 'The variables you measure map onto the scales of measurement that I just described. Some variables are **discrete variables**, which means that they consist of indivisible categories. This means that values fall into distinct categories – for example, whether your main job is scientist or counsellor. However, the rating scales on the Relationship Assessment Scale **(FIGURE 2.2)** are also discrete because you can enter only values of 1, 2, 3, 4 or 5; you cannot enter a value of 3.45 or 1.89. Other variables can be measured at an infinite level of precision – they are not limited to separate categorical responses – these are known as **continuous variables**. A continuous variable would be something like age, which can be measured at an infinite level of precision (you could be 25 years, 6 months, 11 days, 7 hours, 6 minutes, 11 seconds, 122 milliseconds, 3 microseconds, 12 nanoseconds old). The line between discrete and continuous variables can be blurred, though.'

Another message from Milton appeared on my diePad. Genari looked a little annoyed at it breaking his flow. **(MEOWSINGS 2.3)**

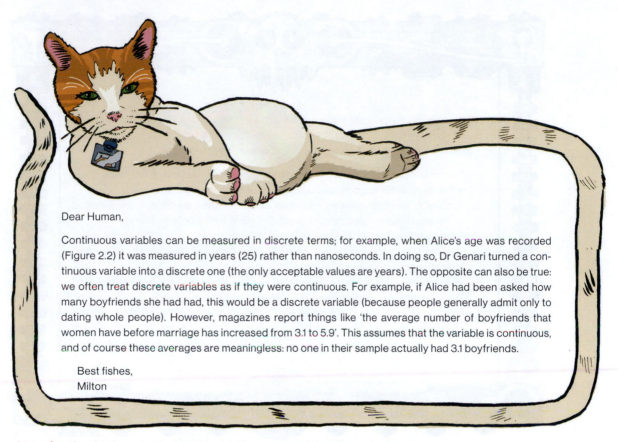

Dear Human,

Continuous variables can be measured in discrete terms; for example, when Alice's age was recorded (Figure 2.2) it was measured in years (25) rather than nanoseconds. In doing so, Dr Genari turned a continuous variable into a discrete one (the only acceptable values are years). The opposite can also be true: we often treat discrete variables as if they were continuous. For example, if Alice had been asked how many boyfriends she had had, this would be a discrete variable (because people generally admit only to dating whole people). However, magazines report things like 'the average number of boyfriends that women have before marriage has increased from 3.1 to 5.9'. This assumes that the variable is continuous, and of course these averages are meaningless: no one in their sample actually had 3.1 boyfriends.

Best fishes,
Milton

Milton's Meowsings 2.3   *Making continuous variables discrete*

2.3.4   Measurement error

I finished reading Milton's message. The doctor's manner was definitely getting more frosty; I guess it was totally rude to read messages when he was trying to talk to me. That was the problem with these things; no one gave each other proper attention any more. I felt bad. I wanted to prove I had listened, so I directed him to look at Alice's notes. **(FIGURE 2.2)** We had discovered that she rated our relationship, overall, at 32 out of 35, and her life satisfaction was 78. This seemed to suggest she was pretty happy with life. I decided to confirm this conclusion with the doctor.

'True, she scored 78 on life satisfaction, but perhaps that is 78 out of 10,000 – have you considered that?' He had definitely become tetchy.

'Err, no. Was it out of 10,000?'

'No, of course not, it was out of 100.'

'So, Alice was pretty satisfied, then.'

'Perhaps,' he begrudgingly agreed. 'But you should consider **measurement error**.'

Oh man! My heart sank. I could feel another lesson coming on. I braced myself and asked him to explain.

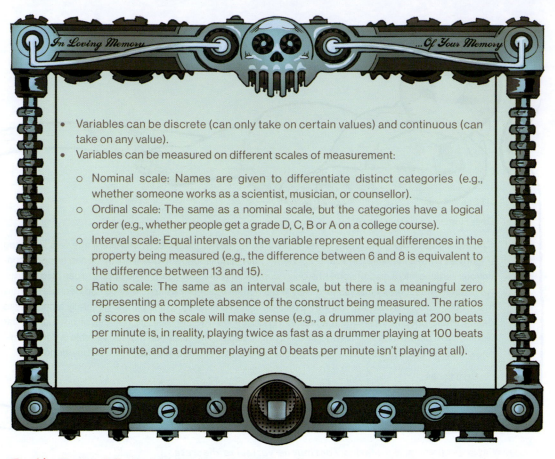

In Loving Memory ... *Of Your Memory*

- Variables can be discrete (can only take on certain values) and continuous (can take on any value).
- Variables can be measured on different scales of measurement:

  o Nominal scale: Names are given to differentiate distinct categories (e.g., whether someone works as a scientist, musician, or counsellor).
  o Ordinal scale: The same as a nominal scale, but the categories have a logical order (e.g., whether people get a grade D, C, B or A on a college course).
  o Interval scale: Equal intervals on the variable represent equal differences in the property being measured (e.g., the difference between 6 and 8 is equivalent to the difference between 13 and 15).
  o Ratio scale: The same as an interval scale, but there is a meaningful zero representing a complete absence of the construct being measured. The ratios of scores on the scale will make sense (e.g., a drummer playing at 200 beats per minute is, in reality, playing twice as fast as a drummer playing at 100 beats per minute, and a drummer playing at 0 beats per minute isn't playing at all).

Zach's Facts 2.3   *Variables and measurement*

'It's one thing to measure variables, but quite another thing to measure them accurately. Ideally we want our measure to be calibrated such that values have the same meaning over time and across situations. Height is one example: we would expect to be the same height regardless of who measures us, or where we take the measurement. It should also be roughly the same over a short time (we don't expect to grow dramatically in a week unless we are a foetus).' The doctor chuckled again. I hoped this was a sign of his mood lightening. 'There will often be a discrepancy between the numbers we use to represent the thing we're measuring and the actual value of the thing we're measuring (i.e., the value we would get if we could measure it directly). This discrepancy is known as measurement error. Imagine we could somehow invent a device that could with complete accuracy and precision measure Alice's life satisfaction. We stick her in this device and it gives a reading of 64%. We then give her a questionnaire and find that her life satisfaction is 78%. There is a difference of 14 between her actual life satisfaction and the satisfaction given by your measurement tool (the questionnaire): this is a measurement error of 14. Self-report measures are likely to have relatively large measurement error (compared to, say, a ruler for measuring length) because factors other than the one we're trying to measure will influence how people respond to questionnaires. For example, if Alice was running late, arrived late for her appointment, felt embarrassed by her lateness and this stressed her out then perhaps this would make her rate her life satisfaction a little lower than she would had she arrived in plenty of time.'

2.3.5 Validity and reliability

'So, what you're saying is that I shouldn't trust Alice's responses to the questions about our relationship?'

'Don't be so melodramatic! What I am saying is that perhaps we can't trust them, but perhaps we can – the measurement error might actually be small.'

"How can we tell?"

'One way to try to keep measurement error to a minimum is to determine properties of the measure that suggest that it is doing its job properly. The first property is **validity**, which is whether an instrument measures what it sets out to measure. The second is **reliability**, which is whether an instrument can be interpreted consistently across different situations. I'll explain. With the Relationship Assessment Scale **(FIGURE 2.2)**, validity asks the question "Do these items, in combination, actually measure relationship satisfaction?" We could look at whether the items seem to relate to the construct that they measure; this is known as **face validity**.'

'The questions *do* seem to ask about relationships.'

'Indeed, so we might say the measure has face validity. We can also compare scores on the measure to objective criteria – ideally real-world observations – to assess its **criterion validity**. For example, we could ask people to complete the Relationship Assessment Scale and then observe them with their partners in natural settings: if their scores on the measure seem to correspond with the way that they behave towards their partner then the scale has criterion validity. If scores on the instrument match real behaviour (or some other objective criterion) measured at the same time then the measure is said to have **concurrent validity**; if scores on the measure also correspond with future behaviours then it has **predictive validity**. Assessing criterion validity (whether concurrently or predictively) can be hard: it isn't always possible to find objective criteria against which to compare. Also, instruments that measure attitudes (like our Relationship Assessment Scale) can reflect the person's perception of reality rather than reality itself. You need a reality prism to disentangle those things and they were abolished after the revolution!' He smiled and I was relieved to see him get back into his stride. 'With self-report measures we sometimes look at **content validity**, which is whether the individual items represent the construct being measured, and cover the full range of the construct. With the relationship questionnaire, we can ask whether those seven items cover all aspects of "relationship satisfaction" and whether each individual item relates to relationship satisfaction.'

'There are some areas of relationship satisfaction that I can think of that aren't mentioned in those seven questions.'

'Perhaps you can question the content validity for lack of breadth then. Validity is a necessary but not a sufficient condition of a measure. We must also consider reliability, which is the ability of the measure to produce the same results under the same conditions. To be valid the measure must first be reliable. One way to test reliability is to test the same people twice: a reliable instrument should produce similar scores at both points in time (**test–retest reliability**). However, it is more complicated than you might think because some things you expect to change over time. Look at Alice's notes; we measured her relationship satisfaction many times, and most likely her scores are different. Does this mean that the scale is unreliable or does it mean that her view of your relationship changed over the months she was coming to see me?'

I had never realized that something as simple as measuring something was so fraught with problems. I also still didn't know what to do with any of this information. Dr Genari sighed. 'I have an appointment soon, and I need to order a new front door; you must leave now. Copy what you want from the file, but I want you gone in 5 minutes … and good luck.'

His abruptness shocked me. I'd started to take for granted that he would help me, and that he would tell me some secret about Alice. All I'd discovered though was how to measure stuff. He'd looked horrified when he'd opened the file and seen Alice's picture, as though he believed that she could be in *serious* danger. I wasn't going to let him get away with abandoning me.

'I really appreciate your help, but we haven't tested either hypothesis about Alice. You know, whether she has left me or someone has taken her. I told you that Alice's ratings of satisfaction and our relationship look good, so does this mean we can rule out her leaving me?'

The doctor shrugged and smiled at me. 'I am a humble counsellor. I deal with emotions, not numbers. Perhaps you should ask an expert.'

'But I don't know any experts,' I pleaded.

'Maybe your new friend Milton can help,' he said sarcastically and walked out, holding up five fingers to remind me of how long I had left in his office.

CHECK YOUR BRAIN: What is the difference between reliability and validity?

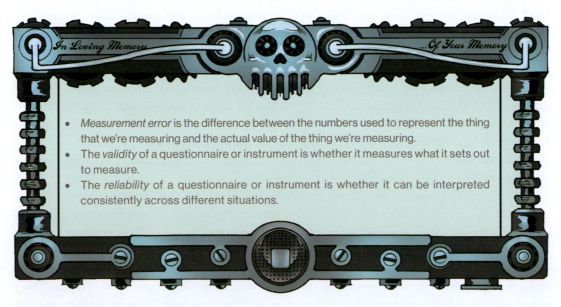

- *Measurement error* is the difference between the numbers used to represent the thing that we're measuring and the actual value of the thing we're measuring.
- The *validity* of a questionnaire or instrument is whether it measures what it sets out to measure.
- The *reliability* of a questionnaire or instrument is whether it can be interpreted consistently across different situations.

Zach's Facts 2.4   *Measurement issues*

KEY TERMS

Binary variable

Categorical variable

Coding

Concurrent validity

Construct

Content validity

Continuous variable

Criterion validity

Dichotomous variable

Discourse analysis

Discrete variable

Face validity

Grounded theory

Interval scale

Levels of measurement

Measurement error

Nominal scale

Operational definition

Ordinal scale

Predictive validity

Qualitative research

Quantitative research

Ratio scale

Reliability

Response bias

Reverse phrasing

Reverse scoring

Scales of measurement

Test–retest reliability

Validity

JIG:SAW'S PUZZLES

1   Describe the main sections of a research report.

2   What is the main difference between qualitative and quantitative research?

3   Look at the variables in Figure 2.2 and complete Table 2.3.

Table 2.3 *Table to classify variables from Figure 2.2*

Variable	Qualitative or quantitative	Level of measurement	Continuous or discrete?
Responses to questions on the Relationship Assessment Scale			
The sum of responses to questions on the Relationship Assessment Scale			
Name			
Occupation			
Significant other			
Age			
Height			
Weight			
College grades			
Depression			
Anxiety			
Life satisfaction			

4 After his conversation with Alice, Zach was wondering how he could sell more of his band's T-shirts. He found an article claiming that sales could be estimated from the price of the T-shirt and how sick the fans thought the design was (from 0 = total junk to 10 = totally on trend):

$$\text{Sales}_i = 20 + \frac{\text{Design}_i^2}{\sqrt{\text{Price}_i + 10}}$$

Use the equation and the values in the Table 2.4 to calculate the sales that would be generated from each combination of price and design. Complete the final column of the table.

Table 2.4 *Possible selling price and design ratings of T-shirts*

Price	Design	Sales
10	0	
10	5	
10	10	
15	0	
15	5	
15	10	
20	0	
20	5	
20	10	
25	0	
25	5	
25	10	

5 Calculate:

$$\sum_{n=1}^{4} n^2$$

6 Calculate:

$$15\left(\frac{2(7+2)^2}{(4\times3)}\right) - 5$$

7 Calculate:

$$20 + \frac{5(8-2)^2}{2} - 7$$

8 Zach measured 10 people's mood score out of 10 (0 = worst ever mood, 10 = best ever mood) after one of his band's gigs (Table 2.5).

Table 2.5   *Mood scores after a Reality Enigma gig*

Person	Mood Score
1	2
2	6
3	7
4	10
5	4
6	2
7	3
8	5
9	5
10	7

Use the values in the table to calculate:

$$\sum_{i=2}^{n} x_i^3$$

$$\sum_{i=4}^{9} x_i^2$$

9   Table 2.6 shows the average minutes per day that 10 Chippers spend on *memoryBank* looking at other people's lives. Using the scores in the table and remembering to use BODMAS, calculate:

$$\sqrt{\sum_{i=4}^{n} x_i}$$

Table 2.6   *Minutes per day spent on memoryBank*

Person	Average Time spent on *memoryBank* (minutes per day)
1	35
2	60
3	20
4	120
5	5
6	15
7	25
8	45
9	60
10	50

10   Nick asked fans on *memoryBank* to rate how likely they thought it was that Alice had been abducted and, also, how likely they thought it was that Alice had dumped Zach. Ratings were from 0 = not at all likely, to 10 = certain (Table 2.7). Using the scores in the table and remembering to use BODMAS, calculate:

$$\sqrt{\sum_{i=5}^{8} \frac{\mathrm{Dumped}_i^2}{\mathrm{Abducted}_i}}$$

Table 2.7 Likelihood (out of 10) of Alice having been abducted vs. her having dumped Zach, as rated by 10 fans

Fan	Abducted	Dumped
1	3	3
2	2	6
3	3	7
4	4	7
5	2	6
6	3	5
7	2	5
8	3	9
9	3	6
10	4	5

IN THE NEXT CHAPTER, ZACH DISCOVERS ...

A cat

Probability distributions

Frequency distributions

Skew and kurtosis

What women (and men) want

3

Summarizing Data

She Loves Me Not?

I wondered why the head in the reception of the Beimeni Centre of Genetics called The Head 'Leni'. I also wondered how they knew each other; was there some secret world of heads that I didn't know about? Now was not the time to worry about this; all that mattered was that he'd got us past the security and into the building. I entered one of the elevators and hit the button to take me to level 2. I'd seen the building many times before: Alice worked here and, until recently, I'd often travel with her to work before going off to our rehearsal space, which was in the same district. Security meant that I'd never been inside the building, but I'd often wondered what the space where Alice spent her days without me looked like. The cylindrical transparent blue glass capsule began to rise and follow the curved structure of the building. As we moved up the outside of the building, I looked at Elpis spreading out below me: a beautiful synergy of Clocktorian technology and modern architecture. It was exactly what I needed to see: Elpis, my home, the city of hope.

As I looked over the city I lost myself in thoughts about the previous day and how we'd ended up here. I'd left Genari's office, my mind and legs racing. I felt that Genari might know more than he let on, but I also felt that I might have played it wrong with him. He seemed concerned, and interested, that something might have happened to Alice but I didn't want to believe that she was in danger, focusing instead on how she viewed our relationship. My rudeness in checking my diePad messages also seemed to upset him. Then there were the messages themselves: why was someone called Milton contacting me, and how did he know what I was talking about at the exact moment before the message was sent? Also, why, if you were going to go to all the trouble of messaging a stranger, and employing whatever device you were using to listen to their conversations, would you send messages about variables and measurement? If he was trying to help me, weren't there more direct ways to do that? These were my thoughts as I ran from Genari's office. I didn't know where I was going, but I felt it was safer for me to get away from somewhere that I'd broken into.

Genari's office was in the district of Janus, where I lived. Elpis was made up of six districts: Postverta sat in the middle and was surrounded to the north by Antevorta, the modernist district. To the east was Porus, where the wealthy lived. Veritas was south, where the universities and hospitals were; and Egestes, the poor district, was in the west. Janus sat between Postverta and Antevorta; it was the bohemian part of town.

I reached the square in front of The Repository in a part of the city called Hallowed Point, in the Postverta district. Many visitors took Postverta to be the oldest part of Elpis because the buildings had been modelled on the Gothic architecture in what was, before the revolution, Europe. In fact it was as new as Elpis itself, but the attention to detail meant that you wouldn't know it. I suppose some people would feel that it was smoke and mirrors, a visual lie, but I liked this part of town best. Buildings define any place, and Postverta was quiet and reverential like the ornate façades that surrounded me. It was the perfect place to gather your thoughts. As I sat on The Repository steps to rest, I noticed a ginger cat scavenging under one of the café tables opposite.

I opened my pocket watch and felt comforted as The Head emerged.

He breathed deeply even though he didn't need air. 'Ah, the fresh Elpis air,' he said. 'Normally I don't get to experience it so much. I am alone in solitude and darkness, while you and the other humans enjoy the Elpis day.'

The Head really knew how to milk it.

'It's not like that,' I said, hoping to avoid his banter.

'No? Maybe you think I *love* being inside that watch? That I like feeling the endless monotony of the cogs gyrating, ticking down the seconds to my death, that I find it so much more invigorating than looking out into the world and seeing the beauty of the Elpis sky, or the carefree smiles of the Elpis children. Oh don't mind The Head, he's doing fine.'

I often enjoyed The Head's banter, but I'd had a wipe of a day already. 'Give it a rest. This is good bonding time for us.'

'The Head ain't superglue, he don't like to bond.'

Usually, the idea of my clockwork watch trying to wind *me* up amused me, but today I wondered if he was actually serious. I always assumed that when I closed the watch he just switched off, like a computer. What if I was wrong, though, maybe he *was* like some kind of electronic genie. Or maybe it was just banter; you could never tell with The Head. I needed him on side, though, so I made a deal: if he helped me out I promised to be more considerate of his needs. It did the trick: his tone lightened. I told him about my meeting with Genari, the messages from Milton and how I was worried that Alice was in some kind of danger.

'You don't *know* Alice is in danger,' he said. 'Maybe you're worrying about nothing.' The Head's empathy was unprecedented and I was touched. 'Maybe she's just dumped you!' The old Head was back before he'd had time to leave.

'Thanks,' I said sarcastically. 'You might be right, though. I don't know which is true: is she in danger or has she just dumped me? Also, there's got to be a reason why this Milton guy is messaging me. Maybe he can help, but who is he?'

The Head span as he gathered information. When he settled he said, 'I'll lay it flat for you. There are *a lot* of Miltons on the planet: 295,765, to be exact.'

My heart sank. I tried to show The Head one of his messages on my diePad, hoping he could trace it or find an address linked to it, but the messages were gone. The Head looked at me with pity as if I were imagining things. Maybe I was. The messages had all been instructing me about science, about variables and measurement. This Milton character knew about these things, so maybe he was a scientist?

The Head acknowledged my logic and span more. 'I crosschecked the Miltons for any with a prefix of Doctor or Professor, because if the guy knows about science, he's probably got a title. There are 4327 Miltons with Doctor or Professor before their name; the nearest one is Professor Milton Tipton. He lives in the city of Solitude, 3000 km from here.'

'There are no scientists called Milton from Elpis?'

The Head looked at me as though I was missing something really obvious. 'Of course there is.' He raised his eyebrows to show me that he was waiting for the penny to drop in my head. He was going to be waiting a long time.

'Professor Milton Grey?' The Head prompted, 'Inventor of the reality prism? Indirectly responsible for the Reality Revolution and the downfall of pre-Clocktorian society?'

Maybe I'd known about him at school, but these clues weren't helping me. The Head gave up. 'You know, most people have heard of him. The guy is pretty famous, and he was born here – well, in the place that became Elpis after he destroyed civilization.'

At last, a lead. 'Does he still live here?' I asked.

'Not so much, Z, he's dead.'

The Head was really annoying me. I was desperate to find Alice and he was frippin' about playing stupid games. 'What is wrong with you?' I asked, 'Why tell me about someone who is dead? A dead person is obviously not the guy sending me messages ... how about for once you do what a reality checker is supposed to do and check reality?'

'Wait up,' The Head interrupted, looking offended by my outburst, 'let The Head finish. After the revolution, Milton Grey worked for the WGA's scientific division, and then the Beimeni Centre of Genetics, but vanished in mysterious circumstances 5 years ago. People have got their theories: he was killed in a genetic experiment, the responsibility for the downfall of society led to his suicide, the WGA whacked him so that he couldn't blow the whistle on their research when he left. It's all speculation.'

'So what? The guy is dead.'

'You missed three important things: *Vanished* is not the same as *dead*, *speculation* is not *proof*, and he worked at the Beimeni Centre of Genetics, the same place that Alice works.'

I still didn't get it, so he spelled it out.

'The only scientist called Milton in Elpis used to work in the same place as Alice, and although he's assumed to be dead it has never been proved, so maybe the dude *is* worm food, but maybe it's worth going to the Beimeni Centre and having a poke about.'

It was too late to go there: it would take ages to get to Veritas, where the University was located, and by the time we arrived everyone would be finishing work. It was frustrating to wait until the morning, but I used the evening to check in with Nick to see how the #NightingaleFlyHome campaign was going. He said it was buzzing, but nothing had come back to him, just a lot of discussion amongst the female fans about how I was single now. Some of the guys were pretty excited about that too, he said. He passed on some messages of support. We had a gig soon and needed to rehearse, but Nick told me to do what I needed to do; they could rehearse without me, and he'd square it with Jessika and Joel.

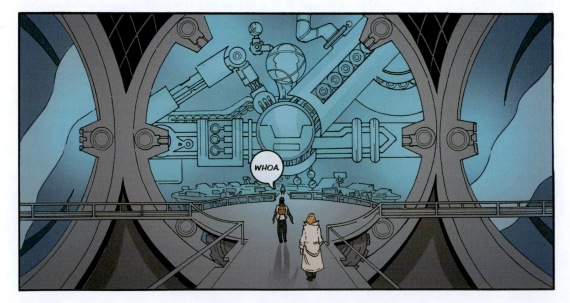

The elevator reached the second floor with a light jolt that brought me back to the here and now. A small hole formed in the transparent wall of the pod. The hole dispersed out like a drop of oil on water, making an increasing gap in the glass. Eventually it left a hole large enough that I could step out – this was programmable matter at its most elegant. I was standing in a large circular room with a corridor that divided the space into two. The walls of the rooms on each side were made of clear blue glass, giving the impression of an enormous open plan space; the light shimmered through the glass, creating a calming blue glow. I headed towards a large laboratory at the end of the corridor. As I got closer I could make out a complex jungle of spinning cogs, belts, computer monitors, fluid-filled pipes, and pistons pushing and pulling at bronze spheres, the shapes of which ebbed and flowed with the metronomic flow of the piston arms. It was like nothing I had ever seen, but mesmerizing and beautiful. The laboratory had no door, just a solid blue transparent wall. I watched as people in white coats walked to the wall and stepped through as it opened up in front of them.

'Slick', said The Head. 'Matter that is programmed to respond only to the thoughts of people that work here.'

'How do we get in?' I asked.

'How indeed,' said a quiet, almost apologetic voice, 'and more to the point, why do you want to?'

I turned around to face a petite, distinguished-looking lady. Her greying hair bobbed around her face as she tried desperately to avoid eye contact. She wore a lab coat that was far too big: the arms overhung her hands, and it was so long that it rippled out around the floor like a really underwhelming wedding dress. Around her neck was a lanyard containing a vortexID that read 'Professor Catherine Pincus'.

'I'm looking for Dr Alice Nightingale. She works here.'

Pincus shuddered slightly, her tone becoming brash. 'Why do you want her? What are you? A reporter? I have not seen Dr Nightingale this morning, and I will not comment further.' She turned and attempted to walk briskly away, but her legs tangled in her lab coat and she started to fall. Instinctively I grabbed her arm to catch her.

'Get your hands off me!' she spat.

'Sorry, I didn't want you to fall. I'm Alice's boyfriend, Zach. She's gone and I'm worried about her.'

'You'd better follow me.'

3.1 FREQUENCY DISTRIBUTIONS

3.1.1 Tabulated Frequency distributions

The Professor took us into her office. She explained that Alice worked alongside her but that she hadn't turned up to an important meeting that morning. She was being cagey; I thought that she was probably lying. I told her about my meeting with Dr Genari, about the information in Alice's file, and about how I thought at first that she had left me, but that lots of things didn't add up and that, having seen Genari, I was convinced she might be in danger. Given that I had turned up unannounced and how busy she must be, I was surprised that the Professor was attentive and sympathetic; at least until I mentioned JIG:SAW and the messages from Milton. Her face turned to stone and she looked very flustered.

I broke the awkward silence by elaborating. 'I noticed that word, JIG:SAW, throughout Alice's file. I've never heard of it. I asked my reality checker last night and he said it's an organization run by the WGA. No other information is listed – is Alice in trouble with the WGA?'

The Professor looked as though she was thinking hard. She composed herself and reassured me that I was letting my imagination get the better of me. She smiled awkwardly at me, although I think she was trying to reassure me. 'I'm no psychologist,' she said, 'but I know from working with the young scientists in my laboratory that relationships dissolve all of the time. I think it much more likely that Alice has perhaps reached a point in life where she is unsure about your relationship. Perhaps she needs some space to think things through. I think that is much more likely than some wild theory about her being in danger, don't you?'

I felt a bit embarrassed that I'd got so carried away, but I also wanted to be sure. 'I'm sorry for wasting your time, I guess you have a lot to do, you're probably right, but I'll go and see what I can find out about JIG:SAW anyway, you know, just to be on the safe side.'

I saw a twinge of panic in the Professor's eye. 'Perhaps you don't need to,' she said. 'You said you had information from Alice's file, perhaps I can help you look at that, maybe we can find some evidence that she was unhappy in your relationship – do you think she might have been?'

It was nice of the Professor to help me, suspiciously nice. Why would she want to? What the frip, though, I needed all the help I could get to untangle what was in the file, so I played along, pointing out as many reasons as I could think of for why Alice might want to leave me: I was a musician who didn't have a proper job, I dropped out of uni, I don't earn much money, I'm not that smart, I don't know about science – the list was depressing.

'... and you think that your job, money, and intelligence are the things that someone like Alice will value?'

'Yeah, isn't that what everyone wants?'

'That's an **empirical question**, one that can be answered through observation and experimentation,' replied the Professor.

'A study by Ha looked at this issue,' The Head piped up. **(REALITY CHECK 3.1)** 'Here are some data from the study about how the women in this study rated those characteristics.'

'You might sometimes wonder what it is that attracts people to each other, Z. It's a question that has played on most people's minds at some point in their life, and it's a question that we can answer with science. Ha and her colleagues conducted a study to see what characteristics 1913 teenagers (aged 13–18) valued in relationship partners.[23] She gave the adolescents a list of 21 characteristics of a future partner (reliable, honest, kind, attractive, healthy, sense of humour, gets along with friends, interesting personality, caring, romantic, flexible, intelligent, ambitious, easy going, educated, creative, wants to have children, high salary, good family, has relationship experience, and religious) and asked them to rate each one along a 10-point scale ranging from 1 (not important at all) to 10 (very important).'

Reality Check 3.1 *What women (and men) want*

'And, for balance, let's look at some of your better characteristics too,' added the Professor. 'What would you say are your three best characteristics?'

'I guess I'm kind, I make Alice laugh, and I'm really passionate and ambitious about my music.'

The Head projected a table of numbers in front of us. *(TABLE 3.1)*

Table 3.1 *A sample of data for 20 randomly selected female adolescents taken from Ha et al.[23]*

High salary	Finished education	Kind	Humour	Ambitious
4	9	10	8	7
5	8	10	10	7
9	5	8	8	8
4	4	9	8	5
5	7	10	10	8
3	3	10	8	7
10	10	10	10	10
10	7	9	9	6
6	6	8	7	7
1	4	7	6	7
3	4	8	6	4
8	8	9	8	6
8	9	9	7	5
2	1	10	8	9
6	7	9	7	7
4	3	9	8	6
8	7	9	5	7
4	6	10	9	8
7	10	10	10	5
7	9	10	9	6

I couldn't see how The Head's table helped, but the Professor explained. 'The problem with data is that you usually have too much for your mind to make sense of them. We need to help our minds by organizing the data into a more manageable form. A popular way to do this is using a **frequency distribution**, which can be either a table or a graph that shows each possible score along with the number of times that score occurred in the data. To create one, we take disorganized data and order the scores from the highest score to the lowest. We then count how many times each score occurs (the **frequency**). If we tabulate the data then we create a column (X) that contains each possible category along the scale of measurement. In this case the scale of measurement was a rating scale from 1 (not important) to 10 (very important), so we have a row for each category along that scale. *(REALITY CHECK 3.1)* We then create a column for the frequency (f), and in this we place the number of times that a score occurred.' The Professor turned and began to draw on the blue glass wall with her finger; as she touched the wall a white trail followed her finger, tracing out lines and numbers as she wrote. 'Looking at this table *(TABLE 3.2)*, we can see, for example, that two women rated high salary as very important (scores of 10), but other women rated it as relatively unimportant (scores of 4). This information is much easier to see in a frequency distribution than it is by looking at the raw data. Frequency distributions provide a visual summary of the entire set of scores. We can see **(TABLE 3.2)** also that every category on the scale of measurement was used: every point along the scale has a frequency of at least 1, indicating that at least one person used that category of the scale. Notice also that if you add up the frequencies ($\sum f$), you get the sample size (N).'

'What would you do if no one had used a particular rating; do you miss it out of the table?' I asked.

'No, you include it, but give it a frequency of 0.'

Table 3.2   *Frequency distribution of females' ratings of high salary as a characteristic in a romantic partner*

Rating (X)	Frequency (f)
10	2
9	1
8	3
7	2
6	2
5	2
4	4
3	2
2	1
1	1
	$N = \sum f = 20$

 CHECK YOUR BRAIN: Create frequency distributions for the ratings of kind, humour, and ambitious from Table 3.1.

I could see that the frequency distribution did make the data easier to understand. Thinking back to what Dr Genari had told me, the ratings we were looking at were measured on an ordinal or perhaps an interval scale. I asked whether frequency distributions could be used for nominal variables.

Professor Pincus looked impressed. 'You know about scales of measurement?' she asked. 'Well, yes, you can construct a frequency distribution for a nominal variable in the same way: you have a column that lists the categories in any order (with each category in a different row) and then in the second column list the frequency with which each entity fell into each category. For example, these ratings come from 20 females; if we wanted a frequency distribution of the nominal variable *sex*, we could list the categories "male", "female" and "non-binary" in the first column, and their frequencies in the second column. **(TABLE 3.3)** Notice that because there were no males or people selecting "non-binary", the frequency is zero, but we still include these categories because they are part of the scale of measurement of the variable *sex*.'

Much as I thought I should play along with the Professor and find out more about whether Alice might have left me, I struggled to see how this was helping. 'The tables look nice,' I said, 'but they don't tell me what people want. How does this help me to understand whether people are looking for partners with high salaries?'

'Bear with me. We can make the data clearer still by looking at the **relative frequency**, rather than the frequency itself. The relative frequency is how often a response is observed relative to the total number of responses. In the case of the salary data, we are asking "what **proportion** of women gave a

Table 3.3   *Frequency distribution of sex*

Sex (X)	Frequency (f)
Female	20
Male	0
Non-binary	0

rating of 10?", that is, how many women gave a rating of 10 relative to the total number of women who responded? We could write this as follows.' Professor Pincus traced an equation **(3.1)** on a fresh piece of blue wall.

$$\text{relative frequency} = \frac{\text{frequency of response}}{\text{total number of responses}} = \frac{f}{N} \qquad (3.1)$$

'To work out the relative frequency of a response', she continued, 'you take the frequency of that response (f) and divide it by the total number of responses (N). If we want to work out the relative frequency of, for example, a response of 10, we look at how many women gave that response – and we can see that 2 did. **(TABLE 3.2)** We then ask how many women in total gave responses, and we can see that 20 did. The relative frequency is, therefore, 2 divided by 20'. The professor scribbled some more. **(EQUATION 3.2)**

$$\text{relative frequency} = \frac{\text{frequency of a rating of 10}}{\text{total number of responses}} = \frac{2}{20} = 0.1 \qquad (3.2)$$

To check that I had understood, the Professor asked me what the relative frequency would be of a rating of 4 for this same rating scale. Looking at the second table **(TABLE 3.2)**, I said, 'the frequency of a score of four was 4, and there were 20 scores in all, so the relative frequency would be 4/20. But I don't know what that is.'

'0.20,' said The Head, looking smug.

'Oh, you've woken up now there's some maths to do, have you?' I glared at The Head, who I felt was trying to make me look stupid in front of the Professor.

'The Head is always awake, Z – *always*,' he said, alluding to our earlier conversation. Was The Head really still awake when I closed the watch? I needed to stay focused. I asked the Professor what a score of 0.2 actually meant.

 CHECK YOUR BRAIN: Calculate the relative frequencies of the remaining scores from the frequency distribution in Table 3.2.

'To make it easier to understand, think of these relative frequencies as percentages, which you do by multiplying them by 100. In other words, 0.2 becomes 20%. Therefore, rather than saying that the proportion of women who rated a high salary as 4 out of 10 was 0.20, we can say that 20% of women rated a high salary as 4.'

I felt my diePad vibrate – it was another message from Milton. **(MEOWSINGS 3.1)** I showed it to the Professor before it had time to disappear. I asked her if there was a Milton working there, someone who might be sending these messages. The message troubled the Professor, but she denied knowing anyone called Milton. When I asked whether it was true that Professor Milton Grey had worked here, she became agitated. 'Professor Grey, as is well documented, is dead – now do you want my help or are you going to continue to ask me impertinent questions?' Before waiting for an answer, she continued: 'The interesting part is if we look at the **cumulative percentage**. Rather than looking at the frequencies of individual categories along the scale, we can look at the **cumulative frequency**, which means that we look at the total frequency of all categories up to and including the category of interest.' The Professor started to add columns to the table she had drawn. *(TABLE 3.4)* 'If we start at the bottom, then a rating of 1 had a frequency of 1; there are no categories before it so the cumulative frequency is also 1. Moving up to the next category (a rating of 2), we see this received one response also, so the frequency is 1, but the cumulative frequency is the frequency of this category and the one before, so it is $1 + 1 = 2$. Moving up to the next category (a rating of 3), this response had a frequency of 2, but the cumulative frequency will be this value added to the frequencies of the previous categories, so it is $1 + 1 + 2 = 4$. Moving up to the next category (a rating of 4), this response had a frequency of 4, so the cumulative frequency will be this value added to the frequencies of the previous categories, so it is $1 + 1 + 2 + 4 = 8$. In general, the cumulative frequency for category n is the frequency of that category added to the cumulative frequency for the *previous* category (i.e., $n-1$). We could write that like this.' The Professor moved across to an untouched part of the blue glass wall and began to write. *(EQUATION 3.3)*

$$\text{cumulative frequency}_n = f_n + \text{cumulative frequency}_{n-1} \qquad (3.3)$$

I still didn't see how this was getting me any closer to finding out whether or not Alice was likely to have left me. I was getting a little frustrated; I felt that I needed to listen in case the Professor suddenly dropped some payload of information, but I also felt empty without Alice. Was it too much to ask to have someone tell me where she was or what was happening? Apparently it was: the Professor was interested only in talking statistics at me as though some unstoppable teaching node had activated in her brain. She didn't pause to think about whether I understood what she was saying; this was exactly why I'd dropped out of uni. 'The cumulative frequency is all very well,' she continued, 'but if we again look at the percentage rather than the raw frequencies then we have a more intuitive way of summarizing scores. Let's look back at the original frequency distribution *(TABLE 3.2)*, now calculate the relative frequencies, and then multiply these by 100 to get the percentages for each category.' *(TABLE 3.4)*

 CHECK YOUR BRAIN: *Calculate the percentages of the scores from the frequency distribution in Table 3.2.*

'We can calculate the cumulative percentages just like we did for the frequencies. Start at the bottom; a rating of 1 had a percentage of 5%, there are no categories before it so the cumulative percentage is also 5%. Moving up to the next category (a rating of 2), we see this received 5% of responses also, so the percentage is 5%, but the cumulative percentage is the percentage of this category and the one before, so it is $5\% + 5\% = 10\%$. Moving up to the next category (a rating of 3), this response had a percentage of 10%, but the cumulative percentage will be this value added to the percentage of the previous categories, so it is $5\% + 5\% + 10\% = 20\%$. Again, in general the cumulative percentage for category n is the percentage for that category added to the cumulative percentage for the *previous* category (i.e., $n-1$).' *(EQUATION 3.4)*

$$\text{cumulative percentage}_n = \text{percentage}_n + \text{cumulative percentage}_{n-1} \qquad (3.4)$$

Dear Human,

Relative frequencies are proportions. A proportion in statistics usually quantifies the portion of all measured data in a particular category in a scale of measurement. Basically, it is the frequency of a particular score or category relative to the total number of scores.

$$\text{proportion} = \frac{\text{frequency of score/category}}{\text{total number of observations}} = \frac{f}{N}$$

Proportions can vary from 0 (this category contains none of the measured scores) to 1 (this category contains all of the measured data). Normally the values fall somewhere in between (it would be rare to find that everyone in your sample had given the same response or score), so you will see values that are decimals, such as 0.15, or 0.54. Decimals are quite unpleasant, and students do not like them very much, so it can be useful to express proportions and relative frequencies as percentages instead. Many students find percentages unpleasant too, but usually less unpleasant than proportions. We can easily convert a relative frequency or proportion to a percentage by multiplying it by 100:

$$\text{percentage} = \text{proportion} \times 100 = \frac{f}{N} \times 100$$

If you have a relative frequency or proportion of 0.15, this equates to 100 × 0.15 = 15%. In other words, this response makes up 15% of all responses (i.e., 15% of people gave this response). You could express this information in two ways:

1   The proportion of women who rated high salary's importance at 8 out of 10 was 0.15.
2   15% of women rated a high salary's importance at 8 out of 10.

Both say exactly the same thing, but arguably the second way, which uses percentages, makes more intuitive sense to most people because they are more familiar with percentages than proportions.

Best fishes,
Milton

Milton's Meowsings 3.1   *Relative frequencies, proportions and percentages*

'Notice that the cumulative percentage will be 100% once we reach the last category on the scale. That means that all of the data are accounted for. We can also calculate the cumulative percentages starting at the highest category and working our way down. Either way is acceptable; it depends what the scale of measurement is and which way around is most useful for the question that you want to answer.' **(TABLE 3.4)**

Table 3.4 Frequency distribution of females' ratings of high salary as a characteristic in a romantic partner, including relative frequencies, percentages and cumulative percentages

Rating (X)	Frequency (f)	Cumulative frequency (up)	Relative frequency (f/N)	Percentage	Cumulative percentage (up)	Cumulative percentage (down)
10	2	20	0.10	10%	100%	10%
9	1	18	0.05	5%	90%	15%
8	3	17	0.15	15%	85%	30%
7	2	14	0.10	10%	70%	40%
6	2	12	0.10	10%	60%	50%
5	2	10	0.10	10%	50%	60%
4	4	8	0.20	20%	40%	80%
3	2	4	0.10	10%	20%	90%
2	1	2	0.05	5%	10%	95%
1	1	1	0.05	5%	5%	100%

CHECK YOUR BRAIN: Compute tables of the relative frequencies, percentages and cumulative percentages for the ratings of kind, humour, and ambitious from Table 3.1.

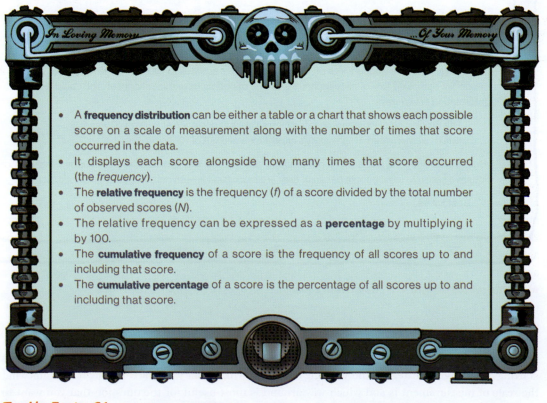

- A **frequency distribution** can be either a table or a chart that shows each possible score on a scale of measurement along with the number of times that score occurred in the data.
- It displays each score alongside how many times that score occurred (the *frequency*).
- The **relative frequency** is the frequency (*f*) of a score divided by the total number of observed scores (*N*).
- The relative frequency can be expressed as a **percentage** by multiplying it by 100.
- The **cumulative frequency** of a score is the frequency of all scores up to and including that score.
- The **cumulative percentage** of a score is the percentage of all scores up to and including that score.

Zach's Facts 3.1 Frequency distributions

At last, she paused for breath. 'I'm sorry Prof, but I still don't see how this tells me what people want.'

Pincus looked excited as though she had reached the pinnacle of her great lecture. 'This is a 10-point scale, ranging from 1 (not important) to 10 (very important). The mid points of 5–6 are the points at which the response changes from 'not important' to 'important'. A 5 is the last rating on the 'not important' side of the scale. What is the cumulative percentage of the response of 5?'

I looked at the table on the wall. **(TABLE 3.4)** 'It's 50%.'

'And what does that mean?' enquired the Professor.

'It means that 50% of women gave a score of 5 or lower, which means that 50% of women thought that a high salary was unimportant to some degree.'

'Excellent, Zach. Does that answer your question?'

'A bit. I mean, it tells me that about half of women think a high salary is important. It doesn't tell me whether Alice is one of those 50%, though.'

3.1.2 Grouped Frequency distributions

'That's a very good point, Zach. We don't know Alice's score, so let's look at some data where we do know her score. For example, what is in her file that you copied from the counsellor?'

'I have her Relationship Assessment Scale (RAS) score – it was 32.' **(SECTION 2.3.4)**

'Perfect. Can your reality checker get us some data from other women on the same scale?'

'I can get you anything you want,' said The Head with a glint in his eye. 'Here are 20 scores on the Relationship Assessment Scale **(FIGURE 2.2)** from females of the same age as Alice: 16, 23, 26, 22, 14, 20, 8, 19, 22, 25, 17, 26, 27, 11, 32, 17, 20, 17, 14, 28'.

'What is the range of this scale?' enquired the Professor.

'According to Dr Genari, it ranges from 7 (someone circles 1 for all seven questions) to 35 (someone circles 5 for every question),' I replied.

'That's quite a range; too much to put in a frequency distribution, because with a highest score of 35 and a lowest of 7 you would need 29 rows in the table to display each score. We will be better off using a **grouped frequency distribution**, which is a frequency distribution where we group scores together. We divide the scale of measurement into equal parts, each one known as a **class interval**. For example, a scale of 1 to 10 could be broken into five equal class intervals of 1–2, 3–4, 5–6, 7–8 and 9–10, or two equal class intervals of 1–5 and 6–10. In both cases the class intervals are equal in size: in the first example every class interval contains two numbers, in the second both class intervals contain five numbers. The quantity of numbers in a class interval is known as the **class interval width**.'

'How do you know how wide to make the intervals?'

'There are some simple rules of thumb. You want enough intervals that you retain the pattern within the data. Imagine for these data that you used a single class interval ranging from 7 to 35. All of the scores are contained within that interval so you would have a frequency of 20 and you'd know nothing about how those scores are distributed. It would be pointless. We need to have enough intervals that we can see the pattern of the data, but not so many that the frequency distribution is unmanageable. Normally you would aim for no fewer than 5 intervals, and no more than about 15; so approximately 10 intervals is reasonable, but how many intervals might be best will depend upon how widely dispersed your scores are. The intervals you create must contain all values of the scale of measurement but should be *mutually exclusive*, which means that they must not overlap. For example, you could not have intervals of 5–7 and 7–9 because both of these intervals contain the value 7, and you could not have intervals of 5–7 and 9–11 because the value 8 is entirely missing. To sum up, the class intervals should cover the entire range of scores, with no gaps and no overlaps. You might consider making the interval width a simple number such as 2, 5, 10 or a multiple of 5 or 10; doing so will help the reader to understand the frequency distribution because people are generally comfortable with multiples of 2, 5 and 10. Finally, the lower boundary of the interval should be a multiple of the width.

For example, if the width is 5, then the intervals should start on 0, or a multiple of 5 such as 5, 10, or 25. Let's turn the RAS data into a grouped frequency distribution. First, we will try an easy interval such as 5. What was the lowest score, Zach?'

'It was an 8.'

'Good, so we need the first interval to contain 8.'

'So, we could start it with 8?'

'We could, but that would not include the lowest *possible* score of 7. Also, if we start it at 5 then the intervals will be easier to follow because we will have 5–9, 10–14, 15–19 and so on; each interval begins with a multiple of 5. The highest score was 32, so we carry on creating intervals until we reach an interval that contains this value, but ideally we'd also have an interval containing the highest possible score of 35. Let me draw a table. **(TABLE 3.5)** Now we count how many scores fall within the boundaries of each interval. With interval widths of 5, we end up with six class intervals, which is perhaps a little on the low side. In fact, the frequencies across intervals are quite similar – half of them have a frequency of 5. An alternative is to reverse the approach and to decide in advance how many intervals we want, and then work back to find out the interval width.' The Professor wrote out an equation **(3.5)** on the wall.

$$\text{interval width} = \frac{\text{range of scores}}{\text{number of intervals}} = \frac{\text{highest score} - \text{lowest score}}{\text{number of intervals}} \qquad (3.5)$$

'Imagine we want 10 intervals,' she continued. 'The highest score was 32 and the lowest 8, so we would get the following'. **(EQUATION 3.6)**

$$\text{interval width} = \frac{32 - 8}{10} = \frac{24}{10} = 2.4 \qquad (3.6)$$

'It would be complicated to have intervals of 2.4, so we can round this number up to 3, and we should find we get about 10 intervals. With what value should we start the first interval?' she asked.

'8 is the lowest score, and 7 was the lowest *possible* score so maybe start with that, but earlier you said to start the intervals with a value that is a multiple of the width. The width is 3, so we could start with 3, 6, 9 and so on. If we start the first interval with 6, then with a width of 3 the first interval would include the values of 6, 7 and 8; this is perfect because it will contain the lowest value in the data, and the lowest *possible* value on the scale.'

'Very good, Zach, very good indeed.' The Professor started scribbling another table, speaking as she drew. 'We would create intervals of 6–8, 9–11, 12–14, and so on. Then we count the frequency with which scores fall into those categories, just like we've done before. **(TABLE 3.5)** You can see that we have ended up with 10 class intervals, and it shows a little more detail about how the frequency of scores tapers off at the extremes of the scale; so the bulk of responses are between 15 and 26, and the frequency gradually declines towards the low extreme of 7 and the high extreme of 35. By comparing these two frequency distributions you can see that with fewer categories you get less detail, so there is a trade-off: although we want to simplify the data to a manageable number of categories, we don't want so few categories that we start to lose too much detail.'

'I don't want to be rude, Prof, but again, how does this tell me about Alice's score?'

'Patience,' she replied a little sternly. 'Let's convert the frequencies in our distribution **(TABLE 3.5)** into percentages, and then let's compute the cumulative percentage going from the lowest to highest scores.'

The Professor added columns to the frequency distribution and filled in the values for each group of scores. **(TABLE 3.6)** 'Remind me what score Alice had?' she asked.

'32,' I replied.

Table 3.5 *Grouped frequency distributions of the RAS data, using different class interval widths*

Width = 5		Width = 3	
RAS (*X*)	Frequency (*f*)	RAS (*X*)	Frequency (*f*)
5–9	1	6–8	1
10–14	3	9–11	1
15–19	5	12–14	2
20–24	5	15–17	4
25–29	5	18–20	3
30–34	1	21–23	3
35–39	0	24–26	3
		27–29	2
		30–32	1
		33–35	0

 CHECK YOUR BRAIN: Convert the frequencies for the grouped frequency distribution with widths of 3 in Table 3.5 into percentages and compute the cumulative percentage going from the lowest to highest score.

'Looking at the percentages, Zach, how many women gave a response of 32?'.

I looked at the table **(TABLE 3.6)** and replied '5%, because that's the percentage for the category 30–32?'

'Very good, but remember that some of this 5% might have had scores of 30 and 31, which are lower than Alice's score of 32. Now look at the cumulative percentage, what percentage of women gave a score *lower* than 32?'

 CHECK YOUR BRAIN: Compute the percentage and the cumulative percentage (from low scores to high) for the grouped frequency distribution with widths of 5 in Table 3.5.

Table 3.6 *Grouped frequency distribution of the RAS data with percentage and cumulative percentage*

RAS (*X*)	Frequency (*f*)	Relative frequency (*f/N*)	Percentage	Cumulative percentage (up)
6–8	1	0.05	5%	5%
9–11	1	0.05	5%	10%
12–14	2	0.10	10%	20%
15–17	4	0.20	20%	40%
18–20	3	0.15	15%	55%
21–23	3	0.15	15%	70%
24–26	3	0.15	15%	85%
27–29	2	0.10	10%	95%
30–32	1	0.05	5%	100%

To find out how many scores were lower I figured that I needed to look at the cumulative percentage up to the category before 30–32. The cumulative percentage of scores up to and including 27–29, was 95%. Wow, that's huge. Did that mean that in a group of women similar in age to Alice, 95% of them rated their relationship lower than she rated our relationship? I asked the Professor.

'Well done; it tells us that relative to other women of her age, Alice was very satisfied with your relationship when she completed this questionnaire.' Professor Pincus looked a little disappointed at the news; it was as if the data hadn't shown what she hoped it might.

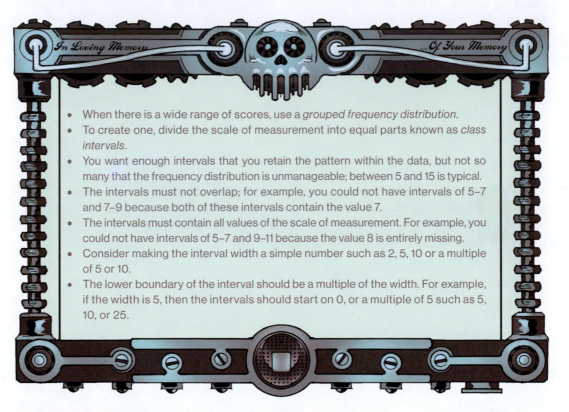

- When there is a wide range of scores, use a *grouped frequency distribution*.
- To create one, divide the scale of measurement into equal parts known as *class intervals*.
- You want enough intervals that you retain the pattern within the data, but not so many that the frequency distribution is unmanageable; between 5 and 15 is typical.
- The intervals must not overlap; for example, you could not have intervals of 5–7 and 7–9 because both of these intervals contain the value 7.
- The intervals must contain all values of the scale of measurement. For example, you could not have intervals of 5–7 and 9–11 because the value 8 is entirely missing.
- Consider making the interval width a simple number such as 2, 5, 10 or a multiple of 5 or 10.
- The lower boundary of the interval should be a multiple of the width. For example, if the width is 5, then the intervals should start on 0, or a multiple of 5 such as 5, 10, or 25.

Zach's Facts 3.2   *Grouped frequency distributions*

3.1.3 Graphical Frequency distributions

'Props and all that, but I'm not being ridiculous. A cat just walked into your office, which in itself is spooks, but then it opened its little cat mouth and said "Hello, Catherine", which takes spooks to a new level.'

'There's no cat,' replied the Professor in a tetchy tone.

'There is. I saw it.'

'Are you calling me a liar?' The Professor spat the words at me. Just like with Genari, I was losing my grip on the situation. It was becoming awkward, and I don't like awkwardness one bit: I avoid it like I avoid tarantulas, and I steer clear of them as a matter of priority. On the other hand, the Professor *was* lying. Or maybe I really was losing it – there were the messages from Milton that were gone when I tried to show The Head, a girlfriend who apparently never existed, and now a talking cat. Maybe my whole existence wasn't real, maybe someone had put a reality prism on my head while I was asleep and I was seeing my actual reality stripped of my subjective experience? I mean, none of our generation had actually worn a reality prism, we'd been told that you see both realities at the same time, but maybe this was a new type of reality prism where you got to live objective reality rather than your subjective one. My mind was on overdrive thinking about what was and wasn't real. The Professor was still glaring at me, waiting for my response. I needed to get her back on side.

'Of course I don't think you're lying to me. You've been so gracious in giving me your time, I trust you completely. It's just that there is actually a cat; look, it's sitting on your desk.'

I pointed to the ginger cat and we both turned to her desk. The cat lifted its paw and waved at us. I thought it might be smiling, but cats don't smile. Perhaps talking ones do – this was new territory for me. It crossed my mind that it was ginger, just like the cat I'd seen outside Dr Genari's window. The Professor looked pale.

'Oh, him,' the Professor said, feigning surprise really unconvincingly. She adopted a faux jovial tone. 'That's just the lab cat. I didn't notice him come in.'

'And you didn't notice him saying "Hello, Catherine"?'

'I think you're stressed about Alice. It is a scientific fact that cats cannot and never will be able to speak.' To prove her point, the Professor addressed the cat while fixing him with a glance that made clear to him that if he spoke his tuna supply was going to dry up. Her eyes narrowed as she spoke, 'Would you be so kind as to tell this young man your name?'

Do cats have eyebrows? I'm not sure, but this one seemed to raise something above his eye. He stared blankly back at the Professor as though engaging her in a secret battle of wills. After a long contemplative pause, he twisted his body and began licking his backside.

The Professor turned back to me and smiled a relieved sort of smile. 'See – just an ordinary cat. Now shall we resume with what women want?'

I agreed. Whatever was going on here the Professor didn't want me to know, and I still felt that I was better off keeping her talking in case something useful came out.

As though nothing had happened, the Professor switched back into teaching mode. I might as well not have been in the room. 'We've looked at frequency distributions as tables, but often it is more appealing to display them as a **graph** (also known as a **chart**). Visually this can give you a very immediate impression of how scores in your data are distributed. Graphs come in lots of different shapes and sizes, but they all have a horizontal and vertical line known as the *axes*. The horizontal line usually displays a predictor variable, or an independent variable, and because these variables are usually denoted with the letter x it is known as the **x-axis**, or **abscissa**. The vertical line usually displays an outcome variable, or a dependent variable, and because these variables are usually denoted with the letter y it is known as the **y-axis**, or **ordinate**. When you have a scale of measurement that is interval or ratio, you can use a **histogram** and **frequency polygon** to display the frequency of scores. These graphs display the possible scores of the measured variable on the x-axis, and the frequency with

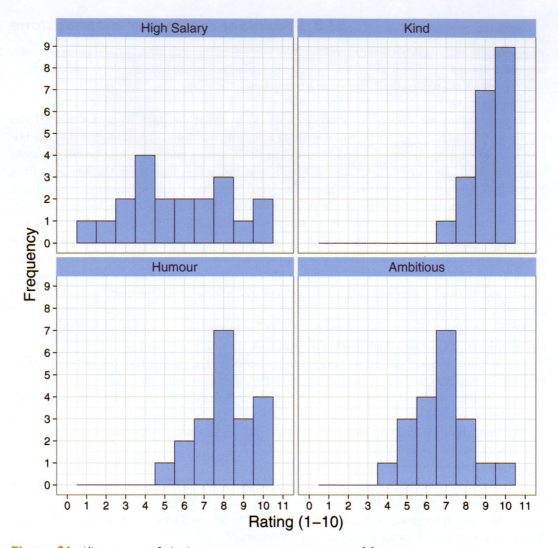

Figure 3.1 *Histograms of the importance to teenage women of four characteristics in their partners*

which each score occurs on the *y*-axis. The difference between these graphs is that a histogram plots the frequencies as bars rising up from the *x*-axis, whereas a polygon plots them as points that are then connected by straight lines. Let me show you some examples.'

The Professor instructed the wall to display histograms of the frequencies of 20 women rating the importance of four characteristics of their partners. **(REALITY CHECK 3.1)** She chose high salary and the three characteristics that I had told her that I had: kindness, humour and ambition. An image appeared on the wall **(FIGURE 3.1)** and the Professor explained it.

'To produce a histogram you put each category of measurement along the *x*-axis. For these data the women rated each characteristic along a scale from 1 (not important at all) to 10 (very important), so we list these categories of response along the horizontal in ascending order. Then for each category we draw a bar that is as tall as the frequency of responses for that category. The width of the bar represents the limits of the category. Look at the values of the bars for high salary in the top left of the figure and compare them to the values in the tabulated frequency distribution; **(TABLE 3.2)** you will see that they are the same. Therefore, these histograms are another way to represent a frequency distribution. However, they make it easier to spot the patterns of the data.'

'What do you mean by patterns?'

'Look at the high salary histogram. It is very flat: the bars are quite similar heights across all of the categories. This suggests that about as many women rated a high salary important as rated it unimportant. In fact, each point along the scale was endorsed by a similar number of women, which suggests that there is no consistent pattern in women valuing a high salary in this sample. Compare this with the kindness ratings in the top right of the figure. What do you notice?'

'Most of the low value categories (i.e., unimportant) have no bars, so few women endorsed those categories, but lots of women endorsed higher values; in fact most women endorsed 9 or 10.'

'And what can you infer from that?'

'The women in this sample consistently thought that kindness was an important characteristic in a romantic partner.'

'You told me that you are kind, so if Alice is like the people within this sample she will value this characteristic.'

'So, we can use patterns in the data to draw conclusions beyond those data.'

'Yes. This is the power that data give us. What might you conclude about attitudes towards humour and ambition?'

CHECK YOUR BRAIN: What can you conclude from Figure 3.1 about the women in the sample's attitudes towards humour and ambition in their relationship partners?

I thought about this question. It seemed to me that the taller bars were mainly at the top end of the scale. In fact, for humour the tallest bar was at 8 and for ambition it was 7, both of which represent 'fairly important'. Also, the bars were very small or non-existent below 5, which means that no one really responded that these characters were very unimportant; the vast majority put their response above 5, which means they thought the characteristic was important to some extent. I gave the Professor my assessment and she looked pleased with me. It made me feel good to have impressed a Professor.

The Professor instructed the wall to produce another image. (FIGURE 3.2) 'Now look at frequency polygons of the same information. Notice that instead of a bar, each frequency is represented by a dot, and these dots are joined by straight lines.'

'Why does the x-axis go up to 11 when the response scale stopped at 10?' I asked.

'That is so that the line can return to zero to create the polygon. It is common with these graphs to have an extra category above and below the limits of the scale so that the polygon can start and finish at zero. What do you notice about the shapes of these polygons?'

'They are roughly the same as the shapes of the bars in the histograms.' (FIGURE 3.1)

'Yes! Let me show you what the histogram of the humour ratings looks like with the polygon superimposed on it. (FIGURE 3.3) The dots of the polygon mark out the midpoint of each bar. Compare the histograms (FIGURE 3.1) and polygons (FIGURE 3.2) of the four characteristics that we have looked at and you will see that the shapes are the same.'

'What do you do if you have grouped data?'

'You can draw both histograms and polygons of grouped data. For example, let's look back at the RAS scores. We produced a tabulated frequency distribution of those scores using a class interval width of 3. (TABLE 3.5) We can draw that as a histogram by having each bar represent each class interval, or as a polygon by having each point located at the midpoint of the interval. (FIGURE 3.4) So, for example, the first interval was 6–8, so the midpoint would be 7. Again, you should see that the histogram and polygon show the same shape, so you would normally draw one of these graphs, not both. What would you conclude about the RAS scores from these graphs?'

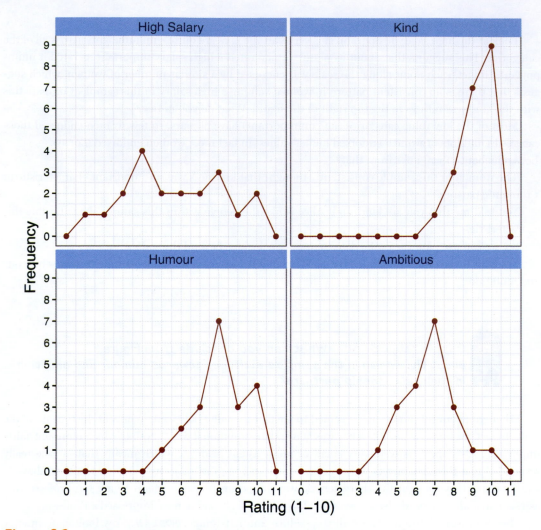

Figure 3.2 Frequency polygons of the importance to teenage women of four characteristics in their partners

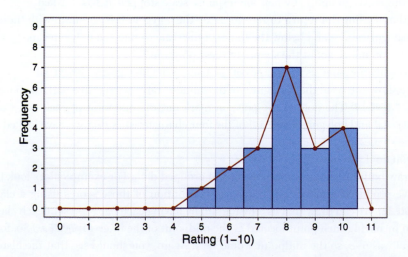

Figure 3.3 Histogram of ratings of humour as a characteristic in a romantic partner with the frequency polygon superimposed

The cat on the table started playing with something sticking out of his collar while looking nonchalantly around the room. Was it a Proteus? My diePad buzzed and a brief notification showed me how to compute the midpoint that the Professor had just mentioned. **(MEOWSINGS 3.2)**

Noticing that I had been distracted, the Professor repeated her question about the RAS scores. Looking at her diagram **(FIGURE 3.4)**, the first three bars looked quite short and so did the last two, but the bars in the middle were relatively high. It looked as though relatively few women were really dissatisfied with their relationships (not many women had scores between 6 and 14) and few were really satisfied (not many women scored above 27). So, the majority of women had satisfaction scores between about 15 and 26.

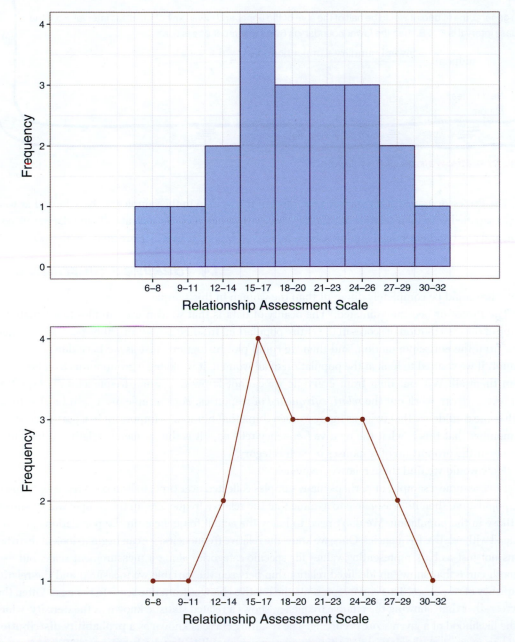

Figure 3.4 *Histogram and frequency polygon of the RAS data*

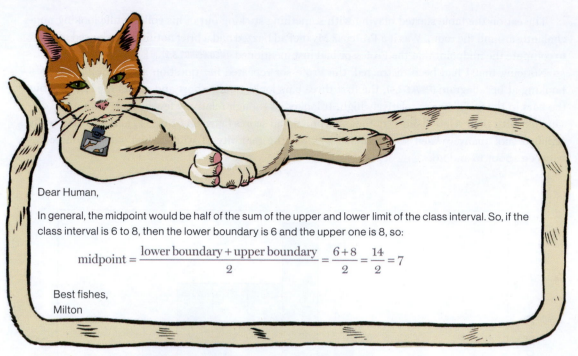

Dear Human,

In general, the midpoint would be half of the sum of the upper and lower limit of the class interval. So, if the class interval is 6 to 8, then the lower boundary is 6 and the upper one is 8, so:

$$\text{midpoint} = \frac{\text{lower boundary} + \text{upper boundary}}{2} = \frac{6+8}{2} = \frac{14}{2} = 7$$

Best fishes,
Milton

Milton's Meowsings 3.2   Midpoints

The Professor agreed. 'Can you see now, most of the women in the samples we have looked at were not as satisfied with their relationship as Alice was with yours, they did not rate a high salary as important, and most of them valued kindness, humour and ambition, all of which are qualities that you have?'

3.1.4 Idealized distributions

'But Alice could be completely different than the women in this sample.'

The Professor became animated. 'The beauty of data is that we can use samples to estimate the shape of the distribution of scores in the entire population. In some cases it might be possible to collect data from the entire population, and then we could plot histograms just as we have done. Often we cannot: if we wanted to look at the population of all women, it is too big a group for us to collect data from them all. Without data from everyone we cannot know the actual frequencies of responses. However, we can work out the *relative frequency* of responses. For example, we might be able to say with some confidence that twice as many women think that humour is important in a partner as don't. Remember that this is what the relative frequency tells us – it is the frequency relative to the entire sample or the proportion of responses in each category.'

'How would we find these relative frequencies?'

'If we assume a sample, or perhaps many samples collected over time, to be a good representation of the population, then it's reasonable to assume that the relative frequencies in the sample will be similar to those in the population. We don't need to know the actual frequencies in the population, we work instead with relative frequencies. Once we know the relative frequencies, we can begin to look at distributions not just as bars representing values for specific categories along a measurement scale, but as a smooth curve that shows an idealized relationship between the variable we measured and the relative frequency of responses. This curve represents the relative changes from one score to the next. Often this curve, rather than showing the relative frequency, shows a related statistic known as the **density**, which is the likelihood of a given score occurring. The resulting curve is known as a **probability distribution** and has an exact mathematical definition known as a **probability density function**.' *(SECTION 7.2.2)*

'How does this help us?'

The Professor turned to one of the few patches of wall that wasn't already covered in tables, graphs or equations, and instructed the wall to produce another graph. **(FIGURE 3.5)** 'Look here. Assuming we can have a continuous measure of humour, the bars show the relative frequency of responses to humour in the sample of 20 people. The curve is an idealized representation of how the relative frequency changes across the rating scale. This idealized shape reiterates the fact that we would expect women's evaluations of humour as a desirable characteristic in a partner to cluster at the top end of the response scale. None of this proves that Alice likes her partner to be funny, but we can start to look at how likely it is that she would, and based on this sample it seems probable that she would like someone funny, kind and ambitious. Someone like you, Zach. If the samples we have looked at are representative of women more generally, and they might not be, then you have the right characteristics to keep most women happy.'

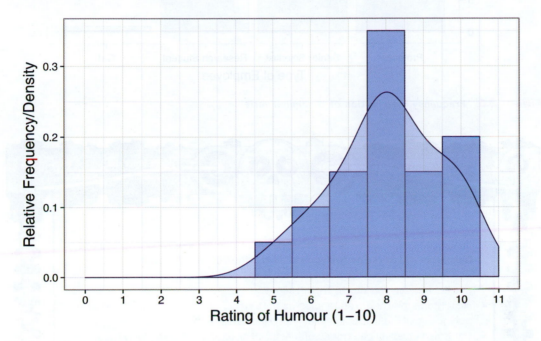

Figure 3.5 *A plot of the relative frequency of ratings of humour and an 'idealized' curve*

3.1.5 Histograms for nominal and ordinal data

I felt a wave of joy; the evidence from Alice's file and from looking at what women want generally seemed to be going against the assumption that Alice had left me. This felt good. I started to daydream about seeing her, about holding her, about being together again, but then it hit me: if she hadn't dumped me then one of the alternatives was that she was in trouble. I felt an urgency to do something – I wasn't sure what, but *something*. A young man walking through the parting wall broke my concentration. He tapped the wall, addressing the Professor as he did.

'I have the latest breakdown of our employees for you to sign off, Professor Pincus,' he said.

'Not now,' she said, urgently trying to usher him out of the room. It was too late, a graph had already appeared on the wall. **(FIGURE 3.6)**

'Is that a histogram?' I asked.

'Of a sort,' the Professor responded.

'Why are there gaps between the bars? In the histograms we looked at before the bars sat directly next to each other. What do you mean, it is "sort of" a histogram?'

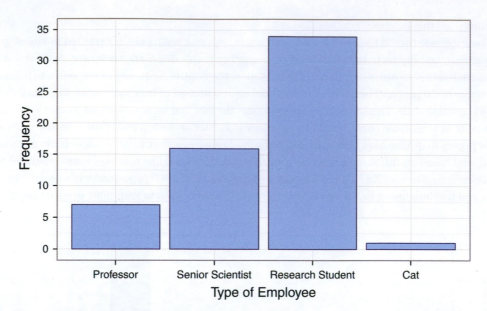

Figure 3.6 *Frequency distribution of a nominal variable*

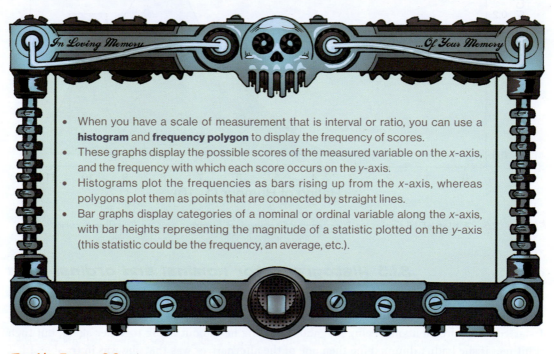

- When you have a scale of measurement that is interval or ratio, you can use a **histogram** and **frequency polygon** to display the frequency of scores.
- These graphs display the possible scores of the measured variable on the *x*-axis, and the frequency with which each score occurs on the *y*-axis.
- Histograms plot the frequencies as bars rising up from the *x*-axis, whereas polygons plot them as points that are connected by straight lines.
- Bar graphs display categories of a nominal or ordinal variable along the *x*-axis, with bar heights representing the magnitude of a statistic plotted on the *y*-axis (this statistic could be the frequency, an average, etc.).

Zach's Facts 3.3 *Histograms, polygons and bar graphs*

She seemed reluctant to dwell on the graph and answered quickly and dismissively, 'It shows the same information as a histogram – the frequency within categories – but these categories do not make up an interval or ratio scale of measurement. These data are the numbers of different types of employees at the Beimeni Centre of Genetics. This is a nominal variable: there are categories of workers: professors, senior scientists and research students. When we display information about a nominal or ordinal variable like this, it's called a **bar graph**. The principle is the same as for a histogram: we display different categories along the *x*-axis, and we use bars to indicate some kind of statistic, in this case the frequency. There are spaces between the bars to indicate that they are independent categories and not points along an interval or ratio scale.'

Something struck me as odd about this graph. At the end there was a category of employee labelled 'cat', with a frequency of 1. The Professor had deliberately not mentioned this category when explaining the graph. I looked at the bar graph, I looked at the cat, then I looked at the graph again, then the cat. He winked at me. At least I thought he did.

3.2 THROWING SHAPES

There was something about the Professor's discomfort with the cat's presence that wasn't right. Why was the Professor so keen to ignore the cat? If she didn't want people to know that she had a cat then why not hide it instead of letting it wander around the place saying 'hello', and even if she couldn't hide it, why not tell me that the cat was on the graph because they employed it to get rid of mice or something? 'Professors,' I thought to myself, 'the most intelligent people on the planet, but no common sense whatsoever.'

I asked the Professor about my earlier conclusion – that the data seemed not to support the hypothesis that Alice would have left me, which left me with the other hypothesis that she was in danger. The Professor looked flustered and, to my surprise, carried on talking about distributions as though I hadn't even mentioned Alice.

'As I mentioned earlier,' the Professor continued, as though the last few minutes had never happened, 'we can create idealized frequency distributions. You will find that certain shapes of distributions are common in the world; that is, some variables have distributions that are similar in shape to other variables. Therefore, we can describe certain distributions that are common to lots of different variables. These "common" distributions have names such as the **normal distribution**, t-distribution, chi-square distribution, uniform distribution, binomial distribution and F-distribution.'

'Catchy names, I might name my children after them.'

The Professor glared at me. 'These idealized distributions have a specific shape that can be described by an equation.'

'I hate equations.'

'Most of you young people do, and fortunately you can ignore the equations and instead focus on properties that describe the shape of the distribution, the position of the centre of the distribution (known as the central tendency), and the width or spread of the distribution (known as the variability). Let me show you some of these characteristic shapes.' The Professor was running out of wall on which to trace out diagrams, and began a brief mission to locate the remaining blank sections. 'This drawing **(FIGURE 3.7)** shows a normal distribution, which you can see looks like a bell. In fact, it is commonly called a bell-shaped curve. This shape tells us that the majority of scores lie around the centre of the distribution (so the largest bars on the histogram are all around the central value). The further we move away from the centre, the smaller the bars get, telling us that the more that scores deviate from the centre the more unlikely, or infrequent, they are. Many naturally occurring things have this shape of distribution. For example, how tall are you?'

'About 180 cm.'

'Which is close to the centre of the distribution of male heights: most men in Elpis are about 175 cm tall, some (like you) are a little bit taller, others slightly shorter, but most cluster around this value. If you venture around Elpis you will encounter very few men who are really tall (i.e., above 205 cm) or really short (i.e., under 145 cm).'

'Unless I'm at a gig trying to watch a band, in which case every person in front will be 250 cm tall.'

'It might seem that way, but unless you possess a gravitational field that draws the small number of really tall people to congregate around you, then statistically that can't be true.'

'I *must* have one of those gravitational thingies … ' I thought to myself.

'There are two main ways in which a distribution can deviate from normal,' the Professor said. 'First, notice that the curve is symmetrical: **(FIGURE 3.7)** if we draw a vertical line through the centre of the distribution then it looks the same on both sides. Not all distributions are like that: some

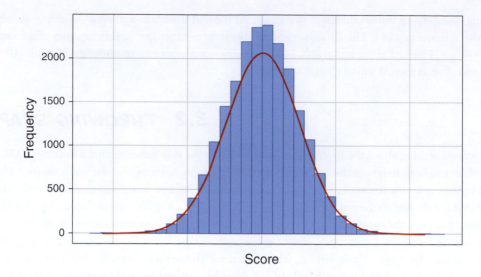

Figure 3.7 *A normal distribution (the curve shows the idealized shape)*

have **skew**. **(FIGURE 3.8)** In a skewed distribution the most frequent scores (the tall bars on the graph) are clustered at one end of the scale. So, the typical pattern is a cluster of frequent scores at one end of the scale and the frequency of scores tailing off towards the other end of the scale. A skewed distribution can be **positively skewed** (the frequent scores are clustered at the lower end and the tail points towards the higher or more positive scores) or **negatively skewed** (the frequent scores are clustered at the higher end and the tail points towards the lower or more negative scores). The second way in which they can be non-normal is in whether there are too many or too few scores in the ends of distribution (the *tails* of the distribution), which is known as **kurtosis**.'

'Isn't that when your flesh rots?' I asked.

'No, that's *necr-osis*.' I was doing a bad job of reining in the flippant remarks, but I was so bored I was starting to wish that my flesh *was* rotting, and carrying me away to the sweet peace of eternal rest. For Alice's sake I needed to concentrate. I apologized and the Professor moved on.

'A distribution with **positive kurtosis** is known as **leptokurtic** and has too many scores in the tails (a so-called heavy-tailed distribution), whereas one with **negative kurtosis** is relatively thin in the tails (has light tails) and is called **platykurtic**.[24] Kurtosis is much harder to spot visually because it is defined by the number of scores in the extremes of the distribution, but leptokurtic distributions can tend to

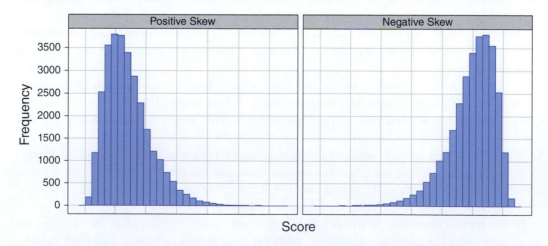

Figure 3.8 *A positively (left) and negatively (right) skewed distribution*

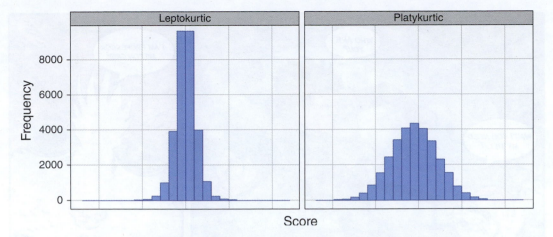

Figure 3.9 *Distributions with a positive kurtosis of +2.6 (leptokurtic, left) and a negative kurtosis of −0.09 (platykurtic, right)*

look pointy, and platykurtic ones tend to look flatter than normal. **(FIGURE 3.9)** However, there are lots of other things that affect how pointy or flat a distribution looks. In a normal distribution the values of skew and kurtosis are 0[1] (i.e., the overall shape of the distribution is as it should be). If a distribution has values of skew or kurtosis above or below 0 then this indicates a deviation from normal.'

'How can I use these shapes to tell me whether Alice dumped me or is in danger?'

'You can't, but I thought it was an interesting way to finish telling you about distributions. I have a very busy day, so it's been very nice to meet you, Zach. I hope that Alice returns to us very soon – she is a much valued part of our team.'

Was she serious? I'd sat through all of that, and at best all I'd found out was that Alice's relationship satisfaction scores were higher than most, and that I had some characteristics that women – in general – seem to like. Now she was giving me the brush-off and coming out with platitudes about Alice being valued. How dare she: Alice was frippin' brilliant. I had the distinct impression that Professor Pincus had deliberately sidetracked me from JIG:SAW by giving me false hope that she could help me to look at the data in Alice's file. My anger spilled over: 'That's it? But I don't know any more about where Alice is than when I walked in!'

The Professor replied, and the rage in her eyes betrayed her calmly spoken words. 'I disagree. I have given you – in the limited free time I have to talk to strangers who come to my laboratory without authorization – some tools to help you to work out the answers for yourself. You have some data from Alice's counsellor's files, you have some real-world data to compare against, we've seen that you can use real data to try to ascertain whether it's likely that she would want to leave you, and you now have a few foundations to use the data that you have. Use those foundations to build on, and don't expect people to give you the answers on a plate!'

Told. I packed up The Head and started to leave her office. As I reached the door I turned and said in passing, 'Maybe someone at JIG:SAW will help me?'

I was testing the Professor, to see whether I could goad her into helping me more. Instead, I shattered her calm. She went cold and her curt response made me shudder: 'You listen to me very carefully, young man. Unless you want your life destroyed, take some advice: some things are best left alone.' With that she turned and accelerated towards the wall, barely giving it time to unfold around her as she left her office.

---

1 Technically it's EXCESS kurtosis that is 0. Expected kurtosis is 3. Different places will report kurtosis vs excess kurtosis, so you may find it useful to know both.

KEY TERMS

Abscissa

Bar graph

Chart

Class interval

Class interval width

Cumulative frequency

Cumulative per cent

Density

Empirical question

Frequency

Frequency distribution

Frequency polygon

Graph

Grouped frequency distribution

Histogram

Kurtosis

Leptokurtic

Negative kurtosis

Negative skew

Normal distribution

Ordinate

Platykurtic

Positive kurtosis

Positive skew

Probability density function

Probability distribution

Proportion

Relative frequency

Skew

x-axis

y-axis

JIG:SAW'S PUZZLES

1 Describe the following terms: frequency, relative frequency, proportion and percentage.

2 Draw the frequency distribution of the RAS scores (with scores not grouped by class intervals).

3 In this chapter Zach looked at 20 women's ratings of how important certain characteristics are in romantic partners. Here are the data for the characteristic 'wants to have children': 1, 1, 9, 1, 10, 3, 7, 6, 7, 2, 2, 9, 8, 2, 8, 6, 9, 2, 9, 6. Produce a frequency table of these data that includes:

    a Frequencies

    b Relative frequencies

    c Percentages

    d Cumulative frequency

    e Cumulative percentage

4 For the data in the previous question, remembering that scores of 0–5 mean 'unimportant' and 6–10 mean 'important', what percentage of adolescent women thought that it was important that their partners wanted to have children in the future?

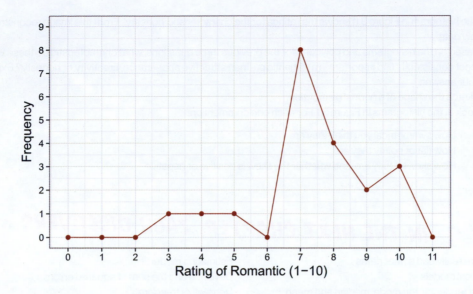

Figure 3.10   *Polygon of the ratings for the characteristic 'romantic'*

5   Zach was worried that he was unappealing to women because he dropped out of college. Here are the ratings of the 20 women in the chapter for the characteristic 'finished education': 9, 8, 5, 4, 7, 3, 10, 7, 6, 4, 4, 8, 9, 1, 7, 3, 7, 6, 10, 9. Draw a histogram of these data. Do you think most of these women think that it is important that their relationship partner finished their college education?

6   The polygon in Figure 3.10 shows the ratings for the characteristic 'romantic'. From this image reconstruct the raw data.

7   Here are the ratings for the same 20 women for the characteristic 'attractive appearance': 4, 10, 9, 8, 7, 8, 10, 8, 7, 3, 9, 10, 8, 10, 7, 9, 9, 9, 8, 7. Draw a frequency distribution of these scores.

8   Here are the ratings for the same 20 women for the characteristic 'creativity': 7, 6, 5, 4, 5, 8, 9, 5, 5, 7, 4, 5, 5, 10, 7, 3, 5, 9, 1, 7. Draw a frequency polygon of these scores.

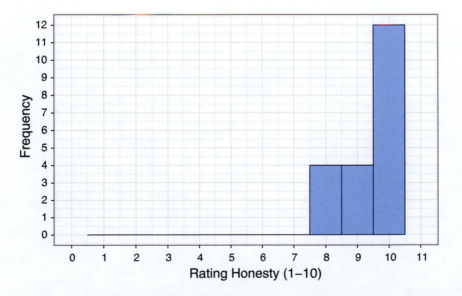

Figure 3.11   *Histogram of the ratings for the characteristic 'honesty'*

9   The histogram in Figure 3.11 shows the ratings for the characteristic 'honesty'. From this image reconstruct the raw data.

10 Based on the histograms and polygons for the previous three questions, what characteristic do these women most consistently find important in a romantic partner: attractive appearance, creativity or honesty? Explain your answer.

11 Sketch the shape of a normal distribution.

12 Look at the histograms in Figure 3.1. For each one comment on:

  a   How symmetrical you think they are
  b   How flat or pointy they are
  c   How skewed they are, and whether the skew is positive or negative

IN THE NEXT CHAPTER, ZACH DISCOVERS ...

Cats are really bad dinner dates
Statistical models
Central tendency: the mode, median and mean
Dispersion: the variance, standard deviation, and interquartile range
Quartiles and percentiles

Estimating model fit
Deviance and the sum of squared errors
Degrees of freedom
Outliers
Chippers are dropping like flies

4

Fitting Models (Central Tendency)

Somewhere in the Middle

I stopped in my tracks and turned to face the cat from Professor Pincus's office. He was licking his chest in that over-purposeful way that cats do when they feel awkward. I had managed to convince myself that I had probably imagined the cat talking in Professor Pincus's office, but unless I'd lost my mind twice it really could talk. I wondered whether Alice knew that she worked somewhere that had a talking cat? If she did then why hadn't she mentioned it to me? If I met a talking cat at our rehearsal studio the first thing I would do is tell her. I'd call her now if she hadn't been wiped from the planet.

The cat stared at me, waiting for my reaction. How could he talk, and why was he claiming to be a dead scientist? If you were going to claim to be a dead scientist wouldn't you pick one who was a bit more popular than the reality prism dude? I had so many questions to ask, but no time to get side-tracked by them.

'That's impossible,' I eventually said, 'Milton Grey died five years ago.' I was aware that this wasn't the most impossible aspect of the situation, but I had to start somewhere.

The cat's rate of cleansing rapidly increased before he stopped and looked up. 'Officially I did, but only because the alternative was to try to explain to everyone that I had become a cat. It transpires that the WGA are reluctant to issue passports and other legal documents to cats, and you can forget anything involving a fingerprint or retina scan. Without official documents I am effectively dead, but with Catherine's help I exist as a cat. It has considerable benefits: I get a lot more time for research, because only a strange person would email a cat.'

If someone told me about a cat that could email, I'd *definitely* message it, I thought to myself. How could a cat be Milton Grey, I wondered? Had his brain been transplanted? That seemed unlikely: a cat's skull was too small for a human brain. Maybe the brain had been shrunk? Was it some kind of mind merge? Was Milton Grey's human body walking around somewhere with the mind of a cat inside it? I needed to establish whether I could trust him, and to do that I needed to know his story, which he was happy to tell.

'After the reality prism nonsense I found myself stripped of my position within the School of Physics here at the University of Elpis, and my reputation made me unemployable. The WGA offered me a position in their Scientific Division, where I helped them to develop technology to rebuild society. Did you know that my colleague Roediger and I invented steam fusion?' The cat paused to take in the awe that he expected from me at this revelation. He looked offended when he got none, and licked his chest to comfort himself. Steam fusion drove so much of the modern world that I took it for granted. I'd never considered what lay beneath it, or how hard it might have been to invent.

'I was quite happy at the WGA,' Milton continued, 'but as their power increased I felt that they were losing their humanitarian principles, so I resigned. It was not easy to convince the WGA that the person they believed brought down society should be given his freedom. They allowed me to go because of my loyal service, but they monitored me constantly: my freedom was an illusion. Worse than that, even the passage of time had not weakened society's ire, and universities still stayed well away from me. I suspect the WGA applied some pressure in that respect. Catherine – Professor Pincus – gave me a lifeline. Although known for my work in physics, for many years I pursued a side interest in genetics. I published an obscure paper on how – theoretically at least –principles of physics could be applied to genetic problems. Catherine was fascinated by the potential of the theory and offered me an opportunity to pursue it at the Beimeni Centre. Catherine put her neck on the line to employ me: in doing so she put the Centre under the WGA's spotlight. I owe her a great deal for her faith, and her unwavering principle to prioritize knowledge and humanity. The first fruits of my work were what I jokingly called the "gene mixer", which was a device for repairing damaged cells; for example, cancer cells. It was a simple enough idea: you turn the damaged cells into programmable matter and then give them a "program" based on healthy cells.'

'That sounds the same as something of Alice's that I read.' **(LAB NOTES 2.1)**

'Alice's work is much more advanced than my gene mixer.'

So he *did* know Alice. Why hadn't she mentioned him to me?

'The gene mixer was crude, difficult to control, and too powerful – a blunt instrument that rampaged through an organism affecting any gene in its path. We have subsequently discovered that you need the human mind to control the process, but at the time, the gene mixer had promise. We had very encouraging preliminary results, but we needed to test it on a human. You cannot go sticking humans in gene mixing machines, not even ones with cancer who you are trying to help. If it goes wrong you might make the disease worse or even kill them. Fortunately, there was one person we knew who had a recent diagnosis of cancer who was willing to take that risk.'

I panicked that it was Alice, before realizing that he was talking about the past, a time before Alice would have worked there. I asked who it was.

'Me. I stepped under the machine, gathered a dish of healthy cells and prepared to have my diseased cells replaced with programmable cells that would take on the behaviour of those healthy cells.'

'What happened?'

'My cat, Erwin, happened. The dish of healthy cells looked a lot like a dish of milk. Like most cats, Erwin was fond of milk. At the point of transmission he jumped onto the table, lapped up the healthy cells, and became caught in the transfer beam. The machine transformed my cells to programmable matter, took Erwin's healthy cat cells and implanted that template into my cells.I became a cat.'

'Over the wall, man! That sucks!'

'On the plus side, my cancer was cured.'

I blurted out a barrage of questions: What happened to the cat? Did Milton's personality change at all? Did the cat's? Milton looked a little upset at my concern for his cat over him.

'Erwin is fine – the transfer was in one direction, so he was unaffected – apart from discovering, much to his disgust, that there was another cat in the house. Cats are not willing cohabiters, so after a few weeks he wandered off to find a new owner. The most surprising thing was that CAT scans' – he paused and smiled at the pun – 'showed that physically my brain had shrunk, but also had become incredibly dense to retain everything within my human mind. I did pick up some cat habits, but on the whole it is a good life: people tickle my chin a lot more than they used to.'

Professor Grey looked at me with vulnerable eyes and I instinctively stroked his chin, pulling away as I realized I was fondling a professor's beard. I still wasn't sure whether to buy his story, but I couldn't deny the evidence of my eyes: he *was* a talking cat. Why would he help me, though, and how could I trust someone who had destroyed society? I asked him whether he felt bad about the Reality Revolution.

'I created the technology, but does that make me responsible for how people used it or their inability to deal with the consequences? Many consider me the modern-day Robert Oppenheimer …'

'Who?'

He gave me a look of disgust, '... the scientist in charge of the creation of the first atomic bomb. I would argue that, unlike Oppenheimer, the consequences of my work were not obvious to me or anyone else. Do I feel bad for inventing the reality prism? No. It was a device that could have been used for great good. Do I regret how people used reality prisms? Yes, but I blame them, not myself. Do I think society is a worse place for the Reality Revolution? For many years it became a more humane place, of that I am certain, but as through all of history it is only a matter of time before someone tries to take advantage of humanity.' Milton looked sad. As detached as he felt from the consequences of his work, he didn't sound evil. I asked him why he wanted to help.

'I have a reputation that makes my apparent death quite convenient for Catherine. It is bad enough that the Beimeni Centre employed the "notorious" Professor Grey, inventor of the reality prism and destroyer of modern civilization, but society forgives them because they seemingly killed me as part of a bizarre genetics experiment. The world believes that justice has been served. Imagine the furore if anyone discovered that instead of being dead I was in fact a rather lovable cat. The Centre would be investigated and probably shut down for good. As I mentioned, the WGA kept a particularly close eye on things while I was working here. Since my "death" they have lost interest in us, and Catherine prefers it that way. I, however, do not, because my activities are restricted. Before I actually die I want to be remembered for something good, I want to erase the false belief in my part in destroying society. As I told you, my work with the gene mixer was getting close to a device that could cure a great many fatal diseases. Perhaps if I can bring that work to fruition the world will forgive me – I can die a hero, not a villain. I can't do that while I'm trapped here, only knowing about the work being done in Catherine's lab. I am forever grateful for all that she has done for me, but I need to expand my horizons. To do that I need someone I can trust. Can I trust you, Zach?'

It was the same question I'd wanted to ask him. 'Of course, I'm a good guy, but why do you think I need your help?'

'Sooner or later you are going to decide that you need to investigate JIG:SAW – '

'Not after what the Prof said,' I interrupted.

'True, only a fool would go there, but sooner or later the fool inside will get the better of you. Catherine is right, it will destroy you; but with my help, you have hope.'

4.1 STATISTICAL MODELS

4.1.1 From the dead

I picked Milton up, put him in my backpack and headed swiftly out of the building. I sheepishly passed the front desk hoping that the head there wouldn't have a change of heart about having let us in and call security. She didn't, but as we moved away from the building my pace quickened until I had broken into a run. I decided to head back to Janus, the area where I lived, and go to Occam's café. Janus was the liberal part of town; if I could take a talking cat anywhere, it was there. Janus was quite a way from Veritas, where the Beimeni Centre was, so I hailed a bubble. Personal transport like cars were a thing of the past; instead the city provided clockwork fusion-powered 'bubbles' that hovered around the city. These transparent spheres could be hailed through *memoryBank* or a Proteus and arrived almost instantly. Once inside, you told it where to go and it hovered you there. We were soon at Occam's.

It was early evening and I was starving. Occam's was a minimalist café that invented 'parsimonious cooking', in which only essential ingredients are used. It tasted better than it sounded. Even in the 'open-minded' part of town I was worried that taking a cat to a café might stretch people's tolerance, so I sat on a long leather couch in one of the many private booths where we'd be less conspicuous. I placed my backpack beside me and Professor Grey wriggled out.

'I'll have a tuna steak please,' he said. 'Now, on to business. Tell me what you know about Alice.' Hearing him speak, in public, made me suddenly self-conscious and scared that someone would discover my talking cat. I understood how Professor Pincus must have felt earlier on when Milton had walked into her office. I told Milton about how Alice had disappeared, how I couldn't contact her, and about my visit to Dr Genari.

'Who is this Genari chap?' Milton asked. As he did, I remembered how I had seen a cat outside Genari's window when I was there. Now I thought of it, the cat was ginger. So that was how Milton could send me messages relating to what Genari was saying: he must have been listening outside. Why would he have known about me? Why would he have followed me? Did Alice send him? Also, Milton said he needed me to help him escape from the Beimeni Centre, but if he was at Genari's then he must be free to come and go from the Centre as he pleased – not the prisoner he made himself out to be. Why was he lying to me? I decided to play along for now rather than confront him: there must be a reason why and the best way to find out was to play dumb.

I told Milton my theories about Alice, about how at first I thought she'd left me, but that after visiting Genari I feared that she was in trouble. I told him how Professor Pincus had helped me to look at data to test this hypothesis, and that she had seemed disappointed when the data we looked at didn't support that idea – as if she'd hoped to convince me that Alice *had* left me. Revisiting the last 36 hours or so made me feel anxious and panicky: why couldn't I just speak to Alice? I wanted to hear her voice, to have her reassure me that she was alright and that this was just some silly misunderstanding. I called her Proteus again and the same cold voice as before told me that her number did not exist.

Milton watched me with interest. I couldn't make out what he was thinking, but you never can with a cat. Finally, he said, 'It doesn't sound as though Catherine, Professor Pincus, really did a good job of evaluating the evidence from Alice: she just looked at general data about what women look for in a man. Perhaps what Alice looks for is a nincompoop like you.'

'We did look at her score on the Relationship Assessment Scale,' I replied. 'Oh, and what note is this?' I sang an F♯.

'A C?' Milton guessed.

'No, it's an F♯ – nincompoop.'

There was an awkward silence while the cat considered his options. Having considered them, he carried on as though nothing had happened. 'You have more data from Alice than you showed Catherine?' he asked.

I showed Milton all of the information from Alice's file. He took it all in, swatting at my diePad screen and screwing up his face in concentration. He licked his lips, again looking like he was trying to decide what to do.

'What you have here', he said, 'are competing hypotheses: she has left you and doesn't want you to find her, or she is in trouble and someone else doesn't want you to find her.' With horror I suddenly had the thought that perhaps Milton and Catherine *were* the people who didn't want me to find her. 'What you need to do is to learn some statistics and put these hypotheses to the test.'

The cat had to be kidding. I hated maths at college, and I wasn't about to voluntarily enrol on a stats module taught by a talking cat in a café. 'Why would I want to do that?' I asked.

'Because statistics is *cool*, that's why. Now listen up, you have two choices. I can send you away to read a book, like the now legendary, genre-defining *Discovering Statistics* ... series by Andy Field[11, 25] ...'

'Alice reckons those books are rubbish,' I interrupted.

'In which case, it's choice number two: listen to me. Oh, and one more thing: nobody can find out who I really am, from now on you refer to me only as Milton. Now go and order my tuna.'

4.1.2 Why do we need statistical models?

Upon my return Milton began his lesson. 'Scientists are interested in the true state of the world.'

'Yeah, Alice mentioned this to me the night before she vanished. She said that scientists want to find out the truth, but because they can't usually get data from the entire population they work with smaller samples from that population.' *(SEE SECTION 1.2.1)*

'Ah, you know the basics already. That is excellent, but you need to know where statistical models fit into all of this. I'll begin with an analogy. You remember the Beimeni Centre building: it looks like three cogs on a spiralling tower of human DNA?'

'Oh, is that what it was supposed to be? I thought it was just a weird spirally coggy thing.'

Milton raised his eyebrow. 'Do you think that the architect who designed it just turned up one day with a truckload of materials and built it?'

'I doubt it. Don't they do drawings and models and stuff?'

'*Purr*cisely. It is expensive and impractical to build the "full building", so instead they build a scaled-down version. This model can differ from the real building in several ways – it will be smaller for a start – but the architect or engineer will build a model that resembles the real one as closely as possible. Once the model is ready, it can be used to estimate what would happen to the real building. For example, they might place it in a wind tunnel to see whether the building is likely to withstand the winter Elpis winds, or they might simulate an earthquake to see if the structure remains intact. To get accurate predictions about the real building, it is vital that the model resembles it as closely as possible, otherwise the architect's predictions about the real building will be wrong.

'Scientists do much the same. They are trying to make predictions about something in the real world – it might be a psychological, societal, biological or economic process to which they do not have direct access. Because they cannot access the process directly they gather data and construct small-scale models of the process and use them to predict how these processes operate under more general conditions. Just like the architect, we want our small-scale model to resemble the real situation as closely as possible so that the predictions we make about the real world are accurate; the statistical model we build must represent the data collected (the *observed data*) as closely as possible. The degree to which a statistical model represents the data collected is called the **fit** of the model.'

Milton started scratching out a picture in the wooden table with his claw. *(FIGURE 4.1)* The noise set my teeth on edge and made me really uncomfortable, but not as uncomfortable as I felt about the criminal damage he was inflicting on the table. 'Look,' he continued, 'I've drawn three models that an architect might have created before building the Beimeni Centre. The first model is an excellent representation of the real building: it is a *good fit*. If the architect uses this model to make predictions about the real building then, because it so closely resembles reality, these predictions ought to be accurate: if the model collapses in a strong wind, then there is a good chance that the real building will too. The second model has some similarities to the real world: the model retains some of the basic structural features, but there are some big differences too (e.g., two of the floors are missing). This model has *moderate fit*: there are some similarities to reality but also some important differences. If the architect makes predictions about the real world based on this model, these predictions could be inaccurate or even catastrophic. For example, the model survives a simulated earthquake but the real building doesn't. The final model bears few structural similarities to the real building – for a start, it is missing the whole top half of the building – and is a *poor fit*. Any predictions based on this model are likely to be completely inaccurate.'

'Is what you're saying that because we can't get data from the whole population and fit a statistical model to it, we instead use samples, and we look at what happens within those samples?'

'Yes, we fit a statistical model to the data from the sample.'

'And that model can be a good or bad fit to the data?'

'Yes, and a good or bad fit to the reality in the population! It's very important to know how well the model fits the data.'

'Is this because – as Alice told me – samples vary from each other; even if you measure the same thing you can get different results in different samples?' *(SEE SECTION 1.2.1)*

'That's true, but also not all samples are equal; we can have greater confidence in some. Now, where's my tuna steak?'

4.1.3 Sample size

The waiter arrived with our food and placed both plates in front of me, assuming that I wasn't weird enough to buy café food for a cat. The smell made me realize that I hadn't eaten since the morning, and I savaged my food.

'Try not to spit food at me, it is undignified,' Milton said as he licked a strand of purry cat dribble from his chin. He picked at his tuna, continuing the conversation as he chewed. 'I have another analogy for you: imagine you are interested in a phenomenon that is trapped inside a cardboard box.'

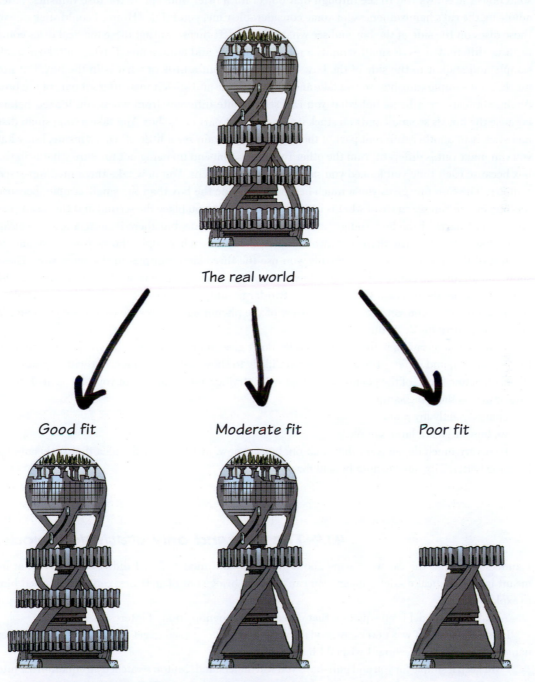

Figure 4.1 Fitting models to real-world data (see text for details)

Milton scratched an image into the table. **(FIGURE 4.2)** It was astonishing that a cat could draw so well. Scientists weren't known for their artistry and I found myself wondering whether Milton's cat might have had some artistic flair that had been wasted on a cat and could now be unleashed with the benefit of a human mind. Milton clawed my shirt to bring my attention back to him.

'The population is this big cardboard box,' he said, pointing at a well-drawn cardboard box. 'You can't see inside the box, but you know that it contains an interesting phenomenon. You really want to see that phenomenon, but you cannot because it is hidden in the box. A very handsome talking cat appears with a suitcase of magical discs that he calls samples. When you stick these discs on any solid object it allows you to see through that object for a brief time before the disc vanishes. After admiring the cat's handsomeness for some considerable time, you think, "Hmm, I could stick one of those discs on the side of the box and see what is inside". It turns out that these magical discs come in three different sizes: a small sample, a medium sample and a large one. First, you take a small sample and stick it to the side of the box. You can make out a little of what is in the box, but not much. That sample vanishes, so you take another small one and stick it to a different part of the box. Again, you can see a little, but what you can see is quite different from when you looked before because the hole is so small and you stuck it to a different part of the box. You take a final small disc and stick it to another different part of the box. You can again see a little of what's inside, but what you can make out is different from the other two times. You end up being not too sure what is in the box because each time you looked you saw something different. You now take three medium-sized samples. The first one gives you a much better view inside the box than the small sample: because it is bigger you can see more of what is inside the box. When you place the second and third samples on different parts of the box, you get a different view each time, but there is quite a lot of overlap with what you saw with the other two samples (because each sample shows you a reasonable amount of the inside of the box). Finally, you use the three large samples in the same way. These show you almost the entire inside of the box and you get a very precise view of its contents: it is the staggeringly handsome cat! With the other two large samples it doesn't matter where you place them on the box – you get a very similar view of the phenomenon, because each time you can see almost the entire inside of the box.'

'So what you're saying is that small samples don't give you a good "view" on the phenomenon in the population, and different small samples are likely to show different things, but with big samples you get a better "view" of the phenomenon that you're trying to study and what you "see" is likely to be similar across these big samples.'

'That is exactly my point.'

'So, how large is a large sample?'

'That very much depends on the situation, but for now, just focus on the idea that with samples bigger is better. The same cannot be said for dogs.'

4.1.4 The one and only statistical model

I understood what the cat was saying about architects and models, but I didn't really get what he meant by a statistical model. I mean, you can't build a bridge out of statistics, can you? I asked him to explain.

'A statistical model is an equation that describes the phenomenon of interest.'

'I hate equations. I was never any good at maths at college – I used to get Alice to help me out.' Her name triggered a sick feeling; I wished I hadn't eaten.

'I will keep it simple for you and purr-haps you will understand.' Milton scratched an equation **(4.1)** into the table. 'Most statistical models are a variation on this one equation. This equation means that for a

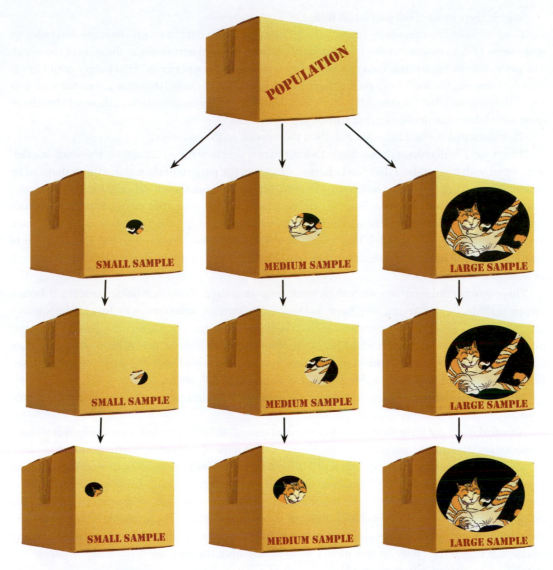

Figure 4.2   Big samples are better

given person, i, we can predict their score on an outcome variable from the model we choose to fit to the data plus some amount of error that is associated to that prediction (for person i).

$$\text{outcome}_i = (\text{model}) + \text{error}_i \qquad (4.1)$$

'For example,' Milton continued while adapting the equation **(4.2)**, 'I noticed some Relationship Assessment Scale (RAS) scores in Alice's file. **(SECTION 2.3)** Imagine that we asked a sample of 100 people to fill in the RAS so that we had a score for each person. The outcome would be the RAS score for person i, so the equation means that for a given person, i, we can predict their score on the RAS from the model we choose to fit to the data plus some amount of error that is associated to that prediction (for person i).'

$$\text{RAS}_i = (\text{model}) + \text{error}_i \qquad (4.2)$$

'Why is there error? Isn't that a bad thing?'

'Error is inevitable because by fitting a model we simplify the data to give it structure and order, to make sense of it, to reduce it down to a summary that encapsulates a truth about the state of the world. The price of reducing the raw data to a summary is that it will not perfectly reflect every entity in the sample: for some, the model will predict their RAS score very accurately (the error associated with that prediction is small), but for others the prediction might be terribly inaccurate, and there will be a large error associated with predicting that score.'

'That does make sense, but what exactly is the "model" in the equation?'

'The "model" will change depending on what you're trying to achieve. Ultimately the word "model" is replaced with an equation that you believe summarizes the pattern of data. Sometimes that can be as simple as a single value that summarizes scores, but other times the model might need to be more complicated. However, no matter how long the equation that describes your model, you can close your eyes and replace its hideous, stress-inducing form with the word "model", which is much less scary. The main thing to understand is that whatever model we choose to represent the phenomenon of interest, there will be error in prediction. Obviously, we want to fit a model where this error is as small as it can possibly be.'

This equation did seem less scary than when I was in college. Perhaps it helped hearing it from a cat, or perhaps he was trying very hard to keep me engaged. I wondered why he cared about me understanding – surely there were easier ways to help me. If this really was the reality prism guy, surely he had other inventions, or he could just split reality and show me where Alice was. I asked him whether we could use a reality prism to find Alice, but his terse reply that I pay attention to the statistics suggested I had broached a subject that he didn't want to talk about.

'Statistical models usually, but not always, contain variables and parameters,' he continued a little grumpily.

'Alice told me about these the night before she disappeared. (SECTION 1.2.1) Variables are things that we have measured and that vary across entities in the sample. I can't remember what parameters are.'

My response got him back on side and Milton adopted a kinder tone. 'Not to worry, it's a tricky concept. Parameters are (usually) constant values believed to represent some fundamental truth about the relations between variables in the model. Unlike variables, which are measured, parameters are estimated from the data. That probably does not mean a lot to you at the moment, but I will explain soon enough. Let's look at the simplest possible model you might fit.' Milton scratched another equation (4.3) into the table. 'In this model we are estimating the outcome from a single parameter, which I have denoted with the letter b.'

$$\text{outcome}_i = \left(b_0\right) + \text{error}_i \qquad (4.3)$$

'Why b? Why not p for parameter?'

'Statististicans try to confuse students by using different symbols for different parameters. For example, $\overline{X}$ tends to be used for the average, which is also called the mean; there's something called a correlation for which they use the letter r or Greek symbol rho, ρ; and in a model called the linear model, they use b or the Greek letter beta, β. Statisticians like Greek letters, but I thought you'd enjoy the simplicity of using the letter b.'

'Won't that upset the statisticians?'

'Probably, but they are easily upset.'

'Why does it have a zero next to it?'

'I put it there to remind you that we are predicting the outcome from zero other variables, that is, just from a single parameter. Can you order me a latte with lactose-free milk please?'

The waiter looked at me as though I was something unpleasant on his shoe as I asked for lactose-free milk in a latte. I guess they weren't used to dealing with cats' lactose intolerances, or perhaps he just didn't like cats eating at the table. Milton got his drink, though, and explained things while his lapping tongue sprayed me.

'The model I have just described is the simplest possible one: we summarize the population using a single parameter, a single value that summarizes the outcome variable. A lot of the time it is more interesting to see whether we can summarize an outcome variable by predicting from scores on another variable. We usually denote predictor variables with the letter X; therefore, our model will look like this.' Milton scratched on the table again. **(EQUATION 4.4)** 'In this model, we are predicting the value of the outcome for a particular entity (i) from its score on the predictor variable (X_i). The predictor variable has a parameter (b_1) attached to it, which tells us something about the relationship between the predictor (X_i) and outcome.'

$$\text{outcome}_i = \left(b_0 + b_1 X_i\right) + \text{error}_i \tag{4.4}$$

'Why is the b_0 still there?'

'We are building up the model, so the b_0 is a parameter estimate that tells us the overall levels of the outcome if the predictor variable was not in the model, and the b_1 is a parameter estimate that tells us about the relationship between the predictor variable and the outcome.'

'So we could, like, predict relationship assessment scores from how long the couple had been together?'

$$\text{relationship satisfaction}_i = \left(b_0 + b_1 \text{length}_i\right) + \text{error}_i \tag{4.5}$$

'Purrfectly true. We could see whether your assessment of your relationship depends upon the length of the relationship. If you did that you could replace the outcome (Y) and predictor (X) in the model with the names of these variables. **(EQUATION 4.5)** We could even take that a step further and add another predictor variable to the model. **(EQUATION 4.6)** Let's say we measured how much effort the couple put into their relationship. Now we're predicting the value of the outcome for a particular entity (i) from its score on two predictor variables (X_{1i} and X_{2i}). Each predictor variable has a parameter (b) attached to it, which tells us something about the relationship between that predictor and the outcome. Again, to help you to see how this works, we could replace some of the letters with the variable names.' **(EQUATION 4.7)**

$$\text{outcome}_i = \left(b_0 + b_1 X_{1i} + b_2 X_{2i}\right) + \text{error}_i \tag{4.6}$$

$$\text{relationship satisfaction}_i = \left(b_0 + b_1 \text{length}_i + b_2 \text{effort}_i\right) + \text{error}_i \tag{4.7}$$

'Sweet, you're summarizing the outcome with other variables that you have measured.'

'Purrcisely, and the beauty of it is that we could carry on expanding the model with more predictor variables. In each case they will have a parameter that quantifies the connection between that variable and the outcome variable.'

'I think I understand all of this, but how can a letter like b quantify the phenomenon we're studying. It's a letter, letters can't quantify anything.'

'Ah, dear human, the letter is just a useful way to represent the parameter in general terms. It helps us to show the form of the model, but we need to replace each letter with a number.' His eyes bulged with excitement at the mention of numbers.

'How do we do that?'

'We use the sample data to estimate the value of the model parameters.'

Estimating seemed a bit wishy-washy, surely we needed something better than an estimate. I must have been screwing my face up because Milton almost read my thoughts.

'Remember that we are interested in drawing conclusions about a population to which we did not have access. In other words, we want to know what our model might look like in the whole population, and to do that we want to know the values of the parameters of that model. The problem is that we cannot calculate the parameters in the population because we did not measure the population, we measured only a sample. What we can do instead is to use the sample data to *estimate* what the population parameters are likely to be. You will hear statisticians use the phrases "estimate the parameter" or "parameter estimates" a lot because it reflects the fact that when we calculate parameters based on sample data they are only estimates (i.e., a "best guess") of what the true parameter value is in the population. Shall we look at some simple models?'

Every atom in my body wanted to say no. I had survived this long without equations, so why would I want to have more of them now? I also thought that there surely had to be an easier way to find out where Alice was and to talk to her. That's all I needed, just to talk to her, and to find out what was going on. However, I had a feeling Milton had other plans, and for now at least, I perhaps needed to go along with him.

4.2 CENTRAL TENDENCY

As I suspected he would, Milton ploughed on. 'After I walked into Catherine's office, you discussed with her a score that reflected Alice's satisfaction with your relationship: the Relationship Assessment Scale (RAS). I noticed when you showed me the information you had from Alice's file that she completed this measure not just once, but many times.'

He was right. I had shown the Professor only Alice's score in the first week of her counselling sessions.

'You have done well to listen to my explanations, but I am certain that you are wondering how this helps you to resolve your little problem. Let us use Alice's ratings to try to see whether we believe the hypothesis about her absence reflecting an over-elaborate exit strategy from her relationship with you.'

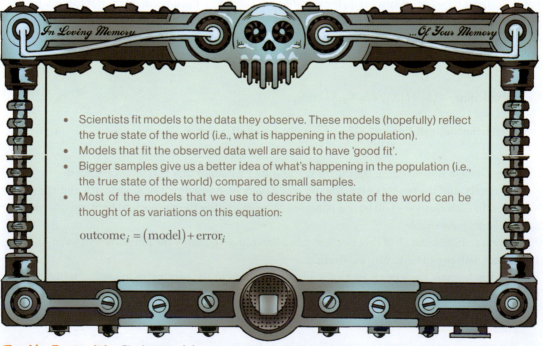

- Scientists fit models to the data they observe. These models (hopefully) reflect the true state of the world (i.e., what is happening in the population).
- Models that fit the observed data well are said to have 'good fit'.
- Bigger samples give us a better idea of what's happening in the population (i.e., the true state of the world) compared to small samples.
- Most of the models that we use to describe the state of the world can be thought of as variations on this equation:

$$\text{outcome}_i = (\text{model}) + \text{error}_i$$

Zach's Facts 4.1 Fitting models

Now we were getting somewhere. I leaned in to listen closely to what the cat had to say. I got out my diePad and we noted Alice's RAS scores over a 10-week block of her counselling sessions: **(FIGURE 4.3)**

32, 30, 28, 30, 30, 29, 31, 29, 31, 11

Milton looked surprised. 'The score of 11 on the last week is really low.' I looked surprised back at him and he explained. 'Most weeks Alice rated your relationship quite highly – close to the top of the scale – but then in the week before her disappearance, last week, it fell to close to the bottom of the scale. Remember that the lowest score on this scale is 7 **(SECTION 2.3)**, so she rated your relationship about as low as it was possible to rate it, whereas the previous 9 weeks she rated it close to the top. A score that is very different from others is called an **outlier**, and if we have one or more of these it can affect the models that we fit. This is one reason why it is important to look at frequency distributions of your data, which Catherine explained to you, because they can show up unusual scores.'

'Should we ignore it if it is unusual?'

'Well, it is true that it can affect our model in bad ways – I can show you some examples in a moment – so for the sake of the model sometimes we try to reduce the impact of these outliers. However, often these scores are telling us something interesting. For example, isn't it interesting that the week before Alice disappears, her relationship rating is low? She was not happy with you and then she vanishes. Read into that what you will.'

I didn't like the knowing look that Milton was giving me, but his argument made sense. The pain in my face must have been obvious because his tone softened.

'Let us not jump to conclusions before we have looked at some simple statistical models.'

He said it as though this were some treat that would cheer me up. It wasn't.

'The simplest model we can fit to these data is one that tries to summarize them in terms of a single parameter. A popular choice would be a parameter that measures **central tendency**: a value that indicates the central point of a distribution of scores. A "typical" score, you might say. If we have data

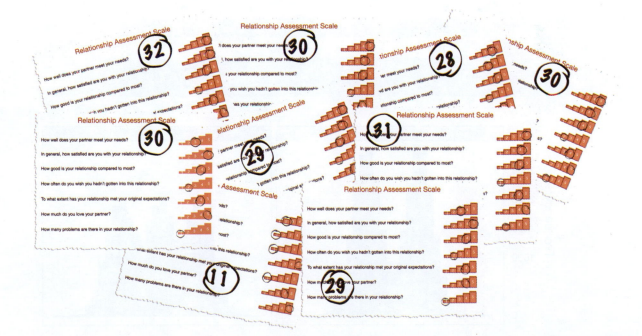

Figure 4.3   Alice's RAS scores over 10 weeks

from the entire population we could compute this value directly, but if we have only a sample then we can estimate the population value from the sample data.'

4.2.1 The mode

'*Purr*haps the simplest way to quantify the centre of a distribution is to use the score that occurs most frequently, which is called the **mode**,' Milton continued. 'This value is easy to spot in a histogram because it will be the tallest bar, and in a tabulated frequency distribution it will be the score with the largest frequency. To take your mind off of Alice, draw the frequency distribution of her RAS scores and tell me which score has the biggest frequency.'

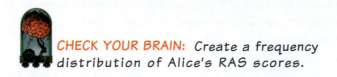

CHECK YOUR BRAIN: Create a frequency distribution of Alice's RAS scores.

I quickly drew up the table; **(TABLE 4.1)** it didn't take my mind off of Alice. The value of 30 had a frequency of 3, which was greater than any other value. I gave this answer to Milton.

Table 4.1 Frequency distribution of Alice's RAS scores over 10 weeks (excluding categories with zero frequencies)

RAS score (X)	Frequency (f)
32	1
31	2
30	3
29	2
28	1
11	1
	$N = \sum f = 10$

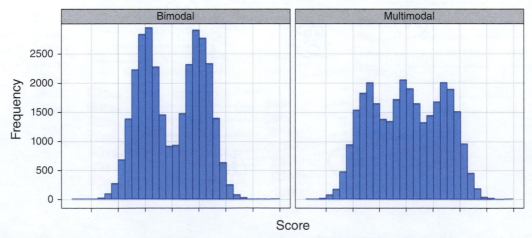

Figure 4.4 Examples of bimodal (left) and multimodal (right) distributions

'*Claw*rect, 30 is the mode of these scores. The mode is useful because it represents the most popular response, and unlike other measures it will always be a value that actually occurred in the data. It does have a downside though, which is that it can often take on several values. Had Alice given another score of 29 then both 29 and 30 would have had a frequency of 3; there would be two modes.' Milton started playing with my diePad, twisting and turning its cogs with his paws until the screen displayed an image. **(FIGURE 4.4)** 'This image shows an example of a distribution with two modes (there are two bars that are the highest), which is said to be **bimodal**, and three modes (data sets with more than two modes are **multimodal**). Another problem is that if the frequencies of certain scores are very similar, then the mode can be influenced by only a small number of cases.'

I was curious about whether this mode had been affected by Alice's unusual score: the low score of 11, which the cat had pointed out. He suggested that I calculate the mode without that score and when I did I found that the mode was still 30: that unusual score had not had an impact.

4.2.2 The median

Milton sat on my diePad, obscuring the data from my view. I asked him what he was doing. He looked puzzled, as though I'd somehow asked him an obvious and idiotic question. 'It's warm on here,' he said.

'But I can't see the screen.'

'Your human needs are insignificant. The diePad is warm. I need warmth. You would think that I would not, what with having a fur coat, but there are many interesting things about cats that you do not realize until you are one. One of them is that we expend an incredible amount of energy keeping the fabric of reality together.'

Milton wasn't making any sense. It was odd that he sometimes referred to me as human, as though he'd never been one, or as if he was proud to be a cat. I wondered whether his personality really hadn't changed. He had an air of superiority about him, which annoyed me, I wondered whether the human Professor Grey had had that arrogance too or whether he inherited it from his cat. My thoughts were soon interrupted.

'Pay attention,' he said abruptly, 'or you will never find Alice. There are other ways to summarize the central point of a distribution. For example, we can look for the middle score when the scores are arranged in ascending order; this value is known as the **median**. To calculate the median for Alice's RAS scores, we first arrange these scores into ascending order: 11, 28, 29, 29, 30, 30, 30, 31, 31, 32. Next, we find the position of the middle score by counting the number of scores we have collected (n), adding 1 to this value, and then dividing by 2. With 10 scores, this gives us $(n + 1)/2 = (10 + 1)/2 = 11/2 = 5.5$. Then, we find the score that is positioned at the location we have just calculated. So, in this example we find the score five and a half positions along the list.'

'Don't be daft! There is a fifth score and a sixth score, but there isn't one in between.'

'Just checking that you have stopped daydreaming. I know how humans like to sleep – they are always dozing off, not like us cats. What a value of 5.5 means is that the median is halfway between the fifth and sixth scores. To get the median we add these two scores and divide by 2. In this example, the fifth and sixth scores in the ordered list are both 30. We add these together ($30 + 30 = 60$) and then divide this value by 2 ($60/2 = 30$). The median score that Alice gave was, therefore, 30.' **(FIGURE 4.5)**

'Is the median affected by the weird score of 11?'

'Let us see, shall we? If we remove the score of 11 we have nine scores left, so the median is even easier to calculate. We find out the middle score as we did before, but now we have nine scores, so this gives us $(n + 1)/2 = (9 + 1)/2 = 10/2 = 5$. The median is the score at position 5 in the ordered list, which is a value of 30.' **(FIGURE 4.6)** It seemed as though the median wasn't affected at all.

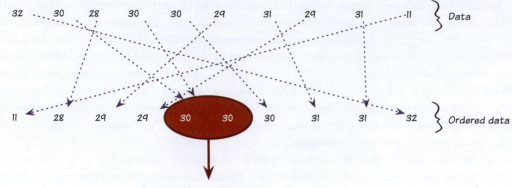

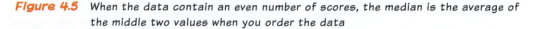

Median = (30 + 30)/2 = 30

Figure 4.5 When the data contain an even number of scores, the median is the average of the middle two values when you order the data

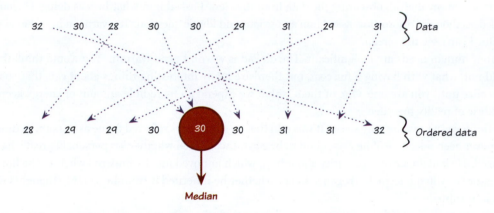

Figure 4.6 When the data contain an odd number of scores, the median is the middle score when you order the data

4.2.3 The mean

Milton did some more scratching on the desk **(EQUATION 4.8)** and said, 'A measure of central tendency that you will have heard of is the **mean**, sometimes referred to as the **arithmetic mean**, but more commonly just called the **average**. To calculate the mean we add up all of the scores and then divide by the total number of scores we have.

Population mean	Sample mean	
$$\mu = \frac{\sum_{i=1}^{n} x_i}{N}$$	$$\bar{X} \,(\text{or } M) = \frac{\sum_{i=1}^{n} x_i}{n}$$	(4.8)

I noticed he had written two equations that looked the same apart from a couple of symbols. I asked him why.

'Very observant. Yes, they are the same, but some of the symbols are different, depending on whether you're calculating the mean of an entire population of scores (the **population mean**) or of just a sample of scores (the **sample mean**). I mentioned earlier that statisticians like to use lots of symbols, and the population mean is represented by the Greek letter mu (μ), which is a Greek lower-case m, which makes it a fairly sensible choice to represent a mean. The sample mean is represented by an X with a bar on top of it, or sometimes the letter M. Also notice that when we have an entire population of scores we typically use a capital N to represent the 'Number of scores', but when we have only a sample we use a lower-case n instead. You are right, though, both versions of the equation are mathematically the same: the top half of the expression on the right-hand side of the equation means 'add up all of the scores' **(SECTION 2.2)**, and the bottom half means divide this total by the number of scores you have added up.'

'I don't understand how you can talk about a population or sample of scores when we have data from a single person: Alice.'

'Good question,' he said with a look of satisfaction as though he should get some credit for my asking a sensible question. 'You can define samples and populations in different ways according to the question you want to address. A population of scores doesn't have to be scores from different entities, and neither does a sample. With the RAS scores we are interested in the population of scores representing Alice's relationship satisfaction; we could define this as the ratings she would give every week of your entire relationship. In which case, the scores we have for the 10 weeks that she completed the RAS are a sample of her relationship satisfaction. Let's calculate the mean for this sample. First, we add up all of the scores.' **(EQUATION 4.9)** Milton again etched the table with his claw. 'We then divide by the number of scores, in this case 10.' **(EQUATION 4.10)**

$$\sum_{i=1}^{n} x_i = 32 + 30 + 28 + 30 + 30 + 29 + 31 + 29 + 31 + 11 = 281 \tag{4.9}$$

$$\bar{X} = \frac{\sum_{i=1}^{n} x_i}{n} = \frac{281}{10} = 28.1 \tag{4.10}$$

I stared silently at his calculation, trying to work out what this all meant for my relationship with Alice. Milton charged on, oblivious to my thoughts.

'Alice's mean assessment of your relationship is 28.1. This value is not one that we observed in the actual data, which illustrates the fact that we are fitting a statistical model: we have reduced the data to a summary that does not perfectly represent the scores we observed. Think back to the equation **(4.2)** I drew for a simple model.' For the umpteenth time the table top was vandalized. 'The model is the value of the mean, so we can replace b with the symbol for the mean, and the outcome we want to predict is the RAS score at a particular time, so we can replace "outcome" with "RAS" to remind us what we are predicting. We have RAS scores at different times, so the i symbolizes a particular point in time that Alice completed the RAS. What does this model mean?' **(EQUATION 4.11)**

$$\begin{aligned} \text{outcome}_i &= (b) + \text{error}_i \\ \text{RAS}_i &= \bar{X} + \text{error}_i \\ \text{RAS}_i &= 28.1 + \text{error}_i \end{aligned} \tag{4.11}$$

'Is it that we predict that Alice's RAS score at a particular time will be the mean, 28.1, but that there is some error attached to that prediction?'

The cat looked pleased. 'You *can* understand equations when you put your mind to it. You can see this error in prediction, because in the first week Alice rated your relationship as 32, but the model predicts 28.1, so it *underestimates* the actual score that Alice gave.'

'I looked at Alice's scores. It seemed to me that the model underestimated most of them: eight of the ten scores were greater than 28. How was that possible if the model is supposed to represent the centre of the distribution? I asked Milton, who said that it was because of the weird score. He called it an outlier – the rating of 11 that Alice gave in the last week. He then said that to see the impact that this score had had, I should compute the mean without including that score.

CHECK YOUR BRAIN: *Compute the mean but excluding the score of 11.*

Milton was still using my diePad as a heat pad, so I grabbed a napkin and pen and tried to add the numbers. The total was 270, and there were nine scores, so I needed to divide 270 by 9. That's the sort of sum my diePad could tackle in nanoseconds if it didn't have a big ginger cat on it. After consulting The Head I had an answer. 'It's 30,' I said. Milton said nothing. He was curled into a ball on my diePad, gently purring. I poked him with my finger. He raised his outer eyelid slightly and made a token attempt to biff my hand away with his paw. I poked him harder. Milton yawned and sat up looking very disgruntled. 'What is it? I'm trying to sleep.'

'The mean without the outlier is 30.'

Milton got up from my diePad, revealing an image on the screen that he had somehow created while sleeping on it. **(FIGURE 4.9)** 'Look,' he said 'you can see the outlier clearly in this histogram. It is a score that is a long way from the others, and the effect it has is to shift the mean towards it. This is because the mean is the balance point of the data.' I noticed that he had also written me a message. **(MEOWSINGS 4.1)**

Dear Human,

The mean is the balancing point of a distribution, which means that adding (or taking away) scores will change the mean unless the score you add (or remove) equals the value of the mean itself. Alice's RAS scores (excluding the outlier) are shown on the left of Figure 4.7; the mean of 30 is the score that keeps these values in balance. If you add a score to the data that is equal to the mean then the mean will not change (Figure 4.7, top row). If you add a score that is greater than the mean then it tips the scores to the right, and the mean shifts that way too (i.e., increases) to compensate and restore balance (Figure 4.7, middle row). Conversely, if you add a score that is smaller than the mean then it tips the scores to the left, and the mean also shifts that way (i.e., decreases) to compensate and restore balance (Figure 4.7, bottom row). A similar thing happens if you remove scores from the data: removing a score less than the mean will increase the mean, and removing a score greater than the mean will reduce it.

In a similar vein, if you change the data by a fixed value, then the mean changes by that value too. For example, if you add 10 to every score then the mean of the new scores will be the mean of the old scores plus 10, similarly it would be 10 less if you subtract 10 from every score; if you multiply all of the scores by a value (e.g., 10) then the new mean will be the old mean times that value, and if you divide scores by a constant (e.g., 10) then the new mean will be the old mean divided by the constant (Figure 4.8).

Best fishes,
Milton

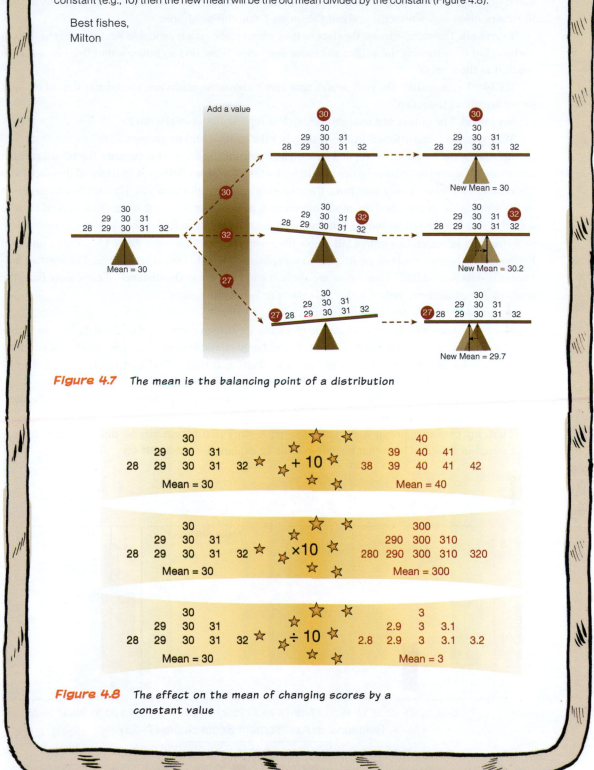

Figure 4.7   *The mean is the balancing point of a distribution*

Figure 4.8   *The effect on the mean of changing scores by a constant value*

Milton's Meowsings 4.1   *Things that affect the mean*

Milton asked me what I noticed about the mean if we exclude the outlier. I looked at the image he had created. **(FIGURE 4.9)** It seemed to me that without the outlier, the mean split the data exactly in two: the distribution was symmetrical about the mean. I said this to Milton.

'*Purr*cisely. The mean divides the data in two, which makes it a reasonable summary of the data as a whole, but if we include the outlier, the mean decreases. What do you notice about this new mean in relation to the scores?'

'It's like I said earlier: the only scores that aren't above the mean are 11 and 28: the other eight scores are above the mean.'

'Very good. The outlier has made the mean less representative of the data.'

'Why was the mean affected by the outlier, but the median and mode weren't?'

'Another good question,' he replied in a slightly patronizing tone. 'It is because the mean, median and mode measure the "typical" score in different ways. The mean defines it in terms of distance from the centre, so a score a long way from the centre can throw the mean off. The median measures it as the score at the centre, and the mode measures it as the most frequent score. The median aims to split the data into two equal halves, but the mean does not try to do this, which is why you can end up in a situation in which two scores fall below the mean and eight above it **(FIGURE 4.9)** – that would not happen with the median because it is based on splitting the data into equal halves. The median balances the data so that half of the scores are above it and half below: the distance of each score from the centre is not considered; only whether it is above or below the centre.'

'So the median is better than the mean?'

'Not necessarily. The mean has many useful features. It uses every score in the data, and so is representative. But most important is that it tends to be quite stable across samples; that is, if you took several samples and measured the same thing in them, you would find that the mean ought to be relatively similar in the different samples – this is less true of the median.'

'Sweet, so we have three "models" of the typical score: the average, the middle score and the most frequent score. Which one should we use?'

'That, my new acquaintance, is another story.' A story that apparently he didn't want to tell me right now, but I noticed later that he had sent me an explanation. **(MEOWSINGS 4.2)**

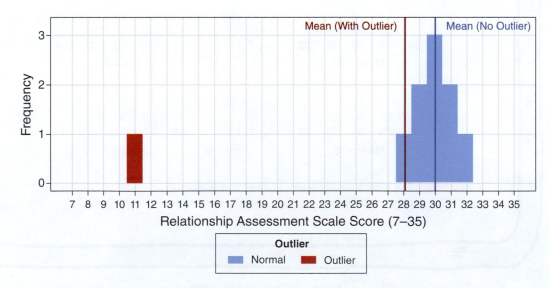

Figure 4.9 *Outliers can affect the mean*

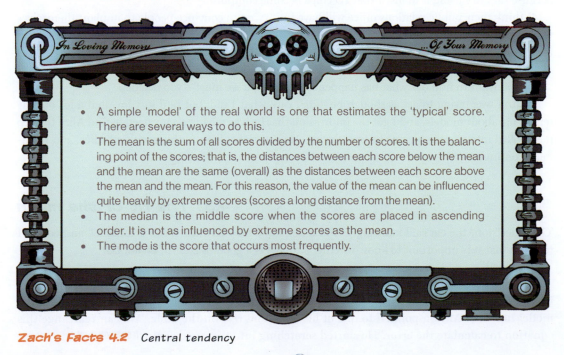

Dear Human,

When considering which measure of central tendency to use, you need to think about the type of data you have (Section 2.3.3). If you have nominal data then you can only use the mode (because the median assumes order in the data, and the mean is based on the distances between scores which doesn't make sense for nominal data). With ordinal data the median is appropriate (because it is based on the scores being ordered) but the mean is not (because it is based on distances between scores and it assumes that the distance between scores is the same at all points along the scale, which is true of interval data, but not ordinal data). With interval or ratio data the mean is appropriate and so is the median (because on an interval scale scores are still ordered).

The other thing to think about is extreme scores or skew in the distribution. The median is less affected by extreme scores at either end of the distribution than the mean. Remember that with our example data, the extreme score (11) did not affect the median but it dragged the mean down. Skewed distributions (Section 3.2) represent a situation in which there are a minority of scores that are a fair bit smaller (negative skew) or larger (positive skew) than the rest. As such, skewed distributions will also affect the mean (negative skew reduces the mean, positive skew inflates it).

Best fishes,
Milton

Milton's Meowsings 4.2 Which measure to use?

- A simple 'model' of the real world is one that estimates the 'typical' score. There are several ways to do this.
- The mean is the sum of all scores divided by the number of scores. It is the balancing point of the scores; that is, the distances between each score below the mean and the mean are the same (overall) as the distances between each score above the mean and the mean. For this reason, the value of the mean can be influenced quite heavily by extreme scores (scores a long distance from the mean).
- The median is the middle score when the scores are placed in ascending order. It is not as influenced by extreme scores as the mean.
- The mode is the score that occurs most frequently.

Zach's Facts 4.2 Central tendency

4.3 THE 'FIT' OF THE MEAN: VARIANCE

'That was strange,' said Milton.

'It's been happening a lot recently. People collapse and don't remember who they are. I was reading about it yesterday: they say there are no known cases of it happening to Clocktorians, only Chippers. The WGA is suggesting a Clocktorian revolution, you know, Clocktorians using some sort of drug to attack Chippers. I don't buy it.'

'Why not?'

'It doesn't make any sense. We don't want to convert everyone else to be a Clocktorian, we just don't want to have ID chips. We don't care if other people have them. It's convenient for the WGA too because they are using it to insist that ID chips become compulsory.'

'I think their public relations office will have fun trying to convince people to implant themselves with something that apparently makes you more likely to forget who you are. Anyway, shall we get back to Alice's data?'

I shrugged.

'If you want to find out what has happened to her then we must – you decide.'

Milton was trying to act as though he didn't care what I did, but he'd just invested a lot of time telling me about models, and I got the impression that he was relying on my need to find Alice to keep me hooked into whatever game he was playing. He was right: I am nothing without Alice, and I willingly continued.

4.3.1 The Fit of the mean

'Good decision,' the cat said knowingly. 'You understand now how the mean is a model, and earlier I told you that it is important to know whether a model is a good or bad fit.' (SECTION 4.1.2)

I nodded.

'We can assess how well the mean, or any other model, "fits" the data by looking at the errors in prediction. Remember, when we use the mean as a model of the typical score, we write the model like this.' Milton pointed to one of his equations (4.11) on the table. 'We can rearrange this equation to calculate the error.' He started scratching into the wood again. (EQUATION 4.12)

$$\text{outcome}_i = (\text{model}) + \text{error}_i$$
$$\text{error}_i = \text{outcome}_i - \text{model}$$
$$\text{error}_i = \text{RAS}_i - \mu \qquad (4.12)$$

'The error for a given observation is the value observed minus what the model predicted. If we are predicting particular RAS scores from the average RAS score, then it is the difference between the particular RAS score and the mean. Imagine we are interested only in the fit of the mean to the scores we have, so we use μ (remember it is just a Greek m) to represent the mean.'

'That's what I said earlier, that the model underestimated Alice's first RAS score because she scored 32 but the mean was only 28.1.'

'Exactly. We can write your observation as an equation, in which we say we are predicting Alice's score in week 1, from the mean (our model). Look,' he said as he destroyed some more table, **(EQUATION 4.13)** 'the error will be 32–28.1, or 3.9.

$$\text{error}_{\text{week1}} = \text{outcome}_{\text{week1}} - \text{model}$$
$$\text{error}_{\text{week1}} = \text{RAS}_{\text{week1}} - \mu \qquad (4.13)$$
$$\text{error}_{\text{week1}} = 32 - 28.1$$

'Can I let you into a secret about statisticians?'

'They are all evil?'

'Oh, so it is not a secret?' Milton joked. 'Legend has it that back in ancient Greece the early pioneers of modern mathematics solved the problem of time travel, but they shared it only with other mathematicians. Mathematicians have been secretly enjoying the privilege of time travel ever since.'

'How do they do it?' I asked, keen to discover the secret so that I could go back to before the revolution and watch some of my favourite bands.

'I do not know. Rumour has it that it involves thinking about some really hard equations.' I wondered whether Milton was lying and did know, but then wouldn't he have gone back in time to prevent his accident? Maybe he liked being a cat? 'In any case,' he continued, sensing my distracted mind, 'the great statistical minds used to gather across time to meet annually at a Victorian café in Soho, London, called Gossett's Tea. They were all there – Fisher, Pearson, Neyman, Gauss, Bayes, and Florence Nightingale. The festivities would kick off with a bun fight between Bayes, Fisher, Neyman and Pearson, after which they would discuss life. They could not understand why all of the other people in the world had wives and husbands, and friends, and lived fulfilled lives. They were also confused about why other people didn't wear glasses and have white beards – especially Florence. They concluded that of all the earthly experiences – friendship, love, a smooth chin – none could compare with the knowledge of statistics. They vowed to keep this experience for themselves, and drew up a pact to obfuscate statistics. They decided that the best way to achieve this was to come up with multiple names for the same thing.'

'Weirds. Alice told me that was because of a guy called Confusius who invented a confusion machine.'

'Don't be ridiculous, that is completely implausible – it is because of time-travelling statisticians. Now *pay attention*. Error is one of these words, because the error in prediction from a model is sometimes known as error, and sometimes as **deviance** or deviation, and other times as **residual**. These terms have subtly different uses, but mean essentially the same thing. The deviance is the value of the outcome minus the value predicted from the model, and when the model is the mean, it is the observed score minus the mean.' **(EQUATION 4.14)**

$$\text{error}_i = \text{outcome}_i - \text{model}_i \qquad (4.14)$$
$$\text{deviance}_i = x_i - \mu$$

Milton continued. 'If we know that this is the error for a particular score, how might we work out how much error there is overall?'

I thought about this question; it seemed that you could work out the error attached to each score and then add them up, but I was scared of making a fool of myself, so I said nothing.

'You are very quiet, I assume that you don't know the answer. I will tell you: if we want to know the total error or total deviance then we could add up the deviances for each data point.' I kicked myself for not having the balls to give Milton an answer, but I was also pleased that I had been right. 'In equation form, we can scratch this into the table as follows.' (EQUATION 4.15)

$$\text{total error} = \sum_{i=1}^{n} \left(\text{outcome}_i - \text{model}_i\right)$$

$$\text{total deviance} = \sum_{i=1}^{n} \left(x_i - \mu\right)$$

(4.15)

'The sigma symbol (Σ) simply means –'

'– add up what comes after, and what comes after is the deviances, so it means add up all of the deviances,' I interrupted.

Milton looked impressed. He had a much more expressive face than the average cat, which I guessed was because it was being controlled by a human mind. 'Let us see what happens when we calculate the deviances for Alice's RAS scores. We will ignore her final score of 11 for now.' Milton sat on my diePad again and wriggled around a bit, before stepping off to reveal an image. (FIGURE 4.10) I didn't even want to think about how he did that. 'This diagram shows Alice's RAS scores over the nine weeks, and also her mean RAS score that we calculated earlier on. The line representing the mean is our "model", and the circles are Alice's observed scores. The vertical lines that connect each observed value to the mean value are the errors or deviances of the model for each observed score. The first week, Alice's score was 32, but the model predicts a score of 30 so the error for week 1 is 2. This error is a positive number, and represents

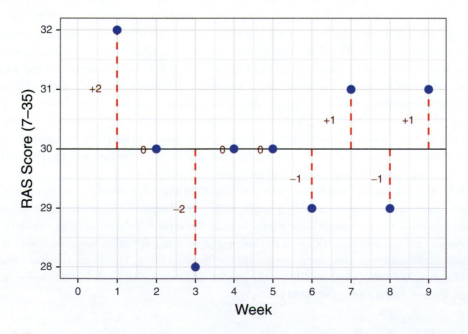

Figure 4.10 Graph showing the difference between Alice's observed RAS scores each week, and the mean RAS score

the fact that our model *underestimates* Alice's actual score. For week 2, the model predicts 30 (again) and the observed score is 30 which means that the error is 0. For week 3, Alice scored 28 but the model predicts a score of 30, so the error is −2; the negative number tells us that our model *overestimates* Alice's actual score. You can see the errors for the other weeks on the diagram.'

'Yeah, you can see how the model sits in the middle of the data, so sometimes it overestimates and sometimes it underestimates the actual scores.'

'Yes, so what do you think might happen when we add up these errors, or deviances, as you suggest?'

'It tells us the total error?'

'Let us see,' the cat said as his claw set to work. *(EQUATION 4.16)*

$$
\begin{aligned}
\text{sum of errors} &= \sum_{i=1}^{n} \left(\text{outcome}_i - \text{model}_i \right) \\
&= (32-30)+(30-30)+(28-30)+(30-30)+(30-30) \\
&\quad +(29-30)+(31-30)+(29-30)+(31-30) \\
&= 2+0+(-2)+0+0+(-1)+1+(-1)+1 \\
&= 2-2-1+1-1+1 \\
&= 0
\end{aligned}
\tag{4.16}
$$

The result was surprising: the total was 0, as though there was no error at all, but that couldn't be true because I could see in the diagram that the mean *was* different from the observed scores; there *was* error. Milton explained.

'Odd, is it not? It happens because the mean is at the centre of the distribution, and so some of the deviances are positive (scores greater than the mean) and some are negative (scores smaller than the mean). Consequently, when we add the scores up, the total is zero.'

'Can't we just ignore whether the error is positive or negative, then?' I asked.

Another impressed look from Milton. 'A sensible idea, and there is nothing wrong with doing that, but generally we square the deviances, which has a similar effect (because a negative number multiplied by another negative number becomes positive). We can add these squared deviances up to get the **sum of squared errors**, *SS* (often just called the *sum of squares*); unless your scores are all exactly the same, the resulting value will be bigger than zero, indicating that there is some deviance from the model (in this case the mean). We can express this like so; *(EQUATION 4.17)* the first equation shows the general principle that we can apply to all models, and the second one shows the equation specifically for the mean.'

$$
\text{sum of squared errors} \left(SS \right) = \sum_{i=1}^{n} \left(\text{outcome}_i - \text{model}_i \right)^2
$$

$$
\text{sum of squared errors} \left(SS \right) = \sum_{i=1}^{n} \left(x_i - \mu \right)^2
\tag{4.17}
$$

'So, as before, the sigma symbol means "add up all of the things that follow", but what follows now is the squared errors.'

'Yes. Can you do this for our nine scores? I will draw a table for you'. *(TABLE 4.2)* Milton again sat on my diePad, wriggled around for a few seconds, then got up and stepped away, revealing a table.

'The first column is Alice's scores. The second column reminds you of the model, in this case the mean. The third column shows the deviance or error for each score. Note that when you add these values the sum is zero. The final column shows the deviance, or error, squared. Note that unlike the

Table 4.2 *Table showing the deviations of each score from the mean*

RAS score (x_i)	Mean (μ)	Deviance ($x_i - \mu$)	Deviance squared ($x_i - \mu)^2$
28	30	−2	4
29	30	−1	1
29	30	−1	1
30	30	0	0
30	30	0	0
30	30	0	0
31	30	1	1
31	30	1	1
32	30	2	4

$$\sum_{i=1}^{n} x_i - \mu = 0 \qquad \sum_{i=1}^{n} (x_i - \mu)^2 = 12$$

raw deviances, none of the values are negative. Therefore, when we add these up we get a positive number, 12. What do you think would happen to this total if we found another 10 scores and added them to the table?'

'Would the sum of squared errors get bigger because we're adding up more squared deviances?' I felt I was getting the hang of this now.

'Su*purr*b. It *would* get bigger, so although we can use the sum of squares as an indicator of the total deviance from the model, its size will depend on how many scores we have in the data. Sometimes this won't matter, but it is a nuisance if we want to compare the total error across samples of different sizes. An easy solution is to divide by the number of scores (N), to give us the "average" squared error, known as the mean squared error. When the model is the mean, the mean squared error has a special name, the **variance**. We can take the previous equation **(4.17)** and add to it by dividing by the number of scores. **(EQUATION 4.18)** The symbol for variance in the population is σ^2. Our total squared error was 12, **(TABLE 4.2)** and that was based on nine scores, so what is the mean squared error, or variance?'

$$\text{mean squared error} = \frac{SS}{N} = \frac{\sum_{i=1}^{n} (\text{outcome}_i - \text{model}_i)^2}{N}$$
$$\text{variance} \left(\sigma^2\right) = \frac{SS}{N} = \frac{\sum_{i=1}^{n} (x_i - \mu)^2}{N} \tag{4.18}$$

Using my diePad I divided 12 by 9. 'It will be 1.33,' I said proudly.

'Yes. Well done. There is one problem with the variance as a measure.'

'Frippin' hell, Milton, is there ever *not* a problem? First the total error is no good, then the total squared error is no good, now the average squared error is no good. Is anything ever going to be good?'

'*Purr*haps "problem" is too strong a word. The mean squared error is fine, but because we squared each error in the calculation it gives us a measure in units squared. For Alice's RAS scores, we would say that the average error of the mean was 1.33 RAS units squared. There is nothing wrong with saying that, but it is sometimes useful to convert back to the original scale of measurement, so we can talk about the error with reference to the RAS scale. To do this, we would take the square root of the variance (which converts the average error back to the original units of measurement). This measure is known as the **standard deviation** and the symbol for it in the population is σ. **(EQUATION 4.19)**

$$\sigma = \sqrt{\text{variance}} = \sqrt{\frac{\sum_{i=1}^{n}(x_i - \mu)^2}{N}} \tag{4.19}$$

$$= \sqrt{1.33}$$

$$= 1.15$$

4.3.2 Estimating the fit of the mean from a sample

This was making some kind of sense to me, and that realization was exciting. I wished Alice was here to see how well I was doing. I felt sure that if she was having doubts about us she'd forget them if she could see me taking in this stuff. Milton had explained that we fit models to data to summarize the general pattern. Like, what's the pattern in Alice's relationship scores? The most basic way to do that is to just look at the middle of the distribution: what is the most common score (the mode), the middle score (the median) or the balancing point of the data (the mean). The mean is a model because it doesn't have to be a value actually observed in the data. It also made sense that if you have a summary then you want to know how good that summary is. With the mean you can do that by looking at the average error between the data and the mean.

I was feeling pretty pleased with myself, but Milton was about to throw me a curve ball of monumental proportions. He rose up, arched his back in an enormous stretch as if preparing himself for something big. Then he dropped the 'degrees of freedom' bomb. More powerful than any nuclear explosion, this was a bomb designed to ruthlessly and precisely destroy all brain matter with which it came into contact. My brain was only centimetres from the epicentre. Batticks!

'Of course,' Milton began, 'I have simplified things a smidge.'

'What do you mean by "a smidge"?'

'I mean, a lot,' replied Milton.

'A lot?'

'An enormous amount, really. Everything I have said about testing how well the mean fits the model is true if you have the population data (i.e., all of the data in which you are interested), but in most situations we have only a sample, and we estimate the population mean and the "fit" from that sample.'

'So, what's the problem?'

'The problem is that if we use the equations that I just mentioned we will underestimate the variance and standard deviation of the population.'

'Why?'

Milton jumped onto my diePad again, his paws moving in a whirlwind around the screen. It was amazing that a cat had such dexterity.

'Look at this drawing. **(FIGURE 4.11)** It shows the histogram of a population of scores on the RAS. You remember what a histogram is?'

'Yes, you have each score listed along the bottom, and the height of the bar tells you how often a score was observed in the data.'

'Ex*scratch*ly, so you can see in the population that most scores cluster around the centre, and scores at the extremes have low bars indicating that these scores do not occur very often in the population. Also, notice that the population uses up the whole of the scale: scores range from the minimum value of 7 on the RAS to the maximum value of 35. If we were to take a sample of scores from this population, it is much more likely that we would select a score from the middle (because there are lots of them in the population) and much less likely that we would sample a score from the extremes (because there are fewer of them). That is not to say that we will not get scores from the extremes in the sample, but it is less likely than getting one from the centre. The resulting sample will, on average, contain lots of scores from the middle of the population and relatively fewer at the extremes. The result is that the sample distribution is typically narrower than the population, as you can see in the drawing. **(FIGURE 4.11)** What that means is that in the sample scores are closer to the middle than they are in the population. Now what does the variance measure?'

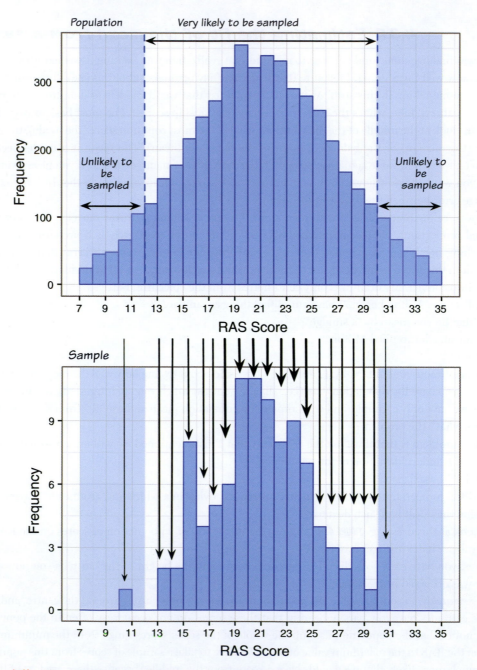

Figure 4.11   *Why do samples underestimate the population variance?*

'It measures the fit of the mean, or the average error between the mean and the observed scores.'

'Yes, and we define the error as the distance between the mean and the score. So, the variance measures the average squared distance of scores from the mean. In a narrow distribution the scores are closer to the centre than in a wide distribution.'

'Which means that the variance, the average squared distance from the middle, will be smaller too in a narrow distribution. So because the sample distribution will be narrower than the population, it's variance will be smaller than the population.'

'Brilliant!' Milton patted my arm with his paw. 'I will make a statistician of you yet! The variance in the sample will underestimate the variance in the population because the sample is likely to be narrower than the population from which it comes.'

'If the sample underestimates the population variance, then doesn't that mean that it sucks?'

'It means that it is a **biased estimator**.'

'Is that statisticians' code for "it sucks"?'

'*Purr*haps. A biased estimator is a statistic taken from a random sample that does not equal its corresponding population parameter, whereas an **unbiased estimator** is a statistic from a sample that does equal the corresponding population parameter.'

'Surely a biased estimate is a bad thing. I mean, if my pocket watch told me the wrong time I'd buy a new one.'

'Would you? What about if your watch always displayed the time exactly 5 minutes behind the actual time? It underestimated the time by exactly 5 minutes. Always.'

'Well, I suppose if I knew the watch was always 5 minutes slow I could add 5 minutes to the time it displays –'

'– and save some money. Exactly, and samples are like this slow watch: they provide a biased estimate of the population variance, but it is always biased in exactly the same way. This means that we can correct it to make it unbiased. Remember that the variance is the average squared deviation from the mean, and to get this average we divided by the number of scores (*N*)? *(EQUATION 4.18)* Well, if we are using the sample to estimate the population variance then we divide by *N* – 1, rather than by *N*.'

'What? That's the only difference?'

'Yes, a small but important difference.'

'We just replace *N* with *N* – 1 in that equation? *(4.18)* Seriously? That's it?'

$$\text{mean squared error} = \frac{SS}{n-1} = \frac{\sum_{i=1}^{n}(\text{outcome}_i - \text{model}_i)^2}{n-1}$$

$$\text{variance}\left(s^2\right) = \frac{SS}{n-1} = \frac{\sum_{i=1}^{n}\left(x_i - \bar{X}\right)^2}{n-1} \tag{4.20}$$

$$= \frac{12}{8}$$

$$= 1.5$$

'Basically, yes. However, because we are now working with a sample, we would also replace the μ, which is the symbol for the population mean, with *M* or $\bar{X}$, the symbol for the sample mean, and we use *n* instead of a capital *N* to show that we are using the number of scores in the sample, rather than in the population. The variance itself we give the symbol s^2 to show that it is based on a sample, rather than using σ^2. *(EQUATION 4.20)* For Alice's RAS scores, if we assume that the nine scores we have are a sample of her scores for the population of all the weeks you have been together, then we could estimate the variance of this population by dividing the sum of squares by 8, rather than 9. This gives us a variance of 1.50, which is slightly higher than before, which illustrates that this correction increases the estimate to counteract the fact that samples typically underestimate the population variance.'

'And the standard deviation of the population is estimated from the sample by taking the square root of this variance estimate?'

'*Purr*cisely, although again we change some of the symbols to show that we are working with a sample. So μ is replaced with M or $\bar{X}$, the symbol for the sample mean, and the standard deviation itself is denoted by s. For Alice's RAS scores we end up with a value of 1.22.' *(EQUATION 4.21)*

$$
\begin{aligned}
s = \sqrt{\text{variance}} &= \sqrt{\frac{\sum_{i=1}^{n}\left(x_i - \bar{X}\right)^2}{n-1}} \\
&= \sqrt{1.5} \\
&= 1.22
\end{aligned}
$$

(4.21)

'I don't understand why dividing by $n-1$ instead of N makes the estimate unbiased. Is it magic?'

'I can see that it seems like magic, but it is not. It does, however, involve some scary maths – even scarier than dogs. With your slow watch, you do not need to know the mechanics of why it is 5 minutes slow; you need only to know that it is and that by adding 5 minutes you get the correct time. It is the same here, we do not need to know the maths, we need only to know that using $n-1$ works, and I can show you that it does.'

It was a boast that Milton followed up on.

'Imagine we have a population of just 5 people, and they gave us RAS scores of 26, 23, 17, 22, and 20.' Milton again started playing frantically with my diePad until he had produced a really complex diagram. *(FIGURE 4.12)* 'The mean of this population is 21.6, and the variance is about 9. Now imagine that we took 10 random samples of 3 scores from this population; because there are only 5 scores in the population, some of these samples will be the same and others different. In each sample, I will compute the variance using both n (in each case this will be 3) and $n-1$ (in each case 2). When calculating the variance using n, the samples give estimates below the actual population value of 9 most of the time. If we use $n-1$ then the estimates are, in general, closer to the actual value of 9. The crucial thing is what happens if we average across the estimates for the 10 samples. The average estimate when we calculate the variance using n is 6.18. In other words, *on average*, we have underestimated the true variance in the population. However, when we calculate the variance using $n-1$ the *average* estimate of the variance is 9.26, which is closer to the true value. This example shows that *on average* estimating the population variance from a sample by dividing by $n-1$ gives us an unbiased estimate of the true value.'

 CHECK YOUR BRAIN: *For each sample of three scores in Figure 4.12, calculate the mean, sum of squares, variance and standard deviation using both n and n – 1.*

I looked at Milton's drawing. It seemed to me that for some samples using $n-1$ made the variance estimate worse. 'Look at the last sample,' I said. 'The variance estimate is 20.33 when you use $n-1$, but only 13.56 when you use n, so it's closer to the true value of 9.04 when you use n.'

The cat stared at me. 'The point is that *on average* the estimate is better, not necessarily for a particular sample. This is important because in the real world we would not know what the population variance is (and if we did we would not need to estimate it), so we have no way of knowing how close the estimate in our sample is to the true value, but by using $n-1$ we know that on average it will be better than using n.'

That was a brain frip, but I had to admit that using $n-1$ did seem to work, even though I didn't understand why.

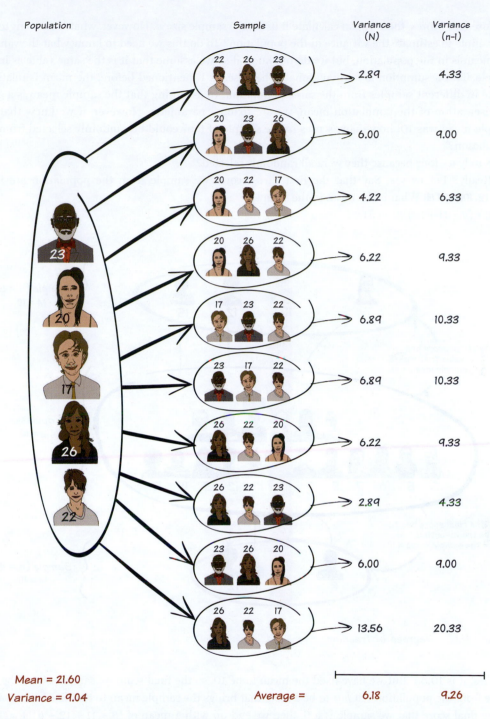

Population	Sample	Variance (N)	Variance (n-1)
	22 26 23	2.89	4.33
	20 23 26	6.00	9.00
	20 22 17	4.22	6.33
	20 26 22	6.22	9.33
	17 23 22	6.89	10.33
	23 17 22	6.89	10.33
	26 22 20	6.22	9.33
	26 22 23	2.89	4.33
	23 26 20	6.00	9.00
	26 22 17	13.56	20.33

Mean = 21.60
Variance = 9.04

Average =   6.18   9.26

Figure 4.12 *Why we use n – 1 when estimating the population variance*

'$n-1$ is known as the **degrees of freedom** for the sample, which is a tricky concept, so concentrate. In statistical terms the degrees of freedom are the number of scores that are free to vary.' Once more Milton attacked my diePad, feverishly creating another visual masterpiece. **(FIGURE 4.13)** 'Imagine we have a population. Of course, we do not actually have the data from the population, so we take a sample of four scores. These scores can be any value – they are free to vary. If we are interested only in the variance of those four scores, then we can calculate it using the sample size *n*. However, what if we want to use the sample to estimate the variance in the population? To do this we need to know what the value of the mean is in the population, but we do not know it so we assume that it is the same value as in the sample. This assumption is fairly reasonable because, as I mentioned before, the mean is relatively stable in different samples from the same population. In assuming that the sample mean is a good representation of the population mean, we are fixing a parameter. However, if we knew that the sample mean was 10, how many scores in the sample of four could be randomly selected from the population?'

'Surely it's four because they were all randomly selected?'

'Really? Let us see. Say that the first three scores we sample from the population are 8, 11 and 12. **(FIGURE 4.13)** What is the mean in the sample?'

'It's $(8 + 11 + 12)/3$, so 31/3.'

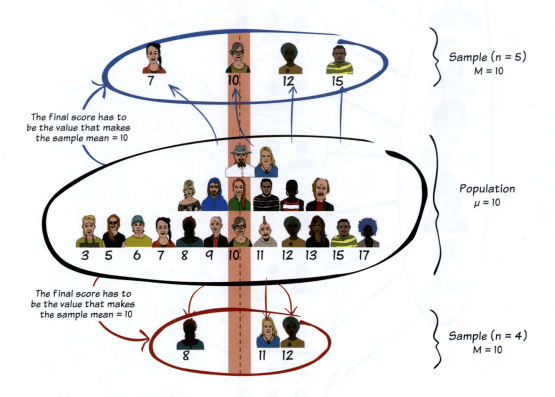

Figure 4.13   *Degrees of freedom*

'Yes, it is 10.33. But we have fixed the mean to be 10, so the final score we sample cannot be any score from the population – it *has* to be a score that brings the sample mean to that fixed value of 10. If the final score that we sample is a 6, then we end up with a mean of $(8 + 11 + 12 + 6)/4 = 9.25$, which is no good because we have fixed the mean to be 10, not 9.25. The only value that will bring the sample mean to the fixed value of 10 is 9: $(8 + 11 + 12 + 9)/4 = 10$. So, in a sample of four, the first three scores can be truly randomly sampled from the population, they are free to vary, but the last score is not: it has to be a score that brings the mean to 10. The same is true if we sampled five people from this distribution: the first four scores can take on any value from the population, but the final score has to be a value that makes the mean, in this case, 10. In general, if we hold one parameter constant then the degrees of freedom must be one less than the number of scores used to calculate that parameter. This fact explains why when we use a sample to estimate the mean squared error (or indeed the standard deviation) of a population, we divide the sums of squares by $n-1$ rather than N: because only $n-1$ scores are truly free to vary, there are $n-1$ degrees of freedom.'

'That made no sense whatsoever.'

'Worry not: nobody understands degrees of freedom.'

4.3.3 Outliers and variance

I was starting to feel stupid again: that whole degrees of freedom nonsense had melted my brain and I felt like I'd got too cocky in thinking I understood everything. Perhaps Milton was putting me back in my place, or perhaps this stuff really was important. I needed to get the conversation back into territory that I understood. I remembered that we'd ignored Alice's extreme score when we calculated the variance. I asked Milton why.

'I did that to keep the maths simple, but you remind me of a very good point. As a bit of practice, compute the variance with that score included and see how it affects the variance.'

'Should I use n or $n-1$?'

'As I said, the vast majority of times we use the sample to estimate the value in the population, so use $n-1$.'

 CHECK YOUR BRAIN: Estimate the population variance of Alice's RAS scores from the sample including the score of 11.

So began the monumental task of working out the variance. Milton jumped off of the table and went on a little tour of Occam's café. He wandered under tables looking for unsuspecting diners to lavish affection upon him. Some looked horrified at the presence of a cat, others simply accepted that he was there and stroked and fussed him. I felt sure that they would have been less enthusiastic if they had known they were tickling a 'dead' physics professor. He returned some time later, by which time I had finished the calculation.

'The variance with the outlier is 37.43,' I said.

'Good, very good. You took a while, but nevertheless correct – well done. Can you remember what the variance was before we added the outlier?' *(EQUATION 4.20)*

'It was 1.5, wasn't it?'

'*Claw*rect.'

'Wow, that's an *insane* difference.'

'Indeed it is. This goes to show you that, like the mean itself, extreme scores influence the variance. In fact the variance is more biased than the mean – the extreme score will not only have a large deviance from the mean, but that large deviance then gets squared when the variance is computed, which makes it disproportionately big.'

4.4   DISPERSION

When I'd woken up yesterday morning I was looking forward to a nice brunch with Alice, but the weekend was broken: I woke up with a broken heart, I broke into someone's office, then this morning I'd sneaked into a high-security research centre and stolen a cat who was now teaching me statistics inbetween licking a cup of lactose-free latte. I'd had my spooks quota for one week. I was feeling out of my depth on every level. We'd been here ages, I was tired, I needed to go home, check in with Nick and actually do something that was going to tell me what the frip was happening. I told Milton I was going home.

'That's very kind of you, I would love to come home with you, rest under your warm radiator and eat all of your food. Thank you for offering.'

'But I ...'

'Before we go, just a few final things,' he said as he padded across my lap to the other side of the bench.

4.4.1 The standard deviation as an indicator of dispersion

Before I could protest, Milton had launched into another monologue. I wondered if his plan was to distract me for so long that I'd forget about Alice.

'I have described the sum of squares, variance and standard deviation to you. I talked about them measuring the "fit" of the mean to the data. Another way to think of "fit" is as the dispersion or spread of data around the mean. I have hinted at this already. Remember that the sum of squares, variance and standard deviation all represent the same thing, but one is a total, one is an average, and one is the average converted back to the original units of measurement. A small standard deviation (relative to the value of the mean) indicates that data points are close to the mean. A large standard deviation (relative to the mean) indicates that the data points are distant from the mean. A standard deviation of 0 would mean that all of the scores were the same.

'I will draw you two pictures *(FIGURE 4.14)* showing some RAS scores for two people over a five-week period. Both people had the same RAS score on average ($M = 20.2$), but their scores are very different. The first person had a standard deviation of 1.6 (very small compared to the mean). RAS scores across the five weeks were consistently close to the mean for this person. Put another way, the scores are not spread too widely around the mean. Contrast this with the second person whose scores had a standard deviation of 12 (fairly high compared to the mean). The second person's scores are spread more widely around the mean than the first: some weeks he rated his relationship very highly but other weeks he was very unsatisfied.'

'I can see that the mean "fits" the scores better for the first person than the second,' I said trying to sound enthusiastic.

'Yes, and this is reflected in the low standard deviation. The variance and standard deviation also tell us about the shape of the distribution of scores. If the mean "fits" the data well then most of the scores will cluster close to the mean and the resulting standard deviation will be small relative to the mean. When the mean is a worse "fit" of the data, the scores will cluster more widely around the mean and the standard deviation will be larger.

'I'll draw you another picture. *(FIGURE 4.15)* These two distributions of RAS scores have the same mean ($M = 21$) but different standard deviations. The one on the left has a large standard deviation relative to the mean ($SD = 6$), and this results in a flatter, more spread-out, distribution. The one on the right has a standard deviation half the size ($SD = 3$). Notice that this gives the distribution a narrower, pointier shape: scores close to the mean are very frequent but scores further from the mean rapidly become increasingly infrequent. The key message is that as the standard deviation gets larger, the distribution gets fatter.'

4.4.2 The range and interquartile range

Milton paused to scratch his ear, and I thought our lesson was over. Instead, and completely oblivious to the desire that his relentless statistics lecture was giving me to pray for sweet death, he carried on.

'You know, there are simpler ways to look at dispersion. A very simple way is to take the largest score and subtract from it the smallest score. This is known as the **range** of scores. If we order Alice's RAS scores we get 11, 28, 29, 29, 30, 30, 30, 31, 31, 32. The highest score is 32 and the lowest is 11; therefore, the range is $32 - 11 = 21$. What happens if we compute the range, but excluding Alice's low score of 11?

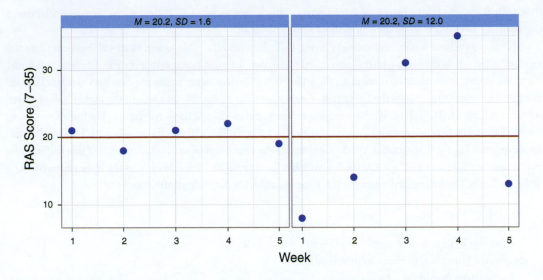

Figure 4.14 *Graphs illustrating data that have the same mean but different standard deviations*

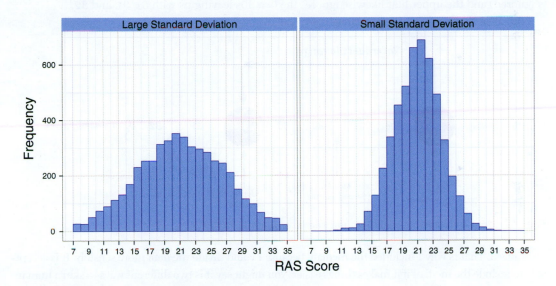

Figure 4.15 *Two distributions with the same mean, but large and small standard deviations*

 CHECK YOUR BRAIN: *Compute the range but excluding the score of 11.*

The highest score was still 32, and the lowest was now 28. It was easy enough to work out that the range would be 32 – 28, or 4.

'Without the extreme score the range drops dramatically from 21 to 4 – less than a quarter the size. This is a problem with the range: outliers can radically influence it. One solution is to calculate the range excluding values at the extremes of the distribution. It is common to cut off the top and bottom 25% of scores and calculate the range of the middle 50% of scores – known as the **interquartile range**. Let us do this with Alice's RAS scores. First we need to calculate **quartiles**, which are the three values that split the sorted data into four equal parts. This is not as hard as it first seems if you understood the median, because it involves computing three medians.'

Milton popped out a claw and started carving a diagram into the table again. **(FIGURE 4.16)** 'First calculate the median of the whole data set, which is also called the *second quartile*, because it splits the data into two equal parts. We already know that the median for these data is 30. Use this value to split the data into two equal halves. For the RAS scores, this means the lower half of scores contains 11, 28, 29, 29 and 30; the higher half of scores contains 30, 30, 31, 31, and 32. We now need to compute the median of these two halves. For the lower scores, the median will be in position $(n+1)/2 = (5+1)/2 = 6/2 = 3$ in the list, which is the number 29. This is called the **lower quartile (Q_1)** or first quartile. We do the same for the upper half of scores: the median of this half is again in position $(n+1)/2 = (5+1)/2 = 3$ in the list, which is the score of 31. This is known as the **upper quartile (Q_3)** or first quartile. The interquartile range is the lower quartile subtracted from the upper one.'

$$IQR = Q_3 - Q_1 \tag{4.22}$$

'So for the RAS scores it would be 31 – 29, which is 2.'

'Su*purr*b. However, there is a complication.'

'I knew there would be ...'

'You see, as a rule of thumb the median value is not included in the two halves when they are split. If we had removed the median then our lower half of scores should have been 11, 28, 29, 29 (and 30 is ignored) and the upper half likewise ignores the two 30s leaving us with 31, 31, and 32.'

'But then the two halves aren't equal.'

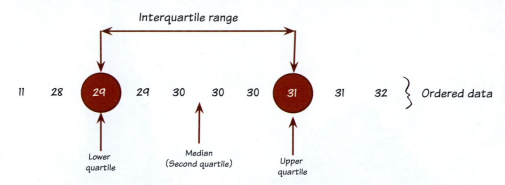

Figure 4.16 *Calculating quartiles and the interquartile range*

'Indeed. That is why I included the median, because I could divide the data more sensibly. It is acceptable to include the median if it makes things easier; you might say it is two different ways to skin a human.' He paused expecting me to laugh, which I didn't. 'How is the IQR affected if we remove the extreme score?'

 CHECK YOUR BRAIN: Compute the IQR but excluding the score of 11. (Hint: you might want to exclude the median when you create the upper and lower halves.)

I thought about this question for a moment. I had worked out before that with 11 removed the median was still 30. Splitting the data in half at 30, I'd get 28, 29, 29, 30 and 30, 30, 31, 31, 32, which is weirds because one half is bigger than the other. I could not think what to do and, not for the first time, I felt a wave of inadequacy come over me.

Sensing my despair Milton prompted me: 'Remember that I said that usually you would *exclude* the median from the halves, perhaps that would help.'

It did help, as Milton well knew. Without including the value of 30 I had a lower half of 28, 29, 29 and an upper half of 31, 31, and 32. The middle scores were easy enough to find: they would be in position $(n + 1)/2 = (3 + 1)/2 = 4/2 = 2$. In other words, the upper and lower quartiles were 31 and 29, the same as before, and the interquartile range would still be 2.

'The interquartile range doesn't change if you exclude the extreme score,' I proclaimed.

'*Purr*fectly true. This is an advantage of the interquartile range: it is not affected by extreme scores at either end of the distribution because it focuses on the middle 50% of scores. Of course, the downside is that you ignore half of your data. It is worth pointing out here that quartiles are special cases of things called **quantiles**, which are values that split a data set into equal portions. Quartiles are quantiles that split the data into four equal parts, but you can have other quantiles such as **percentiles** (points that split the data into 100 equal parts), **noniles** (points that split the data into nine equal parts) and so on. You look awful.'

I felt awful, too. I explained to Milton that, much as I appreciated his time, all of this information had got me nowhere. I felt it was a waste of a day, a day that I could have spent finding out whether Nick had got any leads from our fans, or any clues on *memoryBank*, a day where maybe I could have called the WGA, or done *something* that would get me closer to Alice.

- There are several ways to quantify how well the mean 'fits' the data. The deviance or error is the distance of each score from the mean.
- The sum of squared errors is the total amount of error in the mean. The errors/deviances are squared before adding them up.
- The variance is the average distance of scores from the mean. It is the sum of squares divided by the number of scores. It tells us about how widely dispersed scores are around the mean, and is also a measure of how well the model 'fits' the observed data. If you have all of the population data it can be calculated as:

$$\sigma^2 = \frac{\sum_{i=1}^{n}(x_i - \mu)^2}{N}$$

- If you want to estimate the population variance from a sample of data, then use this formula instead:

$$s^2 = \frac{\sum_{i=1}^{n}(x_i - \bar{X})^2}{n-1}$$

- The standard deviation is the *square root of the variance*. It is the variance converted back to the original units of measurement of the scores used to compute it. For this reason it is the most commonly cited measure of the 'fit' of the mean, or the dispersion of scores around the mean.
- Large standard deviations relative to the mean suggest data are widely spread around the mean (it is a poor 'fit'); whereas small standard deviations suggest data are closely packed around the mean (it is a good 'fit').
- The range is the distance between the highest and lowest score.
- The interquartile range is the range of the middle 50% of the scores.

Zach's Facts 4.3 Dispersion

The cat looked twitchy at the mention of the WGA, but he positioned himself on my lap and looked up at me with his big eyes. If you forgot who he was, he was pretty cute. His tone softened, and he spoke gently. 'I understand. I am sure it is not easy to lose someone who you love.' I wondered whether he had been in love, or whether his work was his love. 'Sometimes, you need to play the long game: a quick fix is not always best. Please try to trust me. I think we have learnt more than you realize: Alice's relationship scores are generally high. When we ignored her extreme score her mean satisfaction was 30, and the standard deviation was very small, 1.22, which suggests that this is a good "fit" of the population of all of Alice's satisfaction scores. It seems that she is very satisfied with her relationship with you. It is understandable when you look at the lengths you are going to in order to find her. Now, she had a very low score on the last week, but even with this score included her average satisfaction was 28.1 out of a maximum of 32. There is, perhaps, a question to ask about why her satisfaction levels were so low in that last week, but the fact remains that over the last 10 weeks, on the whole she is very satisfied.'

I felt a little overwhelmed; I wasn't sure whether it was hearing that Alice liked being with me, or just the stress of the last few days letting itself out, but I hugged the cat, and took a deep breath to control myself. 'Steady on!' he said as he extricated himself from my embrace.

When describing data with a measure of central tendency use M (capital M in italics) to represent the sample mean or mathematical notation ($\bar{x}$). Be consistent: if you choose M to represent the mean then use it throughout your write-up. If you report a summary of the data such as the mean, you should also report the appropriate measure of 'fit': in the case of the mean that would be the spread of scores. Therefore, it's common that when scientists report the mean, they also report the variance or standard deviation. The standard deviation is usually denoted by SD, but it is also common to simply place it in parentheses as long as you indicate that you're doing so in the text. Here are some examples:

- ✓ Zach has 2 'emos' on *memoryBank*. On average, a sample of other users ($N = 11$), had considerably more, $M = 95$, $SD = 56.79$.
- ✓ Alice's average RAS score, $\bar{x} = 30$, $SD = 1.22$, was higher than the national average.
- ✓ On average (SD in parentheses), people spend 3.45 (0.25) hours a day on their Proteus and drink 1.33 (0.25) lactose-free lattes a day.

Note that in the first example, I used N to denote the size of the sample. Although a capital N usually denotes the population size, it is common to see a capital N representing the entire sample and a lower-case n representing a subsample (e.g., the number of cases within a particular group).

When we report medians, a common abbreviation is *Mdn*, and again it is useful to report the range or interquartile range as well (*IQR* is commonly used for the interquartile range). Therefore, we could report:

- ✓ Alice's RAS scores, $Mdn = 30$, $IQR = 2$, were higher than the national average.
- ✓ Alice's RAS scores, $Mdn = 30$, $range = 21$, were higher than the national average.

Alice's Lab Notes 4.1 *Reporting descriptive statistics*

KEY TERMS

Arithmetic mean	Mean	Quartiles
Average	Mean squared error	Range
Biased estimator	Median	Residual
Bimodal	Mode	Sample mean
Central tendency	Multimodal	Standard deviation
Degrees of freedom	Noniles	Sum of squared errors
Deviance	Outlier	Unbiased estimator
Fit	Percentiles	Upper quartile
Interquartile range	Population mean	Variance
Lower quartile	Quantiles	

JIG:SAW'S PUZZLES

1 What does the variance measure?
2 Why does the variance in a sample underestimate the variance in the population?
3 What does a small standard deviation relative to the mean tell us about our data?
4 Milton recruited a group of nine cats and recorded how many lactose-free lattes they drank in a week: 7, 9, 16, 20, 21, 28, 26, 32, 45. Calculate the mean, median and mode of these data.
5 It seems that people are spending more and more time on their electronic devices. Zach asked a group of 20 people how long (in minutes) they spend on their Proteus each day: 65, 125, 34, 90, 45, 25, 10, 22, 22, 24, 30, 50, 60, 65, 34, 90, 100, 15, 20, 35. Calculate the sum of squares, variance and standard deviation of these data.

6   Would you say that the mean in puzzle 5 'fits' the data well? Explain your answer.

7   While Zach was worrying about whether Alice had left him, he ruminated about how successful couples often seem to divorce. Alice is a brilliant scientist and he a brilliant musician, so perhaps their relationship is doomed. To see if his observation might be true he got The Head to check the (approximate) length in days of some celebrity marriages from before the revolution: 240 (J-Lo and Cris Judd), 144 (Charlie Sheen and Donna Peele), 143 (Pamela Anderson and Kid Rock), 72 (Kim Kardashian, if you can call her a celebrity, and Chris Humphries), 30 (Drew Barrymore and Jeremy Thomas), 26 (Axl Rose and Erin Everly), 2 (Britney Spears and Jason Alexander), 150 (Drew Barrymore again, but this time with Tom Green), 14 (Eddie Murphy and Tracy Edmonds), 150 (Renee Zellweger and Kenny Chesney), 1657 (Jennifer Aniston and Brad Pitt). Compute the mean, median, standard deviation, range and interquartile range for these lengths of celebrity marriages.

8   Repeat puzzle 7 but excluding Jennifer Aniston and Brad Pitt's marriage. How does this affect the mean, median, range, interquartile range and standard deviation? What do the differences in values between puzzles 7 and 8 tell us about the influence of unusual scores on these measures?

9   Zach asked Nick to get 15 of their fans on *memoryBank* to rate his new song, 'The Gene Mixer', on a scale ranging from 0 (the worst thing you've ever recorded) to 10 (the best thing you've ever recorded). The ratings were: 3, 5, 7, 8, 2, 4, 10, 8, 8, 5, 5, 7, 9, 10, 6. Calculate the mean, standard deviation, median, range and interquartile range for these ratings of the song.

10 Is the mean in puzzle 9 a good 'fit' to the data? Explain your answer.

IN THE NEXT CHAPTER, ZACH DISCOVERS ...

The cost of striving for perfection
Types of graphs
How to present data

How to avoid chartjunk
Never to show a pie chart to a man who has attacked you with bulldog clips

5

Presenting Data
Aggressive Prefector

'Err, yeah, who are ...?'

'Oh, wow, I *thought* it was you – I can't believe it! I love your band, you're rad. I watch you play all the time. I can't believe that I'm speaking to you ...'

'Thanks, that's awesome, but we're just a band, it's no big deal.'

'You're kidding, you guys are changing music, you have fans around the world, you're huge! Can I take a highsie of us? I've gotta put this on *memoryBank* or no one will believe me.'

I agreed and, with Milton wriggling in my backpack, this bizarrely starstruck young woman grabbed my arm, pulled me towards her and planted a kiss on my cheek. Her Proteus flashed in my eyes to capture the moment. Ten seconds since I'd met her, and already I was dazzled. Whoever this person was, she had no respect for personal space and was far too comfortable in her skin. As she pulled away, doubt momentarily danced around her face.

'You're blushing,' she said.

I was still numb from shock. She started to look worried by my silence.

'I'm sorry,' she said, looking contrite, 'I've made you feel awkward. That's me: I get excitable sometimes.'

'It's standard,' I said. 'Random people kiss me all the time.' She still looked worried, and I felt bad about my sarcasm. 'Chill, it's a nice thing – you like my band, what's to be upset about? I appreciate you being excitable.' All of which was true, but at some level I hoped she would go away so that the awkwardness would end.

'Let's try again, but more calmly,' and with that she extended her hand for a handshake. I met her palm with mine and she gently shook my hand in a mock businesslike way. Suppressing a smile, she said 'Hello, I'm Celia, it's a pleasure to meet you. I very much admire you and your band.'

I tried to laugh and speak at the same time and instead made a 'psthhrrr' noise and shower of spittle. Why did I feel so unsettled? Calming myself, I joined in her mock business meeting game. 'It's nice to meet you, Celia. I'm Zach and I drown people in spittle.'

Her smile broke free. 'Were those guys you were talking to from Zombie Wrath?'

'Yeah, we've gigged with them loads, they're mates.'

'I've seen them supporting you. They were so dull I thought that they actually might be the undead.'

I stifled a laugh. 'They're nice guys. I like them.'

Celia threw me a coy smile. 'So what's the single most important human in the future of rock music doing at a JIG:SAW recruitment event?'

The flattery unleashed another uncomfortable blush. 'The name JIG:SAW keeps popping up recently. Then I was walking home last night and saw the posters, and there was a flyer dropped through my door. It's like the universe told me to come here.'

'Destiny perhaps?' she said, winking at me. Her overfamiliarity was really unsettling. She paused momentarily. 'So, Zach Slade, are you convinced about JIG:SAW?'

I shrugged, 'Honestly? I didn't understand much of that guy's talk.'

'That "guy" is my boss, Rob Nutcot. Hey, let me introduce you.'

'It's all good, really. I'm not good with meeting people, I always make an ass of myself.'

Celia bounced off, linked arms with her boss and bounced back. She really did have issues with personal space. Rob Nutcot did not bounce. He did the opposite: he walked deliberately, raising his knees as though they were connected by string to a puppeteer above his head. Together they looked like a bizarre physiotherapy intervention. The guy's face was fixed in a surprised, but slightly panicked, smile.

'Zach, this is Rob Nutcot, head of JIG:SAW.'

'Zach, great to interface,' he said.

I looked puzzled, and his expression changed to puzzled, too. I could smell a pungent aftershave. At least, I think it was aftershave – he smelt strange, that's for sure. 'Greets Mr Nutcot,' I said.

'Please, call me Rob. Celia told me about you, so I thought I should reach out, see what synergies we have moving forward into the ballpark. Good to meet potential stakeholders, see if we can't go viral with something.'

He spoke like an idiot. The words were English, but not ordered in a meaningful way. I didn't know what the hell he was talking about. I raised my eyebrows. He raised his eyebrows. I looked at Celia, my body language asking for help. He turned to Celia, his body language asking for help. When none was forthcoming, he turned back to me.

'So, how about it, Zach? Maybe we can organically mash up something without the guard-rails; you know, improve the capability bandwidth moving forward?'

I cleared my throat. He cleared his throat. Was he mimicking me? 'Err, I just wanted to find out a bit more about JIG:SAW,' I said. 'You know, what the company does.'

'Sure, we're a global corporation with granular star potential for the next gen. We like to touch base with the people of Elpis, mash up some concepts outside the box. As an employee you enter our genetic enhancement programme, which is a state-of-the-art, bleeding-edge, virally-facing, synthetic-organic, synergistic, top-down, bottom-up, outwardly inward-facing system.'

I shook my head and smiled. He shook his head and smiled. I had another overpowering waft of his aftershave. I coughed. He coughed back. I felt momentarily warmer towards him; perhaps I was misjudging him because he used words that were alien to me. I smiled a reconciliatory smile. He returned it.

'Zach, step back for a moment and see things in the square. Together we could go epidemic. Think about our action potential moving forward.'

5.1   TYPES OF GRAPHS

Rob Nutcot rested one arm awkwardly on my shoulder, and with the other handed me a brochure. I flicked through it and saw that it contained a sheet of the images from his presentation (FIGURE 5.1): a kaleidoscope of colours, lines, dots and bars. Needless to say, it meant nothing to me.

'Thanks,' I said, 'but I'm not good with this sort of stuff.'

'I can explain,' said Celia enthusiastically. 'Ignore the text, and look at the pictures. They're called graphs.'

'I guessed that: a professor recently explained graphs to me. The horizontal line is the x-axis, the vertical one is the y-axis, and each one represents a variable. She gave them posher names than that, but I don't remember them.'

'The x-axis is the abscissa, and the y-axis is the ordinate,' came a muffled voice from my rucksack.

'What was that?' said Celia.

'Nothing,' I replied while elbowing the feline lump on my back. 'So, these graphs. What do they mean?'

'As Rob was saying in his presentation, JIG:SAW are very committed to improving their workforce. That's why he comes out into the community on these recruitment drives, so we can show Elpis what we do for the community. Isn't that right, Rob?'

Rob stood smiling and staring into the distance, as though daydreaming about kittens. I wondered if he even knew there were people next to him, let alone in Elpis generally. Celia's words jerked him out of his stare. 'Yes, we like to open the komodo to the community, peel back the onion and start a sea change of hyperlocal best practice.' He smiled a wide-eyed but very fake smile.

I leant over and whispered in Celia's ear, 'Do you actually understand anything he says?'

She smirked. 'What Rob means is that at events like this, we're trying to show people the benefits of working for JIG:SAW.'

'And those benefits are?'

'We have a free genetic enhancement programme for all of our employees, and these graphs show the benefits of that programme. We measure our employees' maximal push force, visual acuity, and foot-speed.'

'Do you mean how strong they are, how well they see and how quick they are?'

'Yes,' said Rob. 'These are key indicators of a person's physical capabilities and wellness. The graphs show how our employees perform on these measures. Eyeball the top two graphs. **(FIGURE 5.1)** These are bar charts, and they show that our employees are stronger (left) and have better vision (right) than those who don't work for us.' He grinned inanely into the distance.

'How can you tell that?' I asked.

'The height of the bars', replied Celia, 'are taller for the JIG:SAW employees.'

Rob picked up from Celia. 'The graph in the middle left is a boxplot and shows that our employees are faster than those who work elsewhere. The graph in the middle right shows that as our employees get quicker they get stronger too. The graph in the bottom right shows again that our employees are stronger than those working elsewhere.'

'Sweet, I remember you saying some of this in your talk: JIG:SAW employees are stronger, faster and have better vision than the rest of us.'

'Yes, the programme has impact: we holistically empower our employees proactively going forward to facilitate improvement in these core competencies.'

He was talking like an imbecile again. 'What's the graph in the bottom left, then?'

'That's a pie chart,' replied Celia. 'It shows how many people do different types of jobs at JIG:SAW. You can see we have a fairly equal number of scientists, technicians, and people in professional services.'

'What does "code 1318" mean?'

'They are the special ones,' replied Rob, 'the event horizon, the crystallization of our survival strategy ...'

Celia broke him off mid-sentence, put one arm through mine and linked her other arm with Rob, who was still smiling inanely into the distance. 'We'd better go. Rob has meetings,' she said, and bounced forward, pulling Rob and me in the process like Dorothy skipping down the yellow-brick road with her tin man, scarecrow, and – unbeknown to her – the lion in my rucksack.

As we left the building, Celia stopped, unlinked herself from Rob and turned to me. She threw me a mischievous look, as though weighing up whether or not she should say what she was about to say. 'We've got to get back to work, but maybe I can see you again?'

I was about as good at interpreting other people as I was equations – especially, it seemed – women. What did she mean? I didn't want to be rude, so I reluctantly agreed.

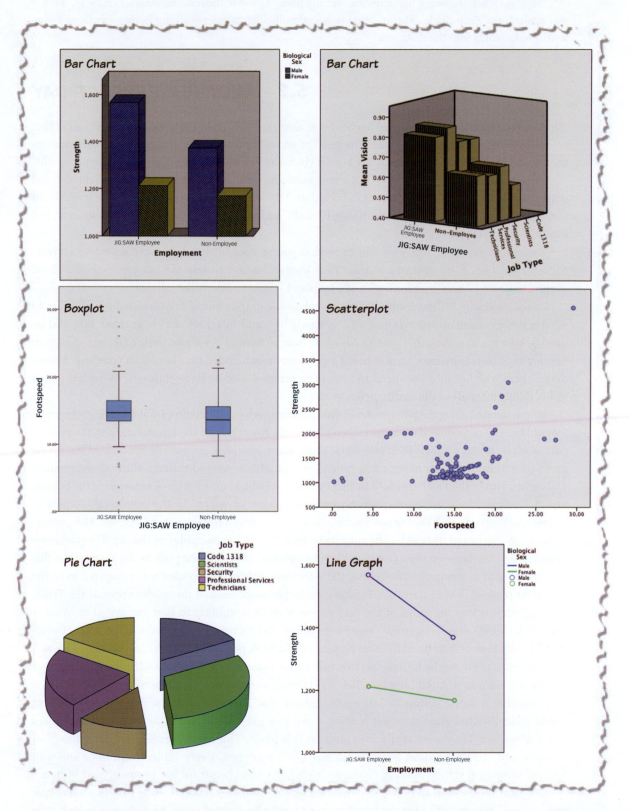

Figure 5.1 Different ways of presenting data

'Yay!' she said, throwing her arms around my neck. As she withdrew she winked and said, 'I'll see you again then, Zach Slade'. She grabbed Rob and pulled his puppet-walking body away from me as it grinned inanely into the distance.

5.2 ANOTHER PERFECT DAY

'That was biz,' I said, as Milton poked his head out of my rucksack, looking glad for some fresh air at last.

'Bizarre indeed. It is strange that the head of an enormous genetics company should speak as though his brain had been wired to his mouth via his anus.' Milton jumped down to the pavement.

'I was talking about the woman – but seeing as you mention him, you're right, I didn't understand what the suit was saying, or the graphs in his report. I thought going there would help me to work out why the counsellor's file on Alice mentions JIG:SAW, and why Pincus was so tetchy about them, but I'm no closer to anything.'

'I wouldn't say that. You seem closer to that young women than you were when we arrived.' Milton raised his furry eyebrow at me. 'Your human mating rituals are not my concern. These graphs are, and I know someone who can help and where to find him.'

I wondered why Milton couldn't simply explain the graphs himself. Everyone kept alluding to what a genius scientist Milton Grey was, so surely he could interpret simple graphs? Why did he need to take me to some other crank? Also, why was he teasing me about Celia? I'd only spoken to her. Perhaps he was jealous. I guess being a cat pretty much ended his chances of true love. I wondered again whether he'd ever been in love, been married. Did he have children? What happened to his family after all of the reality prism stuff?

Milton strutted along the pavement, not even glancing back to see whether I was following – he knew I would be. The recruitment event had taken place in the lower part of the Egestes district, the poorest part of Elpis. It was a labyrinth of alleyways, and it was easy to lose yourself or wind up in the wrong part of town. Even the city of hope has its underworld. Milton weaved through these alleyways until we reached part of the Evil Pockets. 'The Evil Pockets' was a nickname for three areas along the boundary of Egestes. These areas, or 'pockets', evolved because of people in the adjoining districts of Antevorta, Postverta and Veritas not wanting to live near certain rough parts of Egestes. The pockets were uninhabited, and instead had become social areas for the 'undesirables' in the city. The pocket we emerged into was between the Egestes and Veritas districts. Like all of the pockets, I'd heard about this one but avoided it. Being close to Veritas, the 'university district', this pocket was rumoured to be the gathering place of radical scientists, fundamentalist philosophers and those who opposed the WGA. In many ways it was the safest of the pockets – a scientist is unlikely to beat you up – but in other respects it was the most dangerous – there were people there wanting to bring down the WGA. I wondered briefly how Milton fitted in here: he seemed unafraid, perhaps he came here, perhaps he was a fundamentalist? Or maybe he believed that being a cat made him anonymous wherever he went.

We turned into a small lane labelled '6'. Halfway along was a sandblasted glass door with a large number 6 on it. Milton looked up to indicate that I should push the door, which I did, to reveal a sandblasted glass staircase leading down to a glass room, with glass tables, glass chairs and a glass bar. They were really into glass in this place. The room was like an ice palace, but warmer, and one of the most beautiful things I had ever seen. Every table, chair, door and wall had the number 6 etched upon it. 'Welcome to "6", the most beautiful bar in town,' said Milton.

Sitting at the bar was an oldish man wearing an immaculately tailored white suit. His white hair was greased back perfectly over the top of his head – not a hair out of place. As he turned to look at us I noticed his pencil-thin white moustache and goatee. He looked like he was holding a red number 6, but as he swigged it I realized it was a glass containing red liquid. They liked the number 6 almost as much as they liked glass in this place. 'That man', said Milton, 'is Dr Sisyphus Tuff, and he used to be the world expert on displaying data.'

'Used to be?'

'Yes, he was passionate that data could and should be beautiful; he strove for perfection in representing data. However, his desire for perfection eventually consumed him; he became increasingly irritated with every badly drawn graph he saw. One day a student showed him a graph on her laptop to which she had applied a drop shadow effect. He snapped. He grabbed her laptop, turned it towards her and cradling the bottom in one hand, he frantically opened and shut the screen with the other – like a laptop Pac-Man. He chased her around his office, Pac-Manning the laptop screen and screaming "Pac-Man will eat the shadows! Eat the shadows!" The student fled. The university retired him on the grounds of stress-related illness. He spends his days here in the only place he can be calm – a bar designed by mathematicians to be aesthetically perfect. He will tell you everything you need to know about graphs. But tread carefully, because it is only this perfect aesthetic environment that keeps him composed. Anything aesthetically offensive will destabilize him in unpredictable ways.'

'It's all good; I'll just show him these graphs from Rob Nutcot – they look pretty sick to me.'

Milton raised his eyebrow, turned and casually retreated to the opposite end of the bar. Once there he raised his paw and gave me what looked like a thumbs-up sign before curling into a ball on the floor with his paws over his ears. 'Strange cat,' I thought to myself and headed over toDr Tuff.

'Excuse me, Dr Tuff?'

Dr Tuff remained motionless staring into his drink.

'Dr Tuff? Can I please have a few minutes of your time?'

'Leave me alone.'

'Please, Dr Tuff. I'm trying to find Alice, the love of my life: she has disappeared. I have some graphs that might help me out, but I don't understand them. I wouldn't ask if I wasn't desperate.'

'Is she perfect?'

'What?'

'Alice, is she perfect?'

'*I* think she is.'

'You are a lucky man. I have spent my whole life searching for perfection, longing for it, but it has eluded me. I had it once, when I was perhaps your age, a girl called Elspeth. She was the most perfect person both inside and out. Every morning when I woke up and saw her I thought my chest might rupture from trying to contain my love for her. One day she came home with a tattoo: a very pretty pattern along her forearm. It suited her but I found it distracted me from the raw beauty of her arm – it concealed the underlying data of her skin. I became obsessed with why someone would obscure their bodily data by applying a pattern to it. I became incensed by the use of excess ink. One night I left, convinced that a greater perfection existed elsewhere, but I was wrong, and I have paid the price.' He paused to stare into his glass. 'Show me your graphs.'

5.3   THE ART OF PRESENTING DATA

5.3.1 What makes a good graph?

I took out the sheet of graphs in the JIG:SAW report and showed him the first graph. *(FIGURE 5.2)* Dr Tuff started to twitch. Suddenly he sprang from his seat and started waving his arms in a whirlwind of movement. My face felt like it was being stung by bees.

'What is wrong with *me*?' shouted Tuff. 'More to the point, what is wrong with *you*? You must have some sort of illness to present data in this monstrous way! You are broken. Hear what I say? *Broken!*'

I felt shocked. The man had covered my face in bulldog clips – who knew what else he was capable of? I needed to pacify him. 'I didn't draw the graph, I got it from a guy called Rob Nutcot. He's the head of JIG:SAW, a businessman.' The bulldog clip on my lip made 'businessman' sound like 'bisbisban'.

'A businessman, you say? That explains it.'

I removed the clips from my face as he continued. 'Listen carefully to me. This graph you have put in front of me is an abomination. This graph to my eyes is like sunlight to a vampire, it burns them. So many programs make it easy to embellish graphs, to add patterns and shading, or superfluous dimensions, that people lose sight of why they are drawing a graph. It is not to impress people with how many floral gingerbread ducklings you can wallpaper onto the bars on your graph, it is to present information in a clear and concise way. Many years before the Reality Revolution a great man called Edward Tufte set out the foundations of elegant data presentation, and he said that less is more.[26] He set out some principles for good data visualization. He said that graphs should (1) show the data; (2) direct the reader to think about the data being presented rather than some other aspect of the graph.'

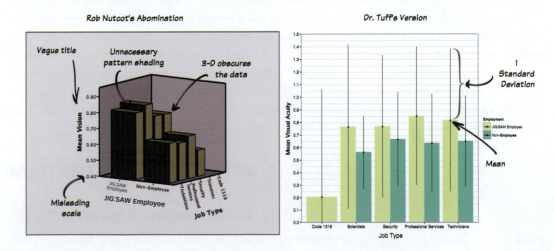

Figure 5.2   A terrible bar graph (left) and a more elegant version (right)

Dear Human,

The message conveyed to an audience can be manipulated by abusing how data are presented. You can find many examples of this practice from politicians, journalists and business people. Imagine you went to the JIG:SAW recruitment meeting and watched Rob Nutcot's presentation at which he talked about the benefits of working for JIG:SAW. Pretend that afterwards there was another talk called 'JIG:SAW in pieces' by another speaker. These two people display the same data relating to the strength of JIG:SAW employees (who have been on the genetic enhancement programme) compared to employees at other companies (who have not been on the programme). The first person, Rob, wants to convey the message that JIG:SAW employees are stronger than controls, and he presents the graph on the left of Figure 5.3. The bars show the average strength of the two groups, and it seems to show a clear effect of working for JIG:SAW because the people in that group seem much stronger (their bar is a lot higher than that of the non-employees). However, the second speaker presents the graph on the right of Figure 5.3. Believe it or not, this graph shows exactly the same data, but with the *y*-axis scaled properly (notice in the right graph the *y*-axis starts at zero, or no strength, but on the left it starts at 1250 N). The graph on the right shows that actually there is quite a small difference between the two groups (although the JIG:SAW group are still higher, the effect looks much less dramatic). This example illustrates how people manipulate the message within the data: Rob has scaled his *y*-axis to make the difference between JIG:SAW employees and controls seem as big as possible. That way, his audience will be more impressed with JIG:SAW and they will be easier for Rob to recruit. Watch out for these cheap tactics when you look at graphs in newspapers and in video transmissions. People often deceive with data, but scientists should never do this; so don't be tempted to scale your graphs to exaggerate your findings (unless, of course, you plan to be a politician at some point in your life).

Best fishes,
Milton

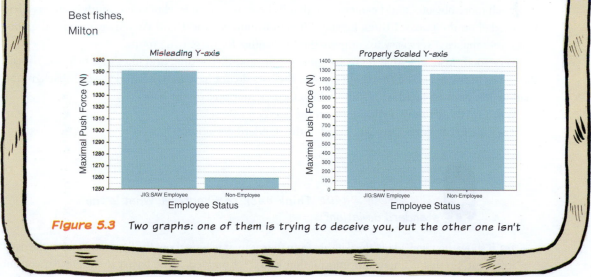

Figure 5.3   *Two graphs: one of them is trying to deceive you, but the other one isn't*

Milton's Meowsings 5.1   *Data deception*

'What, like how many floral gingerbread ducklings there are on it?'

'Precisely. Graphs should (3) avoid distorting the data; (4) present many numbers with minimum ink; (5) make large data sets (if you have one) coherent; (6) encourage the reader to compare different pieces of data; and, perhaps most important, (7) reveal the underlying message of the data.'

I felt the buzz of an incoming message on my diePad: **(MEOWSINGS 5.1)** it was Milton explaining how people use graphs to distort data. I asked Dr Tuff what was wrong with Rob's graph. **(FIGURE 5.2, LEFT)**

'What!? What's wrong? "What's right?" is the more pertinent question. For a start, it is full of **chartjunk**. Look at it, the bars have patterns on them, which distract the eye from what matters (namely, the data). These patterns are completely unnecessary. This is chartjunk. On top of that, by plotting three variables he has created a 3-D monstrosity in which it is difficult to read the values from the y-axis; in some cases you can't even see the bar. What is the strength of JIG:SAW employees who fell into the category of code 1318?'

I studied the graph for a while. 'I can't see a bar for the code 1318 JIG:SAW employees.'

'No, of course you can't, because the idiot who drew the graph has hidden it behind the other bars. The y-axis is misleadingly scaled because it doesn't start at zero and it is badly labelled. What does mean vision mean? How was it measured? Give me your Proteus.'

After Milton's story about the Pac-Man laptop I feared what Tuff was about to do, but if I was to understand why JIG:SAW was linked to Alice, I had no choice but to hand my diePad over. Tuff scanned Nutcot's graph and then his fingers whizzed on the screen like an impassioned pianist. Soon he held the screen towards me and showed me a graph. **(FIGURE 5.2, RIGHT)** 'This is an improvement, don't you agree?'

CHECK YOUR BRAIN: **Why do you think the graph on the right of Figure 5.2 is better than the one on the left.**

'Yes, I agree.' I was so wary of Dr Tuff I'd have agreed to anything – I did *not* want more bulldog clips. 'Why is it better?' he asked.

I thought for a moment. 'It uses two dimensions rather than three, so I can see more clearly the values represented by the bars. Especially, I can now actually see the value for the code 1318 JIG:SAW employees: it's about 0.2. Also, the y-axis is scaled from zero so the real differences between groups are much more obvious, and I can now see that it shows the mean level of visual acuity, so it has a less vague label on the y-axis. I think having different colours for the JIG:SAW employees and the non-employees makes it very easy to compare the bar heights for these two groups.'

'Very good. Also, note that there are some subtle, non-distracting, grid lines that help you to read the values of the bars. The chartjunk is gone: the bars do not have patterns and the grey background shading has been replaced with white, which focuses your eyes on the bars.'

'What are those funny vertical lines on the bars?'

'They are **error bars**. Have you heard of the standard deviation?'

CHECK YOUR BRAIN: **Think back to Chapter 4. What is the standard deviation?**

'Yes, it shows how spread out the data are from the mean; it tells us about the fit of the mean to the data.'

'Excellent. So this is important information isn't it?' I nodded. 'Why hasn't that idiot Nutcot put this information on the graph, then? These error bars can represent different things, but here they represent the standard deviation. The end of the main bar is the mean, and the error bar sticks up one standard deviation from the mean and protrudes down one standard deviation from the mean. If the error bars protrude a long way from the mean then the standard deviation is large, and the mean lacks precision – it is a poor summary of the raw data – but if the bars protrude only a little compared to the mean then the mean is precise and a good fit of the raw data. Let's interpret this graph, shall we? What do you notice when you compare each pair of the differently coloured bars?'

'The lighter bars are always taller.'

'Yes, and these lighter bars represent the JIG:SAW employees, so it tells us that in every category of employee, from scientists to technicians, the JIG:SAW employees had better visual acuity than non-employees.'

'But for code 1318 there isn't a dark bar.'

'Well observed. This suggests to me that they could not find any code 1318 workers outside of JIG:SAW.'

I wondered what a code 1318 worker was, and why only JIG:SAW employed them. Tuff asked me what else I noticed about the error bars, and I told him that they stuck out a really long way from the bars.

'Yes, which tells us that the standard deviation is large compared to the mean in all cases, but they are particularly long for the JIG:SAW workers, which suggests that there might be a lot of variability in the visual acuity of JIG:SAW workers – in other words, the means for JIG:SAW might not be representative of the group as a whole. This is less true for the non-employees because the error bars are shorter than for the JIG:SAW employees.'

5.3.2 Bar graphs

Given that Dr Tuff had been calm for at least a couple of minutes, I felt confident to show him the next graph (**FIGURE 5.4, LEFT**) and to ask him what it meant.

Tuff quivered. His eyes bulged as he stared at the graph, and his cheeks started to blossom. 'What. Is. This?!' he shouted as he span round, removing his jacket and winding it around his head as he did. His head looked like an Egyptian mummy's, tightly wrapped in his white jacket. I could hear muffled screams. He reached out his hands, exploring the air in front of him, searching for something. That something was me. He grabbed my T-shirt and pulled me towards him until my face was touching the

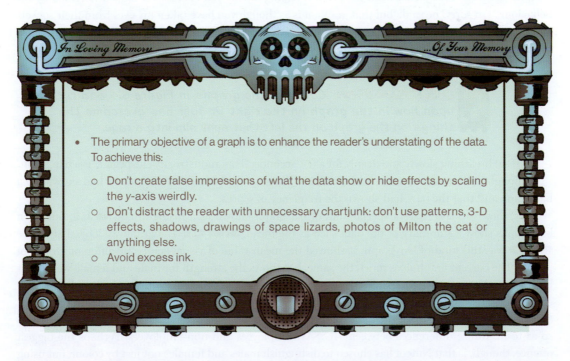

In Loving Memory ... *Of Your Memory*

- The primary objective of a graph is to enhance the reader's understating of the data. To achieve this:
  - Don't create false impressions of what the data show or hide effects by scaling the *y*-axis weirdly.
  - Don't distract the reader with unnecessary chartjunk: don't use patterns, 3-D effects, shadows, drawings of space lizards, photos of Milton the cat or anything else.
  - Avoid excess ink.

Zach's Facts 5.1   *Presenting data*

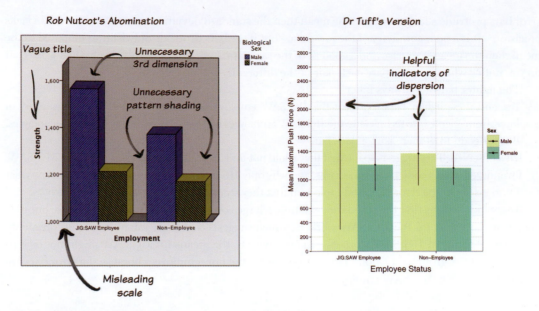

Figure 5.4 Another terrible bar graph (left) and a better version (right)

silk of the jacket lining that currently dressed his face. I was afraid of what he might do next. I wanted to lash out or just run, but an image of Alice came into my mind. She was alone in a room, trapped, scared, her lips mouthing 'Help me'. Of course my imagination was running away with me, but it reminded me to stay calm. However abusive this guy was, hitting him wouldn't get me what I wanted, so I calmly took his hands and removed them from me and told him everything was alright: it was just an image created by a businessman, and I needed to learn how to do these properly. My words pacified him, he unravelled his jacket from his head, revealing sweaty red cheeks. He looked horrified by his behaviour. 'I'm sorry,' he said, 'but that graph, it is as though you have taken my eyes from their sockets and buried them in a cup of dog faeces. I saw red, I'm so sorry, I realize you didn't draw it, but it's hard for me to control my …' his sentence drifted off and he twitched.

 CHECK YOUR BRAIN: Compare the graphs in Figure 5.4 and reflect upon how in the graph on the right Dr Tuff has overcome the things on the graph on the left that sent him into a rage.

Tuff sat breathing slowly and deeply for a few seconds. 'That monstrosity', he began, 'is a bar graph.'

I thought back to my meeting with Professor Pincus. I explained to Tuff that she had shown me a bar graph and that the bars had shown the frequency of scores.

'Yes, they can, and that's a special kind of bar graph known as a histogram **(SECTION 3.1.3)**, but often bar graphs show a summary of the data such as the mean. **(SECTION 4.2.3)** The graph we looked at before **(FIGURE 5.2)** was this kind of bar graph: it showed the mean value of visual acuity for different groups of people. The current graph does much the same, but shows the strength for male and female workers at both JIG:SAW and other companies. However, there are lots of problems with it. The bars have a 3-D effect. Never use 3-D plots for a graph plotting two variables because it obscures the data. In particular, 3-D effects make it hard to see the values of the bars. The *y*-axis is again labelled unhelpfully and is scaled so as to maximize differences between JIG:SAW employees and non-employees. Perhaps the biggest offence, though, is that Nutcot has chosen to distinguish males and females not just by colour, but using a hideous pattern too, and has coloured the background grey; the graph is riddled with chartjunk.'

Tuff repeated his concerto for diePad again and presented me with an alternative version of Nutcot's graph. **(FIGURE 5.5, RIGHT)** He had rescaled the y-axis to start from zero, given it a more precise label, removed the grey background and replaced it with white, added subtle grid lines, and removed the 3-D effects and patterns. It looked slick.

'Now all of the junk is removed, what do you notice about the two bars for JIG:SAW employees?' Tuff asked.

'The bar for males is higher than females, so males were on average stronger than females.'

'Good, and what do you notice for the non-employees?'

'The same: the male bar is taller than the female bar.'

'What do you notice when you compare the two male bars?'

'The JIG:SAW bar is taller than the non-employees one, suggesting that they are stronger.'

'And for the two female bars?'

'They are about the same as each other, although the JIG:SAW females are still a tiny bit stronger.'

'What about the error bars?'

'It's really long for the JIG:SAW males, but relatively short for all of the other groups.'

'Which suggests that there is a lot of variability in the JIG:SAW males. So, putting that all together, it seems that males were slightly stronger than females in general, but JIG:SAW males look stronger than other males, although there is a lot of variability in strength within that group.'

I wondered what that variability would tell us. I asked Tuff.

'It could mean many things, but you would need the raw data to find out. It looks as though in Nutcot's graph he has tried to conceal this variability by not including the error bars. It could be that the group contains some extreme cases, or perhaps just a very wide range of strength, both of which might tell you something interesting about the workforce at JIG:SAW.'

5.3.3 Line graphs

I hesitantly moved onto the next graph in Nutcot's brochure. **(FIGURE 5.5, LEFT)** Tuff again started to quiver and beat his clenched fist on the glass bar at which we sat. I braced myself for his attack, but the beating of his fist started to slow until it eventually stopped. He inhaled deeply and exhaled through puffed cheeks. 'It's OK,' he said, 'this one isn't too bad. It is a **line graph**. Line graphs can be used in the same way as bar charts, except lines connect the means rather than having bars extending up to the means.

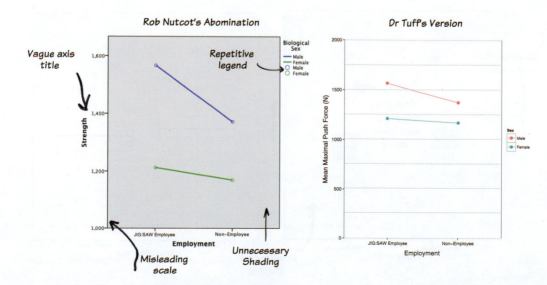

Figure 5.5 Line charts showing the same data

This graph shows the same as the bar chart that we just examined. **(FIGURE 5.4)** So notwithstanding the fact that this character Nutcot is an idiot for producing two graphs of exactly the same data, we can interpret it in the same way. How could we improve it, though?'

Looking at the graph it seemed as though Nutcot had again scaled the *y*-axis to maximize differences. 'We could rescale it to start at zero, and give it a proper label that tells us that it represents the mean and also how strength was measured.'

'Very good. Anything else?'

'Scrub the grey background, and replace it with white and include some subtle grid lines.'

Tuff took my diePad and made these changes. **(FIGURE 5.5, RIGHT)** 'See, this is a very clear way to show the pattern in the data. You can see that the red line is higher than the blue, which tells us that males were, on average stronger than females. The blue line is quite flat, which tells us that the mean strength of females was comparable in JIG:SAW employees and non-employees. Compare this with the red line, it is less flat because the mean for JIG:SAW males is higher than that for the non-employees. Although there aren't any error bars, we could add them, and you'll see that quite often on line graphs.'

5.3.4 Boxplots (box-whisker diagrams)

I showed Tuff the next graph. **(FIGURE 5.6, LEFT)** I tensed up anticipating his berserker rage, and I wasn't disappointed. His head twitched, his hands contorted into bird claws and he started to squawk. I decided to pacify him by impressing him with how much attention I'd been paying. 'These graphs have error bars like the other graphs.'

'*They are not error bars!*' he screamed.

Batticks. Tuff plunged his hands into his pocket and drew out a knife. The blood drained from my legs; I might have mistook the things on the graph for error bars, but this was taking things too far. Before I had time to run, he plunged the knife into a small pot of butter that had appeared in his other hand. He grabbed me by the neck and spread the butter on my face with the knife. I grabbed the knife and told him to get a frippin' grip on himself.

He snapped out of his rage. 'You're right,' he whispered between panted breaths. 'It could be worse: there are no 3-D effects or drop shadows, just a bit of over-shading and vague axis labels. I'm completely overreacting.'

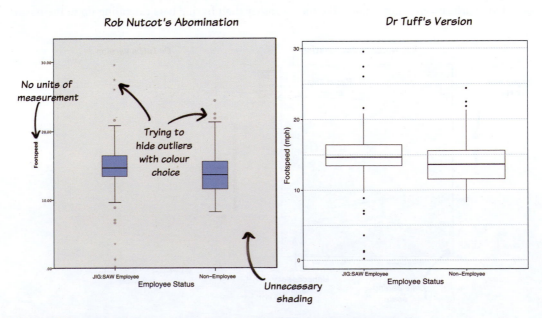

Figure 5.6   Boxplot of the footspeed of JIG:SAW employees and controls

As he released me from the headlock I raised my buttery eyebrows at him. Who the hell did this dude think he was, and what the frip was Milton thinking bringing me here. He said he wanted to help, but it felt like he was wilfully putting me in danger. If Alice and Milton knew each other, which it seemed like they did, what the hell else was she keeping from me? Did she know this guy too – was everyone in her circle so eccentric? For the first time, I didn't feel sorry for Alice, I felt angry at her for putting me in this position, for leaving me – whether deliberately or by force – to deal with these people. But the image returned of her scared, lonely, face and I felt guilty for my anger. Whatever I thought of my situation, I needed this guy's help, so I sucked it up and calmly asked him to explain what the vertical lines were if they were not error bars.

'That, my buttery friend, is a **boxplot** or **box–whisker diagram** and it is perhaps the most useful way to display data. Let's focus on just the boxplot for the JIG:SAW employees and I'll explain what it shows. **(FIGURE 5.7)** It is called a box–whisker diagram because it consists of a box that contains the middle 50% of the scores, and two whiskers that stick out to show the limits of the data, excluding any extreme scores. Let's look at the box first – the shaded area. At the centre of the box is the *median*.'

I remembered Milton telling me that is the middle score when you arrange the scores in order. **(SECTION 4.2.2)**

'The top of the box', the doctor continued, 'shows the upper quartile and the bottom of the box the lower quartile, which means that top and bottom edges of the box are the limits within which the middle 50% of observations fall.'

'That's called the interquartile range (IQR), isn't it?'

'Exactly, so from the box we know the median score, the upper and lower quartiles and the interquartile range. But there is more: now look at the whiskers. The whiskers begin from the upper and lower quartile and extend out from the box. They show us approximately the top and bottom 25% of scores.'

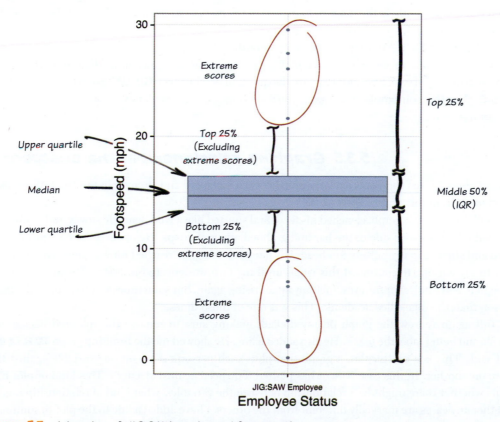

Figure 5.7   *A boxplot of JIG:SAW employees' footspeed*

'Why only approximately?'

'The graph is drawn to take account of any outliers. Do you know what an outlier is?'

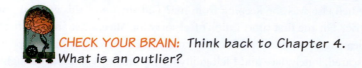

CHECK YOUR BRAIN: Think back to Chapter 4.
What is an outlier?

'It's an unusual score.'

'Very good. So before drawing the whiskers we look for any score greater than the upper quartile plus 1.5 times the IQR, or smaller than the lower quartile minus 1.5 times the IQR. When there are no outliers, the whiskers show the top and bottom 25% of scores exactly; but when there are outliers they show the top and bottom 25% of scores approximately, because the outliers are excluded. The outliers themselves are shown as dots beyond the whiskers, which is good because you get an instant visual impression of how many extreme scores there are in the data. Let's tidy up Nutcot's boxplots.'

Tuff again weaved his magic on my diePad and created a new version of the boxplots. **(FIGURE 5.6, RIGHT)** He removed the background shading, removed the shading from the box, added some non-distracting grid lines and labelled the *y*-axis so that it was clear that footspeed was measured in miles per hour.

'We can use these plots to compare the JIG:SAW employees with the non-employees,' he said. 'First we can see that the median footspeed is slightly higher for the JIG:SAW employees than non-employees.'

'That's what Nutcot said in his talk: JIG:SAW employees are faster.'

'Yes, but look how much the boxes overlap. This shows that the middle portions of both groups of scores are quite similar, and also the whiskers are not dissimilar in the two groups, suggesting that when you exclude outliers the range of footspeed in the two groups is not too different. However, there is one important difference between the groups.'

'Is it that the JIG:SAW group has a lot more outliers?'

'Very good. You can see that the JIG:SAW group has some very quick individuals indeed and some that are painfully slow. These outliers raise the question of why the JIG:SAW group has such extremes compared to the non-employees. Again, you'd need to see the raw data to work out exactly what is happening there.'

5.3.5 Graphing relationships: the scatterplot

'Nutcot also said that there was a relationship between footspeed and strength in the JIG:SAW workers. He showed it on this graph.' **(FIGURE 5.8, LEFT)**

Tuff looked at the graph, clenched his teeth and snorted like a wild boar. He slowly and deliberately reached over the other side of the bar and grabbed a bag of crisps. He opened the bag, picked out a crisp and stuck it to my buttery forehead. His hands shaking, he reached for a second crisp and stuck that to my cheek. He continued this ritual until my face was covered in crisps. He was considerate enough to leave holes for my eyes. I felt my anger rising again, but sometimes you have to be the bigger person than the rage-filled academic. This was one of those times.

Tuff again redrew the graph on my diePad, making sure to remove the coloured background, rescale and better label the *y*-axis. He also added a line. He showed me the resulting graph **(FIGURE 5.8, RIGHT)** and said, 'This is a **scatterplot**, a graph that plots each person's score on one variable against their score on another. In this case Nutcot has plotted footspeed against strength. This kind of plot highlights whether there might be a relationship between the variables, what kind of relationship it is and whether any cases are markedly different from the others. I have added a line to the plot to summarize the trend in the data. What do you notice about the line?'

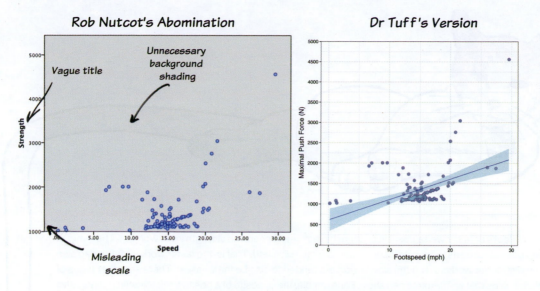

Figure 5.8   Scatterplot of footspeed against strength in JIG:SAW employees

'It points upwards.'

'Exactly, which suggests that low scores on speed tend to accompany low scores on strength, while high scores on speed are accompanied by high scores on strength. This is known as a positive relationship. It can also tell us about outliers: does the line fit most of the dots?'

My diePad buzzed and a notification appeared. It was a message from Milton, who all the while had been curled up on a bench, peacefully sleeping, or so it seemed. **(MEOWSINGS 5.2)** I wondered how he was sending these messages – he must have a Proteus hidden somewhere in his fur, I reasoned. I noticed Tuff staring at me. He was waiting for an answer, so I pointed out the cluster of dots in the middle of the scale for footspeed that are quite close to the line, and noted that below about 10 mph and above about 20 mph quite a few dots were a lot higher than the line.

'Well observed. These dots represent potential outliers. Look, for example, at the person scoring highest on footspeed. That person also scores highest on strength, much higher than anyone else (around 4500 N). This suggests that this person is exceptionally fast and unbelievably strong. This is another example where it could be useful to have a look at the raw data to see what is going on.'

5.3.6 Pie charts

I had one more graph to show to Tuff, but the thought of showing it to him was already making me anxious. He had abused me each time I showed him one of Nutcot's images, and I was scared of what he might do next. My gut told me to leave, but my heart wanted to do anything to find Alice. I told him that I had one more graph to show him, but asked him to please try not to hurt me when he saw it.

'Of course. I am in complete control, I promise you.'

I placed the graph in front of him. **(FIGURE 5.10, LEFT)** He looked at it, and turned to me. Tears streamed from his eyes. He grabbed my shoulders and whimpered, 'Why? Why would you do this to me?' He slid to the floor, his hands trailing from my shoulders down the front of me as he fell. He curled up in a foetal position and sobbed, while gently rocking back and forth on his spine. This was awks, really awks. I edged away towards Milton, who seemed to be chuckling to himself on his glass bench in the corner. As I sat on the chair, he padded across the bench, jumped onto my lap and licked my face.

'Hmm, butter, salt and vinegar. Nice,' he said.

Dear Human,

Rob Nutcot's data showed a positive relationship between speed and strength in his workers. The cloud of data points looked as though it sloped upwards (Figure 5.9, left). That is, the faster workers tended to also be the stronger workers, and the slower workers tended to also be the weakest. There are other types of relationships that scatterplots can show. For example, the opposite of a positive relationship is a negative one. A negative relationship is where high scores on one variable tend to accompany *low* scores on the other. In the case of strength and speed this would be like saying the fastest people tend to be the weakest and the slowest people tend to be the strongest. In this situation the cloud of data points would look as though it sloped downwards (Figure 5.9, middle). The final possibility is that there is no relationship: that is, as one variable changes the other stays exactly the same. In the current example that would mean that at every level of footspeed, strength stays about the same. The cloud of data would not slope up or down but instead looks like a random array of dots around the mean level of strength (Figure 5.9, right).

Best fishes,
Milton

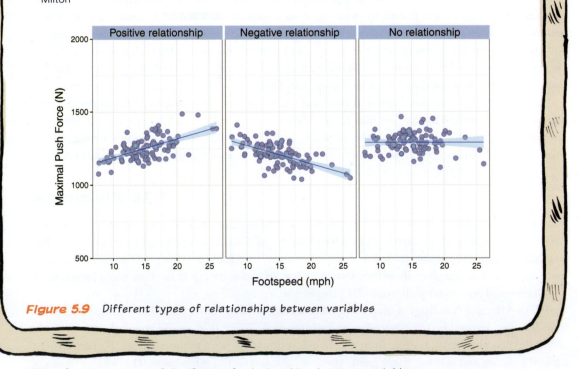

Figure 5.9   *Different types of relationships between variables*

Milton's Meowsings 5.2   *Types of relationships between variables*

'Get lost!'

'But it's so buttery, and salty ...'

I went to the men's room to wash my face, when I returned Milton was looking over at Tuff, still sobbing quietly to himself on the floor.

'You showed him the **pie chart**, didn't you?' the cat asked.

'I might have done. I don't see why that's a problem?'

'Oh, human, you have learnt so much and yet still you are like an innocent baby staring at the world from your swaddling for the first time. Pie charts are not proper graphs, they are the idiocy fodder of business people and politicians.'

'What the frip?'

'They completely obscure the data. Look at your example. It is quite hard to see the relative sizes of the segments: the pointless 3-D effect exacerbates the problem.' Milton fiddled with my diePad and presented me with a different graph. **(FIGURE 5.10, RIGHT)** 'A pie chart shows the frequency or percentage of scores in different categories. It does much the same as a histogram, but in a hideously abhorrent way. Look, I have redrawn the pie chart as a bar graph showing the percentage of cases in each job category. This displays exactly the same information as the pie chart, but it is much easier to see the relative differences in the size of each category with bars than it is using segments of a pie. For example, on the bar graph it is very clear that the majority of JIG:SAW workers are scientists and that the next biggest category is professional service people. The remaining three categories of code 1318, security and technicians are fairly equally sized, suggesting they have roughly equal numbers of people employed in these jobs.'

I could see Milton's point. I asked him why he bought me to meet Tuff when I assumed he could just as easily have told me everything that Tuff had.

'Where would the fun be in doing that?' he replied with an irritating smirk. 'I told you before, to get my freedom I need to trust you. My dilemma is that I do not know you, but the fact that you tolerated Tuff's company so long tells me that you trust me – even when the situation must have made you question that trust. The chances are that if you can place that much faith in me, then I can probably trust you. I was testing you, but you also got what you wanted: more knowledge about JIG:SAW.'

He was right. According to Tuff, these graphs show me that JIG:SAW workers are faster, stronger and have better vision than non-employees. It also seems to be that the faster they are, the stronger

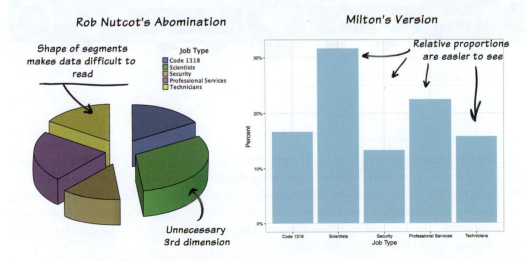

Figure 5.10   *Business people like pie charts, but they shouldn't*

In Loving Memory ... *Of Your Memory*

- **Bar graphs** can be used to present different types of information. They are used to show the frequency of scores (histograms), but the bars can also represent summary statistics such as the mean score for different groups of cases, or the same cases in different situations.
- **Line graphs** are an alternative to bar graphs. They too are often used to display means of groups, or means in different conditions or over time. The means are usually displayed with symbols that are connected by a straight line.
- **Error bars** can be applied to both bar and line graphs when they show means. They are vertical lines that protrude from each mean to show the precision of the mean. One way to indicate precision is to have the error bar show the standard deviation; in other words, the error bar extends 1 standard deviation above and below the mean – for example, if the mean is 5 and the standard deviation is 3, the bar would start at 2 (1 standard deviation below the mean) and stop at 8 (1 standard deviation above the mean). Errors bars can represent things other than the standard deviation, so always note what they show in your figure, and when interpreting graphs check what the error bars show.
- **Scatterplots** show scores on one variable plotted against scores on another variable. They are good for summarizing the relationship between two variables. If the data cloud seems to point upwards, this suggests a positive relationship (as scores increase on one variable they also increase on the other); if the data cloud points downwards, it suggests a negative relationship (as scores increase on one variable they decrease on the other). If the cloud doesn't seem to slope up or down, it indicates a very small or non-existent relationship between the variables.
- **Pie charts** show the relative frequency of cases falling into different categories. It is usually clearer to present this information as a bar chart. If you must use a pie chart, never ever apply a 3-D effect, otherwise Dr Tuff will collapse in a heap and sob, which is just awkward for everyone.

Zach's Facts 5.2 *Graphs*

they are. Something didn't seem right to me, though: Tuff kept pointing out how the JIG:SAW graphs showed a lot of variability in scores, and how there seemed to be lots of extreme scores. He kept saying that he would need to see the raw data to know exactly what was going on. Maybe the key to finding Alice was to work out what these extreme scores were all about. The only way to find out would be to get my hands on the raw data and somehow persuade Milton to show me how to look at them. There was only one way I could think of to get the data.

KEY TERMS

Boxplot

Box–whisker diagram

Chartjunk

Error bars

Line graph

Pie chart

Scatterplot

JIG:SAW'S PUZZLES

1   Dr Tuff was left curled up on the floor in a ball, gently weeping. Zach wanted to coax him out of his emotional hole, and remembered that Edward Tufte set out some principles for good data visualization, which would please Dr Tuff. He felt sure that if he could list as many of Tufte's principles for what graphs should do as he could, then it would cheer Dr Tuff up. The trouble is Zach's forgotten them. Can you help him?

2   What do scatterplots show and how do you interpret them?

3   What do pie charts show and why are they not a good method for presenting data?

4   What are error bars?

5   Zach was interested in the relationship between how much he charged for his band T-shirts at a gig and how many he sold. What type of graph would he use to display the data? What if he wanted to plot the average number he sold when he gave away a free wristband, compared to when he didn't offer a free gift?

6   Zach was curious whether the oddities in the JIG:SAW data had something to do with the fact that JIG:SAW is a genetics research centre. He asked The Head to get him some comparable data from the Beimeni Centre of Genetics, where Alice works, so that he could compare the two. The graph in Figure 5.11 shows the data for the strength of employees.

    a   What type of graph has Zach drawn in Figure 5.11?

    b   According to the graph, which employees are stronger? Explain your answer.

7   Figures 5.12 and 5.13 show the footspeed and visual acuity data for the male and female employees at JIG:SAW and the Beimeni Centre.

    a   What type of graph has Zach drawn in Figures 5.12 and 5.13?

    b   If you showed Figure 5.12 to Dr Tuff, do you think he would adorn your face with bulldog clips? If so, why?

    c   Would Dr Tuff purr gently in delight if you showed him Figure 5.13? Explain your answer.

    d   Is the mean male and female footspeed comparable in the two institutes? Explain your answer.

    e   Is the mean male and female visual acuity comparable in the two institutes? Explain your answer.

157

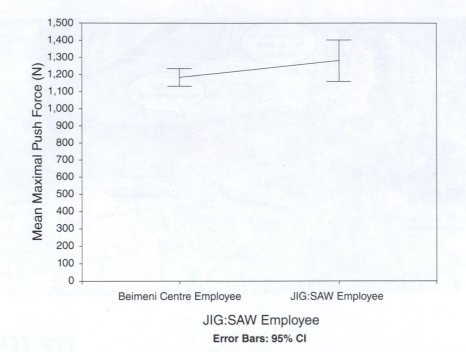

Figure 5.11   *Mean strength of employees at two different genetics institutes*

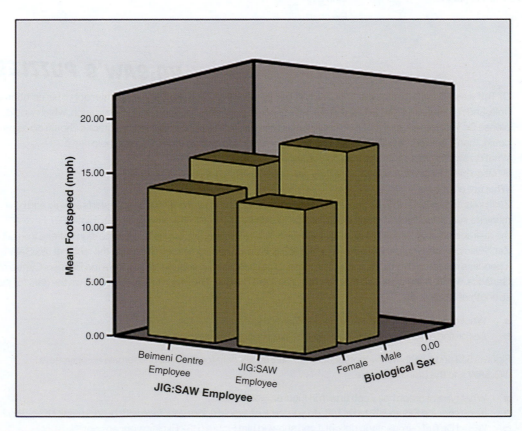

Figure 5.12   *Mean footspeed of male and female employees at two different genetics institutes*

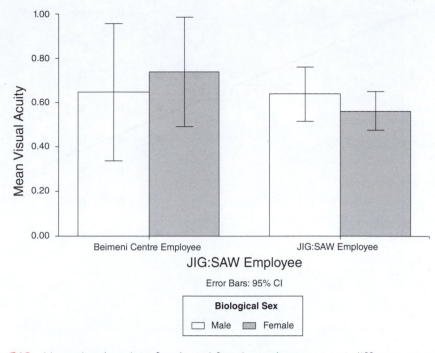

Figure 5.13   Mean visual acuity of male and female employees at two different genetics institutes

8   Zach thought that Alice would rate creativity highly as a characteristic that she likes in her partner. He also worried because he often found it hard to get on with Alice's scientist friends. He wondered whether people who liked creativity in their partner also liked them to get on with their friends. He took another sample of 45 cases from the Ha et al. study data (Reality Check 3.1) and plotted the ratings that this sample of women gave for 'creativity' and 'gets on with friends'. Remember that each woman is rating on a scale from 1 (not important at all) to 10 (very important) how important this characteristic is to her in a romantic partner. A graph of the data is shown in Figure 5.14.

a   What type of graph has Zach drawn?
b   What does the graph suggest about the relationship between women's ratings of creativity and the ability to get on with their friends as characteristics they seek in romantic partners?
c   Are there any cases that look like outliers?

9   Zach was also fairly confident that most people thought he was romantic and had a good sense of humour. He wondered whether if Alice liked a good sense of humour (which she did) then she'd also want a partner who is romantic. To get some idea, Zach again took a sample of the Ha et al. data of women's ratings of characteristics in their partners (from 1 = not important at all to 10 = very important). Again Zach plotted these data (Figure 5.15). Can you help him to interpret the graph? How does the relationship differ from the one in the previous puzzle?

10   After the JIG:SAW recruitment event where Zach saw Rob Nutcot deliver a presentation, he felt none the wiser about JIG:SAW. He put this down to the fact that Rob spoke like an imbecile. However, Zach worried that perhaps everyone else in the room had understood, and it was only he who didn't. Luckily, they collected data at the event to test attendees' knowledge of JIG:SAW before and after Rob's speech. Zach plotted the data in Figure 5.16.

a   What type of graph has Zach drawn?
b   Did people's knowledge of JIG:SAW increase from before to after Rob's presentation? What are the implications?

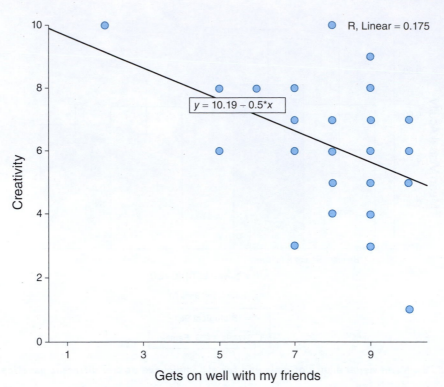

$y = 10.19 - 0.5 \cdot x$

Figure 5.14 *The relationship between women's ratings of 'creativity' and 'the ability to get on with my friends' as characteristics they seek in romantic partners*

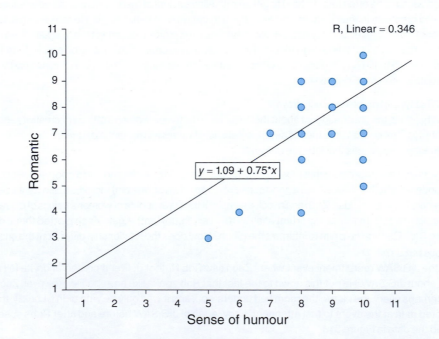

$y = 1.09 + 0.75 \cdot x$

Figure 5.15 *The relationship between women's ratings of 'romantic' and 'sense of humour' as characteristics they seek in romantic partners*

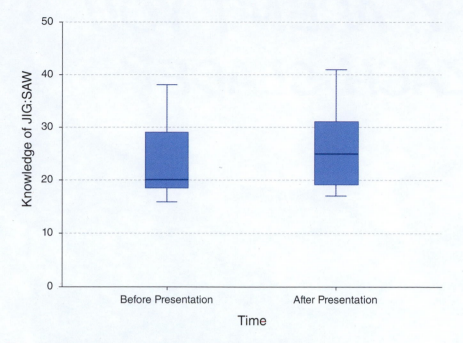

Figure 5.16 *Knowledge of JIG:SAW before and after Rob Nutcot's presentation at the recruitment event*

IN THE NEXT CHAPTER, ZACH DISCOVERS ...

He's not clever enough to get a job

Raw scores and *z*-scores

How to compare scores and distributions

He *is* clever enough to get a job

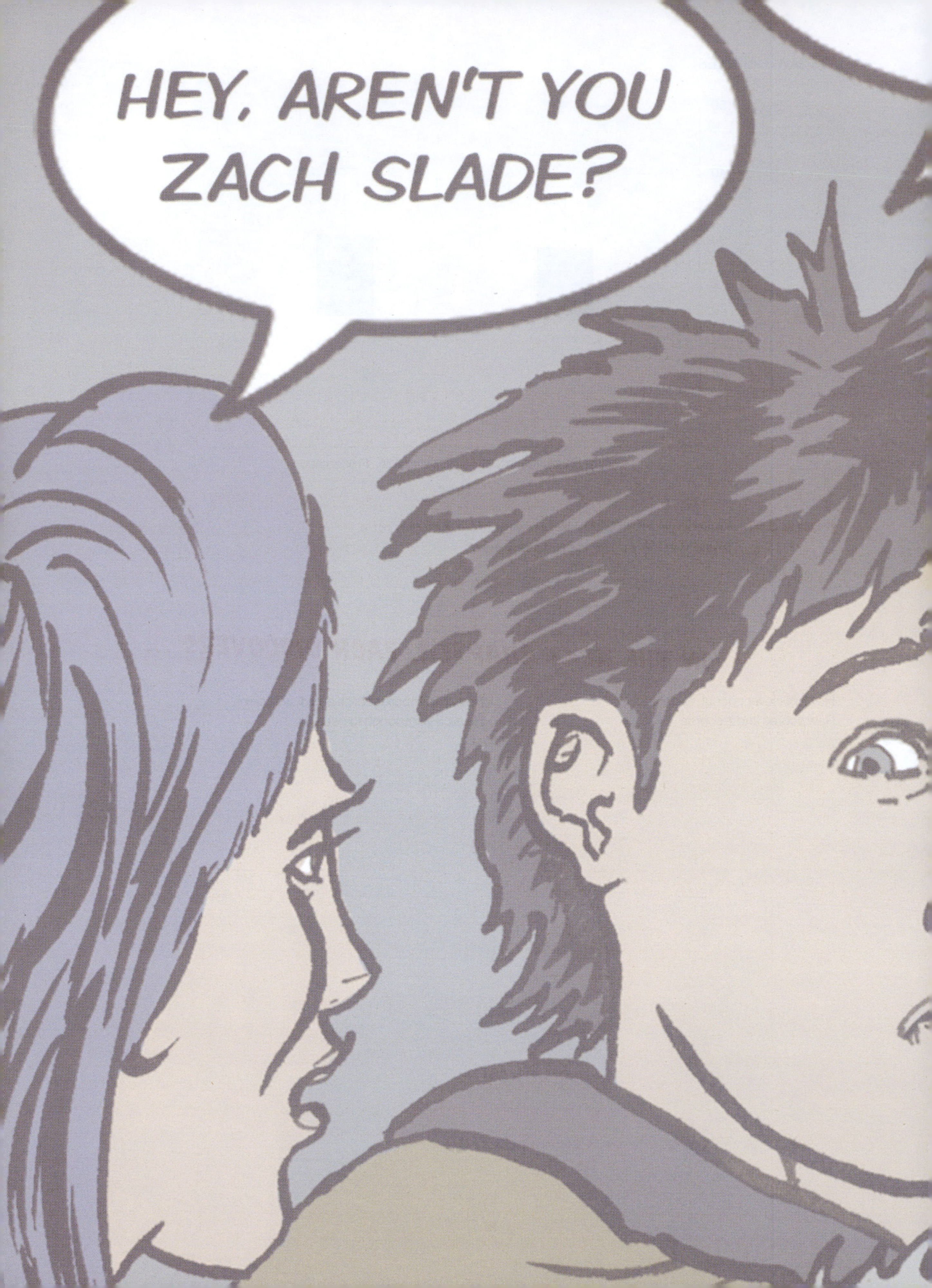
HEY, AREN'T YOU ZACH SLADE?

6

Z-Scores
The Wolf is Loose

Three days passed before I contacted Celia. Milton and I had left the 6 bar and gone back to my apartment. As I took off my jacket I noticed a card in the pocket. It had Celia's vortexID on it; she must have slipped it in my pocket during one of her many invasions of my personal space. She really was very presumptuous. I put the card back into the pocket and sat in the lounge with my guitar. I felt low, and that was always helpful for writing music. Without all the pictures of Alice and me, the apartment felt alien. I looked to replace them, but our photos had been wiped from our constellation. In this world where memories were so redundant, I needed mine more than ever.

The days were erratic. I fluctuated between feeling demoralized and helpless, and determined to find the truth. When I was demoralized the misery proved good for searching my soul. What if the song that Alice had left playing *had* been a farewell message? What if Alice really didn't want me to find her? Sure, Pincus and Genari had helped me to look at some evidence about what women value, but so what? Just because I have some characteristics that women value, doesn't mean Alice values them. Also her relationship ratings *had* dipped just before she vanished. Then there was the other explanation, that someone or something other than Alice didn't want me to find her? Why? Had she been taken? What if she needed my help? Whatever the truth, finding her would help.

When I felt determined, I busied myself with making plans. I checked in with Nick to see if our fans on *memoryBank* had thrown up any clues. Some claimed to have seen someone looking like Alice, but there was no proof. He'd reached out to thousands of people all over the world, but got nothing concrete: it was hopeless. I thought about filing a missing person report with the WGA. Milton pointed out that since the chipping, the WGA could so easily locate Chippers that they didn't have the resources or inclination to locate Clocktorians. I found myself again wondering whether Alice and I might have been better off being chipped.

Every avenue was a dead-end, and I couldn't shake JIG:SAW from my mind. Everything pointed to the conclusion I'd come to when I left the 6 bar: the only way to answer some of the many questions that the last few days had thrown up was to get inside JIG:SAW. I needed to know who the code 1318 workers were and why there was so much variability in the strength, visual acuity and speed of employees there. The biggest question of all was whether they had a connection to Alice and, if so, what it was. Without more information, I couldn't put the pieces of JIG:SAW together. I pestered The Head for maps, floor plans, building layouts, security information and anything that I thought would help. It turned out that, unlike in the movies, major research organizations didn't put detailed floor maps and security plans into the public domain. Even The Head couldn't hack into JIG:SAW. The only thing I discovered was that the company was incredibly good at shrouding itself in mystery.

During my three-day emotional rollercoaster Milton slept. A lot. When not sleeping he paced uneasily about the apartment, bemoaning the stupidity of whatever I was doing: I shouldn't contact the WGA, wallowing in misery wasn't helpful, I couldn't even break into a counsellor's office without being caught – let alone a high-security organization. He never gave me any better ideas though. He complained about other things too: the lack of decent tuna in the apartment, the irritatingly long distance he had to walk from the sofa to the fridge to steal milk, and the lack of genetics research for him to think about. After three days of complaining, he finally said something useful.

'We recently went to a recruitment event for JIG:SAW. If you want to get into JIG:SAW, why not sign up to be recruited?'

It was a sick idea. I remembered the card I'd found in my pocket, scanned the vortexID with my diePad and it uploaded Celia's contact details and opened a connection to her. She didn't seem at all surprised to hear from me. Her last words to me were 'I'll see you again then, Zach Slade.' She had slipped her card in my pocket, knowing I'd contact her, so either she was extremely self-confident or she knew me better than I knew myself. Either way it was unnerving.

Since we'd met, I had compartmentalized the experience of meeting her and Rob into a bucket in my brain reserved for the biz stuff. It was safe and contained, but seeing her again released the experience and all the discomfort I associated with it. There was something else too: it felt good to see her. I'm not sure why – we were strangers – but perhaps because among the over the wall characters I'd met over the past week she seemed the most normal. She was kind to me, and after Milton and The Head's constant mocking, Tuff's abuse, and days of feeling vulnerable that was exactly what I needed.

Celia explained that for security reasons we couldn't meet at JIG:SAW, which had disappointed me – I really wanted to sherlock the place. Instinctively I suggested Occam's, and a week to the day after Alice and I would have had our usual Saturday morning brunch there, I sat with Celia instead. Milton had packed himself in my rucksack and insisted on joining me to 'make sure I didn't do anything stupid'. Celia was everything I remembered: quirky (but only a little), still lacking a basic understanding of personal space, but fascinating, engaging and permanently smiling. Her overfamiliarity still made me squirm, but less so as the meeting went on. Maybe it was time for me to stop avoiding touchy-feely people and accept that others are less aloof than me.

We talked about the sorry state of music, bands we liked, bands we didn't like, clothes we liked, films we liked and guitars we liked. Another person collapsing in the café and waking without their memories prompted a discussion. I thought the seizures were caused by Proteus use, but Celia said that only Chippers collapsed and they don't use a Proteus. I suggested that other people's Proteus devices interfered with the ID chips, and she joked that we could test the theory by zapping Chippers with our Proteuses. I felt relaxed for the first time since Alice had vanished.

Eventually I got to the point. 'I want to join JIG:SAW. I can't survive on what I earn as a musician; I need a proper job.'

Celia looked disappointed, as though this revelation burst part of her bubble. She paused.

'I'd love you to come and work there – we could hang out together, and it'd be so much fun. But I can't just employ you – Mr Nutcot checks everything I do. I've got to give you the recruitment tests.'

She seemed cagey. I asked her what the tests were.

'We use three. The first is Raven's progressive matrices,[27] which measures fluid intelligence, which is commonly known as IQ or just intelligence, and is your aptitude. The second is Carson's creativity scale,[28] which tells us how creative you are. The third is a measure of emotional intelligence, or EI, the TEIQue,[29] which tells us about your people skills.'

Celia asked me to activate my reality checker so I flicked open the lid and The Head emerged from his mist.

The Head turned to look at Celia and floated back jerkily and wide-eyed, as though surprised by what he saw. He floated back above the centre of the pocket watch and turned to me with a slow, affected laugh. 'While The Head is away, Zach will play!'

I glared at him willing him to shut up. He didn't.

'Interesting. Your girlfriend disappears, then the next time The Head emerges you're enjoying a cosy breakfast with a young woman. Seems perfectly innocent.'

Celia became demure, but left the blushing to me. She broke the awkward silence by formally introducing herself to The Head and saying, 'I'm trying to recruit Zach to work at my company. It's about time he got a proper job, don't you think?'

The Head chuckled, 'Yeah, Z sure needs to pay the bills now he's on his own.'

Celia had got the measure of The Head instantly. Alluding to a musician not being a real job was like telling The Head 'We're the same, we mock Zach, so listen to me,' and he fell for her ploy. It had been the same when she met me: she knew how to press my buttons by complimenting my music. Even her boss, Rob Nutcot, obeyed her every command. Whatever this emotional intelligence was that she spoke of, she had it in spades.

Celia addressed The Head in a businesslike tone. 'I want you to give Zach the following tests: Raven's progressive matrices, Carson's creativity scale, and the TEIQue. When you're done, give me his scores.'

With that, she turned away from The Head and gently touched my forearm. Fixing my gaze with a reassuring smile, she said, 'Don't worry, rockstar, I'll be back soon,' and left the table.

The Head spent the next 30 minutes delivering the tests as Celia had asked. This entailed asking me logic questions, showing me images and generally boring the life out of me. When we'd finished he announced, 'Einstein, you got a 30 for creativity, a 125 for IQ and a 165 on emotional intelligence.'

6.1 INTERPRETING RAW SCORES

I noticed Celia was in the opposite corner of the café. She had stretched a Proteus into a large thin screen that she rested on a table, and she swiped and tapped it urgently. Knowing that she would come back soon to find out my scores, I was keen to know how I'd done, so I asked The Head.

'It's hard to say,' he replied. 'Raw scores don't tell you very much in themselves. Take your creativity score, for example. You scored 30. What could you conclude if the mean score on that measure was 10?'

'My score seems a lot higher than the mean, so I'd conclude that I scored quite highly compared to other people,' I said optimistically.

'What if the mean was 29 instead of 10?'

'My score of 30 is still above average, but only just, so perhaps my score is similar to quite a lot of people.'

'And what if the mean was 40?'

'Not so good: my score is less than the average: my creativity is in the lower half of scores.'

The Head beamed. 'Exactly! Your interpretation of your score is affected by knowing about the typical score – the average score. Knowing that you scored 30 doesn't tell you anything about how high or low your creativity is, but if you know the mean then you can start to put your score into context. The mean alone is not enough, though. Imagine you took the creativity test twice and each time you were one of 100 people who took the test. Both times you scored 22. Check this picture. (FIGURE 6.1) It shows histograms of these two sets of imaginary scores. Each square is a person, and the red square is you (a score of 22). In both histograms there are 100 squares, each representing the score of the 100 people who took the test. Let's look at the first time you took the test: the top histogram. The mean score was 18, so you scored 4 higher than the mean.'

'That's good – I'm above average.'

'Yes, but how good is it? Check the top histogram. Remember that each square represents a person, so how many people scored less than you, how many the same, and how many scored higher?'

CHECK YOUR BRAIN: By counting the squares in the top half of Figure 6.1, find out how many people scored less than 22, 22 exactly, and more than 22.

I counted the number of squares below 22, at exactly 22, and above 22 in the diagram: 62 scored less than 22, 7 (including me) scored 22, and 31 scored more. The Head confirmed this and asked me what each score would be as a percentage of the total number of scores. He had said that there were 100 people, so each person's score would be 1 out of 100. I thought back to when I met Professor Pincus, as a proportion this would be 1/100, which is 0.01, so the percentage would be 0.01 × 100, which is 1%. Each square represented 1% of scores.

The Head nodded. 'If each score is 1% of the total number of scores, then if 31 scores were above yours, that means 31% of scores were above yours. Similarly, 62% were below. So, in terms of your place in the distribution, you're about two-thirds of the way along.'

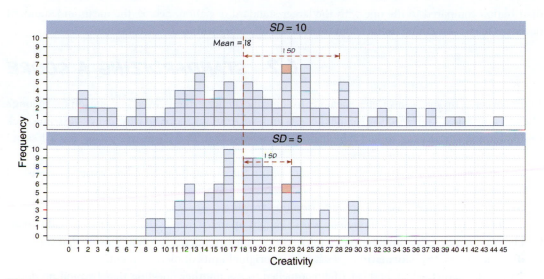

Figure 6.1   A score's location in the distribution can be understood by knowing the mean and standard deviation of that distribution

He asked me to look at the bottom histogram, which showed when I took the test for a second time. He reminded me that we were pretending that I scored 22, and that there were 100 scores in total, and told me to count the squares again and tell him how many scores were less than, the same as, and more than mine. The Head span nonchalantly around, whistling to himself, while I counted. There were 73 people with lower scores, 6 with the same, and 21 with higher scores.

The Head nodded. 'Good work. Again there are 100 people so each score is 1% of the total number of scores, which means that 73% of scores were lower than you, and only 21% were higher. In this situation you're nearly three-quarters of the way up the distribution. In which group are you more creative, compared to the mean of that same group?'

He had asked me to imagine that my score was 22 both times, so I told him that my creativity was the same.

'You didn't listen to The Head. I told you to look at scores *relative to the mean*.'

'Yeah, but you said the mean was 18 in both distributions, so both times my score was 4 above the mean. So, both times my score was 4 higher than the mean, so I was a bit better than average.'

'Don't you find it strange?'

'What?' I paused and stared at The Head. The only thing I found strange was The Head's insistence that I should find something strange. Sensing that I wasn't going to realize what was strange, The Head broke our conversational stalemate.

'Don't you find it strange that you're telling me that you were equally creative according to both tests, and yet on the first test we saw that you scored better than 62% of people but on the second test you scored better than 73% of people? Your second test score marks you out as more creative relative to the rest of the sample than your first test does.'

He was right, that *was* strange.

The Head explained: 'Comparing the score to the mean tells you where the score is relative to the centre of the distribution, but the standard deviation tells us how wide the distribution is **(SECTION 4.4.1)**, so you need to take account of this value too. Check the diagram: **(FIGURE 6.1)** in the top histogram scores are more spread out; it has a standard deviation of 10. Because the scores are more spread out, they extend quite a way beyond 22. In other words, 22 is not a particularly extreme score. In the lower histogram, the scores are more compact around the mean, which shows up in a lower standard deviation of 5. Because the scores are more compact, even the largest scores are relatively close to 22 in this distribution compared to the one with the larger standard deviation. See, Z, the mean and standard deviation tell us something useful about the location of a score within the distribution.'

6.2 STANDARDIZING A SCORE

In the corner of my eye, I saw Celia, speaking to someone on her Proteus. Why had she left for so long? She had only asked The Head to give me the tests and work out my score, so why hadn't she come back yet? Who was she talking to and why hadn't she noticed that The Head was giving me a lesson? Speaking of which, he was in the zone.

'... you've gotta look at the location of a score within the distribution, let it know you ain't satisfied with a **raw score**.' The Head span slowly, thrusting his chin forward like a strutting cock.

'What's a raw score?' I asked hoping to stop the strutting.

He looked embarrassed, as though he was so caught up in his own excitement that he hadn't realized he was strutting. 'It's another name for a score or measurement; the 'raw' tells us that the score hasn't undergone a **transformation** – so, it is in its original units of measurement.'

I wished I hadn't asked, and yet I felt compelled to ask another question that I would no doubt regret. 'What's a transformation?'

'I'm getting there – give The Head a chance. I just explained that it's useful to interpret a raw score within the context of the distribution, and to do that you need to take account of the mean and standard deviation of the distribution from which the score came. You need to **z-score** it ...'

My diePad vibrated to signal a message from Milton. **(MEOWSINGS 6.1)**

'... turn the raw score, X, into a standardized score, which we call z.' The Head projected an equation **(6.1)** onto the table. 'We use this equation, which takes the raw score (X) and subtracts from it the mean of all scores (μ), and then divides by the standard deviation of all scores (σ).'

I wondered why there were two equations, and The Head explained.

'The equation looks different depending on whether you want to calculate a z-score based on the entire population or based on only a sample of scores. The process is the same for both, all that's different are the symbols for the mean (μ for the population and $\bar{X}$ for the sample) and the standard deviation (σ for the population and s for the sample).'

Population

$$z = \frac{X - \mu}{\sigma}$$

Sample

$$z = \frac{X - \bar{X}}{s}$$

(6.1)

'Why would you convert a raw-score to a *z*-score?'

'Have you not been listenin' to The Head? Let me show you what the conversion does. Remember that I showed you two distributions of creativity scores in two tests, and I asked you to imagine that you had a score of 22 for both tests?' *(FIGURE 6.1)*

I did. He'd said that the standard deviation of the distribution affected the relative position of that score. When the standard deviation was smaller, the score of 22 was higher compared to other scores than in a distribution with a larger standard deviation.

'Let's check out those two distributions again.' The Head projected a diagram in front of me. *(FIGURE 6.2)* 'The top of this diagram shows the two distributions I showed you before. *(FIGURE 6.1)* These distributions contain the raw scores, they both have a mean of 18, but in test 1 the standard deviation is 10 (left) and in test 2 the standard deviation is 5 (right). Let's see what the conversion to *z*-scores does. The first part of the conversion *(EQUATION 6.1)* is to subtract the mean from each raw score. This is shown in the middle part of my diagram. *(FIGURE 6.2)* Notice, that this moves the distribution so that the centre is at 0 rather than 18. If the transformed score has a positive value it must be greater than the mean, but if it has a negative score then it is less than the mean.'

It made sense: the distributions hadn't changed shape at all, but the scale at the bottom *had* changed so that the mean (a raw score of 18) was 0, any score originally below the mean had become a negative value and any score originally above the mean had become a positive value.

'Let's see what effect dividing by the standard deviation has,' The Head continued. 'What do you notice when you compare the distributions in the middle of the diagram *(FIGURE 6.2)* to the ones at the bottom?'

I thought about this question for a while. 'It looks like the scale at the bottom has changed, because in the middle it goes from −20 to 28 but at the bottom it goes from −2 to 2.8. But the centre of the distribution is still at 0; the mean has not changed.'

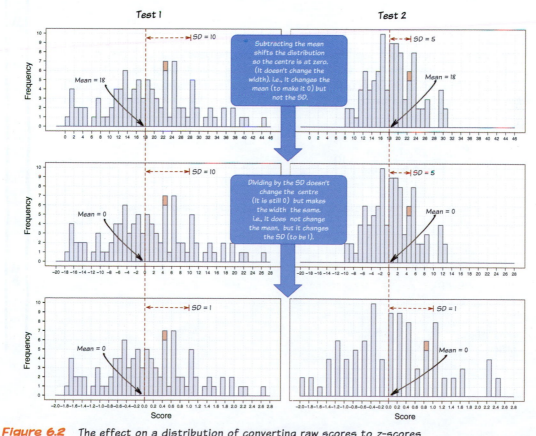

Figure 6.2   *The effect on a distribution of converting raw scores to z-scores*

Dear Human,

It is hot in this rucksack – please hurry up. To speed things along, read this later when I am not stuck in your bag. The equation in (6.1) is not just useful for converting raw scores to z-scores. If we know the mean and standard deviation of a distribution then we can rearrange the equation to convert a z-score back into the original raw score (Figure 6.3). For the creativity example, if we know that the mean of the distribution is 18, the standard deviation is 10, and that the z-score is 0.4, we can work back to show:

$$z = \frac{X - \mu}{\sigma}$$
$$X = z\sigma + \mu$$
$$= 0.4 \times 10 + 18$$
$$= 4 + 18$$
$$= 22$$

In other words, the original score was 22 (which we know from The Head's example). The equation contains four values: the raw score, the z-score, the mean and the standard deviation, so if we know three of the four values we can always work out the fourth by rearranging the equation for z (Figure 6.3). For example, if we know that the raw score is 22, the z-score is 0.4 and the mean is 18, then the standard deviation must be 10:

$$\sigma = \frac{X - \mu}{z} = \frac{22 - 18}{0.4} = \frac{4}{0.4} = 10$$

Finally, if we know that the raw score is 22, the z-score is 0.4 and the standard deviation is 10, then the mean must be 18:

$$\mu = X - z\sigma$$
$$= 22 - 0.4 \times 10$$
$$= 22 - 4$$
$$= 18$$

Best fishes,
Milton

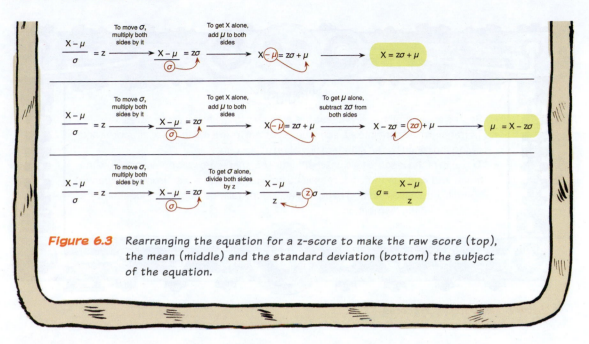

Figure 6.3   *Rearranging the equation for a z-score to make the raw score (top), the mean (middle) and the standard deviation (bottom) the subject of the equation.*

Milton's Meowsings 6.1   *Other uses for the z-score equation*

'The Head is proud of you – that's on the money: dividing by the standard deviation does not affect the mean, it remains at zero. However, it puts both distributions on *similar scales*. If you look at the width of the left distribution, it never changes; however, for the right distribution, it starts off narrower than the left one **(FIGURE 6.2, TOP)**, then when the mean is subtracted from the scores it retains this narrow shape **(FIGURE 6.2, MIDDLE)**, but once you divide by the standard deviation the distribution becomes wider **(FIGURE 6.2, BOTTOM)** and has a comparable width to the distribution on the left. Both distributions now have a standard deviation of 1. Look what happens to the score of 22, which is the red square in the diagram. In both distributions, subtracting the mean does not change the location of that particular score (compare the red square in the top and middle distributions). However, dividing by the standard deviation affects the position of this score (compare the red square in the bottom distributions to the ones above): in the left distribution the position of the red square doesn't change, but in the left one it moves to the right. So, the standard deviation affects the relative position of a score. This is reflected in the z-score. Let's compute the z-score of the value 22 for tests 1 and 2.'

The Head looked to me expectantly. My heart sank. I looked at the equation he'd shown me. **(EQUATION 6.1)** X is the raw score, which in both cases is 22, μ is the mean, which in both distributions is 18, and σ is the standard deviation, which he said was 10 for the first test and 5 for the second test. I plugged these numbers into the equation using my diePad and gave The Head my answers.

$$z = \frac{X - \mu}{\sigma} = \frac{22 - 18}{10} = 0.4$$

$$z = \frac{X - \mu}{\sigma} = \frac{22 - 18}{5} = 0.8$$

He looked very pleased. 'You took a hammer and you nailed that equation,' he chuckled. 'Do you see what's important here? The raw scores were the same – both 22 – but the z-scores are not the same: they reflect the relative position of these scores in the distribution by expressing them

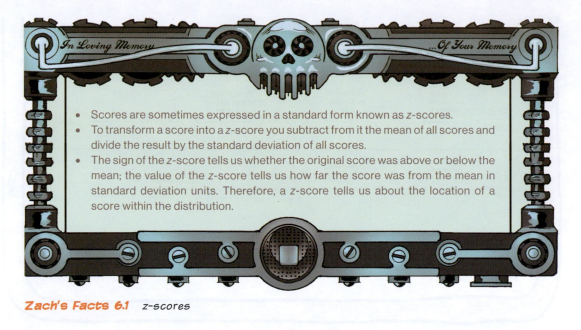

- Scores are sometimes expressed in a standard form known as z-scores.
- To transform a score into a z-score you subtract from it the mean of all scores and divide the result by the standard deviation of all scores.
- The sign of the z-score tells us whether the original score was above or below the mean; the value of the z-score tells us how far the score was from the mean in standard deviation units. Therefore, a z-score tells us about the location of a score within the distribution.

Zach's Facts 6.1 *z-scores*

in standard deviation units. In the first distribution the score 22 is 0.4 standard deviations above the mean, but in the second distribution it is 0.8 standard deviations above the mean. The z-score reflects what we discussed earlier, which is that the score of 22 is relatively better in the second test than in the first, which is why the z-score is larger for the second test than for the first.'

6.3 USING Z-SCORES TO COMPARE DISTRIBUTIONS

I think I understood The Head's point: to get an idea of how big a score is relative to others, a raw score should be interpreted with respect to the distribution of scores, and because the shape of a distribution can be described using the mean and standard deviation, we can look at the raw score relative to these values. That's what a z-score is: its sign tells us where a score is located (whether it is above or below the mean) and its value tells us how far it is from the mean. As I was consolidating my new-found wisdom, a pair of slender arms wrapped themselves around my chest from behind, followed by a pigtail of black hair brushing my face. Celia was back.

'How are we getting on, rockstar?' Celia whispered in my ear. I must have instinctively recoiled because she removed her arms and looked a little upset. I was flustered, dry-mouthed.

The Head stepped in. 'He got a 1-2-5 on IQ, a 3-0 on creativity and a 1-6-5 on emotional intelligence, EI' he said.

'Thank you,' Celia replied. 'Let's see what his strengths are ...' she paused before coyly adding '... apart from excellent cheekbones.' She winked at me before unclipping a Proteus from her wrist and spreading it over the table like a glass mat. She swiped it to open up some data and addressed The Head. 'For IQ the mean is 136 and the standard deviation is 39, for creativity the mean is 32 with an SD of 19, and for EI the mean is 168 with an SD of 32. Can you use those values to give me some z-scores for Zach?'

She had barely finished her sentence when The Head said, 'Those raw scores give us zs of −0.28 for IQ, −0.11 for creativity, and −0.09 for EI.'

'Thank you. It looks like Zach is worst on IQ and about the same on creativity and emotional intelligence. On all of them he's below the mean, though.' In this last revelation I thought I heard a hint of disappointment.

CHECK YOUR BRAIN: Zach got an IQ score of 125, a creativity score of 30 and a score of 165 on EI. Using the information from Celia about the distributions of these measures, calculate the z-scores of each of Zach's scores.

I didn't like Celia having disappointment in her voice, especially when up until now she appeared to love everything about me. 'I don't get it – how can you draw those conclusions? My score on creativity was only 30 but on IQ it was over 100, so how can you say that my intelligence is worse than my creativity?'

Celia adopted an even more disappointed tone. 'I thought The Head might have explained this. Raw scores can't be compared unless they are measured on the same scale.' Celia began to draw on her Proteus. **(FIGURE 6.4)** 'This picture shows the distributions of scores for two of the variables. The top distribution is intelligence or IQ, and the bottom one is creativity. What do you notice about the range of scores for IQ?'

'The lowest is about 75 and the highest is about 200.'

'Yes, and what about creativity?'

'They go from about 0 to 65.'

'Brilliant. So your scores of 125 for IQ and 30 for creativity can't be compared, because they reflect different measurement scales. You couldn't possibly have got a score as high as 125 on creativity because the top of the scale is only 65! We can make the scales comparable, though, by turning each one into a **standardized distribution**. This process is known as **standardization**. A standardized distribution is one that has a predetermined mean and standard deviation. By converting the entire distribution of raw scores to something called z-scores, we get a standardized distribution.'

I explained that The Head had told me about z-scores, but I didn't understand how they made distributions comparable. It occurred to me that perhaps I should tell Celia about Alice. Maybe we could bypass all of these tests and just get straight into JIG:SAW if I did? Celia was keen to help me, so why not? There seemed to be lots of reasons *not* to tell her though. Much as I found it hard to comprehend anyone other than Alice showing a romantic interest in me, and as bad as I usually was at picking up those cues, I thought Celia was flirting with me. If her motivation to help was to spend time with me, would she help me to find Alice? Then there was her relationship with Rob Nutcot: she had almost seemed to be *his* boss, not the other way around, but in any case, she worked closely with him. Perhaps she was loyal to JIG:SAW and at the moment I didn't know what Alice's connection was to them. Perhaps I couldn't trust Celia, but for now I had no choice but to go along with her.

'Think about this,' Celia continued. 'If you convert all of the scores in a distribution to z-scores, what happens to the relative position of the scores – what happens to the order that the scores are in?'

I paused to think. 'I guess the order of scores doesn't change because you do the same thing to each score when you convert them to z-scores: you subtract a value (the mean) and then divide by a value (the standard deviation). So if one raw score is bigger than another it will still be bigger after converting to z because in both cases you do the same thing to the scores.'

'Fantastic, Zach. You're more than just impressive cheekbones! The relative order of scores will not change, and so the overall shape of the distribution does not change either. You can see this in my diagram. **(FIGURE 6.4)** Look at IQ (top) and creativity (bottom): in both cases the shape of the distribution of raw scores (left) is the same as the shape after transformation (right): the heights of the bars are the same as you move along the distribution. So, the shape of the distribution does not change. Now what happens to the overlap of the two distributions, Zach?'

I looked at the diagram **(FIGURE 6.4)** and told Celia what I noticed. For the untransformed scores (left) the distributions for intelligence and creativity did not really overlap: the scores for intelligence began where the creativity scores stopped. For the z-scores, though (right), the distributions overlap almost completely.

CHECK YOUR BRAIN: *The creativity scores in Celia's distribution are 55, 32, 4, 39, 24, 4, 52, 17, 26, 44, 4, 40, 65, 2, 53, 35, 42, 36, 45, and 15. This distribution has a mean of $\mu = 32$ and a standard deviation of $\sigma = 19$. Convert each score to a z-score, and then compute the mean and standard deviation of the resulting scores.*

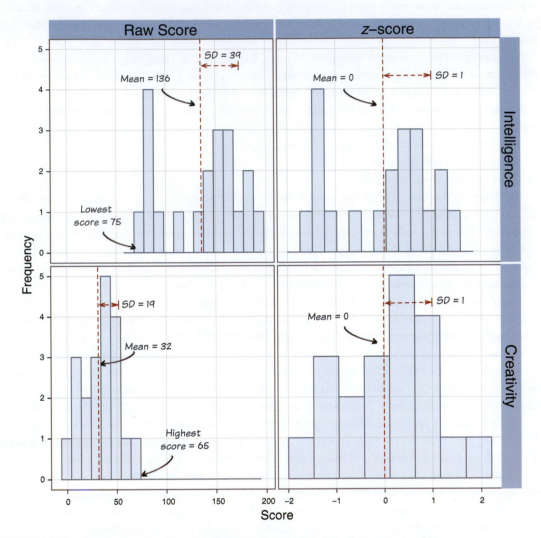

Figure 6.4 *Converting two distributions to z-scores makes them comparable*

'Yes. Converting the entire distribution to *z*-scores relocates the centre of the distribution at zero. Before transformation, the centre of the intelligence distribution as measured by the mean was 136, but after transformation to *z* the distribution is centred on a mean of zero. The same thing happens to creativity: the distribution goes from being centred on 32 to being centred on zero. So, before transformation the distributions have different centres (136 and 32), but after transformation the distributions have the same centres (both 0). Finally, what do you notice about the width of the distributions before and after they are transformed?'

I studied Celia's diagram again. **(FIGURE 6.4)** For the untransformed scores (left) the distribution for intelligence looked wider than the distribution of creativity scores, but for the *z*-scores (right) the distributions seemed a similar width. Feeling that I was on a roll with answering questions correctly, I told Celia what I thought.

'Wow, handsome *and* intelligent!' she replied. Her flattery made me feel good. 'Converting the entire distribution to z-scores places them on the same measurement scale. You told me earlier that, before transformation, IQ scores ranged from about 75 to 200, whereas creativity scores ranged from 0 to 65. However, when converted to z-scores both measures range from about −2 to +2. Before transformation the scales have different units of measurement: one is measured in units of IQ and the other in units of creativity. After transformation both are measured in units of 'standard deviations'. In other words, a z-score of 1 means that the score is 1 standard deviation above the mean, and a score of −1.5 means one and a half standard deviations *below* the mean. For this reason, by converting a whole distribution of scores to z-scores we can compare it to a different distribution of z-scores – because both distributions will be centred on zero and are measured in the same units (standard deviations).

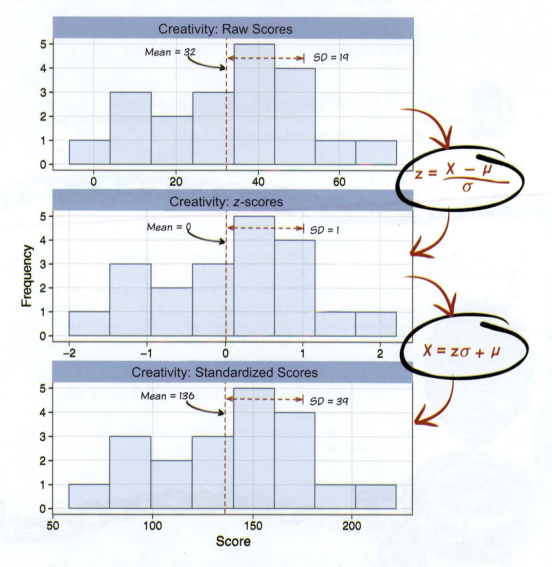

Figure 6.5 *Standardizing a distribution of scores doesn't change the shape of the distribution, but it changes the scale of measurement (note the x-axis changes)*

'Right, so to compare creativity with IQ we'd have to convert both distributions to *z*-scores?'

'Not necessarily,' Celia replied. 'We could change only one of the scales to match the other. For example, we know that our fluid IQ measure has a mean of 136 and a standard deviation of 39, so we could transform the creativity scale so that it also has a mean of 136 and a standard deviation of 39.'

That fripped my head proper.

Celia drew another diagram on her Proteus. **(FIGURE 6.5)** 'Look at the top distribution. These are our raw creativity scores: as we've seen before, they range from 0 to 65 with a mean of 32 and standard deviation of 19. We have just seen that we can convert these raw scores to *z*-scores by subtracting the mean from each score and then dividing by the standard deviation. That's shown in the middle distribution. As we have also seen, the shape of the distribution doesn't change, just the scale of measurement, which now ranges from about −2 to +2 with a mean of 0 and a standard deviation of 1. If we want these scores to have a mean of 136 and a standard deviation of 39, we can rearrange the equation so that *x* is the subject. **(MEOWSINGS 6.1)** If you do that you'll see that you take the *z*-score, multiply it by the standard deviation that you want (in this case 39) and then add the mean that you want (in this case 136). The resulting scores are shown in the bottom distribution. Notice again that the shape of the distribution hasn't changed, but the scale along the bottom has: the mean is now 136 and the standard deviation is 39, which is the same as the IQ measure.'

 CHECK YOUR BRAIN: Take the z-scores for creativity that you calculated before and convert them so that the distribution has a mean of 136 and a standard deviation of 39.

Later on The Head explained what Celia had meant. 'Standardized distributions are used in the real world, Z. For example, intelligence or IQ tests are usually standardized to have a mean of 100 and a standard deviation of 15. About 95% of the population have IQ scores between 70 and 130 (in other words, within 2 standard deviations of the mean) and about 68% of the population have IQ scores between 85 and 115 (i.e., within 1 standard deviation of the mean). Standardizing measures in this way makes it easy to ascertain a person's relative ability from their raw score. For example, Z, if your IQ score is 145, which of course it isn't, then we know that you scored higher than the vast majority of people in the population ('cos 95% of the population score between 70 and 130); if you score 102, then we know you're of about average intelligence.'

Reality Check 6.1 *Standardized distributions*

'Wow, so creativity scores now have the same mean and standard deviation as the IQ scores, so we could compare the two distributions.'

Celia nodded. 'Although we can standardize distributions by converting to z-scores, which have a mean of 0, in the real world scientists sometimes standardize distributions so that the mean is a value that makes every score positive: this is because some people find the negative numbers that you get with z-scores confusing.' **(REALITY CHECK 6.1)**

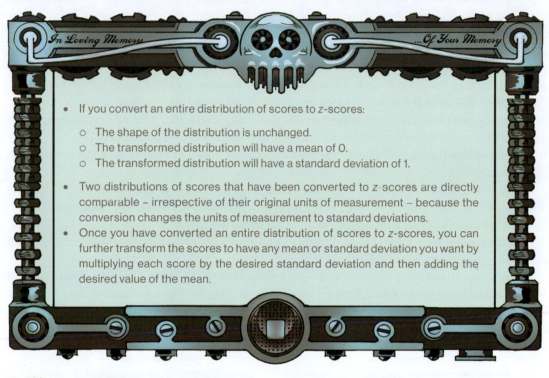

In Loving Memory ... ...Of Your Memory

- If you convert an entire distribution of scores to z-scores:

  o The shape of the distribution is unchanged.
  o The transformed distribution will have a mean of 0.
  o The transformed distribution will have a standard deviation of 1.

- Two distributions of scores that have been converted to z-scores are directly comparable – irrespective of their original units of measurement – because the conversion changes the units of measurement to standard deviations.
- Once you have converted an entire distribution of scores to z-scores, you can further transform the scores to have any mean or standard deviation you want by multiplying each score by the desired standard deviation and then adding the desired value of the mean.

Zach's Facts 6.2 z-score distributions

6.4 USING Z-SCORES TO COMPARE SCORES

As interesting as it was finding out about standardizing distributions – and really, it wasn't interesting at all – I had come here to get into JIG:SAW, not to be educated. I wondered whether it was all part of a more elaborate recruitment strategy: perhaps this meeting *was* the test, and the measures of intelligence and creativity were a smokescreen. I felt relieved that I had been trying to engage with what Celia was explaining, rather than my default of switching off; perhaps in doing so I was passing some sort of aptitude test. I felt ashamed that, after so many attempts by Alice to get me involved in this stuff, it had taken her disappearance to make me listen. I also felt guilty that it was a woman other than Alice that I was listening to.

'Celia ...' I began. The juxtaposition of her pale blue eyes against her black hair and pale skin momentarily stopped me in my tracks. She widened her eyes and smiled as though awaiting something profound. She was going to be disappointed.

'What does any of this tell me about whether I can work for JIG:SAW?'

Celia's smile widened and she grabbed my hand excitedly. 'Sorry Zach, I got carried away! I wanted you to see what your z-scores of −0.28, −0.11 and −0.09 tell me about how you scored *relative to others* on the measures of IQ, creativity and emotional intelligence.'

'You said my IQ sucked.'

'Yes, because these z-scores are all comparable.' Celia drew another diagram. *(FIGURE 6.6)* 'Look at the left-hand side. We started off with three scores on three different scales and with three different distributions. The red values and dots show your scores for each variable. These scores are very different and you can see that, because of this, the red dots are in very different horizontal positions. You can't compare these scores. For example, the distributions of creativity and emotional intelligence do not overlap at all, so it would be impossible to get comparable scores on these measures. The transformation is all about placing the raw score into the context of the distribution of scores so that you can see how close to the mean it is relative to the spread of scores. On the right-hand side, the green values and dots show the same scores after the transformation. These scores are now expressed in terms of how many standard deviations they are away from the mean. After the transformation, the scores are very similar: they line up at roughly the same horizontal position. All three scores are a bit below the mean. Note that after the transformation the distributions completely overlap, so we can compare these transformed scores: by expressing your raw scores as z-scores, they become directly comparable because they are all from distributions with a mean of 0 and a standard deviation of 1.'

'Right, so if we order my z-scores, it reflects the order of how well I did in each test compared to the others.'

'Yes, your z-score of −0.28 for IQ is the smallest of the three − it was the furthest below the mean − so that was your worst score; in the other two you had z-scores of −0.11 and −0.09, which are very similar and both a bit higher than the IQ score.'

'All the z-scores seem fairly similar, though. I mean, there's not much difference between −0.28 and −0.11, they're both very small values.'

'That's true. To put them into context, a z-score bigger than about 3 or smaller than about −3 would be rare, so although z-scores don't have a limited range as such, they have an effective range: it would be very unusual to see values outside of ±3, and extremely rare to see values outside of ±4. So, you're

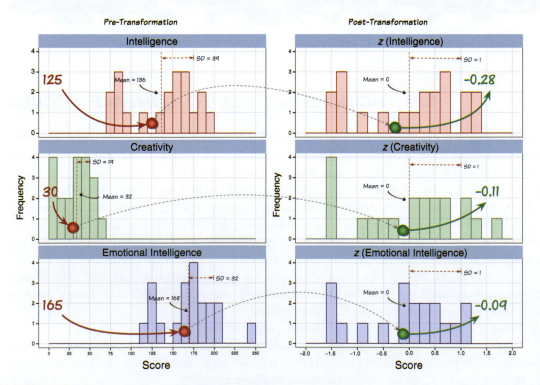

Figure 6.6 *Converting Zach's raw scores to z-scores*

right, in the grand scheme of things all of your scores were quite similar to each other. I think had we tested your handsomeness we might have found a very positive z-score though, maybe even a +4.'

'Was that … a z-score flirt?' I asked.

Celia blushed. 'Glad you noticed, it shows you're learning,' she said trying to salvage the situation.

I played it cool. 'If my z-scores are quite similar then that means my levels of intelligence, emotional intelligence and creativity are similar, so I am a good all-rounder then? So, can I have a job?' I did some ridiculous eyelash fluttering to try to seal the deal.

Celia adopted a mischievous smile. 'It does mean that, but unfortunately all of your z-scores were negative, which means that you are stupid, uncreative and emotionally unintelligent compared to the average person.'

Her bluntness hurt me – I definitely preferred Celia's flattery; I didn't like the now-teasing Celia nearly as much. An awkward silence ensued, but I was too wrapped up in my own feelings to notice it. Celia *had* noticed it and placed her hand affectionately on my shoulder. She fixed my gaze with her bottomless pupils and said, 'I'm just teasing: your scores were negative which means they are all below average, but only a little bit. Look at the right-hand side of my diagram **(FIGURE 6.6)** and you can see each one is only a little bit below average.'

She waited for a response, but I retreated into silence, as I often did with people I didn't know well. She probed my face with her eyes, searching for my thoughts. She squeezed my hand and her tone became serious. 'I'm so sorry, rockstar, but I can't offer you a job at JIG:SAW. At the moment we only have vacancies for technicians – the people who help the scientists – and for those jobs you need *above* average scores. Your scores are all *below* average. I'm sorry, I really am, because I would *love* to work with you.'

'No biggie,' I lied, 'it's standard – there's a reason why I'm a musician.' I smiled a fake smile, but this reminded me of school and college where my teachers always told me I wasn't good enough.

Celia could see she had hurt my feelings and her gaze sank. She looked sad, but was it guilt or was she engaged in some internal battle about whether to say something? She got up, still staring at the floor, and turned to leave. She mumbled 'I'm sorry Zach, you deserve better,' and ran out of Occam's café.

There was turning out to be more to Celia than she let on: along with her playfulness, lack of consideration of my personal space, and her apparent awe of my musical talent, she was impressively clever – a fact that she had seemed keen to hide when we met at the recruitment event. I didn't know what she did at JIG:SAW, but she certainly knew her way around numbers.

Thinking back to the recruitment event had reminded me of something that I'd found odd at the time: she'd asked to take a highsie to put on *memoryBank* as though she were a Chipper, but she used a Proteus device to take a picture, like a Clocktorian. And what was her reaction to my being upset all about? Yeah, she hurt my feelings, but why should she care? She didn't know me. Fans could be biz.

6.5   Z-SCORES FOR SAMPLES

I'd got used to feeling alone in the week since Alice had left, but as I watched Celia rush through the doors into the street I felt hollow, as though she had taken my insides with her. Was it because I had failed to get into JIG:SAW to see whether they were connected to Alice's disappearance? I guessed so, but a little part of me was upset that things had ended badly with Celia. I banged my fist on the table and cursed my stupidity. Resting my elbows on the edge of the table, I closed my eyes and placed my head in my hands. A movement beside me turned into paws on my lap. I opened my eyes to see Milton's staring back at me from between my arms.

'Far be it from me to interrupt your wallowing, but something doesn't add up,' he said.

I looked at him as if to say 'what?'

'Those values for the means and standard deviations of the tests you took are not right.'

I continued my puzzled stare.

'It's well known that IQ tests have a mean of 100 and a standard deviation of 15 **(REALITY CHECK 6.1)**, not 136 and 39 as Celia said. I think it would be wise to check the other values she gave you. Activate your reality checker.' I did as the cat asked.

'Where's the rock princess?' said The Head as he emerged from his clockwork cell.

The Head had been really excited to meet Milton when I first took him home. At first I had told him that I had adopted a cat, but during my three-day hiatus, as I made plans, it became clear to me that I would need both The Head and Milton if I was going to find Alice. After careful negotiation and reassurance, Milton had agreed, and I have never seen The Head as happy as when the cat opened his furry little mouth to speak. He had spun repeatedly through 180 degrees, his eyes and tongue spasming in and out as though on elastic. I wasn't sure whether it was the excitement of a talking cat, or of talking to Milton Grey, but The Head *loved* being with Milton.

'Good evening, Mr Head,' said Milton.

The Head beamed. 'Fuzzball, finally out of the rucksack? What can I do for you?' He was a lot politer to Milton than he was to me.

'Would you be so kind as to tell me what might be reasonable population values for the creativity and emotional intelligence tests that Zach took?'

The head took milliseconds to do this task. 'I went pirate on my database and plundered you some gold,' he said. 'For creativity, I found studies[28] showing a mean of 15 and a standard deviation of 11, and for emotional intelligence a mean of 150 and a standard deviation of 20 are reasonable.[30] **(TABLE 6.1)**

'Interesting,' replied Milton. 'Those means are a lot lower than the means Celia gave you. Let's see what your z-scores would be if we used those values as the population means and standard deviations.'

Milton forced me to make these calculations. It turned out that my new z-scores were 1.67 for IQ, 1.36 for creativity and 0.75 for emotional intelligence.

Milton scratched his chin. 'This is fascinating. When we compare your scores against these population values you come out surprisingly well. Contrary to being below average, as Celia suggested, your z-scores are all positive, showing that you scored above average. What is more, for IQ and creativity you

CHECK YOUR BRAIN: Recalculate Zach's z-scores based on his raw scores, but using these new means and standard deviations: IQ ($\mu = 100$, $\sigma = 15$), creativity ($\mu = 15$, $\sigma = 11$), and emotional intelligence ($\mu = 150$, $\sigma = 20$).

Table 6.1 Distribution means and standard deviations for the measures Zach took in the population, and in two JIG:SAW samples

Sample	Measure	Zach's raw Score	Mean	SD	Zach's z-score
Population	IQ	125	$\mu = 100$	$\sigma = 15$	*1.67*
	Creativity	30	$\mu = 15$	$\sigma = 11$	1.36
	EI	165	$\mu = 150$	$\sigma = 20$	0.75
JIG:SAW (code 1318)	IQ	125	$\bar{X} = 136$	$s = 39$	−0.28
	Creativity	30	$\bar{X} = 32$	$s = 19$	−0.11
	EI	165	$\bar{X} = 168$	$s = 32$	−0.09
JIG:SAW (technicians)	IQ	125	$\bar{X} = 116$	$s = 18$	0.5
	Creativity	30	$\bar{X} = 14$	$s = 9$	1.78
	EI	165	$\bar{X} = 149$	$s = 21$	0.76

were more than a standard deviation above the average because the *z*s are greater than 1. You actually have quite impressive IQ and creativity, and even your emotional intelligence is better than most.'

'Why would Celia's population values differ from the ones that The Head obtained?' I asked.

'Perhaps because she wasn't using population values, but values based on samples at JIG:SAW,' Milton suggested.

'Wouldn't this affect how we compute the *z*-scores?'

'No. Remember that the equation for *z* is the same whether you use population values or sample values. *(EQUATION 6.1)* All that changes are the symbols used to represent the mean and standard deviation. The plot gets thicker, though.'

'Why?'

'While you and the female exchanged mating signals, I was busy under the table investigating her bag. I hoped she might have a tuna sandwich, or perhaps a dead mouse, in there. No such luck, but she *did* have a rather unpalatable report from JIG:SAW. It contained a table of means and standard deviations for the tests you took. I took the liberty of copying it.'

Milton paused momentarily and took off his collar. He flicked his paw at it and it transformed into a screen; his collar was a Proteus device – sick! That was how he'd been able to message me! A table appeared on the screen. *(TABLE 6.1)* 'Look,' he said. 'The population values match those found by The Head. The values that she used to compute your *z*-scores are from a sample at JIG:SAW called code 1318 – their means are much larger than the population.'

'I've seen code 1318 before – I saw it on the graphs in Rob Nutcot's talk. *(FIGURE 5.2)* Dr Tuff didn't know what a code 1318 worker was. Do you?'

'I have no idea. Looking at the table *(TABLE 6.1)*, what other group of workers do you see?'

'Technicians.'

'*Purr*cisely. Celia said they were only recruiting technicians at the moment and yet she compared you to the code 1318 group and *not* the technicians. What are your *z*-scores when you work them out relative to the technician sample?'

CHECK YOUR BRAIN: Convert Zach's raw scores for IQ, creativity, and EI into *z*-scores using the values from the distributions for technicians in Table 6.1.

They were 0.5 for IQ, 1.78 for creativity and 0.76 for EI.

'*Furr*scinating' said Milton. 'If she had compared you to the technicians your z-scores would all have been positive, indicating that you are above average on all measures and *not* below average as she concluded. You met the criteria to work at JIG:SAW!'

KEY TERMS

Raw score

Standardized distribution

Standardization

Transformation

z-score

JIG:SAW'S PUZZLES

1   Milton took the IQ, EI and creativity tests that Zach took. His scores were IQ = 170, EI = 70 and creativity = 55. Calculate the z-scores relative to the population values in Table 6.1. How do Milton's scores compare to Zach's?

2   In the file in Dr Genari's office, Zach also found that Alice had a score of 57 out of 60 on an IQ test (a different one than the one Zach completed). This test had a mean of 32 and a standard deviation of 7. Using this information and the answer to the previous question, who has a larger IQ: Alice or Milton?

3   When Zach met Professor Pincus (Chapter 3), she showed him data from 20 women who rated how important they found various characteristics in men. They rated from 0 (not at all important) to 10 (very important) characteristics such as high salary, humour, kindness and ambition. The data are in Table 3.1. A student outside Occam's asked Celia to rate how important these same characteristics were in a partner. She gave high salary a rating of 5. What is this value as a z-score? (Hint: use the values in Table 3.1 to compute the mean and standard deviation of the distribution of high salary ratings.)

4   For kindness, Celia's rating yielded a z-score of 0.9. What was her raw score? (Hint: use the values in Table 3.1 to compute the mean and standard deviation of the distribution of kindness ratings.)

5   For ambition, Celia gave a rating of 9, which yielded a z-score of 1.56. What was the standard deviation of ambition ratings? (Hint: use the values in Table 3.1 to compute the mean of the distribution of ambition ratings.)

6   For humour, Celia also gave a rating of 9, which yielded a z-score of 0.66. The standard deviation of humour scores was 1.43. What was the mean of the humour ratings?

7   Which of the four attributes did Celia value most? (Hint: use the z-scores.)

8   Celia mentioned Zach's cheekbones a lot. In the data Professor Pincus looked at there were also 20 women's ratings of how important they thought attractiveness was. The scores were: 4, 10, 9, 8, 7, 8, 10, 8, 7, 3, 9, 10, 8, 10, 7, 9, 9, 9, 8, 7. Convert this distribution to z-scores. Celia gave attractiveness a rating of 9. What was the z-score for this raw score?

9   Alice also rated these characteristics of a partner, but using a different rating scale. For kindness, this scale had a mean of 15 and a standard deviation of 7. Alice gave kindness a rating of 21. Who values kindness more: Alice or Celia? (Hint: compare the z-scores.)

10 In the data Professor Pincus looked at there were also 20 women's ratings of how important they thought being romantic was. The scores were: 7, 10, 7, 8, 9, 8, 10, 7, 7, 4, 5, 8, 7, 8, 7, 9, 3, 7, 10, 7. Convert this distribution to z-scores. Celia gave being romantic a rating of 9. What was the z-score for this raw score?

IN THE NEXT CHAPTER, ZACH DISCOVERS ...

A bridge of death

Classical probability and empirical probability

Probability and frequency distributions

Probability density functions

The normal and standard normal distributions

Conditional probability

Bayes' theorem

The cat's murky past

Probability
The Bridge of Death

I stared in awe at the bridge. 'It's like a rainbow reaching out to heaven,' I said to Milton.

'A perfect metaphor if the rainbow is coloured the shades of death, and heaven has taken an interest in genetics research.'

I barely heard him. 'It's magnificent!' I whispered to myself.

'Crocodiles are magnificent, but I don't want to walk across one,' Milton cut me off.

Milton had adopted a steadfastly negative attitude since our meeting with Celia. Perhaps his pride was hurt because she had scuppered his plan for me to sign up to the JIG:SAW workforce, but I sensed it was something else. His remarks about Celia and me were pretty subterranean, as though he didn't approve. Maybe he thought I was flirting with her, but I hadn't been, had I? She made me feel uneasy, so I was pretty sure I had given her freak vibes, not sexy ones. Even if I was a little flattered by Celia's attention, who wouldn't be? It didn't mean anything, and why should he care? Maybe he knew Alice better than I realized?

Since Alice's disappearance I had been surrounded by contradictions. There was Milton, a human trapped in a cat. He had initially tried to put me off of investigating JIG:SAW, but after I suggested contacting the WGA he changed his tune and suggested I get a job there! He had gone as far as hacking Celia's Proteus to access a map of the complex.

Then there was Celia. At face value she was laid-back, emotionally generous and completely fanatic about me and my band, but our recent meeting showed something very different: an intelligent and businesslike side to her that was inconsistent with her apparent free spirit. I wondered whether she really was Rob Nutcot's underling. Also, what was with her flirtations? Fans could be biz, but she was over the wall for sure. Was it real, or was she manipulating me to keep me away from JIG:SAW? Why didn't she want me there – if she liked me as much as she seemed to, then my working for JIG:SAW would give her the perfect opportunity to see me more?

Everywhere I turned, people seemed to be delaying me from finding out what was going on. Genari, Pincus, Milton and Celia – none of them gave me straight answers, and all of them distracted me with explanations about stuff that really wasn't relevant to finding Alice. More than a week had passed and I was no closer to finding her and it frustrated the hell out of me – I started to think about what might have happened to her. If she had been taken, who knows what might have happened to her in a week. She might even be dead.

Milton noticed my eyes watering. He sat by me and rubbed his head on my shin. 'You'll find her,' he said, before wandering off to clean himself of his kind words. How did he know that – did he know where Alice was or was he just being nice? Could I trust him? Genari, Pincus, Milton and

Celia – I had taken them all at face value, trusted their every word, but I knew nothing about them. What if one of them was behind Alice's disappearance? I guess it didn't matter – all I could do was follow my own path and trust myself, and my path was this bridge. A bridge of death.

I stared at it; it was terrifying. Would I cross a bridge of death to find Alice? I could turn back, forget about Alice, or try a different way to find her that didn't involve this bridge. I could, but I felt that the key to the puzzle was in JIG:SAW. If I turned away, I was turning my back on Alice. I had no choice but to trust Milton because the only thing standing between certain death and me was him – a ginger cat nuzzling purposefully into his backside. I hoped he'd never done that as a human.

7.1 PROBABILITY

'Why is it called the bridge of death?' I asked.

'It's not,' Milton replied. 'That's a nickname. It's a probability bridge, and it doesn't have to involve death, although it invariably does. In the wake of the Reality Revolution, and thanks to my perceived part in it, I was seconded to work for the recently formed WGA. They had a plan to isolate the major cities of the world by creating barriers around them. It was a new spin on the centuries-old idea of building a moat around a castle. The cities were the castles, the probability bridge would be the moat: a barrier where the WGA could control who got across.'

'Why would they do that?'

'The world was in chaos before the WGA brought order to it. There were power struggles everywhere, and people willing to do anything to gain a stronghold. Surely you know your history? The WGA built hundreds of enormous cities around the world, the *focities*, filled with people who shared their vision of a united world. They wanted to isolate and protect these cities, which would be the points from which their new ideals would spread. Each focity was to be surrounded by a vast chasm with probability bridges as the entry points to the city.'

'What *is* a probability bridge?'

'It's a bridge along which there are choices to make and you need to use probability to make those choices; without understanding probability you will most likely make the wrong choice and when you do your progress is halted. It is the perfect defence.'

'Why?'

'Because absolutely no one understands probability.'

Milton looked pleased with his quip, but I didn't find it funny because I actually didn't understand probability. Not even a little bit. I asked him how 'progress is halted'.

'It depends upon how the tasks are configured. The best-case scenario is that you have to turn around and go back.'

'And the worst?'

'You die a slow and horrifically painful death.'

'More slow and horrifically painful than learning about probability?'

'I'm afraid so. This was at the heart of why I resigned from the WGA. It became clear to me and some of my colleagues that these bridges would be used to divide society, not protect it. Even as the WGA's agenda of peace was being embraced worldwide, the bridge project continued. Our remit changed from peaceful consequences for failing the tasks to fatal ones. I'm not a fool – they wanted to develop a tool to protect themselves, and ultimately separate the world: to protect the people on their side and cast out those who were not. Take any political or societal institution. Ultimately it is like any organism: its fundamental directive is to thrive, to survive, no matter what the cost. That is why I resigned. We never finished a working bridge. The technology was in place, but a bridge was never built: I hoped that my leaving meant that it never would. This is the first one I have seen, but there is no mistaking what it is.'

'If the WGA developed these bridges then is JIG:SAW run by the WGA?'

'Not necessarily, but it suggests that they have obtained the prototypes that we worked on and finished the job.'

'Can you get us across safely?'

'We cannot answer that question without crossing the bridge and discovering what happens to us. However, we can discuss *potential* outcomes in terms of probability.'

7.1.1 Classical probability

The word 'probability' was like an iceberg to my heart: it sank like the *Titanic*. I remembered my maths teacher at school trying to teach me probability as I gazed out of the classroom window dreaming of music stardom. It had become a great source of comfort to me that having failed my probability coursework, I had never had to think about it again. That comfort was now drowning in the freezing Grand Banks of Newfoundland. Reluctantly, I asked Milton what probability is.

'You already know!' he exclaimed. 'Do you remember what Professor Pincus told you about relative frequencies?' **(SECTION 3.1.1)**

CHECK YOUR BRAIN: What is a relative frequency? If JIG:SAW employed 120 people and 16 of them work in 'security', what is the relative frequency of security workers?

I thought back. 'It's how often something occurs – the frequency – divided by the total frequency of all events, isn't it? Professor Pincus and I looked at women's ratings on a scale from 1 to 10 of how important it was for a potential date to have a high salary. We counted how many women gave each rating on the scale. The relative frequency of how many women gave a rating of 10, for example, was the number of women who gave a rating of 10 divided by the total number of women.'

'Excellent.' Milton looked as pleased as a cat could. 'More formally, the relative frequency is the frequency of a particular outcome relative to the total number of possible outcomes.' He scratched out an equation in the dirt next to us. **(EQUATION 7.1)** 'The fact that you understand this means that you know what a probability is.'

$$\text{relative frequency} = \frac{\text{frequency of outcome}}{\text{total number of outcomes}} = \frac{f}{N} \tag{7.1}$$

This fact surprised me, and I asked Milton to explain.

'The relative frequency is an **empirical probability**, a probability derived from actual observations, so if you understand relative frequency, you understand empirical probability. We can also look at theoretical or **classical probability**, which is a probability derived from probability theory.'

I didn't like the sound of that. Another sound I didn't like was that of Milton scratching out a diagram on a nearby rock. **(FIGURE 7.1)** 'This diagram shows some key concepts in probability,' he said excitedly. 'Imagine that we looked at your Proteus and found that you had five friends in your contacts.'

'That's not very realistic!' I blurted.

Milton looked sad. 'I'm a physics professor – in my world that is completely realistic. Friends are an unnecessary distraction from my work and they invariably let you down.'

It occurred to me that I wasn't so different from Milton. Despite my Proteus being full of names and numbers, most were acquaintances and I had always surrounded myself with just a few close friends. These days, it was perhaps only my band mates and Alice who were true friends, and it was

Nick and Alice who I relied on most. Milton had sounded bitter, and I wondered whether he'd had bad experiences. I asked him about Pincus, and whether he'd had buddies at the WGA.

'In case you had not noticed, I am a cat. Catherine has been very good to me, but she draws the line at socializing with cats and fears my identity being discovered. At the WGA there was a brilliant man, Roediger – we were close, very close,' he said, staring wistfully into the distance. 'He was a phenomenal scientist; if I may say so, we were a quite unparalleled team. My strengths were big theoretical ideas, but I had to force myself to do the tedious intellectual detail. Roediger was the opposite: give him a half-baked set of proofs and he would complete them beautifully. He was technically way above me, but had no original ideas whatsoever. Together we were unstoppable. When I left the WGA it drove us apart: he wanted to stay, I had to go. I have never met anyone like him before or since. He was the only person there who never judged me for inventing the reality prism. He was the only friend I've had since the revolution.'

Milton seemed hurt by his recollections. It was clear he didn't like talking about it, but I asked if he still saw this Roediger guy.

'No,' the cat replied curtly to end the conversation. There was an awkward silence before he continued as though the conversation about Roediger had never happened. 'Pretend you are not an annoyingly popular rockstar and that you have exactly five friends' numbers in your Proteus. Also imagine that you have an app on your Proteus that will select one of these friends. Each selection is known as an **experiment**.'

'The night before she vanished, Alice told me that an experiment was where you compare a situation in which a cause is present, to the same situation but with the cause absent.' *(SECTION 1.3.2)*

'In probability theory the term has a different meaning: it refers to any procedure that can be repeated and that has a well-defined **outcome** or set of outcomes. In the case of the contacts in your Proteus, selecting a friend is an experiment because it has a well-defined set of outcomes: in this example there are only five possible outcomes of selecting one friend because there are only five contacts in your Proteus. The complete set of possible outcomes is known as the **sample space**. A particular instance of the experiment is known as a **trial**, and a particular trial will have a specific outcome that is one of the possible outcomes from the sample space.'

'Hang on there, whiskers – that's a lot of tricksy words.'

The cat sighed. 'Look at the left-hand side of the diagram. *(FIGURE 7.1)* First of all, you have five friends' numbers on your Proteus, so if the experiment is to select one friend, then the size of the sample space is 5: each of the friends. Each time you do the experiment, known as a trial, there is an outcome, which must be taken from the sample space (because the sample space is made up of all of the possible outcomes). Let's imagine the app takes a **random sample**.'

'A what?'

'It means that each of the five contacts in your Proteus has an equal chance of being selected, so the app selects or "samples" a contact on a random basis. For example, perhaps on the first trial, the app selects Jessika, but on the second trial it selects Lemmy, and on trials 3 and 4 it selects Celia. Each time a contact is selected it remains on your Proteus, which is known as **sampling with replacement** because the name that has been selected or "sampled" is replaced back into the sample space so that it can be selected again on a subsequent trial. Sometimes **sampling without replacement** is used, which would be like the contact being deleted from your Proteus if it is selected. Sampling without replacement means that once an item is selected or "sampled" it is *not* put back into the sample space and it cannot be selected on a subsequent trial.'

'Safe: so the contacts on my Proteus are the sample space, and each time I get the app to randomly pick a name, this is a trial of an experiment, and that trial will have an outcome, which will be one of the contacts. Where does probability come into all of this?'

'Simple. We can work out the probability of an **event** associated with this kind of process.' I guessed that by 'event' he didn't mean something rad like one of our gigs. I was right. 'An event is an outcome or set of outcomes of an experiment, and it is something to which we can assign a probability. An event can be a specific single outcome, for example, 'selecting Joel' on a given trial; but it can also be a set of outcomes, for example, 'selecting a woman', which is the same as 'selecting Celia *or* Jessika' on a trial. There are some other examples of events in the diagram: **(FIGURE 7.1)** selecting a man, selecting someone who wears glasses, but you can think of others too, for example, selecting someone with dark hair, selecting someone with no hair. An event can be any outcome that interests you. In classical probability, if we assume that every outcome is equally likely (i.e., the app is equally likely to pick any of the five friends), then the probability of an event is the frequency with which that event occurs divided by the total number of possible outcomes (i.e., the sample space).'

Milton scratched an equation **(7.2)** out on a rock, which brought home the frightening reality of how sharp his claws must be. I made a mental note not to annoy him too much.

$$P(x) = \frac{\text{frequency}(x)}{\text{sample space}} = \frac{f(x)}{\text{sample space}} \tag{7.2}$$

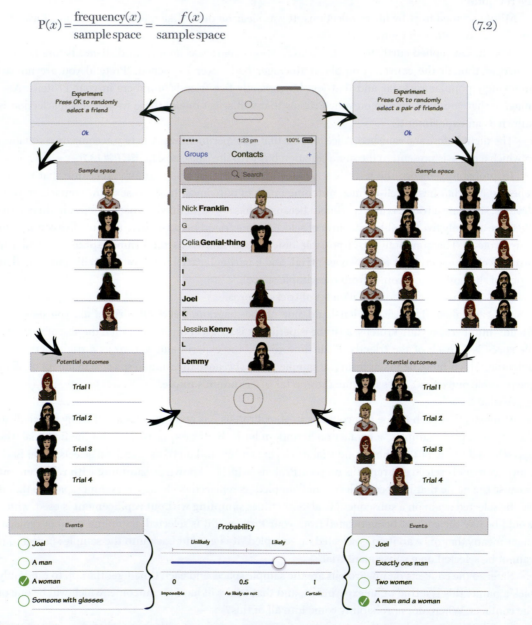

Figure 7.1 An attempt to make probability theory interesting by using social contacts instead of the tossing of coins

'Imagine you are interested in the probability of selecting Joel. *Selecting Joel* is your event. To assign a probability to that event we use the equation *(7.2)*. First, what is the frequency with which Joel's name can occur for a given trial?'

'It can only occur once, can't it – because there is only one Joel in my contacts?'

'Very good. And what is the size of the sample space?'

I looked at the diagram. 'It's 5, the five names in my Proteus.'

'Su*purr*b. So, the probability is 1/5 or 0.2.'

$$P(\text{Joel}) = \frac{f(\text{Joel})}{\text{sample space}} = \frac{1}{5} = 0.2$$

It made sense, but what did it mean? I asked Milton.

'Look at the diagram. *(FIGURE 7.1)* Notice that I have shown probability as a scale that ranges from 0 to 1. A probability of 0 means that an event is impossible, and a probability of 1 means that an event is certain. In the Proteus example, all of your friends are human so the probability of picking a human is 1: it is a certainty that the app will select a human. Conversely, much to your detriment, you do not have my number on your Proteus, nor those of any other cats, so the probability that the app will select a cat is 0: it is impossible because you have no cats in your contacts. A probability of 0.5 means that an event is just as likely to happen as it is to not happen. Therefore, a probability between 0.5 and 1 means that an event is more likely to happen than not, and the closer to 1 it gets, the more likely it is to happen. Conversely, a probability between 0 and 0.5 means that an event is more *unlikely* to happen than to happen, and the closer to 0 it gets, the less likely it is to happen. A probability value is a proportion, and as you have seen before *(MEOWSINGS 3.1)*, you can convert proportions to percentages by multiplying them by 100. Some people find this format easier to understand because you can think of a complete impossibility as having a 0% chance of happening, if something is just as likely to happen as not that would be a 50% chance of happening, and complete certainty is represented by a 100% chance of something happening.'

'So, the probability of the app selecting Joel was 0.2, or 20%, and because that is below 0.5 (or 50%) it means that it is unlikely to happen.'

'Ex*scratch*ly. There is only a 1 in 5 chance of selecting Joel. However, that does not mean that he will not be selected on a particular trial – it is not impossible – it is just that it is more likely that he *will not* be picked than that he *will*. What if the event of interest had been 'selecting a woman' – what would the probability of that be?'

I thought about this question. There were two women in the contacts list (Celia and Jessika), so the frequency of women was 2, and the sample space would still be the five names in the contacts list. So, using the equation, this would give me:

$$P(\text{woman}) = \frac{f(\text{woman})}{\text{sample space}} = \frac{2}{5} = 0.4$$

'Is it 2/5, or 0.4?'

'Excellent work. Yes, there would be a 0.4 or 40% chance that the app selects a woman.'

 CHECK YOUR BRAIN: Using the example of Zach's imaginary Proteus with five contacts in it, what would be the probability of: (a) selecting a male; (b) selecting a bald person; (c) selecting someone with glasses?

Milton looked thoughtfully into the distance. 'I am going to take this up a notch and look now at the right-hand side of the diagram.' *(FIGURE 7.1)*

'Let's not,' I thought. I had been enjoying not looking at the right-hand side of the diagram, which seemed a lot more complicated than the left-hand side.

'The right-hand side', Milton continued, 'shows a different app running a different experiment. This new app, rather than selecting one friend, simultaneously chooses a pair of friends. That is, on each trial it randomly and simultaneously selects two friends out of the five. Now, what will the sample space be?'

'I guess it would be every combination of two friends.' I replied hopefully.

Milton nodded appreciatively. 'Yes, yes it would, and this is shown in the diagram. There are five friends in total, so if we pick a pair each time, then each friend occurs 4 times in the sample space: once with each of the other four friends. A given friend cannot be picked with him- or herself because we pick two of the five friends simultaneously. In total there are 10 possible pairs of friends. This is the sample space. On a given trial of the experiment we pick a pair, and four such examples are shown in the diagram. Again, after a pair is picked, they are replaced back (the contacts are not deleted from the Proteus) so they can be sampled again on the next trial. At the bottom of the diagram there are some example events that might interest us. As with the previous example, we could be interested in the probability of selecting Joel, the probability that we pick exactly one man, but also the probability that we pick a man and a woman, or two women. There are other events you could be interested in that are not listed. So, what is the probability that Joel is picked?'

'Like in the equation **(7.2)**, it would be the number of times that Joel occurs, divided by the number of things in the sample space. So, would it be, 1/10 because Joel appears in the contacts once, and there are 10 possible outcomes in the sample space?'

The disappointment returned to Milton's face. 'Incorrect,' he said.

I felt stupid. This is why I failed probability at school: my brain isn't designed for this stuff. Sensing my feelings of inadequacy, Milton consoled me.

'Try not to hate yourself too much,' he said. 'You made a common mistake. The crucial thing is that it is not the number of times that Joel appears in your Proteus that matters, but *the number of times he appears in the sample space*; in other words, the number of times he *could* have been selected. Looking at the sample space, how many times does Joel appear in a pair?'

I looked at the diagram. **(FIGURE 7.1)** 'He appears 4 times.'

'*Purr*cisely, so he appears in four outcomes out of a possible 10 outcomes, so the probability of Joel being selected is 4/10 or 0.4.'

$$P(\text{Joel}) = \frac{f(\text{Joel})}{\text{sample space}} = \frac{4}{10} = 0.4$$

'OK, so a 40% chance.'

'Yes, now what is the probability of selecting exactly one man?'

'The number of times that a pair has exactly one man is 6: (Nick, Celia), (Nick, Jessika), (Joel, Celia), (Joel, Jessika), (Lemmy, Celia), (Lemmy, Jessika). In all other pairs there are either two men or two women. So it would be 0.6, or 60% chance.'

$$P(\text{exactly 1 man}) = \frac{f(\text{exactly 1 man})}{\text{sample space}} = \frac{6}{10} = 0.6$$

'*Purr*fection! You are better at this than you think.'

CHECK YOUR BRAIN: Using the example of Zach's imaginary Proteus with 5 contacts in it, and an app that randomly chooses pairs of friends, what would be the probability of: (a) selecting two women; (b) selecting two men; (c) selecting a man and a woman?

7.1.2 Empirical probability

When something is named to imply that death is a plausible outcome I find it is best to indulge in any distraction from it, and my relative success with probability was proving just that: a welcome distraction from the bridge of death. It was also good not to be thinking about how slow my progress was towards finding Alice. It was frustrating, but I felt that beyond this bridge was *something* that would get me closer to her. First, though, I had to survive, and to do that I needed to listen and understand how probability could help me to get safely across. I had some thoughts that I put to Milton.

'Am I right that crossing the bridge is an experiment, that the possible outcomes are that we live or we die, and that because there are only two outcomes the probability of death is $\frac{1}{2}$, or 0.5, or 50%, or as likely to happen as not?' As desperate as I was to see Alice, this seemed like a huge risk.

The cat patted my calf with his paw; I think it was an attempt at appreciation. 'You have highlighted the problem with classical probability,' he said. 'You are of course correct, in a classical sense crossing the bridge is a **Bernoulli trial**.'

I looked puzzled. Milton, whose mood I thought was lightening since we started talking about probability, didn't shrug or get annoyed with me, but was apologetic. 'Sorry, I sometimes forget that you are not familiar with these terms. An experiment or trial that has only two outcomes is known as a Bernoulli trial. The most famous, and rather overused, example is that of tossing a coin: it will either land heads up or tails up. If the event of interest can be turned into a question with a yes or no answer then you are probably dealing with a Bernoulli trial. Did the coin land heads up, yes or no? Did he or she die when crossing the bridge, yes or no?'

'Sweet, so what's the problem with classical probability?'

'Ah, yes, well, you are right that the probability of a given outcome for a Bernoulli trial is – according to classical probability which assumes each outcome is equally likely – theoretically, 0.5: one outcome is as likely as the other. If you toss a coin then it is just as likely to land heads up as tails up, assuming that it is a fair coin. We could apply the same logic to the bridge: theoretically the probability of living is 0.5, as is the probability of dying. However, this assumes that each outcome is equally likely. To use the equation that we just used **(7.2)**, we make this assumption. What if this assumption is not true though? The bridge does not randomly select people to kill; instead it sets them challenges. It is probably not realistic to assume that life and death are equally likely outcomes. Therefore, we cannot apply classical probability to this problem; if we do we will certainly get quite an inaccurate answer, and when your life is at stake inaccuracy is to be avoided.'

'What do we do then?'

'I have already told you: empirical probability. We could work out the probability of surviving the bridge by observing people crossing it and then calculating the relative frequency.' Milton started scratching out another diagram. **(FIGURE 7.2)** 'Look, imagine we watched 10 people cross the bridge of death and observed whether or not they survived. The equation for probability stays the same: compare the equation I have just written to the one we used before **(7.2 & 7.3)** – they both say that the probability is the frequency of the outcome relative to the sample space. The thing that changes is the sample space itself. In classical probability it is the set of all possible outcomes, whereas for empirical probability it is the number of outcomes observed. For empirical probability the sample space is N, the number of observations, so the equation becomes the same as that for the relative frequency (compare the first equation with the the the one I have just written). **(7.2 & 7.3)** If we had made the observations in the diagram **(FIGURE 7.2)**, what would the probability of surviving the bridge be?'

$$\text{empirical } p(x) = \frac{\text{frequency}(x)}{\text{sample space}} = \frac{f}{N} \tag{7.3}$$

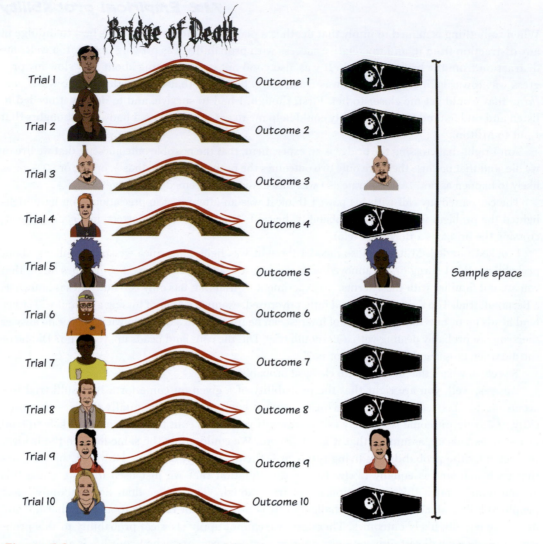

Figure 7.2 An attempt to make probability theory interesting by using bridges of death and skulls instead of coin tossing

'In your drawing we observe 10 people crossing the bridge, so the total number of outcomes is 10, and of those 10 people only 3 survived, so the probability of survival would be 3/10 or 0.3.'

$$p(\text{survival}) = \frac{\text{frequency of survival}}{\text{total number of outcomes}} = \frac{3}{10} = 0.3$$

'Very good. Based on the data in the diagram, we would be well advised not to cross the bridge because it is unlikely that we will survive. The empirical probability (3/10 = 0.3) is worse in this case than the classical probability of 0.5 which makes the potentially incorrect assumption that both options (death or survival) are equally likely. In this situation, that assumption *may* not be appropriate and therefore we *may* not be able to use a classical probability. This difference between the empirical probability and the classical probability illustrates a very important point: probability can only guide us on what we might expect to happen, it does not tell us what actually will happen.'

'Do you mean that although it looks as though death is more likely than survival, that does not mean that we'll certainly die?'

'*Purr*cisely, based on actual data there is a 30% chance we will survive.'

'Excellent, let's do it,' I announced.

Milton buried his face in his paw.

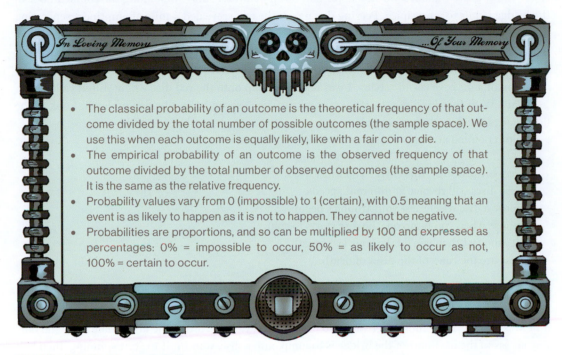

- The classical probability of an outcome is the theoretical frequency of that outcome divided by the total number of possible outcomes (the sample space). We use this when each outcome is equally likely, like with a fair coin or die.
- The empirical probability of an outcome is the observed frequency of that outcome divided by the total number of observed outcomes (the sample space). It is the same as the relative frequency.
- Probability values vary from 0 (impossible) to 1 (certain), with 0.5 meaning that an event is as likely to happen as it is not to happen. They cannot be negative.
- Probabilities are proportions, and so can be multiplied by 100 and expressed as percentages: 0% = impossible to occur, 50% = as likely to occur as not, 100% = certain to occur.

Zach's Facts 7.1 Probability

7.2 PROBABILITY AND FREQUENCY DISTRIBUTIONS

7.2.1 The discs of death

Milton and I stepped onto the bridge of death. I had waited at the edge of it for some minutes, unable to place my foot over the threshold between the cliff top and the bridge. The act of placing my foot forward seemed monumental: the pressure of my toes upon the bridge would start a chain reaction of events that could end my life. When it finally came, though, the first step felt no more a step closer to my grave than every other step I had taken before. A short walk along the cobbled floor of the bridge led us to a precipice. Peering down over the edge revealed a mile of emptiness separating us from the serene waves of the sea. Thirty metres in front of us was the next section of the bridge. Between us was a void within which two horizontal translucent discs floated: a red one on the left and a blue one on the right. The surface of the discs were etched with grooves as if awaiting the attention of a massive cosmic stylus. I was about to jump onto the red disc when Milton called out.

'Wait! With that kind of attitude you won't survive 5 seconds on a bridge of death. Look at the floor – *read* the floor,' he said angrily.

Milton pointed at a mossy stone, etched into which was a rhyme:

To cross the bridge, this rhyme you must heed.
These discs will revolve at different speeds.
Choose a disc wisely, lest your troubles begin:
Because when you jump on, the disc starts to spin,
If it's too fast then you'll take your last breath.
These are the rules of the discs of death.

'Cheery,' I said. 'What does it mean?'

'Must I spell *everything* out?' The cat's grumpiness was back; I wondered if I was annoying him or if he was scared. 'Put simply, there are two discs, as you can see: a red one and a blue one. The only way across to the next part of the bridge is to jump onto a disc, wait for it to start spinning, then half a revolution later – when you reach the other side – jump off.'

'Sick – they're like massive vinyls?'

The cat nodded. 'Massive vinyls that, if you could get a massive needle and pop it into the grooves, would play Chopin's funeral march as they throw you to your death.'

'Freeze, buddy – why do you always have to bring down the mood?' The bad mood was rubbing off: the cat's negativity was irritating me, but my bravado was also a huge act to cover my terror.

'Listen to me, *this isn't a game!*' Milton yelled. 'You step onto the disc, and it starts to spin around. If it spins too fast, the centrifugal force will throw you off and you will fall to your death, taking me with you. It will also make it treacherous to jump off the disc when you reach the other side. I do not want to die before society remembers me for something good, and unless you do want to die *you will listen to me* and stop messing about.'

His reaction shocked me into focus. 'They're not kidding about it being a bridge of death, are they? Isn't this one of those Bernoulli trials you were talking about? There are two choices, the red or blue disc; one means death, the other survival. So the discs represent two outcomes: we have a 50% chance of choosing the disc that kills us.'

'That would be true if we knew for certain that one of the discs leads us safely across and the other does not. I fear that is not the case: look at the writing on the discs.'

I didn't like the sound of this one bit, and I hadn't noticed any writing, but etched into the red disc was 'RPM: $\mu = 33$, $\sigma = 8$', and into the blue one 'RPM: $\mu = 45$, $\sigma = 2$'. I recognized the symbols from an earlier conversation with Milton **(SECTION 4.2.3)**: they represented a mean (μ) and a standard deviation (σ), and I knew that RPM was revolutions per minute. I had no idea why they were etched into the discs, though. I asked Milton.

'Logically it tells us something about each disc,' he replied. 'It looks as though each disc is taken from a population of possible discs and these values tell us the mean speed, in revolutions per minute, and standard deviation of discs in the population.'

'So, you mean that the red disc is taken from a population where on average they spin at 33 rpm, and the blue disc comes from a population where on average the discs spin at 45 rpm? That's obvious then, we choose the red disc because it comes from a population where, on average, discs are slower and so it's less likely to throw us off.'

'You have failed to factor in the standard deviation. We need to estimate the fastest speed you could cope with before being thrown from the disc, and then calculate the probability that each of the discs exceeds that maximum speed.'

'Right, so if I could jump safely on and off a disc spinning at 50 rpm, then we need to work out the probability that each disc is likely to be faster than that speed and if the probability is small we can risk jumping onto it.'

'I could not have put it better myself. Well, I could, but you are correct.'

7.2.2 Probability density functions

I asked Milton how we would work out the probability that each of the two discs exceeds a certain speed.

'First, you need to understand that frequency distributions tell us about probability. Remember when The Head was looking at your creativity score and he gave you an example in which there were 100 scores and you scored 22?' **(SECTION 6.1, FIGURE 6.1)**

I nodded. Milton took off his collar and his Proteus transformed into a screen. **(FIGURE 7.3)** 'I have re-created the bottom histogram that The Head showed you. Each square represents a person's score on creativity. By counting the squares we can see how many people, out of 100, got certain scores. For example, The Head assumed that you scored 22. How many people, including you, scored 22?'

'Six people: there are six squares in that column, it has a frequency of 6.'

'Good, so what is the probability of someone scoring 22?'

I thought back to an equation that Milton had shown me earlier. **(EQUATION 7.2)** The probability is the frequency divided by the size of the sample space. In this case there were six instances of a score of 22, so the frequency is 6, and there were 100 observations, so the size of the sample space is 100. 'The probability that a score is 22 is 6/100, or .06.'

'Excellent. And what is the relative frequency?'

I thought back to the first equation Milton had shown me. **(EQUATION 7.1)** 'It's the frequency of an outcome divided by the total number of observed outcomes. 'It's 6/100, or .06.'

'*Purr*cisely, they are the same thing. Now, what if I wanted to know the probability that a score was higher than 22?'

'I could count the number of squares that fall to the right of 22 on the histogram.'

The cat indicated for me to start counting, and I did, as I had done the previous day. **(SECTION 6.1)** 'There are 21 scores that are higher than a score of 22.'

'And how many scores are there in total?'

'100.'

'So what is the probability that a score is higher than 22?'

'The probability is the frequency divided by the size of the sample space, so it will be 21/100.'

'Excellent, it *is* 0.21. If you think of the histogram **(FIGURE 7.3, TOP)** as an area that is 100 squares big, then the green squares are the part of that area that is greater than a score of 22. By counting the squares as you just have, you have measured the area that is above a score of 22. So, out of the 100 squares, 21 are greater than a score of 22, which is 0.21 as a proportion, or 21% of the area. The key thing is that this demonstrates that the area of any histogram represents probability.'

I still didn't really get it, so Milton tried a different approach.

'Think of it this way: if we cut the histogram into its 100 squares, and placed those squares in a hat, you would have 21 green squares, 1 red square and 78 blue squares. If I stuck my paw into the hat and picked a square randomly, what is the probability that I would emerge with a green square?'

'The sample space is the 100 squares, and 21 are green, so it would be 21/100, or 0.21.' I replied.

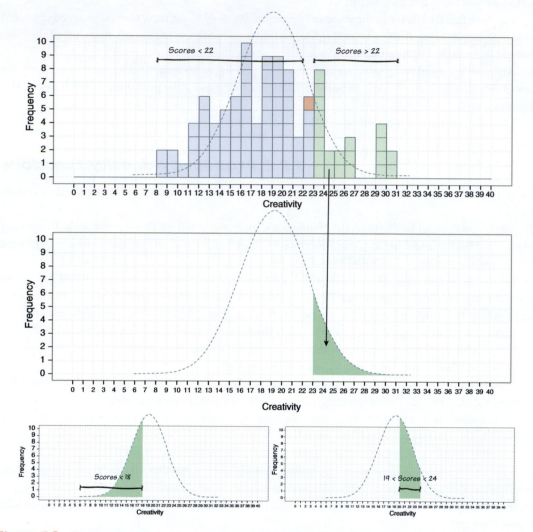

Figure 7.3 Frequency distributions represent the probability of a score

'Yes, and the green squares represent scores greater than 22, so rather than ask "what is the probability of choosing a green square?" we can rephrase the question as "what is the probability of picking a score greater than 22?" You can see, therefore, that the area beneath a histogram represents the probability that a certain score will occur.'

That made more sense, but in this example the number of squares was 100, so it was easy to see that each square is 1% of the total area; I wondered what happens when we don't know what the histogram looks like or if it isn't made up of 100 squares! Milton explained.

'A good point, which takes us back to something Catherine taught you when you visited her: probability density functions. **(SECTION 3.1.4)** Hopefully you remember that Catherine talked about how we could create idealized versions of histograms. These are distributions where we imagine that instead of having discrete scores and their frequencies represented by bars, we can subdivide the scores into infinitely small subdivisions and calculate the frequency of each one. So, for our creativity scale, rather than knowing the frequency of only whole scores such as 20 and 21, we'd know the frequencies for all the potential scores inbetween; for example, 20.01 or 20.0003. If we plotted each frequency value as a dot, these dots would be so close together that they would look like a smooth curve. I've drawn an example of such a curve here,' he said, pointing to his diagram. **(FIGURE 7.3, MIDDLE)** 'It shows an idealized shape of the histogram. The area under that curve is just like the squares on our histogram – it represents probability. In fact, the area under the curve is equal to 1; in other words, the probability of all scores summed together is 1.'

'No one is going to get a score of 20.01, so how can we subdivide a variable like creativity, which is measured in whole numbers, into small enough chunks that we can get a curve?'

'We cannot, but we *can* estimate it with some clever maths. That is what a probability density function is. It estimates the probability of a given score based on the likely shape of the distribution. The clever maths takes a bit of effort, so you would not want to work it out for every variable you measure (although you can if you have a computer), but there are certain shapes of distribution that are quite common. People almost as clever as I am have, at some point in history, done the maths to work out the probability density functions for these common shapes. One such distribution is the normal distribution, which Professor Pincus told you about.' **(SECTION 3.2)**

'Oh yeah, the one that looks like a bell end.'

'You mean a bell.'

'Whatever.'

'Yes, it looks like a bell, and that is the shape that I used to approximate the distribution of creativity. **(FIGURE 7.3, MIDDLE)** The dotted line shows the curve, and you can see it has the same approximate pattern as the bars, which are highest around the centre and shorter in the tails. This curve can be defined for any variable, v, with a mean μ and a standard deviation σ, by using this very rudimentary equation **(7.4)**.'

$$f\left(v, \mu, \sigma\right) = \frac{1}{\sigma\sqrt{2\pi}} e^{-\frac{(v-\mu)^2}{2\sigma^2}} \tag{7.4}$$

'Rudimentary?!! You're an **eisel**.'

Milton raised his whiskery eyebrow. 'The point is that you can use this equation to create a curve that tells you the probability of any value of a variable occurring. With the histogram, when we wanted to work out the probability of a score being greater than 22, you counted the green squares to find out what proportion of the total area of squares they represented. If we use an idealized distribution instead of a histogram, we do exactly the same thing: we measure the area under the curve that falls above 22 and work out what proportion of the total area under the curve that represents. This proportion gives us the probability of getting a score above, say, 22. Similarly, we could work out the probability that a score is smaller than a particular value, or that a score will fall between two values. **(FIGURE 7.3, BOTTOM)** The total area under the curve is 1.'

'Why is it 1?'

'Think about it. If we wanted to know the probability that a score is at least as big as the lowest possible value, what would the green shaded area look like?'

I thought about it. When we looked at scores above 22 Milton had shaded the area under the curve from 22 up to the highest score, so if we were looking at scores as big as or greater than the lowest possible score then we'd shade the area under the curve from that score right up to the highest score. In another words, 'We'd shade the whole area under the curve.'

'Very good. We would shade the area from the lowest to the highest score. And what is the probability that if we pick a score it will be the lowest score or greater?'

'It's certain, isn't it? If we pick a score it *has* to be the lowest score or greater.'

'*Purr*cisely, the probability is 1. Therefore, the area under the curve is 1, representing the fact that if you select a score there is a probability of 1 that the score falls somewhere along the range of the scale. So, to find out the probability of a score occurring, or of a score falling within a certain range of scores, you have to work out what the corresponding area under the curve is. One way to do this is to use the equation that I showed you *(EQUATION 7.4)* to construct the curve for your particular distribution using the mean and standard deviation of that distribution.'

'Surely that would be the slow road to madness?'

7.2.3 Probability and the normal distribution

'Indeed it would,' Milton replied. 'That is why we use the z-scores that you learnt about earlier. Remember that a distribution of z-scores has a mean of 0 and a standard deviation of 1. Some kind soul has used the equation that describes the probability curve *(EQUATION 7.4)* to construct the curve for a distribution with a mean of 0 and a standard deviation of 1, which is called the **standard normal distribution**. Kinder still, they tabulated the probability values *(APPENDIX)* so that others need never experience the same pain that they experienced using that equation. We can convert any distribution of raw scores into z-scores *(SECTION 6.3)*, which means that if we think the distribution has the shape of the normal distribution we can convert our measure to z-scores and then use the table of probability values.'

Milton set to work on his Proteus and presented me with another diagram. *(FIGURE 7.4)* 'Look. If we have the probability density function for the standard normal distribution – the bell-shaped curve – and we know that the area under it equals a probability of 1, then we can start to think about how different areas translate into different probabilities. Remembering that the standard normal distribution is made up of z-scores, what is the standard deviation?'

CHECK YOUR BRAIN: What is the standard deviation of a distribution of z-scores?

'It's 1.'

'Yes, so what is the probability that if we pick a random score it will fall within one standard deviation *above* the mean?'

'Would you look at the dark blue area between the mean and 1 on the horizontal axis?'

'*Purr*fect. Now, it turns out this area is 34.13% of the area under the curve, or .3413 as a probability. What about if we want to know the probability that if we pick a random score it will fall within one standard deviation of the mean?'

'Isn't that what you just asked me?'

'No, I just asked you about a score falling within a standard deviation *above* the mean. I'm now asking about a score falling within 1 standard deviation, so it could be above or below the mean.'

'Oh, we'd look at the area between −1 and 1 then.'

'Yes, and this is double the size of the previous area, because the normal distribution is symmetric, so it is 34.13% + 34.13% = 68.26%. In probability terms we would say there is a .6826 probability of a score falling within a standard deviation of the mean. What is the probability of a score falling within 2 standard deviations of the mean?'

'Two standard deviations would be z-scores of −2 and +2, so we'd look at the area between these two values. So, we'd have 13.59% + 34.13% + 34.13% + 13.59%.'

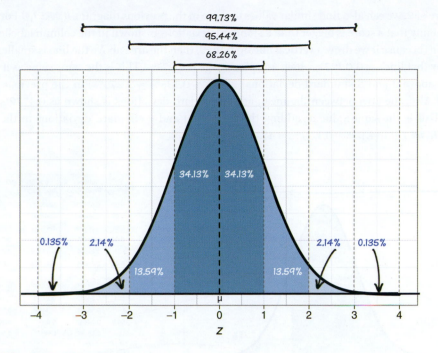

Figure 7.4   Areas under the standard normal distribution

'Yes, which adds up to 95.44%. So, about 95% of scores fall within 2 standard deviations of the mean, and looking at the diagram **(FIGURE 7.4)**, note that 99.73% of scores fall within 3 standard deviations of the mean. In fact, the probability of a score being higher than 2 standard deviations above the mean is only 2.14% + 0.135% = 2.275%.'

'It looks like it is impossible for a score to be greater than 4 or smaller than −4.'

'It is not impossible – z-scores can exceed these values – but it is very *improbable*.'

'Why do we need this table you were talking about?'

'The diagram **(FIGURE 7.4)** shows you some important characteristics of the normal distribution: 68% of scores fall within 1 standard deviation above or below the mean, 95% between two standard deviations, and 99% between three standard deviations. However, we usually want to know about the probability of specific scores. For example, we want to know the probability that the disc we pick will spin faster than your balance can cope with. Provided we can convert the score into a z-score, we can use the table of probability values that I just mentioned **(SECTION A.1)** to calculate the probability that a score will be bigger or smaller than that value.' Milton again frantically worked away on his Proteus, producing another diagram. **(FIGURE 7.5)** 'Notice that the table has four columns. The first lists values of z. If you draw a vertical line from z to split the curve in two, then when z is 0, the mean, you will split the curve into two equal halves, so each half will make up 50% or 0.5 of the area. When z is not 0, the curve will be split into a bigger portion and a smaller one. The second and third columns show the proportion of the area under the curve that is in the bigger and smaller half. For example, if z were 1, then the curve would be split into the blue area in the diagram, which would be the larger area, and the area to the right of the blue, which is the smaller proportion. Reading from the table, the larger portion is 0.8413, or 84.13%. Remember before that we noted how the area between the mean and 1 standard deviation was 34.13%? **(FIGURE 7.4)** That value is shown in the column labelled *mean to z*. The two columns are related because, knowing that the area below the mean is 50% and the area from the mean to z is 34.13%, if we add these values we get the larger area: 50% + 34.13% = 84.13%. Knowing that the area under the curve is 1 or 100%, the portion of the curve above 1 must be 100% − 84.13% = 15.87%, which is shown as a proportion (0.1587) in the column labelled *smaller proportion*. If we look at a *z*-score of 2, we can also find similar values to those in the previous diagram. **(FIGURE 7.4)** For example, the probability that a score is bigger than 2 standard deviations is shown in the column labelled *smaller proportion* (because if we drew a vertical line up from 2, then the area above the line is smaller than the area below that line) as 0.02275, which as a percentage is 2.275%. This is the same value as if we added the areas above 2 and 3 standard deviations (2.14% + 0.135% = 2.275%) in the previous diagram. **(FIGURE 7.4)** Also, the area between the mean and 2 standard deviations is shown as 0.47725, or about 47.72%. This is the same value as adding the areas for 1 and 2 standard deviations in the previous diagram **(FIGURE 7.4)** (34.13% + 13.59%. = 47.72%).'

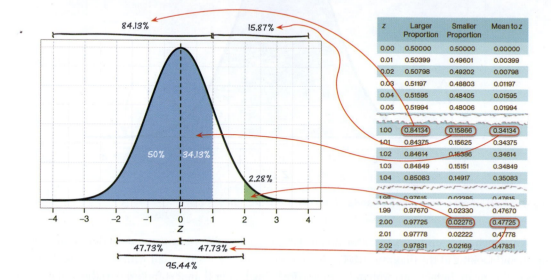

z	Larger Proportion	Smaller Proportion	Mean to z
0.00	0.50000	0.50000	0.00000
0.01	0.50399	0.49601	0.00399
0.02	0.50798	0.49202	0.00798
0.03	0.51197	0.48803	0.01197
0.04	0.51595	0.48405	0.01595
0.05	0.51994	0.48006	0.01994
1.00	0.84134	0.15866	0.34134
1.01	0.84375	0.15625	0.34375
1.02	0.84614	0.15386	0.34614
1.03	0.84849	0.15151	0.34849
1.04	0.85083	0.14917	0.35083
1.98	0.97615	0.02385	0.47615
1.99	0.97670	0.02330	0.47670
2.00	0.97725	0.02275	0.47725
2.01	0.97778	0.02222	0.47778
2.02	0.97831	0.02169	0.47831

Figure 7.5   *Using the table of the standard normal distribution (Section A.1)*

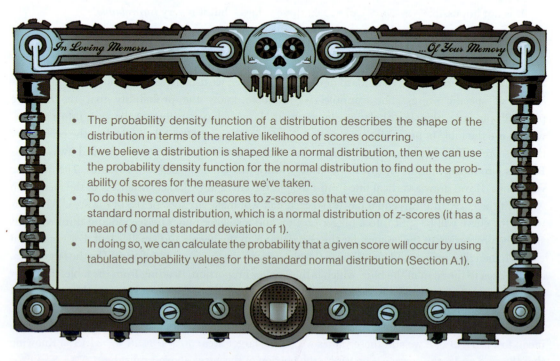

- The probability density function of a distribution describes the shape of the distribution in terms of the relative likelihood of scores occurring.
- If we believe a distribution is shaped like a normal distribution, then we can use the probability density function for the normal distribution to find out the probability of scores for the measure we've taken.
- To do this we convert our scores to *z*-scores so that we can compare them to a standard normal distribution, which is a normal distribution of *z*-scores (it has a mean of 0 and a standard deviation of 1).
- In doing so, we can calculate the probability that a given score will occur by using tabulated probability values for the standard normal distribution (Section A.1).

Zach's Facts 7.2   *The standard normal distribution*

That was a head frip. I told Milton that I didn't understand how this would help us to cross the bridge.

'You will, just as soon as your life depends on it, which it is about to.'

7.2.4 The probability of a score greater than x

Milton's comment drew my gaze to the two enormous discs hovering in the chasm that separated me from the rest of the bridge. The penny dropped. I remembered why we got started talking about all of this probability stuff: the rhyme had said that if the discs spin too fast then they would throw me off (and I'd plummet to my death). So, I needed to pick the disc least likely to throw me off. The two discs have been randomly selected from different populations with a known mean and standard deviation for the spin speed (the revolutions per minute). If the distributions of these populations were normal, then I guessed we could use what Milton had just explained to me to work out the probability that each disc would spin at a speed that would throw me off.

Milton was cleaning his back foot with a lick that occasionally evolved into a frantic nibble. He stopped and raised his eyebrow in that way that cats do when they are trying to feign indifference at your existence.

'What is the maximum rpm that a disc could spin without throwing you off?' he said.

I guessed at 50 rpm.

'Earlier on', Milton continued, 'you said that we should choose the red disc because it comes from a population that on average has slower discs. We can see if you are correct. The red one comes from a population with $\mu = 33$, $\sigma = 8$, and the blue one from a population with $\mu = 45$, $\sigma = 2$.' Milton drew another diagram on his Proteus. **(FIGURE 7.6)** 'Look, the distribution for red has a lower mean than the one for blue, but it is much more spread out. We want to know the probability that a disc from each population will have a speed of 50 rpm or more. I have drawn the line representing 50 rpm, and the coloured area represents the probability of a score of 50 rpm or more. To find out the value of the probability for each, we need to first convert our score of 50 rpm to a z-score.' The cat looked at me expectantly.

 CHECK YOUR BRAIN: Help Zach to convert 50 to a z-score for both distributions. (Hint: use Eq. 6.1.)

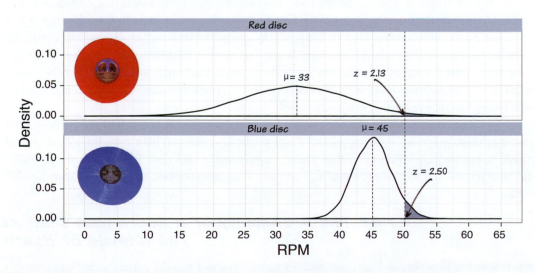

Figure 7.6 *Calculating the probability that a score is greater than a certain value*

I remembered that I needed to take the raw score, subtract the mean from it and then divide by the standard deviation. Using my diePad, I got $z = 2.13$ for the red disc, and $z = 2.50$ for the blue disc. **(EQUATION 7.5)**

Milton seemed pleased. '*Claw*rect. We are interested in the area above this value, so in the table of probability values this will be the "smaller proportion" because, as you can see in the diagram **(FIGURE 7.6)**, if we split the distribution at the dotted line, the shaded region is the smaller of the two parts. So, we look at the table **(SECTION A.1)**, and read down to the values of z that are 2.13 and 2.50, then look at the column labelled "smaller proportion", and this will

z	Larger Proportion	Smaller Proportion	Mean to z
0.00	0.50000	0.50000	0.00000
2.12	0.98300	0.01700	0.48300
2.13	0.98341	0.01659	0.48341
2.14	0.98382	0.01618	0.48382
2.15	0.98422	0.01578	0.48422
2.49	0.99361	0.00639	0.49361
2.50	0.99379	0.00621	0.49379
2.51	0.99396	0.00604	0.49396

tell us the size of the area above these z-scores. This area is the probability of getting a score at least as big as these z-scores. What are the values?'

I looked at the table, which Milton helpfully bought up on my diePad. 'It is 0.01659 for the red disc and 0.00621 for the blue.'

Red disc

Blue disc

$$z = \frac{X - \mu}{\sigma} = \frac{50 - 33}{8} = 2.13 \qquad z = \frac{X - \mu}{\sigma} = \frac{50 - 45}{2} = 2.50 \qquad (7.5)$$

'What are those values as percentages?'

I remembered that you needed to multiply a probability by 100 to get the percentage. 'It would be a 1.66% chance that the red disc is one that spins at 50 rpm or faster, but a 0.62% chance for the blue disc. So, we should go for the blue disc because the probability is smaller – it is less likely to be a disc that goes too fast for me to cope with.'

'Excellent. So, contrary to your intuition, the red disc is not the best choice just because it comes from a population where the mean speed is lower than for blue discs. It is a good job we spent some time learning about probability, or you would more likely be dead in about 10 seconds' time!'

And so, with Milton in my bag, I jumped onto the blue disc and, as the rhyme had foretold, it began to spin. My best strategy was to jump off the first time the disc got me near to the other side of the bridge, but it was going too fast. Had we been unlucky and got an insanely fast disc, or had I seriously overestimated my tolerance of revolving discs? It was too late now. With each dizzying rotation I struggled more against the forces propelling me towards the edge. Each time we reached the other side I bottled it: I fell to my knees and tried to claw at the grooves to latch onto something – anything. Terrified I took a deep breath, screamed '1, 2, 3' and jumped.

My eyes were closed, but the burning in my knees and my grazed hands told me I'd landed on stone. I cautiously opened my eyes, fearing that I might have jumped back onto the side that we'd started on, but we were on the other side. There was no turning back now. I kneeled to stand, and as I did Milton strolled nonchalantly out of my rucksack. 'Luck is on our side, we got a slow disc,' he said.

Eisel.

7.2.5 The probability of a score less than x: The tunnels of death

I was relieved to have survived the discs, and my mood lifted as I saw the entrances to two medieval-looking stone tunnels. Tunnels seemed like an altogether safer prospect than jumping off revolving discs.

Seemed, that is, until I saw 'Tunnel of Death' etched into each of the rusted portcullises that graced the entrances. Carved into the stone between the two gateways was a rhyme. Whoever built this bridge seemed to like rhymes.

To cross the bridge, through a tunnel you go.
But the quicksand floor will make you go slow.
Run through the sand with all of your strength,
Choose a path wisely 'cos they're different lengths.
Sink into the sand if you fail to progress,
These are the rules of the tunnels of death.

'Great, another riddle,' I said. 'Let me guess, these aren't ordinary tunnels, but are tunnels filled with quicksand, which you'll sink into if you don't run fast enough? You don't know how long each tunnel is, so you need to make sure you can get to the other side of the tunnel before sinking. If not you'll be consumed by the sand. That's dark.'

'That would be my interpretation, except I doubt you will be quickly consumed, more trapped under the sand, immobile, choking slowly to death as you gasp for air.'

'That's subterranean.' I was terrified, but what could I do? Behind me were the discs of death and in front the tunnels of death.

'Of course, your task is harder than it seems.'

'Harder than running through quicksand to avoid a slow death?'

'Yes, because you will be carrying me, and I will weigh you down more than your own bodyweight,' he said with a cheerful smile. The cat was bleak.

'Great! You couldn't have mutated yourself into a flea or an ant,' I said sarcastically, 'you had to become a fat, heavy, ginger cat!'

Milton sucked in his stomach. 'I'm big-boned,' he said. 'The question is, how many metres of quicksand can you run through before sinking?'

I was losing the plot. 'You know what, whiskers? My school didn't have a running through quicksand event at sports day, so I'm not entirely sure.' The cat tilted his head waiting for a sensible answer. 'I'm quite fast, so, maybe ... 5 metres?'

'To be safe we need the tunnel to be shorter than 5 metres then. Notice that, like the discs, each gate has a mean and a standard deviation etched upon it. I think it fair to say that we have a similar situation to before: each tunnel is randomly selected from a population of tunnels with a known average length and standard deviation. The left tunnel says $\mu = 4.5$, $\sigma = 1.5$, and the right says $\mu = 4$, $\sigma = 1$. All we have to do is work out the probability that the length of each tunnel is 5 m or less, given the population from which it came.' Milton drew me another diagram. (FIGURE 7.7) 'You see, we again have two distributions from which our tunnels come. The average length of tunnels in each population is different, and so are the standard deviations. We want the tunnel to be 5 m or less, so I have drawn a vertical line at 5 m. We want the length of tunnel to be less than this value, so the area we are interested in is the area below this value. This will tell us the probability of having sampled a tunnel that is 5 m long or less.'

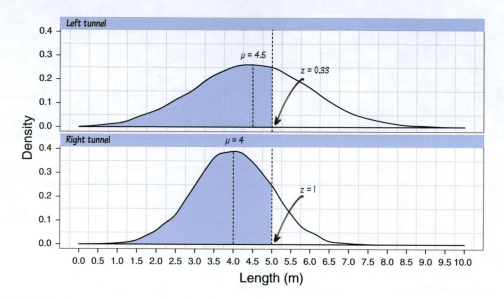

Figure 7.7   *Calculating the probability that a score is less than a certain value*

'Presumably we have to convert the value of 5 m into a z-score so that we can use the table of probability values for the standard normal distribution?'

CHECK YOUR BRAIN: Help Zach to convert 5 to a z-score for both distributions. (Hint: use Eq. 6.1.)

'Yes. For the left tunnel we get $z = 0.33$, and for the right $z = 1$. (EQUATION 7.6) We are interested in the area below this value, so in the table of probability values this is the "larger proportion", as you can see in the diagram. (FIGURE 7.7) You must look at the table (SECTION A.1), and read down to the values of z that are 0.33 and 1, then look at the column labelled "larger proportion" and this will tell us the size of the area below these z-scores.'

'And that tells us the probability of getting a score as big as these z-scores or less.'

'Yes. Look at the table and you will see that these values are 0.6293 for the left tunnel and 0.8413 for the right.'

z	Larger Proportion	Smaller Proportion	Mean to z
0.00	0.50000	0.50000	0.00000
0.32	0.62552	0.37448	0.12552
0.33	0.62930	0.37070	0.12930
0.34	0.63307	0.36693	0.13307
0.35	0.63683	0.36317	0.13683
1.00	0.84134	0.15866	0.34134
1.01	0.84375	0.15625	0.34375
1.02	0.84614	0.15386	0.34614

'So, there is a 62.93% chance that the left tunnel is one that is 5 m or less long, and an 84.13% chance for the right tunnel.'

'Excellent, you are getting the hang of it. Although for both tunnels it is more likely than not that it will be less than 5 m long, the probability is higher for the right tunnel, so that would be the wiser choice.'

Left Tunnel

$$z = \frac{X - \mu}{\sigma} = \frac{5 - 4.5}{1.5} = 0.33$$

Right Tunnel

$$z = \frac{X - \mu}{\sigma} = \frac{5 - 4}{1} = 1 \qquad (7.6)$$

I popped Milton into my rucksack and stepped into the right tunnel. It was filled with steam and I couldn't see the exit. I passed under the gate and stood inches from a stone wall. I wondered whether we had chosen the wrong tunnel, and I turned to leave. As I did the portcullis behind me shut, trapping us, and the stone wall vanished, revealing blackness and a musty smell. The floor already felt soft beneath my feet – surely I couldn't be sinking already?

'Come on! We have *not* got all day,' came an agitated cry from my rucksack.

'Shut it, cat – agghhhhh!' With a scream I drove my legs as hard as I could. The cat was right, we were sinking and I needed to move fast. As I powered forward, my feet sank into a treacle-like fluid. I had no sense of how far we had moved – the mist obscured any sense of distance. I thought of Alice, of how much I missed her, and of how I didn't want this to end here, in a frippin' tunnel with a sarcastic cat. I imagined myself in an Olympic sprint, my arch-rival breathing down my neck, both of us determined to win, but my self-sabotaging mind had other ideas and flooded my head with images of me tripping over and sinking as Milton hopped off of my corpse to safety. I was down to my knees; it was getting so hard to lift my legs. My thighs burned as I drove, and my lungs ached as they fought to get more air. One … final … surge. I screamed, I drove again, and suddenly I felt something solid beneath my feet. It was well below the sand, but with the next step it was a little higher. The sand was getting shallower, I was on a ramp leading out of the tunnel! The end must be near. The black mist evaporated, I emerged from the tunnel and Milton hopped out. At first I didn't register that my legs weren't weighed down in sand and I ran along the bridge with my arms and legs flailing as I screamed. Milton looked on as reality kicked in and I stopped and fell in a heap on the floor.

As I turned back to see him, he said, 'I think I have an idea of why Alice left you.'

Eisel.

7.2.6 The probability of a score between two values: The catapults of death

I was still shaking from the tunnel: my legs literally quivered from the exertion. It had scared me, but not as much as the sight before me. We had had to choose between two discs, then two tunnels, and now I could see two catapults. I could guess what was coming. Sure enough as we reached their enormous structures, a plaque on the floor confirmed my fears.

To cross the bridge, you just need to fathom,
Which of these catapults sends you over the chasm.
Make your choice wisely, pay careful attention,
For the catapult springs vary widely in tension.
Will you survive? It's anyone's guess.
These are the rules of the catapults of death.

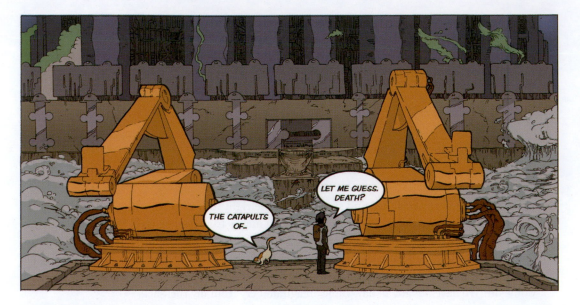

Across the 'chasm', as the rhyme put it, was a narrow platform from which a huge safety net protruded. Beyond the safety net and platform was what looked like another chasm filled with what looked like rocks. My guess was that survival depended upon landing in the net rather than in the sea below or on the bone-breaking stone platform.

'Have you ever wanted to fly?' said Milton in an annoyingly upbeat tone.

'Not really.'

'That is a pity.'

'How do people go to work at JIG:SAW if they have to deal with this batticks every morning just to get to the main entrance?'

'You were not listening. The bridge adapts to who is on it – it's an intelligent bridge. I told you before, bridges like this were designed to keep undesirables out, and you are an undesirable. If they want you to come in then this becomes just an ordinary bridge, no chasms, no rotating discs, no tunnels of quicksand, just a very boring stone bridge.'

'That tech is over the wall. Subterranean, but genius.'

'Thank you,' said Milton, looking pleased with himself. 'Now we have to choose a catapult, and we need to try to make sure that the one we choose does not fire us too far so we overshoot the net, or not far enough so we land in the sea.'

The catapults, like the discs and the tunnel before them, had values suggesting that they had been taken from a population of catapults that shot different distances.

'These plaques on each catapult tell us about the population from which they came,' Milton continued. 'The left catapult says $\mu = 103$, $\sigma = 2$, and the right says $\mu = 97$, $\sigma = 5$. On the floor here, below the rhyme, it tells us the distance to the net is 100 metres, and the net itself is 5 metres wide. We need a catapult that will throw us between 100 and 105 m.' Milton drew a diagram of the distributions. **(FIGURE 7.8)** 'We want a catapult that falls in the shaded area, which starts at the minimum value that we need to be thrown (100 m) and stops at the maximum distance that we can be thrown (105 m). Therefore, any catapult in the shaded zone will fire us between 100 and 105 m, which is the correct distance to hit the safety net. The question is which of the two catapults is more likely to come from that shaded zone. To know that, we have to use the population

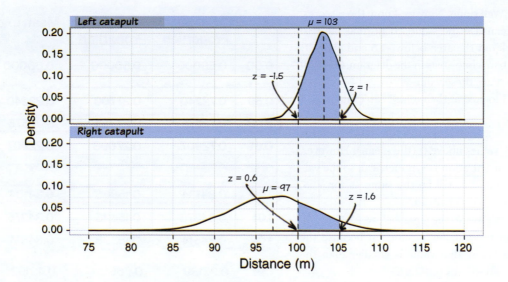

Figure 7.8 *Calculating the probability that a score lies between two values*

values for each catapult to work out the probability that a catapult comes from the shaded zone. It is really the same principle as for the discs and the tunnels.'

'Except we've only ever looked at how to calculate the area at the end of a distribution – above a value or below a value. This shaded area involves us looking at an area in the middle. How can we do that?'

'Think about the area under the curve as a jigsaw puzzle made up of smaller pieces, but we decide what shape the pieces are. The standard normal table **(SECTION A.1)** tells us the areas above or below a value, or the area from the mean to a value. Therefore, we can make pieces of the jigsaw from these areas. For example, look at the left catapult. We could work out the shaded area by taking the whole area under the curve, which we know represents a probability of 1, and subtract from it the two white areas, that is, the area below a distance of 100 m and the area above 105 m. To find the areas below 100 and above 105, we need to convert these values to z-scores in the usual way.'

CHECK YOUR BRAIN: Convert 100 and 105 to z-scores for both the left and right catapult distributions. (Hint: use Eq. 6.1.)

I was getting pretty good with these z-score conversions now, and it didn't take me long to work out that for the left catapult the z-scores were −1.5 and 1, and for the right they were 0.6 and 1.6. **(EQUATION 7.7)**

Distance (m)	Left catapult	Right catapult
100	$z = \dfrac{X-\mu}{\sigma} = \dfrac{100-103}{2} = -1.5$	$z = \dfrac{X-\mu}{\sigma} = \dfrac{100-97}{5} = 0.6$
105	$z = \dfrac{X-\mu}{\sigma} = \dfrac{105-103}{2} = 1$	$z = \dfrac{X-\mu}{\sigma} = \dfrac{105-97}{5} = 1.6$

$$(7.7)$$

'Well done. Now we know the z-scores, we can use the standard normal table to work out the area below −1.5 and above 1: the two white areas in the diagram. (FIGURE 7.8) What are these values?'

I looked at the table. 'I can't find −1.5,' I said.

'No, that is because the table contains only values above 0 (the mean). However, the distribution is symmetrical, so the values for −1.5 will be the same as for +1.5. Look up +1.5 instead.'

'We want the area below −1.5, so we want the smaller proportion because the area below that value is smaller than the area above. It's 0.06681.'

'Excellent. What about the area above 1?'

'Again, the area above the value is smaller than the area below so we'd look in the column for the smaller proportion, which gives us 0.15866.'

'Purrfect. So, the shaded area is the total area, 1, minus the two white areas, so we get 1 − 0.067 − 0.159 = 0.774. There are four other ways we could calculate the shaded area, but we do not have time to get into that now – I will message you about it. (MEOWSINGS 7.1) Whichever way we do it, the shaded area is 0.774. In other words, there is a 77.4% chance that the left catapult will fire us between 100 and 105 metres.'

z	Larger Proportion	Smaller Proportion	Mean to z
0.00	0.50000	0.50000	0.00000
0.59	0.72240	0.27760	0.22240
0.60	0.72575	0.27425	0.22575
0.61	0.72907	0.27093	0.22907
0.62	0.73237	0.26763	0.23237
1.00	0.84134	0.15866	0.34134
1.01	0.84375	0.15625	0.34375
1.02	0.84614	0.15386	0.34614
1.49	0.93189	0.06811	0.43189
1.50	0.93319	0.06681	0.43319
1.51	0.93448	0.06552	0.43448
1.52	0.93574	0.06426	0.43574
1.59	0.94408	0.05592	0.44408
1.60	0.94520	0.05480	0.44520
1.61	0.94630	0.05370	0.44630

'That's not a bad probability.'

'The question is whether the probability for the right catapult is better, and we can find this out in the same way: take the total area, 1, and from it subtract the area below 100 and the area above 105. Alternatively, you could use one of the other methods. (MEOWSINGS 7.1) Work out the size of the shaded area.'

 CHECK YOUR BRAIN: Using the same method as for the left catapult, help Zach to calculate the probability that the catapult will fire Zach and Milton between 100 and 105 m.

I had already worked out that for the distribution of the right catapult the z-scores for 100 m and 105 m were 0.6 and 1.6. (EQUATION 7.7) I needed to know the area below 100 (or 0.6 as a z-score). Looking at the diagram (FIGURE 7.8), this area is bigger than the area above 100, so I would need to look at the value for the larger proportion for $z = 0.6$ in the standard normal table. This value was 0.72575. I then needed to know the area above 105 (or 1.6 as a z-score). Looking at this value in the diagram (FIGURE 7.8), the area above was smaller than the area below so I would need to look up the smaller proportion for $z = 1.6$. This value was 0.05480. The shaded area would then be the total area, 1, minus 0.72575 and 0.05480. I grabbed my diePad and punched in 1 – 0.72575 – 0.05480. 'The shaded area is 0.219, so there is a 21.9% chance that the right catapult will fire us between 100 and 105 m.'

'Very good. So there is a 77.4% chance that the left catapult fires us the distance we want, but only a 21.9% chance that the right ones does.'

'We'd better use the left one then.'

The thought of launching myself with a catapult across an empty void into a safety net wasn't thrilling me. Especially as there was no guarantee of hitting the net. I thought for a moment about the past week and what I was doing. Alice had disappeared. For all I knew she had simply walked out on me, yet I was, for the third time in one morning, about to risk my life for her. Not even for her, but for the chance to find out some information that might help me to find her. But time was running away from me, and whenever I thought of what could have happened to her in the past week, I knew I had to try anything I could. Even if going to JIG:SAW didn't tell me anything, perhaps I could at least rule it out – focus my efforts elsewhere. I was mad for her, and that madness led me to climb up into the cup of a huge catapult. I strapped Milton into my bag and hit a small red button emblazoned with a skull that sat next to the cup. The ferocity of the swing of the throwing arm shocked me into a scream. As I opened my eyes, it occurred to me I hadn't realized they were shut. A long way below was the sea – flying past me – in front I had a fantastic view of the jigsaw-piece-shaped battlements of the complex. I was getting nearer. I felt a brief comfort that vanished when my stomach lurched as I fell towards the net.

Dear Human,

When trying to work out the probability that a score will fall between two values there are usually several ways that you could reach the same answer. If we imagine the area under the curve as a jigsaw that has different pieces, and those pieces add up to an area of 1, then we can find different areas by adding or subtracting pieces. For example, suppose we wanted to calculate the shaded region for the left catapult in Figure 7.8, and we have converted the boundaries of the shaded area to z-scores of –1.5 and 1. We can ignore the minus sign, and, using the table of the standard normal curve (Section A.1), we find that for $z = 1.5$ (or –1.5), the larger proportion is 0.933, the smaller proportion is 0.067, and the proportion from the mean is 0.433; for $z = 1$ (or –1), the larger proportion is 0.841, the smaller proportion is 0.159, and the proportion from the mean is 0.341. We can calculate the shaded area in the four ways illustrated in Figure 7.9, all of which give the same answer:

1   As I explained on the bridge, we could take the whole area (which is equal to 1) and subtract from it the area below the shaded region and the area above the shaded region. In the table of the standard normal curve (Section A.1) these areas are the *smaller* proportion for $z = -1.5$, 0.067, and the *smaller* proportion for $z = 1$, 0.159. The shaded region will be 1 – 0.067 – 0.159 = 0.774.

2   We could calculate the area above the lowest score of the shaded region and subtract from it the area above the highest score of the shaded region. These areas are the *larger* proportion for $z = -1.5$, 0.933, and the *smaller* proportion for $z = 1$, 0.159. The shaded region will be $0.933 - 0.159 = 0.774$.

3   We could do the opposite of option 2. We could calculate the area below the highest score of the shaded region and subtract from it the area below the lowest score of the shaded region. These areas are the *larger* proportion for $z = 1$, 0.841, and the *smaller* proportion for $z = -1.5$, 0.067. The shaded region will be $0.841 - 0.067 = 0.774$.

4   Finally, the shaded area is also made up of the area between the mean and the lowest boundary of the shaded area ($z = -1.5$) and the area between the mean and the highest boundary of the shaded area ($z = 1$). Therefore, we could look up the area between the mean and both z-scores and add them together; the shaded region would be $0.433 + 0.341 = 0.774$.

Best fishes,
Milton

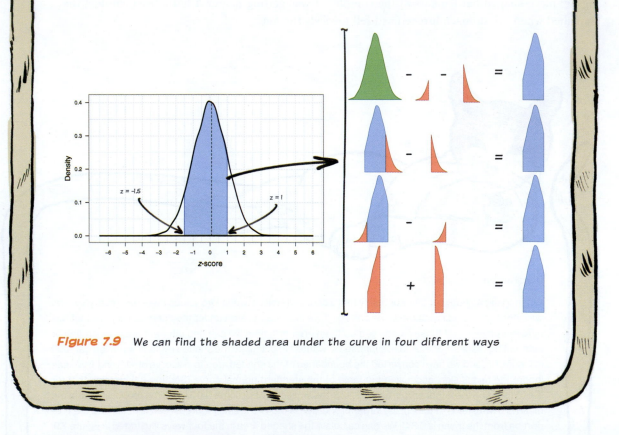

Figure 7.9   We can find the shaded area under the curve in four different ways

Milton's Meowsings 7.1   *There are different ways to skin a cat, but you should never skin a cat*

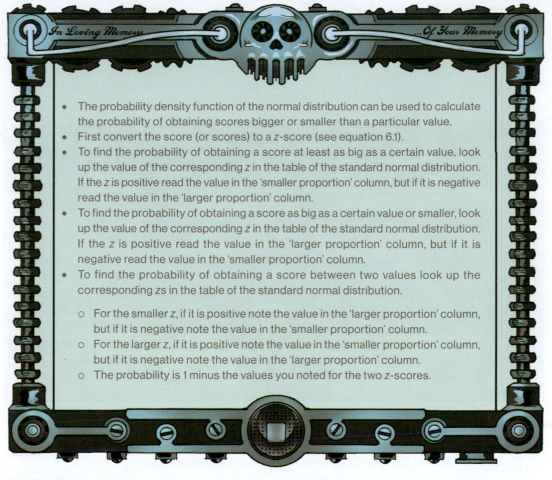

- The probability density function of the normal distribution can be used to calculate the probability of obtaining scores bigger or smaller than a particular value.
- First convert the score (or scores) to a z-score (see equation 6.1).
- To find the probability of obtaining a score at least as big as a certain value, look up the value of the corresponding z in the table of the standard normal distribution. If the z is positive read the value in the 'smaller proportion' column, but if it is negative read the value in the 'larger proportion' column.
- To find the probability of obtaining a score as big as a certain value or smaller, look up the value of the corresponding z in the table of the standard normal distribution. If the z is positive read the value in the 'larger proportion' column, but if it is negative read the value in the 'smaller proportion' column.
- To find the probability of obtaining a score between two values look up the corresponding zs in the table of the standard normal distribution.

  o For the smaller z, if it is positive note the value in the 'larger proportion' column, but if it is negative note the value in the 'smaller proportion' column.
  o For the larger z, if it is positive note the value in the 'smaller proportion' column, but if it is negative note the value in the 'larger proportion' column.
  o The probability is 1 minus the values you noted for the two z-scores.

Zach's Facts 7.3 *Using the standard normal distribution*

7.3 CONDITIONAL PROBABILITY: DEATHSCOTCH

The net absorbed the force of our landing; there was no unpleasant thud as we landed, no rope burns, instead it felt like a pair of soft arms caressing us to safety. I climbed the netting and pulled myself onto the firm floor of the platform. My heart returned to its natural rhythm and I took a deep breath. The platform on which we stood was surprisingly narrow. It occurred to me just how easily we could have overshot or undershot the net. There had not been much room for error. I started to feel a begrudging twinge of gratitude for probability. We were close now: I could see the gates of the JIG:SAW complex towering in front of us. I could also see another break in the bridge. This gap was smaller than the chasm, but it wasn't quite narrow enough to jump. You could get across with the help of the stepping stones scattered within the gap. Some of these stones were heart-shaped and the others were shaped like skulls. I was tempted to assume the obvious and bounce to the other side using some hearts. I knew the bridge too well by now, though; it wasn't going to be that easy. There must be a plaque somewhere warning me of my imminent death, I thought. Oh yeah, there it was.

To cross the bridge, you need to hop,

Onto a heart- or a skull-shaped rock.

Choose a rock wisely: although some will stay put,

Others will vanish from under your foot.

What is your fate at the end of the game?

Deathscotch, the clue's the first half of the name.

I scooped Milton out of my rucksack, and he surveyed the situation. 'Interesting: stepping stones that disappear, or not,' he said.

'Presumably we need to work out whether to hop onto a heart or a skull?'

The cat nodded. 'Look here, next to the plaque – there is a table that gives us some information about the hearts and skulls. **(TABLE 7.1)** This is a **contingency table** and we can use it to calculate some basic probabilities.'

I sighed. Milton could sense my frustration and, not for the first time, patted my calf. 'Stick with it,' he said softly as he looked up at me.

'Look at the column labelled *total*. This tells us that there are 76 stones in total in the gap; 35 are skulls and 41 are hearts. If you closed your eyes and jumped onto a random stone, what is the probability that you'd land on a skull?'

I thought about what Milton had taught me earlier. 'The sample space is 76 stones, and there are 35 skulls, so the probability would be 35/76.'

'Yes, 0.46, or 46%. What about for hearts?'

'That probability would be 41/76.'

'Yes, 0.54 or 54%. What would be the probability of landing on both a skull and a heart?'

Table 7.1   A classification table of stones and outcomes

		Vanishes		
		Vanishes	Remains	Total
Stone	Skull	7	28	**35**
	Heart	16	25	**41**
	Total	**23**	**53**	**76**

'That would be impossible, you can only land on one stone – the probability would be zero.'

'Very good. These outcomes are known as **mutually exclusive** or **disjoint** because they cannot co-occur. You cannot land on both a heart *and* a skull. We can write this situation as an equation *(7.8)*. The ∩ symbol means "and", so the equation means that the probability of *A and B* happening is 0. The probability of two events both occurring is known as the probability of the **intersection**. The *A* and *B* represent events, so we could replace these with our actual events and write $p(\text{Skull} \cap \text{Heart}) = 0$; in other words, the probability of landing on a skull *and* a heart is zero – it can't happen.'

$$p(A \cap B) = 0 \tag{7.8}$$

The cat continued. 'When you have mutually exclusive outcomes, you can work out the probability that one outcome *or* another happens, known as the **union**, by adding the individual probabilities together. This is known as the **additive law**. We can write this law as in this equation.' Milton wrote the equation on my diePad. *(EQUATION 7.9)* 'The ∪ means "or", and it is easy to remember because it looks like a "u" for "union". The equation says that the probability of *A or B* happening is the sum of their individual probabilities. What do you notice if you add the probabilities for skulls and hearts together?'

$$p(A \cup B) = p(A) + p(B) \tag{7.9}$$

'You get a probability of 1.'

'Yes, if you jump on a stone it has to be either a skull or a heart, so the probability that you land on a skull *or* a heart is 1; it is a certainty – you *have* to land on one or the other. We can write this as $p(\text{Skull} \cup \text{Heart}) = 1$. The probabilities of these outcomes are **complementary** because they sum to 1.'

'Won't the additive law always give you a probability of 1?'

'Only if you want to know the probability that one of all possible outcomes will occur. Imagine we considered the probability that you are so uncoordinated that you manage not to land on a stone at all and fall to your death. We have three outcomes: skull, heart, and fall to death. Imagine that their respective probabilities are 0.30, 0.25, and 0.45. The events are mutually exclusive: only one of them can happen. If we ask what the probability is that you will land on a heart, a skull, or fall to your death then the probability will be:

$$p(\text{Skull} \cup \text{Heart} \cup \text{Death}) = p(\text{Skull}) + p(\text{Heart}) + p(\text{Death}) = 0.3 + 0.25 + 0.45 = 1$$

'It is a certainty that one of the events will occur because there are no other possible outcomes. However, we could also ask what is the probability that you land on a skull or fall and die. That probability will be:

$$p(\text{Skull} \cup \text{Death}) = p(\text{Skull}) + p(\text{Death}) = 0.30 + 0.45 = 0.75$$

'which is less than 1.'

CHECK YOUR BRAIN: **What is the probability of landing on a heart or falling to your death?**

'How does this information help us to work out whether to jump onto a skull or a heart?' I asked.

'It does not, but I thought it would be character-building.'

I just didn't get Milton at all. Most of the time he was rude, sarcastic, and intent on delaying me from finding Alice with lessons and diversions, but every so often I'd see a chink of tenderness, or he'd seem impressed with me, maybe even encouraging. He said he wanted my help to be remembered for something good that he had done, yet he designed reality prisms and death bridges. He knew of Alice's work, and it made sense that he knew her too, so was he simply helping me because he also wanted to find her? Why not just tell me that, and why the delays and distractions? I sighed through my gritted teeth. Milton sensed my irritation.

'I apologise for my flippancy. This information is useful background because we need to use **conditional probability** to get us across. It tells us the probability of an outcome, given that something else has happened.'

'Like, what's the probability of a stone vanishing, given it's a skull?'

'*Purr*cisely. We can ask the same question about hearts and compare these two conditional probabilities. We denote the "given that" as a vertical line; for example, $p(\text{vanish}|\text{skull})$ would mean the probability of vanishing *given that* the stone is a skull. There are several ways to calculate conditional probabilities. The first is to calculate them directly from the table. (TABLE 7.1) The "given that" in the conditional probability statement restricts the probability space to a particular outcome. For example, if we want the probability of a stone vanishing given it is a skull, we are restricting the probability space to skulls. How many skull stones are there?'

I looked at the table. '35,' I replied.

'*Purr*fect. That is our probability space. Of those 35 stones, how many vanished?'

'7.'

'Yes, so the conditional probability is 7/35.'

$$p(\text{vanish}|\text{skull}) = \frac{f(\text{vanishing skulls})}{f(\text{skulls})} = \frac{7}{35} = 0.2 \qquad (7.10)$$

Milton drew an equation (7.10) and continued. 'If you think about this equation, you can also express it in terms of probabilities rather than frequencies. Really what you are asking is what is the probability that a stone is a skull and vanishes, $p(\text{skull} \cap \text{vanishes})$ relative to the probability that the stone is a skull, $p(\text{skull})$. Look at this equation (7.11). The probability that a stone is a skull and vanishes is 7/76, because there are 76 stones in total and 7 of them are vanishing skulls; and the probability of a skull is 35/76 because there are 76 stones, 35 of which are skulls. Both probabilities have 76 in the lower half of the fraction, so the conditional probability reduces to 7/35: these equations (7.10 & 7.11) are different ways of expressing the same thing. There is also a third way to calculate a conditional probability known as Bayes' theorem, but *purr*haps you can read about that later.' My diePad pinged as a message from Milton arrived. (MEOWSINGS 7.2) How *did* he do that?

$$p(A|B) = \frac{p(B \cap A)}{p(B)}$$

$$p(\text{vanish}|\text{skull}) = \frac{p(\text{skull} \cap \text{vanishes})}{p(\text{skull})} = \frac{7/76}{35/76} = \frac{0.09}{0.46} = 0.20 \qquad (7.11)$$

So, according to Milton, there was a 0.2 probability that a skull will vanish. I asked whether we could work out the probability that a stone will vanish, given it's a heart, in the same way.

Dear Human,

Bayes' theorem or Bayes' law is an alternative formula for calculating conditional probabilities. It is a law that relates the conditional probability of two events, $p(A|B)$, to the reverse conditional probability of those events $p(B|A)$. It states that

$$p(A|B) = \frac{p(B|A)p(A)}{p(B)}$$

For example, we could work out the conditional probability of a stone vanishing, given it's a skull, $p(\text{vanish}|\text{skull})$, by knowing the probability of a skull:

$$p(\text{skull}) = \frac{f(\text{skull})}{f(\text{all stones})} = \frac{35}{76} = 0.46$$

The probability of any stone vanishing is:

$$p(\text{vanish}) = \frac{f(\text{vanish})}{f(\text{all stones})} = \frac{23}{76} = 0.30$$

We can also work out the reverse conditional probability, that is, the probability of a skull, given that the stone vanished. There were 23 stones that vanished (Table 7.1) and 7 were skulls, so we get:

$$p(\text{skull}|\text{vanish}) = \frac{f(\text{vanishing skulls})}{f(\text{vanish})} = \frac{7}{23} = 0.30$$

Bayes' theorem tells us that the conditional probability of the stone vanishing, given you select a skull, is:

$$p(\text{vanish}|\text{skull}) = \frac{p(\text{skull}|\text{vanish})p(\text{vanish})}{p(\text{skull})} = \frac{0.30 \times 0.30}{0.46} = \frac{0.09}{0.46} = 0.2$$

This value matches the other methods and probably seems more complex than they were, so you might wonder why I am meowsing on it. It is because Bayes' theorem comes in handy for testing statistical models. For example, we can use it to calculate the conditional probability of a hypothesis, given the data we have collected (see Chapter 10).

Best fishes,
Milton

Milton's Meowsings 7.2 *Bayes' theorem*

'Yes, and you will find that you get a probability of 0.39.' *(EQUATION 7.12)*

$$p(\text{vanish}|\text{heart}) = \frac{p(\text{heart} \cap \text{vanishes})}{p(\text{heart})} = \frac{16/76}{41/76} = \frac{0.21}{0.54} = 0.39 \qquad (7.12)$$

'Sweet, so 20% or 1 in 5 skulls disappear, but 39% or about 2 in 5 hearts disappear. So hearts are about twice as likely to vanish than skulls. Rad, I like skulls, let's get hopping.'

And that is what I did. Fortunately, the stones stayed put, and with a couple more jumps I made it to the other side, just a few metres from the gigantic jigsaw-piece-shaped gateway into the main complex. We had chosen to come here on a Sunday, hoping that it would be quiet, but it was too quiet: the entrance had no security and no barriers. Perhaps the bridge was deterrent enough, but I was cautious. We crept past the outer wall of the gateway and, to our relief, we found several recesses between the outer and inner walls of the complex. We scuttled into one and hid in the shadows. I felt safe for the first time since we had set foot on the bridge. The feeling was short-lived.

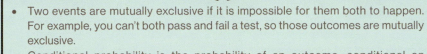

In Loving Memory ......*Of Your Memory*

- Two events are mutually exclusive if it is impossible for them both to happen. For example, you can't both pass and fail a test, so those outcomes are mutually exclusive.
- Conditional probability is the probability of an outcome, conditional on another outcome happening. For example, you could count how many people survive (S) the probability bridge depending on whether they have Milton helping them (M); the conditional probability $p(S|M)$ is the probability of survival, given Milton's help. It is calculated as the probability of surviving *and* having Milton's help, divided by the probability of having Milton's help:

$$p(S|M) = \frac{p(M \cap S)}{p(M)}$$

- Bayes' theorem expresses conditional probability in terms of the reverse conditional probability and the individual probabilities of the individual events. For example, the probability of surviving, conditional on having Milton's help, $p(S|M)$, would be expressed as a function of the probability of Milton helping, given that you survived, $p(M|S)$, the probability of Milton helping, $p(M)$, and the probability of survival, $p(S)$:

$$p(S|M) = \frac{p(M|S)p(S)}{p(M)}$$

Zach's Facts 7.4 *Conditional probability*

KEY TERMS

Additive law	Empirical probability	Probability
Bernoulli trial	Experiment (probability)	Sample space
Classical probability	Event	Sampling with replacement
Complementary	Intersection	Sampling without replacement
Conditional probability	Mutually exclusive	Standard normal distribution
Contingency table	Outcome	Trial
Disjoint	Random sample	Union

JIG:SAW'S PUZZLES

1   Later in the story, Zach and Milton go back to JIG:SAW and have to travel across the bridge again. When Zach reaches the discs of death, the population parameters of the red and blue discs are unchanged (Section 7.2.4), but he decides that the maximum speed he could tolerate is 45 rpm. Should he still choose the blue disc?

2   When Zach reaches the tunnels of death (Section 7.2.5) he decides that his previous estimate of being able to run through quicksand for 5 m was optimistic, so he reduces it to 4 m. The population parameters for left and right tunnels are the same as before: which tunnel should he pick to maximize his chance of survival?

3   If the population parameters for the tunnels of death changed to $\mu = 5$ m, $\sigma = 1.25$ m for the left, and $\mu = 6$ m, $\sigma = 1.75$ m for the right, and Zach still thought he could run through quicksand for 4 m, which tunnel should he choose?

4   When Zach reaches the catapults of death (Section 7.2.6) the distance he needs to travel is still between 100 and 105 m, but the population parameters for the two catapults have changed. The left catapult comes from a population with $\mu = 101$ m, $\sigma = 5$ m, and the right comes from a population with $\mu = 105$ m, $\sigma = 3$ m. Which catapult is most likely to propel him the safe distance of 100–105 m?

5   When Zach and Milton reach Deathscotch (Section 7.3), they see a different table of frequencies (Table 7.2). Should Zach still choose to hop onto a skull?

Table 7.2 A classification table of stones and outcomes

		Vanishes	Remains	Total
Stone	Skull	11	24	**35**
	Heart	15	26	**41**
	Total	**26**	**50**	**76**

6 Using Table *6.1*, what is the probability that someone in the general population has a higher IQ than Zach? (Hint: use a value of IQ one more than Zach's score.)

7 Using Table 6.1, what is the probability that someone in the general population has as much creativity as Zach or more?

8 Using Table 6.1, what is the probability that someone in the general population has the same emotional intelligence as Zach or lower?

9 Using Table 6.1, what is the probability that a JIG:SAW code 1318 worker is at least as intelligent (IQ score) as Zach?

10 Using Table 6.1, what is the probability that a JIG:SAW technician is at least as intelligent (IQ score) as Zach?

IN THE NEXT CHAPTER, ZACH DISCOVERS ...

He looks good in a dress
Estimating parameters
The method of *least squares*
Samples and populations
Sampling distributions
The standard error

The central limit theorem
Confidence intervals
The *t*-distribution
Inferential statistics
How to be better at maths

8

Inferential Statistics: Going Beyond the Data

Humiliative

The first float in the parade of emotions created by seeing Alice was excitement. I went to call out to her, but the pain of a claw in my leg stopped me. 'Don't!' hissed Milton. Of course, he was right: there were zombies everywhere, and shouting would have drawn attention to us. The second float was disappointment that I couldn't communicate with her, that her Proteus number didn't exist, that she didn't turn towards us and notice me, or that she didn't somehow sense that I was there. The final float of betrayal was the worst, though. Alice wasn't being held hostage, because she was walking freely around the complex; nobody was forcing her to be there, she was there by choice. Why hadn't she told me that she was going? After all our years together, didn't I deserve more – an explanation at least? Did she even miss me? My guts churned as I realized that Alice had decided to jettison me from her life, to dispose of me like something as inconsequential as a chocolate wrapper. I felt worthless. Milton put his paw on my calf as though to comfort me.

'At least you know she's safe. Maybe now you can let her go,' he said.

We turned away from JIG:SAW, and as we did the bridge transformed into a regular stone bridge; apparently getting out of there was a whole lot easier than getting in.

I'd moped around the apartment that evening, and the following day I was still consumed by feelings of betrayal and anger at what it seemed Alice had done. Having survived the probability bridge, I felt more alive than I could remember, and yet the person that I wanted to share this newfound life with was gone. Not just gone, but had left without any word of explanation – just a song to decipher. As I sat strumming my guitar, trying to form my feelings into music and words, it hit me how life with Alice had changed since we met. We used to be inseparable, held together by the elastic band of love and shared passions. We could move in different directions but always return to each other. If you stretch an elastic band enough though, it fatigues, and one day I turned around looking for the reassuring pull of Alice only to see a brittle and broken band on the floor. As Alice slowly grew more in love with science she became less in love with her musician boyfriend. Seeing her confidently strutting across the JIG:SAW complex was frightening, like looking at a different person than the one I fell in love with. Alice had abandoned her life with me for a life with science, and she would never leave science without writing a farewell note.

A lot of things made sense to me now. Professor Pincus's reluctance to discuss JIG:SAW and her last words to me: 'Unless you want your life destroyed take some advice: some things are best left alone.' Pincus must have known that Alice had left me, and that if I went to JIG:SAW I would discover that Alice had chosen science over me, and Pincus was right, that discovery was hollowing me out.

The buzz of my diePad interrupted my thoughts. It was Nick checking in with me. He'd had no news back from *memoryBank* on Alice, but that didn't matter now: I knew where she was, and I knew that it was over between us. I needed to get my head straight, and some time with Nick would help, so we arranged to meet at The Repository.

The Elpis Repository was modelled on the ancient library of Celsus and is a series of vast stone rooms over several floors. Stone pillars holding up each floor dominate the central hallway, from which a labyrinth of rooms spread like arteries pumping the blood of the world's artistic history. Catacombs ran like veins from these rooms, dividing endlessly into alleyways leading to small 'pods' where you could immerse yourself in the treasures you had found. You could lose yourself for weeks searching for records or books, and those weeks could turn into months once you'd found a pod to enjoy your selection. It was a world beneath reality, a subculture of introverts, artists, old and young, all with one thing in common: a yearning for a less stagnant relationship with art than offered by a digital file. Nick and I had spent so many days down here, seeking out musical inspiration, huddling together in a pod, pawing our bounty, losing ourselves in the imagery and tactility of the album cover. It was a spiritual experience – they were called catacombs for a reason. We met at Hallowed Point, and as we walked down the stairs into The Repository I told him about the last, unbelievable nine days of my life: the counsellor, the Beimeni Centre, and JIG:SAW. I told Nick that one of Alice's colleagues had been helping me, but I didn't tell him it was Milton – after all, I'd made him a promise.

Nick was unflappable, but even he flapped. 'Bro, that's subterranean. Catapults of death, Deathscotch … over the wall, man, that's sick.' After everything had sunk in a bit, he went quiet. He seemed deep in thought. I asked him what was up.

'I don't buy it,' he said. 'You and Alice, you're like, solid. I've known Alice as long as you have, and she *adores* you, man, just as much as you do her. I know things ain't always silky, but she loves you, I'm sure of it.'

I questioned Nick's faith, but we found records, we sat in a pod and we talked to the continual soundtrack we'd selected on our journey there. Whatever argument I used to persuade him that it was over for Alice and me, he returned to his only point: he'd known Alice since I first met her, he knew both of us, and he knew she wouldn't leave me. I had evidence, he had a gut feeling, it was like Alice and me in reverse. We left The Repository and had our usual farewell embrace. 'Bro, I don't know why she is at this JIG:SAW place, but I *know* she loves you. Don't give up on her,' he said. We pumped fists and went our separate ways.

The walk home gave me time to think. Perhaps Nick was right; perhaps Alice couldn't leave me a note, or tell me why she was leaving. She *had* left a song playing, but I was pretty sure the only way to interpret that was as a farewell, and Nick hadn't had a decent response to that, but he was right about one thing: the evidence I had was circumstantial, and I wouldn't know anything for sure until I'd spoken to her. I walked in to find Milton helping himself to some milk from the fridge.

'I need to know more about JIG:SAW,' I said.

Milton twitched and dropped the milk. 'Why? Surely you know everything you need to know: your girlfriend left you, didn't even leave a note, and then turns up trotting merrily around the JIG:SAW complex. Move on, Zach. Accept that Alice is too good for you and get on with life. It's like you said in your magnificent song this morning: you know what you saw, she don't love you no more.' Milton sounded like he was trying very hard indeed not to be sarcastic.

'Maybe you're right, but there's something subterranean about that place …'

'Perhaps it's the undead army and over-elaborate probability-based security system?' said The Head, who had been quietly spinning above his pocket watch. A few days ago I had promised The Head that I'd release him from his reality checker more often. True to my word, I let him out whenever he wasn't actually in my pocket. I'd feared that The Head would take being released as an invitation for constant banter, but to my surprise he was content to spin and occasionally ask to be moved.

Milton threw The Head a scathing look as if willing him to be quiet. Turning towards me, he adopted a calm but authoritative tone. '*Purr*haps you're right and there is something odd about

JIG:SAW, but if there is, the WGA will no doubt have it on their radar. There is no point in a mentally deficient human, a disembodied head, and a cat – albeit a genius one – trying to uncover whatever it is they might be doing. We are not in a movie, we are not a secret band of superheroes who will come good and overthrow the evil corporation. Admittedly I am a quite remarkable cat, but you, Zach Slade, I'm afraid to say, are a normal and quite unremarkable young man. Write your songs, pursue your dreams, live your life, but do not prove to be even more stupid than I already think you are by trying to save the world when it does not need saving.'

'What if Alice is in trouble? What if she needs me?'

'She looked happy enough. If she needed you she would have called rather than wiping herself from your contacts.'

'Maybe she *couldn't* call, maybe someone else wiped her from my contacts. There's no harm in finding out more about JIG:SAW. If there's nothing strange about them then I'll give up.' Obviously I was lying.

Milton paused. He looked around the room, engrossed in thought, and licked his chest repeatedly as though it helped him to process them. He changed tack. 'We could delve into JIG:SAW, we have some reports from them, perhaps we can get some data – but to do it properly you are going to need to step up to the next level and start to think about how you can use those data to test the hypotheses you have about the organization. Are you really ready to go to the next level, or would you rather just focus on your music, channel these feelings into new songs?'

I sensed Milton was trying to put me off – perhaps to protect his anonymity. After all, he said he didn't want anyone to discover that he was still alive. He was right, though, I didn't want to learn more about statistics, but I did want closure with Alice, even if it was hearing from her own mouth that it was over. 'I don't expect you to understand,' I finally said, 'but I can't give up on Alice. If she doesn't need my help then fine, at least I'll know I didn't let her down.'

Milton continued trying to dissuade me. 'I think the next step will be too hard for you. We are going to get into some complicated concepts that lots of people struggle to make sense of.'

The Head had been keeping his own counsel in the corner. He was gently rotating, taking in the scene. But he rotated to a standstill facing Milton and me, and announced dramatically, 'I have an idea.'

Milton hissed and directed the cat stare of death at him: the stare that cats use when their owners return from holiday, the stare that says 'I will never forgive you.'

The Head continued. 'The cat is right, Z. You're not able to understand these concepts 'cos your brain is constrained by your massive inferiority complex. So, you're gonna have to become someone else.'

'What?' Milton and I chorused.

'Listen. While searching my database I found a study that helps us out. Crack open the nut and in the shell is a message that says that pretending to be someone else makes you better at maths. **(REALITY CHECK 8.1)** It only worked for women, but it's worth a shot.' The Head sported an annoyingly cheeky grin.

Milton raised his eyes to the heavens, and said, in an exasperated tone, 'It is deeply implausible that Zach will understand statistical concepts better simply by imagining that he is a statistics genius.'

The Head fumed. 'Is that so, fur face? Zhang gave women a maths test; some completed it using their own name, and others completed it pretending to be someone else. The mean accuracy on the test of those using their own name was 44.2% with a standard error of 3.10 and a 95% confidence interval of 38.13 to 50.27, but for those using a fake name it was 54.73% with a standard error of 3.35 and a 95% confidence interval of 48.16 to 61.29.'

'Interesting …' said Milton as he scratched his ear.

Everything was getting out of control. None of this was getting me any closer to putting the pieces of JIG:SAW together.

'*Wait!*' I shouted. I rarely shouted, but I needed to take charge. 'I don't have a clue what you two are arguing about. Head, I released you like I said I would, in return for your help – we made a deal. Milton, you promised to assist me. So, both of you, do what you said you would and help me out.'

There was an awkward pause. The Head looked at Milton, who looked at The Head. The Head nodded sideways towards me as if to motion that Milton should explain everything to me. Milton shrugged his shoulders and screwed up his face. After a minute or so of this silent buck-passing, The Head spoke and Milton wandered off.

'We've got your back, I promise. But first we need you to pretend to be Florence Nightingale.'

I wondered if it was a coincidence that he picked someone with Alice's surname.

'Wasn't she, like, some kind of nurse from way back when?' I asked.

'Well, yeah, she was a nurse during the Crimean war – but she was also a gifted statistician who pioneered novel ways to display data'.

The thought crossed my mind that maybe everyone with the surname Nightingale was a genius.

'A bit like Dr Tuff?' I said.

'Sort of,' The Head replied, 'but without the hatred of pie charts.'

8.1 ESTIMATING PARAMETERS

'To understand what we were talking about and why we can use data from samples to test a hypothesis,' began Milton, 'imagine we are interested in whether pretending to be a statistics whizz-kid helps you to perform better on a statistics test. How might we go about finding out? I need you to think back to what I told you about fitting models'. (CHAPTER 4)

'Statistics and maths anxiety are common and affect people's performance on maths and stats assignments,'[31] The Head began. 'Women in particular can lack confidence in mathematics. It does not have to be that way, though. Shen Zhang and her colleagues[12] did an intriguing study in which they asked students to do a maths test. Some students put their own name on the test booklet, while others were given a booklet that already had a name on. They were told that the booklets already had names on to protect their anonymity and that they would be using this other person's name for the purpose of the test. Lo and behold, women who completed the test using a different name performed better than those who completed the test using their own name. It did not matter whether they performed the test under another female name or a male name. Women not using their own name also had fewer self-evaluation concerns and distractions during the test. Zhang concluded that performing under a different name freed women from fears of self-evaluation, allowing them to perform better.'

Reality Check 8.1 How to be better at maths

I thought back to a week ago when I had first met Milton and he had explained about how scientists fit models to the samples of data they collect to try to find out about the true state of the world. The information felt remarkably fresh in my mind – perhaps wearing a Victorian dress and pretending to be Florence was helping already.

I told Milton everything I could remember.

'Scientists want to know about the true state of the world (a population). So in this case they'd want to know about performance in the statistics test in the population. They can't collect data from the whole population, so they'd use a sample instead. The bigger the sample, the more precise the picture you can paint of reality. Having collected a sample of data, they would fit a model, which is an equation made up of parameters and variables. In this case the variable might be whether or not a person pretended to be a stats whizz. Parameters are just numbers that tell us something about the connection between the variables in the model and the outcome that you're trying to predict. Because we don't have access to the population we can't know the true values of these parameters, so we estimate them from a sample taken from the population. One example of a parameter is the mean, which estimates the central score of a population.'

Milton looked bemused. 'Wow – that *is* impressive, Florence,' he replied. 'Can you remember how we measure how well the parameter fits the sample data?'

'Yeah, you take each score that you observed in the sample, and look at the difference between that score and the score predicted using the model. For example, for the mean you could look at the difference between each observed score on the stats test and the mean score. This difference is the error, or deviance, for that score. You do that for each score, and then square them because sometimes the deviance will be positive but other times it will be negative. Then you add up these squared values to get the total error, which is known as the sum of squared errors. You can also divide this total by the number of scores to get the average amount of error, which is known as the variance, or mean squared error. You can then take the square root of the variance to get a similar value known as the standard deviation.' *(SECTION 4.3)*

I was pleased with myself. Milton paced around the bottom of my dress as though looking for the source of my wisdom.

'Yes, we can assess how well a parameter estimate, in this case the mean, "fits" or represents the sample data exactly as you explained. What I have not yet told you is how we work out what the value of the parameter actually is. I feared you could not cope with this information, but I see that I have underestimated your intelligence. I think the time has come to explain estimation – or, at least, one way of doing it.'

I felt proud that I had proved the cat wrong about my intelligence.

'Go to your fridge and you will discover a piece of blue-veined cheese,' he said. '"That's a nice piece of cheese," you will think to yourself, and although you do not remember buying the cheese, you will think that it is fair game to eat because it is in your fridge. So, you will pick a bit off and eat it.'

I did as Milton said, and he was right, there was some Stilton in there. I didn't remember buying it. I took a chunk and ate it. I went back to my living room and Milton continued.

'The tangy, creamy taste of the cheese hits you like a lung-cleansing blast of fresh air, and you start to feel a little disengaged from your body. You suddenly realize that you can see the whole of time and space simultaneously. What is more, by just poking your finger into the space-time vortex before you, you have the power to eradicate anything you like from history. You immerse your hand into the swirling mass of time and space and emerge with the equation for computing the mean. Pausing briefly to consider the enormity of what you are about to do, you squash the equation between your fingertips. "Ha!" you think. "That will stop people computing averages."'

Perhaps this cheese was hallucinogenic. I wondered where Milton was going with the cheese thing.

'My point is this. Imagine that the equation for the mean did not exist. How would we estimate the mean score on the stats test?'

'Why didn't you just say that?'

'I thought the cheese story was more interesting.'

'It was distracting.'

'Cheese is *always* distracting. Back to my question: if the equation for computing the mean did not exist, how might we estimate it?'

'I dunno, maybe look at the frequency distribution of scores and see where the middle is, and sort of guess?'

'Yes, we could have a guess, and then see how well our guess fits the data. Remember at Occam's, when I explained to you about the mean being a statistical model, I said that the mean is the parameter b_0. Here is the equation (8.1) again to remind you.'

$$\text{outcome}_i = b_0 + \text{error}_i \tag{8.1}$$

'I also explained that we could rearrange this equation to look at the error in prediction. Think back – here it is again.' He scratched a familiar equation (8.2) into my wall.

I was beginning to get annoyed with Milton scratching my walls, though he was quite oblivious.

$$\text{error}_i = \text{outcome}_i - b_0 \tag{8.2}$$

'As you recalled just now, if we add the error for each person then we get the sum of squared errors, which we can use as a measure of "fit". So, we can use this equation to work out how well our "guess" fits the sample. To keep things simple, imagine we took a sample of five people and noted their scores on the statistics test: 50, 48, 55, 52, 45. We want to estimate the mean, but because of your cheese-eating antics we do not have an equation to estimate it and instead have guessed that it is 49. We can compute the error for each person by subtracting this value from the score that they actually got on the test. We then square this value to get rid of any minus signs, and we add up these squared errors. The table (8.1) shows this process; by guessing a value of 49, you get a total squared error of 63. Now imagine that you take another guess and this time you guess that b, the mean, is 52. You again compute the sum of squared error as a measure of "fit" of this estimate. You find that the sum of squared errors is 78. Which guess is better: the first one or the second one?'

I thought about this question. The sum of squared error was a measure of the total error so surely the guess that had the lowest value for the sum of squares would be the guess with the best 'fit'. I suggested that the first guess was better because it has a smaller sum of squared error than the second guess.

'*Purr*fect, well done. Is our guess of 49 the best guess we could make, though?'

Table 8.1 *Guessing the mean*

Score on Statistics Test (x_i)	b_{01}	Error $x_i - b_{01}$	Squared error $(x_i - b_{01})^2$	b_{02}	Error $x_i - b_{02}$	Squared error $(x_i - b_{02})^2$
50	49	1	1	52	−2	4
48	49	−1	1	52	−4	16
55	49	6	36	52	3	9
52	49	3	9	52	0	0
45	49	−4	16	52	−7	49

$$\sum_{i=1}^{n} (x_i - b_{01})^2 = 63$$

$$\sum_{i=1}^{n} (x_i - b_{02})^2 = 78$$

I shrugged. 'We'd have to look at other values and calculate their sums of squares to find out if they were smaller than for our guess of 49.'

'Indeed you would, but to look at every other guess you could make would take a long time and would be incredibly tedious, would it not?'

He was right, it was about the most tedious thing I could imagine.

'Which is why', the cat continued, 'it is fortunate that I am a genius and can show you what would happen on your diePad. Look at this image; **(FIGURE 8.1)** it shows the sum of squared error that you would get for various 'guesses' of the parameter *b*. You can see that when *b* is 49 we get a sum of squared error of 63 and when it is 52 the sum of squared error is 78, just as we calculated in the table. **(TABLE 8.1)** The shape of the graph is interesting, though, because the sum of squared error for different guesses is a curve that has a minimum value. That is, there is a "guess" for which the error is the smallest it can be given the data. In other words, there is a "guess" or estimate that minimizes the error – it fits the best, compared to other values we might have chosen. What is the value that has the lowest error?'

I looked at the image. **(FIGURE 8.1)** 'It looks like 50 is the value that is at the lowest point of the curve.'

'*Purr*cisely. Now imagine that you have a pang of conscience and you reinstate the equation for the mean into the space-time vortex. What is the mean of the five scores?'

CHECK YOUR BRAIN: *What is the mean of 50, 48, 55, 52 and 45?*

I added the numbers on my diePad and divided by 5. 'It's 50.'

'Yes, and why does that value sound familiar?'

'It was the value of the guess with the least error!'

'Yes, it was, and this illustrates a process called the **method of least squares**, which is a way of calculating the value of a parameter such that you get the value that produces the least squared error. The equation of the mean, for example, works on this principle – it produces the value that produces the smallest sum of squared error. Values of parameters other than the mean can be calculated using different equations, but these equations all have one thing in common: they produce the value with the smallest sum of squared error.'

'You mean we'll always get a good estimate.'

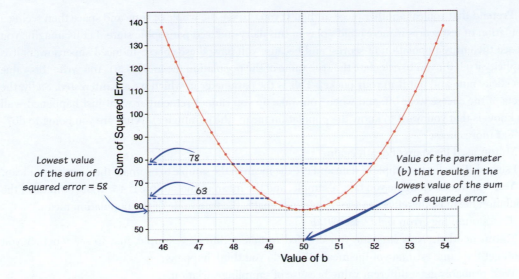

Figure 8.1   Graph showing the sum of squared error for different 'guesses' of the mean (*b*) for five scores on a statistics test

'Not necessarily. Having the least error is not the same thing as the parameter estimate being accurate or representative of the population – it could be the best of a bad bunch. What would you think about the parameter estimate if, despite having the least error in the sample, it was not representative of the population?'

'It would be misleading.'

'*Claw*some. Yes, we want to know how well our estimates represent the population.'

'How do we do that?'

'Funny you should ask that, Florence,' grinned Milton as though reeling in a big fish.

8.2   HOW WELL DOES A SAMPLE REPRESENT THE POPULATION?

8.2.1 Sampling distributions

'What do you know about different samples taken from a population?' asked Milton.

I thought back to what Alice had explained the night before she vanished, and of the image she showed me, which I still had on my diePad. I retrieved it and showed it to Milton. **(FIGURE 1.2)** 'If you take samples from a population then they will be slightly different, which is called sampling variation.'

'*Paw*fectly true. If you estimate a parameter – like the population mean – the estimates from different samples will be slightly different because the samples are slightly different.'

'So, you won't get the same estimate in two different samples?'

'Well, you might, but it is not guaranteed. Therefore, we want to know how representative the estimate in our particular sample is likely to be of the true value in the population. Remember our example: we want to know how people in general do on a statistics test. Now, imagine we could look at the population of scores on the test.'

'But how can we? People keep telling me that you can rarely access the entire population.'

'Use your imagination. Remember that piece of blue-veined cheese that enabled you to see the whole of time and space, simultaneously?'

'Yes.'

'Pretend that you eat another piece of that. If you can see the whole of time and space then seeing a population of test scores is mere child's play in this dairy-induced pansophic state. Let us imagine you can see the entire population of scores, and because you have these cheese-induced superpowers it is simplicity itself for you to calculate the true value of the population mean. It is 50. You write this value on a sticky note and put it in your pocket. This is the parameter in which we are interested. Sadly, the effects of the cheese wear off, and when you wake up you cannot remember what just happened – all you know is that you want to know the population mean (the parameter). What are you going to do?'

'Eat more cheese?'

Milton used his stare of death again.

I sighed. 'I'd collect a sample of data and use the mean in the sample to estimate the population mean.'

'Yes, you would. Imagine you take a sample, and the mean in the sample is 45. Your estimate of the population mean is, therefore, 45 too. It underestimates the true value of the population mean.'

'That's sampling error, right?' **(SECTION 1.2.1)**

Milton nodded. 'Now imagine you decided to take a different sample, just to see whether you would get the same estimate of the mean. What do you think happens?'

'We'd probably get a different value because of sampling variation.'

'Yes. Imagine you work out the sample mean for this second sample and it is 50.'

'So it correctly estimates the population value.'

'Yes, but of course you do not know that because you have forgotten about the sticky note in your pocket. All you know is that your samples have given you two different estimates. Now imagine you are getting really obsessed with this idea of collecting samples, and so you collect scores on the statistics test in seven more samples, giving you nine samples in total.' Milton began to scribble frantically with his paw on my diePad. **(FIGURE 8.2)** 'There, this diagram illustrates your process of taking nine different samples from the population. Notice that in each sample you have computed the sample mean ($\bar{X}$), which is your estimate of the population mean. You can see *sampling variation* and *sampling error* very clearly here because some samples underestimate the population mean (because they contained people who did less well on the test or who were at the lower extreme of population scores), some samples overestimate it (because they contained people who did better on the test or fall at the upper extreme of population scores), and some samples are spot on. Because we have taken nine samples, we now have nine estimates of the population mean. What would happen if we plotted these estimates on a histogram?'

'A histogram shows us how many times each score occurs. The scores here are the sample means, so we'd be able to see how many times a particular value of the sample mean occurs.' **(SECTION 3.1.3)**

'Yes, and because these sample means are our estimates of the population mean, this histogram tells us about how estimates of the population mean vary across samples. I have plotted the histogram for your nine samples in the diagram. **(FIGURE 8.2)** What do you notice about the distribution – what does it look like and what value is at the middle?'

 CHECK YOUR BRAIN: Think about Milton's question. What do you notice about the shape of the histogram in Figure 8.2? What's special about the value at the centre of it?

I looked at the histogram. It reminded me of the normal distribution that Professor Pincus had told me about: **(SECTION 3.2)** it was symmetrical and it had a pyramid shape that looked a bit like a bell. It looked like the value in the middle was 50. I said all of this to Milton and he nodded in appreciation.

'And what is special about the value of 50?' he asked. Then, as if sensing that I needed a clue, he added, 'Remember that you wrote it on a sticky note when you were high on cheese.'

It was the value of the mean for the whole population. I thought about this for a few seconds and then a realization hit me. 'Are you telling me that if you take a load of samples and estimate something from the population in each one, then those estimates will most frequently be right? So, like, if you took different samples of cats and calculated the average amount of time they sleep in a day, then mostly those averages would match the average amount of time that *all cats in the world* sleep?'

Milton nodded and smiled. 'Yes, what the histogram shows is that if you were to take lots of samples and estimate something in the population then mostly they will produce estimates that only have quite small sampling error; that is, mostly their estimates congregate only a small distance from the actual population value. What we have just looked at is called a **sampling distribution**, which is the frequency distribution of sample statistics (i.e., the mean or whatever parameter you are trying to

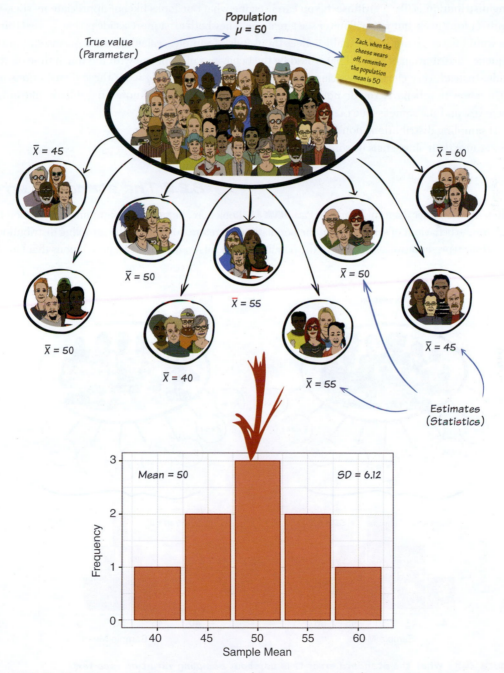

Figure 8.2 Illustration of the standard error (see text for details)

estimate) from the same population. You need to imagine that we are taking hundreds or thousands of samples to construct a sampling distribution – I used nine to keep the diagram simple.'

'Isn't it a bit of a faff having to collect all of those samples just to be able to get the ... err ... what did you call it ... sampling distribution?'

'You miss the point. We do not, in reality, collect lots of samples, we use one (or a small number), but we know that each sample we take came from a sampling distribution. The sampling distribution itself is like a **girifinsect**.'

'Do you mean a griffin?'

'No, a girifinsect – a mythical creature that is a little bit giraffe and a little bit stick insect. A sampling distribution is like a girifinsect: you can imagine what one looks like, or appreciate its stick-like beauty or long neck, but you will never see a real one. They both exist more as ideas than as real things. You would never go out and actually collect thousands of samples, calculate their means and draw a frequency distribution of them. That would be the behaviour of someone with too much time on their hands. Instead, very clever statisticians have worked out *theoretically* what these distributions look like and how they behave. You do not have to have seen a girifinsect to know what it looks like or how it behaves, and the same is true of sampling distributions.'

'If sampling distributions don't exist, why do we need them?'

'Because their shape tells us something important.'

8.2.2 The standard error

Milton drew another diagram on my diePad. **(FIGURE 8.3)** 'Look here,' he said. 'The sampling distribution tells us about the behaviour of samples from the population; therefore, we can use the sampling distribution to tell us how representative a sample is of the population. The diagram shows two populations that have the

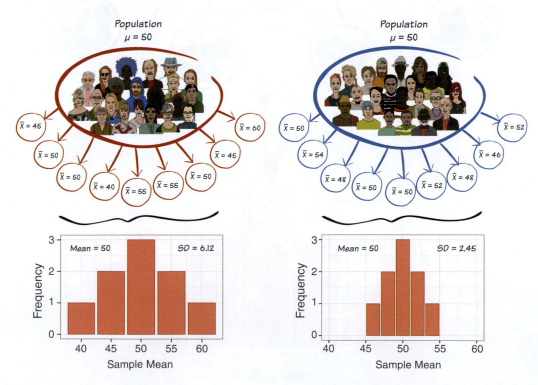

Figure 8.3 What the standard error tells us about sampling variation (see text for details)

same mean (50). As in the previous diagram, we take nine samples from each population and calculate the mean in each as an estimate of the population mean. The sample means in the left population are the same as in the previous diagram (I just have not drawn the people in each sample): the lowest is 40, the highest 60 and the others lie between those values. We get the same histogram as we did before. Now look at the right-hand side. Again we take nine samples and compute the sample mean in each. This time, the lowest sample mean is 36 and the highest is 54. The resulting histogram shows the distribution of sample means. How do the two histograms differ?'

I studied the histograms. The right-hand one looked narrower than the left, but they both had their centre at 50. I told Milton.

'*Purr*fect! Yes, because the population means are the same, the sampling distributions both spread around the same value: the value of the population parameter (50). However, the population on the left gives rise to quite variable samples, which is shown up by how spread out the sampling distribution is; in contrast, the samples from the population on the right give much more similar estimates to each other, which is shown by the narrow histogram.'

'So, samples from the right-hand population are more similar to each other than those on the left?'

'*Purr*cisely, and that also means that samples from that population are more representative of the population than samples from the one on the left. In both cases, the shape of the distribution is the same, and this shows that although most samples will produce estimates that are close to the true value in the population, a small number of samples (the ones towards the tails of the histogram) produce estimates that are quite far from the population value.'

'How do you know if you have a sample that is close to the true value or far away?'

'You do not, because you never know what the true population value is (and if you did know, you would not need to worry about samples or estimating things). However, if the sampling distribution is narrow then you know that even if you did happen to get one of these extreme samples it is not going to be too far from the true value. For example, if you took an extreme sample from the right distribution, the worst scenario is you estimate the population mean to be 46 when it is 50. That is a difference of 4. However, if you took an extreme sample from the left distribution, the worst scenario is you estimate the population mean to be 40 when it is 50, which is a difference of 10. Therefore, the width of the sampling distribution tells us something useful about how close a sample statistic is likely to be to the population value that it is estimating.'

'How do you know the width of the sampling distributions?'

'How do we normally quantify the width of a distribution of scores?'

'Using the standard deviation?' **(SECTION 4.3)**

'*Purr*cisely. The standard deviation of a sampling distribution has a special name, which is the **standard error**. When the parameter you want to estimate is the mean, then we are looking for the standard deviation of sample means, which is known as the **standard error of the mean**. Think back to the standard deviation. We used the standard deviation as a measure of how representative the mean was of the observed data. Small standard deviations represented a scenario in which most data points were close to the mean, and large standard deviations represented a situation in which data points were widely spread from the mean. If our "observed data" are sample means (or some other statistic) then the same logic applies: the standard deviation of sample means (the *standard error*) measures how representative sample means are of the population mean. A small standard deviation represents a scenario in which most sample means are close to the population mean, and a large standard deviation represents a situation in which sample means are widely spread around the population mean. In short, the standard error tells us how widely sample statistics are spread around the population value: it tells us whether estimates from samples are typically representative of the population value.'

'OK, I get that ... I think. But if sampling distributions exist only as ideas then how can we work out their standard deviations?'

'In a different reality where girifinsects exist, the standard error could be calculated by taking the difference between each sample statistic and the mean of all sample statistics, squaring these differences, adding them up, and then dividing by the number of samples. The standard deviation, or standard error, would be the square root of this value. In our reality, we cannot collect hundreds of samples and so we approximate the standard error, using equations devised by exceptionally clever statisticians. The equation is different for different statistics, but for the mean you can approximate its standard error using this equation (8.3) when samples are fairly large.'

$$\sigma_{\bar{X}} = \frac{s}{\sqrt{N}} \tag{8.3}$$

'So, the standard error of the mean is the sample standard deviation divided by the square root of the sample size?'

Milton nodded.

'That equation isn't so hard,' I said.

'No, but it works only when the sample size is fairly large. That is because really the standard error should be computed by dividing the *population* standard deviation (σ) by the square root of the sample size; however, for large samples using the *sample* standard deviation is a reasonable approximation.'

'What's a fairly large sample?'

'Greater than about 30.'

'Why does the equation work only for samples bigger than 30?'

'If our samples are at least this big then the sampling distribution for the mean has a normal distribution with a mean equal to the population mean, and a standard deviation (i.e., the standard error) that can be calculated with the equation (8.3) I showed you. When the sample size is smaller than that, the sampling distribution is not normal: it has a different shape, known as a *t*-distribution. Maybe I will explain that later.'

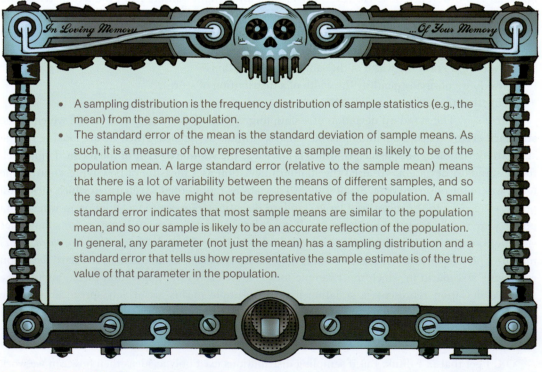

In Loving Memory ...Of Your Memory

- A sampling distribution is the frequency distribution of sample statistics (e.g., the mean) from the same population.
- The standard error of the mean is the standard deviation of sample means. As such, it is a measure of how representative a sample mean is likely to be of the population mean. A large standard error (relative to the sample mean) means that there is a lot of variability between the means of different samples, and so the sample we have might not be representative of the population. A small standard error indicates that most sample means are similar to the population mean, and so our sample is likely to be an accurate reflection of the population.
- In general, any parameter (not just the mean) has a sampling distribution and a standard error that tells us how representative the sample estimate is of the true value of that parameter in the population.

Zach's Facts 8.1 *The standard error*

'But first, you need to explain why the size of the sample makes a difference to the shape of the sampling distribution.' I regretted those words as soon as they left my mouth.

8.2.3 The central limit theorem

Milton asked whether I really wanted him to explain this; his tone suggested he doubted I'd understand. I had my own doubts, but I didn't like the way Milton talked down to me, and backing down would confirm his belief that I was just some stupid human. I wanted to prove him wrong.

'Bring it on, feline,' I said assertively.

'To explain why the sample size matters we need to understand the **central limit theorem**.'

It sounded complicated already but, determined not to let Milton know that the name alone fripped me out, I feigned concentration by frowning and nodding my head.

'Think again of the example where we want to know about whether pretending to be a statistics genius helps you to do better on a statistics test. We just talked about how you might sample from a population of scores on such a test. Imagine that population of scores is not normally distributed.'

'You mean it doesn't have that bell shape?'

'Indeed, imagine that it is highly skewed.' Milton produced a histogram on my diePad. **(FIGURE 8.4)** 'This histogram', Milton continued pointing to the top of his image, 'shows the population of scores. It has a heavy positive skew: most people get scores around 40–60% and relatively few people do really well and get above 70%. This creates a long tail at the top end of the distribution and makes the distribution very skewed. This distribution is far from normal, would you not say?'

I nodded in agreement. It wasn't at all symmetrical and it didn't have that bell shape because the bars of the histogram seemed squashed up the left side of the distribution.

'This is not a trick – this population is as far removed from the bell-shaped normal curve as it looks. Now I am going to take a sample of five randomly selected scores from this population and estimate a parameter – I am going to compute the mean. I will then place the scores back into the population.'

With this, Milton tapped the screen and five numbers appeared out of the population, added themselves up, divided themselves by 5 and produced the mean, which was 51. The scores then flew back into the population histogram and the mean dropped into a new histogram **(FIGURE 8.4, BOTTOM LEFT)** creating a little green line at the value of 51. It clarified the idea of sampling for me: numbers are randomly taken from the population, which make up a sample, these numbers are used to estimate something (in this case the mean) and then return to the population.

'You see how I can take a sample and estimate the mean using that sample. Well, imagine I repeat this process 5000 times,' Milton continued. He tapped the screen again and another five scores appeared, followed by their mean which dropped to form another green mark in the histogram as the scores returned to the population. He tapped the screen again and a third sample of five scores appeared, the mean was computed and another green mark appeared on the histogram below. After I'd got the gist of what was happening Milton tapped the screen again and the process sped up: my diePad screen became a whirlwind of samples appearing from the population, their means being computed and dropping into the histogram below. The bars on the green histogram steadily grew upwards as more means were added. The process got faster and faster until all I could see were the bars of the green histogram creeping upwards. Then it stopped.

'Florence, this green histogram **(FIGURE 8.4, BOTTOM LEFT)** shows the frequency distribution of the means computed from the 5000 samples that I just took from the population. You can see, for example, that the value 51 occurs about 500 times.'

'So, out of the 5000 samples you took, 500 of them had a mean of 51?'

'*Claw*rect. This histogram is the sampling distribution of the parameter estimate (in this case, the mean), which we were just discussing. It shows how often a given value of the mean appears in different samples. The value of 51, for example, occurs in 500 of 5000 samples, or about 10% of the time. What do you notice about its shape?'

I looked at it. **(FIGURE 8.4, BOTTOM LEFT)** It seemed skewed to me, just like the population. I suggested this a little bit apprehensively.

Milton smiled. 'Yes, it is positively skewed, just like the population. That is because when you take small samples from a non-normal population, the sampling distribution is not normal. Let us repeat this whole process but take larger samples. This time, we will take samples of 30.'

Milton tapped the screen and the process began again: samples of 30 scores emerged, the mean was computed and gradually a second green histogram emerged, its bars steadily rising up with each sample that was taken. After 5000 samples had emerged the diePad ground to a halt, showing a second green histogram next to the first. **(FIGURE 8.4, BOTTOM MIDDLE)**

'The process is the same as before,' continued Milton. 'The only difference is that our samples are made up of 30 scores instead of 5. Again, though, we end up with the sampling distribution for the parameter we estimated: the mean. What do you notice about this distribution compared to the one based on samples of five scores?'

 CHECK YOUR BRAIN: Compare the histograms in the bottom left and bottom middle of Figure 8.4. What do you notice about their width and shape?

I studied the two green histograms. 'The one based on 30 samples seems narrower: estimates from these samples ranged from about 45 to 60, whereas those from samples of 5 ranged from 40 to 70. Also, the histogram from the samples of 30 looks more symmetrical and less skewed than the one made up of samples of 5.'

'Well done. Let us do this one last time but with relatively large samples containing 100 randomly selected scores from the population.' Milton's paw set the diePad into action again and for a third time samples of scores appeared, followed by their mean, and with each sample a third green histogram slowly grew, showing how often different values of the mean had occurred. **(FIGURE 8.4, BOTTOM RIGHT)** When 5000 samples had been taken Milton again asked me to compare the final green histogram with the previous two. Again it looked narrower: with samples of 100 scores, the sample means varied between about 47 and 55, with samples of 30 the range was wider (45 to 60) and with samples of 5 the range was wider still (40 to 70). Also, as the sample size got bigger, the distributions looked more normal. Even with samples of 30 the skew from the population was gone.

Milton seemed pleased with my analysis. 'You are correct. I have just illustrated to you some fundamental points about using samples to estimate parameters such as the mean. First, the bigger the sample, the more precise the estimates become. This is illustrated by the fact that in samples of 100 the range of estimates is much narrower than in samples of 5. That means that estimates are more similar to each other in big samples than they are in small samples.'

'Like the cat in the box?'

'What?'

'You told me the other day about trying to find out what was in a box by putting different-sized holes in the box: the bigger the holes, the more you can see and the more likely you are to reach the same conclusion about what's in the box. With small holes you can't see very much so you end up with different ideas about what's in the box. In your example it turned out there was a cat in the box.' **(SECTION 4.1.3)**

'Oh, yes, quite right, well remembered. I *am* making the same point here: bigger samples are better because they give you a more precise (i.e., less variable) estimate of the population value. My second point is that as the sample sizes got bigger the sampling distributions became more normal, until a point

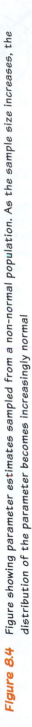

Figure 8.4 Figure showing parameter estimates sampled from a non-normal population. As the sample size increases, the distribution of the parameter becomes increasingly normal

Dear Florence

How big does a sample need to be for the central limit theorem to kick in? The answer most people will give you is 'about 30'. I showed in Figure 8.4 that with samples of this size we start to get a sampling distribution that approximated normal. However, we also know that even bigger samples give us more normal sampling distributions. There is not a simple answer because it depends on the distribution of the population, and of course we never really know the shape of the population. In light-tailed distributions (where outliers are rare) a sample as small as 20 can be 'large enough', but in heavy-tailed distributions (where outliers are common) up to 100 or even 160 might be necessary. If the distribution has a lot of skew and kurtosis you might need a very large sample indeed for the central limit theorem to work. It also depends on the parameter that you are trying to estimate. A book by Wilcox discusses this issue in detail;[32] you should read it.

Best fishes,
Milton

Milton's Meowsings 8.1 *Size matters*

at which the sample is big enough that the sampling distribution *is* normal – despite the fact that the population of scores was very non-normal indeed. This is the central limit theorem: regardless of the shape of the population, estimates in samples of parameters from that population will have a normal distribution provided the samples are "big enough" (and the variance of the population is finite).' A message appeared on my diePad screen, which I'd have to read later. (MEOWSINGS 8.1)

8.3 CONFIDENCE INTERVALS

'Does this all make sense so far?' Milton enquired.

It sort of did, but I was struggling to see exactly where the cat was heading. We'd started off discussing how to demonstrate whether pretending to be a statistics whizz could improve your performance on a statistics test, and I didn't feel any closer to answering that question. Milton sensed that my pause indicated some inner torment, and he grinned to himself as though enjoying my pain.

'I will assume that your silence indicates a complete and thorough understanding of what I have told you so far,' continued the cat, 'but in case not, I shall recap. We usually use a sample value (called a statistic) to estimate the value of a parameter in the population. An example would be using the mean in the sample to estimate the mean in the population. These estimates will vary from sample to sample, and the standard error gives us an idea of the extent to which they do. Large standard errors suggest that sample estimates will vary a lot across samples (low **precision**), whereas small standard errors suggest that different samples will yield relatively similar estimates (high precision). When we use a single value from the sample to estimate a population parameter, it is known as a point estimate.'

This phrase struck a chord. I remembered back to the night before Alice disappeared. She had talked about point estimates. I closed my eyes trying hard to think back to what Alice had said.

'What's wrong?' asked Milton.

'Alice talked about point estimates.' **(SECTION 1.3.4)** Milton raised his eyebrow in disbelief, but I ploughed on. 'I remember her saying that a point estimate was when you used a single value to estimate an effect in the population, but that you could also compute an interval estimate, which would show a range of values that contained the population value ... or something like that.'

Milton clapped his paws. 'This is *purr*cisely where I'm heading. The interval that Alice spoke of is constructed to take account of the degree of inconsistency in estimates across different samples.'

'They take account of how big the standard error is?'

'Yes, in fact they are computed *using* the standard error. These intervals are called **confidence intervals**. Although what I am about to describe applies to any parameter, I will again use the mean as a specific example. Let us again look at this example of how people perform on a statistics test (as a percentage). Look in your pocket.'

'What?'

'Look in your pocket.'

'But my pocket is empty.'

'Humour me.'

I put my hand in my pocket and pulled out a sticky note. It said 'Zach, when the cheese wears off, remember the population mean is 50'. Weird, I didn't remember writing this note to myself.

'Milton, did you put this in my pocket?'

'That *is* your handwriting,' he winked mischievously. 'If we look at the mean accuracy on the statistics test, there is a true mean (the mean in the population, which is the parameter we are trying to estimate). Thanks to your sticky note, we know that this value is 50%. Ordinarily we would not have the benefit of knowing this fact. As we have seen, if we take a sample and calculate the mean, we might find that it is 51, 45, 50 or some other value. Let us say it is 48. Because normally we do not know the true mean, we also do not know whether our sample value of 48 is a good or bad estimate of the population value. Instead of fixating on the single value in the sample, we could use an interval estimate instead: we use our sample value of 48% as the midpoint, but set a lower and upper limit as well.'

Milton produced a diagram on my diePad. **(FIGURE 8.5)**

'For example, imagine that we think the true value of the mean accuracy is somewhere between 45% and 51% (note that 48% falls exactly between these values). This is the red interval in the

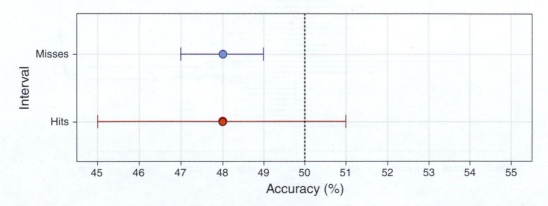

Figure 8.5 Two interval estimates: the red one hits the true population value (dotted line) but the blue one misses it

diagram. Of course, the true value (50%) *does* fall within these limits, as shown by the dotted line crossing the red interval. What if we had set narrower limits, though? For example, imagine that we had thought that the true value fell between 47% and 49% (again, note that 48% is in the middle). This is the blue interval in the diagram, and you can see that this interval does *not* contain the true value of the mean. It misses it, as shown by the dotted line falling outside of the interval. Now imagine that you took 100 different samples, and in each sample you calculated the mean on the test, but also created an interval around this value.'

Milton's paws again worked feverishly on my diePad screen producing an intricate diagram. **(FIGURE 8.6)**

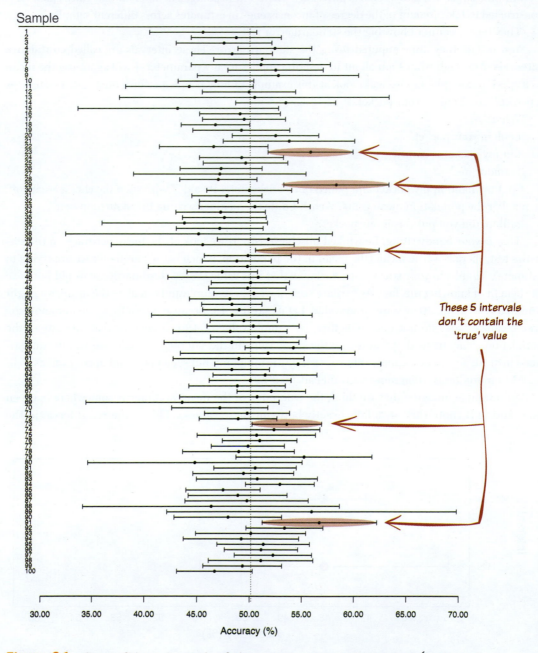

Figure 8.6 *The confidence intervals of the accuracy on a statistics test (horizontal axis) for 100 different samples (vertical axis)*

'This diagram shows this scenario: the dots represent the mean for each sample – the point estimate – and the lines sticking out of them represent the intervals around these means. Thanks to your magic sticky note, we know that the true value of the mean (the mean in the population) is 50%; a vertical line shows this value. The first thing to note is that the sample means are different from the true mean (this is because of sampling variation as we have already discussed). Second, although most of the intervals do contain the true mean (they cross the vertical line, meaning that the value of 50% falls somewhere between the lower and upper boundaries), a few do not. The crucial thing is to construct the intervals such that they tell us something useful.'

'What do you mean by useful?'

'For example, it might be helpful to know how often the intervals hit or miss the true population value in the long run. This is *purr*cisely how we construct these intervals: we calculate them so that we know how often they contain the true value of the parameter that we are trying to estimate (in this case, the mean). Typically we look at 95% confidence intervals, and sometimes 99% confidence intervals, but they all have a similar interpretation: they are limits constructed such that for a certain percentage of samples (be that 95%, 99%, or whatever) the true value of the population parameter falls within these limits. In other words, when you see a 95% confidence interval for a mean, think of it like this: if we had collected 100 random samples in an identical way, and in each of them calculated the mean and a confidence interval for that mean (a bit like in my diagram **(FIGURE 8.6)**), then we would expect that for 95 of these samples the confidence interval contains the true value of the mean in the population.'

8.3.1 Calculating confidence intervals

I was getting into the habit of asking questions that I knew I would regret, and yet I couldn't control the urge. 'How do you make the limits of the confidence interval so you know that 95% of them contain the population value?'

'A good question, Florence. We use two things that you already know something about. First, we use the standard error, because this tells us about the similarity of estimates from different samples. If the standard error is small then it means that different samples produce similar estimates. Remember from the sampling distribution that sample estimates congregate around the true population value. Given that sample estimates congregate around the population value, if they are similar to each other then we know that different samples tend to produce estimates that are very close to the population value. In which case, the interval estimate for each sample can be quite narrow and still capture the population value most of the time. However, if the standard error is large it means that different samples produce very different estimates, which suggests that estimates are spread out widely around the population value. Therefore, an interval that captures the population value in 95% of samples will need to be quite wide because some sample estimates will be very different from the population value.'

'What's the second thing?'

'The normal distribution. We know from the central limit theorem that sampling distributions are normal. We also know that we can use the normal distribution to work out the limits between which a certain proportion of scores fall.'

'Didn't we do that for the catapults of death? We worked out the proportion of scores that fell between two values.' **(SECTION 7.2.6)**

'Yes, in that case we wanted to know the proportion of scores falling between two limits, but we can flip the process on its head and start with a proportion of scores and use the table of the normal distribution **(SECTION A.I)** to work out what z-scores limit that proportion'.

That didn't make sense, and Milton picked up on my silence.

'For example, if we want to know the limits between which 95% of scores fall in a normal distribution, we can use the tabulated values to tell us.'

The power of my Florence Nightingale dress struck again: I was sure I remembered Milton saying earlier that 95% of scores fall within 2 standard deviations from the mean. **(FIGURE 7.4)**

Dear Florence,

As well as using the table of the standard normal distribution to work out the proportion of scores falling above or below a certain z-score (or indeed between two z-scores), you can reverse the process to work out the z-score or scores that cut off a specific proportion of scores. As an example that is helpful in a variety of situations, let us say that we wanted to know what z-scores cut off the middle 95% of scores under a normal curve. Figure 8.7 shows this situation. If we are interested in 95% of scores, then this leaves us with 5% of scores in which we are not interested, and because the normal curve is symmetrical and we are interested in the middle 95% of scores, we would split this 5% across the two tails, each tail having 2.5% of the scores. Note that if we add the areas we get 95% + 2.5% + 2.5% = 100%. The question is what value of z has 2.5% of scores above it. First we convert 2.5% into a proportion by dividing by 100: 2.5/100 = 0.025. In the table of the normal distribution (Section A.1) this 2.5% represents the smaller portion so we look up the value of 0.025 in the smaller portion column. Having found it, we read across to discover that the value of z that cuts of a proportion of 0.025 is 1.96 (Figure 8.7). Therefore, the upper limit is 1.96. The value that cuts of the lower 2.5% will be the same value of z (because the curve is symmetrical) but negative, because we are now looking at the z-scores below the centre of the distribution and these values are all negative. To sum up, exactly 95% of scores fall between z-scores of −1.96 and 1.96 (i.e., within ±1.96 standard deviations of the mean) if the scores are normally distributed.

Best fishes,
Milton

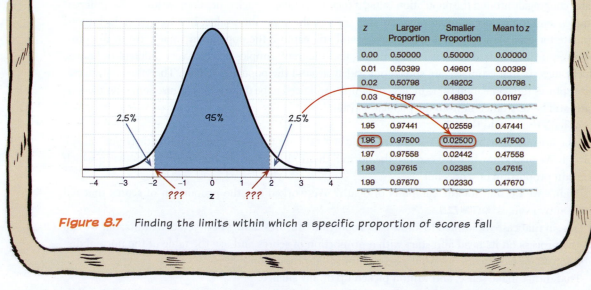

Figure 8.7 Finding the limits within which a specific proportion of scores fall

Milton's Meowsings 8.2 Limits for an area under the normal curve

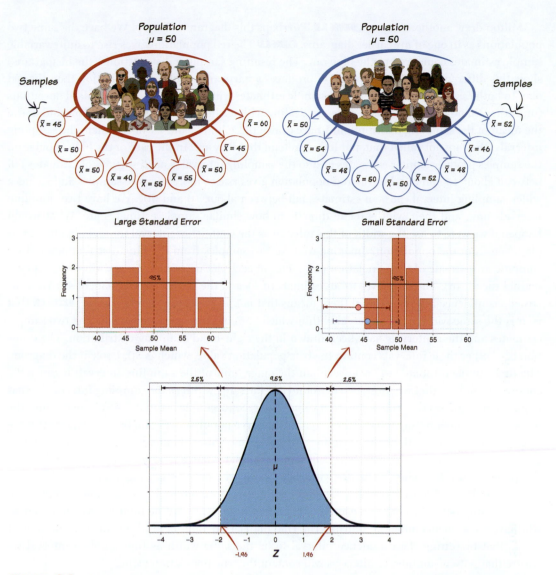

Figure 8.8 *The link between the normal distribution, standard errors and confidence intervals*

Milton looked astonished at my revelation. 'That is extremely well remembered,' he said, 'but to be exact I said *about* 95% of scores fall within 2 standard deviations. If we want to be more precise about it, *exactly* 95% of scores fall within 1.96 standard deviations. In other words, 95% of scores fall between the *z*-scores of −1.96 and 1.96.' My diePad buzzed again, showing another of Milton's seemingly telepathically delivered messages. **(MEOWSINGS 8.2)**

'How does that help us with these confidence interval things?'

The cat explained. 'In a normal distribution we know that an interval containing 95% of scores would stick out 1.96 standard deviations from the mean. In other words, the upper limit will be the mean plus 1.96 standard deviations, and the lower limit will be the mean minus 1.96 standard deviations. The sampling distribution (the distribution of estimates from different samples) is normal, therefore, an interval that contains 95% of sample estimates will similarly have an upper limit of the mean plus 1.96 standard deviations, and a lower limit of the mean minus 1.96 standard deviations.'

'Hang on, didn't you say that the standard deviation of a sampling distribution was called the standard error? And, what "mean" are you talking about?'

Milton drew another diagram. **(FIGURE 8.8)** '*Purr*haps this diagram will help. We have the same two populations as in one of my earlier diagrams. **(FIGURE 8.3)** The red population gives rise to quite variable sample estimates compared to the blue one. The resulting sampling distributions (the histograms) show this difference: the blue population produces a narrower sampling distribution than the red one. In both cases we know that 95% of sample estimates will fall between 1.96 standard deviations (or, rather, standard errors because we are dealing with a sampling distribution) below and above the mean of the sampling distribution. I have drawn these limits, and I will call them the sampling intervals; they are not called that, but let us pretend that they are. In the case of the blue population the samples produce similar estimates and so the sampling interval is narrow (95% of estimates fall between about 45 and 55), but the red population gives rise to more variable samples and so has a wider sampling interval (95% of estimates fall between about 40 and 60). We have two sampling intervals now, and their widths relate directly to how similar sample estimates are. What would happen if we were to use the width of this interval as the confidence interval for an individual sample taken from the population? Imagine we take two samples from the blue distribution, and we compute an estimate of the population parameter in each (let us assume we are interested in estimating the mean). The first gives us an estimate of 44 and the second an estimate of 46. We construct a confidence interval around these means that is 1.96 times the standard error; **(FIGURE 8.9)** that is, it is the same width as the interval within which 95% of sample estimates fall. The two sample estimates and their intervals have been drawn in the right-hand sampling distribution. The question is whether these intervals contain the true population value, which is 50. Look at the diagram. The first sample estimate (44) is lower than the outer limit of the sampling interval; because the confidence interval that we constructed around it is the same width as the sampling interval for that population, it misses the true population value. The second sample estimate (46) is just within the outer limit of the sampling interval, and so it hits the true population (again because the confidence interval is the same width as the sampling interval). Now, think about what the sampling interval means. It is the limits within which 95% of sample estimates fall. So, 95% of samples we take from this population will produce estimates within the boundaries of the sampling interval. We have just seen that if the confidence interval is the same width as what we referred to as the sampling interval, then any sample that produces an estimate that falls within the sampling interval (which 95% will) will have a confidence interval that hits the true population value. Put all of this together and it shows that by setting the confidence interval to be the same width as the sampling interval we ensure that 95% of confidence intervals will contain the true population value.'

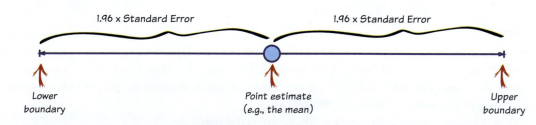

Figure 8.9 The anatomy of a confidence interval

'So, basically you're saying that the confidence interval is calculated by multiplying the standard error by 1.96 and then adding or subtracting that from the value of the sample estimate?' **(EQUATION 8.4)**

$$\text{lower boundary of confidence interval} = \text{estimate} - (1.96 \times SE)$$
$$\text{upper boundary of confidence interval} = \text{estimate} + (1.96 \times SE)$$

$$(8.4)$$

'Yes, Florence, but only for a 95% confidence interval: remember that the 1.96 is the *z*-score that limits the middle 95% of scores from a normal distribution. You can use different values of *z* to compute different confidence intervals and in fact the equation for calculating confidence intervals is directly related to the equation for converting a raw score to a *z*-score.' My diePad flashed another message. (*MEOWSINGS 8.3*)

> **CHECK YOUR BRAIN:** If the mean (estimate) in a sample of people taking the statistics test was 45 and the standard error was 5, what would the 95% confidence interval be?

Dear Florence,

Earlier on (Section 6.2, Eq. 6.1) we used an equation to compute a *z*-score from a raw score and the mean and the standard deviation of the distribution from which the score came. Just to remind you:

$$z = \frac{X - \bar{X}}{s}$$

Remember that we are dealing with a sampling distribution, so the standard deviation is called the standard error, so let us change the *s* in the equation to reflect this:

$$z = \frac{X - \bar{X}}{SE}$$

To keep things as straightforward as possible, let us assume that the thing we are trying to estimate is the population mean (this just means we can leave the $\bar{X}$ as it is). We know that 95% of *z*-scores fall between −1.96 and 1.96. This means that if our sample estimates were normally distributed with a mean of 0 and a standard error of 1, then the limits of our 95% confidence interval would be −1.96 and +1.96. We can replace the *z* in the equation with these values:

$$1.96 = \frac{X - \bar{X}}{SE} \qquad\qquad -1.96 = \frac{X - \bar{X}}{SE}$$

We want to know what raw scores (i.e., what values of *X*) will produce *z*-scores of −1.96 and 1.96 (to differentiate the *X* in the two equations, we will refer to them as X_{Upper} and X_{Lower}). To answer this question we can rearrange the equation.

$$1.96 \times SE = X_{\text{Upper}} - \bar{X} \qquad\qquad -1.96 \times SE = X_{\text{Lower}} - \bar{X}$$

$$(1.96 \times SE) + \bar{X} = X_{\text{Upper}} \qquad\qquad (-1.96 \times SE) + \bar{X} = X_{\text{Lower}}$$

$$X_{\text{Upper}} = \bar{X} + 1.96 SE \qquad\qquad X_{\text{Lower}} = \bar{X} - 1.96 SE$$

As such, the confidence interval is related to the equation we have already used to convert raw scores into z-scores. The confidence interval for the mean can easily be calculated once the standard error and mean are known.

Best fishes,
Milton

Milton's Meowsings 8.3   *Confidence intervals and the equation for z-scores*

8.3.2 Calculating other confidence intervals

I thought about this information and looked at the diagram. **(FIGURE 8.8)** It was difficult to get my head around, but I got the gist: the confidence interval would be wide if estimates varied across different samples from the same population and narrow if different samples tended to produce similar estimates. As such they seemed to tell you something about how likely the sample estimate was to reflect reality. I wondered why we used 95%; at least, I thought I had wondered it, but it turned out that I had said it out loud. Milton smiled an evil kind of smile.

'There is nothing special about 95%; you can construct any confidence interval you like using basically the same equation. All that changes is the value of ±1.96, because those are the z-scores that cut off the middle 95% of scores. If you want a 90%, 99%, or 63% confidence interval you simply find the values of z that contain that percentage of scores.'

'Would someone use a 63% confidence interval?'

'It would be unlikely. The vast majority of times you will see 95% confidence intervals, but 99% and 90% ones are fairly common too. In general, you can calculate any confidence interval using this equation.' Milton scratched it **(EQUATION 8.5)** on my wall.

$$\text{lower boundary of confidence interval} = \text{estimate} - \left(z_{(1-p)/2} \times SE \right)$$

$$\text{upper boundary of confidence interval} = \text{estimate} + \left(z_{(1-p)/2} \times SE \right) \qquad (8.5)$$

'It's the same as before,' I noted, 'apart from all that z and p stuff – what's that about?'

Milton sighed. 'It represents the z-score for the probability value, p, that you want. If you want a 95% confidence interval, then $p = .95$, so you want to look up the value of z for $(1-0.95)/2 = 0.025$. That is what we did before: we looked this value up in the 'smaller portion' column of the table of the standard normal distribution and found that z was 1.96. **(MEOWSINGS 8.2)** What would we do if we wanted a 99% confidence interval?'

'I guess for a 99% confidence interval, p will be 0.99.'

'*Claw*rect.'

'So, we'd want the z for $(1-0.99)/2$, which is ... err ...'

'0.005.'

'Yeah, what you said. So, we look up 0.005 in the smaller portion of the normal table **(SECTION A.I)**, and find a value of …' I looked at the table on my diePad but there wasn't a value of 0.005. Sensing my confusion, Milton prompted me by asking what value in the table was the closest to 0.005. It was 0.00494 and Milton told me to use that value.

'The z-score for that value is 2.58, isn't it?' I asked.

'*Purr*fect. Now replace the z in the equation that I just showed you with that value and it will become …' Milton again vandalised my wall. **(EQUATION 8.6)** 'You can apply the same principle to work out a 90% confidence interval.'

'What, you replace z with the value of z for a probability of 0.9?'

'*Purr*cisely. You would work out the z for (1–0.9)/2, which is 0.05. Look up 0.05 in the smaller portion of the normal table **(SECTION A.I)**, what is the corresponding value for z?'

$$\text{lower boundary of } 99\% \text{ confidence interval} = \text{estimate} - (2.58 \times SE)$$
$$\text{upper boundary of } 99\% \text{ confidence interval} = \text{estimate} + (2.58 \times SE)$$

(8.6)

I looked at the table on my diePad. The closest value to 0.05 in the column labelled smaller portion was 0.0505, which had a corresponding z of 1.64. I offered this value to Milton.

'*Claw*rect. Replace the z in the equation **(8.5)** with that value and you will get …'

Before he could destroy more of my wall, I grabbed my diePad and scribbled out what I thought was the correct equation **(8.7)**. Milton nodded in appreciation.

$$\text{lower boundary of } 90\% \text{ confidence interval} = \text{estimate} - (1.64 \times SE)$$
$$\text{upper boundary of } 90\% \text{ confidence interval} = \text{estimate} + (1.64 \times SE)$$

(8.7)

 CHECK YOUR BRAIN: If the mean (estimate) in a sample of people taking the statistics test was 45 and the standard error was 5, what would the 90% and 99% confidence intervals be?

8.3.3 Confidence intervals in small samples

'You seem to be following all of this, Florence.' The cat teased.

'It sort of makes sense,' I agreed.

'Good, because there is a slight complication.'

I was starting to see a pattern in statistics: just when you thought you understood something, a cloaked, knife-wielding nugget of new information would pop out from around the corner to stab your brain.

'You see, everything I have just described assumes that the sampling distribution is normal,' continued Milton.

'Well, that's true isn't it? That's what the central limit thingie tells us.'

'Does it say that the sampling distribution is *always* normal?'

I thought back to when Milton had explained the central limit thingie. **(SECTION 8.2.3)** 'No,' I replied, 'it's normal when samples are bigger than about 30.'

'Exs*cratch*ly, so what happens if samples are smaller than that?'

'Err … in your diagram, the small samples led to a sampling distribution that looked weird.' **(FIGURE 8.4)**

'Indeed, and that "weird-looking" distribution, as you so articulately put it, is known as a **t-distribution**: a family of probability distributions that change shape as the sample size gets bigger. In fact, when the sample size reaches about 30, it has the shape of a normal distribution.' Yet another message appeared for me. **(MEOWSINGS 8.4)**

'How does that help us?'

'Simple. We use basically the same equation to calculate the confidence interval, but instead of using the value of z from a normal distribution, we use the value of t from the t-distribution appropriate for our sample size.' Milton scratched into my wall some more. 'Notice how this new equation **(8.8)** is the same as for bigger samples **(EQUATION 8.5)** except the z has been replaced with t because we are using the t-distribution instead of the normal.'

$$\text{lower boundary of confidence interval} = \text{estimate} - \left(t_{n-1} \times SE\right)$$
$$\text{upper boundary of confidence interval} = \text{estimate} + \left(t_{n-1} \times SE\right)$$

(8.8)

I asked how we find the value of t.

'Each distribution, Milton replied, 'is defined by degrees of freedom, which are equal to the sample size, n, minus 1. So, we look up the value of t, for the type of confidence interval we want (for example, 95% or 99%) and the degrees of freedom we have.' Milton took my diePad back from me and drew another diagram. **(FIGURE 8.10)** 'This is a table of values of the t-distribution that cut off a certain proportion of scores. **(SECTION A.2)** Imagine we want a 95% confidence interval. Just like with the normal distribution, that would mean that we are interested in the middle 95%, so we want the values that leave us with 5% of scores in the tails – that is 0.05 as a proportion. That 5% must be spread across the two tails, so we want to look in the column that relates to 0.05 as the proportion spread across the two tails. If we had a sample of, say, 5, then our degrees of freedom would be $n-1 = 5-1 = 4$, so we look at the fourth row of that column.'

'And the value is 2.776.'

'*Claw*rect. For a 90% confidence interval we would want the proportion across the tails to be 10% or 0.1, so we look down the column labelled 0.1 instead, and for a 99% confidence interval we want only 1% of scores across the tails, or 0.01 as a proportion, so we look down the final column. In each case, the row we look at depends on the sample size: we look at the row corresponding to the degrees of freedom, which is the sample size minus 1.'

CHECK YOUR BRAIN: If the mean (estimate) in a sample of people taking the statistics test was 45 and the standard error was 5, what would the 95%, 90% and 99% confidence intervals be if the sample contained 5 people? What about if it contained 20 people?

8.4 INFERENTIAL STATISTICS

I got the gist of the central limit theorem, and I thought I could perhaps see how the standard error was useful as a way to get some idea of how similar or different estimates from different samples might be. I even understood how it could be useful to use interval estimates and construct a confidence interval to get some idea of the likely value of something in the population. Something was missing, though, which was why any of this actually mattered. It was a feeling I'd had quite a few times over the past week or so as people had taken it upon themselves to teach me statistics. I didn't want to let on to Milton that I couldn't see the point of everything: I had the suspicion that I was slowly gaining a tiny bit of respect from him, and I didn't want to ruin it. I must have been silently contemplating this issue longer than I realized, because Milton interrupted my thoughts.

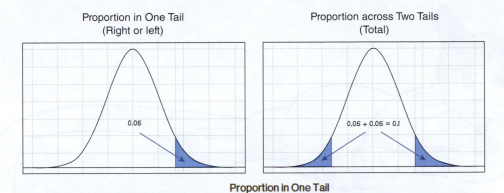

	Proportion in One Tail				
	0.10	0.05	0.025	0.01	0.005
df	0.20	0.10	0.05	0.02	0.01
1	3.078	6.314	12.706	31.821	63.657
2	1.886	2.920	4.303	6.965	9.925
3	1.638	2.353	3.182	4.541	5.841
4	1.533	2.132	2.776	3.747	4.604
5	1.476	2.015	2.571	3.365	4.032
6	1.440	1.943	2.447	3.143	3.707
7	1.415	1.895	2.365	2.998	3.499
8	1.397	1.860	2.306	2.896	3.355
9	1.383	1.833	2.262	2.821	3.250
10	1.372	1.812	2.228	2.764	3.169
11	1.363	1.796	2.201	2.718	3.106
12	1.356	1.782	2.179	2.681	3.055
13	1.350	1.771	2.160	2.650	3.012
14	1.345	1.761	2.145	2.624	2.977

90%
Confidence
Interval

95%
Confidence
Interval

99%
Confidence
Interval

Proportion across Two Tails

Figure 8.10 *Using the t-distribution*

'You are wondering what any of this has to do with anything, aren't you?'

'A little,' I admitted.

'That is to be expected. I am reaching my crescendo, the point at which I deliver you an intellectual epiphany.'

I looked him as if to say 'seriously?'

'Our original question was about whether pretending to be someone else could make a difference to your understanding of statistics. That is why you are dressed as Florence Nightingale.'

It hadn't initially been clear to me why Milton was so insistent that I needed a dress to pretend to be someone else; was he testing what I'd do to find out more about JIG:SAW and Alice? I'd willingly played along to get more information from him, but becoming a brilliant female statistican had freed me of my lack of confidence. Maybe Milton was trying to help me.

Milton produced another diagram on my diePad. **(FIGURE 8.12)** 'Imagine you took three random samples of 6 people from a population. You give all three samples a statistics test, but two of the samples you ask to complete the test pretending to be a great statistician like Florence Nightingale.'

Dear Florence,

The *t*-distribution is a family of probability distributions that describe samples taken from a population that is normally distributed. William Gosset, who worked for the Guinness Brewery, described it in a paper written under the pseudonym of 'Student'; consequently, you will often hear of 'Student's *t*-distribution' but rarely, if ever, 'Gosset's *t*-distribution'. The shapes of the distributions are symmetrical and bell-shaped, like a normal distribution. However, the exact shape of the distribution is determined by the *degrees of freedom*, which are the sample size minus 1 (*n*–1). In small samples (i.e., low degrees of freedom) the distribution is flatter than normal with more scores at the extremes, but as the degrees of freedom increase, the distribution gets closer to normal until it approximates it at a sample size of about 30 (Figure 8.11).

Best fishes,
Milton

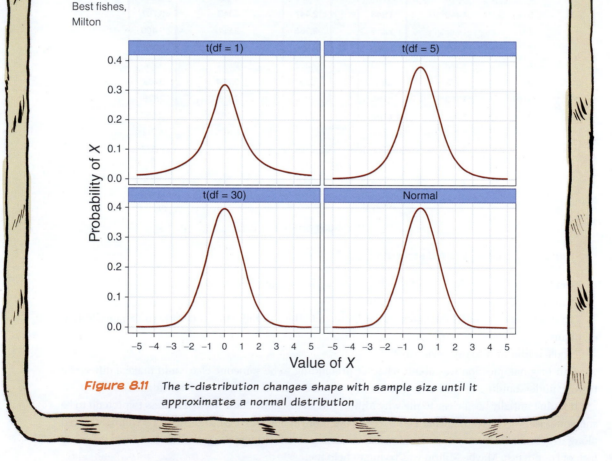

Figure 8.11   The t-distribution changes shape with sample size until it approximates a normal distribution

Milton's Meowsings 8.4   The t-distribution

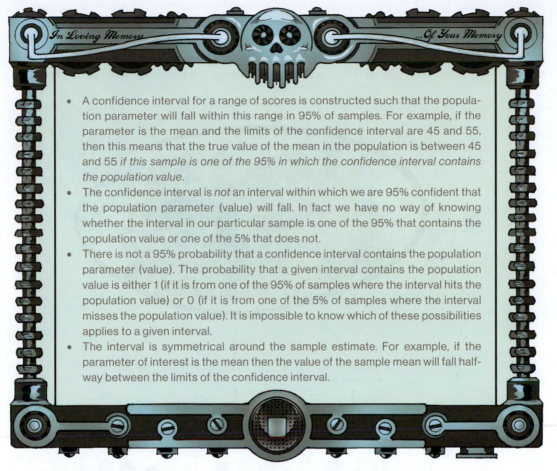

In Loving Memory   *...Of Your Memory*

- A confidence interval for a range of scores is constructed such that the population parameter will fall within this range in 95% of samples. For example, if the parameter is the mean and the limits of the confidence interval are 45 and 55, then this means that the true value of the mean in the population is between 45 and 55 *if this sample is one of the 95% in which the confidence interval contains the population value.*
- The confidence interval is *not* an interval within which we are 95% confident that the population parameter (value) will fall. In fact we have no way of knowing whether the interval in our particular sample is one of the 95% that contains the population value or one of the 5% that does not.
- There is not a 95% probability that a confidence interval contains the population parameter (value). The probability that a given interval contains the population value is either 1 (if it is from one of the 95% of samples where the interval hits the population value) or 0 (if it is from one of the 5% of samples where the interval misses the population value). It is impossible to know which of these possibilities applies to a given interval.
- The interval is symmetrical around the sample estimate. For example, if the parameter of interest is the mean then the value of the sample mean will fall halfway between the limits of the confidence interval.

Zach's Facts 8.2   *Confidence intervals*

'Do they have to wear the Victorian frock?'

'If it helps you to visualize, so be it. Anyway, you find that the two samples that did the test as someone else get an average score of 75, but those that did the test as themselves score, on average, 50. How do you explain this difference in the sample means?'

'It could just be sampling variation, because when you take different samples they can have different means.'

'Very good, but there is another explanation.'

'I guess it could be that some of the samples were told to complete the test as someone who knows about statistics.'

'*Purr*cisely. The question is, which explanation is the correct one? This is where confidence intervals can help us a little. Because the confidence interval tells us the limits within which the population mean might fall, by comparing confidence intervals of different sample statistics we can get some idea about whether they came from the same or different populations. Look at the diagram. **(FIGURE 8.12)** The sample that completed the test as themselves (sample 2) had a mean of 50% on the test, with a confidence interval ranging from 35% to 65%. Therefore, *if* this sample is one of the 95% that has a confidence interval containing the population value, then we know that the population mean is between 35% and 65%. Look at the first sample that completed the test as someone else (sample 1). They had a mean accuracy on the test of 75%, and a confidence interval ranging from 70% to 80%. The confidence interval in sample 1 and sample 2 do not overlap at all, so one confidence interval, which might contain the population mean, tells us that the population mean is somewhere between 35% and 65%, whereas the other confidence interval, which also might contain the population mean, tells us that the population mean is probably somewhere between 70% and 80%. This contradiction suggests two possibilities: (1) our confidence intervals both contain the population mean, but they come from different populations (and, therefore, so do our samples); or (2) both samples come from the same population

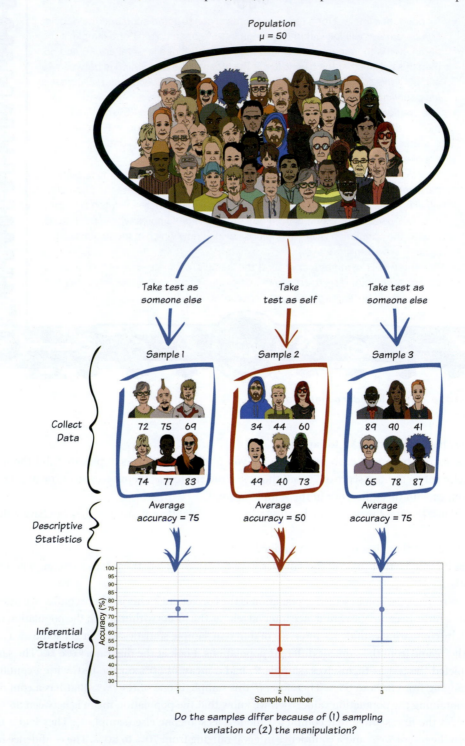

Figure 8.12 *Confidence intervals and inferential statistics*

but one or both of the confidence intervals do not contain the population mean. If we have used 95% confidence intervals then we know that the second possibility is unlikely (only 5 times in 100, or 5% of the time, does a confidence interval miss the true value), so the first explanation is more plausible.'

Milton continued his explanation. 'Look at the other sample that completed the test as someone else. **(SAMPLE 3, FIGURE 8.12)** They also had a mean accuracy on the test of 75%, but a much wider confidence interval ranging from 55% to 90%. This interval overlaps a lot with sample 2, who took the test as themselves. The fact that the confidence intervals overlap tells us that these means could plausibly come from the same population: in both cases the intervals might contain the true value of the mean (because they are constructed such that in 95% of samples they will), and both intervals overlap considerably, so they contain many similar values. Therefore, in this case you would be likely to conclude that you do not have strong evidence that the sample means are different, because the confidence intervals of both samples suggest similar population values for the mean.'

'So what if the samples come from a different population?' I asked.

'*So what?*' Milton sounded irritated. 'It has a very important implication in experimental research. When you do an experiment, you introduce some form of manipulation between two or more conditions. For example, in this case we forced some people to complete the statistics test pretending to be someone else. If we take two random samples of people, and we test them on some measure, then we expect these people to belong to the same population. If their sample means are so different as to suggest that they come from different populations, then this is likely to be because our experimental manipulation has induced a difference between the samples. In the case of the samples where the error bars do not overlap, we might conclude that the lack of overlap is because the first sample is from the population of people completing the test as someone else, whereas the

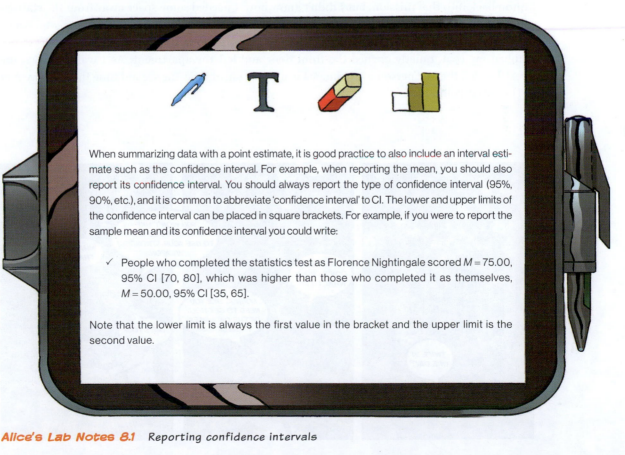

When summarizing data with a point estimate, it is good practice to also include an interval estimate such as the confidence interval. For example, when reporting the mean, you should also report its confidence interval. You should always report the type of confidence interval (95%, 90%, etc.), and it is common to abbreviate 'confidence interval' to CI. The lower and upper limits of the confidence interval can be placed in square brackets. For example, if you were to report the sample mean and its confidence interval you could write:

✓ People who completed the statistics test as Florence Nightingale scored $M = 75.00$, 95% CI [70, 80], which was higher than those who completed it as themselves, $M = 50.00$, 95% CI [35, 65].

Note that the lower limit is always the first value in the bracket and the upper limit is the second value.

Alice's Lab Notes 8.1   *Reporting confidence intervals*

second sample comes from a different population: the population of people completing the test as themselves. As such, the confidence intervals between samples provide us with a principled way to make decisions about whether the two samples come from the same or different populations. This is known as inferential statistics.'

'You know what, fluffy?'

'Don't call me fluffy,' Milton replied tersely.

'Alice explained this to me already the night before she disappeared. She showed me quite a similar diagram but without the confidence intervals. She told me that descriptive statistics summarized the data in your sample, but inferential statistics was about making generalizations about what is going on in the real world based on a sample of data that you have collected.' I compared Milton's diagram to the one Alice had shown me. **(FIGURE 8.12 & 1.3)**

Milton looked surprised. 'Indeed, and confidence intervals are a first step in doing that because they tell us something about the likely value of a parameter in a population that we have never directly measured or tested. This in turn is a useful step in testing hypotheses. However, there is a lot more to know about testing hypotheses.'

Perhaps there was, but I already felt like my brain had been put through a blender. I still wasn't sure whether the dress had been some cruel game to belittle me and fuel Milton's superiority, or if he was testing the lengths I'd go to, but one thing I did know is that he'd hit me with some really over-the-wall concepts. It had been hard, and boring, and I couldn't see why it helped me. It was as though he was trying everything he could think of to put me off of asking more questions about JIG:SAW and Alice – he did seem really uncomfortable when I'd come back and asked about JIG:SAW. I still didn't know whether I could trust him, or what his motives were, but I was quite sure I needed his help. I also needed some way to find out more about JIG:SAW, and to drag Milton back into that mission, but I didn't know how. I needed some space away from the statistical madness, and The Repository was the perfect place. I also needed to talk to someone who I knew I *could* trust. With Milton still babbling about hypothesis testing I took the dress off, grabbed my coat, quietly opened the front door and left the apartment. As I walked down the street I called the one person who I knew I could rely on, and for the second time that day, we met at Hallowed Point.

KEY TERMS

Central limit theorem

Confidence interval

Method of least squares

Precision

Sampling distribution

Standard error

Standard error of the mean

t-distribution

JIG:SAW'S PUZZLES

1   Explain the central limit theorem.

Table 8.2   Female participants' accuracy on a maths test grouped by whether they took the test under their own or a fake name (a subset of the data from Zhang et al.[12])

Own name:	20, 47, 47, 63, 30, 27, 81, 42, 35, 23, 35, 75, 24, 65, 33, 44, 53, 61, 37, 52, 43, 83, 35, 83, 66, 40, 42, 40, 32, 10, 43, 40, 44, 25, 27.
Fake name:	40, 69, 60, 41, 82, 40, 64, 22, 45, 78, 57, 64, 59, 89, 96, 38, 52, 79, 63, 50, 48, 81, 52, 33, 46, 31, 27, 40, 39, 50, 61, 81, 29.

2   Using the data in Table 8.2, what was the mean accuracy in both the fake-name group and the own-name group?

3   Using the data in Table 8.2, what was the standard error in both the fake-name group and the own-name group?

4   What is a 95% confidence interval?

5   Using the data in Table 8.2, calculate the 95% confidence interval for the mean in both the fake-name group and the own-name group.

6   Using the 95% confidence intervals for the own-name and fake-name groups, can you infer anything about whether the accuracy on the maths test was affected by whether the test was taken under their own or a fake name?

7   Using the data in Table 8.2, calculate the 99% confidence interval for the mean in both the fake-name group and the own-name group.

8   Using the data in Table 8.2, calculate the 95% confidence interval for the first 10 scores in the fake-name group.

9   What is a sampling distribution?

10   What is the difference between the standard error of the mean and the standard deviation?

IN THE NEXT CHAPTER, ZACH DISCOVERS …

You shouldn't believe everything that people tell you

Robust estimation

Bias and how to reduce it

Non-normal distributions

The bootstrap

Not to steal from his fans

9

Robust Estimation

Man without Faith or Trust

Nick was right – seeing Alice at JIG:SAW hadn't told me anything. I'd let my heart interpret the situation: seeing her made me feel betrayed and I assumed the worst, but I had no concrete evidence that she was there through choice. Perhaps she had been captured and had decided that her best strategy was to play along and do what they asked her to do. I was sure that the truth about Alice lay in finding out more about JIG:SAW. The more I thought about the past week, the more I felt that everyone was trying to stop me investigating that place: Milton seemed to think that Celia was trying to prevent me from working there and, although he acted as if he was being helpful, he was happy enough to use statistics lectures to slow my progress and quash my enthusiasm. What use had any of these lessons been to me? All they had done was distract me from probing JIG:SAW more. JIG:SAW was a puzzle: it didn't make sense that they had zombie security; it didn't make sense that Celia, a woman who seemed to make every effort to gain my attention, would lie to me to stop me working there when it would mean us spending more time together; and Rob Nutcot didn't make sense full stop.

Nick and I talked into the early hours. I asked Nick what he thought Milton's motives might be, without revealing who or what Milton was. Nick convinced me that I couldn't do much at the moment to uncover the motives of Alice's 'mysterious colleague', but that they didn't matter: he told me to focus on my own motives and take control. He was right, I had relied on other people far too much, and all of them were strangers with their own agendas. I needed to sharpen up, think for myself, and trust my own instincts more. Nick was clear-thinking and rational, pointing out that if The Head couldn't find anything out about Nutcot then no one could, but that I could try to find out more from Celia because, as my fan, she would want to help. Even if she wouldn't talk, I could perhaps get hold of the data in the JIG:SAW report and delve into it. He was right; I hated using Celia, but I was going to do it anyway.

By the time I got home, Milton had helped himself to the contents of the fridge and was curled up on my bed, his front paw twitching as though grabbing for an invisible piece of string. The Head span around peacefully, admiring the inside of the apartment. In a final attempt to avoid lying to Celia, I checked what The Head could find out about Nutcot and JIG:SAW. It was nothing. Nick was right, that was a dead-end. The Head returned to spinning and I went to bed.

The following morning I called Celia's Proteus and arranged to meet her at Occam's. The day dragged on. I was impatient to move forward – if Alice was in danger then I couldn't waste days listening to Milton waffling on about how great he was, but it would be stupid to act without information. Dinner with Celia was nice – too nice. On Nick's advice, I played up to her flirtations. I found it a little too easy. We talked about music, the band, and what life might have been like before the Reality Revolution, but she deflected all of my questions about her past and about JIG:SAW. It was a perfect evening, her only weakness was placing me on a pedestal when she should by now have realized I was leagues below her. Somehow, though, her bubble around me wouldn't burst. As we bid each other goodnight, I drew Celia in for a hug, and positioned myself so that I could slip my hand into her shoulder bag – keeping enough composure to find a memory stone; a memory stone that I hoped contained some answers.

I arrived home late again and found Milton asleep. I was secretly pleased. I had been trying to avoid Milton since the dress incident had made me question his motives, and I was struggling to trust him. As with any conflict in life, I took the easy route and simply avoided him. Perhaps he sensed my distance from him because I woke the next morning to the sound of a knock on my door, which I opened to discover a breakfast hamper.

'You must be hungry after two such long nights,' Milton said as he materialized from the bedroom to take credit for organizing the delivery. 'Unfortunately, I had to use your bank credits – I don't officially exist, remember? I will find a way to pay you back.'

Even if I had paid for it, the breakfast was a nice gesture, and as I ate Milton lowered his guard. Before it could rise again I asked him why he had invented something as destructive as the reality prism.

'Was it destructive?' he asked. 'I told you before, I created the technology, but I do not feel responsible for how people used it or their inability to deal with the consequences. I never imagined what would happen.'

His lack of responsibility irritated me. 'Batticks! It never occurred to you that giving people a tool to split reality into the actual and subjective wouldn't end in tears? Sometimes delusional beliefs about yourself are all that keep you going.'

The cat looked upset by my outburst but he remained calm. 'Sometimes it is the delusional thoughts that make people want to *stop* going,' he said. 'What about people with body dysmorphia who think they are fat when in reality they are painfully thin, or anxious people who perceive threat where there is none, or depressed people whose thoughts immerse them in negative interpretations of reality? A reality prism frees those people from their minds, allows them to see what is real and what is their interpretation of reality. The prism was a tool for good, to help people to strip away the baggage that holds them back, or to see through other people's deceptions. The prism was simply a looking glass to the truth. Think how many people's lives would benefit from knowing the truth. My guess is that if I offered you a tool to see what was real, right now, you would bite my hand off. I invented that tool, and I was vilified for that invention because people used it for the wrong reasons.'

There was a kindness in Milton's tone, a sorrow that his prism hadn't ended up helping people. I felt bad for judging him. 'Do any reality prisms still exist?' I asked.

'Officially, the WGA destroyed them, but can you imagine a governing agency *not* holding onto that type of technology?'

'What about outside of the WGA?'

'I told you – officially, they were all destroyed.'

'What about unofficially?'

'You can destroy *things*, but ideas are much harder to eradicate – and if an idea lives on it is only a matter of time before someone turns it into a reality.'

'Could *you* build a reality prism?'

'It is convenient that the WGA are unaware that I am still alive,' he said avoiding the question. My audience with Milton's lowered guard was over.

9.1 SOURCES OF BIAS

9.1.1 Extreme scores and non-normal distributions

Milton convulsed; he gagged and spluttered as he hopped backwards. He looked like he had been poisoned. Much as I sometimes hated this irascible ginger cat, I certainly didn't want him to die. A long furry projectile heaved its way out of Milton's mouth; it looked like a hairy space caterpillar.

'That is *so* much better,' the cat announced and immediately started to replenish the hair in his stomach by licking his back.

'I stole a memory stone from Celia last night,' I said, trying to regain normality.

'Really? I had assumed you were engaging in more interesting activities than that.'

I ignored his comment. 'I'm hoping it might tell me something about JIG:SAW.'

'About JIG:SAW, or about one of its more attractive members of staff? Why don't you just stalk her on *memoryBank* – that is marginally less criminal than theft.'

'Because I don't have an ID chip in my brain, and in case you hadn't noticed, *cat*, I am trying to track down the love of my life, not find a new one.' I remembered what Nick had said about taking control.

Milton raised his whiskery eyebrow again, and I put the stone into my diePad. It contained thousands of files that, fortunately, were meticulously organized. Alice would have appreciated this filing structure – she was so anally retentive about stuff like that. We located files related to JIG:SAW, and the report we had been given, but the jewel in the crown was a data file containing the raw scores of the graphs in the JIG:SAW recruitment report. I paused for a moment to bask in the horror of the fact that I felt excitement at having found a file full of numbers. Times were changing, that was for sure.

'Remind me,' said Milton. 'What did that idiot Nutcot say at the recruitment event?'

'He said that new employees were put through a genetic enhancement programme that made them stronger, faster and have better vision than those who don't work for the company.'

'Bold claims for a man who made less sense than the transformative hermeneutics of quantum gravity.'

I looked blankly at the cat.

'Never mind. Let us look at these data.' Milton used my diePad and the data file to create some different graphs than the ones presented in the JIG:SAW report. **(FIGURE 9.1)** 'Interesting, very interesting. What do you make of these?' he said pointing to them.

 CHECK YOUR BRAIN: Using what you learnt about boxplots (Section 5.3.4), what do you think about Rob Nutcot's assertion that JIG:SAW employees are faster, stronger and have better vision than employees at other companies?

I thought back to my meeting with Dr Tuff. The memory made me shudder. I recalled that boxplots showed the middle 50% of scores in the box, dots around the plot showed extreme scores, and the whiskers that stuck out of the box showed the top and bottom 25% of scores excluding those extreme scores. The horizontal line within the box showed the median.

Looking first at footspeed **(FIGURE 9.1, TOP)**, I was reminded that for code 1318 workers, there was a boxplot only for JIG:SAW. Tuff had suggested that this was because JIG:SAW might be the only company to employ this kind of worker. In any case, these workers had a box that was much longer than all other categories of workers, and the whiskers stuck out to the very extremes of the scale, from 0 to almost 30 miles per hour. I pointed this out to Milton.

'Fishy, isn't it? That group contains workers who literally do not move at all – they have a footspeed of 0 mph – and some that run at just above the current limit of human ability, which is about 27 mph. That is a very heterogeneous bunch of people.'

'Hetero-what?'

'Heterogeneous – it means diverse, as opposed to homogenous, which means similar. Also notice that the bottom of the box for the code 1318 workers is at the same value as the bottom of the *whiskers* for all the other groups. This suggests that the bottom 25% of the code 1318 workers are slower than the slowest people in every other group. There is a substantial proportion of these workers who are very slow indeed. Unusually slow.'

'Why would that be?'

'Who can tell, apart from perhaps Nutcot and that woman to whom you deny an attraction? However, we cannot ask them. Now, what do you notice about the other groups?'

'Looking at the horizontal lines within the boxes, in all groups they are slightly lower for the non-employees than the JIG:SAW employees, but only by a very tiny amount, and the boxes overlap quite a bit between JIG:SAW and non-JIG:SAW employees. This sort of suggests that their median footspeeds are quite similar.'

'*Purr*cisely, human, and although I did not mention this at the time, that is what Nutcot's boxplot **(FIGURE 5.6)**, which collapsed the data across the different professions, showed too. It showed a lot of extreme scores and variability in the JIG:SAW group, but also that the medians were not a lot different.'

'Doesn't this graph show that the variability in speed comes mostly from the code 1318 workers?'

Milton nodded. 'What do you notice about visual acuity?' **(FIGURE 9.1, MIDDLE)**

'It's all about the code 1318 workers again: their data are really strange. The box and whiskers are all very short suggesting that they have very similar scores, and these scores are all incredibly low. They're all practically blind!'

'*All* of them?' replied Milton, and circled a dot on the graph.

'Man, that's over the wall: that person has insanely good vision; not only miles better than the other code 1318 workers, but even better than any worker in any other group.'

'What about the other groups of workers?'

'The horizontal lines in the boxes are all higher for the JIG:SAW workers than for the non-employees. That's what Nutcot told us: that JIG:SAW workers have better vision.'

'But does it *really* show that? The JIG:SAW scientists contain quite a few extreme scores, and the boxes for the security workers almost completely overlap for JIG:SAW employees and non-employees. The picture is not as clear-cut as you might think – what impact might those extreme scores have? More interesting is the strength data. What do you notice about those scores?' **(FIGURE 9.1, BOTTOM)**

'For all of the professions the boxes for non-employees and JIG:SAW employees overlap almost entirely and the horizontal lines in the boxes are really similar, suggesting no real difference in the median strength between those at JIG:SAW and everyone else. Also, the 1318 worker group are really weird again.'

'If you are going to embrace science then you need to start being more precise than saying things are weird!'

I sighed. 'Fair play – look at the boxplot. The horizontal line in the box is way higher than for any other group, so the median strength is really high in this group. The other thing is that the whisker at the top of the box is really long. Longer than one of yours! In fact, looking from the bottom of the lower whisker to the top of the upper one, the range of scores is over the wall. It looks like a lot of variability in strength. The median (the horizontal line within the box), though, is above the top scores in the other groups. This means that the top 50% of these workers are stronger than the strongest person in the other groups. This group is, like, full of super-people.'

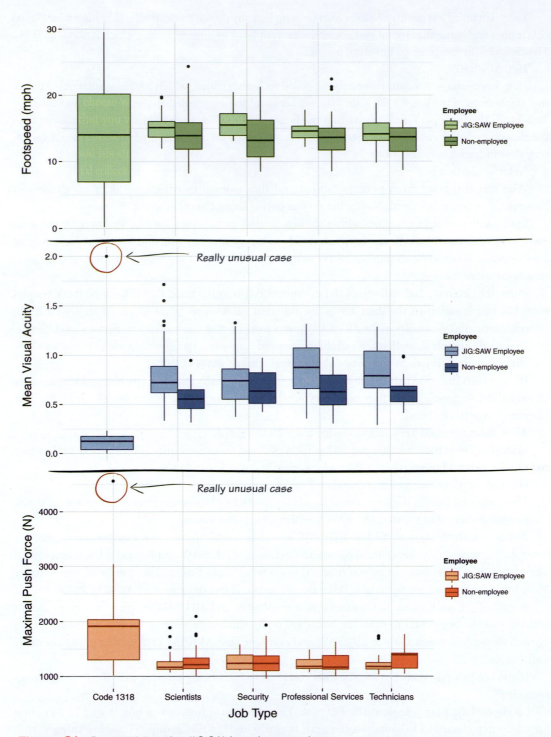

Figure 9.1 *Re-examining the JIG:SAW employment data*

Milton helpfully circled another dot on the graph and looked at me expectantly.

'Frip!' I said as I stared at the dot. 'That person is an extreme score even within this group who are already insanely strong: even the extreme cases in other groups only have scores of 2000, but this freak is more than double that. I wouldn't want to meet that mutant on a dark night – it could rip you in two.'

'The question to ask is whether the person who has exceptional vision is also the person who has inhuman strength? If so, we might also wonder where that person lies in the footspeed data.'

Milton was spooking me. What the hell was Alice involved in at this place? 'Why is Alice working for people who create freaks like that? She's a good person, she would never support a programme like this?'

'Would she not?' questioned Milton. His words fertilized the seeds of doubt already sprouting in my mind. Did I really know Alice at all?

As I contemplated this thought, Milton pawed frantically at my diePad screen, punctuating his activity with deep sighs. Eventually he said, 'These data are very messy. These extreme cases might be biasing the summary results that Nutcot presented at his recruitment event.'

I had my doubts. 'The guy is odd, but he's the head of JIG:SAW, so he must be clever – he wouldn't be daft enough not to spot bias in his data.'

'By the way Nutcot talks, I would think he is daft enough to tie his own shoelaces together before taking a run.'

The cat paused to consider his words. 'You are very naïve – it really is quite endearing. People are not always honest with their data, especially people who want to recruit naïve humans into their company. I have plotted two histograms of the strength data: one showing JIG:SAW and the other the non-employees. Look – it is clear that the summary statistic is biased, especially in the JIG:SAW group. **(FIGURE 9.2)** Let me explain. When we spoke a few days ago, I told you how we use samples to estimate values in the population. For example, we use the sample mean to estimate the population mean. We can do this both with a single value estimate, known as a point estimate, or by constructing a confidence interval around that value.' **(CHAPTER 8)**

'Yes, I remember. A 95% confidence interval will, in 95% of samples, contain the true population value.'

'*Purr*fectly true. The thing is, these estimates can be biased. A biased estimator –'

'– is a statistic, from a sample, that doesn't, on average, equal the corresponding population parameter. You told me this before, when you explained variance.' **(SECTION 4.3)**

Milton looked suspicious, as though I was pulling a confidence trick by remembering something he had already told me.

I felt in the zone. 'I also remember your saying that the mean could be biased by extreme scores.' **(SECTION 4.2.3)**

'Indeed it can, and it has been in these data. Look.' Milton pointed at the diagram he had drawn. **(FIGURE 9.2)** 'The green blocks show the middle 60% of scores, and the blue blocks show the most extreme 20% at the top and bottom of the distributions. What do you notice about the two distributions?'

CHECK YOUR BRAIN: *Using what you learned about histograms (Section 3.1.3), compare the two histograms in Figure 9.2.*

I studied the image. The two histograms were quite similar in that they both had positive skew and the bulk of scores fell between values of 900 and 2100. However, the JIG:SAW data had four extreme cases, one of which we'd seen on the boxplots had a value over 4400. I gave Milton my verdict.

'Well done. Both groups do have skewed distributions, and let us look at how this affects the sample estimate of the mean. The mean is, after all, the summary that Nutcot used to demonstrate that his workforce were stronger than non-employees. On the diagram I have worked out the mean of the whole sample – that is the mean that Nutcot would have used. It is 1351 N for the JIG:SAW group and only 1260 N for the non-employees.'

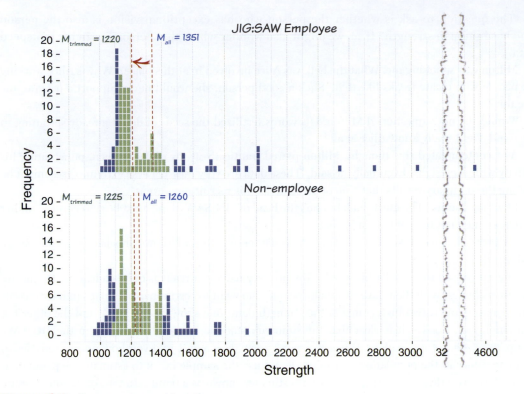

Figure 9.2 *Extreme scores bias the mean*

'So, the JIG:SAW group is stronger.'

'It seems so, but look at what happens if we calculate the mean ignoring the top and bottom 20% of scores.'

'You mean base it on only the green squares – the middle 60% of scores?'

'*Purr*cisely. Notice that for the non-employees the mean falls from 1260 N to 1225 N, so it gets a bit smaller because the extreme high scores are not there to inflate its value. However, this reduction is small in comparison to what happens in the JIG:SAW group, where the mean drops from 1351 N for the whole sample to only 1220 N when we ignore the extremes.'

'Frip! It drops by more than 130 N!'

'Now, what do you conclude if you compare the means that ignore the extremes of the groups?'

The new mean was 1225 N in the non-employees and 1220 N in the JIG:SAW group. I allowed myself a minute for the penny to drop.

'Oh, wow, they're almost the same. There isn't a difference between the groups any more!'

Milton nodded enthusiastically. 'These extreme scores and skewed distributions not only affect point estimates like the mean, they also have a profound impact on the standard error, and therefore the confidence interval. Imagine you have five scores: 1, 2, 3, 4, and 5. The mean of those scores is 3, and the variance is 2.5.' Milton scratched out a diagram on my wall with his claw. **(FIGURE 9.3)** 'Imagine we change the final value from 5 to 6, and then change it to 7, 8, 9 and finally 10, so that with each change it becomes more of an outlier. Also imagine that we recalculate the mean and the variance each time we change that final value. This graph shows the result. As the final value of 5 increases up to 10, the mean steadily increases from 3 to 4, but the variance increases exponentially from 2.5 to 12.5. This happens because the variance is based on the squared difference between each score and the mean, so not only is the distance between

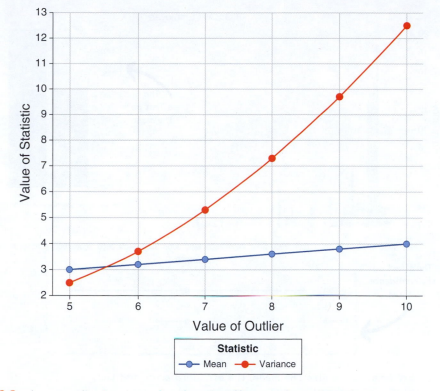

Figure 9.3 *As an outlier increases in value, the effect on the variance is even more dramatic than on the mean*

the mean and the outlier big, but this big difference gets squared, resulting in an even greater bias in the variance. Now, how do we estimate the standard error?'

I thought back to the equation that Milton had taught me. **(EQUATION 8.3)** 'It's the sample standard deviation divided by the square root of the sample size.'

'Yes, and the sample standard deviation is related to the variance.' **(SECTION 4.3)**

'Isn't it the square root?'

'*Claw*rect, which means that outliers bias the variance, then they also bias the standard error, and what do we use the standard error for?'

I thought back to what Milton told me about confidence intervals. **(EQUATION 8.4)** 'The confidence interval is estimated using the standard error, isn't it?'

'Excellent. A 95% confidence interval will fall 1.96 standard errors each side of the mean. All of which means that if outliers bias the variance, which they do, then they also bias the standard error and the confidence interval.'

Milton took his earlier image on my diePad **(FIGURE 9.2)** and, focusing on the histogram for the JIG:SAW group, he added some panels to illustrate how the extreme scores affected the mean and confidence interval. **(FIGURE 9.4)**

'Look. This diagram illustrates what we have already seen about the mean: if we look at only the green scores and trim away the scores at the extremes, the mean is dramatically reduced – but look at what happens to the confidence interval. With all of the data the confidence interval is very wide – it ranges from about 80 points below the mean to 80 points above – meaning that our estimate of the population value is very wide too. It is imprecise because it suggests that the population value might be a value within a very wide range. However, if we trim off the top and bottom extreme scores, the

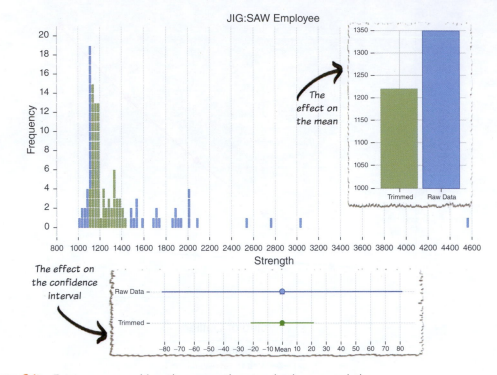

Figure 9.4   *Extreme scores bias the mean, the standard error and the confidence interval*

resulting confidence interval is substantially narrower: it ranges from only 20 points below the mean to 20 above, which is about a quarter of the width of the interval when all of the data were included. By removing the extreme scores we have got a more precise interval estimate of the population value.'

'So, you're saying that extreme scores like in this data set can bias our estimates of the population parameter and also the standard error and confidence interval around those estimates.'

Milton nodded and smiled.

9.1.2 The mixed normal distribution

'If outliers can bias our estimates, it's a good job that they're so easy to spot with histograms and box-plots,' I said, with a relieved sort of chuckle, although I wasn't sure what I was relieved about, given how little I cared about statistics.

'Are they though?' Milton sounded as if he was concealing an evil master plan. 'Most people think of extreme scores as being a small number of obvious scores, but there are ways that unusual scores can hide in the data but still create bias.'

'Don't tell me, there are scores that don little invisibility cloaks and run around the data set causing havoc,' I joked.

'Sort of.'

'Don't be ridiculous – everyone knows that invisibility cloaks don't exist.'

'Do they not?' It was that evil master plan tone again. Not for the first time, I felt that Milton might know a lot more than he let on. 'You are being too literal,' he continued. 'Let me explain. Imagine we looked at the visual acuity scores for the JIG:SAW sample overall. I have produced a histogram, and on the whole it looks fairly normally distributed.' **(FIGURE 9.5)**

'Why are the bars made up of different colours?'

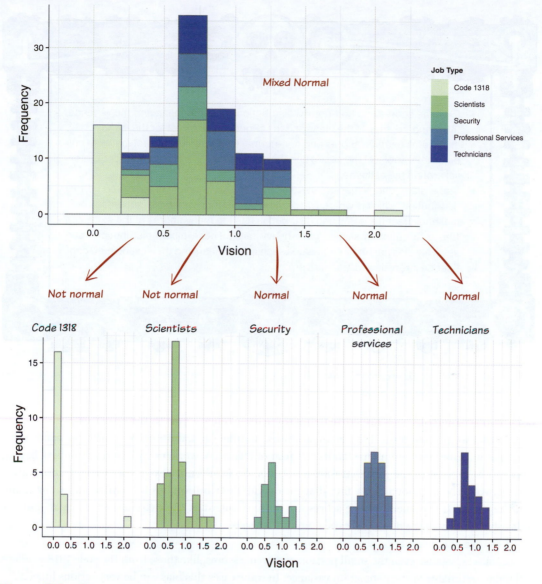

Figure 9.5 *The mixed normal distribution*

'I wanted to show you from which employees the scores come, and below it I have separated out the distributions for each of these groups. Interesting, is it not?'

I wasn't sure what I was supposed to find interesting. Milton filled me in.

'The distribution for code 1318 workers is very obviously not normal, and the distribution for scientists is similarly not normal because it is heavily skewed. However, the distributions for security, professional services and technicians are normal.'

I didn't get it. I must have looked vacant because the cat broke my silence with an explanation.

'Think about it. If we analysed the JIG:SAW data overall, and we tested whether the distribution was normal, we would conclude that it is, but actually it is not. It is what is known as a **mixed normal distribution** or **contaminated normal distribution**.[33] Most of the scores come from normal distributions, but a small proportion do not. The overall distribution is made up of distinct

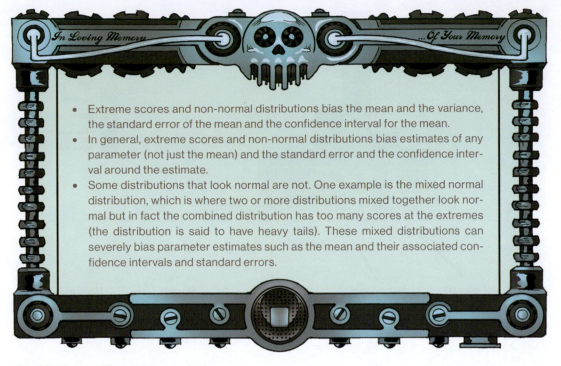

- Extreme scores and non-normal distributions bias the mean and the variance, the standard error of the mean and the confidence interval for the mean.
- In general, extreme scores and non-normal distributions bias estimates of any parameter (not just the mean) and the standard error and the confidence interval around the estimate.
- Some distributions that look normal are not. One example is the mixed normal distribution, which is where two or more distributions mixed together look normal but in fact the combined distribution has too many scores at the extremes (the distribution is said to have heavy tails). These mixed distributions can severely bias parameter estimates such as the mean and their associated confidence intervals and standard errors.

Zach's Facts 9.1   *Sources of bias*

populations, some of which are normal and some of which are not. In this example, we are fortunate in that we can see these distinct populations and their distributions, but often we cannot. For example, imagine we were interested in comparing JIG:SAW workers with non-employees but we were not interested in the jobs that individuals do. We would not have recorded that information and we would be oblivious to the fact that the overall distribution has been affected by, for example, the code 1318 workers, whose scores are more frequent at the extremes of "normal" but not radically different like you might expect an outlier to be.'

'Why does this matter?'

'It matters because even the small portion of extreme scores, like those from the code 1318 workers, will inflate estimates of the population variance. In some cases this bias can be very serious indeed'.[32]

'And we just discussed how the variance is used to estimate the standard error, and the standard error is used to calculate the confidence interval, so if the variance is biased then the standard error and confidence interval will be too.'

'*Purr*cisely.'

I hadn't entirely grasped the consequences of what Milton was saying, but at the very least it was an oversimplification to say that JIG:SAW employees were stronger, faster and had better vision than non-employees. In the case of strength that seemed to be a complete lie, and for vision and speed there was something strange going on with the code 1318 workers. There was also the question of whether the insanely strong code 1318 worker was also the one with remarkable vision.

9.2   A GREAT MISTAKE

Sticking with my vow to take charge of the situation, I decided to confront Celia and Nutcot with what I had found. Milton said that this was 'an act of immense stupidity', because it would play my

hand too soon. I was getting impatient for answers, though, and I didn't know whether Milton could be trusted anyhow. I was sick and tired of not knowing what was happening with Alice. I went from missing her, to anger that she might have left me without an explanation, to feeling sick with worry that something terrible was happening to her. I called Celia's Proteus, and turned on the charm again. Shamefully, I told her that I missed her and how great it would be if we could see each other more, like if we worked together. I said that even though I knew I'd failed their tests I was sure that if I could talk to Nutcot I could convince him that I could be useful to JIG:SAW. I told her I had been learning about data analysis, and we even got into an oddly flirtatious conversation about statistics: I dropped a totally cheesy line about how she'd be an outlier on being clever and interesting, and she rolled straight back with how I was a model she'd like to fit to her data. I was surprised how much I enjoyed the geeky banter, but even more so when she agreed to persuade Nutcot to meet me.

The next day I awoke full of nerves. I hadn't slept well and I was worried. With a bit of distance I could see that Milton was right: meeting Nutcot and confronting him with what we'd found was a dangerous game. We met at the Hermes café at the far edge of Antevorta. Antevorta was the ultra-modern district and was filled with buildings that used programmable matter to change shape to accommodate the spatial demands of the city. It made Antevorta seem alive: like an organism constantly evolving. Janus, where I lived, was sandwiched between this district and the 'old' district of Postverta. Janus was a mix of the two: old-style gothic buildings interwoven with modernist programmable designs and some buildings that merged the two. I'd never been to Hermes – it was too expensive – but it was legendary for its dining booths of programmable matter that changed to match whatever design and ambiance the diners desired.

Milton and I took a bubble to Hermes, and he gave me a pep talk on the way. He told me not to mention our trip to JIG:SAW and that, if Alice had been abducted, mentioning my connection to her might endanger her. Much as I still had doubts about whether to trust the cat, his advice made sense.

Once at Hermes, we were taken to a booth that immediately transformed into my ideal: the chairs and tabletop turned to dark leather with studs and the walls grew backlit photos of my favourite bands from the pre-revolution. I found myself nervously tapping the table, while Milton made himself comfortable in the rucksack beside me.

Soon enough the front doors swung open and I felt my heart pounding as Celia made eye contact and accelerated towards me with a beaming smile. Nutcot followed behind her, his gangly walk making his head wobble with each step, as though he was looking around for some neck muscles. I stood as they reached the table, and Celia threw her arms around me and grabbed me like a long lost friend. 'Hi, rockstar!' she whispered in my ear, as though we were engaged in a conspiracy that needed to be kept from Nutcot. Nutcot held out his hand and smiled, what I assumed he believed to be a genuine and reassuring smile but that actually sent shivers down me. He had the same pungent aftershave on as the last time we met. 'Good to have some face time, Zach,' he said. I thought I heard a 'tut' from my rucksack.

We sat and ordered drinks. I ordered a skinny latte with a dollop of ice cream. Celia positioned herself closely next to me. Too close. Nutcot sat opposite and repeated my order word for word. That was strange, because I was the only person I knew who ever asked for a dollop of ice cream in my coffee.

'Let's boil the fog. Zach, why don't you tee us off,' said Nutcot.

I could feel my arms begin to shake as a wave of nerves crashed through me. Celia, sensing my apprehension, gave my forearm a reassuring squeeze.

Careful to heed Milton's advice not to mention our trip to JIG:SAW, or Alice's disappearance, I focused on a version of reality in which my failure to get recruited by Celia into JIG:SAW had led me to become interested in the data in the report I had been given at the recruitment event. I explained how I had discovered that Celia had compared me to the code 1318 workers and not the technicians, who were the group where there were vacancies. **(SECTION 6.5)** I told them that I had obtained the raw data from the report and that the code 1318 group looked very strange, and that I believed that their data on JIG:SAW workers being stronger, faster and having better vision were biased.

As I talked, Rob Nutcot watched me. He frowned as I frowned, he tilted his head as I tilted my head, and as my eyes dipped to break eye contact – as they often did – his must have too because every time I looked up his eyes followed as though caught in the backdraft of mine. In contrast, Celia's body language became increasingly distant: as I finished, I noticed she'd moved away slightly, her hand was no longer reassuring me, and she stared at the table as though trying to freeze it. She bit her lower lip hard. An awkward silence descended. Nutcot's aftershave seemed to get stronger.

'Great that you want to peel the bunion, Zach. Awesome to mindshare your deep dive into the bricks and mortar of JIG:SAW. You're the kind of proactive, low hanging fruit that we like to pick moving forward into the viral gen.'

I had no clue what he was talking about and, unlike our last meeting, Celia was in no mood to interpret. Her anger was unspoken, but tangible.

'Your analytics are robust in the round. However, you lack the paradigm shift to truly see the headlights.' I thought I heard a puff of air and the aftershave got stronger still. 'Once you break through the clutter, the data provide synergistic mash that shows an organic forward vision of disruptive innovation. I assure you our promise of genetic wellness and fulfilment is mission critical and holds up under scrutiny.'

I felt hypnotized by all these words I didn't understand, and the smell was intoxicating. But then what had seemed like a word salad started to make sense, like actual sentences that created a patchwork of convincing logic. I smiled, he smiled; I nodded, he nodded. He was right: the data supported his claims. I wasn't sure why I had ever doubted him. Celia stared at the table in silence.

9.3 REDUCING BIAS

'That went well,' said Milton sarcastically after Nutcot and Celia had left. Celia had barely spoken as we parted; she offered me a very deliberate handshake and a formal 'Goodbye, Zach'. She looked upset; obviously she realized that I had lied about why I wanted to meet her, but perhaps she realized I'd tricked her to get the data too. One thing was certain; she didn't want to be near me any more. I was surprised by how flat it made me feel – I had been flattered by her attention because in a way she reminded me of how things were when I first met Alice: the unconditional admiration that new love brings, which now lay buried under her science books. I was guilty of burying my admiration for Alice too: I always felt proud of her achievements but rarely told her for fear that it would remind her of my lack of them. Milton interrupted my wallowing.

'Did you really believe Nutcot's reassurances?'

'Yeah, why not?'

'Because morphic resonance makes more sense than that gibbering fool.'

'Morphic what?' The cat stared in disbelief at my not understanding another of his obscure references. 'It's freaks – at first I *did* think Nutcot was talking nonsense too, but then it sort of made sense. Now he's gone I don't know *why* he made sense, and when I think back to his words, they *were* gibberish. I mean, what does "paradigm shift to truly see the headlights" actually mean?'

'It means that your rectum has taken over your speech functions,' Milton replied. 'All we have learnt from this meeting is that it was a terrible idea to speak to them – as I said it would be – and that you would have been better off asking me to help you explore the data.'

'You mean that you know how to overcome bias from extreme scores and weird distributions? Why didn't you tell me?'

'Far be it from me to ruin a perfectly idiotic plan to confront employees of JIG:SAW with conspiracy theories.'

That cat really could be an eisel sometimes.

'There are various ways to correct for bias,' Milton began, 'all of which have pros and cons. The various methods fall into two categories: (1) changing the data; and (2) changing the way you estimate things. You can change the data by changing scores to adjust the shape of the distribution or to reduce the impact of extreme scores. Techniques in this category include transforming the data, trimming the data and winsorizing the data. However, you can also leave the data alone and adjust the way that you estimate the parameter of interest and the associated standard error and confidence interval. Rather than assuming a normal sampling distribution, you can instead use a technique called bootstrapping to estimate the standard error and confidence interval from the data without requiring anything to be normal. Some methods mix and match these techniques – for example, they might trim the data *and* use bootstrapping.[34] A statistic that is reliable even when its assumptions are not met is called robust; for example, estimating the standard error and confidence interval using bootstrapping does not assume that the sampling distribution is normal, so this would be called **robust estimation**, because the estimates are reliable regardless of the shape of the sampling distribution.'

9.3.1 Transforming data

I asked what Milton meant by transforming the data.

'The idea behind transformations is that you do something to every score to correct for distributional problems, outliers, and so forth. For example, the JIG:SAW strength data were very positively skewed and seemed to have a few quite extreme scores.' Milton plotted a histogram of the strength scores on my diePad. **(FIGURE 9.6, TOP)** 'Now, imagine we wanted to try to reduce the impact of the extreme scores, or correct for the skew. We might do that by taking the square root of the strength values and working with these transformed scores.'

'Why would that affect the shape of the distribution?'

'Think about it; what is the square root of 1?'

'It's 1, isn't it?'

'*Purr*fectly correct – taking the square root does not change the score at all. Now, what is the square root of 100?'

Table 9.1 Data transformations and their uses

Transform	Effect	Issues	Before	After
Log: $\log(x_i)$	Taking the logarithm (typically the natural logarithm) of a set of scores reduces positive skew and dampens the impact of extreme high scores by squashing the right tail of the distribution.	You cannot log zero or negative numbers. If your data set contains zeros or negative scores then, before you take the log, add a value to every score that makes the lowest score a positive number (e.g., if the lowest score is −3, add 4 to every score before taking the log so that the lowest score is 1 rather than −3.	1 10 25 50 100	0 2.3 3.2 3.9 4.6
Square root: x_i	The square root reduces large values more than small values; therefore, it reduces positive skew and the impact of extreme high scores.	Negative numbers do not have a square root (see above). If your data set contains negative scores then, before you take the square root, add a value to every score that makes the lowest score a positive number.	1 10 25 50 100	1 3.2 5 7.1 10
Reciprocal: $1/x_i$	Dividing 1 by each score also reduces the impact of large scores and reduces positive skew.	This transformation reverses the scores: scores that were originally large become small (close to zero), but scores that were originally small become large. You can overcome this by reversing the scores before the transformation (Milton's Meowsings 2.1).	1 10 25 50 100	1.00 0.10 0.04 0.02 0.01
Reverse score: $(x_{\text{Highest}} + x_{\text{Lowest}}) - x_i$	Any of the above transformations can be used to correct negatively skewed data, or reduce the impact of low extreme scores, if you reverse the scores before the transformation (Milton's Meowsings 2.1).		0 10 25 50 100	100 90 75 50 0

I sensed Milton was keeping things simple for me. 'Erm, it's 10.'

'Indeed – the square root is a lot smaller than the original value. What this example illustrates is that small scores are relatively unaffected by the square-root transformation but large scores are heavily reduced. The net effect is that the right end of the distribution (where the high scores are) is pushed towards the smaller scores.' Milton drew a histogram of the square root of the strength scores below his original histogram. **(FIGURE 9.6, BOTTOM)**

'So, basically you're saying that extreme high scores will be reduced a lot by taking the square root, but smaller scores will be reduced by only a small amount.'

'*Purr*cisely, and there are other transformations that have a similar effect, such as taking the natural logarithm of scores, or even the reciprocal.'

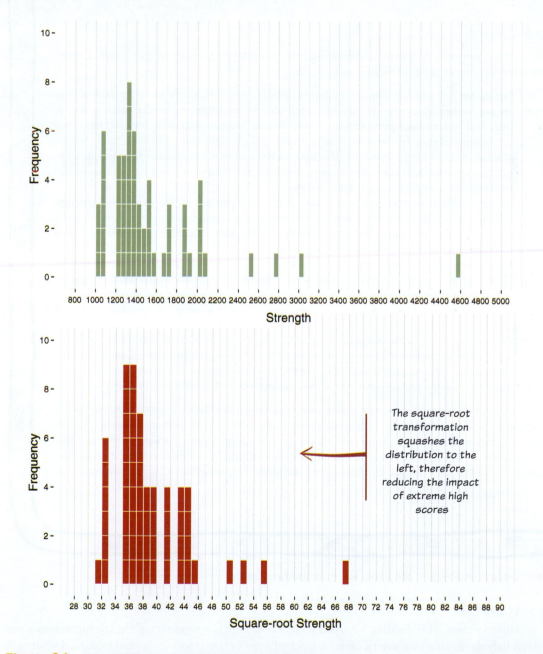

The square-root transformation squashes the distribution to the left, therefore reducing the impact of extreme high scores

Figure 9.6   *The square-root transformation reduces the impact of extremely high scores*

Dear Human,

It is common for researchers to transform their data to correct for problems in the distribution, but here are some reasons not to transform your data.

1. The central limit theorem (Section 8.2.3) tells us that for big samples the sampling distribution is normal irrespective of what the data look like. If our data are not normal but our samples are big, then you need not even worry about normality because the sampling distribution will be normal and that is what matters. There is the issue of how big is 'big'. Early research showed that samples of 40 would do the job in light-tailed distributions; however, with heavy-tailed distributions larger samples are necessary to invoke the central limit theorem.[34] This work suggests that transformations might be useful for heavy-tailed distributions.

2. By transforming the data you change the hypothesis being tested. For example, if you log-transform scores and compare means you are comparing geometric means rather than arithmetic means. Transformation also affects how you interpret the data because the data now relate to a different construct to the one originally measured.[35]

3. In small samples, when transforming data might be most useful because you cannot rely on the central limit theorem, you do not have enough information to know one way or another whether your data are normal. Bootstrapping was designed precisely for the situation of small samples and is a better alternative because it does not rely on your knowing whether the sampling distribution is normal.

4. The consequences for the statistical model of applying the 'wrong' transformation could be worse than the consequences of analysing the untransformed scores. The issue here is essentially that you need to know whether the statistical models you apply perform better on transformed data than they do when applied to data that violate the assumption that the transformation corrects.

On balance, if you are transforming data because you are worried that your data are not normal and that this will bias your confidence intervals and standard errors, then you are probably wisest just to estimate standard errors and confidence intervals with bootstrapping, which does not assume normality. One situation in which transformations can be useful is to change the form of relationship between variables – for example, if you want to make a non-linear relationship linear (see Milton's Meowsings 12.2).

Best fishes,
Milton

Milton's Meowsings 9.1 *Why not to transform data*

'What's that?'

Milton sighed. 'It is dividing 1 by each score. Look, here is a summary of the transformations and what they do.' Milton produced a table of different ways to transform scores and explained what each transformation did. (TABLE 9.1)

It all seemed a bit dodgy to me. You take the data that you actually collected and you change them. Surely that's cheating, because you don't end up analysing the scores that you actually observed? I put this idea to Milton.

'It might seem that way, but you apply the same transformation to every score in the data set, so although you change the form of the relationship between variables that you have measured, the relative differences between scores on a given variable is unchanged. Therefore, we can legitimately quantify those relationships. You do need to be careful if you are interested in *differences* between variables, because the transformation changes the units of measurement.'

Milton noticed me glazing over and tapped my arm. 'Let me explain,' he said. 'Imagine we were interested in the relationship between strength and visual acuity in the JIG:SAW data. If we transform strength, then this does not change the relationship between strength and visual acuity because those who score highly on strength before the transformation will be the same people that score highly after the transformation. However, if we were to compare the mean strength of JIG:SAW workers with that of non-employees and we take the square root of strength only in the JIG:SAW group, then we have changed the mean in that group: we have made it smaller by making each score smaller by taking the square root. If we now compare this mean with that in non-employees then the comparison is nonsense because we have changed the mean in one group (by transforming scores) but not the other (because we did not transform scores). To put it another way, we would be comparing means based on different units of measurement: for the non-employees group the units of measurement would be newtons (N), but for the JIG:SAW group it would be square-root newtons ($\sqrt{\text{N}}$). Therefore, if we want to compare means in different groups we have to apply the same transformation to all groups. Likewise, if we want to compare the same variable measured at different times, then if we transform that variable at one time point we need to transform it at every time point.'

That made sense. I asked Milton which of the transformations would normally be used, or whether people tried them all out to see which one works the best.

'You can use trial and error, but personally I would not use any of them. Get me some milk.'

I returned to find a note on my diePad, which I read. **(MEOWSINGS 9.1)**

'So, you have just spent 10 minutes telling me about something you wouldn't do?'

'*Purr*cisely.'

Eisel.

9.3.2 Trimming data

'If you wouldn't transform the data, what would you do?'

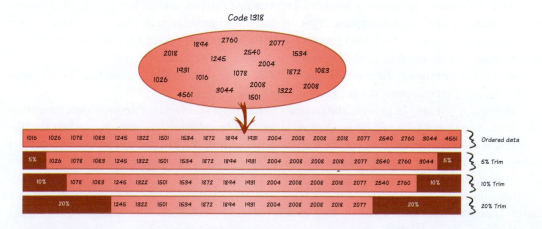

Figure 9.7   Illustration of trimming data

'As we have seen, the problem with extreme scores and non-normal distributions is that they bias estimates of statistics such as the mean, but also their confidence intervals. If we remove or trim these extreme scores then we reduce this bias.'

'Delete the scores that you don't like the look of?'

'No, remove a percentage of scores to stabilize the mean and its confidence interval; for example, delete the 20% of highest and lowest scores.' Milton borrowed my diePad again and produced a diagram. **(FIGURE 9.7)** 'Look, here are the strength scores for the code 1318 JIG:SAW workers. I have also listed them in order. Most of the scores fall between 1000 and 2500, but there is one very extreme score of 4561, another quite extreme score of 3044, and another couple that are above 2500. These four scores especially seem very unusual. There are 20 scores in total, so if we were to trim 5% of the data from either end, this would mean deleting 1 score at each extreme (5% of 20 is 1). The diagram shows that this involves deleting 1016 and 4561. This trimming gets rid of our really extreme score. If we calculate the mean in a sample that has been trimmed in this way, it is called a **trimmed mean**. In this example, the mean for the remaining 18 scores would be called the 5% trimmed mean because it is the mean after the top and bottom 5% of scores have been removed. Similarly, we could trim 10% of scores from either end. With 20 original scores, 10% is 2, so this entails deleting 2 scores from each extreme, as shown in the diagram. Taking the mean of the remaining 16 scores would give us the 10% trimmed mean. Finally, the diagram shows what happens if we trim 20% of the data from the two ends of the distribution. This would entail trimming 4 scores from each end, and the mean of the remaining 12 scores is the 20% trimmed mean. If you take trimming to its extreme then you get the median, which is the value left when you have trimmed all but the middle score.'

CHECK YOUR BRAIN: Compute the mean of the strength scores for the code 1318 workers. Now compute them for the 5%, 10% and 20% trimmed data.

'What effect does trimming the data have?'

'You have already seen the effect,' replied Milton as he flicked through my diePad to one of his earlier diagrams. **(FIGURE 9.2)** 'Remember this diagram shows the strength scores for the JIG:SAW employees and non-employees. The blue blocks are scores in the top and bottom 20% of scores in their respective group, and the green scores are the middle 60% of scores. Look at the means. If we include all of the scores, the mean for the JIG:SAW group is 1351 and for the non-employees is 1260. Both of these means have been inflated by some extreme scores, but the JIG:SAW mean more so than the non-employee mean. If you look at the trimmed means, that is, the mean of just the green blocks, then you find it is 1220 for the JIG:SAW group and 1225 for the non-employees. In both cases the means shift to the left when the data are trimmed.'

'Sick! Before trimming, the mean of the JIG:SAW group is quite a bit higher than for the non-employees, but after trimming the group means are really similar.'

'Interesting, is it not? In general, the accuracy of the mean and variance depends on a symmetrical distribution, but a trimmed mean (and variance) will be relatively accurate even when the distribution is not symmetrical, because by trimming the ends of the distribution we remove outliers and skew that bias these statistics. Some robust methods work by taking advantage of the properties of the trimmed mean.'

'Using the trimmed means, the difference between JIG:SAW employees and non-employees that Nutcot claimed doesn't hold up at all: their means are really similar. I wonder what happens for the visual acuity and speed data?'

Milton set to work on my diePad, tapping away, writing code to process the data, and then producing a series of graphs. **(FIGURE 9.8)** He purred contentedly as he set about his task. 'Here, see for yourself,' he said, passing my diePad back to me with a grin.

CHECK YOUR BRAIN: Compare the difference in the raw and trimmed means for JIG:SAW employees and non-employees in Figure 9.8. Are the patterns different for the raw and trimmed means?

It looked to me like the differences between JIG:SAW employees and non-employees were fairly similar for the raw data and trimmed data when it came to vision and speed; it was only strength where the difference disappeared. Milton confirmed my interpretation.

9.3.3 M-estimators

'How do you know how much of the data to trim?' I asked.

'A good question, human. There is good evidence that in general a 20% trim will produce robust statistics.[32] However, some people use a rule based on the standard deviation, which is not usually a sensible idea.' Milton looked at the clock. 'I'll explain later,' he said as a note appeared on my diePad. **(MEOWSINGS 9.2)** 'A better alternative is to use an **M-estimator.** An M-estimator is similar to a statistic based on trimmed data, except that the amount of trimming is determined empirically. In other words, rather than the scientist deciding before the

Dear Human,

Rather than trimming a fixed percentage of the data, scientists sometimes trim their data using a rule based on the standard deviation. For example, they might trim scores that lie outside 3 standard deviations from the mean. Logically you can understand why, because we know from the normal distribution (Section 7.2.3) that scores more than 3 standard deviations from the mean are very unusual. Unfortunately, we also know that extreme scores inflate the standard deviation (Section 4.3.3). By using a standard deviation rule you are trimming data based on a threshold that has been inflated by the extreme scores that you are trying to exclude. The consequence is that you might retain extreme cases that have fallen below your threshold for exclusion because they have made that threshold higher than it would have been if they had not been there.

Best fishes,
Milton

Milton's Meowsings 9.2   Other trimming methods

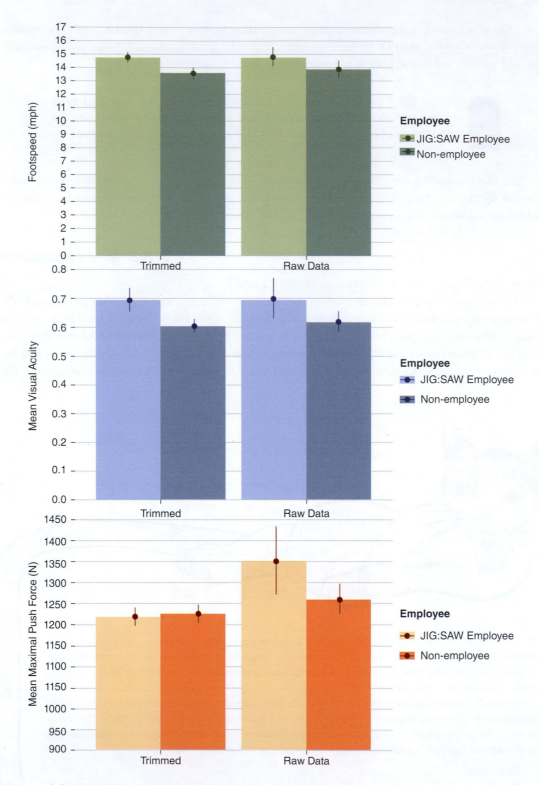

Figure 9.8 The effect of 20% trimming on the JIG:SAW genetics programme data

analysis how much of the data to trim, an M-estimator determines the optimal amount of trimming necessary to give a robust estimate of, say, the mean. This has the obvious advantage that you never over- or under-trim your data. However, the disadvantage is that it is not always possible to reach a solution.'

9.3.4 Winsorizing

It seemed odd to me that you could just discard lots of your data. I put this to the cat.

'Some would agree,' he replied. 'Rather than removing them, an alternative is to replace extreme scores with the nearest score in the data. This is known as **winsorizing**.' Milton produced another diagram. **(FIGURE 9.9)** 'Here is a diagram similar to the one I used to explain the trimmed mean. **(FIGURE 9.7)** I again have the code 1318 strength scores, which I have arranged in ascending order. When trimming the data we would, for example, remove the top and bottom 5% of scores. With winsorizing, rather than deleting the top and bottom 5% of scores, we replace these scores with the next highest and lowest scores. As before, we have 20 scores, so replacing 5% at the top and bottom means replacing 1 score at each extreme of the distribution. The highest score of 4561 is replaced with the next highest score (3044), whereas the lowest score of 1016 is replaced with the next lowest score (1026). A 10% winsorization would involve replacing the top and bottom 10% of scores with the next highest or lowest score. For these data, the top 2 scores (4561 and 3044) are both replaced with the next highest score (2760), and the bottom two (1016 and 1026) are both replaced with the next lowest score (1078). There are other ways to winsorize, but a percentage-based approach is the standard one.' I noticed another message from Milton and resigned myself to spending this evening reading his messages. **(MEOWSINGS 9.3)**

'That *really* seems like cheating – I mean, you're blatantly changing the value of scores!'

'Is it, though? If the score you are changing is very unrepresentative of the sample, to the point that you think it possibly isn't part of the population of interest, and it biases your statistical model, then what is cheating: leaving an extreme case knowing full well that it will bias your findings, or replacing that value to give you a more robust estimate of the parameter in which you are interested? Cheating would be selectively changing scores in a systematic way not because it reduces bias, but for some other nefarious reason, such as to support your hypothesis.'

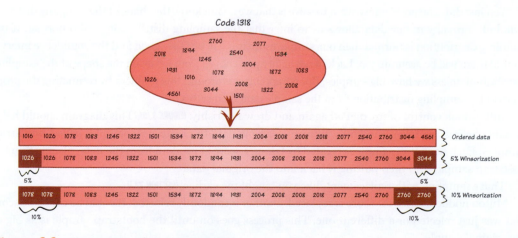

Figure 9.9   Illustration of winsorizing data

9.3.5 The bootstrap

'You mentioned before that you could use methods that don't involve changing your data.'

Dear Human,

There are variations on winsorizing, such as replacing extreme scores with a score 3 standard deviations from the mean. A z-score of 3.29 constitutes an outlier (see Section 7.2.3), so we can calculate what score would give rise to a z-score of 3.29 (or perhaps 3) by rearranging the z-score equation, which gives us $X = (z \times s) + \bar{X}$ (see Milton's Meowsings 6.1). All we are doing is calculating the mean ($\bar{x}$) and standard deviation (s) of the data and, knowing that z is 3 (or 3.29 if you want to be exact), adding three times the standard deviation to the mean and replacing our outliers with that score. As noted for trimming (Milton's Meowsings 9.2), the standard deviation will be biased by extreme scores, so this approach means that you are replacing scores with a value that has been biased by extreme scores.

Best fishes,
Milton

Milton's Meowsings 9.3   *Other winsorizing methods*

'Yes,' replied the cat, 'you can change the way you estimate things. Specifically, you can use a robust estimation method such as the **bootstrap**.'[36]

'Dare I ask what one of those is?'

'You just did. The problem we want to solve is that we do not know the shape of the sampling distribution, but normality in our data allows us to infer that the sampling distribution is also normal. If the sampling distribution is normal then our sample estimates will be fairly good and the confidence interval around them will be accurate too. Lack of normality prevents us from knowing the shape of the sampling distribution unless we have big samples. Bootstrapping gets around this problem by estimating the properties of the sampling distribution from the sample data themselves.'[37]

Milton took control of my diePad again and drew feverishly. **(FIGURE 9.10)** 'This diagram should help,' he said. 'Scores are taken randomly from the sample data to create new samples called **bootstrap samples**. Each bootstrap sample is created by taking a score at random from the data, placing it in the bootstrap sample, and then putting it back into the original data.'

'That's sampling with replacement, like you taught me earlier.' **(SECTION 7.1.1)**

Milton nodded. 'After the score is replaced, another is randomly selected. It could be the same score that was just selected or a different one. This process goes on until the bootstrap sample is as big as the original sample.'

'If it's as big as the original sample, won't the bootstrap sample end up the same as the original one?'

'No, remember that each time we sample a score for the bootstrap sample *it is replaced and so can be sampled again*. In the diagram you can see that some scores are sampled more than once, so the resulting bootstrap sample is different than the original one. It would only ever be the same if, by chance, each score in the original sample was selected exactly once when creating the bootstrap sample.'

'What happens with this bootstrap sample?'

'You calculate the statistic of interest. If you're interested in the mean you compute the mean in the bootstrap sample, if you're interested in some other parameter then you compute that instead. Once you have done that, you generate another bootstrap sample, which will likely be different from the first and you again compute the statistic of interest; for example, the mean. You then generate a third bootstrap sample and compute the statistic of interest. You repeat this process perhaps 1000 times, so you end up with 1000 bootstrap samples, and for each you have an estimate of the thing in which you are interested; for example, the mean.'

'Right, so you have 1000 estimates of the mean. What do you do with them?'

'There are two things. The first is to order them and work out the limits within which a percentage of them fall. For example, in my diagram **(FIGURE 9.10)**, I illustrate the limits within which 90% of bootstrap sample means fall. First, we arrange the sample means in order. To see the limits within which the middle 90% of bootstrap sample means fall we need to ignore the top and bottom 5% (note that 5% + 90% + 5% = 100%). I have done this in the diagram and you can see that the middle 90% of bootstrap sample means fall between 1775 and 2450. We can use these values as an estimate of the limits of the 90% confidence interval of the parameter. The result is known as a **percentile bootstrap confidence interval** (because it is based on the values between which a percentage of bootstrap sample estimates fall). Usually we would have at least 1000 bootstrap samples which enables us to estimate a 95% percentile bootstrap confidence interval by again ordering the bootstrap sample statistics but then ignoring the top and bottom 2.5%. This confidence interval can be adjusted for bias and skew to make it more precise, and when it is, this is known as a **bias corrected and accelerated (BCa) bootstrap confidence interval**. The second thing we can do is to calculate the standard deviation of

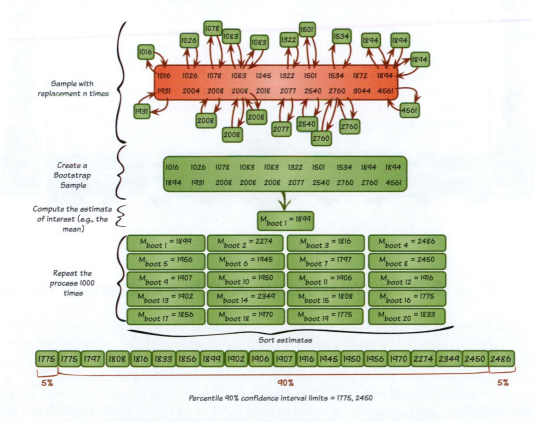

Figure 9.10   Illustration of the percentile bootstrap

the parameter estimates from the bootstrap samples and use this as the standard error of parameter estimates.'

'Doesn't that take ages?'

Milton sighed. 'Obviously you get a computer to do it for you. Unlike you, computers have brains that work very fast indeed. It will take it a few seconds to generate 1000 bootstrap samples and provide an answer for you. What we are doing, in effect, is getting the computer to use our sample data to mimic the sampling process; because bootstrapping is based on taking random samples from the data you have collected, the estimates you get will be slightly different every time.'

'Sounds dodgy.'

'Not as dodgy as wrongly assuming normality.'

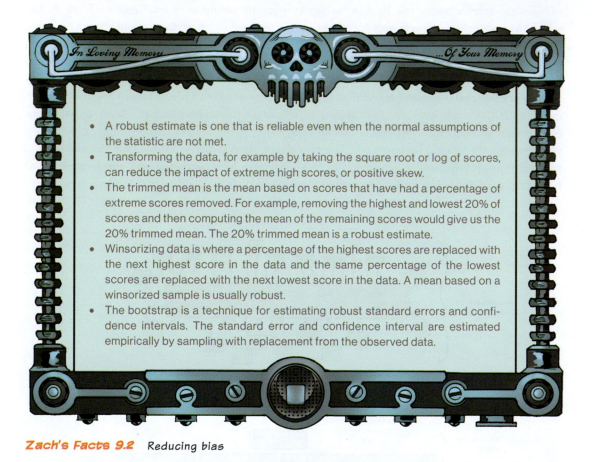

In Loving Memory   ...Of Your Memory

- A robust estimate is one that is reliable even when the normal assumptions of the statistic are not met.
- Transforming the data, for example by taking the square root or log of scores, can reduce the impact of extreme high scores, or positive skew.
- The trimmed mean is the mean based on scores that have had a percentage of extreme scores removed. For example, removing the highest and lowest 20% of scores and then computing the mean of the remaining scores would give us the 20% trimmed mean. The 20% trimmed mean is a robust estimate.
- Winsorizing data is where a percentage of the highest scores are replaced with the next highest score in the data and the same percentage of the lowest scores are replaced with the next lowest score in the data. A mean based on a winsorized sample is usually robust.
- The bootstrap is a technique for estimating robust standard errors and confidence intervals. The standard error and confidence interval are estimated empirically by sampling with replacement from the observed data.

Zach's Facts 9.2   *Reducing bias*

9.4   A FINAL POINT ABOUT EXTREME SCORES

I sighed. It was the kind of sigh where you start to wonder whether it's possible to expel every molecule of air from your lungs. Not for the first time, I felt as though I had learned a lot but understood nothing. I knew a great deal about how to correct for extreme scores, but I wasn't any wiser about whether Nutcot's conclusions from the JIG:SAW data held up to scrutiny. Statistics was frippin' frustrating. Next to me Milton beavered away on my diePad, his paws blurred around the screen as though someone was tracing a laser pointer around it. Just as I was about to get up and leave, the cat clawed my forearm.

'Look, I have made a table –' **(TABLE 9.2)**

'Very pretty,' I interrupted sarcastically.

Milton gave me the cat death gaze. 'It is not intended to be pretty; it is intended to be informative. I have gone to the trouble of working out the mean scores for the JIG:SAW employees and non-employees, and also the trimmed means, an M-estimator, a 20% winsorized mean as well as ordinary and bootstrap confidence intervals. That was no inconsiderable feat, so you might humour me and look at the values and tell me what this tells you about Nutcot's conclusions that JIG:SAW workers are stronger, faster and have better vision.'

CHECK YOUR BRAIN: *Compare the original means and confidence intervals in Table 9.2 with the robust versions. Do the original and robust versions lead you to different conclusions?*

I studied the table. 'For footspeed, the original means of 14.82 and 13.88 really don't change a lot when you trim, winsorize or use an M-estimator, and the bootstrap confidence intervals are basically the same as the raw confidence intervals.'

'Good. What about visual acuity?'

'The same picture really, the means and confidence intervals hardly change when robust estimates are used.'

'*Claw*rect. And for strength?'

'Here it makes a big difference. The mean for the JIG:SAW group gets much smaller when a robust estimate is used, and it wipes out the difference compared to the non-employees as we saw before. The confidence interval isn't affected much though. So, I guess, the conclusion still holds that JIG:SAW employees are faster and have better visual acuity but they are not stronger. So, Nutcot only really lied about strength.'

'Well done – which means that you were premature in rushing off and accusing these people of lying to you. On the plus side, this means that you might never have to endure that imbecile Nutcot again, but I fear you have also set back your mating ritual with the girl.'

I did my best imitation of the cat stare of death. I wasn't sure it was as effective when a human did it, but he deserved it.

There was still something I didn't get about robust estimates. There was one really extreme case who had exceptional visual acuity, and the scientist groups had a lot of outliers **(FIGURE 9.1)**: surely these cases were interesting? Why was it acceptable to ignore them? I asked Milton, and if I hadn't known better I'd have said he looked a little proud of me.

Table 9.2   *Means of JIG:SAW data under various methods for reducing the impact of extreme scores*

Correction	Footspeed		Visual acuity		Strength	
	JIG:SAW	Non-employees	JIG:SAW	Non-employees	JIG:SAW	Non-employees
Raw scores	14.82	13.88	0.70	0.62	1351	1260
20% trim	14.75	13.63	0.69	0.61	1220	1226
M-estimator	14.82	13.65	0.69	0.61	1223	1236
20% winsorized	14.88	13.72	0.69	0.61	1245	1234
95% CI (raw)	14.08, 15.56	13.30, 14.46	0.63, 0.77	0.59, 0.65	1269, 1432	1224, 1297
95% CI (bootstrap)	14.08, 15.53	13.31, 14.45	0.63, 0.77	0.59, 0.65	1272, 1438	1221, 1297

'That is an astute question,' he replied. 'The point is, you ignore them for the purpose of estimation. In the interests of a robust estimate of the mean visual acuity, for example, we sacrifice scores that bias that estimate. However, this does not mean that these scores are not interesting in their own right. By removing them you are effectively suggesting that they are not representative of the population in which you are interested. If that is the case then the interesting point is why they do not represent the population, what is different about that case or cases, and whether they tell you something useful about the phenomenon you are studying.'

'Sweet, so we need to ask why the person with the visual acuity of 2 **(FIGURE 9.1)** and the one with strength of over 4000 N have scores so high?'

'Indeed and, in this case, whether they are in fact the same, rather unusual, person.'

'It's weird that a lot of the unusual cases seem to be in the code 1318 workers, and that group's data seem strange generally. I wonder who they are and what they do at JIG:SAW?'

'We discussed this earlier, and you make a good point that their scores are strange – they seem to be incredibly strong, have exceptionally poor vision, and show enormous variability in their speed: some could barely walk, others were frighteningly fast. I did not pursue the conversation though because you did not seem interested in them.'

'Why did you think that?'

'Because shortly after you asked that idiot Nutcot about them, you said that you were not interested in them.'

'But I didn't ask Nutcot about them ...'

Milton frowned; he looked intrigued. 'Interesting ...,' he said.

I was confused. I thought back to meeting Celia and Nutcot and although I could picture the conversation, I was sure that we hadn't touched on the code 1318 workers at all. The more I tried to remember, the more the phrase code 1318 cycled in my mind. Nothing came to me, nothing – and then something did and it turned me cold.

KEY TERMS

Bias corrected and accelerated (BCa)

confidence intervals

Bootstrap

Bootstrap samples

Contaminated normal distribution

M-estimator

Mixed normal distribution

Percentile bootstrap confidence interval

Robust estimation

Trimmed data

Trimmed mean

Winsorizing

JIG:SAW'S PUZZLES

1   What is a robust estimate?
2   What is the difference between trimming data and winsorizing it?
3   Zach randomly selected 10 scores from the professional services non-employees (see Figure 9.1): 14, 15, 13, 11, 16, 13, 21, 12, 11, 15. Calculate the mean, the 20% trimmed mean, the 10% trimmed mean, and the 20% winsorized mean.
4   Square-root transform the above scores.

Table 9.3 Scientists' strength scores for JIG:SAW employees and non-employees (see Figure 9.1)

JIG:SAW	1161, 1141, 1174, 1112, 1185, 1095, 1102, 1112, 1071, 1244, 1102, 1216, 1884, 1276, 1373, 1145, 1169, 1136, 1313, 1129, 1119, 1197, 1111, 1121, 1274, 1197, 1139, 1233, 1334, 1150, 1138, 1185, 1158, 1445, 1525, 1408, 1128, 1723
Non-employees	1321, 1153, 1072, 1218, 1088, 1373, 1135, 1055, 1096, 1007, 1223, 1291, 1171, 1101 2091, 1308, 1141, 1433, 1141, 1212, 1769, 1071, 1412, 1214, 1031, 1209, 1222, 1241, 1740, 1367, 1313, 1208, 1257, 1376, 1155, 1065, 1147, 1166, 1566, 1436

5   Using the data in Table 9.3, what was the mean strength of scientists in both the JIG:SAW group and the non-employees?
6   Using the data in Table 9.3, what was the 20% trimmed mean strength of scientists in both the JIG:SAW group and the non-employees?
7   Using the data in Table 9.3, what was the 20% winsorized mean strength of scientists in both the JIG:SAW group and non-employees?
8   Using your answers above, how do the robust estimates of the mean differ from those based on the raw data?
9   Log-transform the JIG:SAW data from Table 9.3.
10 Describe the process of bootstrapping.

IN THE NEXT CHAPTER, ZACH DISCOVERS ...

A secret society
Hypothesis testing
Null hypothesis significance testing
Null and alternative hypotheses
The p-value

Test statistics
One- and two-tailed tests
Type I and Type II errors, and statistical power
Statistical significance
Never to mess with a gernal worm

10

Hypothesis Testing

In Reality All is Void

The realization that the code 1318 workers were the zombies that we'd seen patrolling the complex had shaken me. It seemed to prove that JIG:SAW were a nefarious organization, and it made me scared for Alice. What was she involved in? Was she really there willingly? Our look at the JIG:SAW data seemed to confirm that their workers were faster and had better vision, but a lot of the unusual cases seemed to be the code 1318 workers. Were these workers responsible for the differences? Were they the only employees who were given the genetic enhancement programme, or did everyone get it? Also, it looked as though Nutcot had lied about the strength data: these scores did not seem to be higher for JIG:SAW employees. I kept coming back to the idea that to know whether Nutcot had been lying I needed to find out whether the differences between JIG:SAW employees and non-employees were meaningful. I had no idea how to do that.

I needed some time to think, so I headed down to The Repository and straight to my favourite section. This room alone was vast, but I knew what I was looking for: the album Alice had played the night before she disappeared. Of course I could have played the digital file at home, but I needed to connect with my past. Alice and I had listened to this record endlessly in The Repository when we first got together. I wanted to see the sleeve, to touch the vinyl, and to experience the warmth of the analogue sound. More than anything, I wanted to go back in time to a place where I'd never felt more loved or in love.

Despite its 100-year age, this album was the continuity in my life. Not only was it the soundtrack to meeting Alice, but the band that made it were the template for my band, The Reality Enigma: they were eclectic, experimental, and true to a singular musical vision – everything I wanted my band to be. The band was long forgotten, except by me: where the records around them were interred in the dust of neglect, this band's catalogue glistened with the life breathed into them by my many visits. I retreated to the pod where Alice and I used to meet, dropped the needle onto the disc, turned out the lights and was alone with my thoughts.

Hearing these songs, in this pod, rolled back the past decade: I could almost feel Alice's head nestled against my shoulder and I saw us in my drifting mind, wrapped together on this sofa. As the final track, 'Faith in Others' played, it evoked so many memories that had lain undisturbed in my mind when it had looped on repeat in our apartment the morning Alice vanished. I remembered sitting on the same sofa, this song in the background, and telling Alice for the first time that I loved her. I remembered how she'd thrown herself around me, desperate to repeat the words back in my ear.

I remembered how tightly she'd clung to me as though trying to fuse us together. I remembered her thinking that I hadn't felt her tears on my cheek. As the song stopped, I remembered us saying that no matter what, we must always have faith in our love. Had she left the song playing to remind me of that, or to tell me that *her* faith was gone?

And what about my faith? Back then we were 16 and idealistic, and at 26 I knew that even with love, faith is no substitute for evidence. I didn't want to believe that Alice would walk out on me, so I had become wrapped up in trying to prove that JIG:SAW were behind it all. But the more I reflected on recent months, the more evidence I found that Alice and I had drifted apart. Where once she had been fun, carefree, and into gigs and hanging out together, she was now serious, carried the weight of the world on her shoulders, and valued early nights over partying. Worse than that, where she had once loved my creativity and passion for music, she now saw these as things that held us back. She never said so, but whereas once her words bobbed and weaved towards me on the current of her affection, now they shot at me like a Taser. From my side, I had stopped telling her how brilliant I think she is, or how proud I am of her achievements. Perhaps I was even a little jealous that her scientific brilliance is based on a creativity that reveals the smoke and mirrors of my own.

Perhaps the time had come, and maybe cutting me off was the kindest way for Alice to leave me behind. She would have told me to be scientific about it, and I had tried: most of the data suggested that JIG:SAW were what they seemed to be. All the data, that is, except for the overly complicated bridge to get there, the code 1318s who seemed to be zombies prowling the perimeter, and the guy in charge of the company being, well, a bit strange …

I stayed at The Repository late into the night, until I had gone around in circles enough to convince myself that we needed to do more with the JIG:SAW data. We had two samples, one from JIG:SAW employees and the other from non-employees, but so what? Milton had explained to me that samples could be different just because of sampling variation, and even Alice, on our last evening, said much the same thing. (**SECTIONS 8.2 & 1.2.1**) How could I find out whether the differences I'd found between JIG:SAW employees and non-employees were meaningful?

The following morning I explained my concerns to Milton. He looked shifty, then paced around in thought for quite some time. For once he seemed in two minds about the right thing to do. Finally, he told me to follow him. He asked me to hail a bubble and direct it into the Egestes district, which, despite my unease, I did. Egestes was the rough part of town, and I tended to avoid it. The district itself was split into three sub-districts; the main ones were Jerzy and Aylmer. They were fierce rivals. When Elpis was created Egestes was built to contain affordable housing, and people were randomly assigned to either Jerzy or Aylmer; between them was a strip originally called Egon, which contained shared facilities. Very quickly the two sub-districts became embroiled in a rivalry that often broke out into violence. The reason for the hostility was unknown: each sub-district thought it was better than the other for no reason other than that's what was thought. Eventually the strip between them emptied, with Jerzy and Aylmer demanding their own facilities that could be used only by them. Egon became a ghost town that's now called 'the Void'. It's said that the social outcasts moved into it: people with pasts to hide, cults, and statisticians. Milton had heard rumours about a secret society that formed in the wake of the Reality Revolution in pursuit of truth. If you wanted a society to be secret, this was the perfect place to hide it.

We left the bubble in Jerzy, and Milton walked me through the streets and into the Void. I felt anxious. Although Egestes wasn't unsafe as such, you could soon find yourself in trouble if you said the wrong thing: the populations of Jerzy and Aylmer hated each other, but they weren't keen on outsiders either. As for the Void, the stories about its inhabitants were so wild that it was hard to know what might be true. Milton showed no fear; perhaps people in Egestes liked cats more than people.

We stopped by an uninteresting wall next to a homeless guy. He looked in a bad way: pale and coughing, unshaven, and he stank. Milton announced that we had arrived. Arrived where, though? There was no door, no windows, just a wall. Did this society just meet in the street? Milton was infuriating:

he seemed to really enjoy not explaining stuff to me and then acting as though I ought to know what the frip was going on. My thoughts were interrupted by the homeless guy saying he didn't know who he was. I thought maybe he was another Chipper losing his mind, and I offered him help. Before I knew what was happening he'd vanished and I was standing by a Georgian door.

'What was all that about?'

'You will see,' said Milton, walking through the door.

The door led into a narrow pea-green hallway lit by three spectacular rose-like domes in the ceiling. At the end of the hall was a cast iron spiral staircase. Milton led me down it into a large circular meeting room. The walls were lined with books, and a series of engraved curved benches formed concentric circles out from the centre of the room in which there stood a huddle of people with prisms on their heads. Although I'd never seen one for real, they looked exactly like the pictures of reality prisms.

10.1 NULL HYPOTHESIS SIGNIFICANCE TESTING

The pyramid-headed people stared at me, and I felt my brain glowing warmly. It sounds more pleasant than it was.

'What are they doing?' I asked Milton.

'Were you not listening? They are subjecting your soul to scrutiny.'

'What does that involve?'

'They are the Secret Philanthropic Society. They saw the Reality Revolution as a year zero, the point at which society collapsed in on itself because of years of people becoming self-focused instead of humanity-focused. The pursuit of fame, self-affirmation, self-interest and self-promotion took its toll. They believe the reality prism was not an invention of destruction, but an invention of enlightenment: it showed society for the shallow husk it had become, and in doing so pressed the reset button. In the wake of the revolution, and with reality prisms destroyed, they established a society dedicated to seeking truth and the promotion of humanity. As the inventor of the reality prism I'm something of a hero to these people,' Milton's breast swelled a little with pride.

'That's a little self-promoting, self-interested and self-affirming,' I replied, pointing out the cat's hypocrisy.

Milton's breast deflated and he licked it furiously as though trying to cleanse his words from history. Eventually, he continued, 'The society will not interact with anyone who is not philanthropic. That is why their doorway is hidden – to keep society out.'

'But I saw it …'

'You passed their test,' Milton waited for the penny to drop, but it was still floating around doing its own thing.

'The vagrant?' he prompted.

'He was a test?'

'Of sorts. They presented you with a person whom many would judge or ignore, and he begged for your help. The question is: are you a man who passes by, or a Good Samaritan? You helped him, you showed him kindness, and in doing so you revealed the door.'

'Sick,' I felt pleased with myself. 'If I passed the test, why are they heating my brain?'

'One cannot be too careful: anyone is capable of one act of kindness, but we are all essentially a mass of contradictions – perhaps helping the vagrant was one of yours? They are seeing whether you are fundamentally kind and humane, or not.'

'By microwaving my brain?'

'In a manner of speaking: rumour has it that the Society obtained some malfunctioning reality prisms. They are the pyramids on their heads.'

So, they *are* reality prisms, I thought. That's rad. I had always wondered what it felt like to wear one, to really know the truth. I thought about stealing one from them, just to see whether I could find out the truth about Alice. The thought passed quickly as I remembered that they were scanning my thoughts: theft probably wouldn't go down too well.

I turned to Milton. 'You said that all of the reality prisms had been destroyed.'

'I said *officially* they had all been destroyed. The story on the grapevine is that this society has been trying to re-create a working reality prism: one that splits reality into its constituent parts so that you can see the truth. So far they have not succeeded, but they have created prisms that assess the *probability* of different realities. In your case they are using probability to determine whether you are more likely to be humane than not.'

It occurred to me that Milton must be able to help them to rebuild a working prism. I wondered why he didn't help them. Perhaps, despite what he said, he really did regret the effect the prisms had on society. I also wondered why the Society didn't try to persuade him to help. There was no time for these questions; my brain was really aching now.

'Milton, what if I'm not humane?'

'You will find yourself standing by a wall with no memory that you met a vagrant and walked into this building.'

My head was pulsating. It felt as though what they were doing to my brain was fundamentally the opposite of humane. Then the invisible G-clamp on my head felt like it was being unscrewed. The people in front of me spoke in unison.

'We are the Secret Philanthropic Society. You are very welcome, friend. Please, let us help you.'

I explained the past few weeks and my dilemma about the data from JIG:SAW. How could I reveal the truth of the data: were JIG:SAW employees really different from everyone else? The pyramid heads swayed and nodded in unison as I spoke. I realized that they had lost all sense of self and instead existed as a collective: they moved together, spoke together, thought together. It was beautiful, but unnerving. As I finished they formed an inward facing circle, and began chattering to each other. For the first time I heard their individual voices, but not what they said. The circle broke and they addressed me.

'There are different ways to find the truth, friend. We favour the use of probability. These prisms on our heads compare competing versions of the truth and tell us the probability of one truth over another. We determine the truth – or at least, what we believe to be the truth – based on these probabilities. We believe that you can use probability too. We will show you.'

The group shuffled towards me, three taking my left hand and three my right. They sat me in the middle of the room and sat crossed legged beside me.

'Probability is extremely helpful in evaluating evidence. Our approach is called **null hypothesis significance testing**, which is a chimera of two ideas: (1) evaluating evidence using competing hypotheses, and (2) using probabilities to evaluate evidence.'

'You would be wise to remember that chimeras are best avoided,' whispered Milton cryptically.

10.1.1 Types of hypothesis

A member of the Society took the pyramid from her head, revealing long brown hair, a button nose, and deep brown eyes behind square-rimmed geek-chic glasses. She was perhaps in her thirties and looked like she struggled to relax and enjoy herself. Behind her another society member assembled two piles of three identical black cubes, each one about 15 cm square, and with a small finger-hole on the top. Each hole looked as though it had a black rubber film beneath it so that the contents of the box couldn't be seen. The glasses lady spoke to me, her voice sounding lonely without the others joining it. 'Zachary Slade, the boxes in one pile are empty, the boxes in the other pile contain a gernal worm.'

A Society member lifted the lids on the three boxes in one of the piles and beckoned me over to look inside. Inside each box was what looked like a ferret-sized slug: slimy, pulsating, and every bit as disgusting as I'd imagined a gernal worm to be. I shuddered.

The gernal worm was a wonder of modern medicine, but a wonder that you hoped never to meet. Before the revolution people overused antibiotics. They'd take them for anything, even medical problems that they couldn't treat. Over time the bacteria mutated to combat the drugs. The gernal worm was created to contain the drug-resistant bacteria: the worm absorbs and contains them, keeping them safely away from humankind. It is a Russian doll of bacteria. The story of the gernal worm has a sting in its tail – well, its mouth. The worm itself isn't harmful, but inside is a lethal concoction of bacteria; if any of it gets in your blood stream it travels to your heart, where it feasts until your heart is gone. The most likely way for that to happen is from a bite. The only hope of survival is to persuade the gernal worm to reabsorb its own bacteria before it reaches your heart, and if you've annoyed it enough for it to bite you then it's probably in no mood to save your life. Luckily gernal worms are not prone to fits of pique. Typically docile, the gernal worm would bite only if provoked by, for example, a finger poking into the top of a box in which it slept.

'I do not know which pile is which, but fortunately I have psychic powers,' continued glasses lady. 'Do you believe me?'

I was no scientist, but I wasn't stupid. 'No, I don't. Alice – she is my girlfriend, or was – maybe she still is? – anyway, she told me there was no evidence for psychic powers.'

'It is, however, a scientific statement –'

'Alice told me about them,' I interrupted, 'a statement that can be tested with evidence.'

'Yes!' continued glasses lady. 'We can collect evidence to test whether I do have psychic powers, so this is a scientific statement. Two eminent statisticians from the old world, called Neyman and Pearson, believed that scientific statements should be split into testable hypotheses.[38] The hypothesis or prediction from your theory would normally be that an effect exists. For example, "I can tell what is inside these boxes" would be such a hypothesis. This hypothesis is called the **alternative hypothesis** and is denoted by H_1. (It is sometimes also called the **experimental hypothesis**, but "alternative hypothesis" is a more general term that can be applied even if you do not collect evidence using the experimental method.) The opposite hypothesis would be that an effect does not exist. For example, "I cannot tell what is inside these boxes" is a prediction that there is no effect and that my decisions about the boxes will be no better than guessing. This hypothesis is called the **null hypothesis**, which is denoted by H_0. Our reality prisms provide a probability value that we use to determine whether the null or alternative hypothesis is likely to be true. Therefore, we have two competing hypotheses: the alternative hypothesis, "I am psychic/I can 'see' what is inside each box"; and the null hypothesis, "I am not at all psychic/I cannot 'see' what is inside each box".'

'I don't understand why we need the null hypothesis?'

'Neyman and Pearson argued that you can never prove the alternative hypothesis, but you can collect evidence against the null hypothesis. If the observed data give us confidence to rule out the null hypothesis then we might be more inclined to believe the alternative hypothesis.'

'So, if you reject the null hypothesis then the alternative hypothesis must be true?'

'No, it merely means that the alternative hypothesis is supported. You cannot really talk of accepting or rejecting a hypothesis, instead think of it more in terms of the chances of obtaining the data that you observed if the null hypothesis were true. Imagine we randomly selected one box, and I told you that it contained a gernal worm. You open the box and it does contain a worm. Assuming that I have no psychic power (i.e., the null hypothesis is true), what are the chances that I would have correctly identified the contents of the box?'

'Quite high. You have a 50% chance of guessing correctly.'

'Yes, so your observations are quite likely even if I had no psychic powers. What if we randomly selected a box on 10 occasions and each time I correctly identified whether or not it contained a worm. How likely would it be that I could do that if I had no psychic powers?'

'Much less likely than before.'

'Indeed. If the null hypothesis were true – if I had no psychic powers – it would be fairly unlikely that I would correctly identify the contents of 10 randomly selected boxes. Therefore, you would be more confident that I had genuine psychic powers. When we collect data to test theories, we cannot talk about the null or alternative hypothesis being true, we can talk only about the probability of obtaining a particular statistic if, hypothetically speaking, the null hypothesis were true. The question is, what evidence would you need to observe before you believed the hypothesis that I can use my psychic powers to see what's inside these boxes?'

CHECK YOUR BRAIN: What are the null and alternative hypotheses for the following statements:

- JIG:SAW employees are stronger than non-employees.
- T-shirt sales are affected by giving away a free wristband.

10.1.2 Fisher's p-value

Glasses lady put her reality prism back on. A fellow member of the Society placed a black hood on her head so she could not see, and another member took a single box from each of the two piles, and placed them on a desk in a random order.

'I will now play gernal roulette,' glasses lady said, removing the hood. 'I must place my finger into one of the boxes. The question is, can I choose the empty box?'

She said it with a morbid pleasure, but the sinister tone that the meeting was taking filled me with anxiety. Glasses lady studied the boxes in a dramatic and theatrical way – never touching them, just screwing her face in mock concentration. Suddenly, she poked her finger through the rubber seal and into the top of one of them. I waited nervously for her to collapse in a heap of excruciating pain. She didn't.

She turned to me, with a maniacal smile. 'I chose the empty box, do you now believe that I am psychic?'

I felt bad about it, but I didn't believe her. There were two boxes, one with a gernal worm and one empty, so she had a 50% chance of choosing the empty box. 'Even by guessing,' I said, 'you'd pick the right box half of the time. I think you're insane to play gernal roulette, but I don't believe you're psychic.'

'Let's make this more interesting.' The maniacal smile returned to her face, bigger and better than before. Her colleague again placed the hood on her head and behind her another took all six boxes and arranged them on the desk. He moved the boxes around in circling motions like a magician doing the pea under a cup thing that magicians seem to like to do. It was effective because I lost all sense of which box came from which pile. I had a gut-wrenching feeling that the woman in glasses was about to ask me to play gernal roulette.

'Six boxes,' she said, 'arranged in random order. I do not know the order of the boxes, I did not see from which pile the boxes came. All I know is that three of the boxes contain a gernal worm and three do not, and that I must place my finger in half of the boxes and pass on the other three. To survive, I must identify the order of the boxes correctly. There are 20 different random orders in which these boxes can be arranged. If I were to guess, I would get the correct order only 1 time in 20 (or 5% of the time).'

With that, she ripped the hood from her head and turned to face the boxes. She made squatting and gyrating motions with her hips and waved her arms in a circular motion above her head while moaning. It was the kind of extroverted display I had never associated with geek-chic. With a final shrill scream she arched over the boxes, and for each box in turn either pushed it forcefully away with the palm of her hand or stabbed the top with her violently thrusting finger. 'Pass! Poke! Poke! Poke! Pass! Pass!' she screamed in turn at each box, before tearing the prism from her head and taking a dramatic bow. It was over within seconds. I felt pale with stress.

Her colleague led me to the table, and slowly opened each of the three boxes that she had passed on. Curled up in each one, was a gernal worm. Covering those boxes, they opened the three she had poked. They were empty.

Glasses lady grabbed my shoulders and turned me forcefully to face her. 'Now do you believe the hypothesis that I am psychic?'

I had to admit, it was an impressive display. If she were guessing she would have got the order wrong on 95% of attempts, which would mean that by chance I had just witnessed one of the 5% of times she would correctly guess the order. It seemed very unlikely that I had coincidentally been there to witness the 1 time in 20 attempts that someone would guess the order of boxes correctly.

'I think I do believe it, glasses lady. I do believe you're psychic.'

Her grip on my shoulders remained firm. I felt bad that I called her 'glasses lady'; I asked her name. She trembled a little. 'I have no name: I am a society member, part of a collective, no more, no less.'

'Yeah, but before that, what was your name?'

Her eyes were intense, and I felt myself shaking as her trembling increased. She pulled me towards her; I noticed her eyes were full of tears. As they began to stream down her face, her hands relaxed their grip from my shoulders and slid around my back as she clung to my body. It was the embrace of someone who had spent too long sacrificing her individuality to a collective. I could feel her tears as she pressed her cheek onto mine and whispered, 'I'm not sure the Society sees the truth.'

Two of her colleagues quickly but gently pulled her from me and walked her off to a corner of the room. She placed the pyramid back on her head, and everyone pretended that her emotional outpouring hadn't just happened.

The Society spoke to me as a collective voice once more. 'We have demonstrated to you the idea of a ***p*-value**, a value of probability at which you are prepared to believe a hypothesis. Centuries ago, a great statistician called Fisher[39] came up with the idea of using probability to evaluate a claim.[40] We have just shown that process. Only when there was a very small probability that our sister could survive gernal roulette by luck alone would you conclude that she had genuine skill in detecting whether boxes were empty or contained a worm.'

I understood that, but at what point is the probability low enough to believe the claim? They had shown me two examples: in one of them glasses lady had a 50% chance of guessing correctly, but in the other she had only a 5% chance. They're two really different situations. I believed her claim with a 5% chance, but not a 50% chance. What if she had had a 10% chance of guessing correctly, would I have believed the claim then? Well, I think I might, but where do you draw the line? I asked the Society how you know when the probability is small enough to believe a hypothesis.

'You don't,' they replied in chorus. 'Fisher believed it was a subjective decision based on the research context. Although he felt that a probability of 0.01 (in our demonstration a 1% chance of guessing the order of boxes) would be strong evidence to support a hypothesis, and a probability of perhaps 0.20 (a 20% chance of guessing the order of boxes) would be weak evidence, he did not believe that a universal threshold would apply. Despite his advice, scientists often blindly use a threshold of 0.05 (a 5% chance of guessing the order of boxes). This is why we showed you the example of six boxes, because that represented the threshold that many scientists use: our sister had a 5% chance of guessing the correct order.'

'You're saying that when there is only a 5% chance (or 0.05 probability) of getting the statistic they observe if no effect exists, scientists become confident enough to believe that the effect is genuine.'

'Yes,' came the chorus.

'And they do this even though the guy who came up with the idea thought it was daft to apply a universal threshold for believing in an effect.'

'Yes,' came the chorus, slightly more musically this time.

'Frip, for clever people, scientists can be really stupid.'

10.1.3 The principles of NHST

I felt as though my comment had offended the Society: the members paused, as one, and shuffled awkwardly, in unison, on the spot. It was as though the shuffling would somehow dissipate the social awkwardness of confronting me, like they were exorcizing their emotions through their feet and into the floor. It was strange. The shuffling stopped and they spoke, as one, as though nothing had happened.

'The null hypothesis significance testing (NHST) that we mentioned before is a blend of Fisher's idea of using the probability value p as information about the plausibility of a null hypothesis, and Neyman and Pearson's idea of testing a null hypothesis *against* an alternative hypothesis. It follows this logic:

- Make predictions based on your hypothesis (this must happen before any data are collected). **(MEOWSINGS 10.1)**
- Collect some data.
- Assume that the null hypothesis is true (i.e., there is no effect whatsoever).
- Fit a statistical model to the collected data.
- Calculate the probability (the p-value) of getting a model that looks like the one you fit (or one that's even MORE extreme) if the null hypothesis were true.
- If that probability is very small (the usual criterion is 0.05 or less) then conclude that it would be unlikely to get a model like yours if the null hypothesis were true and gain confidence in the alternative hypothesis. Remember, we can never be completely sure that either hypothesis is correct; we can merely calculate the probability that our model would look like it does if there were no effect in the population (i.e., the null hypothesis is true). As this probability decreases, we gain greater confidence that the null hypothesis is not a good fit; it does not mean that the alternative hypothesis is the best model of the data, there could be other hypotheses that fit the data even better.'

I felt my diePad vibrate in my rucksack. **(MEOWSINGS 10.1)**

10.1.4 Test statistics

'When you say "model", what exactly do you mean?' I asked. 'A friend of mine told me that all statistical models were basically a variation on this equation.' I scribbled an equation down. **(EQUATION 10.1)**

$$\text{outcome}_i = \left(b_0 + b_1 X_i\right) + \text{error}_i \tag{10.1}$$

Good day, Human,

Imagine that your friend challenges you to a running race. She proposes that whoever wins gets to keep the other person's mobile device. You know that you can normally run faster than her, so you will probably win. However, you also know that you have a brand new Proteus, whereas she has a pre-revolution Nokia mobile phone.

To keep you both happy, this process needs to be equitable: your friend must feel like she has some chance of beating you (and therefore winning your swanky Proteus), and you need to know you're likely to win (for you to risk your Proteus for a smaller prize). Your friend can offer any reward before the game, but she can't change her mind afterwards – she can't, for example, try to give you a packet of sweets instead of her phone if she loses. Similarly, you can agree to the challenge, but you can't change your mind half-way through the race as she speeds past you into the home straight. Likewise, you both enter the race knowing how good the other person is – that is, you both know the probability of winning the race.

NHST works on the same principle. You can choose any hypothesis before the data are collected, but you cannot change your mind halfway through data collection or after. Likewise, you have to decide on your probability level (the likelihood of winning) before you collect data. Bad scientists cheat: they do not formulate hypotheses before they collect data, they change them once the data are collected (like you refusing to give up your Proteus after losing the race). Similarly, scientists can be guilty of choosing which significance level to use after the data are collected and analysed (this would be like your friend secretly doing lots of sprint training before she challenges you so that you think your probability of winning is higher than it actually is).

To sum up, NHST relies on the researcher generating their hypothesis and setting their probability threshold for believing that an effect is significant before they collect any data. If you change your hypothesis or the details of your analysis you increase the chance of finding a significant result, but you also make it more likely that you will publish results that other researchers cannot reproduce (which is embarrassing). If you follow the rules carefully, and do your significance testing at the 5% level, then in the long run when the null is true only 1 result out of every 20 will give you a p-value <0.05 (which would lead you to incorrectly believe the null is not true).

Best fishes,
Milton

Milton's Meowsings 10.1   *Nobody likes a cheat*

'This is true,' came the harmonious response from the society. Their tone had started to resemble a Gregorian chant. 'The parameters in this model –'

'What, the *b*s?' I interrupted.

'Yes, the *b*s. They represent effects that we want to test. Each parameter is estimated, and there will be some error in that estimation. This error is quantified by the standard error.'

'Right, the standard error tells us how parameter estimates differ across different samples.' **(SECTION 8.2.2)**

Dear Human,

The frequency with which scientists use a 0.05 probability to evaluate hypotheses can make it seem as though it is a magic number, or a mystical threshold that separates the murky underworld of non-significance from the heavenly paradise of a meaningful effect. It is none of these things; it is a number, and a fairly arbitrary one at that. Although Fisher felt that, in general, $p = 0.01$ would be strong evidence, and perhaps $p = 0.20$ would be weak evidence, he was very clear that the observed value of p should be interpreted within the context of the specific research domain. Why, then, is it so common to use 0.05 as a criterion?

It is hard to say exactly why without being impolite, but one contributing factor is probably the time at which NHST was developing: 1900–1940, a long time before computers. Without the benefit of a computer, calculating an exact probability for a test statistic is, to put it mildly, a bit of a pain. Rather than go through that pain, in the days before computers statisticians would calculate critical values for a test statistic using specific probability levels (such as 0.05 or 0.01). For example, in his influential 1935 textbook *Statistical Methods for Research Workers*,[41] Fisher produced tables of these critical values for probability values of 0.05, 0.02 and 0.01.

Fisher's book was hugely influential,[42–44] and researchers used these tables to ascertain whether their test statistic was significant at a certain probability. For example, if your test statistic was 10, you could go to the appropriate table and see whether that value was as big as or bigger than the value that would give rise to $p = 0.05$. If it was, you would conclude that you had a significant result at $p = 0.05$. This all led to a trend to report test statistics as being significant at the now infamous $p < 0.05$ and $p < 0.01$ (because critical values were available at these probabilities).

That all made sense at the time – well, more sense than everyone trying to work their way through complicated probability equations on napkins every time they did an experiment. However, these days a computer (or even your phone) can compute a p-value before you can say 'Fisher'. Therefore, it is slightly puzzling that the trend to accept significance at $p < 0.05$ has continued, given that it started life as a convenience more than anything else.

Best fishes,
Milton

Milton's Meowsings 10.2   Is 0.05 a magic number?

'Yes, so it tells us the potential error in the particular parameter estimate – the particular b – that we have. You can use the parameter estimate and its error to calculate a signal-to-noise ratio. The parameter estimate, b, represents the signal. That is, it represents the size of the effect for the hypothesis you are testing. The standard error tells us the noise – the likely error in that estimate. If we divide the parameter estimate by its standard error then we have a signal-to-noise ratio. That is, an estimate of the size of the effect that represents our hypothesis compared to the error associated with that estimate. In effect, we compare how strong the effect is against how variable or noisy it is (the error).

This signal to noise ratio is called a **test statistic**.' Without any movement from the society members an equation appeared on the wall. *(EQUATION 10.2)*

$$\text{test statistic} = \frac{\text{signal}}{\text{noise}} = \frac{\text{effect}}{\text{error}} = \frac{\text{parameter estimate}\,(b)}{\text{standard error of } b}$$

(10.2)

'What do you do with this test statistic?'

The society shuffled synchronously to the left. 'The exact form of the test statistic differs for different types of model. They all have one thing in common, which is that they have an associated probability distribution. This means that you can compute the probability that you would get a test statistic at least as big as the one you have.'

I looked down at Milton. 'Like when we looked up the probability of getting a z-score at least as big as a certain value when I faced the discs of death?' *(SECTION 7.2.4)* He nodded.

The Society continued. 'Different test statistics have different probability distributions. For example, there is the t-distribution, the chi-square (χ^2) distribution and the F-distribution. Regardless of the exact form of the probability distribution, you can calculate the probability of obtaining a value at least as big as the one you have. This probability is the p-value that Fisher described. The process of NHST therefore entails establishing hypotheses, computing a test statistic and then calculating the probability that you would get a test statistic at least as big as the one you have *if there were no effect* (i.e., the null hypothesis were true). If that probability is low – and as we mentioned, people often use below 0.05 as a threshold – then you gain confidence in the hypothesis you were testing. We say that the effect is *significant*. If the probability is not that low (for example, it is above 0.05) then we consider it insufficient to believe the alternative hypothesis. In this case we say that the effect is *non-significant*.'

'Right, so the test statistic is a bit like the glasses lady playing gernal roulette. The bigger the number of boxes she correctly identified the contents of, the more unlikely it was that she could be guessing. When the number of boxes she got right becomes so big that you wouldn't expect to see her get that many right if the null hypothesis – that she had no psychic powers – were true, you reject that idea and instead believe that she has psychic powers.'

'Yes,' came the reply.

'And the threshold for deciding that it would be highly improbable for her to get so many boxes correct if the null hypothesis were true, is a probability of 0.05 or less?'

'Yeeeees,' they chorused.

'Didn't we decide earlier on that this was stupid?'

The society fell silent. I looked down to Milton, who looked pleased with me. He climbed onto my leg, stuck his paw into my rucksack and handed me my diePad, which contained the message I felt arrive earlier and a new one. *(MEOWSINGS 10.2)*

10.1.5 One- and two-tailed tests

'There is more,' the Society said, pretending they hadn't heard my previous question. 'The alternative hypothesis can be directional or non-directional. A directional hypothesis states the direction of the effect. That is, it specifies whether scores will be higher or lower in certain conditions, or that a relationship between variables is in a specific direction.'

I turned to Milton, 'Like, people who pretend to be Florence Nightingale will get higher scores on a stats test than those who don't?'

Milton nodded, and the Society continued. 'Yes, that would be a directional hypothesis. The opposite is a non-directional hypothesis, which states only that an effect will occur, but not the direction of the effect.'

'Like, people who pretend to be Florence Nightingale will get different scores on a stats test than those who don't?'

'You catch on quickly. That hypothesis is non-directional because you state only that there will be a difference, and not which group will score higher than the other. A statistical model that tests a directional hypothesis is called a **one-tailed test**, whereas one testing a non-directional hypothesis is known as a **two-tailed test**.'

'Why?'

'Let us explain. Imagine we wanted to discover whether listening to music while exercising affects your running speed.[45, 46] If we have a non-directional hypothesis then there are three possibilities. (1) People who listen to music while exercising run faster than those who do not, so the difference (the mean for those listening to music minus the mean for those not) is positive. Put another way, there is a *positive* relationship **(MEOWSINGS 5.2)** between listening to music and speed. (2) People who listen to music while exercising run slower than those who don't, so the difference (the mean for those listening to music minus the mean for those not) is negative. Put another way, there is a *negative* relationship between listening to music and footspeed. (3) There is no difference in speed between those who listen to music and those who do not, so the mean for those who listen to music minus the mean for those who do not is exactly zero. Put another way, there is no relationship between listening to music and speed. This final option is the null hypothesis. The direction of the test statistic (i.e., whether it is positive or negative) depends on whether the difference between listeners and non-listeners is positive or negative. Assuming there is a positive difference or relationship (music results in faster running speed), then to detect this difference we have to take account of the fact that the mean for listeners is bigger than for non-listeners. In other words, the test statistic is positive.'

The society seemed to mentally transmit a diagram onto the wall before continuing. **(FIGURE 10.1)**

'To find this positive difference we would look in the positive end – the positive *tail* – of the distribution in the diagram. We look in one tail only; hence this would be a one-tailed test. However, if we have predicted incorrectly and actually music makes runners slower, then the test statistic will actually be negative, and located in the lower tail, so we will miss it because we have looked only at the upper tail. To avoid this we can look at both ends (or tails) of the distribution of possible test statistics. This

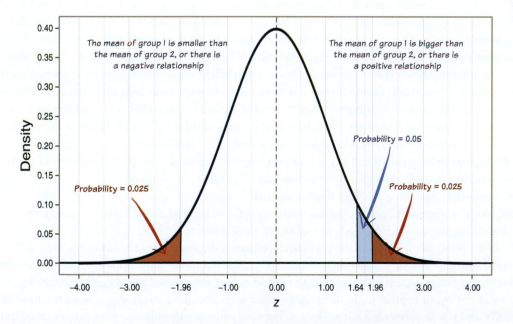

Figure 10.1   Diagram to show the difference between one- and two-tailed tests

would be called a two-tailed test, because we look in two tails of the distribution. This means we will catch both positive and negative test statistics. However, doing this has a price because to keep our criterion probability of 0.05 we have to split this probability across the two tails: so we have 0.025 at the positive end of the distribution and 0.025 at the negative end. The red-tinted areas in the diagram show the areas where test statistics are in the top or bottom 2.5% of the distribution. Combine the probabilities at both ends (i.e., add the two tinted areas together) and we get 0.05, our criterion value.'

'So what you're saying is that if I make a directional prediction, then I'm putting all of my eggs into one basket and I look only at one end of the distribution (either the positive or the negative end, depending on the direction of my prediction). In your diagram, that means that rather than having two small red-tinted areas at either end of the distribution which show what values would be deemed significant, I would end up with the bigger blue-tinted area at only one end of the distribution that shows how big a test statistic needs to be to be deemed significant.'

'Yes.'

'Fine, but the blue area starts further left than the red area, so this suggests that a smaller test statistic would be deemed significant than if we looked in both of the red areas instead.'

'You are correct. If you make a specific prediction then you can get a significant effect with a smaller test statistic (because you are looking in only one tail of the distribution), but if your prediction happens to be in the wrong direction then you will miss out on detecting the effect that does exist. This final point is very important so let us rephrase it: if you do a one-tailed test and the results turn out to be in the opposite direction to what you predicted, you would accept the null hypothesis because you defined the null hypothesis to include effects in that opposite direction. If you don't do this, then you have done a two-tailed test using a different level of significance from the one you set out to use, which is cheating.' **(MEOWSINGS 10.1)**

Milton started furiously tutting and shaking his head.

'What's up, furball?' I asked.

'One-tailed tests, that is what is wrong with me,' he replied grumpily.

'What's the problem? You make a prediction, you look in one tail, and you can find a significant result with a smaller test statistic. Seems legit.'

'No! It's trickier than that, especially when people aren't honest! Did you not hear what they said? If the result of a one-tailed test is in the opposite direction to what you expected, *you cannot and must not reject the null hypothesis*. You must *completely ignore* that result even though you know it is there and it looks interesting and unexpected. Curiosity is going to get the better of you. Like Hansel and Gretel, that result opposite to what you predicted will be like a gingerbread house luring you in, tempting you with its sugary sweetness. Before you know it you will be cooked and eaten by a witch. Also, if you do a two-tailed test and find that your p is 0.06, then you would conclude that your results were not significant (because 0.06 is bigger than the critical value of 0.05). Had you done this test one-tailed, however, the p you would get would be half of the two-tailed value (0.03). This one-tailed value would be significant at the conventional level (because 0.03 is less than 0.05). Therefore, a scientist who finds a two-tailed p that is just non-significant might be tempted to pretend that they had always intended to do a one-tailed test because the "one-tailed" p-value is significant.'

'But scientists have integrity. They'd never do that.'

'You would be surprised! There are documented cases of the widespread invalid use of one-tailed tests.'[47, 48]

'There must be some situation where you'd approve of a one-tailed test?'

'Only if a result in the opposite direction to the expected direction would result in the same action as a non-significant result.[47, 48] One such situation would be if a result in the opposite direction would be theoretically meaningless or impossible to explain even if you wanted to,[49] because that being so, you would not *try* to explain it. To illustrate another such situation, imagine you were the head of JIG:SAW and you implemented a new drug to improve your genetic enhancement programme. You predict that the drug will lead to even greater enhancements in speed, vision and strength than your existing programme can achieve. If the drug turns out to *not* be better than the existing programme (you get a non-significant *p*-value) you would not use it; however, if it produced significantly *worse* outcomes than the existing programme (you get a significant *p* but the effect is the opposite of what you predicted) you would also not use the drug. In both situations, the drug is not used.'

10.1.6 Type I and Type II errors

The Society members had patiently waited for Milton to finish his rant against one-tailed tests. As he finished they started to hum. I turned to Milton, seeking an explanation, but he shrugged his little cat shoulders. The hum reached a crescendo, and then slowly calmed to a quiet murmur. They paused briefly, and then said, 'Mistakes!'

I had to admit, they had a good sense of drama. 'What mistakes?' I asked.

'In the process of NHST, you can make mistakes. Neyman and Pearson identified two types. When we use test statistics to tell us about the true state of the world, we are trying to ascertain whether there is an effect in our population. There are two possibilities: there is, in reality, an effect in the population; or there is, in reality, no effect in the population. We cannot know which of these possibilities is true. However, we can look at test statistics and their associated probability to tell us which of the two is more likely. There are two mistakes we can make: a Type I and a Type II error.

'A **Type I error** is when you believe that there is a genuine effect in the population, when in fact there is not. If we use the conventional criterion then the probability of this error is 0.05 (or 5%) when there is no effect in the population – this value is known as the α-**level**. If the α-level is set at 0.05, then it means that, assuming there is no effect in the population, if you exactly replicated your data collection 100 times you could expect that on five occasions you would obtain a test statistic large enough to make you think that there was a genuine effect in the population even though there is not.'

'And the other type of mistake?'

'It is the opposite: when you believe that there is no effect in the population when, in reality, there is. This is a **Type II error**. In an ideal world, we want the probability of this error to be very small (if there is an effect in the population then it is important to detect it). Cohen[50] suggested that the maximum acceptable probability of a Type II error is 0.2 (or 20%) – this is called the β-**level**. That would mean that if you took 100 samples of data from a population in which an effect exists, you would fail to detect that effect in 20 of those samples; you would miss 1 in 5 genuine effects.'

'Surely there is a trade-off?'

'Yes, the lower the probability of accepting an effect as genuine (i.e., a small α), the more extreme an effect has to be to be significant. Which also means a higher probability that you will reject an effect that does genuinely exist (because you have been strict about the level at which you accept that an effect is genuine). The exact relationship between the Type I and Type II error is not straightforward because they are based on different assumptions: to make a Type I error there has to be no effect in the population, whereas to make a Type II error the opposite is true (there has to be an effect that you have missed). Therefore, although we know that as the probability of making a Type I error decreases, the probability of making a Type II error increases, the exact nature of the relationship is usually left for the researcher to make an educated guess.'[51]

10.1.7 Inflated error rates

'Let me get this straight,' I said. 'Every time I test a hypothesis at a 0.05 level of significance and the null is true, then the chance of making a Type I error is 5%, and presumably the probability of no Type I errors is 0.95 (95%) because these are complementary events.' **(SECTION 7.3)** I winked and smiled at Milton in case he'd missed me dropping some probability terms into my comment.

'Yes,' the Society replied.

'What happens if I want to test more than one hypothesis? The cat and I were looking at some data that showed that JIG:SAW employees were stronger, faster and had better vision than non-employees. They reckon it's 'cos of their genetic enhancement programme. Their hypothesis would be that their genetic enhancement programme improves their employees, but to test this we actually have three hypotheses: one about people's strength, one about their vision and one about their speed.'

Milton nodded approvingly.

'You are right,' the Society began. 'Often scientists need to conduct several tests to get a definitive answer to a question. In your example, you would need three tests. If we assume that each test is independent –'

'What do you mean by that?'

'The results of one test are not related to the results of another.'

'But they will be, won't they? I mean, each one is testing a different outcome from the genetic enhancement programme.'

'True, but pretend for now that they are independent, because doing so means that we can multiply the probabilities of each test. If we do this, then the overall probability of no Type I errors will be 0.95^3 = $0.95 \times 0.95 \times 0.95 = 0.857$, because the probability of no Type I errors is 0.95 for each test and there are three tests. If the probability of no Type I errors is 0.857, then we can work out the probability of making at least one Type I error because, as you correctly pointed out, these events are complementary: their probabilities must add up to 1. The probability of at least one Type I error is, therefore, $1 - 0.857 = 0.143$, or 14.3%.'

I didn't see why this mattered, but the Society weren't done yet.

'Across this group of tests, the probability of making a Type I error has increased from 5% to 14.3%, a value greater than the conventional criterion. This error rate across statistical tests conducted on the same data is known as the **familywise** or **experimentwise error rate**.' The Society paused and an equation **(10.3)** appeared in front of them as though floating on the waves of their collective thought. 'Assuming you use a 0.05 level of significance, this equation shows how the familywise error is calculated. In this equation n is the number of tests carried out on the data. With three tests we saw a modest increase in the Type I error rate, but if we did 10 tests the familywise error rate would be $1 - 0.95^{10}$ = 0.40. In other words, rather than a 5% chance of at least one Type I error there is a 40% chance.'

$$\text{familywise error} = 1 - 0.95^n \tag{10.3}$$

'That's over the wall, man!'

'Yes it is, and that's why sometimes scientists adjust the probability at which they accept a result as supporting a hypothesis such that overall the Type I error rate (α) stays at 5%. A popular (and easy) way to control the Type I error rate is to divide α by the number of comparisons, k.' Another equation appeared before me. **(EQUATION 10.4)** 'This method is known as the **Bonferroni correction**. It is not the only method, but it illustrates the general principle well. All it means is that if we conducted, for example, 10 tests, then rather than accept a result as significant if its probability is below 0.05, we accept it as significant if its probability is below $0.05/10 = 0.005$. In doing so, we ensure that the familywise Type I error remains below 0.05.'

$$p_{\text{crit}} = \frac{\alpha}{k} \tag{10.4}$$

10.1.8 Statistical power

'If you use a smaller criterion for accepting that a result is significant, won't that make it harder to support your hypothesis?'

300

'An excellent question. There *is* a trade-off for controlling the familywise error rate. To explain what this trade-off is, we need to tell you about statistical **power**, which is the ability of a test statistic to detect an effect. It is related to the Type II error, which, as you know, is how often you will miss an effect that genuinely exists in the population. This error is quantified with a probability, the β-level, which is the probability that a given test will *not* find an effect when one exists in the population. It is, therefore, the opposite of power, which is the probability that a given test *will* find an effect when one exists in the population. Therefore, the power of a test is $1 - \beta$. If you follow the commonly used β-level of 0.2, which equates to an effect that exists being missed 20% of the time, then the corresponding level of power is $1 - 0.2$, or 0.8. Scientists, therefore, often try to achieve a power of 0.8, or put another way, an 80% chance of detecting an effect if one genuinely exists.'

'What do you mean "try to achieve"? How can scientists influence what power they have?'

'The power of a statistical test depends on many things. First, it is self-evident that large effects are easier to detect than small ones, so power depends on the size of the effect that you are trying to find. Scientists have no control over this. Second, the stricter a scientist is with their criterion for accepting a hypothesis, the harder it will be to "find" an effect. This strictness is reflected in the α-level. This is the trade-off to which we alluded a minute ago: if you use a more conservative Type I error rate for each test (such as a Bonferroni correction) then the probability of missing an effect that does actually exist is increased. In other words, applying a Bonferroni correction to statistical tests reduces the power of those tests to detect effects. Third, larger samples provide better estimates of the population because they have less sampling error. Test statistics are basically a signal-to-noise ratio and in large samples the "noise" is reduced, making it easier to find the "signal". Finally, as we explained before, if you do a one-tailed test then you focus your attention at one end of the probability distribution.'

I thought back to when we discussed one- and two-tailed tests. 'Yeah, you showed me that you need a smaller test statistic for a result to be significant because you put all of your eggs in one basket.'

'Yes, and another way to think about that is that one-tailed tests have greater power to detect effects.'

'But you should not use one-tailed tests,' grumbled Milton.

The Society ignored Milton. 'To answer your question of how scientists influence power, they could collect larger samples or be less strict with their α-level, but they would not want to do the latter because it trades power off against the chance of making a Type I error. However, power $(1 - \beta)$, the α-level, sample size, and the size of the effect are all linked, which means that if you know three of these things, then you can find out the remaining one. Scientists use this knowledge in two ways.

'First, they can calculate the sample size necessary to achieve a given level of power *before the data are collected*. If a scientist sets the value of α and β to be whatever they want (normally 0.05 and 0.8, respectively), and they use other related research to make a reasonable estimate of the likely size of the effect that they are trying to detect, then from this information they can calculate how big their sample needs to be to detect that effect.

'The second thing that scientists do is calculate the power of a test that they have already done. If they have already done the test then they will have already selected a value of α, they can estimate the effect size from the data, and they will know how many participants were used. From that information they can calculate the power of the test. If this value turns out to be 0.8 or more they can be confident that they achieved sufficient power to detect any effects that might have existed; if, however, the resulting value is less, then they might consider replicating the research but with more participants to increase the power.'

'Isn't that a bit pointless? I mean, surely if you find a non-significant effect then you didn't have enough power, if you found a significant effect then you did?'

'It's not a bit pointless, it's *completely* pointless and frequently misleading', Milton agreed. The Society started to hum again.

10.1.9 Confidence intervals and statistical significance

I hadn't noticed last time, but the apparent monotone of the hum was in fact a complex blend of harmonies. Milton paced around my feet as though needing food. I hadn't brought cat food with me. I'd had other things on my mind, and even if I had, how would I open the tin, and where would I put the food? I decided to distract him from his pacing.

'Fuzzball, remember the other day you were telling me about confidence intervals?'

'Indeed I do – having a memory is one of the most basic of my intellectual talents.'

'I sort of took from what you were saying that if confidence intervals did not overlap then it was likely that the scores on which the intervals are based come from different populations. I thought that you could just look at confidence intervals and use them to make a judgement about your hypothesis, but now these guys are telling me about a much more complex process.'

Milton scratched a diagram **(FIGURE 10.2)** into one of the rather antique looking benches. I wondered whether the Society would be shaken from their humming to punish his vandalism, or whether he ever stopped to consider that a world existed outside of his own experience.

'Look here,' he pointed to his diagram. 'Remember how we looked at how performance on a statistics test might be influenced by whether you take the test under your own name or pretend to be a statistics expert like Florence Nightingale? Well, the diagram shows some possible scenarios. Statistical significance and confidence intervals are related. Three general guidelines illustrate this relationship.[52] (1) The top left of the diagram shows 95% confidence intervals that just about touch end-to-end, and this equates to a p-value of about 0.01 for testing the null hypothesis of no

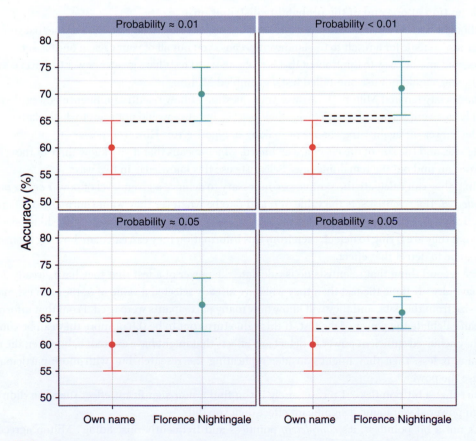

Figure 10.2 *The relationship between confidence intervals and statistical significance*

differences. (2) The top right of the diagram shows a gap between the upper end of one 95% confidence interval and the lower end of another, and this equates to a p-value of less than 0.01 for testing the null hypothesis of no differences. (3) The bottom panels show moderate overlap of the confidence intervals, and this equates to a p-value of 0.05 for testing the null hypothesis of no differences.'

'What is "moderate" overlap?'

'It can be defined as half the length of the average margin of error (MOE).[53] The MOE is the length of the bar sticking out in one direction from the mean (assuming the confidence interval is symmetric). In the bottom left of the diagram **(FIGURE 10.2)** the confidence interval for the own-name sample ranges from 55 to 65 so has a length of 10 and an MOE of half this value (i.e., 5). For the Florence Nightingale sample, it ranges from 62.5 to 72.5, so again a distance of 10 and an MOE of 5. The average MOE is therefore $(5 + 5)/2 = 5$. Moderate overlap would be half of this value (i.e., 2.5). This is the amount of overlap between the two confidence intervals in the bottom left of my diagram.' **(FIGURE 10.2)**

'So when the confidence intervals are the same length, $p = 0.05$ is represented by an overlap of a quarter of the confidence interval.'

'*Claw*rect.'

'But wouldn't it be unusual that the confidence intervals are the same length?'

'Yes, and this makes interpreting the overlap more tricky. In the bottom right of the diagram **(FIGURE 10.2)** the confidence interval for the own-name sample again ranges from 55 to 65 so has a length of 10 and an MOE of 5. For the Florence Nightingale sample, it ranges from 63 to 69, which is a distance of 6. The MOE is half this value, which is 3. The average MOE will be $(5 + 3)/2 = 4$, and moderate overlap is half of this value, which is 2. The two confidence intervals in the bottom left of my diagram do, in fact, overlap by 2 points on the scale, so this again depicts a p of around 0.05.'

10.1.10 Sample size and statistical significance

'There is something else to consider,' said Milton, 'which goes back to the point the Society made about the sample size affecting power.'

I stared in anticipation of Milton's next revelation.

'There is a connection between the sample size and the p-value associated with a test statistic. I will demonstrate this with an example. There is some evidence that people who have been socially excluded will act more pro-socially if they are allowed to touch a teddy bear rather than look at it from a distance.[54] Other scientists claim that touching a teddy bear can reduce anxiety in those with low self-esteem compared to touching a cardboard box.[55] It seems that teddy bears can be quite therapeutic. Imagine we developed a therapy based on cuddling teddy bears. To test whether it worked, we gave a group of 10 people with low self-esteem a teddy bear as a friend and told them to hug it every day. A control group of a different 10 people also got a teddy bear but had to leave it in its cardboard box and hug the box instead. We measured everyone's self-esteem using the Rosenberg Self-Esteem Scale[56] after 8 weeks. We then repeated this experiment but using 100 people in each group.'

Milton drew a diagram on my diePad **(FIGURE 10.3)** while the Society hummed on the far side of the room, seemingly unaware of his actions.

'My diagram shows the results of the two experiments I described. The results are identical: in both cases the box group had a mean of 10 and a standard deviation of 6, and the teddy bear group had a mean of 15 and a standard deviation of 6. The only difference between the experiments is that the first is based on 10 scores per sample, and the other 100 scores per sample. What difference do you notice between the graphs, human?'

CHECK YOUR BRAIN: *Compare the graphs in Figure 10.3. What effect does the difference in sample size have? Why do you think it has this effect?*

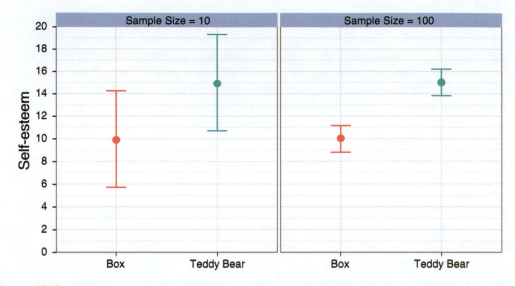

Figure 10.3 *Graph showing two data sets with the same means and standard deviations but based on different-sized samples*

'The confidence intervals are much narrower when the samples contain 100 scores compared to when they contain 10. Why is that – didn't you say that in both experiments the standard deviations were 6? So the bars should be the same shouldn't they?'

'No, they should not, because the bars show the *confidence interval*, not the standard deviation. Do you remember how you compute the confidence interval?'

I thought back a few days to Milton's explanation, and the equations he showed me. The 95% confidence interval for a mean was the mean plus or minus 1.96 times the standard error. **(EQUATION 8.4)** The standard error itself was the standard deviation divided by the square root of the sample size. **(EQUATION 8.3)** So as the sample size (*N*) gets larger, the standard error would get smaller because you divide the standard deviation by the square root of *N*, so as *N* gets bigger you are dividing the standard deviation by a bigger amount. I told this to Milton, adding 'As samples get larger, the standard error gets smaller, and because the confidence interval is the mean plus 1.96 times the standard error, if the standard error is small then the interval will be small too.'

'*Paw*fectly correct. As samples get larger, other things being equal, the confidence interval gets narrower, which reflects the greater precision that the large sample has. I just explained that if the confidence intervals of two samples are the same length then a *p* of around 0.05 is represented by an overlap of about a quarter of the confidence interval. Looking back at my diagram, you can see that even though the means and standard deviations are identical in both graphs, the experiment based on 10 scores per sample is not significant because the bars overlap quite a lot. In fact, the *p*-value is 0.08, which is bigger than the threshold of 0.05 that we use to believe that an effect is significant. Now look at the experiment based on 100 scores per sample. This experiment shows a highly significant difference because the bars do not overlap at all. In fact you would get a *p*-value less than 0.001. It is worth reiterating that the means and standard deviations are *identical* in the two graphs, but the sample size affects the standard error and hence the significance.'

'Why does that matter?'

'Let us take this relationship to an extreme. I am going to show you that with a big enough sample a completely meaningless difference between two means can be significant with $p < 0.05$.' Milton grabbed my diePad and drew another diagram. (FIGURE 10.4) 'Look. This graph again shows means and confidence intervals for a study comparing hugging a box or a teddy, but each group contains *1 million* scores. The box group has a mean of 10.00 ($SD = 3$) and the teddy bear group has a mean of 10.01 ($SD = 3$): a difference of 0.01.'

'That's tiny!'

'Yes, whether you hug a teddy bear or a box makes a difference of 0.01 to your self-esteem. Rosenberg's self-esteem scale ranges from 0 to 30, and it changes in units of 1. That is, you can have a total of 10 or 11 but not 11.5. Therefore a change of 0.01 along that scale has no practical importance at all: it is not possible for an individual to increase their score from 10 to 10.01, they can only change from 10 to 11 (or some other whole number). Therefore, the difference between a score of 10 and 10.01 is, in practical terms, no difference at all.'

I noticed that the graph looked odd because the means looked identical and there were no confidence intervals.

Milton explained, 'The confidence intervals are so narrow that they merge into a single line.' Milton swiped the screen to zoom into the image. I could now see the confidence intervals. 'By zooming in,' the cat added, 'the scale of the vertical axis has changed to range from 9.98 to 10.02. That is, in the zoomed image, the entire range of values displayed is only 0.04. The sample means are 10 and 10.01 as mentioned before.'

'But the mean of the box group looks bigger than 10.'

'That is because I have zoomed in so much that its actual value of 10.00147 is noticeably different from exactly 10. Now, look at confidence intervals. They show an overlap of about a quarter, which equates to a significance value of about $p = 0.05$. In fact, for these data the actual value of p is 0.044.'

'Shut up! How is that possible when the two sample means are almost identical and they have the same standard deviations?'

'It is because of the sample size: there are 1 million cases in each sample, so the standard errors are miniscule.'

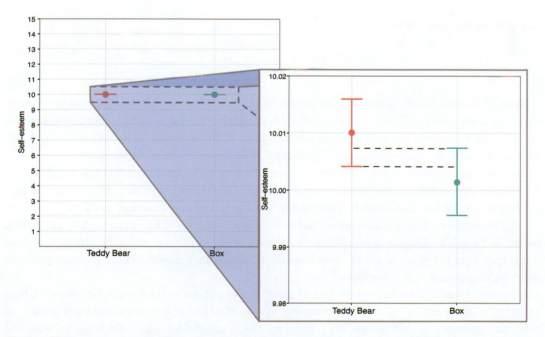

Figure 10.4 A very small difference between means based on an enormous sample size ($n = 1,000,000$ per group)

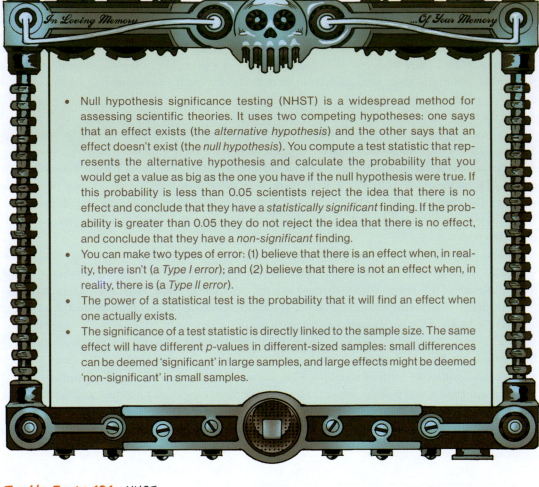

- Null hypothesis significance testing (NHST) is a widespread method for assessing scientific theories. It uses two competing hypotheses: one says that an effect exists (the *alternative hypothesis*) and the other says that an effect doesn't exist (the *null hypothesis*). You compute a test statistic that represents the alternative hypothesis and calculate the probability that you would get a value as big as the one you have if the null hypothesis were true. If this probability is less than 0.05 scientists reject the idea that there is no effect and conclude that they have a *statistically significant* finding. If the probability is greater than 0.05 they do not reject the idea that there is no effect, and conclude that they have a *non-significant* finding.
- You can make two types of error: (1) believe that there is an effect when, in reality, there isn't (a *Type I error*); and (2) believe that there is not an effect when, in reality, there is (a *Type II error*).
- The power of a statistical test is the probability that it will find an effect when one actually exists.
- The significance of a test statistic is directly linked to the sample size. The same effect will have different *p*-values in different-sized samples: small differences can be deemed 'significant' in large samples, and large effects might be deemed 'non-significant' in small samples.

Zach's Facts 10.1   NHST

I spent a moment taking this in. 'Let me straighten this. What you're saying is that the sample size affects whether a difference between samples is significant or not. In large samples small differences can be significant, and in small samples large differences can be non-significant. A difference of practically zero can also be "significant" if the sample size is big enough.'

'Yes, in terms of power, this means that large samples have more power to detect effects. This point is extremely important because it shows that despite what the Society have been drumming into you, a probability value less than 0.05 does not equate to the practical importance of an effect.'

The Society stood facing me, stationary but humming a multilayered harmonic hum. It was getting louder, as though building into something catastrophic. They were supposed to be philanthropic, so surely they were not going to kill me with harmony? Perhaps they considered it a humane death. In any case, they were weirding me out.

'We need to split,' I told Milton, who was gyrating out of time to the hum, a bit like, well, how I used to imagine my college lecturers dancing. We shuffled out of the room, testing the water of whether the society would notice. We backed up the spiral staircase into the long hallway, but when we reached the top and turned to face the front door it wasn't there. Instead, glasses lady sat by the wall curled up on her haunches. Her pyramid hat was gone; instead her hands and a cloak of her unmistakable brown hair hid her face. Her posture personified sadness; I thought she might be trying to protect her soul from the judgement of the world. I knelt beside her, held her hands and gingerly pulled them from her face. Her glasses magnified her tearful eyes into a chasm of sorrow.

'Hey,' I said softly, 'are you all good?'

'I'm so tired … the gernal roulette … it takes it out of you … emotionally.'

I gently put my arm around her shoulders. 'I get it, it was a powerful demonstration, and it really helped me to understand. You were amazing, I'm not surprised you're wiped out.'

She placed her hands on my cheeks and pulled my face into hers. 'Didn't you hear what I whispered?' she said desperately. She was trembling. 'I have doubts,' she stared pitifully into my eyes. 'The Society does not tolerate doubts. All Society members use reality prisms to evaluate the probability of different versions of the truth. We can all play gernal roulette and stand a good chance of surviving, but we are not psychic: we use probability values from our prisms. There is always a chance of death: a small lapse in concentration, a misinterpretation of the probability. It can happen. When visitors come, a member is selected to play the game. In recent months that person has *always* been me. I thought it was chance, but then I worked out the probability of being selected so many times.' Tears started streaming down her face. 'It was less than 0.05.' She tried to regain her composure. 'They do not tolerate doubts,' she repeated. 'Please – help me.'

I didn't know how on earth I could help this poor woman. 'Of course,' I said. 'Tell me how.'

'I hear rumours of other ways of evaluating evidence. I need to find out more, but I can't escape. We are a collective, we hear each other's thoughts.'

'They can hear this conversation then?'

'Not while they are humming. They are in a collective trance. They do that to block out things they don't want to hear. You kept questioning NHST, and they hummed to block out your questions.'

That's pretty childish, I thought to myself. 'Why don't you escape now while they're humming?'

Her arms flapped around her head and she sobbed even more. 'Because I can't see the exit.'

I looked around. 'There isn't one – there *was* a door, but it's gone.'

'It hasn't gone – you can see it only when you accept NHST as the only way to establish reality. *You* can't see it because they didn't convince you about NHST. I *used* to be able to see it, but my doubts shield it. If I could only forget my doubts for a few minutes I will see it again, but my mind is riddled with them.' Her arms flapped desperately like the thoughts flying around her head.

I thought back to her outburst after the gernal roulette, and it hit me. Perhaps I could distract her doubts by freeing her from the collective; perhaps she needed a reminder of what it felt to be an individual. I took her in my arms, and she sank into me revelling in the warmth and kindness of the hug. I gently rested her head on my shoulder and whispered, 'Tell me your name.'

'I don't have a name,' she sobbed.

'Yes you do. Please tell me.'

'I don't have a … I don't have a name.'

'Please, what's your name?'

'I don't … I don't … Emily,' she started convulsing with tears.

'Emily, chill, I'll take care of you.'

She lifted her head and focused her dewy eyes on mine. She looked the opposite of the formidable woman who had plunged her finger into the boxes of death: she was childlike, helpless, and shuddered to hold back more tears.

KEY TERMS

α-level

Alternative hypothesis

β-level

Bonferroni correction

Experimental hypothesis

Experimentwise error rate

Familywise error rate

Null hypothesis

Null hypothesis significance testing (NHST)

One-tailed test

p-value

Power

Test statistic

Two-tailed test

Type I error

Type II error

JIG:SAW'S PUZZLES

1   According to Paul Zak,[57] the hormone oxytocin increases trust in humans. You do an experiment in which groups of people are exposed to oxytocin or not while meeting a stranger. They rate how much they trusted the stranger from 0 (no trust) to 10 (complete trust). What are the null and alternative hypotheses?

2   In a study based on puzzle 1, trust ratings were 8, 95% CI [6, 10], in the oxytocin group and 6, 95% CI [4.5, 7.5], in the non-oxytocin group. What is the value of the MOE? Are trust levels likely to be significantly different in the two groups using an α-level of 0.05?

3   What is the difference between a Type I and Type II error?

4   What are the major problems with null hypothesis significance testing?

5   What effect does sample size have on statistical significance?

6   What are the arguments for not using one-tailed tests?

7   The manager of The Reality Enigma tells Zach that they will sell more albums if they include a free gift with the album than if they don't. What are the null hypothesis and alternative hypothesis? Would you use a one- or two-tailed test to evaluate these hypotheses?

8   In the example above, Zach sold 62, 95% CI [52, 72], albums when he gave away a free gift and 53, 95% CI [50, 56], when he didn't. Are these likely to be statistically significantly different using a criterion of $p = 0.05$?

9   A researcher conducted 15 significance tests on the same data. What is the experimentwise error rate? What p-value would you use as a threshold for significance to correct for this error rate?

10   What is the statistical power of a test?

IN THE NEXT CHAPTER, ZACH DISCOVERS ...

Another secret society

Reasons for not doing null hypothesis significance testing

Effect sizes

Cohen's *d*

Pearson's correlation coefficient

Odds ratios

Bayesian analysis

Everything is better when you hug a Teddy bear

11

Modern Approaches to Theory Testing

A Careworn Heart

If I had ever made a list of things I probably wouldn't do before I die, following some weird druid into a tomb would rank highly on it. Then again, so would talking to cats, loading myself into a giant catapult, and learning statistics. I was concerned that Milton had taken off in the opposite direction. Although I didn't trust him fully, I felt insecure without him. Whatever journey I was on, he had been there from early on and his abandonment left me feeling alone. As I climbed into the tomb and descended the stone stairs leading into the earth, I was aware of how barren and cold death would be. Emily seemed not to share my fear, and bounced down each step. She made strange cooing noises, like a baby noticing something for the first time. She was in a place of wonderment and anticipation, whereas I was confronting a deep, unsettling fear.

The stairs led down into a hallway made entirely of stone. Pews lined the floor, and in front, on a sort of stage, a crescent of druids stood with candles lighting their pale moonlike faces. They all looked the same as the one who had led us here, and each wore an identical pair of glasses. The woman who had led us here scampered onto the stage to take her place in the crescent. In front of them stood a taller lady. She had the same pale, oval face, and the same glasses, but she wore her hood down, revealing two pigtails of shiny white blond hair. She addressed us in a quiet, precise and reassuring voice.

'I am Sister Price, and we are the Doctrine of Chance. You are most welcome.'

Over the wall! Two cults in one day, I thought to myself. I'd heard the rumours about Egestes but I never really believed that this part of Elpis was actually full of spooks, sects and societies. I loved that it was true – I regretted not coming to this part of town sooner because this was next-level sick: a society with disappearing doors and now a cult who lived in a tomb. I definitely had to write some songs about this when I got back – with a sudden panic I thought, *if* I get back.

'What do you want with us?' I asked.

'We want only to provide options.'

What the frip did she mean by that?

'We have long believed in ways of seeking the truth that are, let me say, antithetic to the Secret Philanthropic Society. We are a peaceful doctrine, though: our scouts wait by their building and when someone leaves, we offer them an alternative.'

'You heard my doubts?' said Emily excitedly. 'I knew someone would hear me.'

'We wait, we do not hear,' the lady said firmly but kindly. She was lying because her 'scout' had told Emily that she heard her. It made me suspicious of her, she was too keen to deny that they actively looked for people to 'offer an alternative' to.

Emily didn't seem to care. 'There are things about NHST that don't make sense,'[58] she said.

11.1 PROBLEMS WITH NHST

11.1.1 What can you conclude from a 'significance' test?

Emily started to explain that statistical significance was not the same thing as importance because the p-value is affected by sample size. Milton had made a similar point, I remembered. **(SECTION 10.1.10)** Emily turned to me. 'When you discussed this issue back at the Society, they hummed because they didn't want to hear this truth, but I have suspected the same thing. I believe that we should not be fooled by the phrase 'statistically significant', because even if the p-value is less than 0.05 it tells us nothing about the importance of the effect in the real world. Very small and unimportant effects can be statistically significant just because the test is based on huge numbers of scores **(FIGURE 10.4)**, and very large and important effects can be missed because the sample size was too small. Worse than that, I am troubled by the whole philosophy. What can I really conclude from a significant result?'

I thought back to what the Philanthropic Society had told me. Hadn't they said that you could conclude that the null hypothesis is false? I asked Emily.

'But I don't think you can,' she replied. 'A significant test statistic is based on probabilistic reasoning, which limits what can be concluded.[59] Formal reasoning relies on an initial statement of fact followed by a statement about the current state of affairs, and an inferred conclusion. Take this syllogism:

If someone plays trombone then he or she does *not* play in the band The Reality Enigma.

> *This person plays in The Reality Enigma.*
> *Therefore, this person does not play trombone.*

'The syllogism starts with a statement of fact that allows the end conclusion to be reached because you can deny the person plays trombone (the antecedent) by denying that the person is not in The Reality Enigma (the consequent).'

I really couldn't see what this had to do with hypothesis testing. My mind wandered to how she knew about my band; then I remembered that she had searched my soul. I felt glad that she'd found my band there.

'A comparable version of the null hypothesis', Emily continued, 'would be this:

If the null hypothesis is correct, then this test statistic cannot occur.

> *This test statistic has occurred.*
> *Therefore, the null hypothesis is false.*

'But the null hypothesis is not represented in this way because it is based on probabilities.'

I still couldn't see why Emily was telling me this. I must have looked bemused because she continued without waiting for me to reply.

'The null hypothesis is represented by this reasoning:

If the null hypothesis is correct, then this test statistic is highly unlikely.

> *This test statistic has occurred.*
> *Therefore, the null hypothesis is highly unlikely.*'

Nope, I still hadn't a clue what this had to do with anything.

'To use the example of your band, it would be like saying:

If someone plays guitar then it is highly unlikely that he or she plays in The Reality Enigma.

This person plays in The Reality Enigma.
Therefore, this person is highly unlikely to play guitar.'

I thought about these statements. The first was true: I read somewhere that there were about 50 million guitarists on the planet, and only two of them – Joel and I – play in The Reality Enigma. If someone plays guitar it *is* unlikely that person plays in The Reality Enigma: the probability would be 2 in about 50 million. That's *totally* unlikely. To evaluate the last statement I thought about the probability of someone playing guitar given that they are in The Reality Enigma. There are four of us in the band, and two of us play guitar (if you don't include Jessika on bass) so the probability that someone plays guitar if they are in our band is 2/4, or 50%, which is pretty high. So the final statement isn't true: if the person plays in The Reality Enigma it is not unlikely that they play guitar; it is equally likely as unlikely. Finally, I could see what Emily meant: because significance testing is based on probabilities you can't use these sorts of logical statements to rule out the null hypothesis.

Emily continued, 'Worse than that, I'm not even sure what you can conclude from a non-significant result.'

'That the null hypothesis is true?' I offered.

'No,' said Sister Price, who until now had been passively observing Emily's conversation with me. 'If the *p*-value is greater than 0.05 then you can choose to reject the alternative hypothesis, but this is not the same thing as the null hypothesis being true. The null hypothesis being true implies a zero effect, and a non-significant result tells us only that the effect is not big enough to be detected in the sample that we have taken, not that it is zero. (SECTION 8.1) Even though these differences between samples can be extremely small (e.g., one mean might be 10 and another 10.00001), that is not the same as zero.[60] Even such a small difference would be statistically significant if a big enough sample were used.'

The sister's words resonated with what Milton had explained to me earlier. 'A friend told us much the same,' I said. 'He gave us an example where he developed a therapy based on cuddling teddy bears and tested it by telling a group with low self-esteem to hug a teddy bear every day and comparing them to a control group with low self-esteem who had to leave the teddy in its cardboard box and hug the box. Self-esteem would be measured after 8 weeks of this therapy. He showed that with a large enough sample a meaninglessly small effect could be significant.' (FIGURE 10.4)

'Just as I feared', said Emily. 'A non-significant result should never be interpreted as "no difference between means" or "no relationship between variables".'

'Indeed,' said Sister Price compassionately.

11.1.2 All-or-nothing thinking

Emily became visibly diminished as Sister Price validated each of her concerns, as though each doubt drained a little of her soul. I knew how she felt: over the past few weeks all of my assumptions about the world had been eroded. A couple of weeks ago I thought I was a regular guy, happy with trying to do something with my band, a proud Clocktorian, a man of instinct not evidence, with a girlfriend I loved and admired and who loved me back. I felt secure and happy. Since then everything had changed. Being Clocktorian had made it impossible to find Alice quickly, everyone I met drummed into me to look at evidence and evaluate models of the world, and increasingly I felt sure that my girlfriend couldn't possibly love me back if she treated me this way. I felt detached from and angry with Alice for whatever she was doing; I struggled to hang onto the idea that I should even bother trying to work out what she was messed up with. It would be easier to move on, just like Emily was trying to do. Emily interrupted my thoughts.

'My other concern with NHST is that it encourages all-or-nothing thinking. You could see it in the Society: they would completely believe one version of reality and completely reject another, all based on whether a p-value fluctuated one side of 0.05 or the other.'

This seemed a bit stupid to me. 'For real? If you had two effects, based on the same sample sizes, and one had a p of, say, 0.0499, and the other a p of 0.0501, then you would accept the first effect as significant but not the second?'

'Yes,' Emily replied.

I was astonished; I was no superbrain but even I could see that the ps differ by a tiny amount, 0.0002.

Sister Price inhaled deeply. 'You are correct, there is nothing magic about the criterion of $p < 0.05$. In the scenario you describe the effects would be extremely similar.'

'And yet people who use NHST would come to completely opposite conclusions based on those values?'

'Yes,' replied the sister. 'The recipe-book nature of NHST encourages people to think in this all-or-nothing way. The dogmatic application of the 0.05 rule can mislead scientists. Let me explain using your teddy bear therapy example, in which you measured the effect on self-esteem after 8 weeks of hugging a teddy compared to hugging a box. **(SECTION 10.1.10)** Imagine nine other scientists did exactly the same study. If teddy bear therapy did not work, then there should be a difference of zero between these group means (the null hypothesis), but if it does work then those that hugged the teddy should have higher self-esteem than those that hugged the box. This effect would show up as a positive difference between the groups.'

Sister Price turned to the crescent of druids behind her and raised her arms. They expelled a rasping scream that was simultaneously beautiful and terrifying. Out of the sound waves emerged a projection above their heads. **(FIGURE 11.1)**

As the screams of her choir subsided, Sister Price peacefully explained the image. 'This diagram shows the results of the 10 different studies along with the p-value within each study. Do you think teddy therapy works?'

CHECK YOUR BRAIN: Based on what you have learnt so far, which of the following statements best reflects your view of teddy bear therapy?

A. The evidence is equivocal, we need more research.

B. All of the mean differences show a positive effect of the therapy; therefore, we have consistent evidence that it works.

C. Three of the studies show a significant result ($p < 0.05$), but the other seven do not. The fact that more than half of the studies showed no significant effect means that the therapy is not (on balance) more successful in increasing self-esteem than the control.

D. I want to go for C, but I have a feeling it's a trick question.

Emily responded, 'Only three of the seven studies have a significant result shown by a p less than 0.05. I don't believe that is very compelling evidence for teddy bear therapy.'

'Zach,' said Sister Price, 'do you agree?'

CHECK YOUR BRAIN: Based on the confidence intervals, which of the earlier statements best reflects your view of teddy bear therapy?

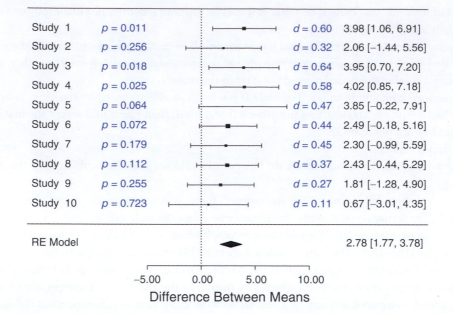

Study 1	$p = 0.011$		$d = 0.60$	3.98 [1.06, 6.91]
Study 2	$p = 0.256$		$d = 0.32$	2.06 [−1.44, 5.56]
Study 3	$p = 0.018$		$d = 0.64$	3.95 [0.70, 7.20]
Study 4	$p = 0.025$		$d = 0.58$	4.02 [0.85, 7.18]
Study 5	$p = 0.064$		$d = 0.47$	3.85 [−0.22, 7.91]
Study 6	$p = 0.072$		$d = 0.44$	2.49 [−0.18, 5.16]
Study 7	$p = 0.179$		$d = 0.45$	2.30 [−0.99, 5.59]
Study 8	$p = 0.112$		$d = 0.37$	2.43 [−0.44, 5.29]
Study 9	$p = 0.255$		$d = 0.27$	1.81 [−1.28, 4.90]
Study 10	$p = 0.723$		$d = 0.11$	0.67 [−3.01, 4.35]
RE Model				2.78 [1.77, 3.78]

−5.00   0.00   5.00   10.00

Difference Between Means

Figure 11.1 Results of 10 different studies looking at the difference between teddy bear therapy and a control group. The squares show the mean difference between groups (a positive number shows that the teddy therapy group had higher self-esteem than the controls)

I thought back to what Milton had told me about confidence intervals (SECTION 8.3), and then I studied them on the diagram. The centre of each interval shows the point estimate of the effect of the therapy compared to the controls, and for all of the studies this point estimate was above zero, showing a positive effect of the therapy. Even though this positive effect was not always 'significant', it was consistently positive. I also noticed that the confidence intervals in different studies overlapped a lot, suggesting that the studies probably sampled the same population. Ninety-five per cent of confidence intervals would contain the effect of the therapy in the population, so across these 10 studies we could expect maybe nine of them to contain the population value and perhaps one to have missed it. The fact that they overlapped so much suggested to me that again there was consistency: the intervals suggest population effects of a similar size. Finally, we know that around nine out of the 10 intervals should contain the actual population value and the biggest part of each interval is above 0; even in the studies that have a confidence interval that includes zero (implying that the population effect might be zero), most of their bars are above zero. I told Sister Price that I thought the confidence intervals showed consistency in the effect of the therapy across different studies. She looked happy.

'Excellent, you are correct. If you look at the confidence intervals rather than focusing on significance it allows you to see the consistency in the data. Rather than the conflicting results implied by the NHST approach, you saw that in all studies the effect of the therapy was positive and, taking all 10 studies into account, there is good reason to think that the population effect is likely to be greater than zero.'

11.1.3 NHST is influenced by the intentions of the scientist

'Another problem with NHST', Sister Price continued, 'is that it is influenced by the intentional state of the scientist. The conclusions you reach depend on what the researcher intended to do before collecting data.'

That was a brain frip right there. How on earth could your analysis be influenced by your intentions before collecting data?

'NHST works on the principle that you will make a Type I error in 5% of an infinite number of repeated, identical, experiments. The associated 0.05 probability of a Type I error is a long-run probability. It is an empirical probability.'

I'd come across empirical probabilities before, on the bridge of death. (SECTION 7.1.2) Milton had explained that the empirical probability of surviving the bridge could be established by counting how many people survived or died crossing the bridge. I told Sister Price about this.

'An empirical probability requires an infinitely large collective of events in which you observe the proportion of events that have the property or outcome in which you are interested.[61] If you define the collective as everyone who has ever crossed the bridge, then the probability of survival is the proportion of those people who survived. The important thing is that the probability applies to the collective and not to the individual events. You can talk about there being a 0.33 probability of surviving the crossing, but the individuals who crossed the bridge either lived or died, so their *individual* probability of survival was either 0 (they died) or 1 (they survived). NHST is based on these long-run probabilities; for example, the 0.05 probability of a Type I error is a long-run probability, and it means that across repeated identical experiments the probability of making a Type I error is 0.05. That probability does not apply to an individual study, because for an individual study you have either made a Type I error ($p = 1$) or have not ($p = 0$). Similarly, the probability of a Type II error (β) is also a long-run probability: if you set it at 0.2 then you are saying that over an infinite number of identical experiments 20% of the time you will miss an effect that genuinely exists, but in an individual study you either have or have not made that error, so the probability for the individual experiment is either 0 or 1, not 0.2.'

My mind wandered back to the bridge, to how scared I'd been, to how proud and relieved I felt when we survived the last challenge, the Deathscotch game, to how lucky I felt to be alive. Sister Price ploughed on.

'Imagine that, in reality, there is no effect – that the null hypothesis is true. Imagine also that you repeated an experiment 1 million times. Each time you compute a test statistic that has arisen from the null hypothesis; I will call this value t_{null}.[62] Therefore, you have 1 million values of t_{null}. You then do another experiment, and you again get a test statistic. The *p*-value for that test statistic is similar to the relative frequency of that value compared to the other 1 million values of t_{null}. The *p*-value is, therefore, a long-run probability: it is the probability of getting a test statistic at least as large as the one observed relative to all possible values of t_{null} *from an infinite number of identical replications of the experiment.* This last part is important. Like determining the likelihood of surviving the bridge by looking at the proportion of people who survived across a collective of all crossings, the *p*-value is the relative frequency of the observed test statistic relative to all possible values that could be observed in the collective of identical experiments. We have a decision rule that if that *p*-value is less than 0.05 then we believe that the null hypothesis is not true, and again this decision rule is a long-run probability: it will control the Type I error rate to 5% across an indefinite set of identical replications of the experiment. Similarly, we set the Type II error rate at 0.2, which again controls this error rate to be 20% across an indefinite set of replications of the experiment. Typically, we use these two probabilities to determine the sample size necessary to detect the effect of interest. (SECTION 10.1.8) Therefore, the usual assumption is that the scientist collects data until they reach this predetermined number of observations; in doing so, the *p*-value is the relative frequency of the observed test statistic relative to all of the t_{null} values that could be observed in the collective of identical experiments with the *exact same sample size*.[62, 63]

I was struggling to keep up with her explanation, but she did her best to look reassuring as she reached her point.

'Imagine that you aim, before the experiment, to collect data from 40 people, but once you start collecting data you find that you can only find 35 people willing to participate. Your decision rule was based on collecting data from 40 people, so the p-value that you want to compute should also be based on collecting data from 40 people. That is, you want the relative frequency of the observed test statistic relative to all of the test statistics that could be observed in the collective of identical experiments that aimed to get 40 observations. However, what ends up happening is that people use the data they have, so they base the p-value on having 35 observations. In doing so the researcher is working out the wrong p-value: they are computing the relative frequency of their test statistic compared to all possible t_{null} values from experiments of size 35 when they ought to look at the relative frequency of their test statistic compared to all possible t_{null} values from experiments of size 40, consistent with their original decision rule. If they do not then they are basing the space of possible t_{null} values on an arbitrary variable such as the *availability of participants* rather than on their original sampling scheme.'[62]

Sister Price inhaled deeply. 'Related to this point, researchers often use different data collection rules than collecting up to a predetermined sample size. For example, they might be interested in collecting data for a fixed amount of time rather than a fixed sample size.[64] Imagine you collect data for two weeks. If you repeated this experiment many times you would get different-sized samples of data (it would be unlikely that you would get exactly the same amount of data in different two-week periods). Therefore, you are interested in the frequency of your observed test statistic relative to all possible t_{null} values from identical experiments where data were collected for two weeks. However, using conventional methods for computing p-values, what you actually get is the frequency of your observed test statistic relative to all possible t_{null} values from identical experiments with the same sample size as yours (not the same duration of data collection).'[62]

I started to grasp what she was trying to tell me: the p-value that is appropriate depends on what your intentions were for collecting data, whether you wanted to collect a certain number of data points or collect data for a specific period of time. The resulting p-values for those two intentions would be different, which means that the scientist's intentions before data collection affect the actual value of p. It seemed insane to me to have the results of your analysis affected by your earlier internal state.

Emily had remained silent for some time; she looked shell-shocked. When she spoke, it was as though her lungs contained no air. 'These were just doubts in my mind, but you talk as though these problems are well known. How can you know so much?'

Sister Price smiled sympathetically but said nothing.

'Tell me more,' Emily asked hesitantly. 'I wanted to escape the Society, to explore the rumours that … that there are better ways to evaluate evidence. But this …. this is … I need to know.'

11.2 EFFECT SIZES

Sister Price squinted through her glasses as though trying to gauge Emily's ability to cope with what she would discover. Emily trembled with excitement, or perhaps it was apprehension.

'Confidence intervals,' Sister Price began. 'You can tell a lot from a confidence interval, and it does not come with all of the logical flaws of competing hypotheses and the unquestioning application of an arbitrary decision rule. Confidence intervals are straightforward in that they can contain the population effect, which allows you to evaluate to what extent you believe that the population effect is zero. A related thing to do is to quantify the population effect, using an effect size. One of the problems with NHST that I have already mentioned is that significance does not tell us about the importance of an effect. One solution is to quantify the size of the effect in a standardized way. Of course, what we want is the size of the effect in the population (that is, the true effect), but because we do not have access to the population we can estimate it from the sample data. When we estimate the size of an effect, whether from an experimental manipulation or the strength of a relationship between naturally occurring variables, we call it an **effect size**.'

'That's an original name,' I said sarcastically.

Sister Price ignored me. 'An effect size is an objective and usually standardized measure of observed effect. Being standardized means that effect sizes can be compared across different studies that have measured different variables, or have used different scales of measurement.'

'So, for the teddy bear treatment we could compare the size of effect on self-esteem even if self-esteem was measured in different ways?' I asked.

'Yes,' Sister Price replied.

'How do you compute them?' Emily interrupted.

'There are lots of different ways,' Sister Price said. 'Some common effect size measures are Cohen's d, Pearson's correlation coefficient, r, and the odds ratio, OR. There are others, but these three are fairly easy to understand.'

11.2.1 Cohen's d

Emily stared as though her eyes were plugholes through which the bathwater of Sister Price's knowledge would travel; she widened them to accelerate the flow. 'Start with Cohen's d,' she said, a little over-enthusiastically.

Sister Price relished Emily's response. 'Think back to the teddy bear therapy experiment. (SECTION 10.1.10) If we wanted to quantify the effect between the teddy bear and box groups, then one place to start, which is easy to understand, is to look at the difference between the means. The teddy bear group had a mean of 15 (on the self-esteem scale), and the box group, the control, had a mean of 10. The effect of cuddling a teddy bear compared to a box is 15–10 = 5 points on the self-esteem scale. This is an effect size. Hugging a teddy bear had a beneficial effect on self-esteem by 5 points on the scale.'

I had to admit it – that *was* easy to understand.

'This raw effect size has two inconveniences. First, the difference in means is expressed in the units of measurement for the particular study. In this particular example, we know that the teddy bear improved self-esteem relative to the box by 5 units. Is 5 units on the Rosenberg self-esteem scale a meaningful change in the real world? Is it clinically meaningful: would it affect how a clinical psychologist viewed your self-esteem? Is it personally significant: is it a noticeable improvement for the individual?

'The second inconvenience is that the difference between means tells us about the "signal" of the effect, but not about the background "noise" in the measure. Is 5 units of self-esteem a lot or a little relative to the "normal" amount of variation in self-esteem experienced?'

Emily stared at Sister Price, enthralled. 'How do you overcome these problems?' she asked.

'You standardize the effect size. The standard deviation is a measure of "error" or "noise" in the mean (SECTION 4.3) and it can be used to convert a raw score to a z-score. (SECTION 6.2) Do you know what are the units of measurement of a z-score?'

Before I had time to think about it, Emily shouted 'Standard deviations!' in a quite unnecessary outburst.

Sister Price nodded as her choir sang their terrifying song again and an equation (11.1) appeared above her head. 'If we divide the difference between means by the standard deviation we get both a signal-to-noise ratio and a value expressed in standard deviation units. This is what **Cohen's d** is, as the equation shows. By expressing the effect in standard deviations we can compare effects in different studies that used different measures. For example, if another study looked at teddy bear therapy but used a different self-esteem scale than the Rosenberg scale, we could still compare the effect sizes from those two studies. Also, we can better determine whether an effect might be meaningful or clinically significant because, for example, a change of 1 standard deviation along a scale would be a fairly large change.'

Population

$$d = \frac{\bar{\mu}_1 - \bar{\mu}_2}{\sigma}$$

Sample

$$\hat{d} = \frac{\bar{X}_1 - \bar{X}_2}{s} \qquad (11.1)$$

I wondered why they had projected two equations, so I asked.

'It is to remind you that the effect size in which we are interested is the population one. That is the difference between population means divided by the population standard deviation. However, we use the sample to estimate this value. The hat on the d for the sample is to show that it is an *estimate* of the effect in the population.'

'So, the hat means "estimate of"?'

'Yes.'

I was on a roll. 'I have a question for you. We take the difference between two means and we divide by the standard deviation. Surely each mean has its own standard deviation, so which one do we use?'

Sister Price raised her arms in appreciation. 'You think like a scientist,' she said dramatically. 'There are three things that are usually done. First, if the group standard deviations are equal, you can pick the value from either one of the groups because it will not affect the calculation too much. Second, if the groups do not have similar standard deviations, you can pool the two values into a single value. Third, if your groups represent an experimental and control group, then you usually use the standard deviation of the control group or baseline. This choice makes sense because any intervention or experimental manipulation should affect not just the mean but also the spread of scores. Therefore, the control group/baseline standard deviation should be a more accurate estimate of the standard deviation for the measure you have used. In our teddy bear study, you would use the box group standard deviation because you would not expect hugging a cardboard box to affect self-esteem. Therefore, d would represent the amount of self-esteem after hugging a teddy compared to after hugging a box relative to the normal variation in self-esteem in people who hug something that should not affect their self-esteem, like a box.'

Sister Price span around, her cloak fanning out as she span. 'Let me show you some examples using the teddy bear therapy data when there were 10 people per group. **(SECTION 10.1.10)** Let's compute d the simplest way first.' Another equation **(11.2)** appeared from the choir. 'The first approach is to compute the difference between means. The experimental group was the teddy bear group who had a mean of 15 and a standard deviation of 6; the control group was the box group who had a mean of 10 and also a standard deviation of 6. Because both standard deviations are 6 we could use the value from either group, but assuming they were different, we can compute d by subtracting the box mean from the teddy mean and dividing by the box group standard deviation. We get an effect size of 0.83.'

$$
\begin{aligned}
\hat{d} &= \frac{\bar{X}_{\text{Experimental}} - \bar{X}_{\text{Control}}}{s_{\text{Control}}} \\
&= \frac{\bar{X}_{\text{Teddy}} - \bar{X}_{\text{Box}}}{s_{\text{Box}}} \\
&= \frac{15 - 10}{6} \\
&= 0.83
\end{aligned}
\qquad (11.2)
$$

'That makes sense, but what about if you do the pooling thing that you were going on about?'

'If groups are independent then you can pool the standard deviations using this equation.' She span again but this time as she came out of the spin she crouched and extended one arm out towards me, while her other formed a sort of claw in front of her mouth. I wondered whether she'd prefer being in the theatre than in a statistics cult. The choir sang a third equation **(11.3)** into the air. 'N is the sample size of each group and s is the standard deviation. For the teddy data, because the standard deviations and sample sizes are the same in the two groups, this pooled estimate is the same as the standard deviation in the individual groups: 6. However, if the sample sizes and standard deviations were different we would get a standard deviation that is a weighted average: it is the average standard deviation, where each standard deviation is multiplied by the sample size. This means that the standard deviation from the larger sample is given more "weight" than the one from the smaller sample.'

$$
\begin{aligned}
s_p &= \sqrt{\frac{(N_1-1)s_1^2 + (N_2-1)s_2^2}{N_1 + N_2 - 2}} \\
&= \sqrt{\frac{(10-1)6^2 + (10-1)6^2}{10+10-2}} \\
&= \sqrt{\frac{324+324}{18}} \\
&= \sqrt{36} \\
&= 6
\end{aligned}
\tag{11.3}
$$

I asked her why you'd give more weight to the larger sample.

'Remember that estimates from large samples are more precise, so the pooled standard deviation gives greater credibility to the more precise estimate of the standard deviation; that is, the one from the larger sample. Using the pooled estimate of the standard deviation changes the meaning of d: we are now comparing the difference between means against all of the background "noise" in the measure, not just the noise that you would expect to find in normal circumstances. In this case the pooled estimate is the same as for the individual groups so we would again end up with $d = 0.83$. This means that if a person hugged a teddy bear rather than a box their self-esteem would increase by 0.83 standard deviations.'

This value meant nothing to me: was that large, small, or what? I just didn't have a clue. I asked how you would interpret that value.

'In a normal distribution,' Sister Price said patiently, '34% of scores fall between the mean and 1 standard deviation. **(FIGURE 7.4)** Remembering that d is measured using standard deviations, a d of 1 is the same as an increase in self-esteem that moves the average score up the distribution past 34% of scores. For example, imagine that you'd hugged a box and got a self-esteem score that was exactly in the middle of the distribution. You would have self-esteem higher than about 50% of scores (because your score is in the middle). A Cohen's d of 1 implies that had you hugged a teddy instead of a box your score would have been 1 standard deviation higher. In terms of the position of your score in the distribution, this means that your self-esteem would now be higher than 50% of scores (your self-esteem had you hugged a box) + 34% of scores (the standard deviation that hugging a teddy adds to your self-esteem); so, higher than about 84% of scores. Cohen[50, 65] made some suggestions about what constitutes a large or small effect: $d = 0.2$ (small), 0.5 (medium) and 0.8 (large).'

It sounded like the merch stand at our gigs, and I sniggered. 'I'll have The Reality Enigma tour effect size in a large, please!' For the first time Sister Price looked displeased. I explained why I was laughing to myself.

Her tone became serious. 'Unlike your, erm, "gigs", you are not selling T-shirts, so, although by these guidelines a d of 0.83 is a large effect, this ignores the context of the effect such as the measurement instruments and the norms in this research area.[66, 67] If we use these benchmarks, we are as guilty of the kind of lazy thinking as those that we criticized for blindly applying a 0.05 decision rule.'

'Sure, but if you can't apply some rules, how do these effect sizes help us?'

'I think I get it,' interrupted Emily. She grabbed my diePad and brought up Milton's graph of the data for the teddy bear study that tested groups of 100 people. **(FIGURE 10.3, RIGHT)** 'What would Cohen's *d* have been had we used the data in this diagram?'

CHECK YOUR BRAIN: Help Zach to compute Cohen's d for the effect of the teddy bear when a sample size of 100 was used.

I looked at the graph and remembered the values Milton had mentioned to me when he originally showed me the figure. The mean for the teddy group was 15, and for the box group it was 10. The standard deviations were both 6. So, *d* would be 15 – 10/6 = 0.83, just the same as Sister Price calculated for the version of the study when the samples contained only 10 scores.

'Well done,' Emily said when I told her my answer. 'The effect size hasn't changed even though the sample size was bigger. This is because the difference in sample size did not affect the means or standard deviations. Unlike *p*-values, other things being equal, effect sizes are not affected by sample size. By using effect sizes we overcome one problem with NHST.' She was beside herself with excitement, but calmed herself. 'I'm sure that the situation is not quite that simple because, like any parameter, you will get better estimates of the population value in large samples than small ones.'

It seemed that what Emily was saying was that although the sample size doesn't affect the computation of the effect size in the sample, it would affect how closely the sample effect size matches that of the population. Before I could dwell on this, Emily was off again.

'Let me show you something else!' She pulled up another of Milton's diagrams on my die Pad. **(FIGURE 10.4)** 'Calculate Cohen's *d* for the effect in this diagram where there were 1 million people in each group and a tiny difference between the means. The exact mean of the teddy group is 10.01, and for the box group is 10.00. In both groups the standard deviation was 3.'

CHECK YOUR BRAIN: Help Zach to calculate the effect size that Emily asked for.

I used my diePad to work out that the effect size was *d* = 0.003 **(EQUATION 11.4)** and gave this answer to Emily.

$$\hat{d} = \frac{\bar{X}_{\text{Teddy}} - \bar{X}_{\text{Box}}}{s_{\text{Box}}}$$
$$= \frac{10.01 - 10}{3}$$
$$= 0.003$$

(11.4)

'Very good. This is a very small effect indeed; it is practically zero.'

'But wasn't that effect significant when we looked at it with Milton?'

'This is my point: when you looked at *p*-values ...'

I felt nauseous as a realization hit me. How did Emily know about these diagrams and these examples? She had left the room when Milton explained them to me. I interrupted to confront her, but her answer did little to reassure me.

'I told you before, the Society members are joined. I may not have been there, but I experienced everything in that room. In any case, Milton showed you that this tiny effect was deemed statistically significant because of the large sample size, but the effect size is again unaffected by the sample size – a tiny effect shows up as a tiny *d* – it allows us to see the effect for what it is.'

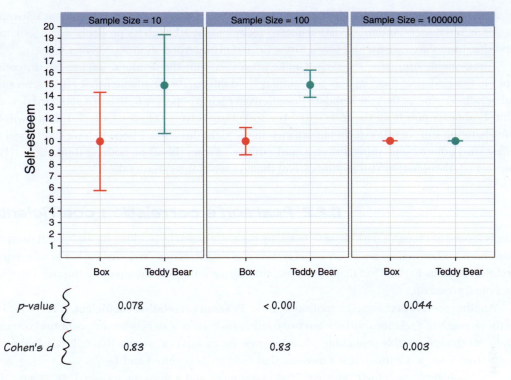

_p_-value	0.078	< 0.001	0.044
Cohen's _d_	0.83	0.83	0.003

Figure 11.2   _Comparing p-values with effect sizes_

I needed to take stock. We'd looked at three different studies that Milton had shown me before. I collected his graphs together **(FIGURES 10.3 & 10.4)** on the screen of my diePad and noted down the _p_-values that Milton had told me and the Cohen's _d_s that we had just calculated. **(FIGURE 11.2)** The first two experiments had identical means and standard deviations but yielded opposite conclusions when using a _p_-value to interpret them: the study based on 10 scores per group was not significant, so hugging a teddy _did not_ seem to have a significant effect, but the study based on 100 scores per group was implying that hugging a teddy _did_ have a significant effect. In the third experiment, two virtually identical means were deemed to be significantly different, implying that hugging a teddy had a significant effect. When we look at effect sizes, our interpretation is quite different: the two experiments with identical means and standard deviations yield identical effect sizes, _d_ = 0.83, and both implied a strong effect of hugging a teddy, whereas the third experiment, which had virtually identical means, produced an effect size that was incredibly small, suggesting that hugging a teddy had virtually no effect, _d_ = 0.003.

This was interesting. I thought back to Sister Price's examples of the 10 different experiments done on teddy therapy. When we looked at only _p_-values we concluded that there was not a lot of evidence that the therapy worked. I wondered what would happen if we looked at the effect sizes instead. **(FIGURE 11.1)**

CHECK YOUR BRAIN: _Help Zach to study the diagram and determine whether teddy therapy works._

Looking at the values of _d_, all of the studies show a positive effect of teddy bear therapy, so they are consistent in showing that the teddy bear therapy group had higher self-esteem than the box group. Nine of the ten studies show an effect size of at least a third of a standard deviation, and six of them show effects of around half a standard deviation. I don't know anything about self-esteem research, but a half standard deviation doesn't seem massive, though it's probably worth looking at, and the studies are consistent. I asked Sister Price if my interpretation was correct.

'A reasonable summary,' she sang. 'Unlike when you study the p-values, you can see the consistency in the evidence: most studies yield similar sized effects. As for whether that effect is meaningful or not, remember that the standard deviations in each group were 6, so half a standard deviation shift is about 3 points on the scale – and the scale ranged from 0 to 30 – which I doubt will be a life-changing shift in self-esteem but is a step in the right direction. I hope to have shown you that effect sizes offer us something different, and can free us from the all-or-nothing thinking of NHST; be warned, though, they still require careful thought when interpreting them.'

11.2.2 Pearson's correlation coefficient, r

Emily looked as though a dark cloud were killing her enthusiasm by blocking its sunlight. It must have been hard for her to have her entire belief system challenged. Sister Price, despite her kindly manner, seemed oblivious to the effect that her tutorial was having on Emily. She squinted through her glasses and bludgeoned on.

'Another useful effect size', she continued, is the **Pearson correlation coefficient**, r. It is a measure of the strength of a relationship between two continuous variables, or between one continuous variable and a categorical variable containing two categories; for example, a variable that tells us whether data come from a cat or a human. It is a measure that can vary between –1 and 1.

The choir broke into their raspy crescendo once more and a diagram appeared. **(FIGURE 11.3)** 'I have drawn different relationships represented by different correlation coefficients,' Sister Price said.

The graphs reminded me of when Milton had highlighted different types of relationships between variables. **(MEOWSINGS 5.2)**

'The top left and top middle panels', Sister Price continued, 'show a negative relationship, which is where as one variable increases the other decreases. For example, the *more* days of the week a teddy is hugged, the *less* self-esteem there is. A perfect negative relationship (top left) has an $r = -1$ and means that as you increase the amount that the teddy is hugged, you decrease self-esteem by a proportionate amount. A slightly smaller negative relationship (top middle) means that an increase in the number of days the teddy is hugged is not matched by a proportionate decrease in self-esteem (although self esteem does go down). Conversely, a positive correlation coefficient (bottom row) occurs when as one variable increases the other increases too: the *more* days of the week a teddy is hugged, the *more* self-esteem there is. A perfect positive relationship has an $r = 1$ (bottom left), which means that as the number of days a teddy is hugged increases, self-esteem increases by a proportionate amount. A positive value less than 1 (e.g., 0.5) shows a situation where as the number of days a teddy is hugged increases, self-esteem also increases but not by a proportionate amount. A correlation coefficient of 0 (top right) shows a situation where there is no relationship at all. For example, as the number of days a teddy is hugged increases there is no change whatsoever in self-esteem; this situation is shown by a completely flat line. Like with d, Cohen[50, 65] suggested some "T-shirt sizes" for r. He said (1) $r = 0.10$ is a small effect because in this situation the effect accounts for only 1% of the total variance; (2) $r = 0.30$ is a medium effect because the effect accounts for 9% of the total variance; and (3) $r = 0.50$ is a large effect because it accounts for 25% of the variance (we get these numbers by squaring r).'

'But we shouldn't use these T-shirt sizes … '

Sister Price swirled her arms. 'Best not to. Also be aware that r is not measured on a linear scale so an effect with $r = 0.8$ is not twice as big as one with $r = 0.4$.'

I asked whether r or d was better.

'It is horses for courses,' the sister replied. 'There are reasons to like r; for example, the fact that it is constrained to lie between 0 (no effect) and ±1 (a perfect effect). However, there are situations in

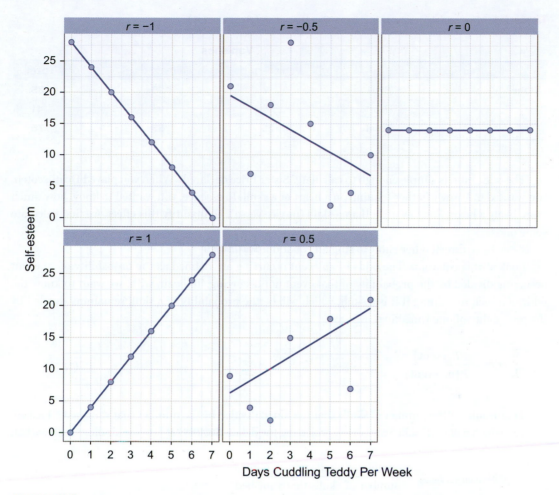

Figure 11.3 *Different relationships shown by different-sized correlation coefficients*

which d may be favoured; for example, when group sizes are very discrepant r can be quite biased compared to d.[68] There are also situations when you might prefer an odds ratio.'

11.2.3 The odds ratio

You've got to be kidding, I thought to myself. It had been a long day, and much as I had enjoyed discovering that there were cults in Elpis hidden under graves and in grand buildings, I was knackered, my brain was frazzled, and I'd become well aware of when someone was about to throw some more statistics at me.

What I lacked in enthusiasm Emily more than made up for. Although she was withering with each revelation from the Doctrine of Chance, she kept wanting more.

Sister Price was on a roll. 'When you have frequency data, the **odds ratio** is often used as an effect size. Effect sizes are most useful when they summarize a focused comparison, and in the case of categorical data that means that they are most useful when quantifying a 2 × 2 contingency table.'

I was pretty sure that this was like the table of frequencies I saw when I played Deathscotch **(SECTION 7.3)** on the probability bridge. To get across I had to decide whether to jump on a heart-shaped stone or a skull-shaped one. The stones could vanish, plunging Milton and me to our death, and the table told us the frequency with which skulls and hearts vanished or remained. I explained the game to Sister Price and drew the frequency table; **(TABLE 11.1)** I remembered it perfectly as though fear had etched it into my brain.

Table 11.1   *The contingency table from Deathscotch (Section 7.3)*

		Vanishes		
		Vanishes	Remains	**Total**
Stone	Skull	7	28	**35**
	Heart	16	25	**41**
	Total	**23**	**53**	**76**

'The odds ratio is simple enough to calculate,' Sister Price declared. 'When you played Deathscotch, you wanted to know whether to jump on a heart or a skull. In essence, you wanted to know how much more likely a heart was to vanish than a skull (or vice versa). To quantify this effect, we first calculate some odds.'

Sister Price directed her choir to sing an equation. **(EQUATION 11.5)**

'Look at this equation. The **odds** of an event occurring are defined as the probability of an event occurring divided by the probability of that event not occurring. To begin with, we want to know the odds of a rock remaining if it is a skull, which will be the probability of a skull remaining divided by the probability of one vanishing.'

$$\text{odds} = \frac{P(\text{event})}{P(\text{no event})} \tag{11.5}$$

'That would be the number of skulls that remained divided by the number that vanished?' I asked. 'Yes, which will be 4,' said Sister Price, projecting the details **(EQUATION 11.6)** into the air directly above her.

$$\begin{aligned} \text{odds}_{\text{skull remaining}} &= \frac{\text{number of skulls that remained}}{\text{number of skulls that vanished}} \\ &= \frac{28}{7} \\ &= 4 \end{aligned} \tag{11.6}$$

'Next, we calculate the odds that a stone remained if it was a heart. This is the number of hearts that remained divided by the number that vanished, which is 1.56.' **(EQUATION 11.7)**

$$\begin{aligned} \text{odds}_{\text{heart remaining}} &= \frac{\text{number of hearts that remained}}{\text{number of hearts that vanished}} \\ &= \frac{25}{16} \\ &= 1.56 \end{aligned} \tag{11.7}$$

'The odds ratio is the odds of a skull remaining divided by the odds of a heart remaining,' Sister Price concluded, as yet another equation **(11.8)** hovered above her. 'This ratio tells us that a skull stone was 2.56 times more likely to remain (than vanish) than a heart stone. This is an extremely elegant and easily understood way to see that you were better off jumping on a skull than a heart. If the odds ratio is 1 then it means that the odds of one outcome are equally as likely as the odds of the other. In this case, if the odds ratio had been 1 then the odds of a skull remaining are the same as the odds of a heart remaining: you would be no better off selecting a skull or a heart.'

$$\text{odds ratio} = \frac{\text{odds}_{\text{skull remaining}}}{\text{odds}_{\text{heart remaining}}} \qquad (11.8)$$

$$= \frac{4}{1.56}$$

$$= 2.56$$

11.3 META-ANALYSIS

Emily's enthusiasm had turned to tears. Much as she had wanted to know about these other ways to test hypotheses, the truth was slowly unravelling her. She looked vulnerable, and I understood: I had the same dilemma. Part of me wanted to know the truth about Alice, but part of me feared it. Although worlds apart, I felt that Emily and I were on similar journeys, and I wished I could make hers less painful. I wished someone could do the same for me too.

'An important part of science is replicating results. It is rare that a single study gives a definitive answer to a scientific question,' Sister Price announced, still completely unconcerned about Emily's emotional state. 'I asked you to imagine earlier that 10 experiments had been done to test whether teddy bear therapy worked. I showed you a diagram (FIGURE 11.1) and evaluated the evidence from these studies in terms of their p-values, confidence intervals and effect sizes.'

Emily looked vacant, as though the strain of having her beliefs undermined was wiping her memory. I held her hand; I felt I needed to remind her of where we were at. I told her that based on p-values we concluded that there were inconsistent results: three studies showed a significant effect of teddy bear therapy and seven did not. Based on the confidence intervals and effect sizes we concluded the opposite: the findings across the studies were quite consistent and suggested that the effect in the population was likely to be positive. The ds ranged from 0.11 to 0.64, all of them were positive and most suggested an effect of around half a standard deviation: no studies showed lower self-esteem after teddy bear therapy compared to hugging a box. Emily thanked me.

Sister Price was impatient to move on. 'Wouldn't it be nice if we could use these studies to get a definitive estimate of the effect in the population? Well, you can!' she said, answering her own question, 'using **meta-analysis.**'

'Sounds tricky!' I said.

'Yes it does, doesn't it?' Sister Price said with a mischievous smile. 'While I think about how to explain something so complicated to you, would you mind just calculating the average of the values of d for the 10 studies in my diagram?' (FIGURE 11.1)

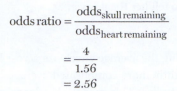 **CHECK YOUR BRAIN:** Help Zach by calculating the average value of the ds.

While Sister Price scratched her brow, shook her head and looked to the skies like a really bad actor pretending to contemplate the most difficult of tasks, I set about calculating the average as she'd asked. I needed to add up all of the ds and then divide by the number of ds I had. Using my diePad I typed in the values to the equation (11.9) for the mean.

$$\bar{d} = \frac{\sum_{i=1}^{k} d_i}{n} \qquad (11.9)$$

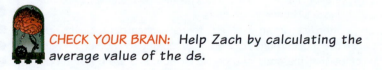
$$= \frac{0.60 + 0.32 + 0.64 + 0.58 + 0.47 + 0.44 + 0.45 + 0.37 + 0.27 + 0.11}{10} = 0.43$$

Pleased with myself, I interrupted Sister Price's performance to tell her the answer.

'Well done,' she said. 'You've just done a meta-analysis.'

'For real?'

'At a simple level, yes. A meta-analysis is a way of calculating the average effect size across lots of similar and comparable studies. In reality, we calculate a slightly more complicated average. Large studies produce better estimates of parameters than small studies. This means that large studies similarly produce more precise estimates of population effect sizes. Therefore, we want to place more importance on effect sizes from large studies than we do on those from smaller (less precise) studies. To achieve this, we weight each effect size by how precise it is, and how precise it is will be a function of the sample size. We can use meta-analysis to combine any effect size – d, r or odds ratios – but within an analysis all effects have to be expressed as the same effect size. We couldn't, for example, combine rs with ds because these are different measures.'

'Right, so you find some studies that have basically tested the same thing. For each study, you calculate the effect size, being consistent about which effect size you use. Then you multiply each effect size by its precision to weight it, and take the average?'

'More or less. There are a lot of other issues to consider and more complex things that you can do, but the essence of it is as you have just described.[69-75] Unlike NHST, meta-analysis seeks merely to quantify the population effect size and not to worry about whether it is significant or not. It is about accumulating evidence for a hypothesis through replication of effects and pooling those replications to get a better idea of what is actually going on in the population.'

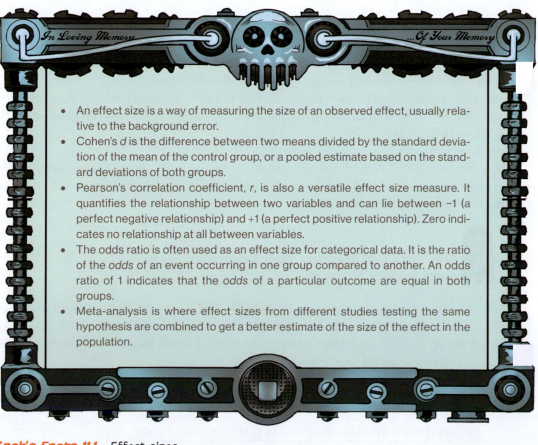

In Loving Memory ...Of Your Memory

- An effect size is a way of measuring the size of an observed effect, usually relative to the background error.
- Cohen's d is the difference between two means divided by the standard deviation of the mean of the control group, or a pooled estimate based on the standard deviations of both groups.
- Pearson's correlation coefficient, r, is also a versatile effect size measure. It quantifies the relationship between two variables and can lie between −1 (a perfect negative relationship) and +1 (a perfect positive relationship). Zero indicates no relationship at all between variables.
- The odds ratio is often used as an effect size for categorical data. It is the ratio of the *odds* of an event occurring in one group compared to another. An odds ratio of 1 indicates that the *odds* of a particular outcome are equal in both groups.
- Meta-analysis is where effect sizes from different studies testing the same hypothesis are combined to get a better estimate of the size of the effect in the population.

Zach's Facts 11.1   Effect sizes

11.4 BAYESIAN APPROACHES

The Doctrine circled Sister Price, and as they moved around her they sang. It was beautiful. It occurred to me that we could use some vocal harmonies like these in our songs: it would add an ethereal feel. In the middle of the circle, Sister Price span, crouched, and postured with jagged arm movements. It seemed as though she was building towards a dramatic crescendo. Then, as suddenly as the display had begun, the choir dispersed behind Sister Price and she screamed 'Bayes!'

Her scream made me jump. She removed her glasses and stared with enormous eyes directly at us. Was she trying to hypnotize us?

'A final approach is completely different than NHST,' she whispered. 'It is the way that the Doctrine of Chance favours.' Sister Price's choir affirmed this by erupting in a magnificent choral tension that resolved into what sounded like the words 'Bayes' theorem'. I knew those words: Milton has explained Bayes' theorem to me when we'd played Deathscotch. **(MEOWSINGS 7.2)**

The choir softened to a silence and Sister Price said, 'Our system of testing hypotheses is called Bayesian analysis.[61, 76–78] We believe in using the data you collect to update your beliefs in a hypothesis. Let me give you an example.[78] Have you heard of gernal roulette?'

I nodded, remembering Emily shoving her finger into the black boxes at the Secret Philanthropic Society. **(SECTION 10.1.2)** Emily shuddered beside me.

'Good. Imagine I have four boxes. No one can see what is inside, but let's assume that we know that two of the boxes contain gernal worms and two do not. I ask you to choose a box. What is the probability that it contains a gernal worm?'

'Half the boxes contain gernal worms, so it would be 0.5.'

'Good. Now I choose a box. Neither of us knows what is inside our box, but I poke my finger in and survive. Therefore, you know that the box I chose did not contain a gernal worm. Does that change your belief that your box contains a gernal worm?'

'No, at the time I picked it I had a 0.5 chance of getting a worm, and that hasn't changed.'

'No, but the information you have about the boxes *has* changed. Imagine that you picked a box with a worm inside, what would be left over?'

'Two boxes without worms and one with.'

'Yes, so what would be the probability of my choosing, as I did, an empty box?'

'It would be 2/3 or 0.67, because there were three boxes and two were empty.'

'Yes. Now imagine that you had picked an empty box, what would be left over?'

'Two worms and one empty.'

'What would be the probability of my picking an empty box?'

'It would be 1/3 or 0.33, because only one of the three boxes was empty.'

'Well done. If you had picked a worm box, then it is more likely that I would pick an empty box ($p = 0.67$) than if you had picked an empty box ($p = 0.33$). Knowing that I did in fact pick an empty box, would you now believe that there was a 0.5 probability that your box contains a worm?'

'I guess not. I'd believe that my box is more likely to have a worm because in that situation you had double the chance of choosing an empty box.'

'Yes!' Sister Price exclaimed. 'Bayesian analysis is based on this idea that you can update your prior beliefs based on the data you observe.'

11.4.1 Asking a different question

'NHST asks an unhelpful question,' Sister Price declared. 'It evaluates the probability of getting a test statistic at least as large as the one you have, given the null hypothesis. It therefore asks, what is the probability of the data we have obtained, given a hypothesis is true: $p(\text{data}|\text{hypothesis})$. Specifically, NHST asks what is the probability of my test statistic (data) given that the null hypothesis is true, $p(\text{test statistic}|\text{null hypothesis})$.'

'Why is that question unhelpful?'

'Because you are not testing the hypothesis, you assume it is true in the first place. More useful things to evaluate are the probability of a hypothesis being true given the data we have collected, $p(\text{hypothesis}|\text{data})$, or whether one hypothesis is more likely than another given the data.'

'Aren't they the same thing?' I couldn't see the difference.

'They very much are *not* the same thing,' she replied. 'The probability that you are a musician given that you have sold millions of songs, $p(\text{musician}|\text{sold millions of songs})$, is very high because to sell songs you must be able to write music; however, the inverse probability that you have sold millions of songs given that you are a musician, $p(\text{sold millions of songs}|\text{musician})$, is likely to be very small because there are thousands of musicians and most of them do not sell millions of songs.'

It was a fair point – I now understood the difference. I still didn't understand why scientists would want to know the probability of a hypothesis being true given the data rather than the opposite. The Sister explained.

'Imagine you have been accused of a murder. The police have a hypothesis that you are guilty. They sample your DNA and compare it to DNA found at the crime scene. It turns out that your DNA matches that at the crime scene.' Sister Price plunged her hand into her cloak, pulled out a piece of chalk, and scribbled a table of numbers on the stone floor. **(TABLE 11.2)** 'Look, here are some data to illustrate your predicament. Let us imagine there are only 1000 people in Elpis. One of those people is guilty of the murder, and his or her DNA will match that at the crime scene. It is not possible to be guilty and for your DNA not to match, so that cell of the table contains a zero. Now, the remaining 999 people are innocent and the vast majority (950) have DNA that does not match that found at the crime scene; however, a small number do (49).

'First off, let us look at the probability of the data given the hypothesis, this is the probability that the DNA matches given that the defendant is guilty, $p(\text{match}|\text{guilty})$. What would that probability be?'

CHECK YOUR BRAIN: Help Zach to calculate $p(\text{match}|\text{guilty})$.

Table 11.2   Contingency table of whether defendants are innocent or guilty of a crime based on whether their DNA matches that at the crime scene

		DNA sample matches crime scene		
		Match	No match	**Total**
Defendant	Guilty	1	0	**1**
	Innocent	49	950	**999**
	Total	**50**	**950**	**1000**

I recognized this situation: it was similar to Deathscotch on the probability bridge, where Milton had explained to me how to calculate a conditional probability. **(SECTION 7.3)** The conditional probability of a DNA match given the person was guilty would be the probability of being guilty and having a DNA match divided by the probability of being guilty. There was one person from the population of 1000 who was guilty and had a DNA match, and there was also one person out of 1000 who was guilty, so the conditional probability would be 1. **(EQUATION 11.10)** In other words, I told Sister Price, given the person is guilty their DNA *must* match that at the crime scene.

$$p(A|B) = \frac{p(B \cap A)}{p(B)}$$

$$p(\text{match}|\text{guilty}) = \frac{p(\text{guilty} \cap \text{match})}{p(\text{guilty})} = \frac{1/1000}{1/1000} = \frac{0.001}{0.001} = 1$$

(11.10)

'Yes! It is a stupid question to ask. If you already know the person is guilty, then the probability that their DNA will match has to be 1: it is a certainty. Also if you knew they were guilty already then you would not need to bother with DNA. This probability does not tell you anything useful about your theory because it relies on you already assuming that your hypothesis is true, which it might not be. NHST follows this logic: we evaluate evidence for the null hypothesis by assuming that it is true in the first place; as I said before, we look at the probability of the data (test statistic), given the null hypothesis is true. Logically this is the same as looking at the probability of a DNA match (data) given that the hypothesis is true (you are guilty). Like NHST, this probability cannot tell us anything about the hypothesis (your guilt) because it assumes the hypothesis is true.

'The more interesting question is what is the probability of the hypothesis (you are guilty) given that your DNA matches that of the crime scene (the data). As a prosecutor, this is the question that matters: given the data (the fact that your DNA matches that of the murderer) what is the probability of the theory that you *are* the murderer. What is that probability?'

CHECK YOUR BRAIN: Help Zach to calculate p(guilty|match).

The conditional probability of a person being guilty given their DNA matched would be the probability of being guilty and having a DNA match divided by the probability of DNA matching the crime scene. There was one person from the population of 1000 who was guilty and had a DNA match, and there were 50 people out of 1000 whose DNA could match that of the killer. **(EQUATION 11.11)**

'The probability would be low, about 0.02,' I replied.

'Oh yes! Yes! You see how important it is to ask the best question for the situation? If the prosecutor followed the logic of NHST, he or she would believe you were certainly the killer because the probability of your having a DNA match given you are the killer is 1. However, by asking the right question – what is the probability that you are the killer given your DNA matches – they would realize that given the data (that your DNA matches) the probability that you are guilty is, in fact, very small: a 2% chance. Bayesian analysis asks a more useful question: it asks what is the probability of my hypothesis being true, given the data I have collected.'

$$p(\text{guilty}|\text{match}) = \frac{p(\text{match} \cap \text{guilty})}{p(\text{match})} = \frac{1/1000}{50/1000} = \frac{0.001}{0.05} = 0.02 \qquad (11.11)$$

11.4.2 Bayes' theorem revisited

Sister Price chalked some more equations **(11.12)** on the wall, one of which reminded me of Bayes' theorem. **(MEOWSINGS 7.2)**

'We can arrive at the same conditional probabilities using Bayes' theorem,' she said. 'Bayes' theorem tells us that we could work out the conditional probability of two events from their individual probabilities and the inverse conditional probability. Rather than thinking of this theorem with abstract letters A and B, we can think of it in terms of the hypothesis we have and the data we have collected. If we rewrite the theorem replacing the letter A with the model or hypothesis that we want to test, and B with the data we have collected, then we can get a sense of how Bayes' theorem might be useful in testing hypotheses.'

$$\begin{aligned}
\text{Bayes' theorem} = p(A|B) &= \frac{p(B|A) \times p(A)}{p(B)} \\[1em]
= p(\text{model}|\text{data}) &= \frac{p(\text{data}|\text{model}) \times p(\text{model})}{p(\text{data})} \\[1em]
= \text{posterior probability} &= \frac{\text{likelihood} \times \text{prior probability}}{\text{marginal likelihood}}
\end{aligned} \qquad (11.12)$$

I looked at Sister Price's equation **(11.2)**, but replacing the probabilities with phrases like 'posterior probability' and 'marginal likelihood' really didn't help me to make sense of anything. Before I could ask, Sister Price picked up her explanation.

'Don't look so scared!' Sister Price wiped her glasses, put them back on, and looked at me. 'I will explain each part of Bayes' theorem and relate them to the example of determining your guilt of murder.

'First, we have the **posterior probability**, which is our belief in a hypothesis or model *after* we have considered the data (hence it is *posterior* to considering the data). In the case of our murder example, this would be our belief that you were guilty given the data that your DNA is a match, $p(\text{guilty}|\text{match})$. This is the value that we are interested in finding out. We can evaluate your guilt given a DNA match both as a single value, and as a **credible interval**. A credible interval is the interval between which a certain percentage of values fall (usually 95%). It tells us the limits between which 95% of values fall in the posterior distribution. In other words, we can be 95% confident that the parameter of interest falls within the limits of the interval.'

'Like a confidence interval?' I said, feeling pleased with myself.

My pleasure was short-lived. 'Noooooo,' came a chorus from the Doctrine. Sister Price's tone hardened.

'Be clear: a confidence interval is set so that before the data are collected there is a 95% chance that the interval will contain the true value of the parameter. Once the data are collected, your sample is either one of the 95% that produces an interval containing the true value, or it is one of the 5% that does not. In other words, having collected the data, the probability of the interval containing the true value of the parameter is either 0 (it does not contain it) or 1 (it does contain it) but you do not know which.

A credible interval is different in that it reflects the *plausibility* that the interval contains the true value. For example, a 95% credible interval has a 0.95 probability of containing the true value.'

'I get it,' I said. I didn't really get it.

'The **prior probability** is our belief in a hypothesis or model *before*, or *prior to*, considering the data. In our example it would be our belief in your guilt before we consider whether your DNA matches or not. This would be the base rate for guilt, p(guilt), which in our example is 1 in 1000, or 0.001. The **marginal likelihood**, which is sometimes referred to as evidence, is the probability of the observed data, which in this example is the probability of matching DNA, p(match). The data show that there were 50 matches in 1000 cases, so this value is 50/1000, or 0.05. The **likelihood** is the probability that the observed data could be produced given the hypothesis or model being considered. In the murder example it is, therefore, the probability that you would find that the DNA matched given that someone was in fact the murderer, p(match|guilty).'

Sister Price wielded her chalk again and spoke as she wrote on the floor. **(EQUATION 11.13)** 'Put all of this together and you can see that our belief in your guilt given that your DNA matches is a function of how likely a match is if you were guilty ($p = 1$), our prior belief in your guilt ($p = 0.001$) and the probability of getting a DNA match (0.05). Our belief, having considered the data, is 0.02: there is a 2% chance that you are the murderer.'

I noticed that the value was the same as we'd calculated a minute ago.

$$p(\text{guilty}|\text{match}) = \frac{p(\text{match}|\text{guilty}) \times p(\text{guilty})}{p(\text{match})}$$

$$= \frac{1 \times 0.001}{0.05} = 0.02$$

(11.13)

Sister Price looked contented. 'This result shows you how Bayes' theorem can be used to update our beliefs about a hypothesis.' She chalked a diagram on the floor. **(FIGURE 11.4)** 'We begin with a certain degree of belief in our hypothesis – this is our prior probability. We then collect some data and look at how likely these data would be if the hypothesis were true. This new information is fed into Bayes' theorem, which uses it to calculate the probability of the hypothesis given the data that you have collected. This posterior probability is an updated version of your prior belief that incorporates the new information provided by the data.'

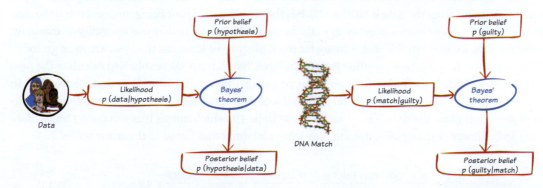

Figure 11.4 *Overview of Bayesian analysis*

Something made me uncomfortable about this example.

'In the murder example, a judge has a certain belief in my guilt, which would be that there is a 1 in 1000 chance that I am guilty (i.e., $p = 0.001$). The judge is then presented with the data, which is that my DNA matches that found at the crime scene. As a result of this new information they update their belief in my guilt, which is that they now think that there is a 1 in 50 chance that I am the murderer (i.e., $p = 0.02$). The judge's probability has increased from 0.001 to 0.02 – they are now more convinced that I am a murderer!'

11.4.3 Comparing hypotheses

Sister Price grinned maniacally. 'Of course, and that is as it should be because your matching DNA makes it more likely you are the murderer than before the judge knew anything about your DNA. Bear with me and let us look at how we might use Bayes' theorem to compare two competing hypotheses. We know the probability that you are guilty given the data is 0.02; in NHST terms, this is the alternative hypothesis, it is the hypothesis that something happened, that you committed the murder. In NHST we also have a null hypothesis, a hypothesis that there is no effect or that nothing happened. The equivalent here is the hypothesis that you are innocent given the DNA match, $p(\text{innocent}|\text{match})$. What would this probability be?'

 CHECK YOUR BRAIN: Help Zach to calculate $p(\text{innocent}|\text{match})$.

Using Bayes' theorem, I would first need to know the probability of a DNA match given the person was innocent, $p(\text{match}|\text{innocent})$. There were 999 innocent people and 49 had a DNA match, so this probability would be 49/999, or 0.049. I would also need to know the probability of being innocent, $p(\text{innocent})$. There were 999 out of 1000 people who are innocent **(TABLE 11.2)**, so the probability would be 999/1000, or 0.999. Finally, I would need the probability of a DNA match, $p(\text{match})$, which I worked out before as 0.05. Putting these values into Bayes' theorem, I'd get a probability of 0.98. **(EQUATION 11.14)**

$$p(\text{innocent}|\text{match}) = \frac{p(\text{match}|\text{innocent}) \times p(\text{innocent})}{p(\text{match})}$$
$$= \frac{0.049 \times 0.999}{0.05} = 0.98$$

(11.14)

Sister Price was impressed with my work. 'Fantastic! What we know, then, is that the probability of your being guilty given the data is 0.02 or 2%, but the probability of your being innocent given the data is 0.98 or 98%. These values allow us to evaluate the evidence of whether you are guilty or innocent, given the data we have. In this case, you are far more likely to be innocent than you are to be guilty.'

Sister Price drew another equation **(11.15)** on the floor. 'We can use these values to calculate the **posterior odds**, which is the ratio of the posterior probability for one hypothesis to that for another. In this example it would be the ratio of the probability of your innocence given the data to the probability of your guilt given the data. The value turns out to be 49, which means that you are 49 times more likely to be innocent than guilty, despite your DNA matching that found at the crime scene.'

$$\text{posterior odds} = \frac{p(\text{hypothesis 1}|\text{data})}{p(\text{hypothesis 2}|\text{data})} = \frac{p(\text{innocent}|\text{match})}{p(\text{guilty}|\text{match})} = \frac{0.98}{0.02} = 49$$

(11.15)

'Over the wall! That's sick – in the movies a DNA match is *always* used as proof of guilt!'

'I wish it were only in the movies,' the Sister said solemnly. 'Even in the real world people do not understand that they should consider how likely it would be for an innocent person to also have matching DNA. The more general point is that we can use Bayes' theorem to compare two hypotheses. The logic of NHST hinges on comparing a hypothesis about there being an effect (the alternative hypothesis) with one stating that the effect is zero (the null hypothesis). Bayes' theorem allows us to compute the probability of both hypotheses given the data, which means we can compute the posterior odds of the alternative hypothesis to the null, that is, a value that tells us how much more likely the alternative hypothesis is given the data relative to null.'

Sister Price began frantically drawing more equations on the floor. **(EQUATION 11.16)** 'You see, if we write out Bayes' theorem for the alternative hypothesis and then divide by Bayes' theorem for the null, then the probability of the data, p(data), which is the marginal likelihood for both the alternative and null hypotheses, drops out. What we are left with are three values.

'The posterior odds, as we have seen, tell us the ratio of the probability of the alternative hypothesis, given the data, relative to that for the null hypothesis.

'We also have the **prior odds**, which tell us the ratio of the probability of the alternative hypothesis to the probability of the null *before* you look at the data. If testing a completely new hypothesis you might set the prior odds to 1, meaning that you are equally prepared to believe the alternative and the null hypothesis. However, if you are testing a hypothesis related to what other scientists have done, you might use past evidence to set your prior belief in the alternative hypothesis over the null.

'Finally, we have the ratio of the probability of the data, given the alternative hypothesis, to that for the null hypothesis. This is referred to as the **Bayes factor**. A Bayes factor less than 1 supports the null hypothesis by suggesting that the probability of the data given the null is higher than the probability of the data given the alternative hypothesis. Conversely, a Bayes factor greater than 1 suggests that the observed data are more likely given the alternative hypothesis than the null. For example, a Bayes factor of 4 means that the observed data are four times more likely under the alternative hypothesis than the null hypothesis. Values between 1 and 3 are considered evidence for the alternative hypothesis that is "barely worth mentioning", values between 3 and 10 are considered "substantial evidence" for the alternative hypothesis, and values greater than 10 are strong evidence for the alternative hypothesis.[79] The Bayes factor also indicates the degree to which your prior beliefs have changed as a result of looking at the data.'

'Isn't it weird that a value of, say, 2 is "barely worth mentioning" but 3 would be "substantial evidence"?'

'Yes, but that is because you are interpreting the word "substantial" in a different way to how it was intended. Three is the value at which the Bayes factor begins to "have substance", you might more accurately describe scores of 3 to 10 as "non-negligible". Although scientists use these category labels, you are better off interpreting the value of the Bayes factor.'

'Let me check this. You're saying that you can use Bayes' theorem to evaluate the relative evidence for the null and alternative hypothesis. How is that better than the NHST stuff?'

$$\frac{p(\text{alternative}|\text{data})}{p(\text{null}|\text{data})} = \frac{p(\text{data}|\text{alternative}) \times p(\text{alternative})/p(\text{data})}{p(\text{data}|\text{null}) \times p(\text{null})/p(\text{data})}$$

$$\frac{p(\text{alternative}|\text{data})}{p(\text{null}|\text{data})} = \frac{p(\text{data}|\text{alternative})}{p(\text{data}|\text{null})} \times \frac{p(\text{alternative})}{p(\text{null})} \tag{11.16}$$

$$\text{posterior odds} = \text{Bayes factor} \times \text{prior odds}$$

11.4.4 Benefits of Bayesian approaches

Sister Price looked uncertainly at Emily, who was silently weeping. She took off her glasses, rubbed them, put them back on and squinted hard at her. 'Is she alright?' she asked.

'Obviously not,' I replied. 'She's really upset!'

'How can you tell?'

'Look at her!'

'I am ... I think my glasses are broken.'

'Your glasses?'

'Yes, they help me to see ... see people's emotions.'

'Is that why you're all wearing identical glasses?'

'Yes, we believe in the objective, in probabilities. This has clouded our ability to interpret the subjective. At times it is useful to judge people's emotional states, and these glasses help us to do that.'

'Scientists!' I muttered under my breath. 'They know everything apart from what actually matters.'

Sister Price studied me, trying to work out what I had said. I hoped her glasses weren't revealing the pity I felt for her Doctrine and their emotional isolation. I thought back to when Alice and I got together. She had been so open, but she had become like them: cold, unable to understand how people felt. Is this what science did to people? I should probably get out while I still had some insight into the emotional world. 'Just tell me how this Bayesian stuff improves upon NHST and I'll be gone,' I said. I'd had enough here.

'Bayesian hypothesis testing asks a more useful question for this situation,' Sister Price reiterated. 'It asks what is the probability of my theory given the data I have collected. Now, what problems did I identify with the NHST approach?'

CHECK YOUR BRAIN: What are the problems with NHST discussed earlier in this chapter?

I thought quickly to our earlier conversation about NHST. I needed to answer fast and bench these people.

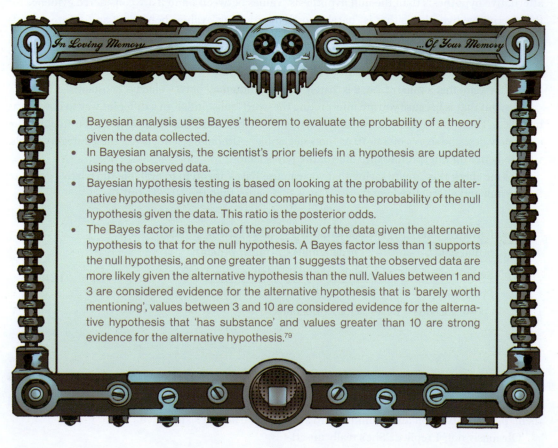

- Bayesian analysis uses Bayes' theorem to evaluate the probability of a theory given the data collected.
- In Bayesian analysis, the scientist's prior beliefs in a hypothesis are updated using the observed data.
- Bayesian hypothesis testing is based on looking at the probability of the alternative hypothesis given the data and comparing this to the probability of the null hypothesis given the data. This ratio is the posterior odds.
- The Bayes factor is the ratio of the probability of the data given the alternative hypothesis to that for the null hypothesis. A Bayes factor less than 1 supports the null hypothesis, and one greater than 1 suggests that the observed data are more likely given the alternative hypothesis than the null. Values between 1 and 3 are considered evidence for the alternative hypothesis that is 'barely worth mentioning', values between 3 and 10 are considered evidence for the alternative hypothesis that 'has substance' and values greater than 10 are strong evidence for the alternative hypothesis.[79]

Zach's Facts 11.2 Bayesian analysis

'I think you said that NHST didn't allow you to draw any firm conclusions about the null hypotheses, significance is affected by the sample size, it encourages all-or-nothing thinking and ... erm ... yeah, it depends on the intentions of the scientist.'

'Solid memory. I assume you are not a Chipper.'

'Why?'

'Because the Chippers fall down, and when they get up their memory is gone.' She said it factually and without any indication that she understood that she was talking about things happening to real people. People with feelings, people with families and lives that they were losing. She was emotionless, without compassion.

'Now think about these problems,' she continued. 'Bayesian approaches, unlike NHST, provide direct evidence about whether the null hypothesis is true. Sample size is not an issue for Bayesian analysis. If you sample more people, all you do is add to the evidence that you use to update your beliefs. You do not need to determine how much data to collect before the analysis, because any prior belief can be updated based on any amount of new information. This point relates to the point about the intentions of the scientist; because Bayesian analysis is not based on long-run probabilities, it does not matter when you stop collecting data or what your rule is for collecting data, because any new data relevant to your hypothesis can be used to update your prior beliefs in the null and alternative hypothesis. Finally, Bayesian analysis is focused on evaluating evidence for a hypothesis and so it does not rely on arbitrary criteria for "significance". Instead, you simply interpret the weight of evidence for one hypothesis over another.'

Emily had taken all of this in and her tears had turned into uncontrollable sobs.

'Are you on the level?' I asked.

'Everything I have spent my life believing has gone. I don't know what is real any more. Years in the Society thinking I could differentiate what mattered from what didn't, but I have been sitting on a house of cards. I used to pride myself on seeing the truth, but I have seen nothing, and consequently I *am* nothing.'

With that she curled up tightly, her head buried in her knees as though switching off from the world. Sister Price shrugged her shoulders, incapable of finding an appropriate response. She tiptoed across the floor, making exaggerated movements with her legs as though that would somehow mute the sound of her movement. The choir followed in a line trying to evacuate the building before they could be contaminated by Emily's emotion.

I had another idea: I ran up the stairs, out of the tomb, down the street several blocks until I found one of Elpis's 24-hour shops. Twenty minutes later I returned and knelt by Emily.

337

KEY TERMS

Bayes factor

Cohen's *d*

Credible interval

Effect size

Likelihood

Marginal likelihood (evidence)

Meta-analysis

Odds

Odds ratio

Pearson correlation coefficient

Posterior odds

Posterior probability

Prior odds

Prior probability

JIG:SAW'S PUZZLES

1   According to Paul Zak,[57] the hormone oxytocin increases trust in humans. You do an experiment in which groups of people are exposed to oxytocin or not while meeting a stranger. They rate how much they trusted the stranger from 0 (no trust) to 10 (complete trust). The oxytocin group had a mean trust of $M = 7.45$ ($SD = 2.67$) and the non-exposed group had a mean trust of $M = 5.13$ ($SD = 1.12$). What is Cohen's *d* for this difference? (Compute it using the pooled variance estimate as well as using the control group variability.)

2   In a different version of the oxytocin study, participants are simply classified according to whether they trusted the stranger or not. The data are in Table 11.3. What is the odds ratio for these data?

Table 11.3   *Number of people who trusted a stranger depending on whether they were exposed to oxytocin or not during the meeting*

		Trusted stranger		
		Trusted	Did not trust	**Total**
Oxytocin	Oxytocin	35	15	**50**
	No oxytocin	27	23	**50**
	Total	**63**	**38**	**100**

3   For the data in Table 11.3, use Bayes' theorem to compute the conditional probability of trusting the stranger given you received oxytocin, $p(\text{trust}|\text{oxytocin})$. What is the conditional probability of trusting given that you didn't receive oxytocin, $p(\text{trust}|\text{no oxytocin})$?

4   For the data in Table 11.3, what are the posterior odds of trusting the stranger when given oxytocin than when not?

5   What does a Bayes factor tell us?

6   Describe the differences between NHST and Bayesian hypothesis testing.

7   What is the difference between a confidence interval and a credible interval?

8   What is a meta-analysis?

9   Zach stole some glasses to help with emotion detection. These were tested on 252 people. Some wore the glasses, some didn't and they had to identify a stranger's emotion from their facial expression. The numbers correct and incorrect in each group are in Table 11.4. What is the odds ratio for these data?

Table 11.4   *Number of people who correctly identified a stranger's emotion depending on whether they were wearing emotion detection glasses or not*

		Emotion detection		
		Correct	Incorrect	**Total**
Glasses	Glasses	68	49	**117**
	No glasses	93	42	**135**
	Total	**161**	**91**	**252**

10   For the data in Table 11.4, use Bayes' theorem to compute the conditional probability of correctly identifying an emotion given you wore the glasses, p(correct|glasses). What is the conditional probability of being correct given that you didn't wear the glasses, p(correct|no glasses)?

11   Using the data in Table 11.4, what are the posterior odds of correctly identifying an emotion in the stranger when wearing glasses than when not?

IN THE NEXT CHAPTER, ZACH DISCOVERS ...

A mysterious fan
The linear model
The assumptions underlying the linear model

Residuals
The power of oxytocin

12

Assumptions

Starblind

I emerged from the Doctrine of Chance in the early hours of the morning and decided to walk the long distance between Egestes and my apartment in Janus. I had a lot of information to take in from my visits to the Secret Philanthropic Society and the Doctrine of Chance. They had conflicting ideas about how to test hypotheses, and I needed to pick the bones out of it all. Knackered as I was, the empty streets gave me headspace. Inevitably my thoughts turned to Alice. Milton had taken me to the Secret Philanthropic Society so that I could test my hypotheses about the JIG:SAW data properly. In my sleep-deprived haze I found it difficult to care. Why should I cling on to some hope that Alice felt something for me when she'd made no effort to contact me, and seemed happy enough at JIG:SAW? If you took Alice out of the mix then I shouldn't care what was happening at JIG:SAW: it wasn't my problem.

I crashed out for the rest of the day, and as a new week began, I had a gig to focus on. Nick had been handling the organization for me: checking in with the promoter, doing publicity on *memory-Bank*, and keeping Joel, the other guitarist, and Jessika, our bassist, up to speed. We had time for one rehearsal, and I walked in feeling at ease for the first time since Alice had gone. I was psyched about playing and hanging out with the band.

My mood was short-lived. Joel and Jessika were distant, and our playing was loose and chaotic. As we faltered through our set list for the gig, tensions rose. Nick was on the level, but Joel and Jessika were annoyed at me for dropping the band before an important show. I didn't have the social skills for this sort of situation. I wanted to apologize, I wanted to ask them to cut me some slack, and I wanted to reassure them everything would be sound, but instead I withdrew into myself. By the time we left only Nick was speaking to me.

Milton was absent from my apartment all week; it felt empty without something else moving about. I missed Alice too, but with no reminders of her in the apartment I started to move on. I stopped feeling angry with her and felt less need to explain why she had gone. The only thing I could control was how I would get on with life, and I vowed to forget about JIG:SAW and Alice and to focus on the band. It worked for a few days, but as Saturday night came around, thoughts of Alice turned up like uninvited guests. My gigs were one of the few things Alice and I had done together recently; however much science steered her away from me, she never, ever, missed my gigs. Tonight would be the first time she had missed one of our shows, and that thought made me unbearably sad.

The gig itself was intense: our lack of practice showed, but what we lacked in tightness we gained in friction between us. Before we hit the stage Joel and Jessika could barely conceal their resentment towards me for our lack of rehearsal time. Once we started to play that tension was spat out through one of the most visceral performances I could remember us giving. The crowd lapped it up, and as I sang I became entranced in a strange, almost transcendental catharsis as I tried to exorcize the emotional turmoil of the past couple of weeks.

The band had a post-gig ritual of coming off stage and into a group hug where we thanked each other. It was cheese, but it reminded us that we relied on each other, that we were greater than the sum of our parts. Tonight I was apprehensive about what would happen as we came off stage, but Joel, Jessika and Nick surrounded me and held me so tight I could hardly breathe. Instead of 'thank you', Jessika and Joel said sorry, and Nick said, 'You were over the frippin' wall tonight, bro!' as he planted a kiss on the top of my head. I said nothing, but inside all I could think about was how much I wished Alice had been here to see it.

After a couple of brews backstage, I was finally winding down. Some fans had joined us and I was enjoying the banter with them and the other bands that had played before us. The show had helped me to get my emotions out. Remembering the week gone by, I resolved again to move forward with my life. That was until Milton walked in. I hadn't seen him since he'd abandoned me outside the Secret Philanthropic Society; I'd thought that was probably the last I'd see of him. After all, he was free from the Beimeni Centre and had no reason to help me. My bandmates joked about the 'stray cat' liking metal music as he strutted in, but Milton's presence unsettled me. He walked through the dressing room nonchalantly, winked at me as he passed, and headed out to the now emptying hallway. I followed.

'Thanks for running off and leaving me in the middle of the Void,' I said.

'Unlike you, I do not need an afternoon in a crypt to understand Bayesian analysis. I get bored with people telling you things that I already know.'

'I didn't ask for a statistics education, I asked you to help me find Alice, which you haven't done.'

My hostility surprised me; I think it surprised Milton too. He paused and considered his words carefully.

'Before an army goes on a mission,' he said, 'it gathers intelligence and runs through training drills to make sure it is as prepared as it can be for a successful mission. I have been training you, and you might not understand the relevance of this training, but perhaps you will once battle begins.'

I didn't like his talk of armies and battles; I didn't believe in violence.

'I have also been gathering intelligence,' he concluded.

I tried to lighten the tone. 'If you've come back for my tuna, you're out of luck: you ate it all before you left.'

The cat didn't laugh. 'I'm confident you will buy me tuna when you see what I have been doing while you have been flouncing about conducting your strange sonic rituals. Do you trust me?'

'Honestly? I'm not sure whom to trust since Alice disappeared. That includes you.' There was a familiar smell, but I couldn't place it.

'You remember when we met Rob Nutcot, and you asked him about the JIG:SAW data that we had analysed and especially the code 1318 workers? You ended up agreeing with him that there was nothing wrong with the data, and you had no recollection of speaking about the code 1318 workers. That has been troubling me, and so has Nutcot's smell.'

That's what the smell was – it reminded me of Nutcot. Someone else must be wearing the same aftershave.

'I noticed the smell the first time we met him,' Milton continued. 'It was very pungent. When we met them at Hermes, I harvested a sample.'

'You harvested his smell?'

'In a manner of speaking, yes. I collected some air, and while you were busy with the Doctrine of Chance I broke down its chemical components to see what his smell contains. I then made some of my own.'

'I'm happy about your new career as a perfumier, but how is that relevant?'

'Do you trust me?'

'Of course I do, implicitly.'

'That is interesting, because 20 seconds ago when I asked, you said that you did not ...'

What was the cat talking about? This was the first time he'd asked me about trusting him. Why did he think he'd asked me before?

'You recall me spraying something in your face though?' he asked.

'Of course I don't, because you didn't do that. Why are you asking me these stupid ques–arghhhhh! What the frip?!' I cried, as I felt a sudden sharp jab in my leg.

12.1 FITTING MODELS: BRINGING IT ALL TOGETHER

Milton had stabbed my leg with a needle. He smiled as he extracted a vial of my blood. He explained that after asking me whether I trusted him the first time, he had sprayed some of Nutcot's aftershave in my face before asking me the same question again.

'My theory', he said, 'is that Nutcot's aftershave contains a chemical that makes people trust him. I needed to test this hypothesis. By now, you should know how I might do that.'

I took my set list from the stage, turned it over and drew on the back. **(FIGURE 12.2)**

The Head burst into song, 'They call me Dr. Love, I am your doctor of love, I've got the cure you're thinkin' of ....' He checked himself. 'I was busting some Kiss, but there really is a neuroeconomist dude who calls himself Doctor Love. His real name is Paul Zak, and he put forward the theory that the hormone oxytocin mediates levels of trust between strangers.[80] In one study,[57] he asked people to invest money in a trustee (a stranger). If they invested, then the total funds for the investor *and* the trustee increased. If the trustee shared the proceeds then both players ended up better off, but if the trustee did not repay the investors' trust by splitting the fund then the trustee ended up better off and the investor worse off. The question was: will investors trust the trustees to split the funds? If they do then they will invest, if not then they won't. The killer thing was that one group of investors were exposed to exogenous oxytocin, whereas a placebo group were not.

'If you believe the article, then the group exposed to oxytocin invested, on average, significantly more than the placebo group: it seems like oxytocin increased trust levels in this group. Listen up, though, the data were messier than a hoarder's bedroom. Some argue that if you inspect those data the effects of oxytocin ain't as clear-cut as they seem.'

(See discoveringstatistics.com/2014/10/31/perhaps-my-oxytocin-was-low-when-i-read-this-paper/.)

Reality Check 12.1 In oxytocin we trust

'I do, actually,' I replied defensively. 'You start off with your hypothesis. What is it that you think the aftershave changes to affect a person's trust?'

'I think it changes oxytocin levels. There was a theory some years ago that oxytocin could increase trust levels. Ask your reality checker about it.' **(REALITY CHECK 12.1)**

'So your hypothesis is that Nutcot is spraying oxytocin?'

'No, he is spraying aftershave containing a chemical that increases oxytocin levels in the recipient's brain.'

'Right, you could test that by collecting some data. You could observe how different concentrations of the chemical in his aftershave correspond to different levels of oxytocin, or you could do an experiment where you spray some people with the chemical in his aftershave and others you don't and measure oxytocin in the two groups. You then fit some kind of model to these data. You did tell me something about models.' **(SECTION 4.1.4)**

Milton interrupted me by taking my diagram and scribbling some equations on it. 'I will refresh your memory,' he said. 'The basic idea is that we are trying to predict an outcome – in this case it would be levels of oxytocin – and we do this from a model, which will have some error in prediction.' I heard a ping in the distance from my diePad. **(MEOWSINGS 12.1)** 'Look at this equation **(12.1)**,' Milton said, pointing to the page. 'It means that for a given person, i, we can predict their oxytocin level (the outcome) from the model we choose to fit to the data plus some error that is associated to that prediction (for person i). The "model" is replaced with an equation that summarizes the pattern of data. These models have variables and parameters. We usually denote predictor variables with the letter X; therefore, we could write a simple model with one predictor variable using this equation **(12.2)**. In this model, we are predicting the value of the outcome for a particular person (i) from their score on the predictor variable (X_i). The predictor variable has a parameter (b_1) attached to it, which tells us something about the relationship between the predictor (X_i) and outcome. And b_0 tells us the value of the outcome if the predictor variable is zero; in other words, if it was not in the model.'

$$\text{outcome}_i = (\text{model}) + \text{error}_i \tag{12.1}$$

$$\begin{aligned} \text{outcome}_i &= (b_0 + b_1 X_i) + \text{error}_i \\ \text{oxytocin}_i &= (b_0 + b_1 \text{Spray}_i) + \text{error}_i \end{aligned} \tag{12.2}$$

'So, we could predict a person's oxytocin level from how much spray they had, or whether they had the spray or not?'. **(EQUATION 12.2)**

'*Purr*cisely,' said Milton scribbling on my diagram some more. **(FIGURE 12.2)** 'The form of the model does not change whether we have used different concentrations of the spray or exposed different groups to different types of sprays (for example, an active spray that contained the chemical or a placebo spray that did not). The equation that describes the model is the same, except we might use words like concentration or group for the predictor variable just to remind ourselves how the data were collected. Although the equation does not change, the look of the model does. If we look at how different concentrations of the chemical relate to different levels of oxytocin, we would look for a linear trend across all of the data points. If my hypothesis is correct then this trend should slope upwards, indicating that as the concentration of the chemical increases so do oxytocin levels. If we looked at oxytocin in two separate groups – one exposed to the spray and the other not – the resulting model would also be a straight line, but this time it is a line connecting the means of the two groups. If my hypothesis is correct then the mean oxytocin levels in the group who were sprayed with the active chemical will be higher than the group that were sprayed with the placebo. Conceptually these models are the same: they are defined by an equation that describes a straight line and are variations of what is known as the **linear model**. We can make the linear model more complicated by measuring a second predictor variable and including that in the model too, like in this equation.' Milton wrote out another equation **(12.3)**.

$$\text{outcome}_i = \left(b_0 + b_1 X_{1i} + b_2 X_{2i}\right) + \text{error}_i \qquad\qquad (12.3)$$

'We could make it more complicated, but let's not,' I replied, taking control of the diagram. 'So we use the sample data to estimate the values of the parameters in these models, like you explained to me before? **(SECTION 8.1)** And for each parameter you can calculate a confidence interval around the estimate to (hopefully) tell you the likely population value? **(SECTION 8.3)** And for each parameter you can calculate a test statistic and p-value to see how significant it is?' **(SECTION 10.1)**

'*Fur*fectly true on all counts. Remember that the parameter attached to the predictor variable, b_1, tells us about the relationship between the predictor variable and the outcome. Therefore, if its value is zero, then it means there is no relationship between the predictor and outcome variable. We can test whether the parameter is significantly different from zero. If it is, then we assume that the relationship between the outcome and predictor in the population is different from zero.'

Dear Human,

Imagine we fitted a simple model to 10 people's data relating to the concentration of chemical in the spray that I sprayed them with and their oxytocin levels. The data for these 10 people are shown in my diagram (Figure 12.1). The red line is the model, which summarizes the general trend in the scores, which is that as the concentration goes up so does the oxytocin level. For each person, there is their actual observed level of oxytocin (represented by the blue dots) and the level of oxytocin predicted from the model (the red dots). In some cases the predicted value is very close to the observed value, such as for the second data point (note that the red and blue dots for this person are almost on top of one another). However, for most people there is an error in prediction. That is, the model either underestimates or overestimates their actual oxytocin levels. Sometimes this error is small, such as for the first, second and eighth cases. However, sometimes it is large, such as for the third and seventh cases, for which there is a large gap between the value predicted by the model (red dot) and the corresponding observed value (blue dot). The difference between the value of the outcome predicted by the model and the value of the outcome actually observed is called the residual. The residual for each participant is represented in the diagram by a vertical black dotted line. In equation form, a residual is defined as:

$$\text{residual}_i = \text{observed}_i - \text{predicted}_i$$

which just means that the residual (or error) for person i is their actual score on the outcome variable minus the score for the outcome predicted by the model.

Best fishes,
Milton

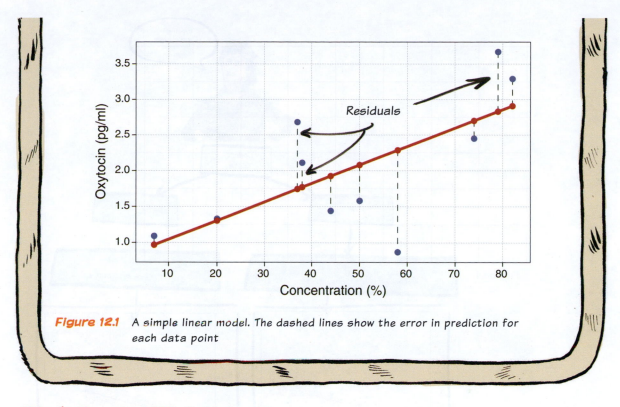

Figure 12.1   A simple linear model. The dashed lines show the error in prediction for each data point

Milton's Meowsings 12.1   Residuals

'In this case, would that mean that the concentration of chemical in the spray had a relationship with oxytocin levels?'

'Indeed it would; however, these models can be biased.'

Milton had told me about bias before when we looked at the JIG:SAW data. **(SECTION 9.1)** I reminded Milton that we'd talked about extreme scores and funny-shaped distributions biasing the parameter estimate and its variance.

'Well remembered,' he replied. 'Since you learned about what biases parameter estimates and their variances, you have subsequently discovered that testing hypotheses also involves looking at standard errors, confidence intervals, test statistics and p-values. Therefore, we must consider what biases these things too. All of them are related. As you said, extreme scores and non-normal distributions bias the parameter estimate and the variance. **(SECTION 9.1.1)** The standard error is estimated from the variance **(SECTION 8.2.2)**, so if the variance is biased the standard error will be too. Confidence intervals **(SECTION 8.3)** and test statistics **(SECTION 10.1.4)** are calculated using the standard error, so if the standard error is biased then these will be too. We compute p-values based on the value of the test statistic, so if the test statistic is biased then the p-value will be too.'

'Right, so if the parameter estimate is biased, then so will its variance be, meaning that the standard error will be, which in turn biases the confidence interval, test statistic and p-value. So, extreme scores and non-normal distributions will bias not only the parameter estimate but also the confidence interval, test statistic and p-value?'

'*Purr*fectly *claw*rect, but it is not as simple as that.'

'It never is,' I interrupted.

'We need to consider the assumptions of the model we are fitting to the data.'

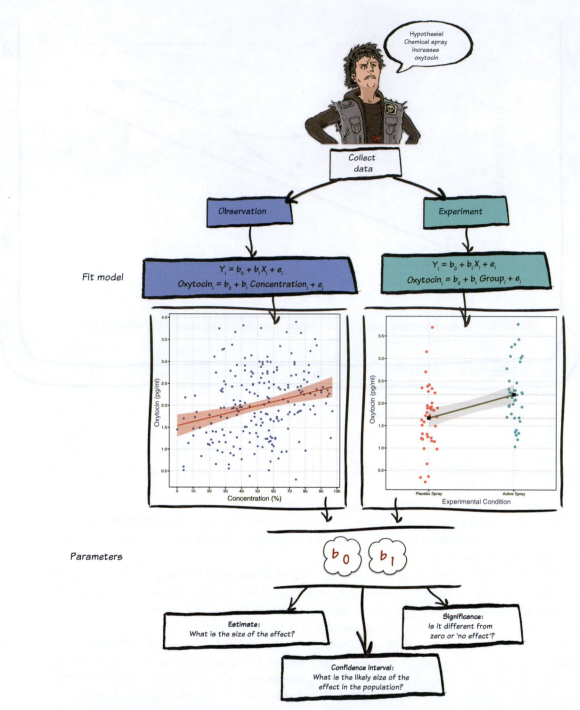

Figure 12.2 Testing hypotheses using a linear model

12.2 ASSUMPTIONS

'An assumption,' continued Milton, 'is a condition that ensures that what you are attempting to do works. For example, when we test a parameter using a test statistic, we have usually made some assumptions, and if these assumptions are true then we know that the test statistic (and, therefore, the *p*-value) associated with it can be taken at face value. However, if any of the assumptions are not true, which is called a *violation*, then the test statistic and *p*-value will be inaccurate and could lead us to the wrong conclusion if we interpret them without question. The model I have been describing – the linear model – has many assumptions.'[81]

'That's tedious ...'

Milton threw me a look. 'Luckily for your startlingly low tedium threshold, we have already discussed some of these assumptions. Here they are, in order of importance.'[82] Milton wrote me a list:

- Additivity and linearity
- Independent errors
- Homoscedasticity
- Normally distributed something or other
- Predictors are uncorrelated with external variables
- Variable types
- No perfect multicollinearity
- Non-zero variance

12.2.1 Additivity and linearity

I had a feeling that Milton was going to explain each of these eight assumptions in turn. That was going to put a serious dampener on an evening that until now had been a welcome break from the knot that Alice's disappearance had placed in my stomach. Never one to pick up on others' emotional states, Milton smiled and continued.

'Shall we look at them one by one?' he said, grinning perversely. I didn't answer. He didn't care. 'Very well, the linear model that we have been talking about takes the form of the equation I already wrote out for you. *(EQUATION 12.3)* In general, we can expand the model to include more and more predictors of the outcome.' Milton adapted his earlier equation to include $b_n X_{ni}$. *(EQUATION 12.4)* 'All this new term means is that we can carry on adding predictor variables until we reach the *n*th one, that is, the last one that we want to include. All predictor variables have a parameter that quantifies the relationship between the predictor variable and the outcome, so b_n is the parameter for the last predictor variable.

$$\text{outcome}_i = \left(b_0 + b_1 X_{1i} + b_2 X_{2i} + \ldots + b_n X_{ni}\right) + \text{error}_i \tag{12.4}$$

'Great, but what is the assumption?'

'The assumption of additivity and linearity is the most important one because it is the assumption that the real-world process that you want to model can, in reality, be described by that equation. Linearity is the assumption that the outcome variable is, in reality, linearly related to any predictors (i.e., their relationship can be summed up by a straight line), and additivity is the assumption that if you have several predictors then their combined effect is best described by adding their effects together. In other words, it means that the equation *(12.4)* accurately describes the process we are trying to model. If the process does not follow a linear pattern then you are fitting the wrong model.' I heard my diePad ping again. *(MEOWSINGS 12.2)*

'Presumably this assumption is the most important because if it is not true then even if all other assumptions are met, your model is invalid?'

'Ex*scratch*ly,' said Milton excitedly. 'It would be like trying to message your friend using a banana instead of a Proteus. You can draw a keyboard on the banana, tap away on its yellow skin, and hold it aloft to try to get a better signal, but your text will not send because you have used the wrong tool for the job. If you have described the real-world process with the wrong statistical model then you have similarly used the wrong tool for the job: there is no point in interpreting its parameter estimates or worrying about significance tests or confidence intervals because the model is just plain wrong.'

Dear Human,

The linear model that we have been discussing is very commonly used by scientists to describe the data they have collected. While you were making a cacophony, I was busy collecting data on oxytocin levels in the audience. I sprayed people with a certain concentration of a chemical and I then measured the oxytocin level in their blood. We could represent these hypothetical data on a scatterplot in which each dot represents an individual's oxytocin level and also how concentrated a dose of the chemical I gave them (as a percentage, so 100% is a pure dose and 0% is no dose at all). Figure 12.3 shows two versions of the same data, but the left-hand one has a linear (straight) and the right-hand one a non-linear (curved) model fitted. Which model do you think better represents the data points?

Although the straight line does fit the data in a general sense, it is nowhere near as good as the curved line. The curved line better reflects the bend in the data points (that is, that initially as the chemical concentration increases so do oxytocin levels, but just before a concentration of 50% that trend starts to reverse and oxytocin levels actually go down). The straight line suggests that overall as the chemical concentration goes up, oxytocin goes down, but it misses the fact that at low concentrations oxytocin actually *increases*. These graphs lie at the heart of what the assumption of linearity is all about: if we fit a linear model to these data then we assume that the relationship between the chemical concentration of the spray and oxytocin levels is, in reality, linear. Figure 12.3 shows that in this example this assumption would not be tenable: the data clearly show a curved pattern, indicating that a curvilinear model is a more realistic model of the relationship.

Best fishes,
Milton

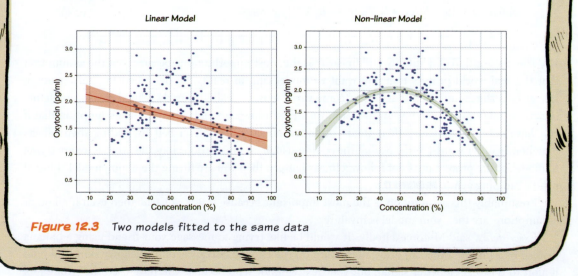

Figure 12.3 *Two models fitted to the same data*

Milton's Meowsings 12.2 *Linear and non-linear models*

'How do you test this assumption?'

'One way is to look at the data using a scatterplot, which Dr Tuff explained to you (SECTION 5.3.5), and see whether a straight line seems like the best summary of the data. You can also look at a graph of the errors in the model, which I will explain in due course.'

12.2.2 Independent errors

With barely a pause for breath, Milton fired into the next item on his list. 'The next assumption is that errors are independent, which means that the error$_i$ for each person in the last equation (12.4) are not related to each other. Imagine you and Alice took part in some research where you had to rate how much you like some songs. If you were to confer about how good each song was then your ratings would not be independent: Alice's rating of a song would depend on your rating. We know that if we estimate a model to predict your responses, there will be error in those predictions. Crucially, because Alice's and your scores are not independent, the errors (or *residuals*) associated with these predicted values would also not be independent. Now, imagine a different scenario where you and Alice hear and rate the songs in soundproof booths where you cannot see or hear each other. Under these conditions, Alice's ratings should not be affected by yours, so the error terms should be independent: the error in predicting Alice's ratings should not be influenced by the error in predicting your ratings.'

'Sure, but why does it matter?'

'It matters because the equation that we use to estimate the standard error (SECTION 8.2.2) is valid only if observations are independent. Remember that the standard error is used to compute confidence intervals and significance tests, so if we violate the assumption of independence then not only will the standard error be incorrect but also our confidence intervals and significance tests

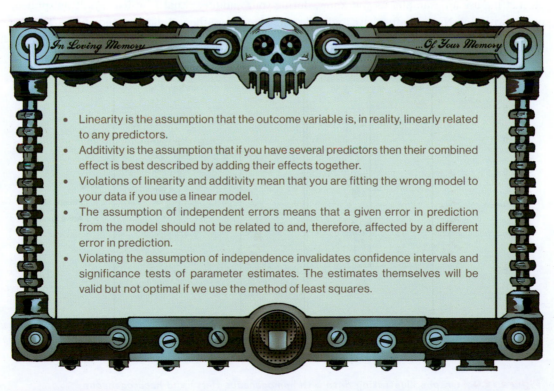

- Linearity is the assumption that the outcome variable is, in reality, linearly related to any predictors.
- Additivity is the assumption that if you have several predictors then their combined effect is best described by adding their effects together.
- Violations of linearity and additivity mean that you are fitting the wrong model to your data if you use a linear model.
- The assumption of independent errors means that a given error in prediction from the model should not be related to and, therefore, affected by a different error in prediction.
- Violating the assumption of independence invalidates confidence intervals and significance tests of parameter estimates. The estimates themselves will be valid but not optimal if we use the method of least squares.

Zach's Facts 12.1 Linearity and independent errors

will be invalid. If we use the method of least squares, then model parameter estimates will still be valid, but not optimal. In other words, there are better methods to estimate the parameters.'

'How do you test the assumption?'

'Some people recommend a test called the **Durbin–Watson test**, which tests whether adjacent residuals are related to each other. However, this test depends on the order of data points so it is useful when the data have a fixed order (for example, a series of observations at different points in time) but it does not really make sense when the data do not have a meaningful order, for example, if you have randomly collected blood samples from 100 different people at the same time.'

'What if you violate this assumption?'

'You can use a different set of models known as **multilevel linear models**, which are rather more complicated but can factor in relationships between errors.'[11, 25]

12.2.3 Homoscedasticity/homogeneity of variance

'This brings me onto the assumption of homoscedasticity,' Milton announced.

'Homosce … what?'

'Homoscedasticity.'

'I can't even spell that, let alone understand it,' I joked.

'It is far easier to understand than it is to spell,' Milton said with a chuckle. 'It is an assumption related to variance. **(SECTION 4.3)** In a design in which you test several groups of participants this assumption means that each of these samples comes from populations with the same variance. In correlational designs, this assumption means that the variance of the outcome variable should be stable at all levels of the predictor variable. In other words, as you go through levels of the predictor variable, the variance of the outcome variable should not change.'

'Whoa, slow down, fuzzball …'

'Let me use an example. As you know, during your auditory ritual I busied myself by spraying people with Rob Nutcot's aftershave and collecting blood from them. I did the study twice. The first

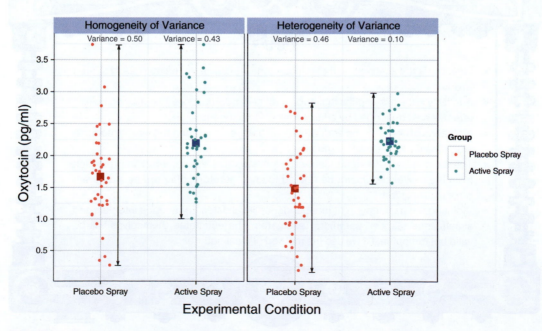

Figure 12.4 *Graphs illustrating data with homogeneous (left) and heterogeneous (right) variances*

time I sprayed people with either the aftershave, which contained the active chemical, or a placebo spray, which smelled the same but did not include the chemical. The second time, I varied the concentration of the chemical within the spray from 0% of the active ingredient to 100%.

'Let us first look at the situation in which a person was sprayed with either the active spray or the placebo.' Milton found another set list from the stage and scribbled on the back. **(FIGURE 12.4)** 'We have two groups: one who had the placebo spray and the other who received the active spray. We also have two graphs, one showing when the assumption is met and the other showing when the assumption is violated. The means the graphs are extremely similar but the spreads of scores around the mean are not. Look first at the left-hand graph. The variance in the placebo group is 0.50, compared to 0.43 in the active group. In other words, the variances in the two groups are very similar, and the spreads of scores in each group are roughly the same. This is what we mean by **homogeneity of variance**: the spread of scores for oxytocin is approximately the same at each level of the spray variable (i.e., the spread of scores is very similar in the placebo and active spray groups).

'Now compare that situation with the one shown on the right-hand side. In the graph on the right, the scores in the active spray group are quite tightly packed around the mean (the vertical distance from the lowest score to the highest score is small), but in the placebo group the scores are a lot more spread out around the mean (the vertical distance from the lowest score to the highest score is large). In fact, the variance in the active spray group (0.10) is four times smaller than that of the placebo group (0.46). This scenario shows **heterogeneity of variance**: the variance of scores in the placebo group is very different than that of the active spray group.

'What about when you didn't have different groups?' I enquired.

Milton scribbled another diagram. **(FIGURE 12.5)** 'The same principle applies. On this diagram, I have again shown when the assumption is met on the left and when it is not on the right. In both figures we see the same general pattern in the data: as the concentration of the spray increases, so do oxytocin levels. The red line shows the model that summarizes this pattern. The assumption relates to the spread of errors around this model. Remember that the errors are also known as residuals and are the difference between what the model predicts (the red line) and the actual observed data point. **(MEOWSINGS 12.1)** The assumption is that the variance of these errors is constant at all levels of the predictor. That is, the variance of the errors at a concentration of 10% should be about the same as at 40% and, say, 80%. In the left diagram the spread of scores around the model is quite consistent. If you draw a shape around the data points then the width of that shape is fairly similar, regardless of which value of concentration we look at. The errors will have a similar shape. This shape is known as **homoscedasticity**. Now compare this situation with that shown on the right. If we look at a concentration of 10%, the scores (and therefore errors) are tightly packed around the model, which would result in a small variance. However, as we move to a higher concentration, say 50%, the scores (and their errors) are now more spread out around the line, and as we move up to a concentration of 80% that spread has increased further still. This gives rise to a characteristic funnel shape; that is, errors are tightly packed around the model at one end of the scale, but widely spread around the model at the other end. This is known as **heteroscedasticity**.'

'What happens if we have heteroscedasticity?' I asked. 'Does Godzilla rise from the sea and destroy us?'

Milton scowled. 'Not quite. As I mentioned earlier, we need to ask ourselves what is the effect on (1) the estimates of parameters, b; (2) their confidence intervals; and (3) their significance tests. In terms of parameter estimation, if we can assume equality of variance (homoscedasticity) then the estimates we get using the method of least squares will be optimal. If variances for the errors differ along the predictor variable (heteroscedasticity) then the estimates of the parameters within the model will not be optimal. All this means is that even if homoscedasticity cannot be assumed, the method of least squares will produce "unbiased" estimates of parameters, but better estimates can be achieved using different methods; for example, by using weighted least squares in which each case is weighted by a function of its variance.'

'What the frip are you going on about?'

The cat looked exasperated with me. 'Put simply, it means that if all you care about is estimating the parameters of the model in your sample then you do not need to worry about homogeneity of variance in most cases: the method of least squares will produce unbiased estimates.'[83]

'So when *do* I need to worry about it?'

'Unequal variances or heteroscedasticity creates a bias and inconsistency in the estimate of the standard error associated with the parameter estimates in your model.'[83]

'And the standard error is used to calculate test statistics and confidence intervals …'

Milton smiled. 'Now, you are getting somewhere! Yes, heteroscedasticity will bias the confidence intervals and significance tests for the parameter estimates in your model. Confidence intervals can be "extremely inaccurate" when homoscedasticity cannot be assumed.'[32]

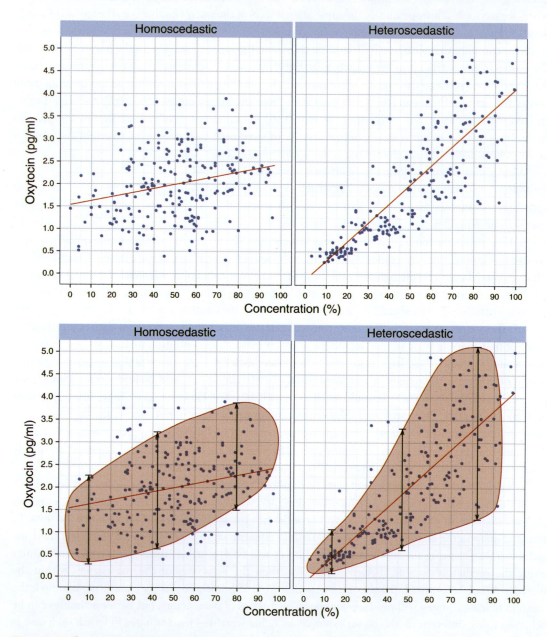

Figure 12.5 *Graphs illustrating data with homogeneous (left) and heterogeneous (right) variances*

'So, if I want to look at the confidence intervals around my model parameter estimates or test the significance of the model or its parameter estimates then homogeneity of variance matters.'

'*Purr*cisely, although in some situations you can correct the test statistic to eliminate the bias created by heteroscedasticity.'

'So how do I know whether or not I have heteroscedasticity?'

'The simplest way is to look at a graph. In fact, this can also help us to check the assumption of linearity, so we kill two assumptions with one graph. Linearity and homoscedasticity both relate to the errors or residuals in the model you have fitted to the data. **(MEOWSINGS 12.1)** We can create a scatterplot of the values of the residuals against the values of the outcome predicted by the model. In doing so we can look at whether there is a systematic relationship between what comes out of the model (the predicted values) and the errors in the model. Normally we convert the predicted values and errors to *z*-scores **(CHAPTER 6)** so this plot is sometimes referred to as *zpred vs. zresid*, meaning the *z*-scores of the residuals plotted against the *z*-scores of the predicted values. If linearity and homoscedasticity can be assumed then there should be no systematic relationship between the errors in the model and what the model predicts. If this graph funnels out, then the chances are that there is heteroscedasticity in the data. If there is any sort of curve in this graph then the chances are that the data have broken the assumption of linearity.'

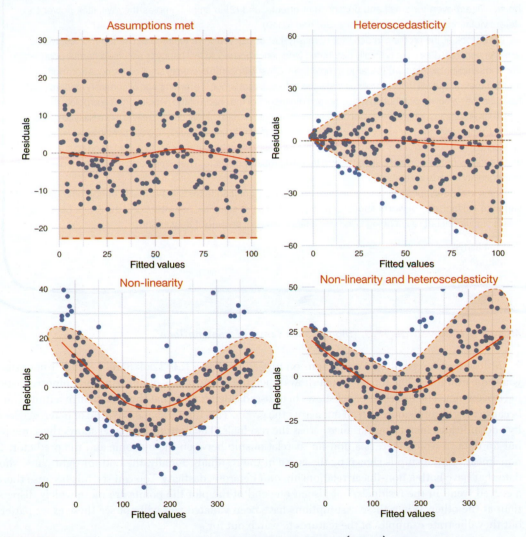

Figure 12.6 *Plots of standardized residuals against predicted (fitted) values*

Dear Human,

There are various significance tests that have been devised to look at whether assumptions are violated. These include tests of whether a distribution is normal (the Kolmogorov–Smirnov (K-S) and Shapiro–Wilk tests), tests of homogeneity of variances (Levene's test), and tests of significance of skew and kurtosis. Although people sometimes use these tests, there is a fundamental problem with doing so. All of these tests are based on null hypothesis significance testing, and this means that (1) in large samples they can be significant even for small and unimportant effects, and (2) in small samples they will lack power to detect violations of these assumptions (Section 10.1.10).

Let us look at the problem in detail for normality. Let us say you were tempted to use the K-S test to see whether your raw data were normally distributed (and hence you would feel happy to assume a normal population and sampling distribution). In a large sample, the K-S test will pick up even very small differences from normality. Also, the central limit theorem tells us that as sample sizes get larger, the assumption of normality matters less because the sampling distribution will be normal regardless of the shape of the population. The problem then is that in large samples, where we do not need to worry about normality, a test of normality is more likely to be significant, which will make us worry about and correct for normality unnecessarily. Conversely, in small samples, where we might need to worry about normality, the K-S test will not have the power to detect it and so is likely to encourage us not to worry about something that we probably ought to. The same basic argument applies for homogeneity of variance tests.

The moral is, if your sample is large then do not use significance tests of normality or homogeneity of variance – in fact, do not worry about normality at all. In small samples, pay attention if the K-S or Levene's test is significant but resist being lulled into a false sense of security if they are not.

Best fishes,
Milton

Milton's Meowsings 12.3   *Significance tests of assumptions*

Milton began scribbling some graphs on my set list. **(FIGURE 12.6)** 'Look here,' he said. 'I have drawn you some examples. The top left panel shows when the assumptions of linearity and homoscedasticity have been met. The top right panel shows heteroscedasticity: note that the points form a funnel shape because they become more spread out across the graph. This funnel shape is typical of heteroscedasticity and indicates increasing variance across the residuals. The bottom left panel shows the same plot, but for data in which there is a non-linear relationship between the outcome and the predictor. The non-linear relationship is shown by the curve in the residuals. Finally, the bottom right panel shows data that have both a non-linear relationship *and* heteroscedasticity. You can see this because there is a curved trend in the residuals, but also at one end of the plot the points are more widely dispersed than at the other. When these assumptions have been violated you will not see these exact patterns, but they illustrate examples of the features to watch out for.'

'Isn't looking at a graph a bit subjective?'

'Perhaps. There are less subjective methods that you can use if you have collected groups of data. In this situation the assumption means that the variance of your outcome variable or variables should be the same in each group. You can test the null hypothesis that the variances in different groups are equal using **Levene's test**.[84] If Levene's test is significant, which means that it has a p-value less than or equal to 0.05, then you conclude that the null hypothesis is incorrect and that the variances are significantly different – therefore, the assumption of homogeneity of variances has been violated. If, however, the test is non-significant (i.e., p is greater than 0.05) then you might conclude that the variances are roughly equal and the assumption is tenable.' For the third time my diePad beeped in the distance. I really hoped these weren't all messages from Milton. **(MEOWSINGS 12.3)** With barely a pause, the cat picked up his lecture. 'There are other ways too: if you have groups of scores, you can look at **Hartley's F_{max}**, which is also known as the **variance ratio**.[85] This is the ratio of the variances between the group with the biggest variance and the group with the smallest variance. For example, in my diagram **(FIGURE 12.4)**, for the homogenous groups the variance ratio was $0.50/0.43 = 1.16$, but in the heterogeneous group it was $0.46/0.10 = 4.6$. These values mean that in the first case the largest variance was 1.16 times as large as the smallest, whereas in the second case the largest variance was 4.6 times as large as the smallest. People sometimes use the rule of thumb that a ratio less than 2 means that variances are similar enough; however, Hartley did publish a table of critical values. The critical values depend on the number of cases per group, and the number of variances being compared. For example, with sample sizes (n) of 10 per group, an F_{max} of less than 10 is more or less always going to be non-significant, with 15–20 per group the ratio needs to be less than about 5, and with samples of 30–60 the ratio should be below about 2 or 3. However, like Levene's test, Hartley's approach relies on significance testing and there are some good reasons not to test assumptions using such tests.' **(MEOWSINGS 12.3)**

'What would you do instead?'

'Look at the graph of the errors like I originally told you!'

- Homogeneity of variance/homoscedasticity is the assumption that the spread of outcome scores is roughly equal at different points on the predictor variable.
- Homoscedasticity ensures that parameter estimates (b) using least squares methods are optimal, and that confidence intervals and p-values associated with those parameters are not biased.
- Look at a plot of the standardized predicted values from your model against the standardized residuals (*zpred vs. zresid*). If it has a funnel shape then you have trouble.
- When comparing groups, a significant Levene's test (i.e., a p-value less than 0.05) reveals a problem with this assumption. However, there are good reasons not to use this test (Milton's Meowsings 12.3).
- The variance ratio (Hartley's F_{max}) is the largest group variance divided by the smallest. This value needs to be smaller than the critical values in the additional material.

Zach's Facts 12.2   *Homogeneity of variance/homoscedasticity*

12.2.4 Normally distributed something or other

We weren't even halfway through Milton's list and I was bored already. I really wanted to get back to the band and have a beer. Every time I went to make my excuses, though, he would talk over me, bludgeoning me with his lecture.

'We have talked a lot about normality before,' he said. 'What things that we have discussed rely on a normal distribution?'

I hated being put on the spot like this, especially when my mind was still on the gig and not really wanting the unpleasant sidetrack of statistics. I thought back to when Milton and I had looked at the JIG:SAW data **(SECTION 9.1.1)** and also when he dressed me as Florence Nightingale and explained sampling to me. **(CHAPTER 8)** Now I thought about it, we had discussed normality quite a bit.

CHECK YOUR BRAIN: Thinking about what you have already learnt in Chapters 8 and 9, what statistical constructs assume a normal distribution?

'The first thing I remember is that when we looked at the JIG:SAW data lots of the distributions were very skewed and not normal and this biased the estimates of the parameter, which at the time was the mean.'

'*Fur*fect. What else?'

'When we calculated the standard error, you said that the equation works only when the sample size is 30 or more, and that's because if it is then the sampling distribution will be normal … oh, and related to that, when you talked about confidence intervals, you also said that we assume that the sampling distribution of means is normal.' **(SECTIONS 8.2.2 & 8.3)**

'*Claw*rect. And do you remember what the central limit theorem tells us?'

'Yeah, wasn't it that if the sample is bigger than about 30 then the sampling distribution will be normal even if the population isn't?' **(SECTION 8.2.3)**

'Well done. So, what we know is that the standard error, confidence interval and parameter estimate itself are all affected by a lack of normality of some kind. For the confidence interval and standard error it is normality of the sampling distribution of the parameter, b, that matters, but for *b* itself it is a lack of normality in the model residuals, that biases the estimate. As I have explained before, any model that we fit will include some error. In other words, it will not predict the outcome variable perfectly. This fact is represented by the error$_i$ in the equation **(12.4)** I wrote out. That means that for each person there is a residual – in other words, the difference between the value of the outcome predicted from the model and the value actually observed for that person. **(MEOWSINGS 12.1)** You can calculate these errors for each person and plot their distribution using a histogram. This assumption really states that if you do plot the residuals you would be hoping to see a normal distribution around 0. A residual of 0 means that the model correctly predicts the outcome value. If the model is a good fit then we would expect that for most people, the error in prediction is zero. Therefore, the frequency of 0 is very high. We would also hope that very extreme over- or underestimations occur only rarely, therefore the frequency of scores a long way from zero should be low. This would give us a characteristic normal distribution, which would tell us that for most people the error in prediction is quite close to zero, and that large residuals occur relatively infrequently. If the residuals *are* normally distributed in the population, then using the method of least squares to estimate the parameters (the *b*s in the equation) **(12.4)** will produce better estimates than other methods.'

'Sweet, so normality matters for parameter estimates, confidence intervals and significance tests?'

'Let us see. First, consider the parameter estimates. The mean is a parameter, and I explained before **(SECTION 9.1)** that extreme scores bias it. The general point is that estimates of parameters are affected by non-normal distributions. Some parameter estimates are affected more than others: the median, for example, is less biased by skewed distributions than the mean. In general, parameters (the *b*s) estimated using the method of least squares, will be optimal when the residuals in the population are normally distributed. The method of least squares will always give you an estimate of the model parameters that minimizes error, so in that sense you do not need to assume normality of anything to fit a linear model and estimate the parameters that define it.[82] However, if the residuals in your model are not normally distributed then it means that there will be better ways to estimate model parameters than the method of least squares.'

'What about confidence intervals?'

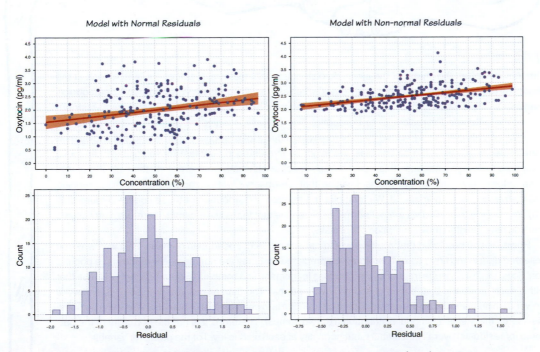

Figure 12.7 Two linear models, one with normally distributed residuals (left) and one with non-normally distributed residuals (right)

'For confidence intervals around a parameter estimate to be accurate, that estimate must come from a normal sampling distribution. This requirement is because we use values of the standard normal distribution to compute the confidence interval **(SECTION 8.3)** and using values of the standard normal distribution makes sense only if the parameter estimates actually come from one. Remember, though, what we assume here is that the *parameter estimate* comes from a normal distribution; that is, the sampling distribution is normal. Crucially, the central limit theorem tells us that in large samples, the parameter estimate will have come from a normal distribution regardless of what the sample or population data look like. Therefore, if we are interested in computing confidence intervals then we should not lose sleep about the assumption of normality if our sample is large enough to invoke the central limit theorem.'[86] **(SECTION 8.2.3)**

'And significance tests?'

'If we want to test a hypothesis about a model (and, therefore, the parameter estimates within it) using the NHST framework that the Secret Philanthropic Society **(CHAPTER 10)** described to you, then we assume that the parameter estimates have a normal distribution.'

'I don't remember the Society mentioning that.'

'Perhaps not, but they did tell you that the test statistics that you use to test hypotheses have distributions (such as the *t*, *F* and *chi-square* distributions). All of these distributions are related to the normal distribution,

Dear Human,

Although it is often the shape of the sampling distribution that matters, researchers tend to look at the scores on the outcome variable (or the residuals) when assessing normality. When you have a categorical predictor variable (such as people falling into different groups) you would not expect the overall distribution of the outcome (or residuals) to be normal. For example, imagine we wanted to break into the JIG:SAW complex. When we visited there before we noticed a lot of security guards who, judging by their state of decay, appeared to be zombies. We might be interested in how fast these zombies can move compared to humans, because this would help us to establish whether we are likely to be able to outrun them before they feast on our brains. Imagine that we observe lots of zombies and humans running 100 metres and note their speed. We then plot the frequency distribution of these speeds (Figure 12.8, left). You decide that the data are not normal because the plot looks like a camel; therefore, you assume that you have violated the assumption of normality.

However, you predicted that zombies would run at a different speed than humans. That was why you collected data in the first place. Therefore, you predicted that they are not members of the same population. So let us plot *separate* frequency distributions for humans and zombies (Figure 12.8, right). Notice that within each group the distribution of scores is very normal. The data are as you predicted: zombies are slower than humans and so the centre of their distribution is lower than that of humans. When you combine the scores this yields a bimodal distribution (i.e., two humps). Therefore, it is not the normality of the outcome (or residuals) overall that matters, but normality at each unique level of the predictor variable.

Best fishes,
Milton

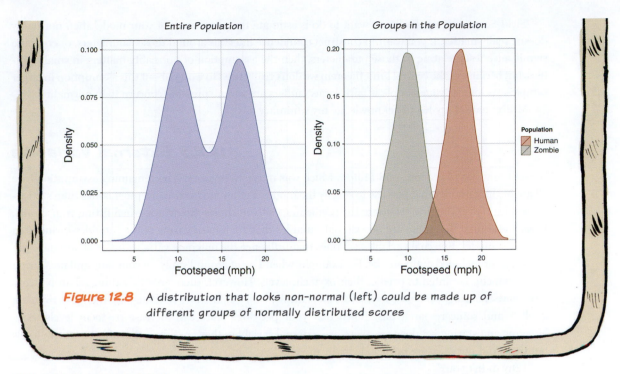

Figure 12.8   A distribution that looks non-normal (left) could be made up of different groups of normally distributed scores

Milton's Meowsings 12.4   The assumption of normality with categorical predictors

so if our parameter estimate comes from a normal distribution then these test statistics and p-values will be accurate. However, again it is the sampling distribution of what is being tested that matters, not the data themselves. As with confidence intervals, the central limit theorem tells us that in large samples this will be true no matter what the shape of the population. Therefore, significance tests are unaffected by the shape of our data provided that our sample is large. However, the extent to which test statistics perform as they should do in large samples varies from one test statistic to another.'

'It sounds as though normality isn't really very important at all!'

'In a sense it is not,' the cat replied. 'If you have a large sample then you can assume that the central limit is doing its work and confidence intervals and significance tests are trustworthy. If you have a small sample you can use bootstrap estimates of the confidence interval and significance **(SECTION 9.3.5)** which are robust and do not assume normality. However, it is worth plotting a histogram of the residuals from the model, because if this graph does not show a normal distribution then it probably means that there are better ways to estimate the parameter of the model than the method of least squares. In small samples, it is worth checking the distribution of the data because if the data are normal then it is reasonable to assume that the population and sampling distribution will be too. When your model involves categorical variables, though, be sure to look at normality within categories separately.' My diePad buzzed yet again. **(MEOWSINGS 12.4)** 'Finally,' the cat concluded, 'you can use two tests: the **Kolmogorov–Smirnov** and **Shapiro–Wilk tests**, which compare your distribution to that of a normal distribution. If this test is significant (i.e., has a p-value less than 0.05) then it means that your data are significantly different from a normal distribution, whereas if it is non-significant then it suggests that there is not sufficient evidence that your data are non-normal.'

'One of your messages said that using these tests was a bad idea.' **(MEOWSINGS 12.3)**

'Indeed it did. When samples are small and you need to establish normality, the K-S test will not have a lot of power to detect deviations from normality. When samples are large and normality is less of a problem the K-S will be overpowered and likely to be significant, leading you to believe that the data are non-normal in a situation where non-normality does not actually matter.'

'Sick! So to sum up, if all you want to do is estimate the parameters of your model then normality doesn't really matter. If you want to construct confidence intervals around those parameters, or compute significance tests relating to those parameters, then the assumption of normality matters in small samples, but because of the central limit theorem we don't really need to worry about this assumption in larger samples. As long as your sample is fairly large, outliers are a more pressing concern than normality.'

Milton patted my leg to acknowledge my summary.

12.2.5 External variables

'That's the worst of it done,' said Milton, which was music to my ears. 'The remaining assumptions are all about the variables that you use to specify the model, so they are more conceptual issues than statistical assumptions. The first relates to the predictors that you choose to include when fitting your model. First, we assume that there are no external variables that are related to any of the variables included in the linear model. External variables are ones that influence the outcome variable but that you have not measured or included in the model. For example, when I went around spraying your fans and measuring their oxytocin, I wanted to predict their oxytocin levels. However, there are other things than Nutcot's aftershave that might increase oxytocin. For example, Paul Zak believes that hugging increases oxytocin levels,[80] and some research has shown that your pet dog's stare can increase oxytocin levels too.[87] Hugging and staring pet dogs are, therefore, external variables: they are things that affect oxytocin levels but that I did not measure or include in my model.'

'Why didn't you?'

'It would have meant hugging some fans and not others, or possibly giving some people multiple hugs. I am a professor and must keep people away from my personal space at all times. What is more, I am a cat and, therefore, capable of affection only when hungry. I ate before I came here.'

'You could have brought some staring dogs with you, though,' I teased.

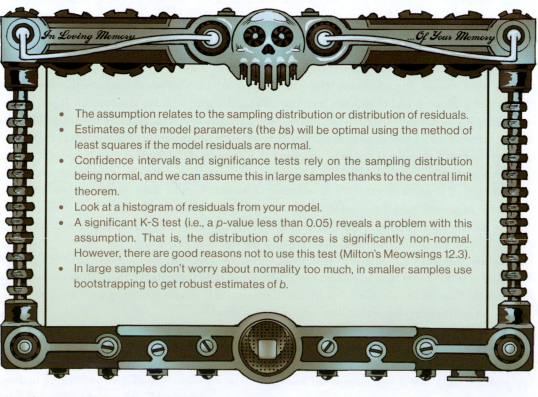

In Loving Memory   ...Of Your Memory

- The assumption relates to the sampling distribution or distribution of residuals.
- Estimates of the model parameters (the *b*s) will be optimal using the method of least squares if the model residuals are normal.
- Confidence intervals and significance tests rely on the sampling distribution being normal, and we can assume this in large samples thanks to the central limit theorem.
- Look at a histogram of residuals from your model.
- A significant K-S test (i.e., a *p*-value less than 0.05) reveals a problem with this assumption. That is, the distribution of scores is significantly non-normal. However, there are good reasons not to use this test (Milton's Meowsings 12.3).
- In large samples don't worry about normality too much, in smaller samples use bootstrapping to get robust estimates of *b*.

Zach's Facts 12.3 *Normality*

Milton's fur pricked up. 'Dogs! Stupid animals! Centuries of domesticity and still they lack even basic skills such as how to train their owners,' he said tersely.

'Why are these external variables a problem?' I asked.

'Think about it. Your model is made up of variables that you hope predict the outcome, and you estimate parameters for any variables in the model. The values of those parameters depend on what other predictors are present. If you have missed out a variable that predicts the outcome, then what is to say that it is not a better predictor than the variables you have included? Perhaps if you had included it, it would have overpowered the other predictors and rendered them less important than they appear to be.'

12.2.6 Variable types

'You must also consider the types of variables that you put into the model. All predictor variables must be quantitative or categorical (with two categories), and the outcome variable must be quantitative, continuous and unbounded.'

'Quantitative means they have to be numbers, right?'

'Yes – but, more than that, they should be measured at the interval level. Do you know what that is?'

I thought back to my meeting with Dr Genari. He had explained that it meant that the intervals between points on the scale are equivalent along the whole scale. Like, the difference between 2 cm and 3 cm is the same as the difference between 10 cm and 11 cm. I explained this to Milton and asked what he meant by unbounded.

'I mean that there are no constraints on the variability of the outcome. If oxytocin levels can, in reality, range from 0 to 5 pg/ml then I should find scores in my data covering that full range. If my scores range from 0 to 3 pg/ml, then my outcome is constrained because it does not include scores as high as are possible to get.'

'In all of your graphs the range seems to be 0–5. Is that the full range of oxytocin levels?'

'No, during childbirth levels can reach as high as 114 pg/ml, but assuming we treat those giving birth as a separate population, 1–3 pg/ml is more or less the typical range for most people, so my data can be considered to be unbounded if we are interested in people who are not pregnant or giving birth.'[88]

12.2.7 Multicollinearity

'That's fine. We should measure everything that could affect the outcome variable, and then we're good,' I said, hoping to end the conversation.

'Not really,' Milton replied. 'You could measure every external variable, I suppose, but no one ever does, and if there are lots of similar variables that predict an outcome you can end up with another problem, **multicollinearity**, which occurs when there is a strong relationship between two or more predictors. The most extreme example would be **perfect collinearity**, which is when at least one predictor is a perfect linear combination of the others. In other words, they are perfectly related: as one variable increases, the other increases by a proportional amount.'

'Like if they had a correlation coefficient of 1?' **(SECTION 11.2.2)**

Milton glanced sideways at me. 'How do you know about that?'

'The Doctrine of Chance explained it to me – you know, when you ran off and left me to be dragged into a tomb by a weird moonfaced person in glasses.'

'I had things to do. You would do well to remember that humans exist to serve cats, not vice versa. In any case, if there is perfect collinearity between predictors it is impossible to obtain unique estimates of the parameters because there are an infinite number of combinations of estimates that would work equally well.'

'Like, if we put two predictors into the model that are perfectly correlated, then the values of b for each variable are interchangeable?'

'Essentially, yes. Luckily, perfect collinearity is rare. Unluckily, less than perfect collinearity is unavoidable. If collinearity between predictors is small, then you do not need to worry, but as collinearity increases there are three problems of which to be aware.

'First, as collinearity increases so do the standard errors of the parameters, *b*. What does the standard error represent?'

'It tells us about the variability of parameter estimates across samples, doesn't it?'

'*Claw*rect. So large standard errors mean that the *b*s are more variable across samples, which in turn implies that the estimate of *b* in our sample is less likely to be representative of the population value.'

'So the parameter estimates for the model are less trustworthy if there is multicollinearity.'

'*Purr*cisely. The second problem is that multicollinearity limits the overall fit of the model. Imagine I analysed the oxytocin data and found that using the concentration of chemical spray as a predictor produced a good fit to the data. Let us also imagine that in an uncharacteristic change of personality I had also gone around hugging people, so I had a measure of how many hugs people were given as well as the dose of chemical that they received. This second variable (hugging) might account for a lot of the variance in oxytocin, which is why I included it in the model. However, imagine that I also inhaled the chemical spray each time so that when I was giving high doses of the chemical my own oxytocin levels increased, making me give lots of hugs, but when I gave low doses my oxytocin was less affected, so I gave fewer hugs. These predictors would be collinear: the amount of chemical and hugs that people received were positively related. When hugging is collinear with the spray concentration the variance in oxytocin that hugging accounts for will be the same variance accounted for by the chemical spray. In other words, once the variance in oxytocin accounted for by the spray has been removed, hugging accounts for very little of the remaining variance in oxytocin. Hence, the overall variance in oxytocin accounted for by the two predictors is little more than when only one predictor was included. Therefore, the fit of the model with two predictors has been limited by the fact that the two predictors are collinear: had they not been collinear then hugging would have been able to add much more to the model in terms of predicting oxytocin levels.'

'So, if the spray and hugging were completely uncorrelated, then hugging would be able to account for different bits of the variability in oxytocin scores than already accounted for by the spray?'

'*Exscratch*ly. Having uncorrelated predictors is beneficial for the overall fit of the model. Now, the final issue is that multicollinearity between predictors makes it difficult to assess the individual importance of a predictor. If the predictors are highly collinear, and each accounts for similar variance in the outcome, then how can we know which of the two variables is important?'

'We can't, can we?'

'No, the model could include either predictor, interchangeably.'

'How do we know if we have collinearity?'

'One simple method is to look at the correlation coefficients between predictors: if they are very high, such as values around 0.8 or more, then that is a reasonable indication that there might be a problem. We can also look at the **variance inflation factor** (**VIF**), which indicates whether a predictor has a strong linear relationship with the other predictor(s) in the model. If the largest VIF is greater than 10 then there is cause for concern,[89, 90] and if the average VIF is substantially greater than 1 then the model may be biased.[89] Some people prefer the **tolerance** statistic, which is the reciprocal of the VIF (1/VIF), and some suggest that values below 0.1 indicate a serious problem and values below 0.2 suggest a *potential* problem.'[91]

12.2.8 Non-zero variance

I shifted towards the backstage area, hoping to escape. Milton stuck a claw in my jeans to prevent me.

'The final assumption is non-zero variance, which is common sense more than an assumption. It means that predictors and the outcome should have some variation in value. In other words, variables should not have variances of 0.'

'Why?' I asked.

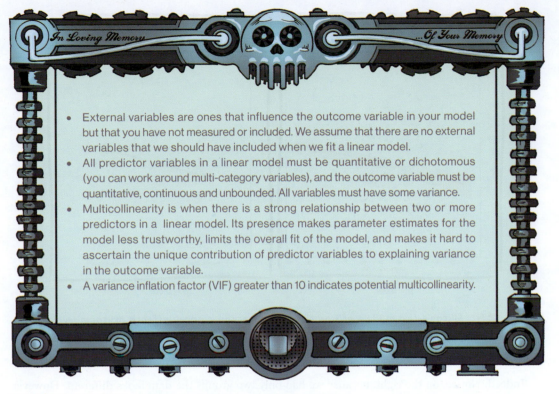

Zach's Facts 12.4 *Other assumptions of linear models*

Milton stared at me as though I had crawled out from under a rock, woken him up from a particularly nice sleep, and then poured iced water on his face.

'To have a variance of zero, every score would need to be the same. How are you going to predict anything with a variable that has the same value for every data point? It is self-evident that variables must contain a variety of scores to be of any use to anyone.'

12.3 TURNING EVER TOWARDS THE SUN

'So what did you find?' Milton looked confused by my question. 'Rather than enjoying our epic musical performance you chose to spend the evening assaulting our fans, so I'm curious what you found. You had a hypothesis that the chemicals in Nutcot's aftershave would affect people's oxytocin levels. Did they?'

Milton looked excited. 'I have already shown you in an earlier diagram **(FIGURE 12.2)**, but let us look more closely at the graphs in that diagram.' Milton drew bigger versions of the graphs showing his data. **(FIGURE 12.9)** 'As I mentioned before, I collected my data in two ways. I started off using different concentrations of Nutcot's aftershave spray and seeing whether, as the dose increased, oxytocin levels in the blood I collected would also increase. These data are shown on the left of the diagram. I also conducted a sort of experiment, where I had two sprays: one containing Nutcot's aftershave (the active spray), and the other containing a mixture that smells the same but lacks the chemical that I think increases oxytocin (the placebo spray). These data are shown on the right of the diagram. In both cases I have fitted a linear model. In the first scenario (left) this model looks at whether we can summarize the relationship between the concentration of aftershave and oxytocin levels with a straight line.'

'It looks like you can, because the red line is sloping upwards. It looks like you were right, the more concentrated the spray, the higher the levels of oxytocin in the blood.'

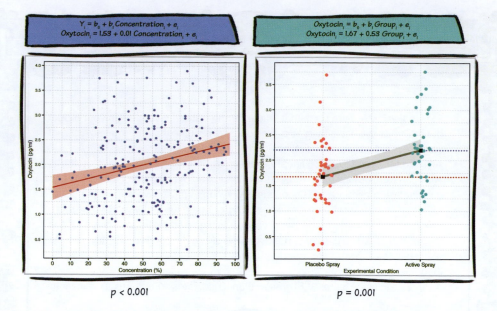

$$Y_i = b_0 + b_1 \text{Concentration}_i + e_i$$
$$\text{Oxytocin}_i = 1.53 + 0.01 \text{Concentration}_i + e_i$$

$$\text{Oxytocin}_i = b_0 + b_1 \text{Group}_i + e_i$$
$$\text{Oxytocin}_i = 1.67 + 0.53 \text{Group}_i + e_i$$

$p < 0.001$

$p = 0.001$

Figure 12.9   Milton's two models of how Nutcot's aftershave spray affects oxytocin levels

'Indeed. Notice, on the right, because we had only two groups the data looks different. However, we can still fit a linear model, but this time it represents the difference between the group means.'

'It is still sloping upwards, so it suggests that the group who had the active spray had higher oxytocin levels than those exposed to the placebo spray.'

'Ex*scratch*ly. Notice that I have estimated the fit of the models too and written the *p*-values for each one below the diagram.'

'Both *p*-values are less than 0.05, so according to what I learnt about NHST that means that the fit is "significant". Does that mean that your hypothesis was supported?'

'Indeed it does. It appears that using the concentration of the spray as a predictor gave rise to significantly better prediction of oxytocin scores than if we do not use this variable as a predictor. Similarly, using group membership (whether or not they were exposed to the active or placebo spray) gave rise to significantly better prediction of oxytocin scores than if we do not use group membership as a predictor.'

'Whatever way you collect the data, the spray seems to increase oxytocin! Why does this matter to me, though?'

'Remember the research I mentioned earlier: **(REALITY CHECK 12.1)** oxytocin is believed to increase trust. When you last met Nutcot, you questioned him about JIG:SAW but by the time you left him you had been placated, and trusted whatever he said, even though what he said was a juggernaut full of nonsense. My data suggest that his aftershave spray contains a chemical that increases oxytocin. In short, he was manipulating you by spraying you with a chemical that made you trust him more.' Milton adopted an earnest pose as he delivered his verdict.

'Basically, I've been zapped with a trust spray?'

Milton nodded before suddenly turning and running away with breathtaking speed. Before I had time to call after him, my attention was drawn to something even more breathtaking.

KEY TERMS

Durbin–Watson test

Hartley's F_{max}

Heterogeneity of variance

Heteroscedasticity

Homogeneity of variance

Homoscedasticity

Independent errors

Kolmogorov–Smirnov (K-S) test

Levene's test

Linear model

Multicollinearity

Multilevel linear models

Perfect collinearity

Shapiro–Wilk test

Tolerance

Variance inflation factor (VIF)

Variance ratio

JIG:SAW'S PUZZLES

Table 12.1 *Values of oxytocin and concentration from Figure 12.1*

Participant	Oxytocin	Concentration	Predicted values
1	2.45	74	2.70
2	3.67	79	2.83
3	0.87	58	2.29
4	2.11	38	1.77
5	3.29	82	2.91
6	1.33	20	1.30
7	1.09	7	0.97
8	2.68	37	1.74
9	1.44	44	1.92
10	1.58	50	2.08

1   In Milton's Meowsings 12.1, Milton presents data from an experiment involving 10 people in which he measured the concentration of a chemical in his spray, and the level of oxytocin in the person he sprayed. Table 12.1 shows these data. What is a residual? Compute the residuals for each participant in Table 12.1.
2   Describe what you understand by the term 'linear model'.
3   Describe the assumptions of additivity and linearity.
4   What is meant by the phrase 'independent errors'?
5   Describe with an example what is meant by homogeneity of variance. Describe the ways in which you can find out whether you have it in your data.
6   What is heteroscedasticity?
7   How does heteroscedasticity affect the linear model?

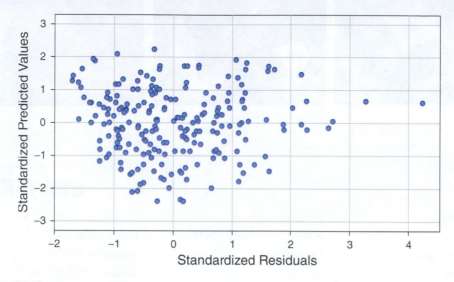

Figure 12.10   *zpred vs. zresid* plot

8   What does Figure 12.10 tell us about whether the assumption of homoscedasticity has been met for this model?
9   What is the assumption of normality and what does it affect in the linear model?
10 The Kolmogorov–Smirnov test can be used to look at whether scores have a normal distribution. Why might we not want to use this test?
11 What is multicollinearity and how do we look for it?

IN THE NEXT CHAPTER, ZACH DISCOVERS ...

The excitement of new love
How to test the relationship between two categorical variables using:

   The chi-square test
   Fisher's exact test
   The likelihood ratio test
   The chi-square distribution

Standardized residuals
Bayes factors
Correlation analysis
Spearman's rho and Kendall's tau
Covariance
Bayesian approaches

He's being followed.

13

Relationships

A Stranger's Grave

I didn't know what to make of Celia's invitation to meet. After our meeting at Hermes she was distant and angry. She had every right to be too: I had deliberately played with her emotions to get what I wanted – the JIG:SAW data – and I felt ashamed. Much as I justified my behaviour with my quest to 'save' Alice, I knew that it was a subterranean move. I'd been an eisel for sure. After her frostiness at Hermes, it was a surprise to see her at our gig, but I was also caught off guard by how pleased I was. The meeting had been off the wall: lots of fans dressed up for our gigs so there was nothing odd about her red hair or make-up, but she walked differently, and the way she asked me to sign something as though we'd never met was biz. It was as if she didn't want anyone to know she was there. I hadn't known it was her until she kissed me. She'd whispered in my ear as though organizing a clandestine meeting. Why was she being so secretive? Who was she keeping it secret from? Was it Milton? After all, he'd run off and she'd asked me not to bring him. That worried me too: I thought I'd been careful to hide him, so it freaked me that she knew about the cat. More than all of that, though, Celia had seemed tense and unsure: as she spoke in my ear I had sensed a lack of confidence that, until then, she had kept well hidden.

I found it difficult to sleep. Partly it was the post-gig adrenalin, but I couldn't get Celia out of my head, and I couldn't work out how to meet her without Milton knowing. By the morning I had a plan: I activated The Head, gave Milton some breakfast and as we sat together I told them about my trip to the Doctrine of Chance. I didn't want to talk about it, but it allowed me to ask them whether NHST or Bayesian approaches were the best. They took the bait and began debating the merits of each. Within minutes they were disagreeing and were so engrossed in trying to prove each other wrong that I could slip away unnoticed.

I went to meet Celia at The Repository; it was Sunday, so we had the freedom of the day. I had butterflies as I waited for her. Last night she had clung to me like I was the sole piece of driftwood in her ocean. Her words had been breathless and staccato, as though she were about to cry. All of which seemed to have activated pupae that had lay dormant within my stomach for some time; I was yet to discover whether today they'd metamorphose into fear or love.

As I spotted her my heart and brain felt as though they had swapped places. My blood pounded in my head, and my mouth felt completely dry. She started to run when she saw me; she greeted me by almost jumping into my arms. My social awkwardness should have rendered me horrified but instead I felt comforted.

We headed into The Repository, chatting as though old friends. I had expected Celia to greet me with a conspiracy story that would explain her secretive behaviour, but instead she launched into a glowing review of our gig. Her eyes glistened as she described the songs, her feelings, and the triumph of the show. I lapped up her enthusiasm, while at the same time telling her every mistake, glitch and close shave of our tense performance. As we wandered past storerooms, we stopped to pick up albums that we loved. We went to a pod deep in the heart of the catacombs; I put on one of the records we'd picked up along the way. The significance of the choice didn't hit me immediately. We sat facing each other cross-legged on a sofa, and I felt truly at peace for the first time since Alice's disappearance.

We soaked up the music and each other. That's when it hit me: I'd chosen the album that Alice had played the night before she left, the one that I'd played the last time I was down here gathering my thoughts. Perhaps that was why I felt so at peace? The music connected me to a happier past, to the visceral awakening of my new love for Alice and to the hope and anticipation of what our future would become. I'd lived that future now, I knew how it turned out, and I still couldn't believe it had ended how it had. When had I stopped trying? When had I forgotten that love is like a living thing: it needs nurturing, feeding, tending, otherwise it withers? When had Alice become so cold? When had science taken her from me, when had logic locked her feelings away? Celia must have sensed my mood changing to melancholy because she reached out to hold my hands.

'What's up?' she asked.

'Nothing, it's just this record ... it reminds me of the past.'

'Yeah, it's a great album,' she said and enthused about it in a way that, ordinarily, would have pressed all of the right buttons. Today, though, I was conflicted: I felt at ease with Celia, but the music connected me to a past that was slipping painfully from me. Maybe it was fitting that the soundtrack to the start of my journey with Alice was also the exit music, and maybe it was the company, not the music, that reminded me of the excitement of a new relationship. No matter how much I tried to convince myself that being with Celia was innocent, it felt wrong sharing my sacred history with another woman.

Celia felt guilty about something too. The glasses I had stolen from the Doctrine of Chance helped me to read her emotional states. It was a cheap move to wear them, but I still didn't know what to make of Celia: one minute she was lying to me about JIG:SAW, the next she was angry at me stealing data from her, yet she came to our gig, and she was keen to meet. That was the definition of mixed signals, and I needed the glasses to make sense of her. I didn't really know how the glasses worked, or exactly what they told me, but it seemed like she had a crush on me for sure, and she was happy and excited to be here. Even to someone as socially backward as me, this information confirmed what her behaviour suggested: her feelings for me, at least, were genuine. She also felt a lot of guilt, sadness and fear. Who was she scared of? Me? What, despite her happiness, was making her sad? What was she feeling guilty about? Lying to me? Or was she betraying someone by being here? Maybe she knew Alice from JIG:SAW and her guilt was because of meeting me behind her back? The glasses raised more questions than they answered, so I took them off. Relying on this objective evidence felt too much like the sort of thing Alice would do; the past few weeks were turning me into something that I was not, and I needed to go with my instinct. Celia asked me something inevitable that brought my wandering mind into sharp focus.

'I bet a rockstar like you has been snapped up by someone gorgeous?' she said, with a hopeful expectation in her eye. I didn't want to tell her about Alice and JIG:SAW, but I wasn't sure why. I was feeling distant from Alice, but part of me couldn't give up on her until I knew for sure she didn't want me. Milton knew this and he had dangled the carrot of Nutcot's aftershave in front of me to reel me back into whatever he was up to with JIG:SAW. Was I reluctant to tell her because she worked for JIG:SAW or because, as much as I didn't want to admit it, I knew I was starting to have feelings for her?

'It's complicated,' I replied.

'Really? The gossip among your fans is all about how Zach Slade is a single man.'

'It's not that simple. There is someone, or was, but I'm not really sure where I stand with her at the moment.'

Celia broke eye contact and stared at the floor; she looked sad. 'And how does she stand with you?'

The question disarmed me. 'Honestly? I love her. Until recently I never doubted that she was my soul mate, but she has been really distant, really dismissive of me, and … well, I guess I'm not sure we're on the same page any more.'

'Tell me about her. How did you meet?'

The question transported me back to when I was 16 years old. 'We met in our final year at school. Even then she was a genius. She blended into the background, keeping her head down, winning science prizes, coming top in the school in everything. She was a true individual: too chic for the geeks, too clever for the sick kids. I was a sick kid. We had our band, and we dressed the part and walked around like stars.'

'And you became one,' Celia said, looking down with a coy smile.

'It was a front though. For real, I worked hard, did my best, and pretended not to care about school. I knew that to get anywhere in the music business I needed to have a brain: the industry is full of people who rip you off, feed you batticks and give you bad advice. Education is the best defence. I met Alice in the school library. She was always there, and I used to hide out there too in a place where I wouldn't be seen. Mainly I worked, but I spent quite some time watching her too.'

'Sounds creepy,' Celia teased.

'Yeah, it does sound freaks.' I laughed at the memory. 'But you know, I dug her mannerisms: you could tell when she was excited by her work because she would open up her beautiful blue eyes into a wide stare and type frantically with two fingers. I became besotted without even knowing it. It creeps up on you, doesn't it? At first, I noticed that I looked forward to seeing her, then I found myself thinking about her as I tried to sleep, and then I couldn't sleep because I would plan in my mind how to get her to stop looking at the floor when she walked by so that I could catch her eye. One day in the library, I was struggling with my maths revision. I always struggled with maths, and usually got frustrated and gave up, but I realized that the solution to getting Alice to notice me had been staring me in the face every day.'

'What was that?'

'Ask for her help, and that's what I did. I'd planned various speeches for when I finally spoke to her, but they all went out of my head.'

'What *did* you say?'

'It was something like this … Hi Alice, I'm Zach. Do you mind helping me? I'm stuck on this maths problem, and you're the smartest, most beautiful, inspiring, amazing person I know, although I don't really know you, but I'd like to get to know you, which is to say, you know, well, I've been watching you for months … but not in a weird way, although I guess it is a bit weird to watch someone in a library, but I can't help it, I just love the way you bite your lip when you're excited about work, it melts my heart.'

'Wow! Way to play it cool, rockstar! She didn't run a mile?'

'No. She gave me a knowing smile and started talking maths as though nothing had happened. A decade later and she is still the smartest, most beautiful, inspiring, amazing person I've ever met.'

'Sounds like you have her on a bit of a pedestal. So what's your problem?'

'We follow different paths, hers science, mine music. Even a small fork in the road becomes a chasm if you walk far enough.'

13.1 FINDING RELATIONSHIPS IN CATEGORICAL DATA

'Perhaps you need to find a relationship?' Celia said playfully.

'What makes you think that?'

'You don't seem very happy, and, according to a study by Mark et al., this means you need some new excitement in your life,' Celia winked at me. 'Ask your reality checker about it.'

Batticks! I'd left him arguing with Milton. I used my diePad to access him remotely, which he hated: he liked being taken places. I asked him if Milton was there, and he said he'd gone out after they'd finished arguing. He asked me where I was, why I hadn't taken him, and who I was with, but I took control by telling him I'd explain it all later, which I had no intention of doing. I asked him about the Mark et al. study. **(REALITY CHECK 13.1)**

Celia took her Proteus and spread it out into large flat sheet. She drew a table of numbers for me. **(TABLE 13.1)** 'Like your reality checker said, we can have a look at the effect of relationship happiness on whether people were open to a little extra fun. Are you up for some fun, Zach?' Celia asked, lingering on the word 'fun'.

I squirmed.

'Look,' she continued. 'The table categorizes the 506 men in the study according to whether they had been unfaithful to their partners or not, and also whether they rated themselves as unhappy or not.'

The table looked like the Deathscotch table I had seen on the probability bridge. Milton had given it a special name.

'That's a contingency table, right?'

Celia looked surprised. 'Yes it is, and it shows us how many people fell into the different combinations of categories. There are four combinations because each of the two variables has two categories: infidelity can be classified as yes or no, and happiness is similarly split into categories of unhappy or happy.'

'Strange thing to be asking The Head about?' The Head said. 'Whatevs though ... Mark et al. wanted to know why people in relationships are unfaithful,[92] because not all scientists study boring stuff, some study sex. They looked at data from 506 men and 412 women in monogamous relationships. They asked them whether they had ever been unfaithful to their partner but also measured how happy they were in their relationship (on a scale from 1 = very happy to 10 = very unhappy), and other variables such as how compatible they felt with their partner (using three items, each with a response ranging from 1 = very compatible to 10 = very incompatible). They converted these rating scales to categories using the median; for example, if the median unhappiness was 4 then anyone scoring above 4 would be categorized as unhappy and anyone scoring 4 or less would be categorized as happy. There are problems with doin' this, but I'll let the cat tell you about that some other time.' (Milton's Meowsings 15.1.)

Reality Check 13.1   *Infidelity and median splits*

Table 13.1 Contingency table showing how many men engaged in infidelity or not, based on how happy they were in their relationship. Data from Table 3 of Mark et al.[92]

		Infidelity		
		Unfaithful	Faithful	**Total**
Happiness in relationship	Unhappy (greater than the median)	56	101	**157**
	Happy (median or less)	62	287	**349**
	Total	**118**	**388**	**506**

'Right, so 56 men were unfaithful and unhappy, but 62 were unfaithful and happy, so they were more likely to be unfaithful if they were happy in their relationship. That seems odd.'

'You are ignoring the fact that many more men were happy than unhappy. If you total up how many happy men there were it's 349, compared to only 157 who said they were unhappy. So, it's actually 56 out of 157 unhappy men were unfaithful, which is about 36% of them. Of the 349 happy men, 62 were unfaithful, which is only about 18% of them.'

13.1.1 Pearson's chi-square test

Celia moved her head to within an inch of mine, tilted it to one side and stared intensely into my eyes.

'You want to see if a relationship is possible?' she said without blinking.

I swallowed what felt like a boulder sized salt crystal. I stuttered, looking for something – anything – to say. Celia just stared expectantly into my soul. The silence was beyond awkward, but every word I'd ever learnt lay at my feet, having fallen out of my head.

She abruptly broke off eye contact and smiled out of the side of her mouth.

'To find out what's going on, you're really asking whether a relationship exists between infidelity and relationship happiness. That is something we can answer with these numbers.' She smiled to herself. 'If you want to see whether there's a relationship between two categorical variables you can use Pearson's **chi-square test**.'[93, 94]

'What does it do?'

Celia paused. 'Well, that could take a long time to explain. It lets you differentiate between two hypotheses, one that says that a relationship exists –'

'Yeah, and the null hypothesis, which is that there is no relationship at all.' I interrupted. Celia's jaw dropped slightly. 'Look, I know you probably think I'm an airhead musician, but I've had a really biz few weeks where everyone I meet tries to explain statistics to me.'

Celia chose her words carefully. 'I would never think you are an airhead, but this isn't the sort of stuff I expect rockstars to have any interest in.'

I smiled. 'Well, I didn't say I was interested, but the world seems hell bent on teaching me it, so I'm going with the flow.'

'What do you know?'

'I know that to test hypotheses you fit a model to the data, which represents the hypothesis that you want to test. So, in this case, I assume we'd fit a model that represents there being a relationship between infidelity and happiness.'

Celia smiled sweetly at me. 'It's sort of the opposite, the model represents what we would expect if there were no relationship. In other words, we want to work out the frequencies that you might expect to get in each combination of categories by chance and then compare this to the actual frequencies that we observed. The frequencies you'd expect if there were no relationship between the variables are called the *expected frequencies*.'

'How do you work those out?'

'One simple way would be to say we've got 506 men in total, and four categories, so the expected value is simply 506/4, or 126.5. That approach would be fine if, for example, we had the same number of men that were happy as were unhappy, but we didn't: we had more than twice the number of happy men as unhappy men. Likewise there are not equal numbers that were faithful or not. The expected frequencies need to take account of these inequalities, and this is done by using the column and row totals for a particular cell to calculate the expected value.' Celia wrote out an equation *(13.1)* for me on her Proteus.

$$\text{model}_{ij} = E_{ij} = \frac{\text{row total}_i \times \text{column total}_j}{n} \tag{13.1}$$

Celia gave me a reassuring look. 'In this equation, n is the total number of observations (in this case 506). Now each of the four categories occupies a unique cell in the contingency table, so it can be identified by a unique combination of the row and column to which the cell belongs. Therefore, for each cell, we use the total for the row and column to work out what the expected frequency should be.'

'What do the i and j represent?'

'They represent the different levels of the variables that make up the rows and columns. For example, the i means "the relevant level of the variable represented in rows"; for example, if we're working out the expected frequency for those who were unfaithful and unhappy then i would refer to the row category 'unhappy', whereas j would refer to the column category of "unfaithful". Let's calculate the expected frequencies for the four cells within our table.'

CHECK YOUR BRAIN: Can you work out the expected frequencies for the four cells in Table 13.1?

It wasn't as much fun as she tried to make it sound, but we did it nevertheless. Celia seemed to enjoy explaining this all to me: I periodically caught her smiling to herself. We worked through each of the cells in the table, calculating the expected frequencies *(EQUATION 13.2)*, and, at Celia's request, put these values in a new table. *(TABLE 13.2)*

$$
\begin{aligned}
\text{model}_{\text{Unhappy, Unfaithful}} &= \frac{\text{RT}_{\text{Unhappy}} \times \text{CT}_{\text{Unfaithful}}}{n} = \frac{157 \times 118}{506} = 36.61 \\
\text{model}_{\text{Unhappy, Faithful}} &= \frac{\text{RT}_{\text{Unhappy}} \times \text{CT}_{\text{Faithful}}}{n} = \frac{157 \times 388}{506} = 120.39 \\
\text{model}_{\text{Happy, Unfaithful}} &= \frac{\text{RT}_{\text{Happy}} \times \text{CT}_{\text{Unfaithful}}}{n} = \frac{349 \times 118}{506} = 81.39 \\
\text{model}_{\text{Happy, Faithful}} &= \frac{\text{RT}_{\text{Happy}} \times \text{CT}_{\text{Faithful}}}{n} = \frac{349 \times 388}{506} = 267.61
\end{aligned}
\tag{13.2}
$$

Table 13.2 *Contingency table showing the predicted values from the model for each cell in Table 13.1*

| | | Infidelity | | |
		Unfaithful	Faithful	**Total**
Happiness in relationship	Unhappy (greater than the median)	36.61	120.39	**157**
	Happy (median or less)	81.39	267.61	**349**
	Total	**118**	**388**	**506**

'This second table' *(TABLE 13.2)*, Celia said, 'shows us the values we'd expect to get in each cell. We can compare these values to those that we actually observed. These values are really predicted values; they are the values we predict from the model. The question is how well they predict the values we actually observed. Do you know how you look at the error in prediction in a model?'

'Don't you look at the difference between the value that the model predicts for each case and the actual value, and then you add these errors up. It's like variance, isn't it? The mean is used to predict each person's score, and the error in the mean is calculated by looking at the difference between the actual value and the mean value for each case and then squaring the differences because some will be positive whereas others will be negative.'

'Brilliant!' Celia exclaimed. 'There is certainly more to you than those irresistible cheekbones!'

I wondered if she knew how patronizing she was being, or how much I liked the attention.

'You're right,' she said. 'To calculate the fit (or total error) of a model, you add up the squared differences between the observed values of the outcome, and the predicted values that come from the model. In this case that would entail looking at the difference between the expected frequency and the observed frequency for each cell of the table.'

'And squaring these differences?'

'Yes!' Celia said excitedly as she drew another two equations. *(13.3 & 13.4)* 'So, just like with the mean, or any other model of the observed scores, we square the difference between the value predicted by the model and the value that was observed. *(EQUATION 13.3)* However, there is a slight variation in that we divide these squared differences by the model scores.'

$$\text{total error} = \sum_{i=1}^{n} \left(\text{observed}_i - \text{model}_i\right)^2 \tag{13.3}$$

'Why do you do that?'

'Because we need to place context on the error by looking at whether it is large or small relative to the number of observations we have made. If the model predicts a value of 10 and the observed value is 6 (so the error is 4) this error is relatively large compared to a situation where the model predicts a value of 100 and the observed value is 96, which also has an error of 4. By dividing by the value predicted by the model we're standardizing the deviation for each observed frequency. If we add all of these standardized deviations together the resulting statistic is Pearson's chi-square, χ^2. Here is the equation *(13.4)*.'

$$\chi^2 = \sum \frac{\left(\text{observed}_{ij} - \text{model}_{ij}\right)^2}{\text{model}_{ij}} \tag{13.4}$$

I stared at it. 'And I'm right to think that the i represents the rows in the contingency table and j represents the columns?'

'Sure. Let's work out what it is for this table of frequencies, shall we?'

Ordinarily, I could think of nothing worse, but I was happy that Celia was enjoying being with me.

'All we need to do is take each value in each cell of the table of observed frequencies *(TABLE 13.1)*, subtract from it the corresponding model value in the table of expected frequencies *(TABLE 13.2)*, square the result, and then divide by the corresponding model value. Once we've done this for each cell in the table, we add them up!' *(EQUATION 13.5)*

$$\begin{aligned}
\chi^2 &= \frac{(56-36.61)^2}{36.61} + \frac{(101-120.39)^2}{120.39} + \frac{(62-81.39)^2}{81.39} + \frac{(287-267.61)^2}{267.61} \\
&= \frac{19.39^2}{36.61} + \frac{-19.39^2}{120.39} + \frac{-19.39^2}{81.39} + \frac{19.39^2}{267.61} \\
&= 10.27 + 3.12 + 4.62 + 1.40 \\
&= 19.41
\end{aligned} \tag{13.5}$$

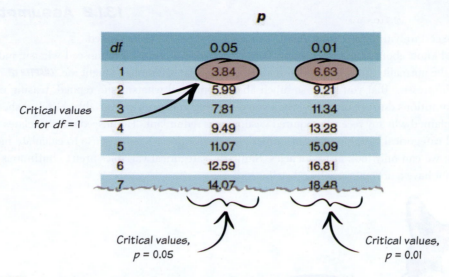

Figure 13.1 Finding out the critical values for a chi-square statistic

'Sweet, so we have a value of 19.41. What does that mean?'

'It is a test statistic and so we need to find out what the p-value associated with it is. Do you know what I'm talking about?'

'Yeah, the test statistic represents our hypothesis about there being a relationship between happiness and infidelity, and the p-value will tell us the probability of getting a test statistic at least as big as the one we have if there were no relationship between those variables. But how do we find that p-value?'

'Well, normally you just get a computer to do it for you. It calculates the probability of getting a test statistic at least as big as the one you have in a special distribution called the **chi-square distribution**. The shape of this distribution is affected by the degrees of freedom, which are calculated as $(r-1)(c-1)$ in which r is the number of rows and c is the number of columns.'

'Right, so it is the number of levels of each variable minus one, multiplied together.'

'Yes, in this case the df will be $(2-1)(2-1) = 1$. If you didn't have a computer, then you would find the critical value for the chi-square distribution with $df = 1$. Some statistics books print critical values. You can probably download an illegal copy of one. If the observed value is bigger than this critical value, you would say that there was a significant relationship between the two variables.'

Celia showed me a table of numbers (SECTION A.3) and highlighted the row of values for the distribution with 1 degree of freedom, like we had for this example. (FIGURE 13.1)

'For $df = 1$ the critical values are 3.84 ($p = 0.05$) and 6.63 ($p = 0.01$),' she said. 'Because the chi-square value that we calculated is bigger than these values it means that the probability of getting a value at least as big as 19.41, if there were no association between the variables in the population, is less than 0.01. With a computer we'd be able to work out the exact value of the probability. In any case, the probability is small enough that we might reject the possibility that infidelity and relationship happiness are not related at all.'

My diePad pinged; it was a message from Milton. (MEOWSINGS 13.1) It made me panic: how had he found out I was here, let alone that I'd be discussing the chi-square test? I looked quickly around to see if he was in the room, but I saw nothing. Celia noticed both my spasmodic movements and the note. I distracted her by asking whether the chi-square test could be biased. I remembered spending a fairly tedious part of a couple of days being told to think about bias, so it seemed a reasonable question.

13.1.2 Assumptions

'There are certainly things to think about with a chi-square test,' Celia replied.

'Yeah, I know about all of those assumptions of statistical models like homosced-whatsit, independence and the normality stuff,' I replied, thinking back to what Milton had taught me. **(CHAPTER 12)**

'It *is* impressive that you know so much about homosced-whatsit,' she replied, teasing me, 'but those assumptions don't really apply when you're looking at categorical variables.' I felt disheartened as she explained why my recently acquired wisdom was redundant. 'Homoscedasticity relates to variance, and categorical variables are not numeric, and so it doesn't make sense to calculate means or variances; we can only look at frequencies. Similarly, categorical variables aren't continuous and so they cannot have a normal sampling distribution.'

Dear Human,

I thought you might need some help. The χ^2 distribution is a family of probability distributions that describe the probability of chi-square values from all possible *independent* random samples. If samples are independent, it means there should be no relationship between them; to put it another way, it means that the null hypothesis is true. As such, the χ^2 distribution describes the probability of chi-square values when the null hypothesis is true. The exact shape of the distribution is determined by the *degrees of freedom*, which are related to the number of cells in your contingency table: they are $(r-1)(c-1)$, in which r is the number of rows and c is the number of columns. The different shapes of the χ^2 distribution are shown in the diagram (Figure 13.2). Note that although they differ they share common features:

- The chi-square statistic is a sum of squared values, so the minimum value is zero (it is not possible to have a negative value).
- They are all positively skewed, indicating that small values are relatively common whereas large values are relatively uncommon. This makes sense if you think about what the chi-square statistic represents. It is the squared discrepancy between the expected frequencies in each cell of the contingency table, and the observed frequencies. If the variables are independent and there was no relationship between them (i.e., the null hypothesis is true) then the expected and observed frequencies would be the same and the resulting chi-square would be zero. Remember that the distribution represents the probability of different chi-square values *when samples are independent*, that is, when the null hypothesis is true. When the null hypothesis is true and the variables are not related, then small chi-square values (which represent a small relationship) should happen frequently; conversely, when the null hypothesis is true and the variables are not related, we would expect large chi-square values (which represent a strong relationship) to happen very infrequently. Therefore, if the chi-square value that we observe is as large as or larger than a value that we would expect to occur in only 5% of independent samples then we assume that we have obtained such a large value because our samples are not independent; that is, there is a relationship between them.

Stay out of trouble with your new fan.

Best fishes,
Milton

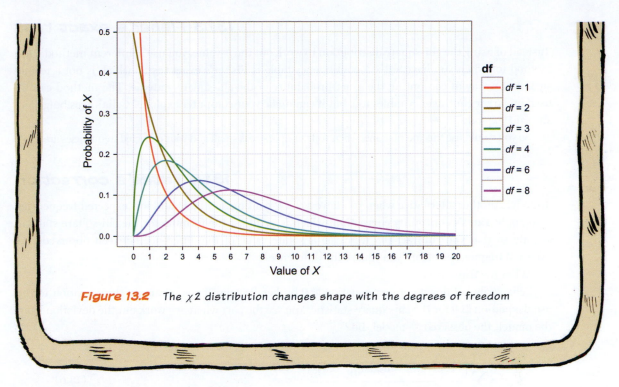

Figure 13.2   *The χ2 distribution changes shape with the degrees of freedom*

Milton's Meowsings 13.1   *The χ2 distribution*

I thought back to what Dr Genari had told me about variables, and Celia's explanation made sense. **(SECTION 2.3.3)**

'Having said that,' she continued, 'the assumption of independent errors *is* relevant: **(SECTION 12.2.2)** the chi-square statistic is based on the assumption that categories are independent, which means that each entity that you classify contributes to only one cell of the contingency table.'

'And that's true for our data isn't it? I mean, each guy could be faithful or unfaithful but not both, and could be unhappy or happy but not both, so, every guy was classified into exactly one of the four cells of the table.'

'Fantastic!' Celia's eyes glistened at me. 'The other thing that matters relates to the sample size, and it is that you need to have large enough expected frequencies. In a 2 × 2 contingency table like the one we have, no expected frequency should be below 5. In larger tables, and when looking at associations between three or more categorical variables, all expected frequencies should be greater than 1 and no more than 20% of cells should have expected frequencies less than 5. If the expected frequencies are too small then the test statistic will have very poor power.'[51]

'You mean it won't be very good at detecting relationships between variables?'

'Exactly.'

'Why does the test not have much power if the expected frequencies are small?'

'Good question! It is because the sampling distribution of the test statistic only *approximately* follows a chi-square distribution. The larger the sample, the closer this approximation is to the actual chi-square distribution; when the sample is large enough the approximation is so close to an actual chi-square distribution that we can forget that it is an approximation. In small samples, though, the approximation will be so bad that by evaluating the test statistic with a chi-square distribution we are effectively using the wrong distribution. Remember that we use the chi-square distribution to ascertain the *p*-value of the test statistic, so in small samples this *p*-value will be wrong too.'

'Whoa, heavy. What can you do?'

13.1.3 Fisher's exact test

'Instead of using the chi-square distribution to work out the p-value, you use a different method. One method for when you have a 2×2 contingency table is **Fisher's exact test**,[93] which is not a test as such, but a way of computing the exact probability of the chi-square statistic. The method can be used on larger contingency tables too, but it can make your computer explode.' Celia's eyes bulged as she said 'explode'.

'So you would use this method only when your sample size is small and your expected frequencies are low?'

13.1.4 Yates's correction

'Exactly! Another alternative when you have a 2×2 contingency table and low expected frequencies is to apply **Yates's continuity correction**, which is to adjust the formula for the chi-square statistic slightly so that you subtract 0.5 from the absolute value of the difference between observed and expected frequencies before you square the difference.'

'What the frip ...?'

Celia scribbled down another equation *(13.6)* on her Proteus. 'Look, compare this equation to the usual equation *(13.4)* for the chi-square statistic. You see the part where we work out the deviation from the model: the observed$_{ij}$ – model$_{ij}$ bit?'

$$\chi^2 = \sum \frac{\left(\left|\text{observed}_{ij} - \text{model}_{ij}\right| - 0.5\right)^2}{\text{model}_{ij}} \tag{13.6}$$

'Yeah.'

'Notice that in the new equation this part has vertical lines around it, which means that we ignore whether the value is positive or negative. This is known as the absolute value. So, we take the absolute value of the difference between observed and expected frequencies, and then we subtract 0.5 from this value. Then we square it. See what effect this has on the infidelity data.'

 CHECK YOUR BRAIN: *Use the formula to recalculate the chi-square statistic for the data in Table 13.1, but applying Yates's correction. Hint: use Eq. 13.5 to help you.*

Celia worked through the equation with me. *(EQUATION 13.7)* We ended up with a test statistic of 18.42, which was lower than 19.41 – the value when the correction wasn't applied.

'The fact that the test statistic has got smaller', Celia said, 'means that the exact p-value will be larger. The correction makes the test stricter.'

'Which means that you can stop worrying about low expected frequencies?'

Celia paused and inhaled deeply. 'Probably not. There's a lot to suggest that this procedure *overcorrects*, producing a test statistic that is too small.'[51]

'Excellent, I'm glad we just spent 10 minutes discussing it then,' I said sarcastically.

$$\chi^2 = \frac{(19.39 - 0.5)^2}{36.61} + \frac{(19.39 - 0.5)^2}{120.39} + \frac{(19.39 - 0.5)^2}{81.39} + \frac{(19.39 - 0.5)^2}{267.61}$$
$$= 9.75 + 2.96 + 4.38 + 1.33$$
$$= 18.42 \tag{13.7}$$

13.1.5 The likelihood ratio (G-test)

Celia tried to diffuse my sarcasm by frowning at me. Then, as if a thought had popped into her head, she sprang into highly animated life again.

'Actually, there is another way to test for relationships between categorical variables, which is called the **likelihood ratio test**, or **G-test**. This test is based on the idea that you collect some data and create a model for which the probability of obtaining the observed set of data is maximized, then you compare this model to the probability of obtaining those data under the null hypothesis. This is known as maximum-likelihood estimation.'

Celia wrote out another equation **(13.8)**. 'The *i* and *j* are the rows and columns of the contingency table, just like they were in the equation for the chi-square test. The test statistic compares the observed frequencies with those predicted by the model. We take the natural logarithm (ln) of this ratio. Let's see what we get for the infidelity data.' She said this with a huge grin of excitement on her face. I did not feel excited, but I did admire her endless supply of positivity. It was infectious, and made the ensuing calculation bearable. **(EQUATION 13.9)**

$$L\chi^2 = 2\sum \text{observed}_{ij} \ln\left(\frac{\text{observed}_{ij}}{\text{model}_{ij}}\right) \tag{13.8}$$

$$L\chi^2 = 2\left[\begin{array}{l} 56\times\ln\left(\dfrac{56}{36.61}\right) + 101\times\ln\left(\dfrac{101}{120.39}\right) \\[2mm] +62\times\ln\left(\dfrac{62}{81.39}\right) + 287\times\ln\left(\dfrac{287}{267.61}\right) \end{array}\right]$$

$$= 2\left[56\times0.425 + 101\times-0.176 + 62\times-0.272 + 287\times0.070\right]$$

$$= 2\left[23.80 - 17.78 - 16.86 + 20.09\right]$$

$$= 18.50 \tag{13.9}$$

'How do we know if this value is significant?' I asked.

'The same way as for Pearson's chi-square. The test statistic has a chi-square distribution, and it has degrees of freedom that are the same as before, that is, $(r-1)(c-1) = 1$. We could look up the critical value of chi-square for the number of degrees of freedom that we have. We did this before and saw that the critical values with 1 *df* were 3.84 ($p = 0.05$) and 6.63 ($p = 0.01$). Because our test statistic is larger than those values, we could again conclude that there is a significant relationship between infidelity and relationship happiness.'

'So basically it's told us the same thing as the chi-square test?'

'Yes, in fact in large samples the G-statistic will be roughly the same as Pearson's chi-square, but it is preferred when samples are small.'

13.1.6 Standardized residuals

I could see where Celia was heading with this example: the significant test statistic suggested that infidelity is related to relationship happiness, and because I'm unhappy in my relationship I'd be more likely to be unfaithful, but the result seemed unspecific. I asked her how we could know specifically which categories differed, hoping that it might derail her argument.

She looked excited by the question and spoke quickly and enthusiastically. 'You can break down a significant chi-square test using the standardized residual. The residual is just the error between what the model predicts (the expected frequency) and the data actually observed (the observed frequency)'. Celia scribbled residual$_{ij}$ = observed$_{ij}$ – model$_{ij}$ onto her Proteus screen. 'To standardize this equation, we divide by the square root of the expected frequency.' Celia paused to write out an equation (13.10). 'Does the equation seem familiar?'

$$\text{standardized residual} = \frac{\text{observed}_{ij} - \text{model}_{ij}}{\sqrt{\text{model}_{ij}}} \qquad (13.10)$$

It seemed to me that it contained part of the equation for the chi-square statistic. (EQUATION 13.4) Celia enjoyed my revelation. 'Yes, it's basically part of that equation. The only real difference is that we're look-ing at the pure deviation, rather than the squared deviations. The only rationale for squaring deviations is to make them all positive, which means that they can be added up without cancelling each other out. Because the chi-square statistic is based on adding values together, it matters that the deviations are squared. However, if we're not planning to add up the deviations or residuals then we can inspect them in their unsquared form. There are two important things about these standardized residuals.'

I sighed: her enthusiasm was exhausting.

'First off, the chi-square statistic is, sort of, the sum of these standardized residuals. Therefore, if we want to decompose what contributes to the overall association that the chi-square statistic measures, then looking at the individual standardized residuals is a good idea because they have a direct relation-ship with the test statistic. Second, these standardized residuals behave like any other: each one is a z-score (provided your sample size is sufficient). (CHAPTER 6) This helps us because, by looking at a stand-ardized residual, knowing it is a z-score enables us to assess its significance. A z-score with a value outside of ±1.96 will be significant at $p < 0.05$, whereas a z that lies outside ±2.58 is significant at $p < 0.01$, and if it lies outside ±3.29 then it is significant at $p < 0.001$. Let's calculate the standardized residuals.'

 CHECK YOUR BRAIN: Help Zach to calculate the standardized residuals.

Celia again walked me through the calculations (EQUATION 13.11) and we even put the values in a new contingency table. (TABLE 13.3) We were looking at the table and equations on her Proteus. She moved closer to me and put her arm around me. She pointed at the table.

'When the person was unfaithful in their relationship, the standardized residual was significant for both those that reported being unhappy ($z = 3.20$) and those that didn't ($z = -2.15$), because they fall outside of ±1.96. The plus or minus sign tells us the direction of the effect, as do the counts and expected counts within the cells. For the guys who were unfaithful, significantly *more* than expected reported being *unhappy* in their relationship, and significantly *fewer* reported being *happy*. For the guys who were faithful, the standardized residuals were not significant for both those who reported being unhappy ($z = -1.77$) and those who didn't ($z = 1.19$). This tells us that for the guys who were faithful, as many guys as expected reported being unhappy or not. The association between unhappiness and infidelity is driven

Table 13.3 Contingency table showing the standardized residuals for each cell in Table 13.1

		Infidelity	
		Unfaithful	Faithful
Happiness in relationship	Unhappy (greater than the median)	3.20	–1.77
	Happy (median or less)	–2.15	1.19

by more unfaithful guys than expected reporting being unhappy and fewer unfaithful guys not reporting being unhappy than expected. She smiled again and whispered, 'The take-home, rockstar, is that you said you weren't happy in your relationship, and these data show that guys who aren't happy are more likely to engage in infidelity.' She tossed me a knowing look.

$$z\ \text{residual}_{\text{Unhappy, Unfaithful}} = \frac{\text{observed}_{U,\,U} - \text{model}_{U,\,U}}{\sqrt{\text{model}_{U,\,U}}} = \frac{56 - 36.61}{\sqrt{36.61}} = 3.20$$

$$z\ \text{residual}_{\text{Unhappy, Faithful}} = \frac{\text{observed}_{U,\,F} - \text{model}_{U,\,F}}{\sqrt{\text{model}_{U,\,F}}} = \frac{101 - 120.39}{\sqrt{120.39}} = -1.77$$

$$z\ \text{residual}_{\text{Happy, Unfaithful}} = \frac{\text{observed}_{H,\,U} - \text{model}_{H,\,U}}{\sqrt{\text{model}_{H,\,U}}} = \frac{62 - 81.39}{\sqrt{81.39}} = -2.15$$

$$z\ \text{residual}_{\text{Happy, Faithful}} = \frac{\text{observed}_{H,\,F} - \text{model}_{H,\,F}}{\sqrt{\text{model}_{H,\,F}}} = \frac{287 - 267.61}{\sqrt{267.61}} = 1.19$$

(13.11)

13.1.7 Calculating an effect size

Celia broke the awkward silence by saying, 'We can calculate an effect size for categorical data called the odds ratio.'

The Doctrine of Chance had explained the odds ratio to me **(SECTION 11.2.3)**, so this was an opportunity to impress Celia. I told her that I knew that the odds ratio tells you the odds of one outcome relative to another. She added that the odds ratio would work really well for a 2×2 contingency table like this one because it will quantify a focused comparison; for example, the odds of being unfaithful if unhappy compared to the odds of being unfaithful if happy. I took charge, wanting her to see that I was legit.

'So presumably, comparing the odds of being unfaithful if unhappy to the odds of being unfaithful if happy is focused because it compares only two things, so the resulting odds ratio will tell us how much more likely it is that a guy will be unfaithful if unhappy than guys who were happy?'

Celia gave me a thumbs up. I started by calculating the odds of a guy being unfaithful if he reported being unhappy. This was the number of guys who were unfaithful and unhappy, divided by the number of guys who were unhappy but faithful.

$$\text{odds}_{\text{unfaithful if unhappy}} = \frac{\text{number that were unhappy and unfaithful}}{\text{number that were unhappy and faithful}}$$
$$= \frac{56}{101}$$
$$= 0.554$$

(13.12)

I showed Celia the calculation **(EQUATION 13.12)** and then worked out the odds that a guy was unfaithful but was happy in his relationship. This was the number of guys who were happy in their relationship but unfaithful, divided by the number of guys that were happy and faithful.

$$\text{odds}_{\text{unfaithful if happy}} = \frac{\text{number that were happy and unfaithful}}{\text{number that were happy and faithful}}$$
$$= \frac{62}{287}$$
$$= 0.216$$

(13.13)

I wrote out the calculations on Celia's Proteus. **(EQUATION 13.13)** I then calculated the odds ratio as the odds of being unfaithful if a guy reported being unhappy divided by the odds of a guy being unfaithful but reporting being happy. **(EQUATION 13.14)**

$$\text{odds ratio} = \frac{\text{odds}_{\text{unfaithful if unhappy}}}{\text{odds}_{\text{unfaithful if happy}}}$$
$$= \frac{0.554}{0.216}$$
$$= 2.56$$

(13.14)

Not for the first time, Celia leaned in and whispered as though imparting a great conspiracy. 'See what this means, rockstar? If a guy reported being unhappy in his relationship, like you do, the odds of his being unfaithful were 2.56 times bigger than if he reported ... happiness. There is hope for me yet.' She kissed my cheek and I blushed.

13.1.8 Using a computer

Celia started fiddling with her Proteus and presented me with the screen. It showed a bunch of numbers. I asked what it was.

'Honey, that's what you get when you get a computer to calculate all of this for you. There are lots of different software packages that you can use to do statistics. Some of them are free, like R,[95] JASP[96] and PSPP, whereas others cost money, like IBM SPSS Statistics, SAS, Systat and STATA. At JIG:SAW I use R and SPSS mainly. On the screen is some output from SPSS that shows lots of the things we have just calculated. **(OUTPUT 13.1)** Notice that it combines the information from our three tables **(TABLES 13.1–13.3)**, so that each cell of the contingency table contains the observed frequency, the expected frequency and the standardized residual.'

'Yeah, and the chi-square statistic is 19.41, the same as you calculated, but what are the *Asymp. Sig.* and *Exact Sig.*?'

'These are the *p*-values. The values in the column labelled *Asymp. Sig.* reflect the *p*-value based on the chi-square distribution. Remember that I said that the larger the sample, the closer the distribution of the test is to a chi-square distribution? Well, this is the *p*-value based on that distribution. I mentioned that in smaller samples, the test statistic will only approximate a chi-square distribution and so Fisher's method for computing the exact significance can be applied. That is the *p*-value in the columns labelled *Exact Sig.* In both cases, the values are given as 0.000, which means that the *p*-value is smaller than 0.001: because the output used three decimal places, any value less than 0.001 appears as 0.000.'

When reporting Pearson's chi-square test, report the value of the test statistic with its associated degrees of freedom, sample size and significance value. The test statistic is denoted by χ^2. It's also useful to reproduce the contingency table and to quote the odds ratio. For our example, you could report:

- There was a significant association between whether a man reported being unhappy or not in his current relationship and whether he had been unfaithful, $\chi^2(1, n = 506) = 19.41$, $p < 0.001$. Based on the odds ratio, the odds of a man being unfaithful were 2.56 times larger if he reported being unhappy compared to if he did not.

Alice's Lab Notes 13.1 *Reporting a chi-square test*

'Sweet, so the probability of the chi-square value is less than 0.001 ...'

'... which tells us that if there were no association between infidelity and happiness then the probability of getting a chi-square value of 19.41 or larger is smaller than 0.001 ...'

'... in other words, very small indeed.'

We were becoming like a statistics tag team, and I was enjoying it.

'Yes, and smaller than 0.05, which is the usual threshold for deciding that an effect is significant. Notice that the output also contains the continuity-corrected value of the chi-square, which is 18.42, like we calculated earlier, and this also has a *p*-value well below 0.05. It also calculates the odds ratio of 2.56, which matches the value we calculated, and tests whether this value is different from 1.'

'Because, if the odds ratio is 1 it means that the odds of being faithful if happy are the same as the odds of being faithful if unhappy?'

'Yes. How did you know that?'

'It's a long story involving a tomb and some druids in funky glasses.' **(SECTION 11.2.3)**

Celia looked confused. 'Let's save that story for another day – there *will* be another day, won't there?' She looked forlorn at the possibility that there might not. I said there would be and she carried on. 'The table contains a confidence interval for the odds ratio, which suggests that if this sample is one of the 95% for which the confidence interval contains the true value, then this value lies somewhere between 1.68 and 3.93. The important thing is that both of these values are greater than 1, which means that the odds of being faithful if happy might be greater than the odds of being faithful if unhappy.'

'An unhappy man is an unfaithful man.'

'Exactly, rockstar,' Celia replied, staring intensely.

13.1.9 Bayes Factors for contingency tables

Celia was still staring. I needed a distraction, so I asked whether you could use Bayes' theorem to test this theory. I remembered the Doctrine of Chance getting very excited about Bayes, and I hoped it might be the curveball to break Celia's gaze. I was right. She blinked slowly and deliberately to make her surprise clear. She played with her Proteus before waving an output in front of me.

'I have computed a Bayes factor for the test of independence using some reasonable default prior beliefs.' **(OUTPUT 13.2)**

I must have looked confused. Celia sighed, 'You *did* ask!' She smiled. 'Do you know what a Bayes factor is?' she asked.

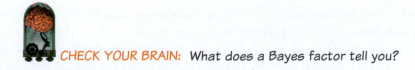

CHECK YOUR BRAIN: What does a Bayes factor tell you?

I had been told, but I couldn't really remember, so she explained.

'The Bayes factor tells you the probability of the data given the alternative hypothesis relative to the probability of the data given the null hypothesis. In this case, the value is about 1312, which means that the data are 1312 times more likely given the alternative hypothesis compared to the null. In other words, you should shift your belief towards the hypothesis that there is a relationship between happiness and infidelity by a factor of 1312.'

She stared intently at me again. 'I know all about your unhappiness, I just need the data point about your infidelity'.

My heart thumped.

13.1.10 Summary

All of this intense eye contact was doing my head in. I shuffled awkwardly away and put my emotion glasses back on. As a further distraction, I sketched the process on my diePad. **(FIGURE 13.3)**

Happiness * Infidelity Crosstabulation

			Infidelity		Total
			Faithful	Unfaithful	
Happiness	Happy	Count	287	62	349
		Expected Count	267.6	81.4	349.0
		Std. Residual	1.2	-2.1	
	Unhappy	Count	101	56	157
		Expected Count	120.4	36.6	157.0
		Std. Residual	-1.8	3.2	
Total		Count	388	118	506
		Expected Count	388.0	118.0	506.0

Chi-Square Tests

	Value	df	Asymp. Sig. (2-sided)	Exact Sig. (2-sided)	Exact Sig. (1-sided)	Point Probability
Pearson Chi-Square	19.411[a]	1	.000	.000	.000	
Continuity Correction[b]	18.423	1	.000			
Likelihood Ratio	18.533	1	.000	.000	.000	
Fisher's Exact Test				.000	.000	
Linear-by-Linear Association	19.373[c]	1	.000	.000	.000	.000
N of Valid Cases	506					

a. 0 cells (0.0%) have expected count less than 5. The minimum expected count is 36.61.
b. Computed only for a 2x2 table.
c. The standardized statistic is 4.401.

Risk Estimate

	Value	95% Confidence Interval	
		Lower	Upper
Odds Ratio for Happiness (Happy / Unhappy)	2.567	1.675	3.932
For cohort Infidelity = Faithful	1.278	1.127	1.450
For cohort Infidelity = Unfaithful	.498	.366	.678
N of Valid Cases	506		

Output 13.1 Output for a chi-square test using IBM SPSS Statistics

```
Bayes factor analysis
--------------
[1] Non-indep. (a=1) : 1311.697 ±0%

Against denominator:
  Null, independence, a = 1
---
Bayes factor type: BFcontingencyTable, independent multinomial
```

Output 13.2 Output for a Bayes factor for independence in a contingency table using R

'For real, if I want to look for a relationship between two categorical variables, then I'd first make a contingency table and then calculate the expected frequencies. If I have a 2×2 contingency table then the expected frequencies need to be above 5, but if I have a larger table then 80% need to be above 5 and all must be greater than 1. If this is true then I do a chi-square test or a G-test, but if it's not true then I should use Fisher's method to get the exact p-value or consider applying the continuity correction. Having done all of that, if I find a significant relationship between variables I should look at the odds ratio and standardized residuals to make sense of what the finding means.'

Celia affectionately hugged my shoulders and said, 'Spot on, rockstar.'

13.2 WHAT EVIL LAY DORMANT

My awkward reaction to Celia's advances had flattened the mood. I liked Celia a lot – despite her using a statistics lesson to try to convince me to betray Alice and start something with her. I was tempted by the excitement of a new relationship, but deep down I knew I couldn't do it – perhaps I clung to the belief that what I had with Alice was better and that I needed to find out if that really was over. I didn't want to hurt Celia's feelings, and the only way around that was to explain why I felt so awkward, to tell her that

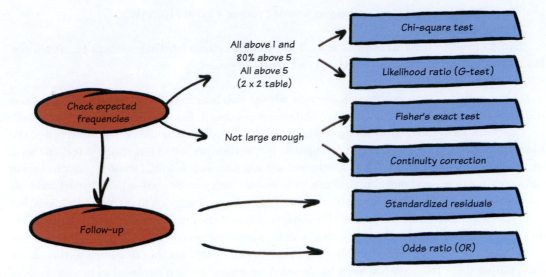

Figure 13.3   *The general process for fitting a model looking for a relationship between two categorical variables*

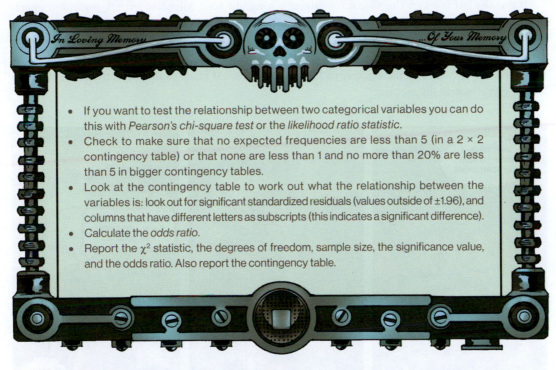

- If you want to test the relationship between two categorical variables you can do this with *Pearson's chi-square test* or the *likelihood ratio statistic*.
- Check to make sure that no expected frequencies are less than 5 (in a 2 × 2 contingency table) or that none are less than 1 and no more than 20% are less than 5 in bigger contingency tables.
- Look at the contingency table to work out what the relationship between the variables is: look out for significant standardized residuals (values outside of ±1.96), and columns that have different letters as subscripts (this indicates a significant difference).
- Calculate the *odds ratio*.
- Report the χ^2 statistic, the degrees of freedom, sample size, the significance value, and the odds ratio. Also report the contingency table.

Zach's Facts 13.1   *Relationships between categorical variables*

Alice had disappeared, that I'd seen her at JIG:SAW, that until I'd spoken to her I wouldn't know for sure that it was over between us, and that I stole data from her because I thought it would help me to find out more about JIG:SAW. I was pretty sure that coming clean was a terrible idea, but I did it anyway.

Celia wasn't affected in the way I expected: my glasses registered low values for anger, and increasing sadness, guilt, fear and a new emotion registered on the display: sympathy. She reached out for my hand, took it between both of hers and pulled me towards her. Our eyes were fixed. She was trembling like she had when she whispered in my ear the previous evening. She fixed my gaze and took a long and deliberate intake of breath, the fear value in my glasses spiked, and she spoke.

'You're right, I *did* lie to you so that you wouldn't pursue a job at JIG:SAW.'

'Why?' I asked.

'Isn't it obvious?' It wasn't obvious at all. 'I like you, rockstar. *A lot*. There's things I can't tell you, but please don't get involved in JIG:SAW. I lied to protect you.'

'Do you know Alice?'

'... Not really, just that she's the new scientific adviser. Rob Nutcot was very excited to get her. There is strange research happening at JIG:SAW, and she's overseeing it. I'm sorry to be the one to tell you.'

I shivered. This didn't sound like my Alice; she was kind, dedicated to making the world better. Did I know her at all? Was Celia trying to manipulate me, to convince me to forget Alice? It didn't seem so, my glasses told me that she felt sympathy and she was genuinely fearful. I wanted to ask more, but Celia drew me to her and said, 'I'm risking a lot to be here with you.' She paused and looked suddenly vulnerable, as though thinking twice about whether to continue. 'I'm trying to get out of JIG:SAW, but ... it's not easy: Rob Nutcot follows me. He's suspicious; that's why I had to meet you here on a Sunday, on a day when he doesn't work.' The fear value in my glasses increased.

Why on earth would Nutcot be following Celia? Before I could ask, her face lifted as though the conversation about JIG:SAW had never happened. A happiness emotion displayed an increasing value in my glasses as Celia beamed, took my hands and pulled me up into a swaying embrace.

'I *love* this song,' she said.

It was the last track on the album, my favourite song, the song Alice had left playing in our apartment, and the song that concluded this vinyl wormhole to my past. This song seemed to be following me around recently; perhaps it was telling me to let go of the past, or perhaps it was coincidence. It certainly swept me away from thinking about JIG:SAW and Alice. Instead we swayed together to the music like old friends, and the mystery of JIG:SAW was buried beneath the joy of the moment. Celia knew exactly how to distract me.

Bumping into Nutcot unnerved me. Celia had said that he followed her, and here he was, on a Sunday in the same place as her. That was too big a coincidence, surely? It also spooked me that my glasses hadn't registered any emotions. Had they malfunctioned, or was he actually emotionless? First zombies, and now the head of the company lacks emotions. Celia wasn't wrong when she said there was biz stuff happening there. Why was Alice involved with this company? At least Celia was trying to get out. Alice had done the opposite and got herself in.

My first problem was that Nutcot recognized me. If he was following Celia then I didn't want to lead him to her. Luckily, I knew The Repository inside out. Some of the Repositorians who worked here were fans of the band, and over the years I'd got to know them. They liked hanging out with me in pods that only they had access to, and they'd shown me the network of service twittens that they use to get to these secret parts of The Repository. I led Nutcot out towards the exit, then turned out of his view and doubled back through one of these concealed twittens. When I got back to Celia she sensed my unease: her fear registered in my glasses. At least I knew they still worked. I took them off so she could see my urgency.

'Hey, what's up, rockstar?'

'Shh, follow me,' I whispered.

I led her quickly through the service twittens to a pod that I had been to with some of the Repositorians. It was a safe room designed to protect workers in an emergency like a fire, or if The Repository were under attack or something. Each safe pod was practically indestructible and was connected to an equally indestructible exit tunnel. Of course, the likelihood of The Repository being under siege was small, so Repositorians congregated in these pods away from the public to relax. We reached one of the safe pods, and I let us in. My Repositorian friends liked having a 'cool' musician hanging out with them, and they'd logged my biomarkers in the security system. The pod was empty.

'We'll be safe here,' I said.

'Safe from what?'

'Nutcot: he's here.'

Celia looked spooked; she shuddered. 'Are you sure we're safe here?' she whispered. I wasn't sure.

'What's going on, Celia? You said you'd come here on a Sunday so Nutcot wouldn't follow you, but here he is. What aren't you telling me about JIG:SAW?' She didn't respond, her lips tightening; her reluctance to tell me what she knew was obvious. 'Come on,' I demanded, 'help me out or I can't do anything. I know something isn't right at JIG:SAW. When I looked at your data, there were people who scored abnormally high on their footspeed, their visual acuity and strength. I kept wondering whether it was the same people who were strong, fast, and have exceptional vision. If they are, then there are some really freaky people working for JIG:SAW. Fill me in: are there people who have super-human strength, speed and vision?'

'I don't know. Honestly,' she replied sadly. She paused as though considering whether or not to continue. 'You could fit a statistical model to test it, but you wouldn't know how to do that, so maybe it's best to just leave it.'

'You assume wrong. People in my life have recently taken great pains to tell me about fitting a linear model.' (CHAPTER 12)

13.3 MODELLING RELATIONSHIPS

'Wow, for real? You know how to do this already then.' Celia drew a diagram. (FIGURE 13.4) 'Look, this diagram shows the general procedure that you'd use. First, you'd check that the assumptions of the linear model are met (CHAPTER 12), and you could do that by using graphs; for example, draw a scatterplot to see whether the relationship looks linear, and histograms will show whether the data are normally distributed, which would suggest that the sampling distribution is too. Remember that normality of the data only really matters if the sample is small. These graphs can also help you to identify outliers and extreme scores. (SECTION 9.1) If the assumptions are met and there are no extreme cases, then you plough ahead with the linear model. In fact, you can use a special case of the linear model known as Pearson's correlation coefficient. If, however, the assumptions are violated, then use a robust method (SECTION 9.3) to estimate the correlation, confidence interval and p-value of the model parameters.'

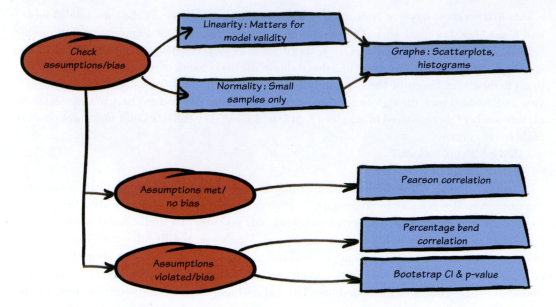

Figure 13.4   *The general process for conducting correlation analysis*

A message from Milton popped upon my diePad **(MEOWSINGS 13.2)**, with spooky timing as always. I checked again to see whether he had somehow got into the locked room we were in, but the cat was not there.

'I know a bit about Pearson's correlation,' I said. 'It's a measure of an effect size isn't it? But how is it a linear model?'

'Well, rockstar, I'm going to blow your mind here. Everything in statistics boils down to this one simple idea.' Celia drew an equation that I'd seen several times before:

$$\text{outcome}_i = (\text{model}) + \text{error}_i$$

'Consider my mind not at all blown,' I replied cheekily. 'I've seen this equation lots of times. **(SECTION 4.1.4)** It just means that the data observed can be predicted from the model fitted to the data plus some error. The "model" in the equation varies: it represents the design of your study and how you are modelling the outcome. For example, are you just modelling a typical value of the outcome, or using other variables to predict the outcome? If you are predicting the outcome from another variable then your equation looks like this.' I wrote out a new equation **(13.15)** hoping desperately that I had remembered it properly.

$$\text{outcome}_i = (b_0 + b_1 X_i) + \text{error}_i$$

$$(13.15)$$

Celia was grinning from ear to ear. 'I must say, you are *full* of surprises! You're right, this model shows that we're predicting the value of the outcome for a particular entity (i) from its score on the predictor variable (X_i). The predictor variable has a parameter (b_1) that tells us the strength of the relationship between it and the outcome. The b_0 tells us the average level of the outcome if the predictor variable was not there.'

'So how does Pearson's correlation coefficient fit into all of this?'

'Imagine that we converted the outcome variable and predictor variable into z-scores so that they had the same units of measurement. **(CHAPTER 6)** The b_0 tells us the average level of the outcome if the predictor variable was not there. Well, what would be the average value of the outcome if it consisted of z-scores?'

Dear Human,

How is the mating ritual progressing? Do not answer, I am feigning interest. I thought I might distract you from doing something unbelievably daft by telling you about some alternatives to the Pearson correlation coefficient.

When data have outliers or are not normal (and the sample is small), people often quantify the relationship between two variables using statistical procedures that work on ranked data. **Ranking** data transforms the raw scores into numbers that represent their position in an ordered list of those scores. For example, the scores 24, 36, 6 could be transformed into ranks of 2, 3 and 1; that is, the lowest score (6) receives the lowest rank (1) and the highest score (36) receives the highest rank (3).

The Pearson correlation coefficient computed on the ranks of two variables is called **Spearman's rho**, and when samples are small a variant called **Kendall's tau** is sometimes used. Although by working with ranks instead of the raw scores you reduce the impact of outliers, you have also transformed the data, which has its own problems (Milton's Meowsings 9.1). These methods were useful before computers existed, but given that they do now exist we can use robust methods that do not rely on transforming the data to estimate the correlation (such as the percentage bend correlation), and use bootstrapping to get robust estimates of confidence intervals and *p*-values.

Also, do not get too close to Celia.

Best fishes,
Milton

Milton's Meowsings 13.2 *Spearman and Kendall*

I can't tell you how much I wanted to get this question right to impress her. 'It would be zero, wouldn't it; *z*-scores have a mean of zero, right?'

'Absolutely, they do. So, what value will b_0 be?'

'It'll be zero as well because it's the average level of the outcome variable.'

'Yes, it drops out of the model. So, if we standardize the scores first, then the model becomes this.' Celia amended her equation **(13.16)**.

$$z(\text{outcome})_i = b_1 z(X_i) + \text{error}_i \tag{13.16}$$

'In other words,' she continued, 'if we predict the standardized outcome from the standardized predictor we end up with one parameter that represents the relationship between the two variables. This parameter *is* the Pearson product-moment correlation coefficient, which is usually denoted by the letter *r* rather than b_1, but it is the same thing.'

13.3.1 Covariance

Celia's explanation seemed to make sense, but I still didn't really understand how you'd find out the value of these parameters that everyone kept telling me about, so I asked her.

'What do you know about variance?' she replied.

'It's the average amount that the data vary from the mean.'

Celia wrote out an equation **(13.17)** that I'd seen before. 'Yes, the variance is described by this equation, in which the mean of the sample is represented by $\bar{x}$, x_i is the data point in question and N is the number of observations. Now, if two variables are related, then if an observation is far from the mean on one variable, would we expect it to be close or far from the mean on the second?'

$$\text{variance}\left(s^2\right) = \frac{\sum_{i=1}^{n}\left(x_i - \bar{x}\right)^2}{N-1} = \frac{\sum_{i=1}^{n}\left(x_i - \bar{x}\right)\left(x_i - \bar{x}\right)}{N-1} \qquad (13.17)$$

'If they're related it would be far from the mean too, wouldn't it?'

'The brains of science haven't just looked at what makes a relationship fail, they also try to ascertain what makes it work,' The Head said. 'Kurdek et al. measured six dimensions of relationship commitment:[97] the advantages (*Rewards*) and disadvantages (*Costs*) of the relationship, whether the relationship matched the person's ideal standard (*Ideal*), how open the person was to alternatives (*Alternatives*), how invested people were in their relationship and what barriers there were to ending it. You know, like, is your partner going to stick your favourite guitar on the fire if you flee the nest?

'Not content with measuring attitudes to relationships, they wanted to check out the person's personality. Like, The Head is all cool and chilled, but some people, like you, Z, are knotted up like a party-balloon dinosaur. They measured 'the big five' personality characteristics: neuroticism (whether you tend to feel negative emotions), extroversion (if you're like The Head and seek social stimulation), openness (intellectual curiosity, creativity and appreciation of novelty), agreeableness (your compassion and cooperation), and conscientiousness (are you organized and dependable?). One oversight was that they didn't measure resemblance to a dinosaur balloon. Their question was whether personality characteristics predict relationship commitment.'

Reality Check 13.2   *Relationship commitment*

'Yes. An example will help to explain. I've got some data based on a study by Kurdek et al.,[97] who looked at how personality affects your commitment to a romantic relationship.' While Celia found the data file on her Proteus, I used my diePad to contact The Head to find out more about the study. **(REALITY CHECK 13.2)**

Celia showed me the data **(TABLE 13.4)**, and also the mean and standard deviation (*s*) of each variable.

'Let's look at the relationship between people's responses to questions about how much their partner matches their ideal standard (**ideal**) and questions about how appealing they find alternatives to their relationship (**alternatives**). Am I an attractive alternative?'

I was a little shocked that telling Celia more about Alice hadn't stopped her flirting, so I ignored the question.

In the meantime, Celia drew a diagram **(FIGURE 13.5)** and said, 'Look, here are the data for each participant. The red circles represent the responses to being asked about their partner matching their ideal standard, and the blue circles represent the responses to questions about the attractiveness of alternatives. The horizontal black lines are the means for each variable. The vertical lines are the differences (the *deviations* or *residuals*) between the observed values and the mean of the relevant variable. If there is a relationship between these variables, then as one variable deviates from its mean, the other variable should deviate from its mean in the same or the directly opposite way. Is that happening?'

I studied the diagram and it seemed to me that it *was* happening. The first participant's responses to questions about ideals and alternatives were both above the mean; but for the remaining nine participants, if their score on ideals was above the mean then their score on alternatives was *below* the mean. It seemed like there was a directly opposite pattern: for 9 out of 10 people, those scoring above the mean on one variable would score below the mean on the other, and similarly if they were below the mean on one variable they would be above the mean on the other. I told Celia my thoughts, and she looked pleased.

'Yes. Now when we calculate variance we don't look at the total deviation from the mean, because some deviations are positive and others are negative, so they'll cancel out. Instead we square the deviances before adding them up. We want to do something similar here, but at the same time gain some insight into whether the deviations for one variable are matched by similar deviations in the other. The answer is to multiply the deviation for one variable by the corresponding deviation for the other. If both deviations are positive or negative then this will give us a positive value (indicative of the deviations being in the same direction), but if one deviation is positive and the other negative then the resulting product will be negative (indicative of the deviations being opposite in direction). The

Table 13.4   *Data on neuroticism and relationship commitment based on Kurdek et al.*[97]

Person	Neuroticism	Rewards	Costs	Ideal	Alternatives
1	28	4	2	4	4
2	22	5	3	4	1
3	31	5	3	5	2
4	49	3	4	1	3
5	15	5	1	4	2
6	53	1	2	3	5
7	43	2	4	2	5
8	30	4	2	4	3
9	15	4	1	4	1
10	18	3	1	3	3
Mean (SD)	**30.40 (13.83)**	**3.60 (1.35)**	**2.30 (1.16)**	**3.40 (1.17)**	**2.90 (1.45)**

deviations of one variable multiplied by the corresponding deviations of a second variable are known as the **cross-product deviations**. If we want the total of these cross-product deviations we can add them up, which gives us the sum of cross-product deviations, or SCP.' *(EQUATION 13.18)*

$$SCP = \sum_{i=1}^{n} (x_i - \bar{x})(y_i - \bar{y})$$ (13.18)

I drew up a table, *(TABLE 13.5)* and copied the values for the variables *ideal* and *alternatives* from Celia's Proteus.

'So what you're saying is that I should first calculate the difference between each person's score on *ideal* and the mean of *ideal*. This is the fourth column in my table. Next, I should calculate the difference between each person's score on *alternatives* and the mean of *alternatives*. This is the fifth column of the table. Finally, I should multiply the deviations from *ideal* by the corresponding deviations for *alternatives*; these multiplied values are the cross-product deviations.'

'Excellent, well done,' Celia replied. 'We could use the sum of cross-product deviations, but, like the variance, the SCP isn't that helpful because the more data points you have the greater the SCP will be. Therefore, like the variance, rather than using the total cross-product deviation we use the average. To get the average cross-product deviation, we divide the SCP by the number of observations; however, because we are estimating the value in the population, we divide by the degrees of freedom, $N-1$. *(SECTION 4.3.2)* This averaged sum of cross-product deviations is known as the **covariance**.'

Celia wrote an equation *(13.19)* that summarized what we'd been discussing. It was the same as the equation *(13.17)* for variance, except that instead of squaring the deviations, we multiply them by the corresponding deviation of the second variable.

$$\text{covariance}(x,y) = \frac{SCP}{N-1} = \frac{\sum_{i=1}^{n} (x_i - \bar{x})(y_i - \bar{y})}{N-1}$$ (13.19)

'Let's calculate it,' Celia said excitedly. She took the sum of cross-product deviations *(TABLE 13.5)* from my table and divided by 9, the sample size minus 1. *(EQUATION 13.20)*

$$
\begin{aligned}
\text{covariance}(x,y) &= \frac{\sum_{i=1}^{n} (x_i - \bar{x})(y_i - \bar{y})}{N-1} \\
&= \frac{-7.6}{N-1} \\
&= \frac{-7.6}{9} \\
&= -0.84
\end{aligned}
$$ (13.20)

Celia's energetic explanations seemed freaks, given the predicament we were in. 'A positive covariance shows that as one variable deviates from the mean, the other variable deviates in the same direction. However, ours is negative, which means that as one variable deviates from the mean (e.g., increases), the other deviates from the mean in the opposite direction (decreases).

'There is a problem with the covariance, which is that it is not a standardized measure: it depends upon the scales of measurement. For example, if you multiply the data above by 10 and recalculate the covariance, you'll find that it increases to −84.44. In other words, although the relationship between the variables hasn't changed, the covariance has. This dependence on the scale of

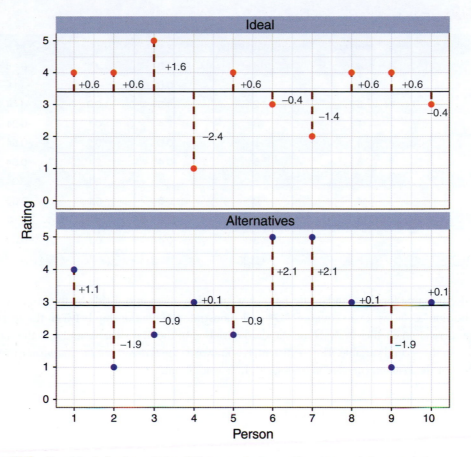

Figure 13.5 *Graphical display of the differences between the observed data and the means of two variables*

measurement is a problem, because you cannot interpret covariances in an objective way – you cannot say whether a covariance is particularly large or small relative to another data set unless both data sets were measured in the same units.'

13.3.2 Pearson's correlation coefficient

'What do you do, then?' I asked.

'You convert the covariance into a standard set of units. Essentially, you turn it into a *z*-score by converting it into standard deviation units. If you divide any distance from the mean by the standard deviation, it gives us that distance in standard deviation units. For example, for these data **(TABLE 13.4)**, the standard deviation for responses to the question about your ideal partner was 1.17. In my diagram **(FIGURE 13.5)** the observed value for participant 1 was 4, and the mean was 3.4, so there was an error of 0.6. If we divide this deviation, 0.6, by the standard deviation, we get a value of 0.6/1.17 = 0.51. This tells us that the difference between participant 1's score and the mean was about half a standard deviation. We can express the deviation from the mean for a participant in standard units by dividing the observed deviation by the standard deviation.'

'How does this help?'

'Well, rockstar, if we want to express the covariance in a standard unit of measurement, we can do much the same thing: divide by the standard deviation. There are two variables contributing to the covariance, though, and the covariance reflects two deviations (one for each variable) that are multiplied.

Table 13.5 *Calculating cross-product deviations*

Person	Ideal (x)	Alternatives (y)	$x_i - \bar{x}$	$y_i - \bar{y}$	$(x_i - \bar{x})(y_i - \bar{y})$
1	4	4	0.6	1.1	0.66
2	4	1	0.6	−1.9	−1.14
3	5	2	1.6	−0.9	−1.44
4	1	3	−2.4	0.1	−0.24
5	4	2	0.6	−0.9	−0.54
6	3	5	−0.4	2.1	−0.84
7	2	5	−1.4	2.1	−2.94
8	4	3	0.6	0.1	0.06
9	4	1	0.6	−1.9	−1.14
10	3	3	−0.4	0.1	−0.04
	$\bar{x} = 3.40$	$\bar{y} = 2.90$			$\sum(x_i - \bar{x})(y_i - \bar{y}) = -7.60$

So we do the same for the standard deviations: we multiply them and divide by the product of this multiplication.' Celia wrote an equation **(13.21)** to demonstrate the relationship between the covariance and the correlation coefficient. 's_x is the standard deviation of the first variable and s_y is the standard deviation of the second variable. The coefficient, r, is known as the *Pearson product-moment correlation coefficient* or the Pearson correlation coefficient. Let's work it out.'

$$r = \frac{\text{cov}_{xy}}{s_x s_y} = \frac{\sum_{i=1}^{n}(x_i - \bar{x})(y_i - \bar{y})}{(N-1)s_x s_y} \tag{13.21}$$

Celia helped me to convert the covariance into the correlation coefficient by dividing it by the two standard deviations **(TABLE 13.4)** for each variable multiplied together. We ended up with a correlation coefficient of −0.50. **(EQUATION 13.22)**

$$r = \frac{\text{cov}_{xy}}{s_x s_y} = \frac{-0.84}{1.17 \times 1.45} = -0.50 \tag{13.22}$$

'This is a large effect, isn't it?' I asked. **(SECTION 11.2.2)**

'You shouldn't think of r too much in this way, but, yes, some regard values of ±0.1 as representing a small effect, ±0.3 a medium effect and ±0.5 a large effect. By standardizing the covariance we get a value that lies between −1 and +1. A coefficient of +1 indicates that the two variables are perfectly positively correlated, so as one variable increases, the other increases by a proportionate amount. A coefficient of −1 indicates a perfect negative relationship: if one variable increases, the other decreases by a proportionate amount. A coefficient of zero indicates no linear relationship at all and so if one variable changes, the other stays the same. **(SECTION 11.2.2)** The correlation we have just computed is a **bivariate correlation**, which is a correlation between two variables; you can also compute a **partial correlation**, which quantifies the relationship between two variables while "adjusting" the effect of one or more additional variables.'

13.3.3 The significance of the correlation coefficient

Minus a half seemed a reasonable effect. It meant that as people give higher ratings to items about their partners being more like their ideal, the less they are tempted by alternatives. But I wondered how we'd know whether this effect was big enough to matter? I asked Celia if it was possible to look at significance or a confidence interval or something.

'We could do that, rockstar. We can test the hypothesis that the correlation coefficient is not zero.'

'You mean, the null hypothesis would be that the correlation is zero, that there is no relationship, and we'd pit this against an alternative hypothesis that it is different from zero, or that there *is* some relationship?'

Celia looked gobsmacked. 'How do you know all of this stuff? Aren't you supposed to spend all day writing songs and pottering about down here listening to records?'

Her comment made me laugh. 'I wish ... I've had to learn a lot of stuff to try to get to the bottom of what's happened to Alice.'

'You must really love her if you're prepared to learn statistics.' Celia's tone was softer, sadder even.

'She's my soul mate, but I'm not sure that I'm hers.'

'Maybe she loves you more than you realize.'

I didn't believe that, and I reacted defensively. 'Seeing as she didn't leave me a note when she disappeared, I guess I won't know until I can speak to her, and to do that I probably need to work out what's going on at JIG:SAW. So let's get on with this.'

I was agitated by the situation. If I'd met Celia at a different time I'd be thanking fate for bringing me someone who shared my passion for music, with whom I felt completely at ease, and who made me feel – well, special. The thought hit me hard, because that was how I felt 10 years ago when I met Alice. Celia made me feel like I used to feel. It was exciting, dangerous, and it was the first time in ages I'd felt really wanted. After 10 years, though, how could I expect Alice to make me feel special every day? We soak up each other's love until it is absorbed into us, existing in our cells, but invisible and unspoken. The things you appreciate become things you expect, and the perfection you saw so vividly becomes a ghost occasionally catching your eye. How I felt with Celia was vibrant and colourful, but what I felt for Alice was embedded into the fibres of my body.

Celia broke into my thoughts. 'Hey, you're miles away. I was saying that you can test the hypothesis that the correlation coefficient is not zero. If our observed coefficient is very unlikely to be as big as it is if there was no effect in the population, then we gain confidence that the relationship that we have observed is statistically meaningful. There are two ways to do this: (1) use z-scores, or (2) use a t-statistic. Do you know about z-scores?'

I was distracted by my thoughts, and I couldn't care less about z-scores. I looked at Celia's face, though, and her eyes glistened with excitement. They begged me to be interested, so I ploughed on.

'They are scores expressed as standard deviations, so the distribution has a mean of 0 and a standard deviation of 1.'

'Excellent. They are useful because we know the probability of a given value of z occurring, if the distribution from which it comes is normal. Now, Pearson's r does not have a normal sampling distribution, but it can be transformed so that it does.'[98] Celia wrote out an equation (**13.23**). 'This looks a bit complicated, but isn't as bad as it looks ...'

'Nothing is as bad as *that* looks,' I quipped.

'... You take 1 plus the value of r and divide by 1 minus the value of r, then you take the natural logarithm of that value. It's a mathematical transformation, you get it by using the ln button on your calculator or Proteus. Finally, you multiply that value by a half. In this case it gives us −0.54.'

$$
\begin{aligned}
z_r &= \frac{1}{2}\ln\left[\frac{1+r}{1-r}\right] \\
&= \frac{1}{2}\ln\left[\frac{1+(-0.50)}{1-(-0.50)}\right] \\
&= \frac{1}{2}\ln\left[\frac{0.50}{1.50}\right] \\
&= -0.55
\end{aligned}
\tag{13.23}
$$

'It's made r a bit bigger.'

'Yeah, -0.50 **(EQUATION 13.22)** has become -0.55. **(EQUATION 13.23)** The important thing about this z-transformed version of r is that because it is normally distributed, it has a known standard error that is related to the sample size, N, on which r is based.' Celia wrote out another equation **(13.24)**. 'In this case we had 10 observations, so we can replace N with the value 10 and find that the standard error is 0.38.'

$$SE_{z_r} = \frac{1}{\sqrt{N-3}} = \frac{1}{\sqrt{10-3}} = \frac{1}{\sqrt{7}} = 0.38 \qquad (13.24)$$

'How does this help us to work out the significance of r?'

'What do you know about test statistics?'

'They are a signal-to-noise ratio, aren't they – often the parameter divided by its standard error?' **(EQUATION 10.2)**

'Yes! In this case the parameter we've been estimating is r, which we have transformed to z_r, which has a known standard error. So, we can calculate a test statistic by dividing z_r by its standard error, which in this case gives us -1.45.' Celia wrote out this equation too. **(EQUATION 13.25)** 'The test statistic is a z-score, so we can find out the probability of getting a score at least as big as the one we have by comparing this value to known values of the normal distribution.' **(SECTION 7.2.4)**

$$z = \frac{z_r}{SE_{z_r}} = \frac{-0.55}{0.38} = -1.45 \qquad (13.25)$$

Celia dragged up a table on her Proteus; **(SECTION A.1)** I'd seen something similar before on the probability bridge.

'I ignore the minus sign, and read down to the value of z that is 1.45, then look at the column labelled "smaller proportion" and this will tell me the size of the area above this value?'

'Brilliant!' Celia clapped her hands. 'That area is the probability of getting a score at least as big as the z-score that you have observed.'

CHECK YOUR BRAIN: **What is the p-value of getting a z-score of −1.45?**

I looked up the value of 1.45 in the table. 'The p-value is 0.07353,' I told Celia.

'That is the one-tailed significance, because we looked at the area above the observed value at one end of the distribution. We usually want to know the two-tailed significance **(SECTION 10.1.5)**, and this means assuming that we are also interested in an area of the distribution that is the same size but is situated at the tail of the distribution that we haven't looked at. To get the combined p-value that included both tails of the distribution we would need to add these two areas together: $0.07353 + 0.07353$, which is 0.147.'

'Right, so you double the one-tailed p-value.'

'Yes. There is a second way to find a significance value for r using a different distribution from the normal distribution.' Celia wrote down another equation **(13.26)**. 'Look, you can use the value of r and the sample size on which it's based to calculate a test statistic that has a t-distribution.'

CHECK YOUR BRAIN: **What is a t-distribution? (Think back to Milton's Meowsings 8.4.)**

Milton had told me about the *t*-distribution: it's a bit like the normal distribution, but it changes shape with the sample size, so with big samples it's basically normal.

Celia continued, 'We can get a computer to calculate the probability of getting a value of *t* at least as big as the one we have. If you want to be old school you can also look up the probability in a table; however, unlike the normal distribution, the *t*-distribution changes shape as the degrees of freedom (which is related to the sample size) increases, which means that you would need a different table of probabilities for each *t*-distribution. That would be a lot of tables, so it is common to find that books publish just one table that contains the values of *t* at the threshold of certain commonly used probabilities (for example, $p = 0.05$ and 0.01). These critical values of *t* tell you how big *t* would need to be for there to be, for example, a 0.05 probability of getting a value at least that big if the null hypothesis were true. If the value of *t* that we observe in the data is bigger than the corresponding critical value from the table, then people conclude that the test statistic is significant at that probability value.'

$$t_r = \frac{r\sqrt{N-2}}{\sqrt{1-r^2}}$$

$$= \frac{-0.50\sqrt{10-2}}{\sqrt{1-(-0.50)^2}} = \frac{-0.50\sqrt{8}}{\sqrt{0.75}} = \frac{-1.40}{0.87} = -1.62 \tag{13.26}$$

$$df_t = N-2$$

Celia showed me a table on her Proteus. **(SECTION A.2)** 'Look, here's one of these tables. Now, the *t*-value we got was -1.62 and this was based on a sample of 10. The degrees of freedom for *t* are the sample size minus two ($N-2$), so that means that we have to look up the critical value for a *t*-distribution with 8 degrees of freedom. Let's focus on that part of the table. **(FIGURE 13.6)** Read across the row for 8 degrees of

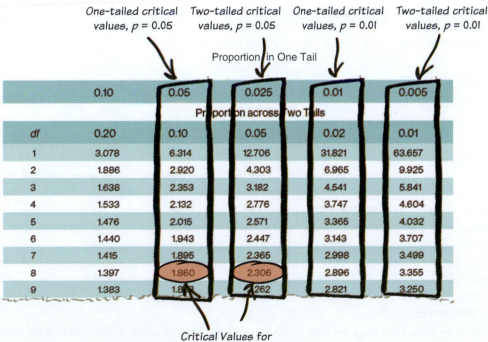

One-tailed critical values, $p = 0.05$	Two-tailed critical values, $p = 0.05$	One-tailed critical values, $p = 0.01$	Two-tailed critical values, $p = 0.01$

Proportion in One Tail

	0.10	0.05	0.025	0.01	0.005

Proportion across Two Tails

df	0.20	0.10	0.05	0.02	0.01
1	3.078	6.314	12.706	31.821	63.657
2	1.886	2.920	4.303	6.965	9.925
3	1.638	2.353	3.182	4.541	5.841
4	1.533	2.132	2.776	3.747	4.604
5	1.476	2.015	2.571	3.365	4.032
6	1.440	1.943	2.447	3.143	3.707
7	1.415	1.895	2.365	2.998	3.499
8	1.397	1.860	2.306	2.896	3.355
9	1.383	1.8__	2.262	2.821	3.250

Critical Values for
$df = 8$, $p = 0.05$

Figure 13.6 Using the *t*-distribution

freedom, and we can see that the critical value for a two-tailed test with a p equal to 0.05 is 2.306. The value of t that we observed was –1.62, and we can ignore the minus sign because that just tells us the direction of the effect. The question is whether our observed value of 1.62 is bigger than the critical value of 2.306.'

'It's not, so does that mean that the effect is not significant?'

'Totally! The value of r is not significantly different from zero using 0.05 as the alpha level.' **(SECTION 10.1.6)**

'So, there is not a significant relationship between how much your partner matches your ideal and your willingness to explore alternative relationships.'

'Yes, sweetie, there's hope for me yet: Alice's perfection doesn't rule out your exploring alternatives.'

13.3.4 Confidence Intervals For r

I quickly changed the subject by asking about confidence intervals for r. It crossed my mind that statistics was turning out to be a useful life skill in diffusing sexual tension.

'You can calculate a confidence interval for r,' Celia replied. 'Do you know much about them?'

'If it's a 95% confidence interval, then in 95% of samples the confidence interval will contain the true value of the parameter. You calculate them by adding and subtracting 2 times the standard error of the parameter.' **(SECTION 8.3)**

'Wow! It's actually 1.96 times the standard error,' Celia teased, feigning a wide-eyed surprise, 'but that's otherwise a flawless explanation. Because z_r has a normal distribution we can work out a confidence interval in the same way.' Celia wrote out some more equations **(13.27)**. 'You see, it's the same idea: we take the z-version of the correlation coefficient and we add or subtract 1.96 times the standard error, and once we have done that we can convert the values from z back to r by using this other equation **(13.28)**.'

$$\text{lower boundary of confidence interval} = z_r - \left(1.96 \times SE_{z_r}\right)$$
$$\text{upper boundary of confidence interval} = z_r + \left(1.96 \times SE_{z_r}\right)$$

(13.27)

$$r = \frac{e^{2z_r} - 1}{e^{2z_r} + 1}$$

(13.28)

'What's the weird e thing?'

'Remember that to convert r to z we had to take the natural logarithm? This is the opposite, it does the reverse of taking the natural logarithm of a number. So this equation **(13.28)** is the opposite of the one we used to convert r to z.' **(EQUATION 13.23)** Celia frantically wrote out some more equations, biting her lip with concentration as she calculated values and wrote out her workings. When she had finished, she put her arm around my shoulders as though about to share some great conspiracy with me.

'Look,' she said quietly, 'If we replace z_r with the value of –0.55 that we worked out earlier, and replace SE_{z_r} with the value 0.38, we find that the upper limit of the 95% confidence interval is –1.29 and the lower limit is 0.19. If we convert these limits back to r, then we can say that the confidence interval is from –0.86 to 0.19.' **(EQUATION 13.29)**

'It contains zero. That suggests that, if this is one of the 95% of samples that contains the population value of the relationship between how much your partner matches your ideal and considering alternatives, then that relationship might be zero or no relationship at all.'

'Like I said, I have reason to hope,' Celia said with a grin.

$$\text{lower boundary } 95\% \text{ CI}_{z_r} = -0.55 - (1.96 \times 0.38) = -1.29$$

$$\text{upper boundary } 95\% \text{ CI}_{z_r} = -0.55 + (1.96 \times 0.38) = 0.19$$

(13.29)

$$95\% \text{ CI lower, } r = \frac{e^{2z_r} - 1}{e^{2z_r} + 1} = \frac{e^{2(-1.29)} - 1}{e^{2(-1.29)} + 1} = \frac{-0.924}{1.076} = -0.86$$

$$95\% \text{ CI upper, } r = \frac{e^{2z_r} - 1}{e^{2z_r} + 1} = \frac{e^{2(0.19)} - 1}{e^{2(0.19)} + 1} = \frac{0.480}{2.480} = 0.19$$

13.3.5 Using a computer

Celia fiddled with her Proteus and pulled me closer to her to look at the screen.

'Here's some output for the correlation between the variables showing how much your partner matches your ideal and openness to alternative relationships,' (OUTPUT 13.3) she said, pointing to the screen. 'Notice that the correlation coefficient is –0.496, which rounds to the value of –0.50 that we calculated. It also displays the exact probability of getting a value at least as big as the one we have if there were a correlation of zero in the population. When we did the calculations by hand we could see that this probability was higher than 0.05 because the t-value was smaller than the critical value of t, but with a computer we can see just how much bigger the probability is than 0.05. It is equal to 0.144; because this value is above 0.05 people would regard the relationship between these variables as non-significant.'

Correlations

		Closeness to ideal standard	Openness to alternative relationships
Closeness to ideal standard	Pearson Correlation	1	-.496
	Sig. (2–tailed)		.144
	N	10	10
Openness to alternative relationships	Pearson Correlation	-.496	1
	Sig. (2–tailed)	.144	
	N	10	10

Output 13.3 Output for a correlation analysis using SPSS

13.3.6 Robust estimation of the correlation

'Earlier on you mentioned using robust methods if the assumptions of the linear model are broken. I know about the bootstrap to get confidence intervals and p-values (SECTION 9.3.5), but what about the correlation itself?'

'You can calculate something called the **percentage bend correlation**, which is known to be robust to outliers and extreme cases. It is much more tricky to calculate by hand than the Pearson correlation, but it is straightforward enough to do on a computer.' Celia typed some commands into her Proteus and another output (OUTPUT 13.4) appeared. She pointed at the output and said, 'Look, this shows a stronger association than the Pearson correlation of –0.50: the percentage bend correlation is –0.62, with a t-value of –2.26, which has a p-value of 0.053.'

'That means it is right at the threshold of significance: it is only just non-significant.'

'More important, the effect is quite strong if the value of r is –0.62. Also, neither of the bootstrap confidence intervals contains zero, suggesting that the population effect might not be zero or no effect.

401

```
          r.bp          t*      P(T>t*)
1  -0.6247012 -2.262778 0.05348993

BOOTSTRAP CONFIDENCE INTERVAL CALCULATIONS
Based on 1906 bootstrap replicates

CALL :
boot.ci(boot.out = rpb.out, type = c("perc", "bca"))

Intervals :
Level      Percentile           BCa
95%     (-0.8885, -0.1289 )    (-0.8944, -0.1583 )
Calculations and Intervals on Original Scale
```

Output 13.4 *Output of a percentage bend correlation using R*

The output shows both percentile and BCa confidence intervals, but BCa ones are typically better in that they contain the true effect closer to the 95% of times that they are supposed to. This confidence interval tells us that if this is one of the 95% of confidence intervals that contain the true value then this value is somewhere between –0.89 and –0.16.'

I thought about this, it seemed to contradict the non-robust analysis. 'Actually, then, this robust analysis suggests that how much your partner matches your ideal *is* negatively associated with being open to alternatives; the more committed you are to one relationship the less open you are to alternatives ... Bad luck, Celia.' I gave her an affectionate smile, but she seemed deflated.

13.3.7 Bayesian approaches to relationships between two variables

'If you're going to be like that, then I will inflict a Bayesian approach on you,' Celia said defiantly as she played around some more with her Proteus. 'This is a very simplified version of what a Bayesian analysis of this situation would look like,' she said pointing to a new output. *(OUTPUT 13.5)* 'Essentially we have an estimate of the correlation, which is slightly smaller than Pearson's *r*, it is –0.44, but most important we have a credible interval. Do you know what that is?'

 CHECK YOUR BRAIN: What is the difference between a 95% confidence interval and a 95% credible interval? (Think back to Section 11.4.)

'The monks with the funky glasses *did* tell me. Aren't they intervals for which there is a 95% probability that they contain the true value of the thing we're interested in; so, they're different from a confidence interval, because for those we know that for 95% of samples they will contain the true value but for the particular sample we have we don't know whether the confidence interval is one that does contain the true value or one that doesn't.'

'Very true. In this case the credible interval ranges from –0.89 to 0.15, which suggests that the true size of the relationship falls within that range. In other words, there is a reasonable chance that the relationship is negative, but it is not guaranteed, and it could be zero or even positive.' Celia pointed to the screen again. *(OUTPUT 13.6)* 'This shows the Bayes factor for the relationship too and it is 1.02, in other words the probability of the data given the null hypothesis is about the same as the probability of the data given the alternative. This means we shouldn't update our belief about the hypothesis much; there is equal evidence for both. Don't be so quick to say I'm out of luck, rockstar.' The glow returned to Celia's face.

```
Bayesian First Aid Pearson's Correlation Coefficient Test

data: Alternatives and Ideal (n = 10)
Estimated correlation:
  -0.44
95% credible interval:
  -0.89 0.15
The correlation is more than 0 by a probability of 0.096
and less than 0 by a probability of 0.904
```

Output 13.5 *Output for a Bayesian correlation test using R*

```
Bayes factor analysis
--------------
[1] Alternatives : 1.018349 ±0.01%

Against denominator:
  Intercept only
---
Bayes factor type: BFlinearModel, JZS
```

Output 13.6 *Output for the Bayes factor for the relationship between two variables using R*

13.3.8 Correlation and causation

'If the correlation between how much your partner matches your ideal and openness to alternative relationships had been significant, would that mean that Alice's perfection would make me less likely to pursue alternative relationships?' I asked.

Celia viewed me suspiciously. 'No, it wouldn't; there are two issues. The first is that the correlation tells us nothing about the direction of causality. So, although you might be tempted to think that how much your partner matches your ideal reduces the appeal of alternative relationships, it is equally valid to interpret the correlation as the appeal of alternative relationships reducing how much your partner matches your ideal. The other problem is the third variable problem or the **tertium quid**.'

I thought back to my last night with Alice. 'Isn't that where an unmeasured variable affects the things you've measured?'

Celia nodded. 'The relationship between two variables might actually be explained by a third variable that you haven't measured. For example, if you are someone who likes stability and security, this might make you both view your partner as matching your ideal (because he or she makes you feel stable and secure) and also make you less open to alternative relationships (because that would be destabilizing and create insecurity). Therefore, the apparent relationship between how much a partner matches someone's ideal and openness to alternatives is driven by having a personality that is drawn towards security and stability.'

13.3.9 Calculating the effect size

'The other thing to remember when interpreting the correlation is that it is an effect size,' Celia continued. 'Although most of our analyses seemed to suggest that there was not a significant relationship between how much your partner matches your ideal and openness to alternatives, the coefficients themselves were quite large.'

'The druids in shades said that values of ±0.1 represent a small effect, ±0.3 is a medium effect and ±0.5 is a large effect. So, the size of our relationship was large.' **(SECTION 11.2.2)**

'If only it were ...,' said Celia wistfully. 'We observed large correlation coefficients, but we shouldn't blindly use the benchmarks without thinking about our research literature. We can square the correlation coefficient to get the **coefficient of determination**, R^2, which is a measure of the amount of variability in one variable that is shared by the other. Our two variables had a correlation of −0.50 and so the value of R^2 will be $(−0.50)^2 = 0.25$, which means that 0.25 of the variability in how much a partner matches an ideal is shared by openness to alternative relationships. You can think of this value as a percentage by multiplying by 100. In this example, then, how much your partner matches your ideal shares 25% of its variability with openness to alternative relationships, meaning that 75% is not shared.'

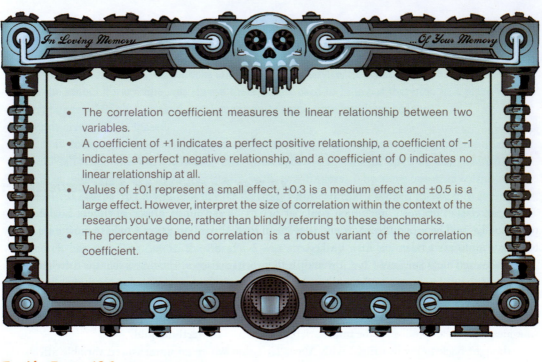

In Loving Memory   ...Of Your Memory

- The correlation coefficient measures the linear relationship between two variables.
- A coefficient of +1 indicates a perfect positive relationship, a coefficient of −1 indicates a perfect negative relationship, and a coefficient of 0 indicates no linear relationship at all.
- Values of ±0.1 represent a small effect, ±0.3 is a medium effect and ±0.5 is a large effect. However, interpret the size of correlation within the context of the research you've done, rather than blindly referring to these benchmarks.
- The percentage bend correlation is a robust variant of the correlation coefficient.

Zach's Facts 13.2   *Correlations*

13.4 SILENT SORROW IN EMPTY BOATS

We had got onto the subject of correlations because I'd been wondering whether it was the same people at JIG:SAW who were strong as had good vision and were fast. If it was the same people who scored high on strength, footspeed and vision, wouldn't you expect there to be a significant correlation between those variables? I asked Celia, who looked annoyed that I was dragging the conversation back to JIG:SAW.

'Not necessarily,' she said, 'but, yeah, a significant correlation could point to that.'

I was excited. 'Can you work out the correlations on your Proteus? You have the data, right?'

'I told you before, Zach, leave JIG:SAW alone.'

'Please.' I fluttered my eyelashes shamelessly.

Celia screwed up her mouth. 'Really, rockstar? You're going to flutter your eyelashes at me?' She paused, and huffed in reluctant acceptance of what she was about to do. She tapped away on her screen before waving the results at me. **(OUTPUT 13.7)** 'Happy?' she said with some exasperation.

Reporting correlation coefficients is easy: report how big they are, their confidence intervals, and their significance value (although the significance value isn't *that* important because the correlation coefficient is an effect size in its own right). Some general points: (1) different coefficients have different symbols – Pearson's correlation has the symbol r, whereas ρ_m is used for the percentage bend correlation; (2) often the correlation coefficient and probability value are reported with no zero before the decimal point; (3) coefficients are usually reported to 2 or 3 decimal places, which is a reasonable level of precision; (4) typically 95% confidence intervals are reported; and (5) report exact p-values. For example:

✓ There was not a significant association between how much your partner matches your ideal and open-ness to alternative relationships, $r = -.50$, 95% CI [−.86, .19], $p = .144$.
✓ A percentage bend correlation was computed with bias corrected and accelerated bootstrap 95% CIs. There was a significant association between how much your partner matches your ideal and openness to alternative relationships, $\rho_m = -.62$, 95% CI [−.89, −.16].

When there are lots of correlations a table can be useful. For example, if you correlated all of the variables in Table 13.4 then it would be more efficient to tabulate their correlations as in Table 13.6. Note that you place correlation coefficients above the diagonal and use symbols to represent different levels of significance. The confidence intervals are reported directly below each estimate. The legend below the table tells readers what the symbols represent. In the lower part of the table report the sample sizes, which in this example are all the same (10), but when you have missing data it is useful to report the sample sizes in this way. You could alternatively use the bottom part of the table to report exact p-values.

Table 13.6 *An example of reporting a table of correlations*

	Neuroticism	Rewards	Costs	Ideal	Alternatives
Neuroticism		−.73* [−.93, −.18]	.68* [.08, .92]	−.62 [−.90, .02]	.72* [.17, .93]
Rewards	10		−0.20 [−.74, .49]	0.67* [.08, .91]	−.82** [−.96, −.39]
Costs	10	10		−0.51 [−.86, .18]	0.28 [−.42, .78]
Ideal	10	10	10		−0.50 [−.86, .19]
Alternatives	10	10	10	10	

*$p < .05$, **$p < .01$, ***$p < .001$. 95% CIs reported in brackets

Alice's Lab Notes 13.2 *Reporting correlations*

CHECK YOUR BRAIN: Interpret the three percentage bend correlations in Output 13.7.

I studied the output. 'Footspeed and strength are significantly correlated, with ρ_m = 0.36, and a p-value less than 0.001. Footspeed isn't significantly correlated with vision, because ρ_m = 0.13 and the p-value is 0.17, which is greater than 0.05. Vision and strength are significantly negatively correlated, with ρ_m = −0.20 and a p-value of 0.03, which is less than 0.05. So, the faster people tend to be the stronger ones, but the stronger ones tend to have worse visual acuity. That sort of suggests it *is* the same people who are strong who are also fast but have terrible vision.'

I thought back to when I'd looked at the JIG:SAW data with Milton. **(FIGURE 9.1)** I remembered that the code 1318 workers scored higher than other workers on strength but lower on visual acuity, and weren't much different on speed. Putting these pieces of information together, it occurred to me that this would mean that the stronger workers would tend to be the code 1318s and the stronger ones would tend to be faster, but they'd also tend to have worse vision. I was feeling compelled to go back to JIG:SAW to see whether I was right.

Celia was perplexed by my silence. Not for the first time this weekend, her usual overconfidence was taking a nap.

'Whatever you're thinking, rockstar, don't think it. Just trust me, please, and leave JIG:SAW alone.'

'Why should I trust you, when I don't even know your real name?'

She looked puzzled. 'What do you mean? Of course you do!'

'What, so "Genial-Thing" is your actual surname? Once upon a time, two people met in a bar. One's surname was "Genial" and the other's "Thing" and they thought, "Hey, let's get married – it'd make a fun surname"?' I immediately felt guilty at being so flippant about her name.

'Not exactly.' Celia looked to the floor solemnly and paused in thought. After a long sigh, she said, 'My real surname is Spector. I changed it to Genial-Thing. ... I needed to ... to reinvent myself.'

'Reinvent yourself? What does that even mean? Why?'

'Something happened ...,' and with that Celia leaned slowly in to kiss my lips.

'Sorry,' I said, 'I can't do this. I love Alice and I need to know whether she still loves me too.'

Celia's composure broke completely for the first time. I could feel her trembling as though fighting back a lifetime of suppressed emotion. A solitary tear had carved a track down the make-up on her cheek. Her chin quivered as she said, 'How could she not love you, rockstar?'

They were the last words we spoke that night. I led her down one of the secret exits of The Repository. As we hit the street, she hugged me tightly and kissed my cheek. We parted silently in

```
Footspeed - Strength:
        r.bp       t*        P(T>t*)
1  0.3609127  4.203857  5.130962e-05


Footspeed - Vision:
        r.bp       t*        P(T>t*)
1  0.1251186  1.369901  0.1733188


Strength - Vision:
        r.bp        t*        P(T>t*)
1  -0.1963253  -2.174967  0.03162753
```

Output 13.7 *Percentage bend correlations for the relationships between footspeed, strength and vision in the JIG:SAW sample*

opposite directions. I turned back for a final look at her and caught her wiping her eyes. Seeing her sorrow made me feel desolate – the situation was fripped up – but I had to keep my resolve. I walked slowly back to my apartment to give myself time to think, all the while wondering what on earth could have happened to make her want to reinvent herself.

KEY TERMS

Bivariate correlation

Coefficient of determination

Covariance

Chi-square distribution

Chi-square test

Cross-product deviations

Fisher's exact test

G-test

Kendall's tau

Likelihood ratio test

Partial correlation

Percentage bend correlation

Ranking

Spearman's rho

Yates's continuity correction

JIG:SAW'S PUZZLES

Table 13.7 Contingency table showing how many women engaged in infidelity or not, based on how happy they were in their relationship. Data from Table 3 of Mark et al.[92]

		Infidelity		
		Unfaithful	Faithful	**Total**
Happiness in relationship	Unhappy (greater than the median)	34	70	**104**
	Happy (median or less)	45	263	**308**
	Total	**79**	**333**	**412**

Table 13.8 Contingency table showing how many women engaged in infidelity or not, based on how compatible they felt with their partner. Data from Table 3 of Mark et al.[92]

		Infidelity		
		Unfaithful	Faithful	**Total**
Compatibility with partner	Compatible (greater than the median)	42	154	**196**
	Incompatible (median or less)	37	177	**214**
	Total	**79**	**331**	**410**

Table 13.9 Contingency table showing how many men engaged in infidelity or not, based on how compatible they felt with their partner. Data from Table 3 of Mark et al.[92]

		Infidelity		
		Unfaithful	Faithful	**Total**
Compatibility with partner	Compatible (greater than the median)	87	228	**315**
	Incompatible (median or less)	31	160	**191**
	Total	**118**	**388**	**506**

1 Table 13.7 shows the infidelity data from the Mark et al.[92] study but for *women*. Compute the chi-square statistic and standardized residuals for these data.

2 Table 13.8 shows the number of women who were unfaithful or not, based on whether they felt sexually compatible with their partner (data from Mark et al.[92]). Compute the chi-square statistic and standardized residuals for these data.

3 Table 13.9 shows the number of men who were unfaithful or not, based on whether they felt sexually compatible with their partner (data from Mark et al.[92]). Compute the chi-square statistic and standardized residuals for these data.

4 For puzzles 1–3 calculate the chi-square test using Yates's correction.

5 For puzzles 1–3 calculate the likelihood ratio.

6 For all of the puzzles above compute the odds ratio.

7 Using the data in Table 13.4, compute the Pearson correlation, confidence interval, and *t*-statistic for the relationship between *Neuroticism* and each of *Rewards, Costs, Ideal* and *Alternatives*.

8 Using the data in Table 13.4, compute the Pearson correlation, confidence interval and *t*-statistic for the relationship between *Rewards* and each of *Costs, Ideal* and *Alternatives*.

9 Using the data in Table 13.4, compute the Pearson correlation, confidence interval and *t*-statistic for the relationship between *Costs* and each of *Ideal* and *Alternatives*.

10 What is the relationship between the covariance and the correlation coefficient?

IN THE NEXT CHAPTER, ZACH DISCOVERS …

Why you should never wake a sleeping cat

The general linear model

Simple regression

Multiple regression

Robust regression

How to incapacitate zombies

14

The General Linear Model

Red Fire Coming Out From His Gills

'I'm not describing our predicament,' I said to the cat. 'Those zombies are my mates from the band Zombie Wrath.'

'Do not let me spoil your emotional reunion,' Milton said tersely.

'We met those guys at the JIG:SAW recruitment event and now decaying, living dead, versions of them are patrolling the complex. What the hell is going on? And since when did garlic not repel zombies?'

'Since always – idiot!'

A second trip across the probability bridge had put Milton in a foul mood, although he'd been tetchy ever since I woke him yesterday morning.

'It is unwise to disturb a sleeping cat,' he had said, contorting his face with irritation.

'Why?'

'Since my transformation from human to cat I have discovered many unknown secrets about cats. The most important one being that sleeping cats form a telepathic connection that binds the fabric of reality together.'

'What are you talking about?'

'You've heard of parallel universes?'

'The idea that infinite "versions" of the universe exist in which every possible eventuality is played out?'

'Basically, yes. In better versions of my current universe, you did not just wake me. These infinite universes coexist in the same time and space, which is extremely confusing. Cats have long been protecting humanity from this confusion by keeping the universes separate through a hugely powerful telepathic network. An enormous amount of energy is required to keep universes apart. Cats generate this energy by sleeping: the *potential* energy that they would have expended if they were moving about is channelled into the telepathic network. To maintain the minimum amount of energy required to separate the universes, millions of cats need to be asleep simultaneously. If they are not, other universes will start to seep into this one and confusion will reign. The safest way to avoid that is to ensure a critical mass of concurrently sleeping cats at all times. If all cats sleep most of the day then it guarantees that a lot of cats will be telepathically linked at any given time. This is also why cats hate each other: if two cats touch, the network short-circuits. The hissing and yowling is to remind the other cat not to come too close.'

Milton constantly acted as though I was an idiot, but he must really think I was dumb to spin me this story.

'For real? You expect me to believe that the only reason that I get to experience a single coherent reality is because of sleeping cats?'

'Yes, but there's no need to thank us.'

'That's utter batticks!'

'Is it?' The cat raised an eyebrow. 'Have you ever known that you did something but you cannot remember doing it?'

'Sure, that happens to everyone.'

'That is two of the universes leaking – you did something in one universe, but the feeling of having not done it is bleeding through from another universe in which you did not do it.'

'Why would that happen?'

'Probably because some idiot woke a sleeping cat. So never do it again.'

I wasn't sure what to make of this. It wouldn't be the first time Milton had been dishonest – like when he pretended not to know who Dr Genari was, or when he said he needed my help to escape from the Beimeni Centre. But he had given me a lot of help, and although I didn't know what his agenda was or even if I could really trust him, he explained the sleeping cats with such conviction that I felt that it might be true. You couldn't invent something that biz. The truth was that although he could be spiky and patronizing, I had warmed to Milton's insulting banter. Every so often during his lessons his guard would drop and I thought I could see genuine concern for me, and sometimes a little pride in how I was taking all of his information in. I wondered if his rudeness was a front, a forced distance he tried to place between himself and other people, because underneath the tetchy exterior he was a pussycat, literally. This morning, though, there was no soft underbelly to his mood. I didn't know whether he was annoyed at me for disappearing for a day, or that I'd met Celia (which he must've known about because of the messages he sent while I was with her). Whatever – the tense start to the morning made me uneasy, and feeling uneasy made me talk, so I told Milton about my night in The Repository and my visit to Celia's grave. The grave part really cheered him up.

'One missing girlfriend and one dead mistress?' he chuckled. 'Your love life gets more entertaining by the day.'

His improving mood was tempered by my announcing that I was going back to JIG:SAW. Celia telling me that Alice was overseeing some strange research there had unsettled me: that wasn't *my* Alice. On top of that, I needed to know why Celia had a grave. Had I been talking to the dead for the past few weeks? Maybe the 'strange research' involved resurrection? I didn't know, but I felt sure that the only place to find out was JIG:SAW.

'You have finally lost your microscopic human mind,' Milton had said. 'Did you notice when we were there last that the living dead patrol their courtyard?'

'They're just zombies.'

'They were dribbling and smelt putrid,' moaned Milton as he licked fetid fishy drool from his chin.

I raised my eyebrows at the irony.

'What?' he dribbled.

Milton paced around grumbling to himself about 'ending his association with a deranged monkey intent on ending his life by being eaten by zombies.' He paused and looked up at me. It was amazing how cute he looked when he wasn't speaking.

'There is something inexplicably endearing about your indefatigable stupidity,' he said. 'It is predictable too. I anticipated this moment and have been reading a book about how to kill zombies.'

'No need,' I replied dismissively. 'I've done my own research and I have a plan.' Milton looked deeply suspicious. 'These guys on the internet have collated information about how to survive the zombie apocalypse. There's the usual stuff about destroying their brains, but I'm not sure I'm comfortable killing people.'

'You realize that zombies, by definition, are already dead,' Milton said, rolling his eyes to the sky.

'Accept it, I'm not a killing type of guy. Not even killing the dead.' Milton planted his face into the wooden floor and slowly and deliberately banged his head as though this would somehow knock some sense into me. I picked up my diePad and showed Milton a website. 'Look, these guys have collated 10 reports of people who repelled zombies using the smell of garlic. In each case they report how many bulbs of garlic they wore, and for how many seconds the zombie was repelled. I think there's a pattern, and I think I could use a correlation to measure it.'

'You could,' the cat replied dramatically. 'Or we could do something rather more interesting.'

14.1 THE LINEAR MODEL WITH ONE PREDICTOR

Milton noted down the numbers from the website and arranged them into a table **(TABLE 14.1)** that showed, for each person, the number of bulbs of garlic that they had worn (*Garlic*) and the amount of time it took the zombie to approach them (*Latency*).

'I have explained to you at least twice that if we want to look at the relationship between an outcome and a predictor then we use the linear model. **(EQUATION 14.4)** When we have measured only one predictor variable this is sometimes called **simple regression**.' Milton wrote this familiar equation **(14.1)** on my diePad. 'Do you remember?'

$$\text{outcome}_i = (b_0 + b_1 X_i) + \text{error}_i$$
$$Y_i = (b_0 + b_1 X_i) + \varepsilon_i$$

(14.1)

I did. 'You'd be impressed with me,' I replied, 'because I remembered that equation when Celia spoke to me about the correlation coefficient.' **(SECTION 13.3)**

'I might have been impressed had I been there, but I cannot guarantee it.'

So, as I thought, he hadn't been at The Repository, so how had he known to send me messages to my diePad?

'This equation,' he continued, 'keeps the fundamental idea that an outcome for a given entity can be predicted from a model (the bits in brackets) and some error associated with that prediction (ε_i). An outcome variable (Y_i) is predicted from a predictor variable (X_i) and a parameter, b_1, which quantifies the relationship that the predictor has with the outcome variable. There is a second parameter, b_0, which tells us the value of the outcome variable when the predictor is zero. These parameters b_1 and b_0 are known as the **regression coefficients**, and you may see them referred to generally as b (without any subscript) or $\boldsymbol{b_n}$ (meaning the b associated with variable n).'

'It looks like the equation of a straight line that I learnt at school.'

Milton raised his eyebrow. 'It *is* the equation of a straight line. I call it the linear model, but linear is just another way of saying straight line.'

'At school though, we talked about the gradient and intercept, not regression parameters.'

Table 14.1   *Some data about repelling zombies*

Person	Latency to approach (Y)	Garlic bulbs (X)
1	13	0
2	15	2
3	30	14
4	16	0
5	19	13
6	23	9
7	15	1
8	16	4
9	26	3
10	23	7
	$\bar{y} = 19.60$	$\bar{x} = 5.30$
	$s_y = 5.62$	$s_x = 5.21$

'When the model contains only one predictor it is common to use those terms, but the linear model can contain more than one predictor and those descriptions make less sense with several predictors. Instead people tend to refer to the bs attached to predictor variables as regression coefficients, and the intercept, b_0, as the constant.' Milton drew a diagram. **(FIGURE 14.1)** 'Look, these graphs show what the regression coefficients tell us. The left-hand one shows two models that have the same intercept but different gradients. In other words, the values of b_0 are the same in the models but the values of b_1 differ. You can see that the different values of b_1 result in models that have a different shape: in this case one slopes upward and the other downward.'

'Right, and an upward slope means a positive relationship between the variables, whereas a negative slope means a negative relationship.' **(MEOWSINGS 5.2)**

'*Purr*cisely. b_1 quantifies the relationship between the predictor variable and the outcome – both how strong the relationship is, and the direction that it takes. The right-hand side of the diagram shows three models that have the same gradient but different intercepts; in these models the values of b_0 are different but the values of b_1 are the same. Notice that the shape of the model stays the same (all three models slope up at the same angle) but the location of the model changes, reflecting differences in the average level of the outcome in the three models.'

'So, the regression coefficient (b_1) tells us what the model looks like (its shape) and the constant (b_0) tells us where the model is located with respect to the outcome.'

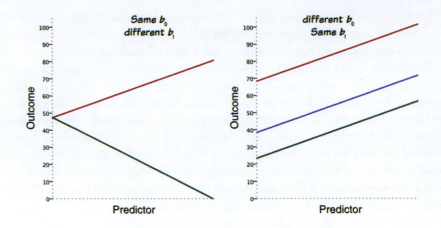

Figure 14.1   Models that share the same value of b_0 but have different values of b_1 (left), and models that share the same value of b_1 but have different values of b_0 (right)

'*Fur*fect. Now, we can use such a model to test whether the data you have about garlic repelling zombies shows up a relationship that can help us to predict how much time we can repel a zombie for by wearing a certain number of bulbs. We could summarize this relationship using a linear model by replacing the X and Y in the model **(EQUATION 4.4)** with the names of our predictor and outcome. Our predictor is the number of garlic bulbs, let us call this variable *Garlic*, and the outcome is the time taken for the zombie to approach, let us call this variable *Latency*. I will replace the X and Y with these variable names.'

Milton wrote out a new equation **(14.2)** and continued, 'Once we have estimated the values of the bs we can use this model to predict the latency of approach of a zombie based on the number of bulbs of garlic we wear. All we need to do is to replace the variable name, *Garlic*, with the number of bulbs we intend to wear and solve the equation. For example, imagine that b_0 turned out to be 15.62 and b_1 turned out to be 0.75, our model would become this equation.' Milton replaced the b values in the model with these values. **(EQUATION 14.3)**

$$Y_i = b_0 + b_1 X_i + \varepsilon_i$$
$$\text{Latency}_i = b_0 + b_1 \text{Garlic}_i + \varepsilon_i \tag{14.2}$$

$$\text{Latency}_i = 15.62 + (0.75 \times \text{Garlic}_i) + \varepsilon_i \tag{14.3}$$

'Now that we know the values of the bs, we can make a prediction about how long we can repel a zombie for based on wearing a certain number of bulbs. How many bulbs do you think you might want to wear?'

I shrugged.

'For goodness' sake, just pick a number!' Milton was getting exasperated.

'Chill, furball! ... Ten.'

'Thank you! We can replace the variable name, *Garlic*, with this value and solve the equation to predict for how many seconds a zombie will be repelled.' Milton showed me how. **(EQUATION 14.4)**

$$
\begin{aligned}
\text{Latency}_i &= 15.62 + (0.75 \times 10) + \varepsilon_i \\
&= 15.62 + 7.5 + \varepsilon_i \\
&= 23.12 + \varepsilon_i
\end{aligned}
\tag{14.4}
$$

'You see?' Milton continued. 'Our model predicts that if we wear 10 bulbs of garlic we can stave off a zombie for 23.12 seconds. Certainly long enough to run a respectable distance away. This value of 23.12 seconds is a **predicted value**.'

'Why is the error term still in the model?'

'Because the value is a prediction; it is not necessarily what will actually happen. Remember that the model is a summary of lots of data, and the predicted value is a prediction based on that summary; in reality, if we walked up to a zombie wearing 10 cloves of garlic it might repel them for 20 seconds, or perhaps 29 seconds, or possibly only 5 seconds. There is likely to be some error in prediction. Therefore, it is important to try to get some indication of how well the model fits the data on which it is based, but also to try to quantify how well the model generalizes beyond the sample of data on which it is based.'

14.1.1 Estimating parameters

Milton had made up some values for b, so I asked him how we'd find out the real values.

'You forget that I am a genius,' he replied modestly. 'Those values were not made up: I did a little mental arithmetic when you were not paying attention. The short answer to your question is that we can use the method of least squares, which I have explained to you before.' (SECTION 8.1)

 CHECK YOUR BRAIN: On what general principle is the method of least squares based?

I thought back. It seemed so long ago now, but I remembered him telling me that this method finds the value of b that gives you the least squared error between the model and the data you collected. When he'd explained it before, he'd used the mean, so I asked how it worked for the linear model.

'The principle is the same. When I explained it before, I showed you that we could look at the deviations between the model and the observed data. These deviations are the vertical distances between the value of the outcome predicted by the model and the observed values of the outcome. We already looked at these deviations when the model fitted is the mean, but the same principle applies when the model is the linear model.'

Milton drew a diagram for me (FIGURE 14.2) and pointed at it. 'Look, here are your garlic and zombie data, and the line through the data points is a linear model. Pretend for a minute that we already know the values of b_1 and the constant, b_0, and they are the values that I said before: 0.75 and 15.62, respectively. For each value of the predictor that we observed, we could compute a value of the outcome predicted by the model. We do this exactly as we did before: we replace the word *Garlic* with a value of that variable. For example, the 8th zombie was repelled for 16 seconds by 4 bulbs of garlic. (TABLE 14.1) If we replace the word *Garlic* with the number 4, we can find out the predicted latency.' Milton showed me his calculation. (EQUATION 14.5)

$$\begin{aligned} \text{Latency}_i &= 15.62 + (0.75 \times 4) + \varepsilon_i \\ &= 15.62 + 3 + \varepsilon_i \\ &= 18.62 + \varepsilon_i \end{aligned} \qquad (14.5)$$

The cat pointed to his equation. 'The model overestimates the latency because it suggests that with 4 bulbs of garlic a zombie will be repelled for 18.62 seconds, but in our data the zombie was repelled for only 16 s. Look at the diagram (FIGURE 14.2) and you can see these values. Look on the horizontal axis for 4 bulbs of garlic and then look up from that point and you will see that the actual data (the blue dot) shows a latency of 16 s, but the model predicts a latency of 18.62 s (the red dot that falls on the line). This difference between the red dot and blue dot is the same as the *deviation* that we encountered when we discussed the mean (SECTION 8.1): it is the difference between what the model predicts and what actually happened. In the context of the linear

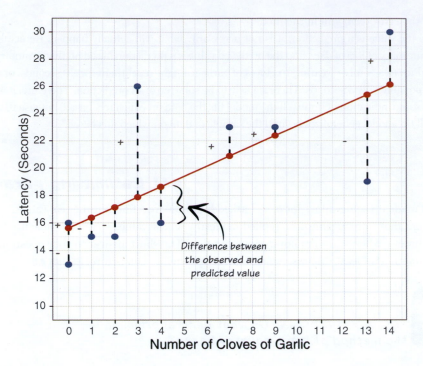

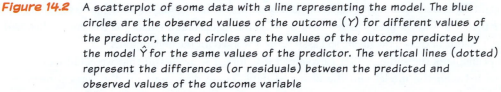

Figure 14.2 A scatterplot of some data with a line representing the model. The blue circles are the observed values of the outcome (Y) for different values of the predictor, the red circles are the values of the outcome predicted by the model $\hat{Y}$ for the same values of the predictor. The vertical lines (dotted) represent the differences (or residuals) between the predicted and observed values of the outcome variable

model, this difference is called a *residual* rather than a deviation. I have also explained residuals to you before **(MEOWSINGS 12.1)**: they are the values of ε_i in the model. If the model were a perfect fit to the data then it would perfectly predict the outcome for each value of the predictor. This would mean that in our diagram, the blue dots (the observed data) would fall in the same location as the red dots (the predicted values). However, it would be very unusual for this to happen. There will always be error in prediction, but we want the model we fit to have the least amount of error possible. How could we work out the total error in the model?'

I thought back to when Milton told me about how we estimated the error associated with the mean. **(SECTION 8.1)** 'Could we use the sum of squared errors? You know, work out the residual for each data point, then square them and add them up?'

'*Purr*cisely. Let us do it!' Milton scribbled down a table of values excitedly. **(TABLE 14.2)** The first three columns replicated the data we'd copied from the internet. In the fourth column he noted down the equation for the model, but in each case replacing the value of X with the value in the data from the third column. The fifth column showed the solution for each of these equations, which was the predicted value of the outcome (Y), which he labelled $\hat{Y}$ so that I would know it was a predicted value, not the observed value. The sixth column showed the difference between the predicted values and the observed values of the outcome ($Y_i - \hat{Y}_i$). Some of these residuals were positive (the model underestimated the outcome) and others negative (the model overestimated the outcome). If we added these residuals they would cancel out, so the final column showed each residual squared, and then the total of these values added up, the total sum of squared errors.

Milton was enthused by his mathematical escapades. 'See, just as I told you before, if we want to calculate the total error in a model we do so by looking at the squared differences between the observed

Table 14.2 *Calculating the sum of squared residuals*

Zombie	Latency to approach (Y)	Garlic bulbs (X)	Model	$\hat{Y}$	Residual $(Y_i - \hat{Y}_i)$	Squared Residual $(Y_i - \hat{Y}_i)^2$
1	13	0	15.62 + (0.75×0)	15.62	−2.62	6.88
2	15	2	15.62 + (0.75×2)	17.12	−2.12	4.51
3	30	14	15.62 + (0.75×14)	26.13	3.87	14.98
4	16	0	15.62 + (0.75×0)	15.62	0.38	0.14
5	19	13	15.62 + (0.75×13)	25.38	−6.38	40.69
6	23	9	15.62 + (0.75×9)	22.38	0.62	0.39
7	15	1	15.62 + (0.75×1)	16.37	−1.37	1.88
8	16	4	15.62 + (0.75×4)	18.62	−2.62	6.89
9	26	3	15.62 + (0.75×3)	17.87	8.13	66.03
10	23	7	15.62 + (0.75×7)	20.88	2.12	4.51
					$\sum (Y_i - \hat{Y}_i)^2 = 146.91$	

values of the outcome (Y_i) and the predicted values ($\hat{Y}_i$) that come from the model. You can sum this up in this equation **(14.6)**, and all I have done in the table is to work through what this equation represents: you calculate the residual for each person, square them and add them up. This total is the *sum of squared residuals* or **residual sum of squares** (SS_R) and it quantifies how well a particular model fits the data: if the squared differences are large, the model is not representative of the data; if the squared differences are small, the model is representative. In this case we get a value of 146.91.' **(TABLE 14.2)**

$$\text{Total error in model, } SS_R = \sum_{i=1}^{n}\left(\text{observed}_i - \text{model}_i\right)^2 = \sum_{i=1}^{n}\left(Y_i - \hat{Y}_i\right)^2 \qquad (14.6)$$

'I don't understand how this helps us to estimate the values of b?'

'Ah, well, it does not, but it helps me to illustrate the principle through which least squares estimation works. If the residual sum of squares tells us the total amount of error in the model, then the "best model" will be the one for which residual sum of squares is minimized. The method of least squares is a way of estimating the values of the bs that result in the smallest residual sum of squares.'

'Safe, so it does what it says on the tin: it is a method that results in the least squared error. That still doesn't tell me how this method estimates the value of the bs.'

'The regression coefficient, b_1, quantifies the size and direction of the relationship between the predictor and the outcome. If there is a positive relationship then as the predictor goes up then so should the outcome, and if there is a negative relationship then as the predictor goes up the outcome should go down. What we are really saying here is that a relationship will be shown up by the degree to which as the predictor deviates from its mean, the outcome shows a corresponding deviation from its mean.'

'What, like the cross-product deviation?'

Milton stared at me wide eyed and flapped his mouth unable to form words. It was a satisfying spectacle. Finally, he composed himself. 'You know about cross-product deviations?'

'Sure, Celia told me about them when she explained correlations. You take the deviation from the mean of one variable and multiply it by the deviation from the mean for a second variable. You add these cross-product deviations to get the total or sum of cross-product deviations, the SCP.' **(SECTION 13.3.1)**

'Interesting that you remember what *she* tells you', the cat remarked pointedly. 'It does make my life easier if you already understand what the SCP is.' I was fairly sure I did. 'It represents the total relationship between two variables, right?'

'Yes, and that is what we want the regression coefficient to represent. However, think back to what I said a few minutes ago: *a relationship will be shown up by the degree to which as the predictor deviates from its mean, the outcome shows a corresponding deviation from its mean*. In other words, if the predictor shows a lot of deviation from the mean, if it varies a lot, we would expect the outcome to show a lot of deviation from its mean too. Conversely, if the predictor deviates only a little from its mean (it has little variance) then the outcome should likewise show only small deviations from its mean. Therefore, what we expect to happen with the outcome depends on how much the predictor deviates from its mean. If the predictor deviates a little from the mean, then the SCP should be smaller than if the predictor deviates a lot from the mean. Therefore, we need to factor in how much the predictor deviates from its mean: we want the regression coefficient to reflect the total relationship between the predictor and outcome *relative to how much the predictor deviates from its mean*. For a single variable, how do we quantify the total degree to which it deviates from its mean?'

I thought back to when Milton first explained the mean. **(SECTION 4.3)** 'You use the variance.'

'Yes, but the variance is the *average* deviation from the mean and we want the *total* deviation to match the fact that we have used the total (not average) relationship between the predictor and outcome.'

'Oh, in which case you'd use the sum of squares for the predictor.'

'*Claw*rect,' Milton said with a smile as he scribbled an equation **(14.7)**. 'I have put a funny hat above the *b* to remind you that it is an *estimated* value. Now, to estimate the regression coefficient we divide the sum of cross-product deviations by the sum of squares for the predictor. In other words, we divide the total relationship between the predictor and outcome by the total deviation of the predictor from its mean. Of course, the SCP is related to the covariance and the sum of squares to the variance, so there are other ways to think about what the regression coefficient represents. I will message you about that.' **(MEOWSINGS 14.1)**

$$\hat{b}_1 = \frac{\text{sum of cross product deviation}}{\text{predictor sum of squares}} = \frac{\text{SCP}}{SS_x} \qquad (14.7)$$

Milton twitched into action creating another table of numbers. **(TABLE 14.3)** The first three columns again replicated the data from the internet. In the fourth column Milton noted down the deviation between each value of the predictor and its mean, and in the fifth column he squared these values so that we could add them together to get the sum of squares for the predictor (SS_x). In the sixth column, he noted down the deviation between each value of the outcome and its mean. In the final column he calculated the cross-product deviation for each observation, that is, the deviation of the predictor from its mean (column 4) multiplied by the deviation of the outcome from its mean (column 6). We could add the values in this last column to get the sum of the cross-product deviations.

'The table, I hope, makes it easy to see how we calculate the two values we need,' Milton said as he finished writing. 'The sum of the cross-product deviations is 183.20, and the sum of squares for the predictor is 244.10 **(TABLE 14.3)**, and we divide these values to give us the least squares estimate of the regression coefficient.' The cat helpfully showed me the equation **(14.8)**.

$$\hat{b}_1 = \frac{\text{SCP}}{SS_x} = \frac{183.20}{244.1} = 0.75 \qquad (14.8)$$

Table 14.3   *Calculating cross-product deviations*

Zombie	Latency to approach (Y)	Garlic bulbs (X)	$x_i - \bar{x}$	$(x_i - \bar{x})^2$	$y_i - \bar{y}$	$(x_i - \bar{x})(y_i - \bar{y})$
1	13	0	−5.3	28.09	−6.6	34.98
2	15	2	−3.3	10.89	−4.6	15.18
3	30	14	8.7	75.69	10.4	90.48
4	16	0	−5.3	28.09	−3.6	19.08
5	19	13	7.7	59.29	−0.6	−4.62
6	23	9	3.7	13.69	3.4	12.58
7	15	1	−4.3	18.49	−4.6	19.78
8	16	4	−1.3	1.69	−3.6	4.68
9	26	3	−2.3	5.29	6.4	−14.72
10	23	7	1.7	2.89	3.4	5.78
	$\bar{y} = 19.60$	$\bar{x} = 5.30$		$SS_x = 244.10$		$SCP = 183.20$

I was impressed: the value was the same as Milton had used earlier. 'It comes to 0.75, just as you said it would,' I exclaimed.

Milton looked pleased with himself. 'Mental arithmetic when you were not paying attention ...' he repeated with a knowing nod.

'Now, onto the constant, b_0. This value tells us about the overall level of the outcome variable. Now remember that the model is this equation' **(14.9)**. Milton scribbled more equations as he spoke. 'Again, I have put hats on the bs to remind you that these are estimated values. If we wanted to make the constant b_0, the subject of this equation, we could rearrange it by subtracting $\hat{b}$ from both sides of the equation. If we did this we would get this equation,' he said pointing to another equation **(14.10)**.

$$Y = \hat{b}_0 + \hat{b}_1 X \tag{14.9}$$

$$\hat{b}_0 = Y - \hat{b}_1 X \tag{14.10}$$

I looked at Milton's equations; I could see how he had rearranged the model so that the constant was now the subject. I also could see that we knew the value of b_1, so we could replace that in the equation with a value, but what values would we use for X and Y? I asked him.

'A good question, human. What makes sense is to use the average values of the predictor and of the outcome because these represent the middle, or typical, scores in the data. Now, if we replace the X and Y with the symbols for their respective means, this gives us the equation that we use to estimate the constant.' **(EQUATION 14.11)**

$$\hat{b}_0 = \bar{Y} - \hat{b}_1 \bar{X} \tag{14.11}$$

Having written down this equation for me, Milton pointed back to one of his tables. **(TABLE 14.1)** 'Look, I already worked out the mean latency (19.60) and the mean number of bulbs of garlic (5.30) when I originally tabulated the data, so we can replace these values into the equation and you'll see that the constant is 15.62, just as I said it would be.' **(EQUATION 14.12)** Milton puffed out his chest, raised his chin and strutted in a circle as if waiting for applause.

$$\hat{b}_0 = \bar{Y} - \hat{b}_1 \bar{X}$$
$$= 19.60 - (0.75 \times 5.30) \tag{14.12}$$
$$= 15.62$$

Dear Human,

The equation for estimating the regression coefficient, b_1, gives us a clue as to what it represents, but we can use what we already know about the relation between different statistical constructs to think about what it represents in slightly different ways, which might (or might not) make more sense to you. The equation we have used (Eq. 14.7) shows that b is the total relationship between the outcome and predictor variables (i.e., the total of the cross-product deviations) divided by the total variability in the predictor (i.e., the total sum of squared errors for the predictor). In other words it is the ratio of the total relationship between the predictor and outcome to the total spread of scores in the predictor.

Think back, and you might remember that the covariance between variables is the *average* relationship between variables, or the sum of cross-product deviations divided by the sample size minus 1 (Eq. 13.19). Similarly, the variance of the predictor variable is its sum of squared errors divided by the sample size minus 1 (Eq. 4.20). Therefore, we could change the equation for b by dividing both the top and bottom of the equation by $N - 1$. Doing so does not affect the result of the equation because we are doing exactly the same thing to both the top and bottom half, but it shows you a different way to think about what b represents conceptually:

$$\hat{b}_1 = \frac{\text{SCP}/(N-1)}{SS_x/(N-1)} = \frac{\text{covariance}(x,y)}{\text{variance}(x)}$$

The equation has not changed, except that we have gone from working with total values, to average values. This shows us that b can also be thought of as the covariance between the predictor and outcome expressed as a function of the variance in the predictor variable. In other words, it is the average relationship between the predictor and outcome scaled to the average spread in the predictor variable.

We also know that Pearson's correlation, r, is the covariance divided by the standard deviation of the predictor and outcome multiplied (Eq. 13.21), which means that by rearranging this equation we can express the covariance as r multiplied by the standard deviations of the predictor and outcome:

$$r = \frac{\text{cov}_{xy}}{s_x s_y}$$
$$\text{cov}_{xy} = r\left(s_x s_y\right)$$

We also know that the standard deviation of the predictor is the square root of its variance, which, if we put it another way, means that the variance of the predictor is the standard deviation of the predictor multiplied by itself. We can, therefore, express b in terms of the correlation coefficient by replacing the covariance and variance in the equation with standardized versions such as r and the standard deviations of the variables:

$$\hat{b}_1 = \frac{\text{covariance}(x,y)}{\text{variance}(x)} = \frac{r\left(s_x s_y\right)}{s_x \times s_x} = \frac{r\left(s_y\right)}{s_x}$$

One of the standard deviation terms for the predictor (s_x) cancels out of the top and bottom of the equation, leaving us with a simple way to express b in terms of the correlation coefficient. That is, b is the standardized relationship between the predictor and outcome expressed as a function of the ratio of the spread of scores in the outcome to the predictor. If the predictor and outcome have similar spreads then b and r will have similar values, but this is rare.

Best fishes,
Milton

Milton's Meowsings 14.1   *What the regression parameter (b) represents*

14.1.2 Interpreting regression coefficients

Although I had grasped how we arrived at the estimate of the regression coefficient, I still wasn't sure exactly what it told me. Sure, it quantifies the relationship between the predictor and outcome variables, but then a correlation coefficient also quantifies the relationship between two variables. The correlation coefficient has limits that are helpful: we know that 0 means no relationship, and that +1 is a perfect positive relationship, I asked Milton whether b_1 was the same.

'Yes and no,' was his unhelpful response. 'Yes in that they both quantify the size and direction of relationship between two variables, and that a value of 0 would mean no relationship at all; but no, in that – unlike the correlation coefficient – b is not a standardized measure, its size depends on the units of measurement of the predictor variable. The value of b represents the change in the outcome resulting from a unit change in the predictor. In our model, where b_1 was 0.75, that would mean that as garlic bulbs increases by 1, the number of seconds for which a zombie is repelled increases by 0.75.'

That would come in useful for visiting JIG:SAW, I thought – for every extra bulb of garlic we wore we'd gain an extra 0.75 s of time to escape.

14.1.3 Standardized regression coefficients

I asked Milton whether we could compare regression coefficients, like we can correlations.

'No, because they depend on the spread, or variance, of the predictor. What we *can* do, is standardize b by multiplying it by the ratio of the standard deviation for the predictor (s_x) to the standard deviation of the outcome (s_y). This has the effect of scaling the regression coefficient by the spread of scores in the predictor relative to the spread in the outcome. By including information about the spread of both the predictor and outcome we end up with a version of b that is in standard deviation units, a bit like a z-score. **(CHAPTER 6)** These **standardized regression coefficients** are often denoted by the Greek letter β_i to distinguish them from the raw coefficients.' Milton showed me the equation **(14.13)**.

$$\hat{\beta}_i = \hat{b}_i \frac{s_x}{s_y} \tag{14.13}$$

He pointed to one of his tables. **(TABLE 14.1)** 'We have the standard deviations for the predictor and outcome here, and if you place these values into the equation you'll see that we get a standardized beta of 0.695.' Milton showed me his working. **(EQUATION 14.14)**

$$\hat{\beta}_1 = 0.75 \times \frac{5.21}{5.62} = 0.75 \times 0.927 = 0.695 \tag{14.14}$$

'How is this different from the normal b?' I asked.

'The standardized version of b has a different interpretation because it is b but expressed in standard deviations rather than the original units of measurement. In this case, as the predictor variable changes by 1 *standard deviation*, the outcome changes by 0.695 *standard deviations*. The standard deviation for garlic was 5.21 and for latency it was 5.62, so it means that if you wear 5.21 more bulbs of garlic a zombie will be repelled for 0.695×5.62, or 3.91, more seconds. When the model has only one predictor the standardized beta is the same as the correlation coefficient (r), and you can see that the equation we used to calculate it **(EQUATION 14.13)**, is a rearranged version of the equation I messaged to you earlier to explain the link between the regression parameter and r.' **(MEOWSINGS 14.1)**

14.1.4 The standard error of b

Milton paused and scratched his furry chin. 'Of course it's all very well estimating the parameters in our model, but we need to know whether they are representative of the population values. Just like with any parameter, we can calculate a standard error for b, which gives us some idea of how estimates might differ across samples. For the regression coefficient, our starting point is to look at the standard error for the whole model. Remember that I said earlier that the total error in the model could be quantified using the residual sum of squares. **(EQUATION 14.16)** This value is the total squared differences between the observed values of the outcome, and the values predicted by the model. We could convert this total error into an average error by dividing by the number of scores on which it is based.'

'What, like when we convert a sum of squares to a variance?' **(SECTION 4.3)**

'Ex*scratch*ly. Remember, when we did that, though, we divided by the degrees of freedom rather than the number of scores, and this was to correct for the fact that we are using a sample to estimate values in the population.'

To my amazement I was remembering lots of what I'd been taught. 'Didn't you say, back when you talked about variance, that we assume that our estimate of the mean is the population value, and by doing that only $N-1$ scores are free to vary?' **(SECTION 4.3.2)**

'*Purr*cisely. For b we still divide the sum of squares by the degrees of freedom, but this time the degrees of freedom are $N-p$, where p is the number of parameters you have estimated. **(EQUATION 14.15)** With the variance, we estimate one parameter, the mean, therefore the degrees of freedom ($N-p$) are $N-1$. However, with a linear model with one predictor, we estimate two parameters: b_0 and b_1. In the same way that we assume that the sample mean *is* the population mean, we assume that these bs *are* the population values. Therefore, there are two things we have estimated, and for each one there will be a score that is not free to be sampled randomly; therefore, the degrees of freedom ($N-p$) for the model are $N-2$.'

'And you divide the sum of squares by these degrees of freedom?'

'Indeed. To get the average error we divide the residual sum of squares by the sample size (in this case 10) minus the number of parameters in the model (in this case 2). We calculated the residual sum of squares in our earlier table **(TABLE 14.2)** and it was 146.91, and the degrees of freedom will be 8, which means that the average error in the model is 146.91/8 = 18.36.'

$$\text{mean squared error in model} = \frac{SS_R}{df} = \frac{\sum_{i=1}^{n}\left(Y_i - \hat{Y}_i\right)^2}{N - p} \tag{14.15}$$

Milton was on an unstoppable roll. 'This gives us the average error in the model, but if we want to express this in standard units, we need to square root it, which reverses the fact that we originally squared the errors.'

'Like when we convert the variance to the standard deviation?'

'Ex*scratch*ly. The standard error for the model will be the square root of the average error **(EQUATION 14.16)**, which in this case is $\sqrt{18.36} = 4.29$.'

$$\text{standard error in model} = \sqrt{\text{mean squared error}} = \sqrt{\frac{\sum_{i=1}^{n}\left(Y_i - \hat{Y}_i\right)^2}{N - 2}} \tag{14.16}$$

'Got it; the standard error in the model is 4.29.'

Milton became animated, waving his paws about as though chasing a laser. 'We can use this value to calculate the standard error of b for the predictor. To get the standard error of b for the predictor we scale the standard error for the whole model to that predictor by using the spread of its scores. This is done by dividing the model standard error by the sum of squares for the predictor. However, we first square root the sum of squares so that it has comparable units of measurement to the standard error for the model.' Milton drew another equation **(14.17)**.

$$SE_b = \frac{SE_{\text{model}}}{\sqrt{SS_x}} \tag{14.17}$$

'You see,' Milton concluded, 'if you divide the standard error for the model, which we just calculated as 4.29, by the square root of the sum of squared errors for the predictor, which we calculated as 244.10 in the last table **(TABLE 14.3)**, we get a value of 0.274. This is the standard error for the b attached to the predictor.' **(EQUATION 14.18)**

$$SE_b = \frac{SE_{\text{model}}}{\sqrt{SS_x}} = \frac{4.29}{\sqrt{244.10}} = 0.274 \tag{14.18}$$

14.1.5 Confidence Intervals For *b*

Milton braced himself to continue by taking a long breath in that turned into an even longer sigh. I was grateful for the break to try to absorb what he was saying.

'Of course, if we know the standard error of the parameter, then we can calculate a confidence interval for it too,' he said.

I thought back to that unpleasant day when confidence intervals entered my life. **(SECTION 8.3.3)** 'Would you do that by taking the parameter and adding or subtracting from it 1.96 times the standard error?'

Milton bounced in a circle as though the floor was hot. 'Yes! Yes! *Purr*fect! For a 95% confidence interval, assuming a normal sampling distribution, that is what you would do. For small samples we use the *t*-distribution, so the value is not 1.96, but the critical value of *t* for the degrees of freedom that you have.' Milton wrote out an equation *(14.19)*, which seemed very familiar. *(EQUATION 8.8)* 'In fact, as the sample size gets bigger the *t*-distribution approximates a normal distribution anyway, so we can use *t* regardless of the sample size: for small samples it will give us better estimates than assuming a normal sampling distribution, and for large samples you will get the same solution anyway. The question is what degrees of freedom do we use?'

$$\text{lower boundary of confidence interval} = \text{estimate} - \left(t_{n-p} \times SE \right)$$
$$\text{upper boundary of confidence interval} = \text{estimate} + \left(t_{n-p} \times SE \right)$$

$$(14.19)$$

'You said earlier that the model has degrees of freedom equal to the sample size (N) minus the number of parameters (p). We have 10 observations, and 2 parameters (b_0 and b_1), so the degrees of freedom would be $10 - 2$, which is 8.'

'You were paying attention, well done! For a 95% confidence interval we would look up the value of *t* that has 8 degrees of freedom and yields a two-tailed *p*-value of 0.05 in the table of critical values.' Milton showed me the table of values.

Celia had shown me how to use this table *(FIGURE 13.6)*, so I quickly found that the value with 8 *df* was 2.306. Milton plugged this value into the equations and solved them. *(EQUATION 14.20)*

$$95\% \text{ CI lower boundary} = b - \left(t_{n-p} \times SE \right) = 0.75 - \left(2.306 \times 0.274 \right) = 0.118$$
$$95\% \text{ CI upper boundary} = b + \left(t_{n-p} \times SE \right) = 0.75 + \left(2.306 \times 0.274 \right) = 1.382$$

$$(14.20)$$

14.1.6 Test statistic for b

'We can also use the *b* to test whether the relationship between a predictor and an outcome is significantly different from zero,' Milton said. 'Remember that the value of *b* represents the change in the outcome resulting from a unit change in the predictor; if it is zero it means that as the predictor changes, the outcome does not change at all. In other words, there is no relationship. In keeping with the logic of NHST, which the Secret Philanthropic Society told you about *(CHAPTER 10)*, we have a null hypothesis that there is no relationship, and an alternative hypothesis that there is. A value of *b* equal to 0 is our null hypothesis, and a value different from 0 is our alternative hypothesis. We can construct a test statistic that compares our alternative hypothesis to the null and then expresses this difference relative to the error in our estimate.' Milton produced yet another equation *(14.21)*. 'The top half of the expression on the right-hand side is the hypothesis: it asks what the difference is between the estimate of *b* that we observed, and the value we would expect under the null hypothesis. Of course the value we expect under the null hypothesis is 0, so this top half ends up being the estimate of *b* itself. The bottom half is the error or noise in that estimate, which is represented by the standard error because this is a gauge of how much estimates vary across different samples. Notice that the resulting equation follows the general format explained to you by the Society.' *(EQUATION 10.2)*

$$t_{N-p} = \frac{b_{\text{observed}} - b_{\text{expected}}}{SE_b}$$
$$= \frac{b_{\text{observed}} - 0}{SE_b} = \frac{b_i}{SE_{b_i}}$$

$$(14.21)$$

I nodded and Milton continued. 'For our data, b is 0.75 and the standard error for b is 0.274, so what would the value of t be?' With the aid of the calculator on my diePad I concluded it would be 2.74. **(EQUATION 14.22)**

$$t_{N-p} = \frac{0.75}{0.274} = 2.74 \qquad\qquad (14.22)$$

'*Purr*fect,' replied Milton. 'This value of t again has $N–p$ degrees of freedom.'

'The same as when we calculated the confidence interval? Eight degrees of freedom?'

'Yes. Now you can either get a computer to work out the exact probability value for a t of 2.74 with 8 *df*, or you can look up the critical value of t for a two-tailed significance level of 0.05.'

'Like we did for the confidence interval? The value was 2.306.'

'*Claw*rect. Now because the observed value of 2.74 is greater than the critical value of 2.306, we know that a t at least as big as the one we have would have a probability less than 0.05 if the null hypothesis were true. Put another way, if the null hypothesis is true this value of t is very unlikely, which might make us believe that the relationship between the predictor and outcome is significantly different from 0.'

'So, the amount of garlic you wear significantly predicts how long it takes a zombie to approach.'

'That would be a reasonable summary of the situation.'

14.1.7 Assessing the goodness of fit

Milton paused again as though considering whether I might have had enough. 'Of course,' he began tentatively, 'having estimated the parameters, we need to know whether the model is a reasonable fit to the data. Just because the method of least squares gives us estimates that are the best available using that method, it does not guarantee that the model fits the data well. The model might actually be lousy despite having the best estimates that the method can find.'

Milton showed me a diagram. **(FIGURE 14.3)** 'I explained before that the residual sum of squares is a measure of how much error there is in the model. Although it tells us how much error there is in prediction, it does not tell us whether the model is better than nothing. If we did not fit a model representing the relationship between the predictor and outcome to the data, all we would have to predict the outcome would be its mean. If you use the mean to predict the outcome then no matter what the value of the predictor variable, you are always predicting the same value of the outcome. This is shown in the top left of my diagram. The blue line is the mean of the outcome. Notice it is flat and horizontal because the mean is a single value, so for every value of the predictor variable we predict the same value of the outcome. As such, the mean of the outcome is a good baseline: it represents no relationship and a completely flat line. If our model of the relationship between the predictor and outcome variable is good then we would hope that it improves upon this baseline: we should be able to better predict the outcome from our model than from simply using the mean of the outcome.'

'How do we know whether our model has improved the prediction of the outcome variable?'

'Look at the diagram. First, using the mean as a model, we can calculate the difference between the observed values, and the values predicted by the mean using one of our earlier equations **(14.6)**. This is the difference between the observed value of the outcome (the red dots), and what the model predicts for each of those values (the blue line). These differences are the dotted lines, and you should be familiar with the idea that we square these deviations and add them to get a measure of the total squared error. When we use the mean as our model, this sum of squared differences is known as the **total sum of squares**, SS_T. It is the total amount of error present when we predict the outcome from its typical value – the mean – rather than from a predictor variable.

'The next step is to estimate the model of best fit, and we have already discussed how we do that. Once we have fitted this more sophisticated model to the data, we use the same equation *(14.6)* to work out the differences between what this new model predicts and the observed data. This is shown in the top right of the diagram, which shows the same thing as one of my earlier diagrams. *(FIGURE 14.2)* As we have seen, the value we get when we add these squared errors is the residual sum of squares (SS_R), which we have discussed. This value represents the error in prediction when the best linear model is fitted to the data.

'Finally, we can use these two values to calculate how much better the best linear model is than using the mean (i.e., how much better at predicting the outcome our model is compared to a model representing no relationship). The improvement in prediction resulting from using the best model instead of the mean is the difference between SS_T and SS_R. This difference is the reduction in the error of prediction that results from fitting the linear model to the data. This improvement is the **model sum of squares**, SS_M, and it is shown in the bottom of the diagram *(FIGURE 14.3)* as the difference, for each observed data point, between what the model predicts and what a flat line (the mean) predicts. If the value of SS_M is large then the linear model has made a big improvement to how well the outcome variable can be predicted. However, if SS_M is small then using the linear model is little better than using the mean.'

'How large is large?'

'One way to answer that question is to use an *F*-test. You have seen that test statistics are typically the effect compared to the error *(SECTION 10.1.4)*, and *F* is no exception: it is based upon the ratio of the improvement due to the model (SS_M) relative to the error that still remains in the model (SS_R). I say *based upon*, because the sums of squares depend on the number of values that we have added up, and so *F* is calculated using the average sums of squares (referred to as the **mean squares** or MS). To work out the mean sums of squares we divide the sum of squares by the degrees of freedom.' *(EQUATION 14.23)*

$$MS = \frac{SS}{df} \tag{14.23}$$

Milton looked at me, seeking an unspoken indication that I was following what he was saying. I nodded and he continued. 'We convert the model and residual sums of squares to the mean squares for the model (MS_M) and the residual mean squares (MS_R) by diving by their respective degrees of freedom. The details of calculating the mean squares are not important for now, provided you understand that the **F-ratio** *(EQUATION 14.24)* is a measure of how much the model has improved the prediction of the outcome compared to the level of inaccuracy of the model. If a model is good, then we expect the improvement in prediction due to the model to be large (so MS_M will be large) and the error within the model to be small (so MS_R will be small); this will yield a large *F*-ratio (greater than 1 at least) because the top of the equation *(14.24)* will be bigger than the bottom. The probability of finding an *F*-ratio at least as large as the one we have can be calculated, and if this *p*-value is less than 0.05 we tend to conclude that the model has significantly improved our ability to predict the outcome.'

$$F = \frac{MS_M}{MS_R} \tag{14.24}$$

Milton wrote out another equation *(14.25)*. 'There is another way we can use the sums of squares,' he said. 'If we divide the sum of squares for the model by the total sum of squares then it gives us the improvement due to the model expressed as a proportion of how much error in prediction there was to begin with. The value is called R^2 and it can be expressed as a percentage by multiplying it by 100. R^2 represents the amount of variance in the outcome accounted for by the model (SS_M) relative to how much variation there was to explain in the first place (SS_T).'

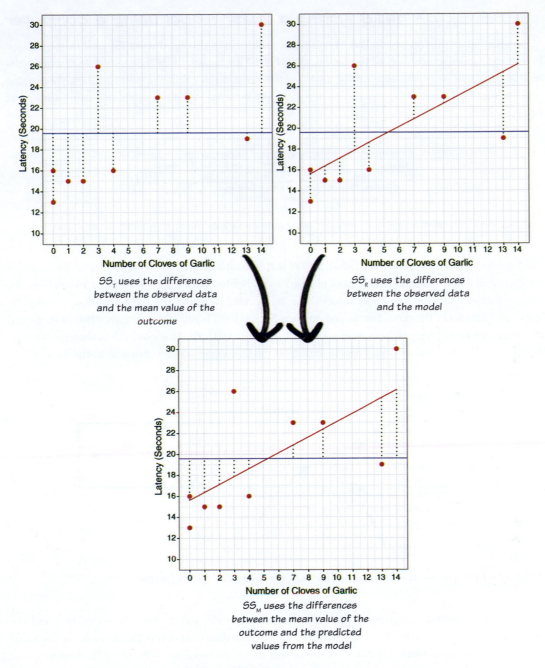

Figure 14.3   Diagram showing from where different sums of squares derive

'Celia told me about an R^2 **(SECTION 13.3.9)**, the correlation coefficient squared.'

'It is the same thing. We can take the square root of this value to obtain Pearson's correlation coefficient for the relationship between the values of the outcome predicted by the model and the values of the outcome we actually observed. Put another way, it is the correlation between the red and blue dots in a previous figure. **(FIGURE 14.2)** With only one predictor in the model this value will also be the same as the Pearson correlation coefficient between the predictor and outcome variable.'

$$R^2 = \frac{SS_M}{SS_T}$$

$$(14.25)$$

14.1.8 Fitting a linear model using a computer

Milton loaded an app on my diePad. 'A computer can do all of this hard work for you,' he said. 'Look here. First we see a summary of the model. **(OUTPUT 14.1)** This table tells us that R^2 is 0.483, which tells us that the garlic worn can account for 48.3% of the variation in zombie approach times. We are also told the standard error of the model, which is 4.29, the same value that we calculated using a previous equation **(14.16)**.'

Model Summary[b]

Model	R	R Square	Adjusted R Square	Std. Error of the Estimate	Durbin–Watson
1	.695[a]	.483	.419	4.285	2.044

a. Predictors: (Constant), Number of Bulbs of Garlic Worn
b. Dependent Variable: Latency to Approach Victim

Output 14.1   *Output model summary for regression analysis using IBM SPSS Statistics*

'Next we see a table that shows the F-test. **(OUTPUT 14.2)** The table shows the various sums of squares that we discussed **(FIGURE 14.3)** and the degrees of freedom associated with each. From these two values, the average sums of squares (the mean squares) can be calculated by dividing the sums of squares by the associated degrees of freedom. I explained how the F-ratio itself is calculated already **(EQUATION 14.24)**, and the computer provides us with an exact p-value for F, which is 0.026. This value is less than the conventional cut-off of 0.05, so we would conclude that overall the model is a significant fit to the data.'

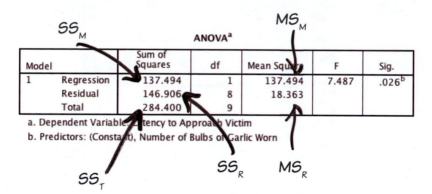

ANOVA[a]

Model		Sum of Squares	df	Mean Square	F	Sig.
1	Regression	137.494	1	137.494	7.487	.026[b]
	Residual	146.906	8	18.363		
	Total	284.400	9			

a. Dependent Variable: Latency to Approach Victim
b. Predictors: (Constant), Number of Bulbs of Garlic Worn

Output 14.2   *The F-ratio for regression analysis using IBM SPSS Statistics*

'The next table **(OUTPUT 14.3)** gives us the estimates of the model parameters (the b-values) and the significance of these values. From the table, b_0 (labelled as the constant) is 15.62, which is the value we calculated earlier. **(EQUATION 14.11)** This value means that if we wore no bulbs of garlic then we could expect a zombie to take 15.62 seconds to approach us. The table tells us that b_1 is 0.751, which also matches the value we calculated earlier. **(EQUATION 14.7)** As we know, this value means that as our predictor variable is increased by one unit (we wear one more bulb of garlic), then our model predicts that a zombie will take an extra 0.751 seconds to approach us. The confidence interval for this value ranges from 0.118 to 1.383, which matches our calculation too. **(EQUATION 14.20)** This means that if our sample is one of the 95 out of 100 for which the confidence interval contains the population value, then we can assume that the population value of b lies between 0.118 and 1.383. The table also gives us the standardized beta value of 0.695, which again matches our own calculation. **(EQUATION 14.13)**

'The t-test tells us whether the b-value is different from 0, and the computer computes the exact probability that the observed value of t would occur if the value of b in the population were zero. For both ts, the probabilities are less than 0.05, meaning that the probability of obtaining t-values at least

Coefficients[a]

Model		Unstandardized Coefficients		Standardized Coefficients	t	Sig.	95.0% Confidence Interval for B	
		B	Std. Error	Beta			Lower Bound	Upper Bound
1	(Constant)	15.622	1.987		7.861	.000	11.039	20.205
	Number of Bulbs of Garlic Worn	.751	.274	.695	2.736	.026	.118	1.383

a. Dependent Variable: Latency to Approach Victim

Bootstrap for Coefficients

Model		B	Bootstrap[a]				
			Bias	Std. Error	Sig. (2-tailed)	95% Confidence Interval	
						Lower	Upper
1	(Constant)	15.622	.042	1.735	.004	12.965	19.461
	Number of Bulbs of Garlic Worn	.751	.022	.308	.099	.199	1.248

a. Unless otherwise noted, bootstrap results are based on 1000 bootstrap samples

Output 14.3   Main output for regression analysis using IBM SPSS Statistics

as extreme as these (if the values of b in the population were zero) is low enough for us to assume that these bs are significantly different from 0. In the case of the b for garlic, this result means that the garlic makes a significant contribution ($p = 0.026$) to predicting zombie approach times.'

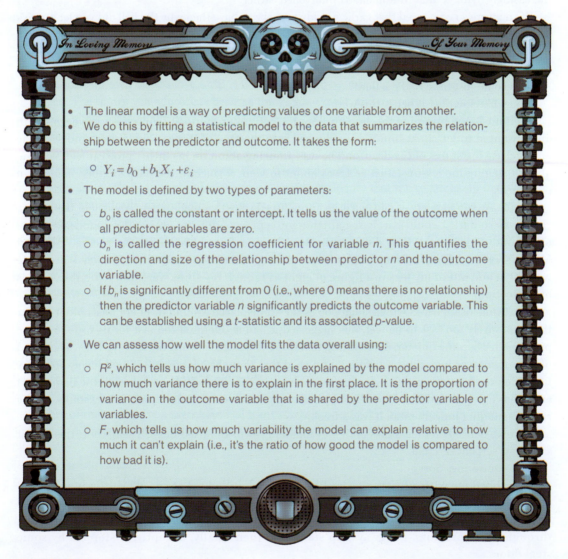

- The linear model is a way of predicting values of one variable from another.
- We do this by fitting a statistical model to the data that summarizes the relationship between the predictor and outcome. It takes the form:

  ○ $Y_i = b_0 + b_1 X_i + \varepsilon_i$

- The model is defined by two types of parameters:

  ○ b_0 is called the constant or intercept. It tells us the value of the outcome when all predictor variables are zero.
  ○ b_n is called the regression coefficient for variable n. This quantifies the direction and size of the relationship between predictor n and the outcome variable.
  ○ If b_n is significantly different from 0 (i.e., where 0 means there is no relationship) then the predictor variable n significantly predicts the outcome variable. This can be established using a t-statistic and its associated p-value.

- We can assess how well the model fits the data overall using:

  ○ R^2, which tells us how much variance is explained by the model compared to how much variance there is to explain in the first place. It is the proportion of variance in the outcome variable that is shared by the predictor variable or variables.
  ○ F, which tells us how much variability the model can explain relative to how much it can't explain (i.e., it's the ratio of how good the model is compared to how bad it is).

Zach's Facts 14.1   The linear model

I stood like a rabbit in headlights and Milton steamrollered on through his explanation. 'The bootstrap confidence interval tells us that, assuming this is one of the 95% of intervals that contain the true value, the population value of b for garlic falls between 0.199 and 1.248 and because this interval does not include zero we might conclude that there is a genuine positive relationship between garlic and zombie approach times in the population. However, the significance associated with this confidence interval is $p = 0.099$, which is greater than the 0.05 threshold. The bootstrap confidence intervals and significance values are useful to report and interpret because they do not rely on assumptions of normality or homoscedasticity.'

That is how, armed with the knowledge from our linear model, we ended up in the JIG:SAW complex two days later wearing quite a bit of garlic.

14.1.9 When this Fails

As we cowered behind the mesh that separated our brains from those wishing to devour them, I felt increasingly irritated that Milton hadn't intervened earlier.

'If you were so convinced that garlic wouldn't repel zombies, then why the hell did you let me risk death by coming here with loads of bulbs draped around my neck?'

'Because it teaches you a valuable lesson: no matter how well your model fits your data, it does not mean that reality will turn out as your model predicts.'

'You could just have told me that!'

'You will remember it better this way.'

I felt my blood pumping through my temples. Milton's superiority complex was wearing thin and I wanted to let rip at him. I'd just looked into the face of three of my mates, and seen the empty decaying stares of the dead, and he was prancing about on his little tiptoe cat feet bleating about teaching me lessons. Just as I was about to vent, a voice in the dark stopped us both in our tracks.

'I will take you to safety,' it said in a deep, raspy, lisped voice that made 'safety' sound like 'thafety'.

It was so dark I could barely see anything except two glowing eyes and a vague silhouette of an undulating mass that didn't indicate a human form. My heart was racing. I caught Milton's eye and for the first time I saw something other than arrogance. He was scared. He weaved in and out of my legs in a figure of eight as though my shins were indestructible shields of protection.

The thing disappeared with a small pop as the air displaced around it. There was a pitter-patter that was surely too fast to be feet, but suggested it had accelerated too fast for us to follow. The pitter-patter became quieter, decelerating to a stop before accelerating back towards us. The speed of movement was incredible – before I'd finished that thought a large mass stood inches from my face. I felt the heat of a red fire glowing through gills on its neck. With each breath the flames cast an amber light around its bulbous head, revealing pointed ears, and eyes on sinewy stalks. At the risk of sounding judgemental, it was a freak.

Its eyes danced on their stalks until they found my own, and fixed them, 'I said, come this way,' it said in its serpentine croak.

I was quivering. 'Sorry ...'

It grabbed me with a bristly, gecko-like hand and pulled me at speed. Milton jumped and attached himself to my jacket with his claws. The thing pulled me faster than I could run, and I used every physical resource I had not to fall. It dragged us deeper into the building, through dark corridors, gangways, up stairs and then finally, abruptly, it stopped by some steel doors.

'I am Clint Vue: one of the code 1318s. Don't let my appearance deceive you; trust me. We are in the waste disposal centre, the zombies won't come here, the stench of waste repels them.' His forked-tongue lisp made his attempt to say 'waste disposal centre' entertaining, but having seen him bend a steel door with his bare hands, I swallowed the urge to snigger. Composing myself, I asked him why the code 1318 workers were zombies.

'The code 1318s are those entered into JIG:SAW's genetic enhancement programme. Mostly the enhancements work, for a few weeks, but then their bodies reject the gene manipulation and enter a state of living death.'

'That happens to me when people try to teach me statistics,' I said, trying to comfort myself with humour.

Milton was staring intently at Clint. 'You seem to be very much alive,' he said.

'I underwent a different type of genetic enhancement. In general, they try to enhance the minds and destroy them in the process, but with me they targeted the physical. I am the best of the animal kingdom. I can hear like a bat, I have a wild cat's agility, a dog's sense of smell, the footspeed of a cheetah, the eyesight of a mantis shrimp, gecko-enhanced hands and feet, I can expel toxins like a bombardier beetle, and I am as flexible as an octopus.'

'Impressive, but can you bootstrap a model parameter?' said Milton defiantly.

The thing ... Clint ... looked confused, and turned to look out of the window as though keeping watch for us. Milton looked pleased by Clint's confusion and did a celebratory cat parade. I was confused too, confused by why my garlic idea had failed to repel the zombies. Thinking about that was more comforting than thinking about being trapped with a massive chimera of the animal world.

I turned to Milton. 'Why would you have a model that fits well but doesn't turn out to be much use in the real world?' I asked.

Milton's face contorted into a strange mix of admiration and dejection. 'I spent a great deal of time telling you about sources of bias that can influence the linear model. Must you subject me to the utter tedium of explaining all of that again?' *(CHAPTERS 9 & 12)*

'I wasn't asking you to explain it all again,' I replied indignantly.

14.2 BIAS IN THE LINEAR MODEL

Milton made no apology. 'Having produced a model based on a sample of data, and assessed the fit,' he continued, 'there are two questions to ask. First, is the model influenced by a small number of cases? Second, can the model generalize to other samples? These questions are sequential because only a fool would want to generalize a bad model. You are *claw*rect, though, that just because a model fits the observed data well, that does not mean we can apply it beyond our sample, or that it is unbiased. **Generalization** is a critical additional step: if our model is not generalizable, then any conclusions based on the model must be restricted to the sample used. Generalization is established by making sure that the assumptions of the model are true. Can you remember what those assumptions are?'

 CHECK YOUR BRAIN: What are the main assumptions and sources of bias in the linear model and what effect do they have?

I noticed Clint pacing about by the window. It troubled me. I thought back to Milton's explanation of assumptions. **(SECTION 12.2)** That troubled me in a different way. 'They are additivity and linearity; independent errors; homoscedas ...'

'Homoscedasticity,' Milton added.

'Normally distributed something or other; predictors are not correlated with external variables; you can only include certain types of variables; predictors shouldn't be too highly related to each other ...'

'In other words, no multicollinearity,' interjected the cat.

'And the variables need to have some variance. Oh, and of course we'd need to look for cases that bias the model like outliers.' As I concluded my list I looked at Milton with eyes that dared him to be unimpressed.

'An adequate summary,' replied the eisel. 'But what are the implications of violating those assumptions?' Milton raised his nose rather snootily, which made me want to kick him.

'I guess the general message was that violating these assumptions biases significance tests and confidence intervals around b; the estimates of bs themselves are not dependent on the assumptions.'

'True, but remember that least squares estimates will be optimal when the assumptions are met.'

'Err, thanks. Anyway, the confidence interval for a b is the boundaries within which the population value of that b is likely to fall. So if the confidence interval is biased we cannot accurately estimate the likely population value.'

'Good. This brings us back to generalization. When the assumptions are met then *on average* the regression model from the sample is the same as the population model, which means that it is reasonable to generalize your model beyond the sample. To be clear, though, even when the assumptions are met, a single model obtained from a sample will be different than the population model – but when the assumptions are met we can trust our sample to be close most of the time and, on average, if we looked at many models we would be accurate.'

'Safe, and presumably outliers affect the linear model just like they affected the mean?'

Clint was still pacing by the window seemingly oblivious to our conversation, but I remembered what he had said about hearing like a bat and wondered if he was paying more attention than he let on. Milton drew out two models on my diePad based on the JIG:SAW data that we had examined when we first discussed outliers. **(FIGURE 14.4)** 'This scatterplot shows the relationship between employee strength and vision for the code 1318 workers. You remember how we speculated that perhaps the workers who were really strong might also be the ones with good vision? Well, the diagram partly answers this question.'

'And so did the correlations that Celia and I worked out. It seemed to suggest a relationship between strength and speed and strength and vision.'

'Well, for strength and vision we certainly have one worker who excels on both. Look at this outlier; this is a person with almost inhuman strength and perfect vision.' I could almost sense Clint's ears twitch as Milton spoke. His eyes, protruding on their sinewy stalks, peered around the side of his head to look at us before his head turned.

'I am that outlier,' he said enigmatically and turned back to face the window. Proof, although I scarcely needed it, that he was listening to everything.

Milton carried on, apparently less perturbed than me by the large genetic deformation in the room. 'Look how this outlier affects the model. I have plotted the model including this outlier (the red line) and excluding it (the blue line). These lines show how cases can affect the estimates of the regression coefficients. With the outlier included, the line becomes more positive and steeper (i.e., b_1 gets larger and more positive) and the intercept decreases (i.e., b_0 is smaller). If outliers affect the estimates of the bs that define the model, then it is important to detect these cases.'

'How?'

'The first way is to use residuals, which we have seen reflect the difference between what the model predicts for a case, and the actual value of the outcome. **(MEOWSINGS 12.1)** We can use residuals to look generally at the fit of the model. If a model fits the sample data well then all of the residuals will be small because it should predict all cases fairly accurately. If a model is a poor fit of the sample data then the residuals will be large.'

'How do you tell if the residuals overall are large or small?'

'The *normal* or **unstandardized residuals**, which are the values I have referred to up until now, are measured in the same units as the outcome variable, so all you can do is look for residuals that stand out as being particularly large; I cannot give you a universal value that constitutes a large residual. However, we can convert residuals to z-scores **(CHAPTER 6)**, and these are known as **standardized residuals**. Standardized residuals are the residuals expressed in standard deviations, and have a mean of 0 and a standard deviation of 1. By converting to z-scores we can apply the rules of a standard normal distribution to them. For example, I have explained to you that, in a normally distributed sample, 95% of z-scores should lie between −1.96 and +1.96, 99% should lie between −2.58 and +2.58, and 99.9% (i.e., nearly all of them) should lie between −3.29 and +3.29. This yields some general rules: (1) a case with a standardized residual with an absolute value greater than 3.29 should be looked at because a value this high occurs rarely (signalling to us that this value may not be a part of the population we want to measure); (2) if more than 1% of the sample cases have standardized residuals with an absolute value greater than 2.58, or more than 5% of cases have standardized residuals with an absolute value greater than 1.96, then the level of error within our model is getting larger than we would expect.'

'So if a case has a standardized residual greater than 3.29, then it's an outlier?'

'Perhaps. It certainly follows that if a case is an outlier, then we might expect it to have a large residual (that is, the model will predict the outcome for that case badly). However, it is not as simple as that because if an outlier has had a large influence on the model, then it might not have a large residual. You can see, for example, in my diagram **(FIGURE 14.4)** that if we were to fit the blue line model the residual for the outlier would be almost twice as large as when we use the red line model. This is because the outlier is influencing the model and dragging the line towards it. In this case, even with the red line model the outlier has a fairly large residual, but it is possible to have a model where a case has had so much influence that the model predicts that case quite well and the residual is small. Therefore, as well as looking for outliers we need to try to ascertain whether certain cases exert undue influence over the parameters of the model. So, if we were to delete a certain case, would we obtain different values for the bs?'

'Like in the diagram **(FIGURE 14.4)** in which including the outlier changes both b_0 and b_1?'

'Yes, there are numerous ways to look at influence,[11] and if I explain them all I think we will find our brains being devoured by zombies before I can finish, so I will explain only one: **Cook's distance**. We just discussed how if you delete a case and calculate the model then if that case has had an influence then the estimates of the bs will change. That also means that the

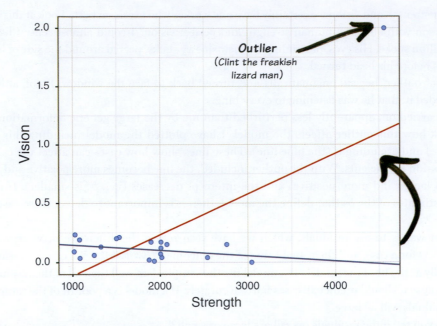

Figure 14.4 *Graph demonstrating the effect of an outlier or influential case. The blue line represents the model excluding the outlier, whereas the red line represents the model when the outlier is included*

predicted values from the model will change. For a given case we can compute a Cook's distance, which is the sum of the differences between the predicted values for the model with that case included and excluded. Therefore, it is the total difference in predicted values that results from including or excluding that case. This total is then standardized by dividing it by a function of the mean squared error of the model. *(EQUATION 14.15)* If a case has a Cook's distance greater than 1 then it is worth inspecting further,[99] because a value of 1 means that the total difference in predicted values when the case is included or excluded is greater than the error in prediction.'

14.3 A GENERAL PROCEDURE FOR FITTING LINEAR MODELS

'Let me get this straight,' I said, as I sketched out a flow diagram. *(FIGURE 14.5)* 'If we want to fit one of these linear model things we first draw scatterplots to get some idea of whether the assumption of linearity is met, and also to look for obvious unusual cases. Thinking back a few days to when we talked about correcting bias, we might transform the data to make the relationship linear. *(CHAPTER 9)* Having screened for problems, we fit the model, and if we want to generalize our model, or we are interested in interpreting significance tests and confidence intervals, then we examine the residuals of this model to check for homoscedasticity, normality, independence and linearity (again). If there's a problem, we take corrective action like running a robust test or using bootstrapping to estimate the confidence intervals and *p*-values.'

'I could not have put it better myself ... well, I could, but your version will suffice.'

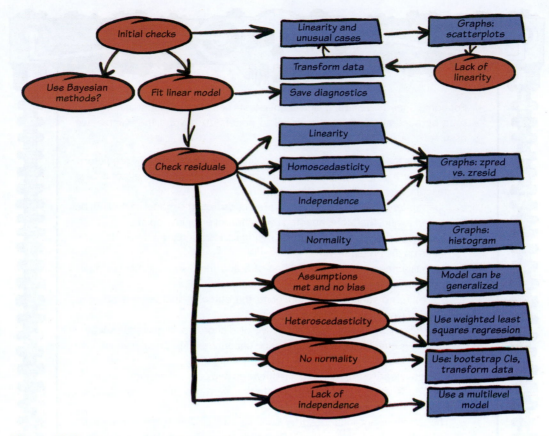

Figure 14.5   *The process of fitting a linear model*

14.4   MODELS WITH SEVERAL PREDICTORS

Clint was still pacing impatiently by the window.

'You are wasting time!' he said.

He moved his body away from the window revealing a small party of zombies with their faces pressed up to the green glass. It was only a matter of time before a critical mass was reached. He was right: our garlic hadn't deterred the zombies, but the real issue now was not whether our garlic model had been biased, but how we were going to get out without resorting to killing them. We needed a plan and none of us had one.

The Head would know what to do. I opened my reality checker and explained our predicament to him. As I told him how I'd planned to repel the zombies with garlic he laughed uncontrollably.

'Are you out of you tiny mind? I bet you didn't even check the science!'

'I checked the internet.'

'The internet!' The Head exclaimed. 'Even a goldfish knows that the internet is as reliable as a politician. My goldfish knows that, and he's got a one-second memory!'

'Don't you get *your* information from the internet?' I asked.

The Head looked indignant. 'It ain't the same: I *own* the internet.'

I mock-apologized for questioning his knowledge, and moved us onto how to incapacitate a zombie.

'Trouble is, Z, a lot of the information about zombies is speculation – like what happens in the movies. I'm struggling to find proper research on how to kill dead people. It's as though scientists don't perceive a need for that valuable work. You could give rTMS and Tasers a whirl though.' **(REALITY CHECK 14.1)**

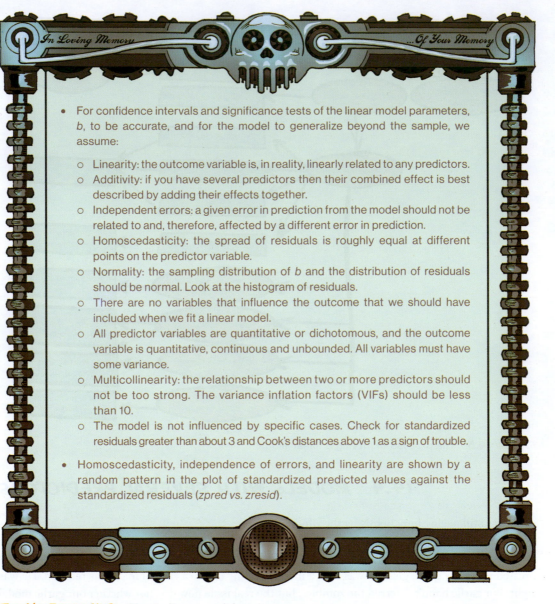

In Loving Memory ... *Of Your Memory*

- For confidence intervals and significance tests of the linear model parameters, b, to be accurate, and for the model to generalize beyond the sample, we assume:

  o Linearity: the outcome variable is, in reality, linearly related to any predictors.

  o Additivity: if you have several predictors then their combined effect is best described by adding their effects together.

  o Independent errors: a given error in prediction from the model should not be related to and, therefore, affected by a different error in prediction.

  o Homoscedasticity: the spread of residuals is roughly equal at different points on the predictor variable.

  o Normality: the sampling distribution of b and the distribution of residuals should be normal. Look at the histogram of residuals.

  o There are no variables that influence the outcome that we should have included when we fit a linear model.

  o All predictor variables are quantitative or dichotomous, and the outcome variable is quantitative, continuous and unbounded. All variables must have some variance.

  o Multicollinearity: the relationship between two or more predictors should not be too strong. The variance inflation factors (VIFs) should be less than 10.

  o The model is not influenced by specific cases. Check for standardized residuals greater than about 3 and Cook's distances above 1 as a sign of trouble.

- Homoscedasticity, independence of errors, and linearity are shown by a random pattern in the plot of standardized predicted values against the standardized residuals (*zpred vs. zresid*).

Zach's Facts 14.2   *Bias in linear models*

'So, basically you're saying I should zap their brains or zap their hearts?'

'You should definitely zap something, or else they're gonna feast on your brain.'

'Slim pickings,' said Milton looking very serious indeed. 'Head, get some data and test these predictors, and for goodness' sake find some proper scientific data and not garbage from Zach's internet friends.'

Milton jumped up onto the desk, shot out a claw and started unscrewing just about everything electronic that he could find. The Head whizzed around searching for, well, whatever Milton had asked him to search for, and with frightening efficiency Milton dismantled just about everything in the room. He removed a side panel from a large computery-looking thing and quietly but purposefully started to drag wires and circuit boards into it. Once inside, he set to work ... on something. All the while Clint continued his vigil at the window, every so often extending his sausagey eye stalks around his head to peer at Milton's carnage.

The Head whizzed round and settled with a bemused look. 'Some scientists are wild,' he said. 'Check out this tongue-in-cheek study from 1994 that looked at whether garlic can repel vampires.[100] They didn't use actual vampires, because in 1994 they hadn't yet discovered the 2 billion vampires living in an underground colony below North America. They used leeches instead. They smeared their hands with either water or garlic and measured how quickly the leeches attached. Guess what? The leeches exposed to the garlic hand attached quicker. I ain't saying that zombies are the same as leeches, but to the extent that you can generalize from a leech to other organisms that want to eat your blood, this might explain why your garlic plan was doomed.

'Looking at other things that might incapacitate a zombie, you could try zappin' their brains. Repetitive transcranial magnetic stimulation (rTMS) is where you apply a train of pulses of current through a special magnetic coil that looks a bit like a massive key from a gigantic clockwork toy.[101] The pulses can vary in frequency from high (> 10 Hz) to low (< 1 Hz). These pulses disrupt movement, but more relevant to your situation is what happens after the rTMS is applied. One study on healthy humans blasted their motor cortex with either low (1 Hz) or high (10 Hz) frequency rTMS before a kinematic evaluation that consisted of them tracing their finger from one object to another on a TV screen. Those that had low-frequency rTMS were slower to do this than those who had high-frequency rTMS.[102] Maybe a low frequency blast of rTMS would slow down the zombies?

'You could also Taser them. Scientists have used case studies and mathematical simulations to argue that Tasers can cause heart attacks,[103, 104] but not everyone agrees. Other research studies have measured how the body reacts to being Tasered and showed no adverse effects.[105] But if you ramp up the voltage on a Taser maybe it'll knock out their cold, dead hearts.'

Reality Check 14.1   *How to incapacitate zombies and vampires*

14.4.1 The expanded linear model

The Head spun briefly and then stopped with a wide-eyed grin. 'I've got data,' he announced proudly. 'Let's model this funk! The furry one has already explained about the linear model. That model is versatile: it expands like a circle pit at a metal gig, consuming any predictors standing around trying to watch the band.'

'Oh, do get on with it – I have explained this at least twice before,' Milton spat from beneath a pile of wires and circuit boards. **(SECTION 4.1.4 & 12.1)**

The Head threw him an annoyed look. 'I'll do my job, you stick to yours!'

He turned back to me. 'I'll keep the recap brief. To add a predictor to the linear model, you place it into the model and give it a *b*, so that it don't get lonely. When you have more than one predictor, people sometimes call this model a **multiple regression**.'

'Safe, so the *b* is like when there is one predictor, it estimates the relationship between that predictor and the outcome?'

'You got it. So, if we build a model that predicts zombie immobility from rTMS frequency and Taser voltage, we expand the equation.' The Head projected an equation onto the desk. **(EQUATION 14.26)**

$$Y_i = \left(b_0 + b_1 X_{1i} + b_2 X_{2i}\right) + \varepsilon_i \tag{14.26}$$

It looked as though the linear model with one predictor **(EQUATION 14.2)** had changed to include a second predictor (X_2) that had an associated parameter (b_2).

'Let's make things more concrete and replace those Xs with the names of our predictors.' The Head's equation transformed before my eyes. **(EQUATION 14.27)**

$$\text{Immobility}_i = b_0 + b_1 \text{rTMS}_i + b_2 \text{Taser}_i + \varepsilon_i \tag{14.27}$$

The Head projected an image onto the desk. **(FIGURE 14.6)** 'Look. This diagram shows what the model looks like. The trapezium is the model, which some call the regression *plane*. Equation 14.27 describes the shape of this model. Notice that the constant, b_0, is where the model touches the *y*-axis; it is the value of immobility when both predictors are zero. The *b*-value for Taser voltage describes the slope of the left- and right-hand sides of the regression plane, and the *b*-value for rTMS frequency describes the slope of the top and bottom of the regression plane. Like with one predictor, where we had a straight line for a model, knowing the two slopes tells us the shape of the model and the constant locates the model in space.'

'So, the *b*-values for each predictor show the relationship to the outcome variable in terms of direction and strength. It looks like Taser voltage has a positive relationship because the model slopes up along that axis, but rTMS frequency has a negative relationship because the model slopes downwards along that axis.'

'*Zach*ly,' The Head smirked, pleased with his pun. 'The dots are the observed data. Like when we had one predictor, the model aims to best predict the observed data, but there will be errors. The vertical distances between the model and each data point are the errors in prediction or *residuals*.'

'That's the same as for one predictor: the residual is the distance between each data value and the model, it's just that the model is a plane rather than a line.'

'*Zach*ly.' I rolled my eyes at The Head.

'What about if we had another predictor? Let's say we wanted to include garlic to see its zombie immobilizing power.'

'You'd be a fool 'cos you've already seen that it don't immobilize a thing. If your foolish mind wanted to add it though, it's easy enough. Like I said, the model is versatile: it can rock a trilby or a

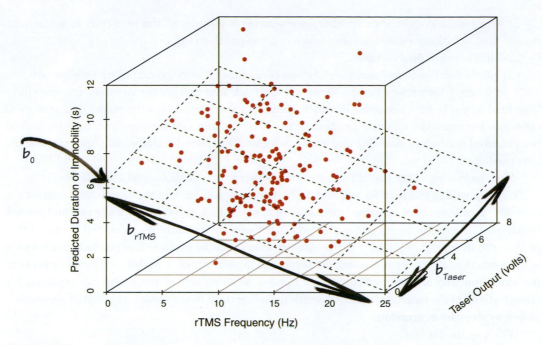

Figure 14.6 *Scatterplot of the relationship between zombie immobility, rTMS frequency and Taser voltage*

fedora. You want to add predictors, then you got it: the linear model will expand accordingly. You add each predictor as an X in the equation, and assign it a parameter, b.' The Head transformed the equation on the desk again. **(EQUATION 14.28)**

$$Y_i = b_0 + b_1 X_{1i} + b_2 X_{2i} + \cdots + b_n X_{ni} + \varepsilon_i \tag{14.28}$$

'I guess Y is the outcome variable, b_1 is the coefficient of the first predictor (X_1), b_2 is the coefficient of the second predictor (X_2), and ε_i is the error for the ith entity, but what are b_n and X_{ni} and why are there three dots?'

'The dots show that you can expand the model as much as you want by adding predictors and parameters, Xs and bs, until you get to the final one that you want to include, which is denoted as n. That final, nth, predictor is X_{ni} and it has a parameter of b_n.'

14.4.2 Methods for entering predictors

'When you model several predictors,' said The Head, 'you gotta think carefully about how you put them into the model. Let me explain. The best way to build your model is to select predictors based on past work, so the researcher decides in which order to enter the predictors into the model. Known predictors (from past research) are entered into the model first in the order of their importance in predicting the outcome. Once these predictors are entered, you can add new predictors to the model. This method is known as **hierarchical regression**, and it is good because an educated brain makes the decisions about when to enter predictors.'

'Unless Zach is building the model,' came a familiar cat-like voice from inside a large machine that had wires spewing from its insides like it had been disembowelled.

We ignored the cat. 'Another way to enter predictors is to force them in simultaneously,' continued The Head. 'You shouldn't do this willy-nilly; you need good theoretical reasons for including predictors. This method is called **forced entry regression** or **simultaneous entry regression**.'

'So, that's like hierarchical except that the researcher just bungs all the predictors in at the same time instead of making a decision about which order to put them in.'

'*Zach*ly. There is a final method ...'

'Oh, please don't go there!' said the disembowelled machine with the cat tail sticking out of it.

'I go where I like, when I like!' shouted The Head, irritated by the constant interruptions. 'The final way is to base the order in which predictors are entered into the model on a statistical criterion. For example, imagine we start off predicting using only the constant, then we look at the potential predictors available and we ask which of them would, statistically speaking, be the best predictor.'

'What, by looking at the size of the correlation between each predictor and the outcome?'

'Yeah, something like that. So, you find the best one, and you put it in the model. Now, some of the outcome variable has been explained but not all of it, so you look at your predictors again and you ask which one can explain the biggest part of what's left over by the current model. You then add that predictor to the model. A bit more of the outcome should now be explained, so you look at what's left and ask whether any of the remaining predictors can explain any of it, and if so, which one explains the most. You stop adding predictors when none of those outside of the model can explain a big enough chunk of the outcome to make it worth including them in the model. This sort of approach is known as **stepwise regression**.'

'Which method is best?'

'Not stepwise!' shouted an aggravated feline head as it emerged from the eviscerated machine. 'Stepwise methods take important methodological decisions out of the hands of the researcher. Stepwise methods use statistical criteria to make decisions, and bear in mind that the values of the statistics they use will vary from sample to sample, so the decisions about the model are based on values that will not be the same in a different sample. That means that the order of entering predictors in one sample will likely be different than if you replicated the study in a different sample. Also, slight differences in the statistic for a particular predictor make the difference between it being entered in favour of another or vice versa. In other words, slight statistical differences may contrast dramatically with the theoretical importance of a predictor to the model. As if these were not reason enough, there is also the danger of having too many variables in the model that make little contribution to predicting the outcome (over-fitting) or of leaving out important predictors (under-fitting).'

'I can't argue with that,' The Head conceded. 'They're all good points. Some scientists believe that forced entry and hierarchical entry are the only methods appropriate for theory testing.[106] Of the two, hierarchical is better because the decisions are based on past research and theory.'

14.4.3 Estimating parameters

'How are the parameters estimated when there are several predictors?'

The Head began to chuckle, and that chuckle turned into a bellowing laugh. 'Oh, Z, you crack The Head up.'

'No, seriously,' I asked. 'How is it done?'

The Head stopped laughing and gave me a quizzical look.

'For goodness' sake,' said Milton. 'It is perfectly simple, you take what we learned earlier about estimating parameters with one predictor but apply a quite simple matrix algebra generalization of that method.'

The Head tried to be helpful. 'What the hairball is trying to say is that it's the same principle that you already know, but let a computer do it for you.'

'I thought he was trying to say that he is a massive eisel,' I quipped.

14.4.3 Using a computer to build more complex models

Milton took hold of my diePad. 'We have several predictors, and The Head has got us some data from 156 zombies. A great deal of care should be taken in selecting predictors for a model because the parameter estimates depend upon the predictors in the model. *Do not select hundreds of predictors, put them all into a model and hope for the best.* Instead, select predictors based on a sound theoretical rationale or on well-conducted past research that has demonstrated their importance. We have done this: we asked The Head to scan the evidence and suggest some theoretically grounded predictors of immobilizing zombies. He came up with rTMS frequency and Taser voltage. Theoretically there is good reason to think that these methods will immobilize a zombie; therefore, we might include predictors in the model that represent these methods. Next we would collect some data, and in doing so we need to think about how much data to collect. *(MEOWSINGS 14.2)* Once the data are collected, we fit the model. Because there is no particular reason to prioritize one predictor over another, we might force them both into the model and evaluate them simultaneously. Then we get a computer to fit the model for us.'

Milton tapped the screen and presented me with some tables of output. 'The first table *(OUTPUT 14.4)* summarizes the overall model. It tells us the outcome variable (immobility) and what the predictors were (Taser output and rTMS frequency). The column labelled R shows the value of the correlation coefficient between the predicted values of immobility from the model and the observed values. The next column squares this value (R^2), which tells us the proportion of variance in immobility that is shared with the predictors (overall). If we multiply this value by 100, then we conclude that 18.7% of the variance in immobility times can be accounted for by Taser output and rTMS frequency. This is quite a lot, but it is worth considering that this still leaves 81.3% that is unexplained.'

Model Summary

Model	R	R Square	Adjusted R Square	Std. Error of the Estimate
1	.433[a]	.187	.177	2.194

a. Predictors: (Constant), Taser Output (KV), rTMS Frequency (Hz)

Output 14.4 *Output model summary for multiple regression analysis using IBM SPSS Statistics*

What's the adjusted R^2?' I asked.

'It is an estimate of what R^2 would be in the population. If it is similar to the unadjusted value then it means that the sample value is close to the population value; in other words, the sample value is likely to generalize across other samples. If the adjusted and unadjusted values are very different it implies that the value will be variable across samples; in other words, you should not generalize the model beyond your sample. For this model, the difference between the values is 0.187 − 0.177 = 0.01 (about 1%). This shrinkage means that if the model were derived from the population rather than a sample it would account for approximately 1% less variance in the outcome, which is a fairly modest reduction and suggests we can generalize the model.'

ANOVA[a]

Model		Sum of Squares	df	Mean Square	F	Sig.
1	Regression	169.576	2	84.788	17.615	.000[b]
	Residual	736.443	153	4.813		
	Total	906.019	155			

a. Dependent Variable: Immobility (Seconds)

b. Predictors: (Constant), Taser Output (KV), rTMS Frequency (Hz)

Output 14.5 *F-ratio for multiple regression analysis using IBM SPSS Statistics*

'What's the next table all about?' *(OUTPUT 14.5)*

'Remember we talked about the *F*-test?'

'Yeah, it tests the overall fit of the model.'

'*Fur*fect, yes, and this table contains that test. It tells us the value of the sum of squares for the model (SS_M), which we discussed earlier.'

'It represents the improvement in predicting the outcome that you get from using the model compared to if you used the mean of the outcome?'

'*Claw*rect, well done. The table also reports the residual sum of squares (SS_R).'

'The total difference between the values of the outcome predicted by the model and the observed values; the error in prediction?'

'*Fur*bulous! The table also has the degrees of freedom (*df*) for each of these sums of squares. For the model sum of squares, this value is equal to the number of predictors, and for the residual sum of squares it is, $N-p$, the number of observations (156) minus the number of parameters in the model, which is 3 (the constant plus one for each of the two predictors). That gives us 153 degrees of freedom. The average sum of squares (MS) is calculated by dividing each SS by its *df* *(EQUATION 14.23)*, and the

Dear Human,

It is important to collect enough data to obtain a reliable regression model. Also, because of the central limit theorem (Section 8.2.3), we know that larger samples enable us to assume that our *b*s are from a normally distributed sampling distribution. In general, bigger sample sizes mean more precise estimates of the model parameters and their confidence intervals. If you also want to conduct significance tests, then the sample size will affect the power that you have to detect effects. The minimum sample size required to detect effects in a linear model depends on the size of the effect (i.e., how big you expect the *b*s in the model to be), how much statistical power you want (Section 10.1.8), and whether you are testing the significance of the *b*-values or the model overall. Figure 14.7, taken from an ancient text,[11] shows the sample size required to achieve a high level of power (0.8) to test that the model is significant overall (i.e., R^2 is not equal to zero). The author varied the number of predictors and the size of expected effect: he used $R^2 = 0.02$ (small), 0.13 (medium) and 0.26 (large). Broadly speaking, when testing the overall fit of the model you'll need hundreds of cases of data if you expect a small effect; a sample size of 77 and 157 will always suffice (with up to 20 predictors) for a large and medium effect, respectively. Other books provide more detailed tables.[107]

Best fishes,
Milton

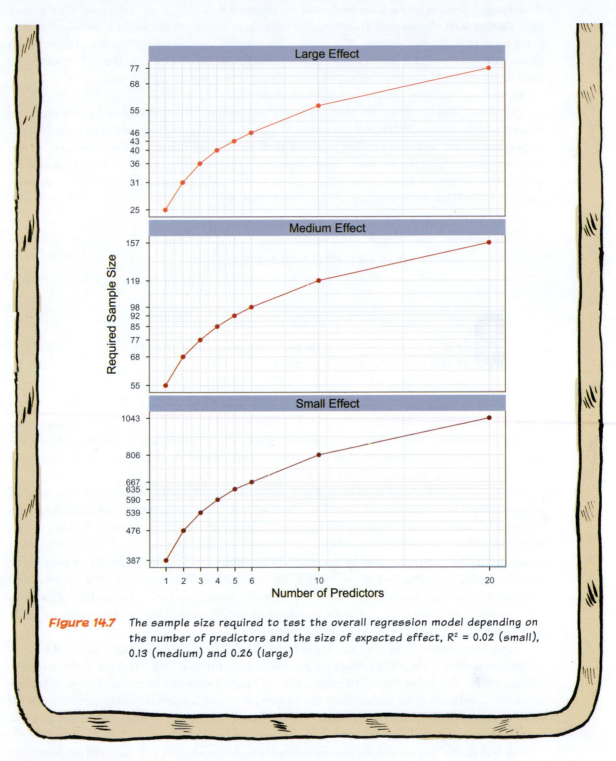

Figure 14.7 The sample size required to test the overall regression model depending on the number of predictors and the size of expected effect, $R^2 = 0.02$ (small), 0.13 (medium) and 0.26 (large)

Milton's Meowsings 14.2 *Sample size in regression*

F-ratio is the average improvement in prediction resulting from fitting the model (MS_M) divided by the average difference between the model and the observed data (MS_R) – you remember the equation for *F* **(EQUATION 14.24)**, do you not? Therefore, it is the ratio of how good the model is compared to how much error in prediction remains. The *F*-value has a specific probability of less than 0.001, which means that if the model made no improvement to prediction (in other words, the null hypothesis is true) then we would expect to find an *F* at least this big with a probability less than 0.001.'

'In other words, the model is a significant fit to the data.'

'*Purr*cisely!' said the ginger cat, slapping my leg and smiling. 'The next table shows the estimates of the model parameters. **(OUTPUT 14.6)** Remember that the model takes the form of this equation.' Milton swiped the screen back to an earlier equation **(14.27)** before continuing. 'The equation has several unknown parameters (the *b*-values). The computer estimates these values using the least squares method that we have discussed before. We can rewrite the model, replacing the *b*s with the estimates from the table. What do these *b* values tell us?' **(EQUATION 14.29)**

$$\text{Immobility}_i = b_0 + b_1\text{rTMS}_i + b_2\text{Taser}_i$$
$$= 6.380 + (-0.251\,\text{rTMS}_i) + (0.342\,\text{Taser}_i) \tag{14.29}$$

 CHECK YOUR BRAIN: Interpret the *b*-values for both of the predictors in the model.

'They tell us about the relationship between zombie immobility and each predictor, don't they?' I asked. Before Milton could answer, I tried to interpret the values. 'For these data Taser voltage has a positive *b*-value indicating a positive relationship, whereas for rTMS it is negative. So, as rTMS frequency increases, the amount of time a zombie is immobilized decreases; but as Taser voltage increases, so does the amount of time for which a zombie is immobilized.'

'*Fur*fect, human. They tell us to what degree each predictor affects the outcome *if the effects of all other predictors are held constant*. For rTMS the *b* is −0.251, which means that as rTMS frequency decreases by one unit (1 Hz), zombies will be immobilized for an extra 0.251 seconds. This interpretation is true only if the effect of Taser is held constant. Similarly, for Taser voltage, the *b* is 0.342, which means that as the voltage increases by one unit (1 kV), zombies will be immobilized for an extra 0.342 seconds. Again, assuming that the effect of rTMS is constant.' Milton paused for a moment and scratched his ear. 'The standardized beta values tell us the same thing but in standard deviation units (i.e., *z*-scores), which makes it possible for us to compare the effects of rTMS and Taser voltage directly because they are expressed in the same unit of measurement.'

'Sweet, these standardized betas are −0.384 for rTMS and 0.214 for Taser voltage.' **(OUTPUT 14.6)**

Milton nodded. 'The rTMS effect on zombie immobility is a little stronger than the Taser voltage effect. The value for rTMS means that as rTMS frequency decreases by one standard deviation, zombies will be immobilized for an extra 0.384 of a standard deviation, whereas for Taser voltage as it increases by one standard deviation, zombies will be immobilized for an extra 0.214 of a standard deviation.'

'You said earlier that we test the unstandardized betas to see whether they are different from zero, or no effect.'

'Indeed. Each *b*-value has an associated standard error indicating to what extent its values vary across different samples. These standard errors can be used to construct a confidence interval around *b*, but also to create a *t*-statistic. **(EQUATION 14.21)** Let us look at the *t*-tests first. Remember that these tests have $N - p$

degrees of freedom, where p is the number of parameters being estimated. In this model, there were 156 cases (N) and three parameters (the constant and the bs for two predictors), so the degrees of freedom are 153. For this model both rTMS, $t(153) = -5.27$, $p < 0.001$, and Taser voltage, $t(153) = 2.94$, $p = 0.004$, were significant predictors of zombie immobility. These t-tests are accurate only if the assumptions of the linear model that we discussed earlier are met.'

Coefficients

		Unstandardized Coefficients		Standardized Coefficients			95.0% Confidence ...		Collinearity Statistics	
Model		B	Std. Error	Beta	t	Sig.	Lower Bound	Upper Bound	Tolerance	VIF
1	(Constant)	6.380	.666		9.573	.000	5.064	7.697		
	rTMS Frequency (Hz)	-.251	.048	-.384	-5.268	.000	-.345	-.157	.998	1.002
	Taser Output (KV)	.342	.116	.214	2.939	.004	.112	.571	.998	1.002

a. Dependent Variable: Immobility (Seconds)

Bootstrap for Coefficients

					Bootstrap[a]			
						Sig. (2–tailed)	BCa 95% Confidence Interval	
Model		B	Bias	Std. Error			Lower	Upper
1	(Constant)	6.380	-.001	.653		.001	5.108	7.646
	rTMS Frequency (Hz)	-.251	.000	.044		.001	-.336	-.162
	Taser Output (KV)	.342	.001	.120		.005	.086	.569

a. Unless otherwise noted, bootstrap results are based on 1000 bootstrap samples

Output 14.6   *Main output for multiple regression analysis using IBM SPSS Statistics*

 CHECK YOUR BRAIN: Based on what you have learned about confidence intervals, interpret the confidence intervals for the b-values for both predictors in the model.

'The confidence intervals suggest the same,' I said. 'They're constructed so that in 95% of samples they contain the true population value. So, assuming that our sample is one of those 95%, the actual b for rTMS in the population lies between −0.345 and −0.157, and for Taser voltage it lies between 0.112 and 0.571, which in both cases suggests that the b is not zero and that there is, in reality, a negative relationship between rTMS and immobility and a positive relationship between Taser voltage and immobility.'

'*Purr*fectly *claw*rect, although it is possible that our sample is one of the 5% that completely misses the population value.'

'Why are cats so frippin' negative all of the time?'

'It is because we are not appreciated for holding the fabric of reality together,' Milton quipped. 'Most of what we have looked at so far is what scientists would report when they summarize their results in research papers (*LAB NOTES 14.1*), but the output tells us many other interesting things. This table (*OUTPUT 14.6*), for example, evaluates collinearity, which is when predictor variables are too highly correlated.'

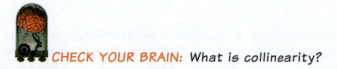 CHECK YOUR BRAIN: What is collinearity?

The table showed two measures of collinearity: the VIF and tolerance statistics. I remembered Milton saying that the VIF should be less than 10. (*SECTION 12.2.7*) He confirmed this and added, 'A tolerance below 0.1 also indicates a serious problem and below 0.2 a potential problem. The values for our predictors are 1.002 for the VIF and 0.998 for tolerance.'

'So, the VIF is well below 10 and tolerance is well above 0.2, so there's no sign of a problem at all.'

Milton agreed. 'The final stage of the general procedure that we discussed **(FIGURE 14.5)** is to check the residuals for evidence of bias. We do this in two ways. First, we can examine the standardized residuals and Cook's distances for each case. After that we can look at some graphs.' Milton drew my attention to a table. **(OUTPUT 14.7)** 'This table shows the maximum and minimum values for the standardized residual and Cook's distance. Cases that have a Cook's distance above 1 are worth inspecting as potential influential cases, but the maximum value in our sample is 0.07, which is well below this threshold.'

'Does that suggest that no individual case influenced the parameters of the model?'

'*Claw*rect. Also, the standardized residuals, which are z-scores, ranged from −2.17 to 2.07.'

'And they should lie between −3.29 and +3.29?'

Milton nodded. 'This suggests that the model has not been unduly biased by any particular case of data. We also need to check the assumptions of the model, which we reminded ourselves about earlier.'

Residuals Statistics

	Minimum	Maximum	Mean	Std. Deviation	N
Std. Residual	−2.171	2.075	.000	.994	156
Cook's Distance	.000	.070	.006	.010	156

a. Dependent Variable: Immobility (Seconds)

Output 14.7 *Residual statistics for multiple regression analysis using IBM SPSS Statistics*

'How do we do that?'

'Graphs! I told you before, graphs! Remember at your concert we discussed how you could look at a histogram of the standardized residuals from the model to check that they are normal, and we plot the standardized residuals against the standardized predicted values from the model to look for heteroscedasticity and non-linearity?' **(SECTIONS 12.2.3 & 12.2.4)**

That was an overload of jargon if ever I heard one, but it did tingle my memory cells enough for a recollection of Milton showing me funnel-shaped data and clouds of dots that looked like sausages. Just as I was losing myself in thoughts of sausage, Milton tapped my arm and said, 'Here are the graphs from our statistics software.'

'I don't think Dr Tuff would like them.'

'Agreed, it is best he never sees them. However, they do the job we need them to do. Now, look first at the histogram. **(FIGURE 14.8, LEFT)** Does it look normal to you?'

 CHECK YOUR BRAIN: Based on the histogram (Figure 14.8, left), do you think the residuals of the model are normally distributed?

'Yeah. It has roughly the characteristic bell shape, it's symmetrical, and there isn't any obvious skew.'

'Agreed. Of course we cannot be sure, but the residuals do look normally distributed. The plot on the right is a plot of standardized residuals against standardized predicted values, or *zpred vs. zresid* for short. This graph should look like a random array of dots. Remember that I showed you the other day **(FIGURE 12.6)** that if it funnels out then that is a sign of heteroscedasticity, and any curve suggests non-linearity.'

'It looks like a fairly random array to me.'

'Indeed it does. In summary, the assumptions of the model are probably met.'

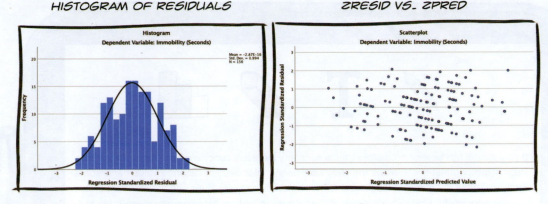

HISTOGRAM OF RESIDUALS   ZRESID VS. ZPRED

Figure 14.8 Plot of the histogram of standardized residuals (left) and the scatterplot of standardized predicted values against standardized residuals (right)

'Which means we can generalize the results beyond the sample. And *that* means we can use rTMS or Tasers to zap the sample of zombies that is about to eat our brains, because the model applies beyond the sample of data we just analysed.'

'*Claw*rect. Which is just as well, because I have been busy recycling everything in this room into a rather splendid Taser and rTMS device.'

Milton beamed from ear to ear as he produced what looked like two single-shot pistols made out of copper pipes soldered together, and a steaming oversized key to a toy soldier.

14.5 ROBUST REGRESSION

The question I ought to have asked was about these gadgets that the cat had somehow fashioned by vandalizing every piece of technology in the room, but instead I found myself asking what we would have done if the model assumptions had been broken. It seemed important: my brain did not want to be eaten.

'You could apply a robust procedure to estimate the significance and confidence intervals of the predictors,' Milton replied. 'The most straightforward way is to use bootstrapping **(SECTION 9.3.5)** to generate confidence intervals and significance tests of the model parameters. These bootstrapped values can be seen in a separate table from the main estimates. **(OUTPUT 14.7, BOTTOM)** The bootstrapped versions tell us that both rTMS, $b = -0.251$ $[-0.336, -0.162]$, $p = 0.001$, and Taser voltage, $b = 0.342$ $[0.086, 0.569]$, $p = 0.005$, significantly predict zombie immobility. The confidence intervals for both rTMS and Taser voltage do not change a lot when estimated using bootstrapping because the assumptions of the model were met, so the non-robust estimates are not biased. When the assumptions are not met, though, these bootstrap confidence intervals and significance values give us a robust estimate of the true population value of b for each predictor, because they do not rely on assumptions of normality or homoscedasticity.'

14.5.1 Bayes factors for linear models

'A different approach to looking at confidence intervals and significance tests is to use Bayes factors to compare models,' continued the cat. **(SECTION 11.4)** 'One approach, for example, is to add predictors to or remove predictors from the model and at each step compute a Bayes factor that compares the model to a baseline that includes only the intercept.[108, 109] The output shows the Bayes factor when we include only rTMS as a predictor, or only Taser voltage, or when both are included. **(OUTPUT 14.8)** The questions to ask are which model has the largest Bayes factor and whether it is big enough to provide evidence for the hypothesis that the model predicts the outcome better than the intercept alone.'

If your model has several predictors then a summary table is a concise way to report the model. Report the parameter estimates (*b*), their confidence intervals, significance values and some statistics about the model fit (such as R^2). The standardized beta values and the standard errors are also very useful. For the zombie immobility data, you might produce something like Table 14.4, which is based on the information in Output 14.6.

Some general points about presentation: (1) round numbers to a sensible level of precision (I've used 2 decimal places); (2) some journals (i.e., those using APA style) ask that you do not place zeros before the decimal place if the numbers can't exceed 1, which is why I have done this for the standardized betas; (3) the significance of the variable is often denoted by an asterisk with a footnote to indicate the significance level being used but it's better practice to report exact *p*-values; (4) the R^2 for the model is reported below the table; and (5) I mention in the title that confidence intervals and standard errors are computed using bootstrapping because this information is important for readers.

Table 14.4 *Linear model of predictors of zombie immobility, with 95% bias corrected and accelerated confidence intervals reported in parentheses. Confidence intervals and standard errors based on 1000 bootstrap samples.*

	b	*SE B*	*β*	*p*
Constant	6.38 (5.11, 7.65)	0.65		*p* = .001
rTMS (Hz)	−0.25 (−0.34, −0.16)	0.04	−.38	*p* = .001
Taser voltage (kV)	0.34 (0.09, 0.57)	0.12	.21	*p* = .005

Note. R^2 = .19.

Alice's Lab Notes 14.1 *Reporting linear models*

All of the models had huge Bayes factors, well above 1.

'The largest Bayes factor is for when rTMS and Taser are both included as predictors, and it is gigantic. Taser voltage still has a reasonable effect (the evidence for the model is 3.14 times that of the null) but much smaller than for rTMS alone (BF = 10,810.52). Including both predictors produces a Bayes factor nearly 10 times greater than for rTMS alone (BF = 105,901.60). Therefore, we may as well try using both devices to immobilize zombies.

```
Bayes factor analysis
--------------
[1]  rTMS         : 10810.52  ±0%
[2]  Taser        : 3.135408  ±0%
[3]  rTMS + Taser : 105901.6  ±0%

Against denominator:
  Intercept only
---
Bayes factor type: BFlinearModel, JZS
```

Output 14.8   *Bayes factors for multiple regression models using R*

'The other thing we can do is estimate the parameters in the model using Bayesian methods. The second output shows this, and the values to focus on are the means for rTMS and Taser. The Bayesian estimate of b for rTMS is −0.2421, and for Taser is 0.3295.' *(OUTPUT 14.9)*

I noted that the values were really similar to those we'd got using least squares estimation, which were −0.251 and 0.342. *(OUTPUT 14.6)*

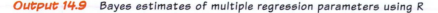

	Mean	SD	Naive SE	Time-series SE
rTMS	-0.2421	0.04778	0.0004778	0.0005001
Taser	0.3295	0.11541	0.0011541	0.0011541
sig2	4.8885	0.56915	0.0056915	0.0061181
g	3.1899	113.98500	1.1398500	1.1398500

Output 14.9   *Bayes estimates of multiple regression parameters using R*

The cat acknowledged this. 'This again suggests that whatever way we approach fitting the model, we get evidence for Taser voltage and especially rTMS as a means to predict the amount of time for which a zombie will be immobilized.'

I grabbed Milton's strange rTMS clockwork key thing and set it to low frequency. My heart was pounding with fear, but I felt overwhelmed with a mindless bravado.

'Right, so I just pop this over the zombie's head and press the switch?' I asked.

'Yes. Be careful not to activate it over your own head, or mine for that matter,' the cat replied.

Something in me snapped; I was fed up with Milton treating me like an idiot. Had I not proved to him that I was more than just a brainless musician? It had been more than two weeks and still I hadn't spoken to Alice, or found out what the hell was going on here. I'd endured hours of tedious lectures, in the hope it would get me closer to the truth. I'd been catapulted across bridges, sent down tombs full of people in weird glasses, and now I was stuck in a room with a freaky lizard, surrounded by unrepellable bloodthirsty zombies. It was time for me to take charge. I needed to talk to Alice. And that was what I was going to do. I took Milton's paw and Clint's gecko-like hand, and drew them into a huddle. Looking them straight in the eyes, I said, 'We are *doing this now*: I'll zap, you freaks follow me.'

'Insanity! There's too many of them, we won't make it!' Clint objected.

'Yes. We. Will,' I said defiantly. 'Because I came here to see Alice and I'm not dying until I do.'

I pushed open the door to face the zombie horde. As I did, I saw Celia's unmistakable figure across the courtyard, hurrying into the adjacent building called 'Research 1'. That spurred me on. I felt sure she'd help us, so with zapper in hand, I ran like a soldier across no man's land into the fray.

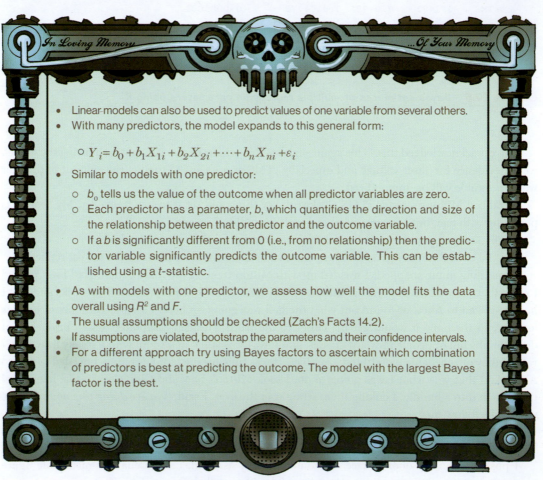

- Linear models can also be used to predict values of one variable from several others.
- With many predictors, the model expands to this general form:

  ○ $Y_i = b_0 + b_1 X_{1i} + b_2 X_{2i} + \cdots + b_n X_{ni} + \varepsilon_i$

- Similar to models with one predictor:

  ○ b_0 tells us the value of the outcome when all predictor variables are zero.
  ○ Each predictor has a parameter, b, which quantifies the direction and size of the relationship between that predictor and the outcome variable.
  ○ If a b is significantly different from 0 (i.e., from no relationship) then the predictor variable significantly predicts the outcome variable. This can be established using a t-statistic.

- As with models with one predictor, we assess how well the model fits the data overall using R^2 and F.
- The usual assumptions should be checked (Zach's Facts 14.2).
- If assumptions are violated, bootstrap the parameters and their confidence intervals.
- For a different approach try using Bayes factors to ascertain which combination of predictors is best at predicting the outcome. The model with the largest Bayes factor is the best.

Zach's Facts 14.3 *Linear models with several predictors*

KEY TERMS

b_i	Mean squares	Simple regression
b_n	Model sum of squares, SS_M	Simultaneous entry regression
β_i	Multiple regression	Standardized regression coefficients
Cook's distance	Predicted value	
F-ratio	Regression coefficient	Stepwise regression
Forced entry regression	Regression line	Total sum of squares, SS_T
Generalization	Regression model	
Hierarchical regression	Residual sum of squares, SS_R	

JIG:SAW'S PUZZLES

1   In Chapter 13, we looked at an example of how big a correlation there was between openness to new relationships (*alternatives*) and the extent to which your partner matched your ideal (*ideal*). The data are in Table 13.4. Calculate the parameters of the linear model for openness to new relationships being predicted from how closely a partner matches the person's ideal.

2   Compute the confidence intervals for the parameters of the model in puzzle 1.

3   Compute the standardized beta for the parameter for the variable *ideal* in the model in puzzle 1. What do you notice about this value and that of the correlation coefficient between the variables *ideal* and *alternatives* in Chapter 13?

4   Write out the model in puzzle 1. What value of *alternatives* would you expect if someone had scored 6 on the variable *ideal*?

5   Calculate the model sum of squares, total sum of squares and residual sum of squares for the model in puzzle 1. What do these values each represent?

6   Use the values in puzzle 5 to calculate the F-ratio. Is the model a significant fit to the data?

7   Use the values in puzzle 5 to calculate R^2. What does R^2 represent, and how would you interpret the value for this specific model?

8   In Chapter 13 Celia tried to convince Zach that there was not a meaningful relationship between how closely your partner matches your ideal and your willingness to entertain other relationships. She did this knowing that Alice closely matched Zach's ideal. The model summarized in Output 14.10 shows what happens when you build a model to predict openness to alternative relationships (*alternatives*) from both how much your partner matches your ideal (*ideal*), and also the benefits you see in your current relationship (*benefit*). This model uses the data in Table 13.4. How might Celia use this model to get Zach to consider a relationship with her instead of Alice?

9   Write out the model in puzzle 8. What value of *alternatives* would you expect if someone had scored 6 on the variable *ideal*, and 7 on *benefit*?

Coefficients[a]

Model		Unstandardized Coefficients		Standardized Coefficients	t	Sig.	95.0% Confidence Interval for B		Collinearity Statistics	
		B	Std. Error	Beta			Lower Bound	Upper Bound	Tolerance	VIF
1	(Constant)	5.903	1.000		5.905	.001	3.539	8.267		
	Closeness to ideal standard	.122	.360	.099	.340	.744	−.729	.974	.547	1.829
	Benefits of current relationship	−.950	.313	−.885	−3.033	.019	−1.690	−.209	.547	1.829

a. Dependent Variable: Openness to alternative relationships

Output 14.10

10   A Bayes factor version of the model in puzzle 8 is shown in Output 14.11. What three models have been tested, and which one should we choose?

```
Bayes factor analysis
--------------
[1] Ideal              : 1.018349  ±0.01%
[2] Rewards            : 10.15071  ±0%
[3] Ideal + Rewards    : 3.939688  ±0%

Against denominator:
  Intercept only
---
Bayes factor type: BFlinearModel, JZS
```

Output 14.11

IN THE NEXT CHAPTER, ZACH DISCOVERS ...

The secret of invisibility
How to compare two means with the *t*-test in an independent experimental design
How to compare two means with the *t*-test in a repeated-measures design

Alternative approaches to comparing two means
That everything you believe is wrong (sorry!)

15

Comparing Two Means

Rock or Bust

It wasn't the joyful reunion I'd dreamt about. On seeing Alice, I instinctively went to embrace her; perhaps if I squeezed her tightly enough we'd merge and dissolve the past few weeks. Her reaction was biz, as though my being there agitated her. Perhaps The Head was right, she had left me, and now I was just a fool who had catapulted myself not once, but twice, across a chasm to rescue her. She definitely didn't look like someone who needed rescuing.

As Alice led us onto the glass and cast iron mezzanine of the spectacular circular laboratory, my awe at the building's splendour turned to horror as I looked over into the faceless circle of people below. The Alice I thought I knew was compassionate and humane, not the orchestrator of horror. What had science turned her into?

I had so many questions, but they seemed unimportant compared to asking Alice what the hell was happening in this lab.

Alice's tone was brittle. 'Zach, what are you doing here, and since when did you travel with a cat and a ...' she looked at Clint with confusion, '... with him?'

Milton and Alice eyed each other suspiciously.

'Sorry, I'm so rude,' I said, seething inside. 'Introductions. Alice, this is Clint. We ran into him in the complex and he's been proper sick as our lookout.'

'Pleased to meet you,' Clint lisped as he cupped Alice's hand and drew her fingers towards him to kiss her knuckles. She manoeuvred their hands sideways turning the kiss into a firm handshake. 'Nice to meet you, Clint.'

'And this is Milton; he's been helping me. I freed him from the Beimeni Centre. I thought perhaps you might have met there.' I was pretty sure they had and I wanted to put her on the spot.

Milton and Alice looked at each other as though neither of them knew what to say.

'And how exactly can a *cat* help you, Zach?' asked Alice.

I wasn't going to let her get away with making me sound stupid.

'He's been teaching me statistics.'

'Yes,' said Alice, rolling her eyes, 'and a rabbit has been cooking your dinner.'

'He cooks his own dinner,' said Milton.

'A *talking* cat – that makes complete sense,' said Alice, glaring at Milton.

Alice turned to me, her tone softer. 'I really wouldn't pay much attention to what a cat has to say. They can't be trusted,' her voice hardening, 'not even to follow the most basic instructions.'

Placing my hands gently on her shoulders, I turned Alice towards me. 'Honey, what is going on here?'

'What is going on is that you are going to leave here and forget about me,' she replied with a quiver in her chin.

I was angry now. 'Not an option, Alice. I'm here to find you, to know the truth, and even if you don't care for me any more I want to know that you are safe.'

'I am safe. I am happy and I have all that I want here. Do as I ask, Zach: turn around and leave.'

'A room full of faceless people doesn't cry out "safe" to me. I'm not leaving until you tell me what you're doing here.'

Alice took her Proteus and spread it into a screen for me. 'Very well. *This* is what I have been doing,' she said, placing it in my hands.

The Proteus showed a report outlining different pieces of research across different research buildings. I swiped to the report for the building we were in **(LAB NOTES 15.1)** and read.

'Invisibility! You compare the effect of a mask made of calcite with a paste containing calcite, and in the second study you look at this calcite paste but also manipulate what people think they have seen by using their ID chips?'

'Not bad, Zach.' Alice looked impressed. 'Maybe the cat isn't as useless as he seems.'

This was the opportunity I needed. If I could use what I'd learnt over the past few weeks to talk to Alice on *her* wavelength, about *her* work, maybe it would buy me some time; she might even stop telling me to leave. My newfound statistical skills were my route into her world. Perhaps this was the reason why Milton had gone to such lengths to teach me this stuff. Alice was right: the cat *wasn't* as useless as he seemed.

'The thing I don't understand', I said, 'is how you could tell whether the mask was better than the paste, or whether manipulating the images sent to the ID chips had an impact. It looks like you used null hypothesis significance testing **(CHAPTER 10)**, and I know about linear models, and how we can predict one variable from another, but this looks like you were comparing the average recognition scores in two conditions, so it isn't a linear model, right?'

15.1 TESTING DIFFERENCES BETWEEN MEANS: THE RATIONALE

I was right, my question reeled Alice in. She couldn't resist the bait to tell me more about her work.

'Actually it is a linear model, but let's take a step back, Zach. Do you remember the last night we spent together when I explained two types of research design to you that are used to test a hypothesis?' **(SECTION 1.3.2.1)**

I did. We had looked at testing whether a free gift would improve T-shirt sales at gigs, and Alice had said that we could either use different bands and have some bands give out free gifts and others not, or use the same bands but look at two different gigs: one where they give out a free gift and one where they don't. I told Alice that I remembered.

'Good. The first design I told you about was an independent design: you test different entities in different experimental conditions. The first experiment I report uses this kind of design. We had a group of participants who, for 20 different people, had to identify which of two photos showed the person they were looking at, when those people wore a calcite mask. The masks bend light, making the faces of the people wearing them ambiguous. Just like the people in the room below. A different group of participants did exactly the same, except that the people they looked at wore a calcite paste on their face rather than a mask. For all participants, the outcome was how many of the 20 people who they saw they could correctly identify; they got a score out of 20. Our hypothesis was that calcite paste would make recognition harder, that is, scores would be lower than for the calcite masks.'

'And your null hypothesis would be that there was no difference in recognition in the two conditions,' I interrupted, keen to keep her talking.

Notes on recent experiments in Research Building 1 by Dr Alice Nightingale

Introduction

Humans have been enchanted by the idea of invisibility for centuries. From H. G. Wells's tale of a scientist who makes himself invisible (Wells, 1897), to Harry Potter's cloak of invisibility (Rowling, 1997). In the years since these fictional tales, scientists have tried to make the science fiction of invisibility a science fact. For example, Di Falco, Ploschner, and Krauss (2010) created a flexible material (Metaflex) that had optical properties that meant that layers of it might cause light to bend around it. Chen et al. (2011) produced a calcite lump of invisibility, which could hide small objects (centimetres and millimetres in scale). These studies laid the foundations for calcite-based flex materials that would bend light. Hogarth, Rothery, Kelly, Trewavas, and Mosley (2104) developed the first calcite invisibility cloak, and showed that its light-bending properties were sufficient to blur the object beneath beyond recognition, but without making it invisible. This has led to the possibility of pastes containing calcite micro-crystals that have the same properties but are less easily detected by the naked eye. The current two studies develop this work to see whether calcite flex materials can be used as a mask to obscure facial features (Experiment 1) and, if so, whether viewers can be made to perceive a different face through information passed to the optical circuits of the brain via ID chips (Experiment 2).

Experiment 1: Summary

Twenty-eight participants were tested individually. Each participant sat on a revolving chair in the middle of a circle of 20 people. The 20 people all wore a light-deflecting aid on their face. For half of the participants ($N = 14$) the 20 people wore a standard calcite-based mask, whereas the other half ($N = 14$) saw people wearing 'invisibility paste', a transparent cream containing calcite micro-crystals. Participants looked at each person and were given two photographs, one depicting the person they were looking at and one depicting a different person matched for age and sex. Participants had to decide which person they were looking at, before turning to the next person and being given two different photographs. Participants scored a point for each person they identified correctly: a score of 0 would mean they always chose the incorrect photo, while a score of 20 would mean that they always chose the correct photo.

We predict that the invisibility paste will be more effective than the calcite masks: the paste will make it harder to identify people, resulting in lower recognition scores than for the mask. Figure 15.1 and the analysis showed this trend: recognition was significantly lower when recognizing people with invisibility paste on their face than when recognizing people wearing calcite masks, $t(26) = -2.07$, $p = 0.049$. This finding suggests that invisibility paste is better at concealing faces than a calcite mask.

Experiment 2: Summary

In an extension of Experiment 1, we asked whether we could manipulate the face perceived by the participant when viewing someone wearing calcite invisibility paste. Participants were all so-called Chippers, who had ID chips installed in their brains. Each participant met 40 people who had calcite paste on their face. For each of these people we took a photo of their face (the 'actual' face), and found a photo of a different face matched for sex and age (the 'different' face). We could send these images to the participant's visual cortex using their ID chip.

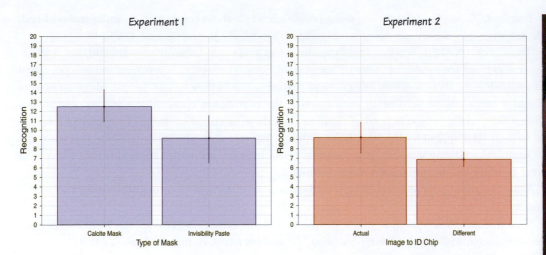

Figure 15.1   Mean (and 95% confidence interval) recognition in Experiments 1 and 2

For 20 of the encounters an image of the person's 'actual' face was transmitted to the participant's ID chip during the encounter, for the remaining 20 encounters the 'different' face was sent to the chip. During each encounter the participant was shown the photos of the actual and different face and pointed to the one depicting whom they thought they had just met.

As in Experiment 1, participants scored a point for each person they correctly identified: a score of 0 would mean that they never chose the correct photo, while a score of 20 would mean that they always chose the correct photo. We predicted that the visual ambiguity created by the paste should make recognition scores low generally, even when the actual face was beamed to their ID chip. However, when the 'different' face was beamed to their ID chip this additional interference would make recognition even harder: participants would more often respond in line with the information beamed to their chip than what they actually saw. In other words, they would more often choose the wrong picture as being the person they met, resulting in lower recognition scores.

Figure 15.1 and the analysis showed this hypothesis was supported: recognition was significantly lower after meeting people when a 'different' face was transmitted to the ID chip than when the 'actual' face was, $t(19) = 2.14$, $p = 0.046$. This finding suggests that invisibility paste in combination with manipulating input to people's ID chips could be a viable way to conceal a face.

References

Chen, X. Z., Luo, Y., Zhang, J. J., Jiang, K., Pendry, J. B., & Zhang, S. A. (2011). Macroscopic invisibility cloaking of visible light. *Nature Communications, 2*(1), 176. doi: 10.1038/ncomms1176

Di Falco, A., Ploschner, M., & Krauss, T. F. (2010). Flexible metamaterials at visible wavelengths. *New Journal of Physics, 12*, 113006. doi:10.1088/1367-2630/12/11/113006

Hogarth, S., Rothery, S., Kelly, M., Trewavas, P., & Mosley, I. (2104). The invisible man. *Proceedings of the Garden Party Society, 67*, 1984–1988.

Rowling, J. K. (1997). *Harry Potter and the philosopher's stone.* London: Bloomsbury.

Wells, H. G. (1897). *The invisible man. A grotesque romance.* London: C. Arthur Pearson.

Alice's Lab Notes 15.1   Invisibility

'Excellent, Zach, yes. In these situations people often talk about conducting an **independent *t*-test**, although what they are actually doing is using a linear model, like you mentioned.' **(CHAPTER 14)**

'The second type of design that I told you about was a repeated-measures design, and that is where the same entities are measured under different conditions. The second experiment in my report used this methodology: there was only one group of participants and they met 40 people whose faces were painted with calcite paste. During each meeting the participant chose which of two photos they believed showed the person in front of them. On half these meetings an image of the correct face was sent to their ID chip, but for the other half a different face was sent. The hypothesis was that when the face sent to the ID chip was different, then this would interfere more with them choosing the correct photo. In other words, recognition would be lower.'

'Again the null hypothesis would be that there was no difference in recognition in the two conditions,' I said.

Alice nodded. 'You sometimes hear people talk about comparing two means from a repeated-measures design with a **paired-samples *t*-test**, **dependent *t*-test**, or **matched-pairs *t*-test**.'

'What's the difference?'

'Nothing, they're different names for the same test. Now, regardless of whether the design was independent or repeated-measures, and whether you're therefore using an independent *t*-test or a paired-samples *t*-test, there is a similar rationale behind the test. First, two samples of data are collected and the sample means calculated. In our experiments, these are the mean recognition scores. These means might differ by either a little or a lot.'

'Because of sampling variation.' Every interruption seemed to make Alice lighten up a little more.

'Exactly, Zach. If the samples come from the same population, then their means should be more or less equal. Although it is possible for their means to differ by chance, we expect large differences between sample means to occur infrequently.'

'Right, and Milton told me that the standard error of the mean tells us how variable sample means are; so, it tells us whether different samples are likely to have similar means or quite variable ones.' **(SECTION 8.2.2)**

'The cat *has* been busy,' she replied, throwing Milton a less hostile look than before. 'Of course, you're right: if the standard error is small, then we expect most samples to have very similar means, but if it is large then bigger differences in sample means are more likely. Now, under the null hypothesis we assume that the experimental manipulation has no effect on the participants; that is, recognition scores are not affected by our manipulations, and therefore, means in the two conditions will be very similar. How similar they ought to be is indicated by the standard error. If the difference between the sample means that we have collected is larger than we would expect based on the standard error, then there are two possibilities. First, there is no effect and we have, by chance, collected two samples that are atypical of the population from which they came; or second, the two samples are typical of their parent population but they *come from different populations*. In other words, the difference between sample means represents a genuine difference between the samples (and so the null hypothesis is unlikely). The larger the difference between the sample means gets relative to the standard error, the more probable it is that this difference has been created by our experimental manipulation.'

'You'd use a test statistic, right?' I said, still keen to impress Alice. 'The Secret Philanthropic Society told me about them. **(SECTION 10.1.4)** They're basically a signal-to-noise ratio, so in this case the signal would be the difference between means, and the noise would be …' I stopped as I realized that I'd waded in too deep.

Alice helped me out. 'The noise, or error, would be the **standard error of differences** between the two means, because this value tells us by how much we could expect two sample means from the same population to differ. So, the test statistic, the *t* in the *t*-test, tells us how different our two means are relative to how variable we could expect the means of two random samples from the same population to be.' Alice wrote an equation **(15.1)** on her Proteus screen.

'Look, as you said, test statistics are a signal-to-noise ratio: the variance explained by the model, divided by the variance that the model can't explain. In other words, the effect divided by the error.

The top half of the equation is the "model", and represents the hypothesis: it asks whether the difference between our sample means is bigger than the expected difference, and under the null hypothesis the expected difference is 0, so the top half becomes the difference between means. The bottom half is the "error": it is the estimate of how variable two means can be from the same population.'

$$t = \frac{\text{observed difference between sample means} - \begin{array}{c}\text{expected difference between population means} \\ \text{(if null hypothesis is true)}\end{array}}{\text{estimate of the standard error of the difference between two sample means}} \tag{15.1}$$

$$= \frac{\bar{X}_1 - \bar{X}_2}{\text{estimate of the standard error}}$$

15.2   MEANS AND THE LINEAR MODEL

'I don't understand,' I said. 'Milton showed me that a t-statistic was used for testing whether a model parameter, b, was zero, and that parameter represents a straight line, so how can we also use a t to compare means?'

Alice looked unsettled by my knowledge, as though she couldn't believe it was real. 'Comparing differences between the means of two groups is simply asking how well you can predict an outcome based on which of two groups an entity belongs to.'

'But don't base the two groups on a median,' shouted Milton, who had been nosing about the mezzanine while Alice and I spoke. Having made his enigmatic contribution, he turned away to continue his investigations. Seconds later a message appeared on my diePad. **(MEOWSINGS 15.1)**

I asked Alice to explain what she meant with the data from the first experiment. She pulled up the data. **(TABLE 15.1)**

'There are two groups, and we measured their ability to recognize 20 different people; the two groups differed in whether the 20 people were wearing calcite masks or calcite paste on their faces. In effect, we're asking how well we can predict recognition scores based on whether participants had to recognize people in calcite masks or with calcite paste on their face. This is a linear model with one dichotomous predictor. If Milton told you what a linear model is, you'll know the equation.'

CHECK YOUR BRAIN: Write out the general equation for the linear model with one predictor. (Hint: see Chapter 14.)

If Alice was testing me, then I was up to it. I wrote out the equation **(15.2)** and explained that the model is defined by parameters: b_0 tells us the value of the outcome when the predictor is zero, and b_1 shows the relationship between the predictor (X_i), and outcome (Y_i).

$$Y_i = b_0 + b_1 X_{1i} + \varepsilon_i \tag{15.2}$$

'Excellent,' she replied. 'But let's make the model more concrete. We can replace the outcome, Y, with what we measured, recognition scores, and replace the predictor, X, with the group to which a person belonged (we'll call this variable *Mask*).' Alice adapted my equation. **(EQUATION 15.3)**

$$\text{Recognition}_i = b_0 + b_1 \text{Mask}_i + \varepsilon_i \tag{15.3}$$

Dear Human,

Alice seems remarkably indifferent to the sight of you. I bet you are glad you crossed the probability bridge not once, but twice, to discover this fact!

Researchers often analyse their data using a 'median split'. For example, imagine you wanted to know whether fans of your band, The Reality Enigma, were less intelligent than non-fans. You might test this by measuring how many downloads of your songs each person had, and then measuring their intelligence. You might then take the median number of The Reality Enigma downloads and classify anyone with a score above the median as a 'Reality Enigma fan', and those below the median as a 'non-fan'. In doing so, you 'dichotomize' a continuous variable.

This practice is quite common, but rarely sensible[110] for the following reasons:

1. Imagine there are four people: Alice, Milton, Celia and Zach. We measure how many Reality Enigma songs they have downloaded, and find Zach has them all (72 songs), Celia has 55, Alice has 49 and Milton has 0, because he has taste. Let us say the median was 50 songs. If we split these four people at the median, we are saying that Zach and Celia are identical (they both get a score of 1 = fanatic) and Alice and Milton are identical (they both get a score of 0 = not a fanatic). In reality, Celia and Alice are the most similar of the four people, but they have been put in completely different groups. Median splits, therefore, dramatically change the original information: Alice and Celia are originally very similar but become opposite after the split; Milton and Alice are relatively dissimilar originally but become identical after the split.
2. Effect sizes get smaller. If you correlate two continuous variables then the effect size will be larger than if you correlate the same variables after one of them has been dichotomized.
3. There is an increased chance of finding spurious effects.

When there is a clear theoretical rationale for creating distinct categories based on a meaningful break point, then dichotomizing a continuous variable may be justified; for example, having groups of 'high risk' or 'low risk' for diabetes based on a doctor's assessment of body mass index, family history, and lifestyle.[110-112]

Best fishes,
Milton

Milton's Meowsings 15.1   *Median splits*

'What *is* the variable that you've called *Mask*?' I asked.

'It is a dichotomous variable – in other words, a nominal variable with two categories: participants recognized people wearing calcite masks or calcite paste. We can't put words into a statistical model, so we must convert these two categories into numbers. The numbers you use depend upon what you want your model to test, but a common method is to use **dummy coding**. Dummy coding involves converting your categories into a series of variables that contain zeros and ones. In the case of two groups, like we have here, it means we code a baseline category with a 0, and other category with a 1.'

Table 15.1 *Data comparing recognition of people wearing calcite masks or calcite paste*

Person	Recognition (*calcite mask*)	Person	Recognition (*calcite paste*)
1	11	15	10
2	11	16	4
3	10	17	9
4	9	18	11
5	7	19	9
6	11	20	14
7	12	21	16
8	14	22	13
9	19	23	7
10	11	24	12
11	19	25	0
12	11	26	10
13	17	27	13
14	13	28	0
	$\bar{x}_{Mask} = 12.50$		$\bar{x}_{Paste} = 9.14$
	$s^2_{Mask} = 12.88$		$s^2_{Paste} = 23.98$
	$s_{Mask} = 3.59$		$s_{Paste} = 4.90$

'What's the baseline category?'

'It would be the control group. In this case, there was past work looking at calcite masks that showed that it interfered with people recognizing the person behind the mask, but our new innovation was to develop calcite paste, which we thought would be better than a mask at concealing the face. Our baseline was, therefore, calcite masks because these masks had been proven to work, and so our new invention, calcite paste, needed to be better than the masks. So we could assign participants who met people in calcite masks a 0 for the variable *Mask*. The "experimental" group was made up of participants who met people with calcite paste on their faces, and we could assign these participants a value of 1 for the variable *Mask*.'

15.2.1 Estimating the model parameters

Alice swiped her fingers around her Proteus before showing me a diagram. **(FIGURE 15.2)** 'Look,' she said. 'This diagram shows the model described by our equation **(15.3)**. The dots show individual participants' recognition scores. The means of the two groups are shown by the large squares, and these are connected by a straight line. This line is the linear model and it has two parameters, b_0 and b_1, that need to be estimated.'

'If it's a linear model then I know how to calculate these parameters.' Alice looked sceptical. 'Don't give me that look,' I said. 'Milton taught me that to compute b_1, we calculate the total relationship between the predictor and outcome, the sum of cross-products (SCP), and divide this value by the total deviation of the predictor from its mean, SS_x.' **(EQUATION 14.7)**

Alice visibly recoiled in surprise, and burst into a huge smile. It was the first time her guard had properly lifted, but she soon caught herself and lowered it again. She swiped at her Proteus screen and her serious expression returned. Finally, she found what she was looking for: a rather unpleasant looking table of values. **(TABLE 15.2)**

'The first three columns show the data from Table 15.1 but rearranged. Note that I have included a variable *Mask*, which contains the value of 0 for those in the calcite mask condition and 1 for those in the calcite paste group. For this variable and the recognition scores in the second column I have computed the mean in the bottom row. In the fourth column I have computed the deviation between each value of the predictor and its mean, and in the next column I have squared these values so that we can add them together to get the sum of squares for the predictor (SS_x), which is 7. The sixth column shows the deviation between each recognition score and the mean of all recognition scores (10.82). The final column shows the cross-product deviation for each observation; that is the deviation of the predictor from its mean (column 4) multiplied by the deviation of the outcome from its mean (column 6). If you add the values in this last column you get the sum of the cross-product deviations (SCP), which is −23.50.'

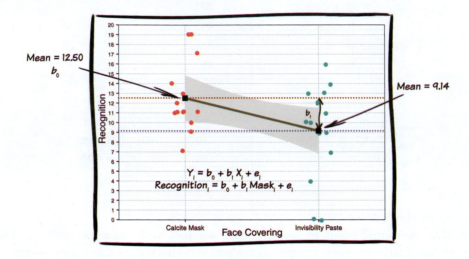

Figure 15.2   *The linear model with a single categorical predictor*

I looked at Alice's table **(TABLE 15.2)** and said, 'That looks exactly like what Milton did when he explained the linear model, except that the predictor variable is made up of 1s and 0s. If I use the values from your table in the equation **(14.7)** that Milton showed me then I can work out what b_1 will be.' I wrote out my workings. **(EQUATION 15.4)** 'It's −3.36.'

$$\hat{b}_1 = \frac{\text{SCP}}{SS_x} = \frac{-23.50}{7} = -3.36 \qquad\qquad (15.4)$$

'Well done, and what is the difference between the group means in my first table?' **(TABLE 15.1)** Alice asked.

'It's $9.14 - 12.50$,' I said, unable to compute that in my head.

'Yes. Which, of course, is −3.36: the same value that you just calculated.'

'Safe, so when we apply the equation for the linear model to estimate the parameter b_1 and the predictor is a dummy variable, b_1 turns out to be the difference between the two group means. Can we use the same equation that Milton showed me to calculate b_0 too? He taught me that the constant is the mean of the outcome minus the mean of the predictor multiplied by the estimate of b_1.' **(EQUATION 14.27)**

'That's correct. You have all of the values you need in my table.' **(TABLE 15.2)**

I took the mean values of recognition and mask from the table, and the value of b_1 that I had just calculated and plugged them into the equation Milton had shown me earlier that day. **(EQUATION 14.27)** The end result was 12.50. **(EQUATION 15.5)** I told Alice.

'What do you notice about that value?' she asked.

I looked back at the original data **(TABLE 15.1)**, and saw that 12.50 was the mean of the control group, the calcite mask group.

'b_0 is the same as the mean of the group that we coded as zero,' I said.

$$\hat{b}_0 = \bar{Y} - \hat{b}_1 \bar{X}$$
$$= 10.82 - 3.36 \times 0.5$$
$$= 10.82 + 1.68$$
$$= 12.50$$

(15.5)

Table 15.2 *Calculating cross-product deviations*

Person	Recognition (Y)	Mask type (X)	$x_i - \bar{x}$	$(x_i - \bar{x})^2$	$(Y_i - \bar{Y}_i)$	$(x_i - \bar{x})(y_i - \bar{y})$
1	11	0	−0.5	0.25	0.18	−0.09
2	11	0	−0.5	0.25	0.18	−0.09
3	10	0	−0.5	0.25	−0.82	0.41
4	9	0	−0.5	0.25	−1.82	0.91
5	7	0	−0.5	0.25	−3.82	1.91
6	11	0	−0.5	0.25	0.18	−0.09
7	12	0	−0.5	0.25	1.18	−0.59
8	14	0	−0.5	0.25	3.18	−1.59
9	19	0	−0.5	0.25	8.18	−4.09
10	11	0	−0.5	0.25	0.18	−0.09
11	19	0	−0.5	0.25	8.18	−4.09
12	11	0	−0.5	0.25	0.18	−0.09
13	17	0	−0.5	0.25	6.18	−3.09
14	13	0	−0.5	0.25	2.18	−1.09
15	10	1	0.5	0.25	−0.82	−0.41
16	4	1	0.5	0.25	−6.82	−3.41
17	9	1	0.5	0.25	−1.82	−0.91
18	11	1	0.5	0.25	0.18	0.09
19	9	1	0.5	0.25	−1.82	−0.91
20	14	1	0.5	0.25	3.18	1.59
21	16	1	0.5	0.25	5.18	2.59
22	13	1	0.5	0.25	2.18	1.09
23	7	1	0.5	0.25	−3.82	−1.91
24	12	1	0.5	0.25	1.18	0.59
25	0	1	0.5	0.25	−10.82	−5.41
26	10	1	0.5	0.25	−0.82	−0.41
27	13	1	0.5	0.25	2.18	1.09
28	0	1	0.5	0.25	−10.82	−5.41
	$\bar{y} = 10.82$	$\bar{x} = 0.50$		$SS_x = 7.00$		$SCP = -23.50$

15.2.2 How the model works

Alice looked as though she was trying hard to conceal her delight. 'Good work, Zach,' she said. 'You see, it turns out that in the equation **(15.3)** that describes the model shown in my diagram **(FIGURE 15.2)**, b_0 is the mean of the group coded with a zero (in this case the calcite mask group) and b_1 is the gradient of the line connecting the two group means, which is the difference between those means.'

'Is that coincidence?' I asked.

'No, it will always be the case when the predictor consists of two categories that are coded as either 0 or 1; we can show this by using the equation.'

Alice wrote out the model again and replaced the values of *Recognition* and *Mask* with numbers. **(EQUATION 15.6)** 'Imagine someone is in the calcite mask condition,' she said. 'What would be the best prediction we could make of the number of people that person recognized?'

$$\text{Recognition}_i = b_0 + b_1 \text{Mask}_i$$
$$\bar{X}_{\text{Calcite Mask}} = b_0 + (b_1 \times 0)$$
$$b_0 = \bar{X}_{\text{Calcite Mask}} \tag{15.6}$$
$$b_0 = 12.5$$

I thought about this for a second. It seemed to me that if we knew which group they were in then we could use the group mean as an estimate of their score. I cautiously offered this suggestion to Alice.

'Well done. Our predicted value *would* be the group mean, so let's replace *Recognition* in the equation with the group mean for that participant, $\bar{X}_{\text{Calcite Paste}}$. Given we know that the person was in the calcite mask group, our baseline, we can also replace the value of *Mask* with 0, which is the code that we decided to assign for this group. If we ignore the residual term, then you can see that b_0 (the constant) is equal to the mean of the baseline group (i.e., the group coded as 0), which in this case is the calcite mask group. This mean was 12.50 for the data I collected.' **(TABLE 15.1)**

'Sweet, and that's the value that we calculated.'

'Exactly. Now let's see what happens when we use the model to predict recognition scores in participants who evaluated people wearing calcite paste. If we knew someone was in the paste group, what might we predict as their recognition score?'

My response of the group mean had gone down well last time, so I thought I would try my luck again.

'Yes. The outcome we'd predict for someone in the paste group would be the mean of the paste group, $\bar{X}_{\text{Calcite Paste}}$, and because they were in the paste group, the value of *Mask* is 1.' Alice started modifying the model again. **(EQUATION 15.7)** As she wrote, she said, 'The mean of the paste group can be predicted from b_0 added to b_1. We know that b_0 is equal to the mean of the calcite mask group ($\bar{X}_{\text{Calcite Mask}}$), so let's replace it with that and rearrange the equation. You end up showing that b_1 represents the difference between the group means. In this case the mean of the calcite mask group was 12.50 and for the calcite paste group it was 9.14 **(TABLE 15.1)**, so b_1 is the difference between these two values: $9.14 - 12.50 \lceil 12.50 \rceil = -3.36$.'

'Which is also the value that we calculated.'

$$\text{Recognition}_i = b_0 + b_1 \text{Mask}_i$$
$$\bar{X}_{\text{Calcite Paste}} = b_0 + (b_1 \times 1)$$
$$\bar{X}_{\text{Calcite Paste}} = b_0 + b_1 \tag{15.7}$$
$$\bar{X}_{\text{Calcite Paste}} = \bar{X}_{\text{Calcite Mask}} + b_1$$
$$b_1 = \bar{X}_{\text{Calcite Paste}} - \bar{X}_{\text{Calcite Mask}}$$

'Yes. What I've shown you is how the parameter values and dummy variable codes fit into the equation. The predicted values from the model are the group means, the predictor variable can take a value of either 1 or 0, and by rearranging the equation you can show that the values of the parameters that we calculated do indeed represent the mean of the group coded as 0 (b_0) and the difference between the group means (b_1). By rearranging the equation for the model, as I just have done, we can see that this last point will always be true when the predictor consists of two categories that are coded as either 0 or 1.'

15.2.3 Testing the model parameters

'Presumably you can test the significance of the parameters in the same way as when the predictor variable is not made up of categories?' I asked.

'Yes, the *t*-test is used to ascertain whether the parameter (b_1) is equal to 0 **(SECTION 14.1.6)**; given that b_1 is the difference between means, the *t*-test evaluates whether the difference between group means is equal to 0.'

I thought back to when Milton explained this to me. We had started off by working out the error in the model by looking at the difference between the observed values of the outcome and the values predicted by the model. He called it the residual sum of squares. I asked Alice if this was what we'd do. **(SECTION 14.1.4)**

Alice was sucked in completely now. 'Yes. If we replace the *b*s with the parameter estimates that we just calculated, what would the model become?'

 CHECK YOUR BRAIN: Use the values of the parameter estimates to write out the model for predicting recognition scores from which group a participant belonged to.

I wrote out the model for her. **(EQUATION 15.8)**

$$\text{Recognition}_i = b_0 + b_1 \text{Mask}_i + \varepsilon_i$$
$$\text{Recognition}_i = 12.50 - 3.36 \times \text{Mask}_i + \varepsilon_i$$

(15.8)

'Great. Now if we replace the variable *Mask* with the values that we have in the data for each participant, we can calculate the predicted values of recognition. Now, *Mask* could take on two values: a 0 for people in the calcite mask group and a 1 for those in the calcite paste group. If you replace *Mask* with these two values, what are the corresponding predicted values of recognition?'

 CHECK YOUR BRAIN: What are the predicted values of recognition for those in the calcite mask group and those in the calcite paste group?

After some fiddling with the calculator on my diePad, I responded, 'You get 12.50 for everyone in the calcite mask group and 9.14 for everyone in the calcite paste group.'

'Yes, and looking at my original table of data **(TABLE 15.1)**, what do you notice about those values?'

I studied the table and noticed that these values were the means of the two groups.

'Exactly,' Alice said. 'The values predicted by the model, as I suggested earlier, will be the means of the two groups. Therefore, for each person, the error in prediction will be the difference between their recognition score and the average recognition score for the group they were in.' Alice created a table on her Proteus and showed it to me. **(TABLE 15.3)**

'Look, I have rearranged the data in this table. For each participant, I have their recognition score, and the number that I assigned to denote the group to which they belonged, which is either a 0 or a 1. I used the model, just like you did, to compute the predicted score ($\hat{Y}$) for each person. Because the predicted score is based on group membership, everyone in the calcite mask group has the same predicted score (12.50), as does everyone in the calcite paste condition (9.14). As you just discovered, these predicted scores are the group means. In the penultimate column I calculate the residual: the difference between the predicted score and the score that the participant actually got, and because some of these values will be positive and others negative, we square them in the final column.'

'And you add the squared residuals to find the total error, the residual sum of squares, SS_R. I remember Milton telling me this,' *(EQUATION 14.6)* I added.

Alice's face softened into a reluctant smile. 'Brilliant. Yes. We can turn this total error into an average ...'

Table 15.3 *Calculating the sum of squared residuals*

Person	Recognition (Y)	Mask Type (X)	Model	$\hat{Y}$	Residual $(Y_i - \hat{Y}_i)$	Squared residual $(Y_i - \hat{Y}_i)^2$
1	11	0	12.50 + (−3.36×0)	12.50	−1.50	2.25
2	11	0	12.50 + (−3.36×0)	12.50	−1.50	2.25
3	10	0	12.50 + (−3.36×0)	12.50	−2.50	6.25
4	9	0	12.50 + (−3.36×0)	12.50	−3.50	12.25
5	7	0	12.50 + (−3.36×0)	12.50	−5.50	30.25
6	11	0	12.50 + (−3.36×0)	12.50	−1.50	2.25
7	12	0	12.50 + (−3.36×0)	12.50	−0.50	0.25
8	14	0	12.50 + (−3.36×0)	12.50	1.50	2.25
9	19	0	12.50 + (−3.36×0)	12.50	6.50	42.25
10	11	0	12.50 + (−3.36×0)	12.50	−1.50	2.25
11	19	0	12.50 + (−3.36×0)	12.50	6.50	42.25
12	11	0	12.50 + (−3.36×0)	12.50	−1.50	2.25
13	17	0	12.50 + (−3.36×0)	12.50	4.50	20.25
14	13	0	12.50 + (−3.36×0)	12.50	0.50	0.25
15	10	1	12.50 + (−3.36×1)	9.14	0.86	0.73
16	4	1	12.50 + (−3.36×1)	9.14	−5.14	26.45
17	9	1	12.50 + (−3.36×1)	9.14	−0.14	0.02
18	11	1	12.50 + (−3.36×1)	9.14	1.86	3.45
19	9	1	12.50 + (−3.36×1)	9.14	−0.14	0.02
20	14	1	12.50 + (−3.36×1)	9.14	4.86	23.59
21	16	1	12.50 + (−3.36×1)	9.14	6.86	47.02
22	13	1	12.50 + (−3.36×1)	9.14	3.86	14.88
23	7	1	12.50 + (−3.36×1)	9.14	−2.14	4.59
24	12	1	12.50 + (−3.36×1)	9.14	2.86	8.16
25	0	1	12.50 + (−3.36×1)	9.14	−9.14	83.59
26	10	1	12.50 + (−3.36×1)	9.14	0.86	0.73
27	13	1	12.50 + (−3.36×1)	9.14	3.86	14.88
28	0	1	12.50 + (−3.36×1)	9.14	−9.14	83.59
					$\sum(Y_i - \hat{Y}_i)^2 =$	**479.21**

'By dividing by the degrees of freedom,' I interrupted. 'Milton told me that too, and that the degrees of freedom will be $N - p$, where p is the number of parameters.' **(EQUATION 14.15)**

Alice's smile widened a little. 'Yes, and there were 28 participants, N, and two parameters (b_0 and b_1), so we divide the residual sum of squares, 479.21, by 28 – 2, which is 26. The resulting mean squared error in the model is 18.43.' **(EQUATION 15.9)**

$$\text{mean squared error in model} = \frac{SS_R}{df} = \frac{\sum_{i=1}^{n}\left(Y_i - \hat{Y}_i\right)^2}{N - p} = \frac{479.21}{26} = 18.43 \qquad (15.9)$$

'And the standard error of the model is the square root of this value.' **(EQUATION 14.16)**

'Is there anything Milton *didn't* teach you?' Alice affectionately mocked.

For the first time I felt a glimmer of hope that, whatever was going on, the real Alice, the Alice that I fell in love with, was allowing herself to have the conversation not because she cared that I knew about linear models, but because at some level she wanted me here.

'You're correct,' she continued. 'If we take the square root of the mean squared error we get the standard error, which for these data is 4.29. **(EQUATION 15.10)** We can use this value to ....'

$$\text{standard error in model} = \sqrt{\frac{\sum_{i=1}^{n}\left(Y_i - \hat{Y}_i\right)^2}{N - 2}} = \sqrt{18.43} = 4.29 \qquad (15.10)$$

'I've got this, Alice – calculate the standard error for the b. Milton said that we take the model standard error and scale it to the spread of predictor variable scores, dividing by the square root of the sum of squares for the predictor.' **(EQUATION 14.17)**

It felt good to be finishing Alice's statistical sentences for her, and she seemed to be enjoying it too. I looked back to the table Alice had constructed to calculate the sum of cross-products **(TABLE 15.2)**, and noticed that she had calculated the sum of squared errors of the predictor and it was 7. Therefore, all I needed to do to get the standard error for the b was to divide the standard error of 4.29 by the square root of 7, which gave a value of 1.62. **(EQUATION 15.11)**

$$SE_b = \frac{SE_{\text{model}}}{\sqrt{SS_x}} = \frac{4.29}{\sqrt{7}} = \frac{4.29}{2.65} = 1.62 \qquad (15.11)$$

'You *have* been busy over the last 3 weeks, Zach,' Alice said, and I allowed myself a playful look of mock satisfaction. 'Presumably then, you know that we can calculate a t-value to test the hypothesis that b is zero by dividing b by its standard error?' **(EQUATION 14.21)**

'Yes,' I said proudly. 'You divide an expression that represents the hypothesis that b is zero, that is, the "signal" or "effect", by an expression that represents the "noise" or "error" in estimating that effect.' **(SECTION 14.1.6)**

'True, but there's something more important than that. Let's return to where we started. When I explained my rationale for this test, I ended up saying that what we needed was a test statistic that compared the differences between means to the error in estimating that difference. **(EQUATION 15.1)** Now, what does b represent in this example?' Alice asked.

'It's the difference between means, isn't it?'

'Exactly, so what we are doing here is dividing b, the difference between means, by the standard error associated with that difference (in other words, the standard error of b).'

The penny dropped. 'Right, so we've come full circle. By applying the linear model to a categorical predictor, the t-statistic that we end up with tests whether the difference between means is 0, and it does this in the same way that it would test whether a relationship between a continuous predictor and an outcome was significantly different from zero.'

'Exactly, Zach. The linear model that Milton taught you is very flexible. The t we get in this case is the difference between means (-3.36), which is also the value of b, divided by its standard error of 1.62, which ends up being -2.07.' **(EQUATION 15.12)**

$$t_{N-p} = \frac{b_i}{SE_{b_i}} = \frac{\bar{X}_{\text{Calcite Paste}} - \bar{X}_{\text{Calcite Mask}}}{SE_{\bar{X}_{\text{Calcite Paste}} - \bar{X}_{\text{Calcite Mask}}}} = \frac{-3.36}{1.62} = -2.07 \qquad (15.12)$$

'Now we'd need to look up the critical value for t **(SECTION 13.3.3)** at the 0.05 significance level with 26 degrees of freedom.'

'Yes, it's 2.056.' **(SECTION A.2)**

'And because our observed of -2.07 is smaller than the critical value, we have a significant result.'

'No,' said Alice abruptly. 'Remember that the distribution is symmetrical and the table contains only the positive values. With a two-tailed test, the table is really saying that the critical value is 2.056 or -2.056 because we need to look at both ends of the distribution. Therefore, we want to know whether our observed value falls outside of the interval from -2.056 to 2.056 and, of course, it does, because -2.07 is smaller than the lower limit. It is simpler, in real life, to do all of this on a computer, which will work out the exact probability value for the observed t.'

15.2.4 The independent t-test on a computer

Alice took her Proteus back and, after some tapping and swiping, she showed me some output. **(OUTPUT 15.1)** 'Here's what the results of the test look like on a computer. Notice that there are two rows containing values for the test statistics: one labelled *Equal variances assumed*, and the other labelled *Equal variances not assumed*. The rows of the table relate to whether or not the homogeneity of variance assumption has been broken.' **(SECTION 12.2.3)**

Independent Samples Test

		Levene's Test for Equality of Variances		t-test for Equality of Means					95% Confidence Interval of the Difference	
		F	Sig.	t	df	Sig. (2-tailed)	Mean Difference	Std. Error Difference	Lower	Upper
Number of Faces Recognised	Equal variances assumed	.836	.369	-2.069	26	.049	-3.357	1.623	-6.693	-.022
	Equal variances not assumed			-2.069	23.841	.050	-3.357	1.623	-6.707	-.007

Bootstrap for Independent Samples Test

				Bootstrap[a]		
		Mean Difference	Bias	Std. Error	BCa 95% Confidence Interval	
					Lower	Upper
Number of Faces Recognised	Equal variances assumed	-3.357	.016	1.619	-6.882	-.214
	Equal variances not assumed	-3.357	.016	1.619	-6.882	-.214

a. Unless otherwise noted, bootstrap results are based on 1000 bootstrap samples

Output 15.1 *The independent t-test using IBM SPSS Statistics*

'You mean whether the variances in the two groups were roughly the same?'

'Exactly. My Proteus has produced Levene's test to see whether variances are different. The significance of this test is $p = 0.369$, and because this value is bigger than 0.05 it suggests that the variances are not significantly different, in other words we can assume that they are equal. Therefore, we can read the test statistics in the row labelled *Equal variances assumed*. Had Levene's test been significant, then we would have read the test statistics from the row labelled *Equal variances not assumed*. The value of *t* is as we calculated, −2.07. The mean difference between groups is −3.36, which is the same as our value of *b*, and the standard error of this value is also the same as the value we calculated, 1.62. You can also see that the degrees of freedom are 26. The key thing is that we get an exact *p*-value for the *t*-statistic, which is 0.049. This means that if the null hypothesis were true and there was no difference at all between groups, then the probability of getting a *t*-value at least as big in magnitude as the one we have is 0.049. Because this value is less than 0.05, I concluded that recognition scores were significantly different when the calcite paste was used compared to the calcite masks, and the means tell me that recognition was significantly worse when the calcite paste was used.'

'You mean that the calcite paste made it harder for people to recognize who they were looking at than the calcite masks?'

'Yes, Zach, and that is what my report concludes. Notice that the values I give in my report match those that we just calculated.' **(LAB NOTES 15.2)**

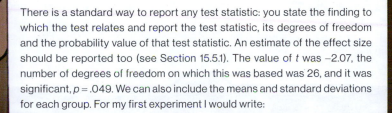

There is a standard way to report any test statistic: you state the finding to which the test relates and report the test statistic, its degrees of freedom and the probability value of that test statistic. An estimate of the effect size should be reported too (see Section 15.5.1). The value of *t* was −2.07, the number of degrees of freedom on which this was based was 26, and it was significant, *p* = .049. We can also include the means and standard deviations for each group. For my first experiment I would write:

✓ On average, participants were significantly worse at recognizing people wearing calcite paste (*M* = 9.14, *SD* = 4.90), than those wearing a calcite mask (*M* = 12.50, *SD* = 3.59). This difference, −3.36, BCa 95% CI [−6.88, −0.21], was significant, *t*(26) = −2.07, *p* = .049, *d* = 0.78.

Note how I have reported the means in each group (and standard deviations), the mean difference and its bootstrapped confidence interval, Cohen's *d*, and the test statistic, its degrees of freedom and *p*-value.

Alice's Lab Notes 15.2   Reporting the independent t-test

15.2.5 Assumptions of the model

'Did you check that nothing biased your results? **(CHAPTER 12)** I mean, Milton taught me all about the assumptions of the linear model and the general procedure for conducting one. **(SECTION 14.3)** Would all of that apply to this model?'

'Yes, of course. Everything I have just talked about is a special case of the linear model, so we have the same assumptions and the same process we'd go through to fit the model.'

'Right, so did you do anything like check the assumptions or use bootstrapping to get robust estimates?'

Alice recoiled in astonishment. 'Erm, well, you can see in the output that the bootstrap confidence intervals are displayed. The difference between means was −3.36, and the confidence interval ranged from −6.882 to −0.214. Assuming that this is one of the 95% of confidence intervals that contains the true value of the effect, then the true difference between means lies between −6.88 and −0.21 – that's to say, it is not zero. Therefore, this bootstrap confidence interval confirms our conclusion that calcite paste is better for hindering recognition than a calcite mask.'

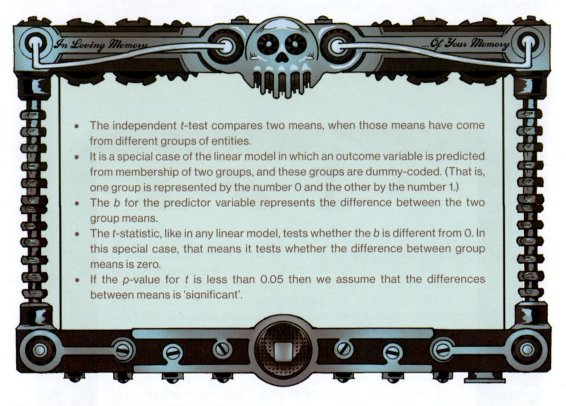

- The independent *t*-test compares two means, when those means have come from different groups of entities.
- It is a special case of the linear model in which an outcome variable is predicted from membership of two groups, and these groups are dummy-coded. (That is, one group is represented by the number 0 and the other by the number 1.)
- The *b* for the predictor variable represents the difference between the two group means.
- The *t*-statistic, like in any linear model, tests whether the *b* is different from 0. In this special case, that means it tests whether the difference between group means is zero.
- If the *p*-value for *t* is less than 0.05 then we assume that the differences between means is 'significant'.

Zach's Facts 15.1 *The independent t-test*

15.3 EVERYTHING YOU BELIEVE IS WRONG

Clint had remained silent throughout. He hovered by the edge of the mezzanine and rested on the iron guardrails. He stared into the distance, looking sad and uninterested in our discussion. He looked as though he might be considering how life had turned out so unfortunate for him. I still wanted to hug Alice, but despite her occasional lapses, her vibe was frosty enough that I kept the urge suppressed. Seeing me had brought on an emotional winter in her – after 10 years, weeks of tracking her down, and two trips across a probability bridge to find her I thought I deserved better. I pulled her to one side.

'Alice, what's going on?'

'I just told you, Zach.'

'No, I mean, with us, what's going on with us? I wake up one day and you're gone. No note, no goodbye, nothing. Ten years, and you leave me nothing, Alice.'

'I left you a song.'

She was right, there had been a song playing on repeat, but I hadn't been sure what it meant. I felt anger that she would leave me something so ambiguous.

'What did you think that song was going to tell me about why you left?'

'Nothing. I thought it would tell you something much more important than that.' Alice looked disappointed in me. She shook her head and sighed; she was the master of ambiguity. 'I'm not chained up here,' she said. 'There are great opportunities for me. Nutcot knew about the work I was doing and, yes, I was a little scared by their interest in me because trying to find out anything about this place is impossible, and where there is secrecy there is usually cause for worry ...'

'So, that was what you wanted to talk to me about all those weeks ago – that Nutcot was interested in your work?'

Alice ignored me. 'Once I got here, and saw the opportunity to be involved in this fantastic research, I had to stay. Look at the facilities, Zach, look at the *opportunity*. I couldn't let it pass me by.'

'But you could let *me* pass you by?'

'Look around you, Zach. This is everything I ever dreamed of.'

'There was a time that *I* was everything you ever dreamed of.'

'You need to leave: the director of JIG:SAW won't appreciate people snooping around.'

Alice was evading the issue of *us* again, so I benched it for now. I took a different tack and asked who exactly was the director.

Alice stared at Milton, who stared back. I thought they might be competing to see who would blink first. Finally, Alice said, 'The director is Rob Nutcot.' She intensified her glare, inviting Milton to keep his silence.

'Vic Luten is the director,' the cat said, raising the stakes with his glare. Alice, her rage poorly concealed behind pursed lips, broke their stare off.

'Who the hell is Vic Luten?' I asked.

'When I worked for the WGA,' the cat explained, 'Vic Luten's name was legend – for the wrong reasons. Nobody I knew had met him, but the stories about him were inescapable. They say that in his youth he was a businessman who started the Reality Revolution by mass-producing affordable reality prisms and giving them away to the poor. Having destroyed society, he led one of the largest rebel groups outside of the WGA's focities. When it became obvious that the WGA would win the battle to

471

unify the world, he deserted his group to join them. He seemed to have an amazing knack for getting people to trust him, and he quickly and easily worked his way into a position of power at the WGA. He formed an agency called YIN, whose agenda was carefully managed evil. He convinced the directors of the WGA that their ethically driven policies to improve the lives of the majority were only viable in the short term, because in time people would take their comfortable lives for granted. He reasoned that world harmony was achievable only through the balance of good and evil: people needed bad experiences so that they could appreciate the good that the WGA did. Under his spell, the WGA gave him a free reign to develop YIN, a vehicle to introduce carefully managed evil into society. Anything evil or annoying in society is probably down to Vic Luten.'

'He invented *memoryBank* then?' I quipped.

'After the hell I experienced in being blamed for the Reality Revolution, I was desperate to find out whether the Vic Luten stories were true. If I could prove that *he* was the one who kick-started the revolution, that I was an innocent inventor whose device had been misused, then perhaps I could find redemption. I put every resource that I could into discovering what I could about Vic Luten and YIN, but he was surrounded by a wall of mystery built on the implicit trust of those around him. It was hopeless, and in time I left the WGA, YIN was dissolved, and it appeared as though Vic Luten had disappeared for ever. I am a scientist, and without evidence I had to resign myself to the fact that I would never find Vic Luten or support my hypothesis that he had used me as a scapegoat for creating the Reality Revolution. However, when mysterious organizations protect themselves with WGA technology such as probability bridges, conduct nefarious research using ID chips, and appear to be led by someone who has a knack for making people trust him, you *do* start to wonder.'

Alice sighed. 'I think your need for atonement is making you get carried away. I have worked here for weeks now, and there is no Vic Luten. I can assure you that Rob Nutcot directs the company. That is the unexciting truth.'

15.4 THE PAIRED-SAMPLES T-TEST

Something wasn't right: Alice was shutting the door on the conversation as though she knew more than she wanted to say. I needed a way to get her talking again. When we'd talked about her research report she had relaxed a little and showed a glimmer of the Alice I knew beneath her guarded exterior. Perhaps the way to a woman's heart was through statistics ...

'You're right,' I said. 'Nutcot is dirgey: men in suits running organizations is about as dull as it gets. Your second experiment sounds way more interesting; you had participants look at people wearing calcite paste on their face, right? The paste made their faces look ambiguous. Then you transmitted to the participant's ID chip either a picture of the face of the actual person they were meeting or a different person of the same age and sex. The participant chose from the two pictures which person they had just met. Is that about right?'

Alice eyed me suspiciously but couldn't help herself. 'Yes, we used a repeated-measures design. Doing so changes the model a bit. What do you know about the assumptions of the linear model? Have you heard of the assumption of independent errors?'

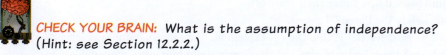

CHECK YOUR BRAIN: What is the assumption of independence? (Hint: see Section 12.2.2.)

'It's something about when the errors of the model are related to each other. Milton said if you and I rate how much we like some songs, then our ratings would be influenced by each other so they would be dependent. This would mean the error in prediction of our scores would also be dependent.'

I didn't want to put Alice off by admitting that I couldn't remember why it was important, but luckily she butted in.

'Yes, and it's important because the equation that we use to estimate the standard error is valid only if errors are independent. If errors are dependent then the estimate of the standard error is wrong.'

'Safe, and that would make confidence intervals and significance tests wrong too because they depend on the standard error.' I was back in the zone.

'Yes – fantastic! Also, if scores are dependent there are better ways to estimate the model parameters than the method of least squares.'

'I think Milton mentioned multilevel something or others ...'

'Multilevel linear models,' Alice helpfully responded. 'Those models are very complicated, so sometimes we use simpler approaches that are limited to specific situations. You *can* apply a multilevel model to the data in our second experiment, but we used one of these simpler methods. When the same entities have been tested under two conditions, so they have contributed two scores, we still want to know whether the means of the two conditions are different. What we're effectively asking is this: if we calculate the difference between people's scores in the two conditions and we average these differences, do we get a value different from zero? Therefore, rather than thinking about means of samples of scores from a population that have an associated sampling distribution, we think instead of means of samples of *difference scores* from a population of *difference scores* that have an associated sampling distribution. If there were no effect in the population then we would expect that population to have a mean of zero; in other words, difference scores in the population are, on average, 0. We take a sample of difference scores by testing people under two conditions and working out the differences between their scores, and then use the average of these differences as an estimate of the value in the population.'

'So, everything is the same process of sampling that Milton taught me **(CHAPTER 8)**, except that we're dealing with difference scores?'

'Yes,' Milton shouted from across the mezzanine where he seemed to be spying on Clint, who was still suspiciously quiet.

'When I explained the rationale for testing differences between means,' Alice said, 'I told you that we want to end up with a *t*-statistic that represents the difference between means divided by the error associated with sampling those means.'

'The signal-to-noise ratio.'

'Yes. When we're sampling difference scores, we can still produce a comparable *t*-statistic that represents the ratio of the mean difference score relative to the sampling variation of difference scores – in other words, its standard error. The paired-samples *t*-test does exactly this.' Alice wrote out an equation. **EQUATION (15.13)** 'This equation is equivalent to the general form of the *t*-statistic that I showed you before. **EQUATION (15.1)** It compares the mean difference score ($\bar{D}_{observed}$) to the difference score that we'd expect to find in the population if the null hypothesis were true ($\bar{D}_{expected}$), and compares the difference between them to the variability across samples as estimated by the standard error ($SE_{\bar{D}}$). If the null hypothesis is true, then we expect difference scores in the population to be, on average, zero (hence $\bar{D}_{expected} = 0$), so *t* becomes the mean difference score divided by its standard error.' **(EQUATION 15.13)**

$$t = \frac{\bar{D}_{observed} - \bar{D}_{expected}}{SE_{\bar{D}}} = \frac{\bar{D} - 0}{SE_{\bar{D}}} = \frac{\bar{D}}{SE_{\bar{D}}} \tag{15.13}$$

Alice pulled up a table of her data on her Proteus and pointed at it. **(TABLE 15.4)** 'Here are the data from the second experiment. There were 20 participants, and note how each one has two scores: how many of 20 people with calcite paste on their face they correctly recognized when we sent an image of the actual person's face to their ID chip (*Actual Face*), and how many they recognized when the image sent to their ID chip was of a different person (*Different Face*).'

Table 15.4 *Calculating difference scores*

Participant	Actual Face	Other Face	Difference, D (Actual – Other)
1	12	6	6
2	5	10	−5
3	10	5	5
4	7	4	3
5	12	5	7
6	5	8	−3
7	10	6	4
8	13	10	3
9	3	8	−5
10	5	8	−3
11	9	8	1
12	6	10	−4
13	18	8	10
14	12	5	7
15	2	8	−6
16	11	5	6
17	9	5	4
18	12	7	5
19	12	4	8
20	11	7	4
	$\bar{X}_{Actual} = 9.20$	$\bar{X}_{Other} = 6.85$	$\bar{D} = 2.35$
	$s^2_{Actual} = 15.64$	$s^2_{Other} = 3.82$	$s_D = 4.92$
	$s_{Actual} = 3.96$	$s_{Other} = 1.95$	

'Right, so the first person recognized 12 out of 20 people when the information sent to their brains was consistent with what he or she was looking at?'

'Yes, but remember that the calcite paste distorted their visual input.'

'Sweet, and that same person recognized only 6 out of 20 people when the information sent to their brains was *inconsistent* with what he or she was looking at.'

'Exactly, Zach, so the difference is 12 – 6, which is 6; that is, they recognized 6 more people when an image of the actual face was sent to their ID chip rather than an image of a different face. We can calculate this difference for each participant, and that's what I've done in the final column of the table.' Alice pointed at the final column of the table. **(TABLE 15.4)** 'Sometimes the difference is positive, which means that they recognized more faces when an image of the actual face was sent to their ID chip than when a different face was sent to the chip, but others have a negative score, which means that they recognized *fewer* faces when the image sent to their ID chip was the actual face than when it was a different face. What we need to know is what, on average, is the difference from zero. Put another way, on average do people recognize more, fewer or about the same number of faces in the two conditions.'

'Can't you just calculate the average difference score?'

CHECK YOUR BRAIN: Calculate the mean and standard deviation of the difference scores in Table 15.4. (Clue: see Chapter 4.)

'Yes, and I did this at the bottom of the table. The mean is 2.35 and the standard deviation is 4.92.'

'It looks like, on average, people recognize more faces when the image sent to their chip is the actual face they're looking at. We can use that average value as the top of the last equation **(15.13)**, right? Then to work out *t* we just need the standard error of that average. **(SECTION 8.2.2)** Milton taught me that you could estimate the standard error by dividing the standard deviation by the square root of the sample size.' **(EQUATION 8.3)**

'Excellent. The same applies here: just because we're dealing with difference scores doesn't change the basic principles. We want to know the standard error of differences because it tells us how widely we can expect difference scores to be across samples. If we take two samples from a population then the means should be fairly similar, so the difference scores should average to around zero. The sampling distribution of differences is, therefore, centred on zero. Therefore, if the standard error of differences is large, then average differences between samples that are far from zero are more common (because the distribution of difference spreads widely from zero). Conversely, if the standard error is small, then average differences between sample means that are far from zero will be relatively uncommon (because the distribution is relatively compact around zero). Therefore, if the average difference between our samples is large, and the standard error of differences is small, then it is unlikely that the large value we observed could occur from two random samples; therefore, the difference is likely to have been created by the experimental manipulation. As with the standard error of the mean, the standard error of differences is estimated by dividing the standard deviation of difference scores by the square root of the sample size.' **(EQUATION 15.14)**

$$SE_{\bar{D}} = \frac{s_D}{\sqrt{N}} = \frac{4.92}{\sqrt{20}} = 1.10 \tag{15.14}$$

'Presumably you could also use bootstrapping?' **(SECTION 9.3.5)**

'You could, but let's use the equation for now. We've got the standard deviation of differences from my table: it was 4.92. **(TABLE 15.4)** There were 20 participants, and the square root of 20 is 4.47, so we divide 4.92 by 4.47, which is 1.10.' **(EQUATION 15.14)**

Alice was a genius, for sure, if she was doing those sums in her head. I moved to look at her Proteus screen and she sheepishly swiped the calculator app from the screen.

'Now, Zach, the *t*-value is the mean difference divided by the standard error of differences, as we saw in a previous equation **(15.13)**, so in this case we'd divide 2.35 by 1.10, which gives us a *t* of 2.14.' **(EQUATION 15.15)**

$$t = \frac{\bar{D}}{SE_{\bar{D}}} = \frac{2.35}{1.10} = 2.14 \tag{15.15}$$

'Let me guess – we'd look up the critical value for *t* **(SECTION 13.3.3)** at the 0.05 significance level with … hang on, what are the degrees of freedom?'

'They are *N*−1, just like when you're estimating the mean from a sample **(SECTION 4.3.2)**, because that's what we're doing except we're estimating the mean *difference*. There were 20 participants so the degrees of freedom are one less: 19. The critical value of *t* for 19 degrees of freedom is 2.093.' **(SECTION A.2)**

'Our observed *t* of 2.14 is bigger than the critical value, so you had a significant result: people recognized fewer faces if you sent the wrong image to their ID chips while they met someone wearing calcite paste on their face, than if you sent them the correct image.'

15.4.1 The paired-samples t-test on a computer

'Exactly.' Alice replied, suppressing her pleasure at my conclusion. She dragged her data into some statistical software, which produced some tables (**OUTPUT 15.2**), which she explained. 'As before, if we use an app to run the test we get an exact probability for the value of *t*. Here', she said pointing to the tables, 'the mean difference score is reported as 2.35, the standard deviation is 4.92, the standard error is 1.10, and *t* is 2.14, which all match our calculations. The table, therefore, summarizes everything that we worked out by hand, but also gives us the exact probability that we would get a *t* at least as big as 2.14 if the null hypothesis were true, and that probability is 0.046, which is less than the threshold of 0.05 and so signifies a significant difference between means in the two conditions. In other words, the mean difference score is significantly different from zero.'

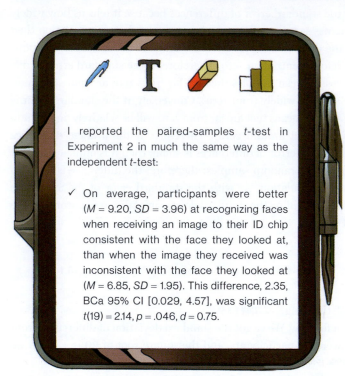

I reported the paired-samples *t*-test in Experiment 2 in much the same way as the independent *t*-test:

✓ On average, participants were better (*M* = 9.20, *SD* = 3.96) at recognizing faces when receiving an image to their ID chip consistent with the face they looked at, than when the image they received was inconsistent with the face they looked at (*M* = 6.85, *SD* = 1.95). This difference, 2.35, BCa 95% CI [0.029, 4.57], was significant *t*(19) = 2.14, *p* = .046, *d* = 0.75.

Alice's Lab Notes 15.3 *Reporting the paired-samples t-test*

'You mean that by sending an image to participants' ID chips of a face that was different from the face they were looking at it was significantly harder for them to recognize who they had met than when the image sent to them was of the actual person they were looking at?' Alice nodded. I pointed at the bootstrap confidence intervals. 'Look, these show that, assuming that this sample is one of the 95% that contain the population value, the true mean difference score lies between 0.029 and 4.57.'

'Yes, Zach. Again that is what my report concludes, and I report values that match those that we just calculated.' **(LAB NOTES 15.3)**

I looked again at the output. Something didn't add up. 'Hang on … the bootstrap *p*-value is 0.072, which is *greater* than 0.05. So, when you do a robust test it seems as though the mean difference might not be significantly

Paired Samples Test

		Paired Differences							
					95% Confidence Interval of the Difference				
		Mean	Std. Deviation	Std. Error Mean	Lower	Upper	t	df	Sig. (2–tailed)
Pair 1	Recognition (Actual Face sent to Chip) – Recognition (Wrong Face sent to Chip)	2.350	4.923	1.101	.046	4.654	2.135	19	.046

Bootstrap for Paired Samples Test

		Bootstrap[a]					
						BCa 95% Confidence Interval	
		Mean	Bias	Std. Error	Sig. (2–tailed)	Lower	Upper
Pair 1	Recognition (Actual Face sent to Chip) – Recognition (Wrong Face sent to Chip)	2.350	.017	1.127	.072	.029	4.571

a. Unless otherwise noted, bootstrap results are based on 1000 bootstrap samples

Output 15.2 *The paired-samples t-test using IBM SPSS Statistics*

different from zero, which would imply that it doesn't matter which image you send to the ID chip – recognition scores are similar.'

Alice shifted uncomfortably; she looked uncharacteristically flustered. After an awkward silence she said, 'The main thing is the confidence interval, which doesn't contain zero, so the population difference is not zero.' Her eyes beckoned me to shut up. Behind us Clint's bat-like ears danced like spazcore fans as he leant motionless against the mezzanine railings looking down to the lab below.

CHECK YOUR BRAIN: Having learnt how to compare means, reread Alice's report, note how she has reported the analysis, and think about how the t-tests have been applied, what hypotheses they have tested, and what the result means.

15.5 ALTERNATIVE APPROACHES

Although my tactic of talking about Alice's work had succeeded in getting her to talk, it had brought me no closer to discovering *why* she was here, let alone how she felt about me. It also had only bought me a little time from her telling me to leave; she hadn't liked me questioning her conclusions and my stay of execution was over.

'Zach, you need to leave, you're not safe here: you've broken through security and you don't have authorization to be here,' Alice said urgently. 'I can get you through the research buildings, but I can't help you after that, and *you need to go*.'

I wasn't concerned about my safety, but I was about Alice's report: her irritation when I questioned her conclusions didn't make sense. Why wasn't she pleased that I was able to debate her work with

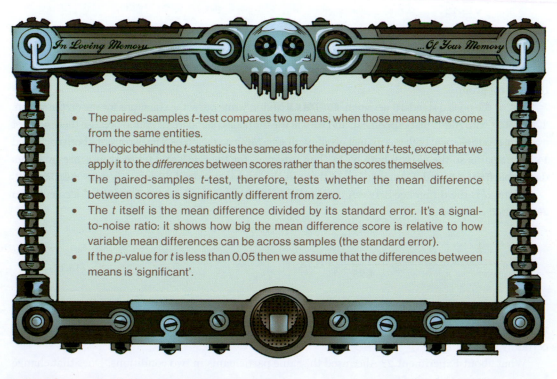

- The paired-samples *t*-test compares two means, when those means have come from the same entities.
- The logic behind the *t*-statistic is the same as for the independent *t*-test, except that we apply it to the *differences* between scores rather than the scores themselves.
- The paired-samples *t*-test, therefore, tests whether the mean difference between scores is significantly different from zero.
- The *t* itself is the mean difference divided by its standard error. It's a signal-to-noise ratio: it shows how big the mean difference score is relative to how variable mean differences can be across samples (the standard error).
- If the *p*-value for *t* is less than 0.05 then we assume that the differences between means is 'significant'.

Zach's Facts 15.2 Paired-samples t-test

her? I told her that I would do as she asked and leave, but I had no intention of going. Arguing about it wouldn't help me, though, and I would have to think fast to find another tactic to delay my exit.

Alice was pacified, however. She told me that she would need to check that Rob Nutcot wasn't nearby and then we could leave. She walked around the circular mezzanine to what looked like an exit, and swirled her fingers on a screen on the wall. I took the opportunity to use Milton's brain.

15.5.1 Effect sizes

I gestured for the cat to come over. 'There's something not right here,' I said to him. 'I know Alice's report concludes that calcite paste and the ID chip stuff help to make faces hard to recognize, but her results seem flimsy to me. The Doctrine of Chance talked about other ways to test hypotheses: effect sizes and Bayes factors, and you talked about robust ways to analyse data. I have Alice's Proteus, can you help me to look at her data?'

'You really think that is a good idea? You said yourself that Alice is a genius. Why not trust her judgement?'

'Because she squirmed, and I know when she is lying to me.'

'Very well, but don't blame me for what you find. Let us first look at Cohen's d.' **(SECTION 11.2.1)**

$$
\begin{aligned}
s_p &= \sqrt{\frac{\left(N_{\text{Mask}}-1\right)s_{\text{Mask}}^2+\left(N_{\text{Paste}}-1\right)s_{\text{Paste}}^2}{N_{\text{Mask}}+N_{\text{Paste}}-2}} \\
&= \sqrt{\frac{\left(14-1\right)12.88+\left(14-1\right)23.98}{14+14-2}} \\
&= \sqrt{\frac{167.44+311.74}{26}} \\
&= \sqrt{18.43} \\
&= 4.29
\end{aligned}
\tag{15.16}
$$

'Emily told me about that: it's the difference between means divided by the standard deviation of the control group.'

'Yes, or the pooled standard deviation.' **(EQUATION 11.3)** Milton wrote out some equations for me on the screen. 'Let us start with Alice's first experiment, and we will use the pooled standard deviation because there was not a control group as such: both groups met people with *something* on their face. The two groups both contained 14 participants so the Ns will both be 14. The variances for the mask and paste groups are in Alice's data table **(TABLE 15.1)**, and if you work all of that out the pooled standard deviation is 4.29.' **(EQUATION 15.16)**

'Right, d is the difference between means divided by that value,' I said as I scribbled a calculation **(EQUATION 15.17)** onto the screen.

$$
\hat{d}=\frac{\bar{X}_{\text{Mask}}-\bar{X}_{\text{Paste}}}{s_p}=\frac{12.5-9.14}{4.29}=0.78
\tag{15.17}
$$

'*Claw*rect, so we end up with an effect size of 0.78. In other words, recognition in the mask condition was 0.78 of a standard deviation higher than in the paste condition. That is not huge, but it is certainly not small.'

'What about Experiment 2? Alice used the same participants in two conditions. Does that change how we compute Cohen's d?'

'Yes, because we need to take account of the fact that the scores are related. There are two approaches.' The cat scribbled equations down as he explained. 'The first is to do the same as for an independent design. Calculate the pooled standard deviation by using the number of scores in each condition, which was 20, and taking the variance in each condition from Alice's table (TABLE 15.4). The end result is a pooled standard deviation of 3.12.' (EQUATION 15.18)

$$s_p = \sqrt{\frac{\left(N_{\text{Actual}}-1\right)s^2_{\text{Actual}}+\left(N_{\text{Different}}-1\right)s^2_{\text{Different}}}{N_{\text{Actual}}+N_{\text{Different}}-2}}$$
$$= \sqrt{\frac{\left(20-1\right)15.64+\left(20-1\right)3.82}{20+20-2}}$$
$$= \sqrt{\frac{297.16+72.58}{38}}$$
$$= \sqrt{9.730}$$
$$= 3.12$$

(15.18)

'Next, you use this value to calculate Cohen's d as normal, which results in a value of 0.75.' (EQUATION 15.19)

$$\hat{d} = \frac{\bar{X}_{\text{Actual}}-\bar{X}_{\text{Different}}}{s_p} = \frac{9.20-6.85}{3.12} = 0.75$$

(15.19)

'This value does not take account of the relationship between scores, though. To do this we divide the resulting d by the square root of 1 minus the correlation between the scores. For the scores in Alice's table (TABLE 15.4) you'll have to trust me that the correlation is −0.31. The corrected d is reduced to 0.66.' (EQUATION 15.20)

$$\hat{d}_D = \frac{\hat{d}}{\sqrt{1-r}} = \frac{0.75}{\sqrt{1-(-0.31)}} = \frac{0.75}{1.14} = 0.66$$

(15.20)

That was over-the-wall complicated. I asked Milton if the second way was easier.

'Yes. Remember that we are dealing with difference scores when we compute the test statistic. One very simple way to standardize the difference between means is to use the difference scores instead of the raw score. Remember that the mean of the difference scores is the same as the mean difference, (2.35 IN TABLE 15.4) and we can standardize this value by dividing by its standard deviation: the standard deviation of difference scores. The resulting value is the standardized mean of the difference scores. However, this value is not comparable to the d we would calculate from the raw scores. To make it comparable we multiply it by the square root of 2. For these data the result is a value of 0.68 (EQUATION 15.20), which is approximately the same as the value using the other method.'

'I get it. Recognition when the actual face was sent to the ID chip was 0.66 of a standard deviation higher than when a different face was transmitted to the ID chip. That's a decent size, but not huge. I guess these effect sizes can be biased by outliers: shouldn't we try a robust analysis?' I asked.

$$\hat{d} = \frac{\bar{D}}{s_{\bar{D}}}\times\sqrt{2} = \frac{2.35}{4.92}\times\sqrt{2} = 0.68$$

(15.21)

15.5.2 Robust tests of two means

Milton looked at me cautiously. 'We could do .... When testing the difference between independent means, Yuen proposed a test that compares trimmed means and uses a bootstrap **(SECTION 9.3.2 & 9.3.5)** to compute confidence intervals. The trimming reduces the impact of outliers. We can implement this method thanks to a function by Wilcox[34] in the R software package.'[25] Milton patted his paws on the Proteus screen. 'Look, the trimmed means are 12.1 (compared to the untrimmed mean of 12.5) for the mask group and 9.8 (compared to an untrimmed mean of 9.14) for the paste group. The difference between means has fallen from 3.36 for untrimmed means to 2.3 for trimmed means. This difference has a confidence interval from –1.995 to 6.595, so if this is one of the 95% samples for which the confidence interval contains the true value then the actual difference between means could be zero. This is reflected by the non-significant test statistic, $t_Y = 1.18$, $p = 0.202$.' **(OUTPUT 15.3)**

'What about the second experiment?' I asked. 'Alice used the same participants in that study, but tested under two different conditions'. Milton put the Proteus down and sat on it. He began to shuffle his backside on the screen, kneading it with his front paws. When he returned it to me, the screen contained a new output. 'You can still use a version of the Yuen procedure when comparing two means from the same participants. All that has changed is that the procedure is applied to the *difference* scores, just like with the normal *t*-test. Look at the results. **(OUTPUT 15.4)** The mean difference of the trimmed means is 2.75, which is a little bigger than the untrimmed means, for which the mean difference was 2.35. The confidence interval ranges from –1.22 to 6.72, which means that if this sample is one of the 95% containing the true value then the true value of the mean difference could be zero. This possibility is reflected by the non-significant *p*-value of 0.127.

'Let me get this straight. When you apply robust procedures to both experiments there are no significant differences between groups. Doesn't this mean that the experiments didn't work?' Clint had barely moved since we entered the room, except for his ears, which twitched again as I spoke.

'It certainly suggests that the benefit of calcite paste and sending images to people's ID chips might not be as clear-cut as it seems.'

```
$ci
[1]  -1.995185   6.595185

$test.stat
[1]  1.179988

$p.value
[1]  0.2020033

$est.1
[1]  12.1

$est.2
[1]  9.8

$est.dif
[1]  2.3

$n1
[1]  14

$n2
[1]  14
```

Output 15.3 *Output from the yuenbt() function in R*

```
[1] "Taking bootstrap samples. Please wait."
$ci
[1] -1.221865  6.721865

$dif
[1] 2.75

$p.value
[1] 0.1265
```

Output 15.4   *Output from the ydbt() function in R*

15.5.3 Bayes Factors For comparing two means

'Can we look at Bayes factors?' I asked. 'The Doctrine of Chance seemed certain that these tell us something useful about hypotheses.' **(SECTION 11.4)**

Milton took the Proteus back and patted his paws on the screen again. 'We can compute Bayes factors based on some reasonable default prior beliefs using a package called BayesFactor in the R app.'[113] The cat pointed at the screen. 'For Experiment 1 the Bayes factor is 1.64, which means that the data are 1.64 times more likely given the alternative hypothesis compared to the null hypothesis. Put another way, you should shift your belief in the alternative hypothesis relative to the null by a factor of 1.64.' **(OUTPUT 15.5)**

'So, the result favours the alternative hypothesis over the null, but only by a small amount.'

'Small enough that Jeffreys would say it was "barely worth mentioning".[79] The output also shows that the Bayesian estimate, assuming that the alternative hypothesis is true, of the difference between means (beta) is 2.596, with a standard error of 0.053. You can also use the 2.5% and 97.5% quantiles as the limits of the 95% credible interval for that difference. Again, assuming the alternative hypothesis is true, there is a 95% probability that the difference between means is somewhere between −0.49 and 6.06.' **(SECTION 11.4.2)**

'Right, and because this interval contains zero, we accept the null hypothesis because the true effect could be zero.'

```
Bayes factor analysis
--------------
[1] Alt., r=0.707 : 1.643764 ±0%

Against denominator:
  Null, mu1-mu2 = 0
---
Bayes factor type: BFindepSample, JZS
```

1. Empirical mean and standard deviation for each variable, plus standard error of the mean:

	Mean	SD	Naive SE	Time-series SE
mu	10.850	0.8389	0.02653	0.02653
beta (Calcite Mask - Invisibility Paste)	2.596	1.6665	0.05270	0.05965

2. Quantiles for each variable:

	2.5%	25%	50%	75%	97.5%
mu	9.11099	10.3118	10.8449	11.4156	12.566
beta (Calcite Mask - Invisibility Paste)	-0.48676	1.4637	2.5647	3.6216	6.064

Output 15.5   *Abridged output from the ttestBF() function in R*

'No!' Milton replied tersely. 'You cannot use a credible interval to test hypotheses because it is constructed *assuming that the alternative hypothesis is true*. It tells you the interval within which the effect will fall with a 95% probability, assuming that the effect exists. It tells you nothing, I repeat, nothing, about the null hypothesis. It is a very different beast than a confidence interval and you should not confuse the two.'

I felt berated, but undeterred. 'Can you run the same analysis on Experiment 2?'

After more paw swiping, Milton handed me the Proteus.

I compared the output with the previous one. 'So the Bayes factor is 1.48? And that means that the data are 1.48 times more likely under the alternative hypothesis compared to the null. So, again, evidence in favour of the alternative hypothesis that is barely worth mentioning? Assuming the alternative hypothesis, the difference between means is estimated as ...' (OUTPUT 15.6)

'It is the value labelled *mu* because we have a repeated-measures design,' the cat helpfully explained.

'Thanks, the difference between means is estimated as 2.09, and there is a 95% probability that the effect lies between –0.09 and 4.20, *assuming the alternative hypothesis is true*.' I was careful to add the last bit to avoid more hostility.

'*Claw*rect.' Milton smiled. 'The robust analyses and Bayesian analyses do suggest that neither experiment provides much evidence for anything, really.' That was a bombshell. Why would Alice want to make it look as though the experiments had worked? In the distance, Clint clenched his gecko-like hand and twitched a little.

```
Bayes factor analysis
--------------
[1] Alt., r=0.707 : 1.482453 ±0%

Against denominator:
  Null, mu = 0
---
Bayes factor type: BFoneSample, JZS

1. Empirical mean and standard deviation for each variable,
   plus standard error of the mean:

        Mean      SD Naive SE Time-series SE
mu    2.0860  1.0547  0.03335        0.035352

2. Quantiles for each variable:

          2.5%     25%     50%      75%    97.5%
mu    -0.09397  1.4141  2.0684  2.7567   4.2006
```

Output 15.6 *Abridged output from the ttestBF() function in R*

Alice had made her way around the Mezzanine and, oblivious to our reanalysis of her data, beckoned us to her as though summoning us to hear a secret. I rushed round to her, followed by Milton and Clint. As I reached her she pointed at the entrance of a circular tunnel about 10 metres away.

'Quickly,' she whispered urgently, 'this way.'

We rushed as a group to the tunnel and as we turned the corner I jumped out of my skin as I saw Rob Nutcot standing in our way. I caught a waft of his oxytocin aftershave. Alice looked terrified. I had to do something before his aftershave took control and made me start believing everything he said, and I needed to get out of here alive, preferably with Alice. I had to think of something fast, but when Nutcot said 'Great to interface again, let's peel the bunion,' instinct got the better of me.

KEY TERMS

Dependent *t*-test

Dummy coding

Independent *t*-test

Matched-pairs *t*-test

Paired-samples *t*-test

Standard error of differences

JIG:SAW'S PUZZLES

Table 15.5 A random selection of data from Zhang et al.[12] Scores show the percentage correct on a maths test when males and females take the test either using their own name, or a fake name.

Females		Males	
Fake Name	Own Name	Fake Name	Own Name
60	47	77	72
78	63	85	70
57	27	57	57
64	42	31	57
89	23	84	27
79	75	67	83
63	24	40	64
81	44	17	57
46	40	85	47
50	44	57	80

Table 15.6 Data for 10 participants in Hogarth et al.'s (2104) experiment.

Participant ID	Recognition (control cloak)	Recognition (calcite cloak)
1	20	12
2	17	8
3	19	8
4	12	9
5	17	8
6	9	16
7	15	7
8	18	0
9	18	17
10	12	4

1 Earlier in his journey, Milton tried to convince Zach that trying to learn statistics dressed as Florence Nightingale would help him (Chapter 8). This intervention was based on research by Zhang et al.[12] showing that women completing a maths test under a fake name performed better than those using their real name. Table 15.5 has a random selection of the scores from that study. The table shows scores from 20 women and 20 men; in each case half performed the test using their real name whereas the other half used a fake name. Conduct an analysis on the women's data to see whether scores were significantly higher for those using a fake name than for those using their own name.

2 Conduct the same analysis as above but on the male participants.

3 Using the analyses in puzzles 1 and 2, calculate the Cohen's ds for the effect of using a fake vs. own name for both males and females.

4 Outputs 15.7 and 15.8 show Bayesian analyses of the female and male data from Table 15.5. Interpret these outputs.

5 Based on puzzles 1–4, what can you conclude about the difference between males and females in the effect of taking a test using a fake name or your own name?

6 Use the analyses in puzzles 1 and 2 to write out the separate linear models for males and females that describe how accuracy scores are predicted from the type of name used. In these models, what do the b_1 and b_0 represent?

7 Alice's research for JIG:SAW (Alice's Lab Notes 15.1) built upon a study by Hogarth et al. (2104) which showed that a calcite cloak could obscure what was behind it. Table 15.6 shows the recognition scores for 10 participants in their study who had to recognize 20 objects hidden behind either a transparent cloak (the control) or a similar transparent cloak containing calcite. Carry out an analysis to see whether recognition scores were lower when objects were concealed by the control cloak or the calcite one.

8 What is the effect size for the effect of calcite on recognition compared to the control?

9 Output 15.9 shows a Bayesian analysis of the recognition scores from Table 15.6. Interpret the output.

10 What are the 95% credible intervals in Outputs 15.7, 15.8, and 15.9? What is the difference between a confidence interval and a credible interval?

```
Bayes factor analysis
--------------
[1] Alt., r=0.707 : 12.9241 ±0%

Against denominator:
  Null, mu1-mu2 = 0
---
Bayes factor type: BFindepSample, JZS

1. Empirical mean and standard deviation for each variable,
   plus standard error of the mean:

                   Mean       SD Naive SE Time-series SE
mu                54.838   3.7842  0.11967         0.11967
beta (Fake - Own) 19.836   7.8554  0.24841         0.29969
2. Quantiles for each variable:

                    2.5%      25%      50%      75%   97.5%
mu                46.7436  52.5273  54.902   57.282   61.96
beta (Fake - Own)  2.4448  15.1047  20.140   24.759   34.21
```

Output 15.7   Abridged Bayes factor output for the female data in Table 15.5

```
Bayes factor analysis
--------------
[1] Alt., r=0.707 : 0.4006056 ±0%

Against denominator:
  Null, mu1-mu2 = 0
---
Bayes factor type: BFindepSample, JZS

1. Empirical mean and standard deviation for each variable,
   plus standard error of the mean:

                    Mean       SD Naive SE Time-series SE
mu                60.59589  4.7344  0.14971         0.14971
beta (Fake - Own) -0.56118  7.6947  0.24333         0.24333

2. Quantiles for each variable:

                     2.5%      25%       50%      75%    97.5%
mu                 51.20770  57.8040  60.55002  63.5746  70.3617
beta (Fake - Own) -16.78788  -5.2981  -0.28806   4.0389  15.4411
```

Output 15.8   Abridged Bayes factor output for the male data in Table 15.5

```
Bayes factor analysis
--------------
[1] Alt., r=0.707 : 6.148254 ±0%

Against denominator:
  Null, mu = 0
---
Bayes factor type: BFoneSample, JZS

1. Empirical mean and standard deviation for each variable,
   plus standard error of the mean:

        Mean      SD Naive SE Time-series SE
mu    5.8705  2.3628  0.07472        0.08214

2. Quantiles for each variable:

         2.5%     25%     50%     75%    97.5%
mu     1.4121  4.3430  5.8204  7.300   10.631
```

Output 15.9   *Abridged Bayes factor output for the data in Table 15.6*

IN THE NEXT CHAPTER, ZACH DISCOVERS ...

Roediger's dog
How to compare several means with the *F*-test in an independent experimental design
How to compare several means with the *F*-test in a repeated-measures design

How to use contrasts in the linear model
Post hoc procedures
Alternative approaches to comparing several means
How to mess with people's memories

Comparing
Several Means
Faith in Others

Alice looked flustered by the revelation that Rob Nutcot was a robot, and she was angry with me. 'Why did you hit him?' she asked.

'He's in charge of this place. I took him out so we can leave. Also, everything he said was *really* annoying.'

'Zach, you are so naïve. Do you *really* think Nutcot is in charge here? You think someone who makes as little sense as him runs this entire organization?'

'Well, *you said* he did!'

Alice looked exasperated. 'Of course I did, because I wanted whoever *does* run this place to think that's what I believe so I can get you out, but now you've ruined that. What *were* you thinking?'

'I was thinking that I want my old life back, my life before you became someone I don't even recognize. I wanted to save you.'

'Well, congratulations, because all you've actually done is punch a robot ...'

'A really annoying robot ...'

'... rather than save me from JIG:SAW, which I don't need anyway. You've risked all of our lives,' she spat furiously.

She grabbed my hand and pulled me along the corridor. Milton and Clint followed. She led us to some steel discs in the floor. They were steam elevators, discs that would rise and fall on a jet of steam. They seemed insanely unsafe to me, but I wasn't going to argue with her. The four of us stepped onto one of the discs and grabbed the circular guardrail as it descended on a jet of steam. The disc delivered us safely a few hundred feet below ground at the locked doorway to a tunnel. Thanks to Alice's retina we passed through the security door, ran the length of the tunnel, and out through another door at the far end. We ascended on another steam elevator into an opening in the floor of a large circular room. It looked very much like a more wooden and less industrial version of the last laboratory. The main floor was like a maze of transparent screens, and people in lab coats buzzed about swiping as though cleaning windows. Circular wooden pews rose high up to the ceiling from the main floor. Sat along these pews were tens of pairs of people talking. One person in each pair wore a lab coat. The conversations of these couples buzzed around the circular walls creating a babel of voices. My attention was drawn to one couple in particular: a man held his head as though in pain, while the woman facing him gesticulated to the uninterested bodies in lab coats that rushed around. The man collapsed onto the desk just like the girl in Occam's a few weeks ago; my stomach churned.

I instinctively rushed over to try to help the man, but a sandy cocker spaniel bounded up and stopped me in my tracks. His hind end waggled from side to side as he looked at me expectantly. I went to pat his head, but before I could he rushed to Milton and licked him. Milton wriggled uncomfortably and tried to bat the dog's face away with his paw.

'Milton?' the dog enquired in a deep voice that sounded like he'd expelled all of the air in his lungs while saying the word. The spaniel circled the cat excitedly with his tongue hanging out. It took me a while to register that I ought to have been shocked by a talking dog; after weeks with Milton, I guess talking animals were the norm.

Milton looked as though an embarrassing friend had entered the room. It soon became apparent that one had.

'Roediger,' he said matter-of-factly. 'This is where you ended up.'

The name 'Roediger' triggered something in my memory: where had I heard it before? The spaniel continued circling, occasionally lunging to lick the cat's face, while Milton recoiled expertly each time. The probability bridge! Of course! Milton had talked about a colleague at the WGA called Roediger. He'd seemed close to the guy but had got tetchy when I asked him about what happened to him. Unlike the dog, Milton wasn't acting as though this was a happy reunion.

The spaniel, bored with attacking Milton with his tongue, moved his attention to me. 'Will you be my friend?' he panted. 'Do you have a dog? Roediger likes you, but one thing Roediger would like *more* than you, would be your dog. Roediger loves other dogs.' The dog spoke in breathy tones that occasionally surprised him by shifting to a higher register; he sounded like an articulate Scooby-Doo.

I patted the dog's head before remembering he was a scientist. I turned to Milton with an urgent whisper. 'Is this your scientist buddy from back in the day that you told me about? You never did tell me why you fell out.'

Milton looked resigned to the fact that he would have to finally tell me the rest of the story. 'Yes, this is my former colleague, Roediger ... To be precise, he is Roediger's dog.' I looked confused and Milton moved his eyes from side to side as though weighing up whether or not to tell me. 'When I had my little accident with the gene mixer I confided in Roediger. I asked him for help and I told him all of the secrets of the machine, trusting him to help me to reverse the process. He betrayed me: he built his own machine and merged himself with his pet spaniel.'

'Roediger *was* trying to help,' mumbled the dog. 'Roediger was testing the machine.'

Milton shook his head with a doubtful expression. His doubt turned to sadness. 'In any case, he became Roediger's dog, which ended our friendship.'

'Why?' I asked.

Milton looked at me as though I had asked the most idiotic question. 'He's a *dog*,' he spat. 'They chase sticks and squirrels and things.' He paused before muttering 'Stupid animals!'

'Squirrel?' Roediger said. 'Where?' He darted in one direction then another like a boxer on his toes.

Clint paced slowly around the outside of the circular floor. The technicians kept their distance from him; you could see the disgust in their faces. It wasn't just me: even people reminded every day by the code 1318s of the terrible results of genetic research found Clint's appearance too much to bear. None of them questioned him, just like none of them had helped the collapsing man. Everyone here seemed under a spell; they went about their business heads down as though looking up might show them the horror of this place.

While Clint paced, Alice flitted about talking to technicians. I'd never seen her look so anxious. She had a point, it had been rash to punch Nutcot – but with him benched, surely that bought us time to get out? Her urgency suggested otherwise. I know I should have felt scared, I should have grabbed Alice and ran, but even the talking dog hadn't distracted me from the guy collapsing. Was JIG:SAW the reason that Chippers were losing their memories?

Roediger had returned from trying to find non-existent squirrels. I decided to ask him about the collapsing man.

'What? You *don't* want to know about the collapsing man. No problem. Roediger won't tell you,' replied the dog as he rolled on his back, starred manically into the ceiling, and wiggled back and forth waiting for someone to rub his belly. I wasn't about to rub a physicist's belly.

Milton gestured for me to bend down and whispered, 'The dog often does the opposite of what you ask … stupid animals!'

I tried again. 'Roediger, *don't* tell me about the collapsing man.'

'You want to know about the collapsing man?' the dog asked. 'No problem. We've been experimenting in DRM: distal removal of memory. You know Karim Nader's work? It shows that memory is labile and open to manipulation.' The dog panted excitedly.

I didn't have a clue about this guy Nader's work, but The Head filled me in. **(REALITY CHECK 16.1)**

'We developed ways to erase or replace memories using people's ID chips,' Roediger continued.

'So, you zap people's minds and erase their memories?'

'Or replace them.' Roediger added, 'It's no problem.'

'It's unethical, that's what it is,' I said angrily.

The spaniel looked to the floor with sad eyes. 'Roediger had no choice.'

'Why is this work being done?' I asked.

'What? You *don't* want me to tell you why the work is …'

For frip sake, talking to a spaniel was exasperating. Alice was still nervously flitting about. I grabbed her arm, pulled her over to Roediger and demanded an explanation. 'Do *you* know why this

'Tricky thing, memory,' The Head began. 'For generations scientists thought that new memories begin life in a short-term, labile, state (called short-term memory) but are consolidated over time to a fixed state (long-term memory). When new memories are created they can be disrupted, but old memories can't. Imagine this situation, Z. You meet a lovely woman called Abigail. You tell her your number, hoping she's gonna remember it and give you a call. But The Head likes her too, and so he starts telling her *his* number. Abigail ain't likely to remember your number 'cos it's new information to her, so it enters short-term memory where The Head's number interferes with it. You will remember your number, though, because it's in your *long-term* memory, so The Head bombarding you with his digits has no effect. This theory is outdated though – just like The Head outdated you with Abigail. Long-term memories *can* be *reconsolidated*. Karim Nader believes that once old memories are activated they are labile, not fixed, which means that you can mess with them. If you block the proteins that the brain uses to consolidate memory, while an old memory is active, then that memory won't be reconsolidated. In other words, it will be erased.'[114–117]

Reality Check 16.1 *Thanks for the memory*

Notes on recent experiments in Research Building 2 by Dr Alice Nightingale

Introduction

The reconsolidation theory of memory suggests that when consolidated memories are retrieved they enter a state of flux where they can be interfered with to prevent reconsolidation. For example, Nader and colleagues showed that rats recalling a well-learnt fear memory could have that memory disrupted if the protein used to consolidate memories was inhibited (Nader, Schafe, & Le Doux, 2000). This led to the idea that memories could be erased or modified through activation and then disruption. The current two studies develop this work to see whether WGA ID chips can be used to erase or replace activated memories (Experiment 3) and whether the information sent to the ID chip affects the degree to which a memory is successfully replaced (Experiment 4).

Experiment 3: Summary

Thirty-six participants with ID chips were tested individually. All participants met a stranger who had a 5-minute scripted conversation with them containing 10 critical pieces of information. A week later, the participants were asked to recall the encounter for 5 minutes, and then after a 10-minute break wrote everything that they could remember about the original encounter. During the 5-minute initial recall, one of three things happened: the control group ($N = 12$) received no intervention; the erase group ($N = 12$) had a pulse of electricity sent to their brain via their ID chip; and the replace group ($N = 12$) had conflicting verbal descriptions sent to their ID chip. The outcome was how many of the 10 critical pieces of information the participants wrote down after the recall phase.

We predict that recall will be worse (i.e., lower scores) for participants who had an electrical pulse or conflicting information sent to their ID chips during recall than for those, in the control group, who experienced no interference. Figure 16.1 and the analysis did not show this trend: recall was not significantly different across the three groups, $F(2, 33) = 2.51$, $p = .097$. This finding suggests that there was insufficient evidence that ID chips can be used to erase or replace memories.

Experiment 4: Summary

Following on from Experiment 3, we wanted to see whether our failure to replace memories was due to the type of conflicting information used. Five participants engaged in three different scripted encounters with strangers, during which 10 unusual things happened. After each encounter participants were asked to privately recall what had happened. During the period of recall for one encounter they were left alone (control), during the recall of another their ID chip was used to implant a verbal description of the encounter in which the 10 unusual events were replaced with different events, and during the recall of the final encounter their ID chip was used to implant visual images of 10 different things than what they actually experienced. Each participant, therefore, experienced three encounters and a different type of recall manipulation followed each one; the type of manipulation associated with a particular encounter was counterbalanced. Finally, participants recalled the event for a second time, and we measured how many

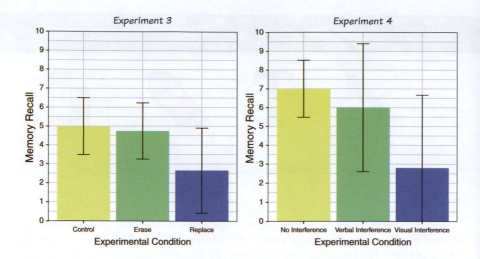

Figure 16.1 Mean (and 95% confidence interval) recall in Experiments 3 and 4

of the 10 unusual events they originally experienced they could recall. We predicted that, as in Experiment 3, verbal information might not be enough to replace a memory but that memory recall would be poorest when visual images were used to replace existing memories.

Figure 16.1 and the analysis showed this hypothesis was not supported: recall was not significantly different after verbal, visual or no interference, $F(1.01, 4.06) = 3.33$, $p = .142$. This finding suggests that there is not sufficient evidence that ID chips can be used to implant new memories over old.

References

Nader, K., Schafe, G. E., & Le Doux, J. E. (2000). Fear memories require protein synthesis in the amygdala for reconsolidation after retrieval. *Nature, 406*(6797), 722–726. doi:10.1038/35021052

Alice's Lab Notes 16.1 *Memory implanting*

work is being done? Is this why Chippers have been collapsing: because JIG:SAW have been trying to erase their memories remotely?'

'Of course not!' she replied, pulling her arm from my grip. 'This is provisional research. We don't have any authority to do anything to anyone outside of this complex.'

Roediger started whining and circling with a guilty look on his face. 'Mr Nutcot had the authority,' he said. Alice looked horrified. 'Mr Nutcot made Roediger conduct case studies: we've been removing memories using people's ID chips. It's no problem.'

Alice exploded. 'It *is* a problem, Roediger. Why wasn't I told about this? I'm the chief scientist – you answer to me! This is completely unacceptable.'

The dog whimpered. 'No choice ... Roediger didn't mean to hurt anyone.'

'What do you mean, you had no choice?' Alice spat.

For the first time Roediger's tail stopped wagging. His back legs quivered in fear. 'Schrödinger's prison ...' he whined.

Alice went pale, Milton's hair stood on end, and the room fell silent except for the sound of Clint slowly pacing.

I had no idea what a Schrödinger's prison was, but it sounded bad.

The babel of voices started up again, and Alice berated Roediger about these case studies. She said that her studies had convincingly shown that implanting memories didn't work, so there was no need for case studies. Roediger just kept quivering and repeating the phrase 'Schrödinger's prison'.

The more they argued, the more certain I felt that something wasn't right here, and that I needed to do something to stop it. After Deathscotch, zombies, and catapulting myself across chasms, I was tired of being scared, and I was sick of people not telling me the truth. I remembered Alice's reports on her Proteus, and while she continued her argument, I took it and found the section **(LAB NOTES 16.1)** relating to the work in this building.

I finished the report. Alice was still in discussion with Roediger. I pulled her away.

'I've read your report. In the first experiment, you had a bunch of people meet a stranger who dropped 10 bits of scripted information into their conversation. A week later those people were asked to remember those encounters, which got them to reactivate the memory. While the memory was reactivated, some of them were zapped via their ID chip, others had verbal information sent to their chips, and the control group were left alone. They then recalled the encounter for a third time and you measured how many of the 10 bits of information from the initial encounter they recalled. Let me guess, you fitted a linear model. I mean, that seems to be the general theme – whatever you do, fit a linear model.'

16.1 GENERAL PROCEDURE FOR COMPARING MEANS

'That's a good summary,' Alice said. She still looked nervous, but perhaps sensed that it might be useful to have an ally. She pulled up the data on her Proteus screen. **(TABLE 16.1)** 'You can see in the table that we had three groups: the control where nothing was done while they first recalled the conversation, a group where we tried to erase the memories with a blast of electricity to their ID chip, and a final group where we tried to replace the memory with something different using a verbal description – and, yes, just like when comparing two means, we can fit a linear model to predict the outcome based on membership of these three groups. When you predict an outcome from one predictor variable and that variable is made up of groups people often refer to the model as a one-way independent **analysis of variance** (**ANOVA**).'

'So, we can follow the same procedure as for any other linear model?' **(SECTION 14.3)**

Alice drew a diagram. **(FIGURE 16.2)** 'Yes. This figure shows a summary of the process. The starting place is always exploring the data, looking for unusual cases, problems with the assumptions of the model that you plan to fit. **(CHAPTER 12)** For example, some people use tests like Levene's test **(SECTION 12.2.3)** to check whether variances are equal (homogeneity of variance).'

Table 16.1   Data on erasing or replacing memories

	Control	Memory Erasing	Memory Replacing
	8	10	0
	2	5	5
	7	3	2
	8	4	1
	1	3	0
	5	7	10
	7	8	0
	4	3	0
	4	4	1
	4	3	1
	7	4	3
	3	3	9
$\bar{X}$	5.00	4.75	2.67
s	2.374	2.340	3.525
s^2	5.636	5.477	12.424

Grand Mean = **4.139**
Grand SD = **2.919**
Grand Variance = **8.523**

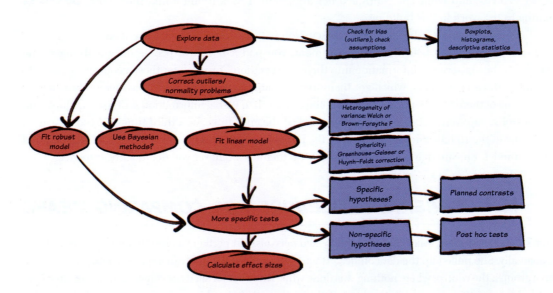

Figure 16.2   Overview of the general procedure for comparing several means

As Alice mentioned Levene's test, a message appeared on my diePad from Milton. **(MEOWSINGS 16.1)**

'If you find any problems you should correct them if you can before fitting the model,' Alice continued, 'or estimate the model using robust methods. **(CHAPTER 9)** You can choose to apply Bayesian methods when fitting a model to test your hypotheses. The model we fit, as you will see, tests a general hypothesis about whether you can predict the outcome from group membership, but often we want to test more specific hypotheses about which groups differ from which others – in other words, which groups contribute most to being able to predict the outcome variable. The next step is to do this more

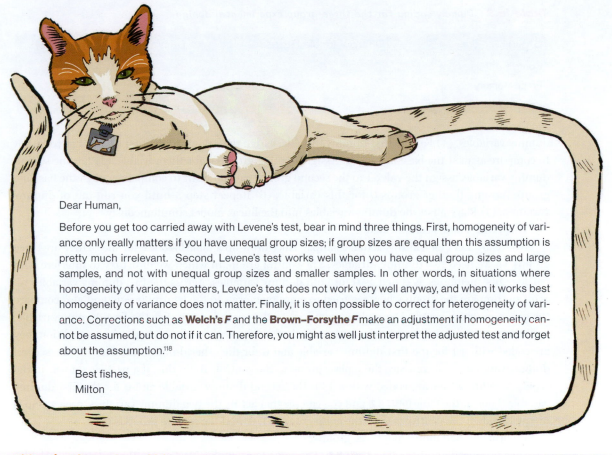

Dear Human,

Before you get too carried away with Levene's test, bear in mind three things. First, homogeneity of variance only really matters if you have unequal group sizes; if group sizes are equal then this assumption is pretty much irrelevant. Second, Levene's test works well when you have equal group sizes and large samples, and not with unequal group sizes and smaller samples. In other words, in situations where homogeneity of variance matters, Levene's test does not work very well anyway, and when it works best homogeneity of variance does not matter. Finally, it is often possible to correct for heterogeneity of variance. Corrections such as **Welch's F** and the **Brown–Forsythe F** make an adjustment if homogeneity cannot be assumed, but do not if it can. Therefore, you might as well just interpret the adjusted test and forget about the assumption.[118]

Best fishes,
Milton

Milton's Meowsings 16.1   Is Levene's test worth the effort?

specific analysis by either using planned contrasts or *post hoc* tests. *You would interpret these specific tests only if the overall model is significant*. I'll explain that later. The final stage is to quantify the size of effects.'

16.2 COMPARING SEVERAL MEANS WITH THE LINEAR MODEL

'Do you remember what I explained in the previous building about what the model looks like when we include a predictor variable containing two categories in the linear model?' Alice asked.

'Yeah, then the resulting *b* for that predictor compares the difference between the mean score for the two categories.'

16.2.1 Dummy coding

'When we have a predictor variable made up of more than two categories, we can do something similar by recoding that variable into several categorical predictors, each of which has only two categories. It's an extension of the dummy coding that we used to code two categories. There are seven steps. (1) Create one fewer dummy variables than the number of categories. (2) Choose one of your categories as a baseline against which to compare all other categories. Normally you'd pick the control group, or, if you don't have one, the largest group. (3) Assign the baseline group values of 0 for all of the

Table 16.2 *Dummy coding for the three-group experimental design*

Group	Dummy Variable 1 (Erase)	Dummy Variable 2 (Replace)
Control	0	0
Erase Memory	1	0
Replace Memory	0	1

dummy variables. (4) For the first dummy variable, assign the value 1 to the first group that you want to compare against the baseline group. Assign all other groups 0 for this variable. (5) For the second dummy variable, assign the value 1 to the second group that you want to compare against the baseline group. Assign all other groups 0 for this variable. (6) Repeat step 5 until you run out of dummy variables. (7) Place all of the dummy variables into the linear model simultaneously.'

'Wow, that sounds complicated.'

'Not really. Let's look at this actual example.' Alice drew up a table **(TABLE 16.2)** for me. 'There are three groups, so we need two dummy variables. The control group, in which we didn't try to interfere with participants' memories, is coded as 0 for both dummy variables. Across the two dummy variables we want to compare the group where we tried to erase memories to the control group, and also compare the group in which we tried to replace memories to the control group. For the first dummy variable, we'll compare the erase group to the control. To do this, if a participant was in the erase condition they are coded with a 1 for the first dummy variable and 0 for the other dummy variable. For the second dummy variable, we'll compare the replace group to the control. To do this, if a participant was in the replace condition they are coded with a 1 for the second dummy variable and 0 for the first dummy variable. Look at the table **(TABLE 16.2)** and you can see that across the two dummy variables, each group is uniquely coded: the control is 0, 0; the erase group is 1, 0; and the replace group is 0, 1.'

'What if you had more than three groups?'

Alice produced another table. **(TABLE 16.3)** 'The same logic applies. We create three dummy variables because that is one fewer than the number of groups we want to code; we specify one category as a base category (a control group), and assign this category a code of 0 for all dummy variables. The remaining three conditions will have a code of 1 for the dummy variable that compares that condition to the base category and a code of 0 for the other dummy variables.'

'How do these dummy variables fit into a linear model?'

Table 16.3 *Dummy coding for the four-group experimental design*

	Dummy Variable 1	Dummy Variable 2	Dummy Variable 3
Group 1	1	0	0
Group 2	0	1	0
Group 3	0	0	1
Group 4 (base)	0	0	0

'If we want to predict the number of items recalled from the experimental group to which someone belonged then we can use the general equation for the linear model with two predictors: the two dummy variables.'

CHECK YOUR BRAIN: What is the equation for the linear model with two predictors?

I thought back to Milton's explanation of the linear model **(SECTION 12.1)** and wrote out an equation **(16.1)** for Alice. 'We'd use this model, then?' I asked expectantly.

$$\text{outcome}_i = b_0 + b_1 X_{1i} + b_2 X_{2i} + \text{error}_i \tag{16.1}$$

Alice's tension seemed to drop a little; she edited my equation **(16.2)** to make the model clearer.

$$\text{Recall}_i = b_0 + b_1 \text{Dummy } 1_i + b_2 \text{Dummy } 2_i + \varepsilon_i$$
$$\text{Recall}_i = b_0 + b_1 \left(\text{Erase vs. Control}\right)_i + b_2 \left(\text{Replace vs. Control}\right)_i + \varepsilon_i \tag{16.2}$$

'I've replaced the Xs and outcome to make the model clearer. We are predicting recall scores from the two dummy variables. I've called the first dummy variable *Erase* because it represents the erase group compared to the control, and the second dummy variable we could label as *Replace* because it represents the replace group compared to the control.'

'So, a person's recall can be predicted from knowing their group code (i.e., the code for the erase and replace dummy variables) and the intercept (b_0) of the model.'

'Exactly, Zach. We can code the dummy variables in different ways, but this is a good place to start. Let's look at what the parameters in the model represent. Like we saw when we compared two groups, the predicted values from the model **(SECTION 15.2.2)** will be the group means because for a given individual the best guess of their score will be the mean of the group to which they belong. Let's start by looking at the model for the control group. In this group both the *erase* and *replace* dummy variables are coded as 0. The predicted value for the model will be the mean of the control group. Therefore, if we ignore the error term (ε_i), the regression equation becomes this.' Alice wrote out an equation **(16.3)**.

$$\text{Recall}_i = b_0 + \left(b_1 \times 0\right) + \left(b_2 \times 0\right)$$
$$\text{Recall}_i = b_0 \tag{16.3}$$
$$\bar{X}_{\text{Control}} = b_0$$

It seemed to me that the erase and replace groups had been excluded because they were coded with 0. We were looking at predicting the level of recall when both experimental manipulations are ignored, and so the predicted value would be the mean of the control group because all other groups had been excluded.

'The intercept of the model, b_0, is the mean of the base category, the category you coded as zero for both dummy variables,' I said.

Alice confirmed. 'In this case the mean of the control group was 5, so b_0 will be 5.'

'Now, let's look at the erase group. The dummy variable *Erase* is coded as 1 and the dummy variable *Replace* is coded as 0. If we replace the values of these codes into the model **(EQUATION 16.2)**, we get the following.' Alice wrote out another equation **(16.4)**.

$$\text{Recall}_i = b_0 + \left(b_1 \times 1\right) + \left(b_2 \times 0\right)$$
$$\text{Recall}_i = b_0 + b_1 \tag{16.4}$$

'And we know that b_0 is the mean of the control group.'

'Brilliant!' Alice looked pleased with me. 'And if someone is in the erase group then the model predicts that their recall will be the mean of the erase group.' Alice developed the equation **(16.5)** by replacing some of the values. 'You see? b_1 represents the difference between the means of the erase and control groups, which will be $4.75 - 5 = -0.25$.'

$$\text{Recall}_i = b_0 + b_1$$

$$\bar{X}_{\text{Erase}} = \bar{X}_{\text{Control}} + b_1 \tag{16.5}$$

$$b_1 = \bar{X}_{\text{Erase}} - \bar{X}_{\text{Control}}$$

'Sweet, so what happens in the replace group?'

Alice wrote two more equations. 'In the replace group, the dummy variable *Replace* is coded as 1 and the dummy variable *Erase* is coded as 0. So, recall is predicted from the constant, b_0, plus b_2. **(EQUATION 16.6)**

$$\text{Recall}_i = b_0 + (b_1 \times 0) + (b_2 \times 1)$$
$$\text{Recall}_i = b_0 + b_2 \tag{16.6}$$

'Presumably, we can again replace b_0 because we know it is equal to the mean of the control group?' **(EQUATION 16.3)**

'Yes, and the predicted recall value for someone in the replace group is the mean recall in the replace group. If you replace these values into the model, you see that b_2 represents the difference between the means of the replace group and the control group.' **(EQUATION 16.7)**

$$\text{Recall}_i = b_0 + b_2$$

$$\bar{X}_{\text{Replace}} = \bar{X}_{\text{Control}} + b_2 \tag{16.7}$$

$$b_2 = \bar{X}_{\text{Replace}} - \bar{X}_{\text{Control}}$$

'Sick! So, looking back at the data **(TABLE 16.1)**, the parameter for the first dummy variable, b_1, is the difference between the means of the erase and control groups, or $4.75 - 5 = -0.25$, and the parameter for the second dummy variable, b_2, is the difference between the means of the replace and control groups, or $2.67 - 5.00 = -2.33$.'

'Yes, although there are other ways in which the dummy variables can be coded to test different hypotheses.' **(SECTION 16.4)**

16.2.2 The F-ratio as a test of means

Alice drew a diagram on her Proteus. **(FIGURE 16.3)** 'Look, this shows the model that we have fitted to the data by using the dummy coding scheme that I explained. We want to test the hypothesis that the means of three groups are different, so the null hypothesis is that the group means are the same. The coloured horizontal lines show the three group means. What would these lines look like if the null hypothesis were true?'

I told her that I thought that they would all line up vertically, so there would be no vertical gaps between them.

'Exactly, Zach. They would line up, creating one single flat line, and that line would be the value of the mean of all scores, the *grand mean*: the black horizontal line in the diagram.'

'So, the grand mean represents the null hypothesis?'

'Yes, and because the coloured horizontal lines are in different vertical positions – not aligned with each other – it suggests that the group means differ. The question is whether these differences are due to sampling variation or because of what happened to participants in the different groups. I just told you that the parameter, b_1, represents the difference in means between the erase and control group, and b_2 represents the difference in means between the replace and control groups; in my diagram b_1 represents the distance between the red and green horizontal lines, and b_2 the distance between the

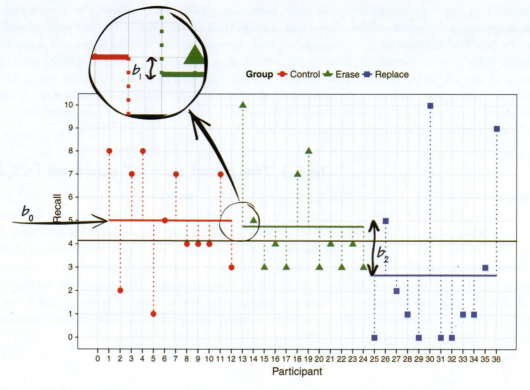

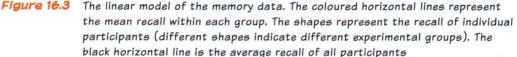

Figure 16.3 *The linear model of the memory data. The coloured horizontal lines represent the mean recall within each group. The shapes represent the recall of individual participants (different shapes indicate different experimental groups). The black horizontal line is the average recall of all participants*

red and blue horizontal lines. If the null hypothesis is true and all the groups have the same means, then these b coefficients would be zero.

'To test whether the means are different from each other we need some way to test whether predicting recall from the group means results in better prediction than predicting them from the mean of all scores (the null hypothesis). The logic is fairly straightforward. (1) The grand mean represents the null hypothesis, or no effect, or no relationship between the predictor variable and the outcome. (2) We fit a different model to the data that represents our hypotheses. (3) The intercept and one or more parameters (b) describe the model. (4) The parameters determine the shape of the model, but in experimental research they also represent differences between group means. (5) If the differences between group means are large enough (compared to the error in the model) – in other words, the bs are large enough – then the resulting model will be a better fit to the data than the grand mean. (6) This would suggest that predicting scores from the group means is better than predicting scores from the grand mean, or null hypothesis. Put another way, the group means are significantly different.'

'What you're saying is, if the group means are significantly different then using them to predict recall scores, like we do in the linear model, will give us a good fit of the model to the data.'

'Yes, and do you know how to assess whether a linear model is a good fit?'

I thought back to when Milton was explaining to me how to see whether garlic would repel zombies. **(SECTION 14.1.7)** We had calculated various sums of squares: the total sum of squares told us how much variability in outcome scores there was, the model sum of squares told us how much of this variability was accounted for by the model, and the residual sum of squares told us how much variability the model could not explain. We used these sums of squares to work out the mean sums of squares: the mean squares for the model told us the average variability in the outcome accounted for by the model, and the residual mean squares told us the average variability in the outcome that is not accounted for by the model. The *F*-ratio was the mean squares for the model divided by the residual mean squares **(EQUATION 14.24)** – it was the signal-to-noise ratio of the model, how good the model was compared to how much error there was within it. I explained this to an increasingly captivated Alice.

16.2.3 The total sum of squares (SS_T)

Alice set to work on her Proteus, creating a monstrous diagram. **(FIGURE 16.4)** 'You're absolutely right,' she said urgently. 'We can use the sums of squares to assess the fit of the model. My diagram shows the three sums of squares that you mentioned for our current model. The top image shows the total sum of squares, and this is the sum of the squared distances between each observation and the mean of all observations, the grand mean. You can also think of this as the squared distances between each observation and the null hypothesis.' Alice paused to write out an equation. **(16.8)** 'This equation shows how to calculate the total sum of squares. You take each score, x_i and subtract from it the mean of all scores, $\bar{x}_{grand}$. These are the coloured vertical lines in the diagram. We square these values because some are positive and others negative, and we add them up.'

$$SS_T = \sum_{i=1}^{N} \left(x_i - \bar{x}_{grand} \right)^2 = 298.306 \tag{16.8}$$

'Right, that's similar to when you calculate the variance.' **(SECTION 4.3.2)**

'Exactly,' Alice replied as she brought up a table on her screen. **(TABLE 16.4)** 'This table shows the process. In the second column we have the recall scores, and in the third column we have the grand mean. This value is 4.139 and is the same for every participant because it is the mean of everyone's recall scores. The first step is to take each person's recall score and subtract the grand mean from it. The result is in column 4; for example, the first person had a recall score of 8 and when we subtract 4.139 from this value it leaves us with 3.861. This value is the error from the grand mean for that person. Some of these errors will be positive and others negative so we square them in column 5. For example, for the first participant 3.861^2 gives us a value of 14.907. This value is the squared error for the first person. To get the sum of squared errors we complete this process for every person and then add the results together. Column 5 shows the squared errors for each person, so to get the sum of squared errors we add up the scores in this column. The result is 298.306. This means that there are 298.306 units of variation in recall scores for which the model can potentially account. Before we move on, what do you know about degrees of freedom?'

The truth was not a lot, except that I had some vague memory of Milton telling me something about it. **(SECTION 4.3.2)** After staring at my blank, helpless face for a few seconds, Alice broke the silence.

'All that matters is that you have some appreciation that when we estimate population values from a sample, the degrees of freedom are typically one less than the number of scores used to estimate the population value. This is because to get these estimates we have to hold something constant in the population (in this case the mean), which leaves all but one of the scores free to vary. Every sum of squares has an associated degrees of freedom, which is one less than the number of things used to compute it. For the total sum of squares, we used the entire sample of 36 scores to calculate it, so the total degrees of freedom (df_T) are one less than this total sample size ($N - 1$). That's 35 for these data.'

SS_T uses the differences between the observed data and the overall (grand) mean value of the outcome

SS_R uses the differences between the observed data and the predicted values from the model

SS_M uses the differences between the mean value of the outcome and the predicted values from the model

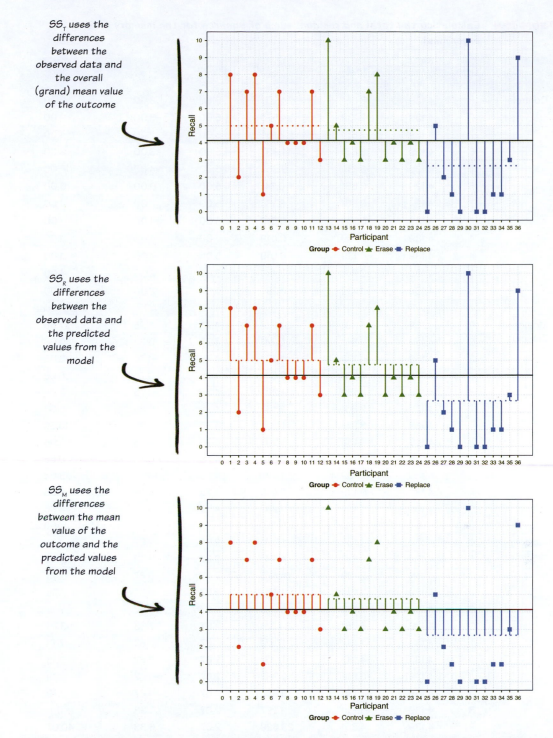

Figure 16.4 *Graphical representation of the different sums of squares when predicting an outcome from group membership*

Table 16.4 Calculating the total and residual sums of squares for the memory erasing experiment

	Recall	Grand Mean	$x_i - \overline{x}_{grand}$	$(x_i - \overline{x}_{grand})^2$	Group Mean	$x_i - \overline{x}_{group}$	$(x_i - \overline{x}_{group})^2$
Control	8	4.139	3.861	14.907	5.00	3.00	9.00
	2	4.139	−2.139	4.575	5.00	−3.00	9.00
	7	4.139	2.861	8.185	5.00	2.00	4.00
	8	4.139	3.861	14.907	5.00	3.00	9.00
	1	4.139	−3.139	9.853	5.00	−4.00	16.00
	5	4.139	0.861	0.741	5.00	0.00	0.00
	7	4.139	2.861	8.185	5.00	2.00	4.00
	4	4.139	−0.139	0.019	5.00	−1.00	1.00
	4	4.139	−0.139	0.019	5.00	−1.00	1.00
	4	4.139	−0.139	0.019	5.00	−1.00	1.00
	7	4.139	2.861	8.185	5.00	2.00	4.00
	3	4.139	−1.139	1.297	5.00	−2.00	4.00
							$SS_{Control} = 62$
Memory Erasing	10	4.139	5.861	34.351	4.75	5.25	27.56
	5	4.139	0.861	0.741	4.75	0.25	0.06
	3	4.139	−1.139	1.297	4.75	−1.75	3.06
	4	4.139	−0.139	0.019	4.75	−0.75	0.56
	3	4.139	−1.139	1.297	4.75	−1.75	3.06
	7	4.139	2.861	8.185	4.75	2.25	5.06
	8	4.139	3.861	14.907	4.75	3.25	10.56
	3	4.139	−1.139	1.297	4.75	−1.75	3.06
	4	4.139	−0.139	0.019	4.75	−0.75	0.56
	3	4.139	−1.139	1.297	4.75	−1.75	3.06
	4	4.139	−0.139	0.019	4.75	−0.75	0.56
	3	4.139	−1.139	1.297	4.75	−1.75	3.06
							$SS_{Erase} = 60.25$
Memory Replace	0	4.139	−4.139	17.131	2.67	−2.67	7.13
	5	4.139	0.861	0.741	2.67	2.33	5.43
	2	4.139	−2.139	4.575	2.67	−0.67	0.45
	1	4.139	−3.139	9.853	2.67	−1.67	2.79
	0	4.139	−4.139	17.131	2.67	−2.67	7.13
	10	4.139	5.861	34.351	2.67	7.33	53.73
	0	4.139	−4.139	17.131	2.67	−2.67	7.13
	0	4.139	−4.139	17.131	2.67	−2.67	7.13
	1	4.139	−3.139	9.853	2.67	−1.67	2.79
	1	4.139	−3.139	9.853	2.67	−1.67	2.79
	3	4.139	−1.139	1.297	2.67	0.33	0.11
	9	4.139	4.861	23.629	2.67	6.33	40.07
							$SS_{Replace} = 136.67$
Σ				**298.306**			**258.92**

16.2.4 The model sum of squares (SS_M)

Alice was getting into her stride. 'We know that the total amount of variation in recall scores is 298.31 units. The interesting question is how much of this can be accounted for by our model. The model sum of squares is calculated by taking the difference, for each observation, between the values predicted by the model and the grand mean. This is shown by the coloured vertical lines in the bottom image of my diagram.' **(FIGURE 16.4)**

The diagram looked familiar: it was similar to one that Milton had shown me **(FIGURE 14.3)**, except that the model was now made up of the group means rather than a single straight line.

'For each participant, the value predicted by the model is the mean for the group to which the participant belongs,' Alice explained. 'The predicted value for the twelve participants in the control group will be 5, for the twelve participants in the erase condition it will be 4.75, and for the twelve participants in the replace condition it will be 2.67. The model sum of squares requires us to calculate the differences between each participant's predicted value and the grand mean. These differences reflect the differences in prediction from using the model (the group means) compared to using the overall mean. Another way to think about it is they are the differences in prediction arising from when prediction is based on the null hypothesis (the grand mean) and the alternative hypothesis (the model).' Alice wrote another equation **(16.9)** for me. 'In equation form, we're taking the mean of each group, $\bar{x}_k$, and subtracting from it the mean of all scores, $\bar{x}_{grand}$. We square these differences because some will be positive and some negative. This distance is the same for each participant in a group, so we multiply the squared difference by the number of people in the group, n_k. This tells us the model sum of squares for a group, and we repeat this process for each group that we have.'

$$SS_M = \sum_{k=1}^{k} n_k \left(\bar{x}_k - \bar{x}_{grand} \right)^2 \tag{16.9}$$

'I suppose you want me to calculate this?' I asked reluctantly, and she broke into an affectionate and mock evil grin. It made me feel like we were a team, and any match for whatever JIG:SAW threw at us. The feeling faded after much swearing at my calculator app, but I had an answer: the model sum of squares was 39.38. **(EQUATION 16.10)**

$$
\begin{aligned}
SS_M &= 12(5.000 - 4.139)^2 + 12(4.750 - 4.139)^2 + 12(2.667 - 4.139)^2 \\
&= 12(0.861)^2 + 12(0.611)^2 + 12(-1.472)^2 \\
&= 8.896 + 4.480 + 26.001 \\
&= 39.38
\end{aligned}
\tag{16.10}
$$

'The degrees of freedom,' Alice said, 'are one less than the number of things used to calculate the sums of squares, just like before. However, this sum of squares is based on group means, so the model degrees of freedom (df_M) are the number of group means minus one, which you'll see denoted as $k-1$. We used three group means, so the degrees of freedom are 2.'

16.2.5 The residual sum of squares (SS_R)

'So we know that there are 298.31 units of variation in recall scores to be explained, and the model accounts for 39.38 of them. That doesn't seem like a lot.'

'Perhaps not, but we need to compare it to how much error there is in the model. That is what the middle picture in my diagram shows. **(FIGURE 16.4)** The residual sum of squares is the difference between what the model predicts and what was actually observed. When our model is based on group means, the predicted values are those means (the coloured dashed horizontal lines in the diagram). The residual sum of squared error is the sum of the squared distances between each observation and the predicted value from the model (the group mean). In equation form (EQUATION 16.11), we calculate the difference between the observed value, Y_i, and the predicted value, $\hat{Y}_i$, for each observation, square these differences and add them up. In this case, because we're using the mean as predicted values, we're looking at the difference between each observation in each of the k groups, Y_{ik}, and the mean of the particular group to which an observation belongs $\bar{Y}_k$. Does any of this seem familiar?'

$$\text{total error in model}, SS_R = \sum_{i=1}^{n} \left(\text{observed}_i - \text{model}_i\right)^2 = \sum_{i=1}^{n} \left(i - i \right)^2$$

$$SS_R = \sum \left(ik - k \right)^2 = 258.917$$

(16.11)

Actually it did. The middle picture in the diagram (FIGURE 16.4) reminded me of when Milton had explained to me how to calculate the variance within a set of scores (FIGURE 4.10): it looked like we just calculate the sums of squares within each of the three groups. It also reminded me of when Milton explained the residual sum of squares for the linear model (SECTION 14.1.7) – the only difference was that the predicted values were now made up of group means. I explained this to Alice, and she put her arm around me briefly before something stopped her and she retracted her brief display of affection. I felt hurt.

'You're right. We can calculate the residual sum of squares by adding up the sums of squares *within* each group (in other words, $SS_{Control} + SS_{Erase} + SS_{Replace}$). The sum of squares within each group is calculated by looking at the difference between each score in a group and the group mean.' Alice swiped her Proteus screen and her earlier table appeared. (TABLE 16.4) 'Remember that the second column contains the recall scores. In the sixth column I have placed the group means. This value will be the same for each person in the same group. For example, everyone in the control group has a group mean of 5. The first step is to take each person's recall score and subtract the *group* mean from it. The result is in column 7; for example, the first person had a recall score of 8 and when we subtract the group mean of 5 from this value, it leaves us with 3. This value is the error from the *group* mean for that person. As before, because some of these errors are positive and others negative we square them in column 8. For example, for the first participant 3^2 gives us 9. This value is the squared error for the first person within the control group. We repeat this process for every person in the control group (column 8) and add the results together to get the total sum of squares for that group ($SS_{Control}$). We then do the same for the people in the erase group: calculate their errors from the group mean, square them and add them up to get SS_{Erase}. Finally, do the same for the people in the replace group to get $SS_{Replace}$. When you have the sums of squared errors within each group you add the values up to get the residual sum of squares for the model.' Alice wrote the equation and added the values for me. (EQUATION 16.12)

$$\begin{aligned} SS_R &= SS_{Control} + SS_{Erase} + SS_{Replace} \\ &= 62.00 + 60.25 + 136.67 \\ &= 258.92 \end{aligned}$$

(16.12)

'What about the degrees of freedom?' I asked.

'Each time you calculated a sum of squares within a group, you used $n - 1$ degrees of freedom.'

'Yeah, each group sum of squares was based on 11 degrees of freedom.'

'Right, and you calculated the total residual sum of squares by adding the sum of squares within each group, so to get the residual degrees of freedom, df_R, you similarly add the degrees of freedom for each group.'

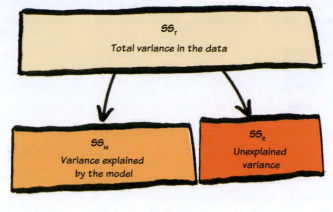

$$SS_T = SS_M + SS_R$$
$$df_T = df_M + df_R$$

Figure 16.5   *Partitioning variance*

'So, it will be $11 + 11 + 11$, which is 33?'

'Exactly. You will also find that it is $N - k$: the total sample size, $N = 36$, minus the number of groups, $k = 3$.'

16.2.6 Partitioning variance

Alice drew me another diagram. **(FIGURE 16.5)** 'All we have done so far is take the total variance in recall scores and split it into two portions: the portion accounted for by the model, and what's left over, the error in the model. As such, the sums of squares should add up such that the model sum of squares added to the residual sum of squares, gives us the value of the total sum of squares.'

'With our model, that means that if we add 39.38 to 258.92 we should get 298.306.'

'Which, of course, we do to within rounding error. Similarly the degrees of freedom should add up too, so the model degrees of freedom, 2, when added to the residual degrees of freedom, 33, should give us the total degrees of freedom, 35, which again it does.'

16.2.7 Mean squares

I was getting frustrated and impatient. Fun as it was to have some time with Alice, I was eager to find out what was happening here with all of the memory zapping. I asked her how we know if the means are different.

'Hang on in there,' she implored. 'The model sum of squares tells us the *total* variation in recall scores that is accounted for by the model, and the residual sum of squares tells us the *total* variation in recall scores that is not accounted for by the model. Because both of these values are totals they depend on the number of scores that were summed: SS_M used the sum of only three different values (the group means), while SS_R used the sum of all 36 values. To eliminate this bias we can calculate the average sum of squares (known as the *mean squares*, MS), by dividing both the SS_M and SS_R by their associated degrees of freedom. The reason why we divide by the degrees of freedom is that we are trying to extrapolate to a population and so for each sum of squares some parameters within that population have been held constant.'

Milton had mentioned mean squares to me already. **(SECTION 14.1.7)**

Alice wrote out some more equations for me. **(EQUATION 16.13)** 'See, the average variation in recall scores attributable to the model is bigger than the average amount that remains unexplained.'

$$MS_M = \frac{SS_M}{df_M} = \frac{39.38}{2} = 19.69$$

$$MS_R = \frac{SS_R}{df_R} = \frac{258.92}{33} = 7.85$$

(16.13)

16.2.8 The F-ratio

'The final step,' Alice continued, 'is to look at the ratio of the variation in recall scores accounted for by the model and the variation explained by unsystematic factors, in other words, the error in prediction. This is the F-ratio.' Alice wrote down an equation **(16.14)**, which I had seen before. **(EQUATION 14.24)** 'Think of it like this if you like: it is the ratio of how good the model is to how bad it is (how much error there is).'

$$F = \frac{MS_M}{MS_R} = \frac{19.69}{7.85} = 2.51$$

(16.14)

'So, like any test statistic, the F-ratio is the signal-to-noise ratio: it's a measure of the ratio of systematic variation to unsystematic variation; or, in experimental research, it is the ratio of the experimental effect to the individual differences in performance. How big does it need to be before we know that our model is a good fit?

'At an intuitive level, we know that if its value is less than 1 then, by definition, it represents non-significant differences between means. This is because if the F-ratio is less than 1 it means that MS_R is greater than MS_M, which in real terms means that there is more unsystematic than systematic variance. Our value is 2.51, so we at least know it's bigger than 1. To discover if the value is big enough to represent a significant fit of the model – or, in other words, significant differences between means - we can either get a computer to calculate the probability of getting an F at least as big as the one we have if the null hypothesis were true, or we can compare the obtained value of F against the maximum value we would expect to get, if the null hypothesis were true, in an F-distribution with the same degrees of freedom.' Alice accessed a table of numbers on her Proteus. **(SECTION A.4)** 'This table shows the critical values of F at the 0.05 level of significance in distributions with different degrees of freedom. The columns show the degrees of freedom for the model (the top of the F-ratio) and the rows show values of the residual degrees of freedom (the bottom of the F-ratio). We had 2 model degrees of freedom and 33 residual degrees of freedom,

df_R							df_M							
	1	2	3	4	5	6	7	8	9	10	15	25	50	100
1	161.45	199.50	215.71	224.58	230.16	233.99	236.77	238.88	240.54	241.88	245.95	249.26	251.77	253.04
2	18.51	19.00	19.16	19.25	19.30	19.33	19.35	19.37	19.38	19.40	19.43	19.46	19.48	19.49
3	10.13	9.55	9.28	9.12	9.01	8.94	8.89	8.85	8.81	8.79	8.70	8.63	8.58	8.55
4	7.71	6.94	6.59	6.39	6.26	6.16	6.09	6.04	6.00	5.96	5.86	5.77	5.70	5.66
5	6.61	5.79	5.41	5.19	5.05	4.95	4.88	4.82	4.77	4.74	4.62	4.52	4.44	4.41
6	5.99	5.14	4.76	4.53	4.39	4.28	4.21	4.15	4.10	4.06	3.94	3.83	3.75	3.71
7	5.59	4.74	4.35	4.12	3.97							3.40	3.32	3.27
28	4.20	3.34	2.95	2.71	2.56	2.45	2.36	2.29	2.24	2.19	2.04	1.91	1.79	1.73
30	4.17	3.32	2.92	2.69	2.53	2.42	2.33	2.27	2.21	2.16	2.01	1.88	1.76	1.70
33	4.14	3.28	2.89	2.66	2.50	2.39	2.30	2.23	2.18	2.13	1.98	1.84	1.72	1.66

Figure 16.6 *Using the F-distribution*

so we read down the column for 2 until we get to the row for 33. The value in that cell is the critical value, which is 3.28.' **(FIGURE 16.6)**

'So, in an F-distribution with 2 and 33 degrees of freedom the minimum value of F that is significant at the 0.05 level of probability is 3.28.'

'Yes, and our observed value of 2.51 is smaller than this critical value, which suggests that prediction based on group means is no better than prediction based on the overall mean.'

'In other words, the means are not significantly different at $p = 0.05$.'

16.2.9 Comparing several means using a computer

Alice swiped her Proteus screen as though conducting an orchestra. 'Here,' she said passing me the device. 'This is what happens when we fit the model using a statistics app. The first table **(OUTPUT 16.1)** shows the descriptive statistics; the means and standard deviations correspond to those I originally showed you. **(TABLE 16.1)** The standard errors and confidence intervals for each mean are shown too. For example, assuming that this sample is one of the 95% for which the confidence interval contains the population value, the true value of the mean of the control group is between 3.49 and 6.51. These diagnostics will help us to interpret the analysis. The output also reports Levene's test, which can be used to assess the homogeneity of variance assumption.' **(SECTION 12.2.3)**

'Isn't it the case that if it is significant then the assumption is broken?'

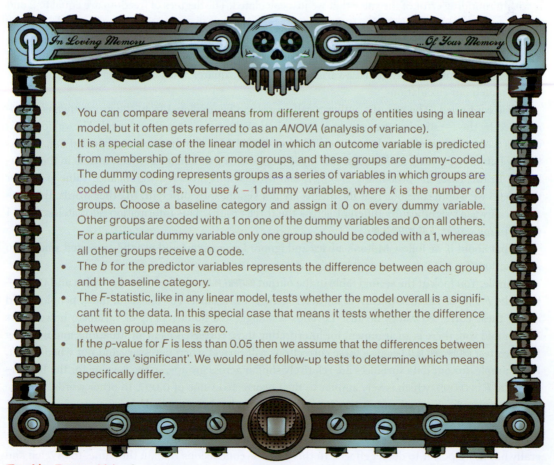

- You can compare several means from different groups of entities using a linear model, but it often gets referred to as an *ANOVA* (analysis of variance).
- It is a special case of the linear model in which an outcome variable is predicted from membership of three or more groups, and these groups are dummy-coded. The dummy coding represents groups as a series of variables in which groups are coded with 0s or 1s. You use $k - 1$ dummy variables, where k is the number of groups. Choose a baseline category and assign it 0 on every dummy variable. Other groups are coded with a 1 on one of the dummy variables and 0 on all others. For a particular dummy variable only one group should be coded with a 1, whereas all other groups receive a 0 code.
- The b for the predictor variables represents the difference between each group and the baseline category.
- The F-statistic, like in any linear model, tests whether the model overall is a significant fit to the data. In this special case that means it tests whether the difference between group means is zero.
- If the p-value for F is less than 0.05 then we assume that the differences between means are 'significant'. We would need follow-up tests to determine which means specifically differ.

Zach's Facts 16.1   *Comparing more than two means*

Descriptives

Memory Recall (Out of 10)

	N	Mean	Std. Deviation	Std. Error	95% Confidence Interval for Mean		Minimum	Maximum
					Lower Bound	Upper Bound		
Control	12	5.00	2.374	.685	3.49	6.51	1	8
Erase	12	4.75	2.340	.676	3.26	6.24	3	10
Replace	12	2.67	3.525	1.018	.43	4.91	0	10
Total	36	4.14	2.919	.487	3.15	5.13	0	10

Test of Homogeneity of Variances

Memory Recall (Out of 10)

Levene Statistic	df1	df2	Sig.
1.083	2	33	.350

Output 16.1   *Descriptive statistics using IBM SPSS Statistics*

'Yes, and in this case the *p*-value is greater than 0.05, so it is not significant and we assume that variances are equal across groups.'

'Milton said you might as well just correct the analysis and ignore this test.' **(MEOWSINGS 16.1)**

'Well, the next tables show us both the uncorrected and corrected result. **(OUTPUT 16.2)** The first table shows the uncorrected version, and if we take Levene's test at face value, we'd use this table because the test suggested that variances were approximately equal. The row labelled *Between Groups* is the overall experimental effect. We are told the sums of squares for the model ($SS_M = 39.39$), and this value is within rounding error of the value that we just calculated. The degrees of freedom are equal to 2 and the mean squares for the model is 19.69, which again matches the value that we calculated. The row labelled *Within Groups* details the unsystematic variation within the recall scores. It displays how much variation the model can't explain (the residual sum of squares, SS_R, which is 258.92 units, and the average amount of unsystematic variation, the mean squares (MS_R), which is 7.85. Again these values match our calculations.'

Alice continued, 'The test of whether recall scores can be predicted from the group means is represented by the *F*-ratio; in other words, it tests whether the group means are equal. The value of this ratio is 2.51, which corresponds to our calculation. **(SECTION 16.2.8)** The final column labelled *Sig.* tells us the probability of getting an *F* at least this big if there wasn't a difference between means in the population. In this case, the probability is 0.097, and because this observed significance value is greater than 0.05 we would conclude that the means are not significantly different. In other words, the average recall wasn't significantly different across the three groups. This information all matches what I wrote in my report.' **(LAB NOTES 16.1)**

'What about if we follow Milton's advice and ignore Levene's test and use the corrected analysis in all situations?'

'Simple. You look at the second table in the output **(OUTPUT 16.2)**, which shows the Welch and Brown–Forsythe *F*-ratios. These both correct for heterogeneity of variance. For our data, many people would ignore these corrected values because Levene's test suggested homogeneity of variance; however, as Milton told you, there is an argument for interpreting these corrected *F*s in all situations and ignoring Levene's test **(MEOWSINGS 16.1)** because these corrections will correct when necessary and not when it isn't. For example, for our data variances are relatively similar across groups, so the *p*-value for the Brown–Forsythe *F* is 0.099, which is very similar to the uncorrected value of 0.097. In other words, because variances were fairly equal, only a very minor adjustment has been applied.'

'Which correction should you look at?'

'Either is fine, but Welch's *F* is often preferred to the Brown–Forsythe correction because it generally has more power to detect effects. In this case the conclusions remain the same, the Welch and Brown–Forsythe corrections are both non-significant because their *p*-values are greater than 0.05.'

ANOVA

Memory Recall (Out of 10)

	Sum of Squares	df	Mean Square	F	Sig.
Between Groups	39.389	2	19.694	2.510	.097
Within Groups	258.917	33	7.846		
Total	298.306	35			

Robust Tests of Equality of Means

Memory Recall (Out of 10)

	Statistic[a]	df1	df2	Sig.
Welch	1.896	2	21.452	.174
Brown–Forsythe	2.510	2	28.197	.099

a. Asymptotically F distributed.

Output 16.2 *The overall fit of the model using IBM SPSS Statistics*

Alice drew my attention to a final table (OUTPUT 16.3), 'The model parameters are what I said they would be: b_0 is the value of the mean for the control group, 5; b_1 is −0.25, the difference between the means of the erase and control groups; and b_2 is −2.33, the difference between the means of the replace and control groups.'

'The beta for the replace variable is significant. Does this mean that the replace group mean was significantly different from the control group mean?'

'It does, but because the model overall is not a significant fit to the data you should not interpret these individual parameters. If you do, then (1) you're interpreting a model that you know poorly fits the data; and (2) you're in danger of making a Type I error.'

Coefficients[a]

Model		Unstandardized Coefficients B	Std. Error	Standardized Coefficients Beta	t	Sig.	95.0% Confidence Interval for B Lower Bound	Upper Bound
1	(Constant)	5.000	.809		6.184	.000	3.355	6.645
	Erase_Dummy	−.250	1.144	−.041	−.219	.828	−2.577	2.077
	Replace_Dummy	−2.333	1.144	−.382	−2.040	.049	−4.660	−.007

a. Dependent Variable: Memory Recall (Out of 10)

Output 16.3 *The model parameter estimates from IBM SPSS Statistics*

16.3 CONTRAST CODING

I thought about what Alice had just explained. It seemed to me that you used the *F*-ratio to test overall whether the means were significantly different, and the model parameters told you more specifically which means were different. I asked her if this was true.

'Yes, that's exactly right. By default we used dummy coding, but we can also use *contrast coding*, which is where the numbers that you use in the dummy variables ensure that the *b*-values represent differences between groups that relate to your specific hypotheses, while controlling for Type I errors.'

There it was again, Type I errors. I didn't understand why you would make this kind of error. Alice explained.

'As you said, Zach, the *F*-ratio tells us only whether the model fitted to the data accounts for more variation in the outcome than it can't explain. It doesn't tell us where the differences between groups lie. The *b*s do tell us where differences lie, but when you use dummy coding these *b*s are not independent or **orthogonal**, which means that it is like doing two tests on the same scores, which inflates the familywise error rate.'

I had learnt about that before (SECTION 10.1.7), but I didn't understand why the *b*s aren't independent.

Alice explained. 'Let's take our example. We used the control group as a base category; that means that both b_1 and b_2 use the mean of the control group. In other words, the control group data are being used twice when estimating the bs, and this means that the familywise error rate will creep above 0.05. To make sure that it doesn't you can do one of two things: (1) adjust the tests to be stricter; or (2) use a coding scheme that keeps the bs independent. The first option is an example of a more general process known as ***post hoc* tests**, whereas the second option is known as planned comparisons or **planned contrasts**.'

'So for the bs we looked at **(OUTPUT 16.3)**, we could interpret them if we correct for the number of tests we have done?'

'Yes, so you could use a basic Bonferroni correction **(SECTION 10.1.7)** and instead of using 0.05 as a critical value for p, use 0.05 divided by 2 (because you have done two tests). Therefore, you'd accept an effect as significant if the p-value was less than 0.025.'

'And the b for the replace group would not be significant using this criterion.'

'Exactly, which is consistent with the overall poor fit of the model.'

I asked whether we could use planned contrasts.

16.3.1 Generating contrasts

'We could, because this experiment had very specific hypotheses that were generated before the data were collected (known as *a priori* hypotheses). We had two groups where we tried to manipulate memories (the erase and replace conditions) and one where we did not try to influence memory (the control). Therefore, we would predict that recall in the control group should be better than in the groups where we tried to influence memory. However, we would also expect recall to be different in people where we tried to erase their memories compared to those where we tried to replace them. The question is whether these hypotheses can be tested using a set of dummy variables that are independent of each other.'

Alice drew a diagram for me. **(FIGURE 16.7)** 'Think back to my earlier diagram,' **(FIGURE 16.5)** she said. 'The F-ratio is based upon splitting the total variation in recall scores into two component parts: the variation due to the experimental manipulation, which is accounted for by the model we fit to the data, SS_M; and the variation due to unsystematic factors, which is the error in prediction of the model, SS_R. The model sum of squares, though, is made up of several group means. If we want to know which means differ from

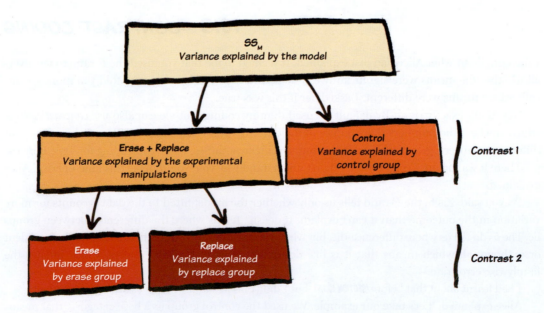

Figure 16.7 *Partitioning experimental variance into component comparisons*

which, then we need to break it down further in a way that tests our hypotheses about how we expect the means to differ. This new diagram shows how we might achieve this for the memory study: first we divide the model sum of squares up into the part that is accounted for by the two groups where memory was manipulated and compare that to the part that is accounted for by the control group (*contrast 1*); then we subdivide the variance explained by the memory manipulations to compare the variance explained by erasing memory to the variance explained by trying to replace memories (*contrast 2*).'

'How do you know that these contrasts are independent?'

'Remember I told you that when using dummy coding the contrasts were not independent because the control group was used in both contrasts? The key is that variance must not be reused: every group must be singled out once, and only once. Imagine that the model sum of squares is a cake, and you are dividing it up into slices. Once a slice has been cut from the cake you can cut it into smaller slices, but you can't reattach it. So, we cut off the control group in contrast 1, and to ensure that the contrasts are independent we must not reuse the control group and we cannot subdivide it any further. However, the memory groups in contrast 1 can be subdivided, and that is what we do in contrast 2. Also notice that in both contrasts we compare only two things. In contrast 1 we compare memory groups with the control, in contrast 2 we compare erasing with replacing. Why do you think it is important to compare only two things at a time?'

 CHECK YOUR BRAIN: Why do you think Alice's contrasts both compare only two things at a time?

I thought about Alice's question. I guessed that when we had looked at the fit of the model, we had tested something very general: is there a difference between means? That question then needed to be broken down further. These contrasts, on the other hand, by comparing only two things, were testing something very specific: that two things were different. I suggested to Alice that by comparing two things at a time we could clearly interpret the result, unlike with the *F*-ratio. She looked very pleased.

'Exactly, Zach – brilliant! Now, if you keep your contrasts independent by following the rules of (1) comparing two things at a time, and (2) never reusing a mean once it has been singled out, then you should always end up with one less contrast than the number of groups; there will be $k-1$ contrasts. With three groups you should end up with 2 contrasts, with four groups it will be 3, and so on.'

'How do you know what contrasts are correct?'

'It's not about there being correct contrasts, Zach: there is a correct way to make sure the contrasts are independent, but it's more about testing hypotheses and making sure that these hypotheses can be tested before you collect data. For example, look at this.' Alice drew another diagram for me. **(FIGURE 16.8)** 'Imagine an experiment in which you had a control group, and three groups where you had tried different memory manipulations. Now, generally, the first sensible contrast is likely to be to compare the experimental groups to the control group, because the function of a control group is to act as a control. However, contrast 2 could be constructed in several ways, all of which are correct in the sense that they compare two chunks of variation and they do not reintroduce the control group. On the left, the chunk of variation containing the experimental groups is broken down by first separating off group E3 from groups E1 and E2, and then in the third contrast separating out groups E1 and E2. On the right, the chunk of variation containing the experimental groups is broken down by first separating off group E1 from groups E2 and E3, and then in the third contrast separating out groups E2 and E3. Both sets of contrasts are independent, so both are correct, but which one you would choose would depend upon what the experimental groups represent and what it makes sense to compare. Note that in both cases we have three contrasts, which is one less than the number of groups, and that every group is singled out once and only once.'

Example I
Example 2

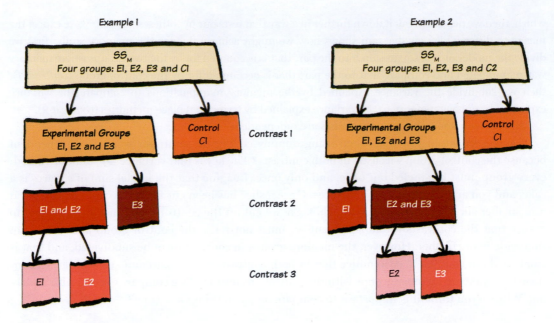

Figure 16.8 *Two examples of contrasts that might arise from a four-group experiment*

The take-home messages seemed to be to compare experimental groups with controls in the first contrast, that to keep contrasts independent each group should be singled out once and only once, and that each contrast should compare two chunks of variation.

16.3.2 Devising weights

'Once you know what comparisons you want to make,' Alice continued, 'you need to work out what numbers to assign to each group in the dummy variables to do the contrasts that you have designed. The numbers you assign to groups are known as **weights**.'

'You mean the 0s and 1s in the dummy coding scheme were weights?'

'Yes, but to code contrasts we need to use different numbers, or weights, that reflect the comparisons that we want to make. You do that by following some fairly simple rules. (1) Groups coded with positive weights will be compared against groups coded with negative weights. The first thing to do, then, is to arbitrarily assign one chunk of variation positive weights and the opposite chunk negative weights. (2) If a group is not involved in a comparison, assign it a weight of 0 to eliminate it from the calculations. Contrasts work by multiplying the group means by their weights, and anything multiplied by zero becomes zero. (3) For a given contrast, the magnitude of the weight assigned to the group(s) in one chunk of variation should be equal to the number of groups in the opposite chunk of variation. Let's see how this works in practice for the memory data.'

Alice drew me a diagram **(FIGURE 16.9)** before continuing. 'The first contrast we chose was to compare the two experimental groups against the control. So the first chunk of variation contains the two memory groups, and the second chunk contains only the control group. The first rule says that we arbitrarily assign one chunk positive weights, and the other negative. It doesn't matter which way round we do this, so I'll assign chunk 1 positive weights, and chunk 2 negative weights. The next question is what magnitude of weight to use. The third rule answers this question: the weight we assign to the groups in chunk 1 should be equivalent to the number of groups in chunk 2, and vice versa. There is only one group in chunk 2 and so we assign the groups in chunk 1 a weight of 1. Likewise, there are

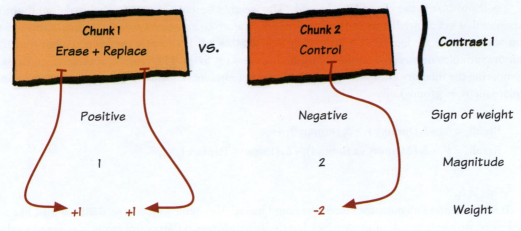

Figure 16.9   Defining the weights for contrast 1

two groups in chunk 1 so we give the control group (chunk 2) a weight of 2. By combining the sign of the weight with its magnitude we get weights of −2 (control), 1 (erase memory) and 1 (replace memory). What would the weights for the second contrast be?'

I drew a similar diagram to Alice's to help me think through the steps I needed to use to work out the weights. **(FIGURE 16.10)** The second contrast we devised compared the two memory groups, which meant ignoring the control group. The second rule told me that I should assign this group a weight of zero to eliminate it from the contrast. This left me with two chunks of variation: chunk 1 contained the erase group and chunk 2 contained the replace group. Just like Alice had done before, I started by assigning the first chunk a positive weight and the second chunk a negative. To work out the magnitude, I looked at the number of groups in the opposite chunk. Both chunks 1 and 2 contained only a single group; therefore, in both cases the opposite chunk contained one group. The magnitude would be 1 for both chunks. Combining the weight with the magnitude, I thought that the erase group should be assigned a weight of +1, the replace group a weight of −1 and the control group a 0.

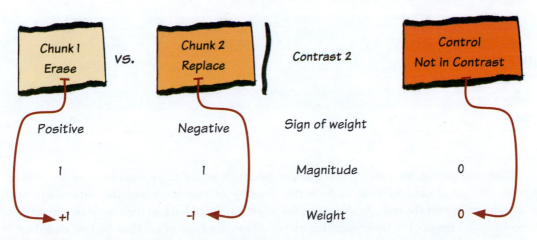

Figure 16.10   Defining the weights for contrast 2

16.3.3 Contrasts and the linear model

My response seemed to imbue Alice with a frantic enthusiasm to tell me more.

'Yes. Now, *this* is the clever bit,' she said. 'The weights we have just generated make up dummy variables that act as predictors in the linear model.' She wrote an equation (*16.15*). 'Compare this equation with the one we looked at a little while ago. (*EQUATION 16.2*) It's exactly the same, except that the dummy variables now represent the contrasts that we want to do. Therefore, b_1 represents contrast 1 (comparing the memory groups to the control), and b_2 represents contrast 2 (comparing the erase and replace memory groups).'

$$\text{Recall}_i = b_0 + b_1 \text{Dummy}\,1_i + b_2 \text{Dummy}\,2_i + \varepsilon_i$$
$$\text{Recall}_i = b_0 + b_1 (\text{Memory vs. Control})_i + b_2 (\text{Erase vs. Replace})_i + \varepsilon_i \tag{16.15}$$

'What is b_0?'

'It is the mean of all outcome scores, the grand mean.' Alice pulled up a table. (*TABLE 16.5*) 'Just like we did before, we create two dummy variables, but this time, anyone in the control group is assigned a value of −2 for the first variable and 0 for the second, anyone in the erase group will be assigned a value of 1 for both variables, and anyone in the replace group will be assigned a 1 for the first dummy variable and a −1 for the second. You can also do a useful double check of whether your contrasts are independent.'

'How?'

'First, add up the weights within a contrast; they should sum to zero. For contrast 1 we get −2 + 1 + 1, which is equal to zero. For contrast 2 we get 1 − 1 + 0, which is also equal to zero. Next, you multiply the weights of the two contrasts and then add up the results. The sum should again be zero. The final column of the table (*16.5*) shows these products: for example, for the control group you multiply −2 by 0, which results in zero. When we add up these products we get 0 + 1 − 1, which is equal to zero. If the weights within a contrast sum to zero and their products also sum to zero then the contrasts are independent.'

'So if you add the weights for a contrast, or multiply the weights, and the sum isn't zero you should have a meltdown?' I joked.

'You could just go back and redesign your contrasts,' Alice said with mock exasperation.

Table 16.5 *Orthogonal contrasts for the memory data*

Group	Dummy Variable 1 (Contrast$_1$)	Dummy Variable 2 (Contrast$_2$)	Product Contrast$_1$ × Contrast$_2$
Control	−2	0	0
Erase	1	1	1
Replace	1	−1	−1
Total	**0**	**0**	**0**

Alice's excitement increased further as she feverishly wrote more equations on her Proteus screen. My gut started to twist at both the quantity of equations and the enthusiasm with which she embraced the task. As she wrote, my mind wandered back in time to when we met. The innocence and freedom of those days, before real life took a hold of us. How had we ended up in a laboratory surrounded by unethical research, a menagerie of talking animals, and a lisping chimera? That word – chimera – jogged a memory of something Milton said when I was learning about significance testing: 'You would be wise to remember that chimeras are best avoided.'

Alice pulling my arm disrupted the thought. 'Stop daydreaming and look here,' she said, pointing to an equation (*16.16*). 'First let's see what b_0 represents. Remember that b_0 is the value of the outcome when the predictors are zero, so when using contrast coding this means it is the value of the outcome when both dummy variables are zero. When both dummy variables are zero it means that we do not know to which group a case belongs (because no groups are represented by codes of zero on both dummy variables). What is the predicted value of the outcome if group membership isn't known?'

'I don't know.'

'It would be the overall mean of the outcome, in this case the mean of all recall scores regardless of group. If we know nothing about group membership then we'd predict the mean value of all scores to be the outcome. When group sizes are equal, as they are for our memory data, this grand mean would be the same as the average of the group means. Does that make sense?'

$$\text{Recall}_i = b_0 + b_1 \text{Dummy} 1_i + b_2 \text{Dummy} 2_i$$
$$\overline{\text{Recall}}_i = b_0 + b_1 \times 0 + b_2 \times 0$$
$$\frac{\bar{X}_{\text{Erase}} + \bar{X}_{\text{Replace}} + \bar{X}_{\text{Control}}}{3} = b_0$$

(16.16)

I nodded.

'Let's look at the control group. We use the same equation; however, if we know someone is in the control group, then the predicted value from the model for that person is the mean of the control group. We can replace the dummy variables with the codes we devised to represent the control group: −2 for the first dummy variable and 0 for the second. If we rearrange the equation (*16.17*), then b_1 is proportionate to b_0 minus the mean of the control group.'

$$\text{Recall}_i = b_0 + b_1 \text{Dummy} 1_i + b_2 \text{Dummy} 2_i$$
$$\bar{X}_{\text{Control}} = b_0 + (-2 \times b_1) + (b_2 \times 0)$$
$$\bar{X}_{\text{Control}} = b_0 - 2b_1$$
$$2b_1 = b_0 - \bar{X}_{\text{Control}}$$

(16.17)

'But we know what the value of b_0 is, so can't we use that?'

'Yes, we know that b_0 is the average of the group means, so we can replace it with this average. If we rearrange this equation (*16.18*) and multiply everything by 3 to get rid of the fraction, you can see that b_1 is a function of the group means.'

$$2b_1 = \left(\frac{\bar{X}_{\text{Erase}} + \bar{X}_{\text{Replace}} + \bar{X}_{\text{Control}}}{3} \right) - \bar{X}_{\text{Control}}$$
$$6b_1 = \bar{X}_{\text{Erase}} + \bar{X}_{\text{Replace}} + \bar{X}_{\text{Control}} - 3\bar{X}_{\text{Control}}$$
$$6b_1 = \bar{X}_{\text{Erase}} + \bar{X}_{\text{Replace}} - 2\bar{X}_{\text{Control}}$$

(16.18)

Alice looked at me with wide-eyed anticipation of some kind of penny dropping in my head. The equation meant nothing to me, a fact that must have become apparent because she stepped in. 'Maybe it will help if we rearrange things,' she said. 'Let's divide everything by 2, first, which tells us what three times b_1 is, and then divide everything by 3 to get the value of b_1.' *(EQUATION 16.19)*

$$3b_1 = \left(\frac{\bar{X}_{\text{Erase}} + \bar{X}_{\text{Replace}}}{2} \right) - \bar{X}_{\text{Control}}$$

$$b_1 = \frac{1}{3} \left[\left(\frac{\bar{X}_{\text{Erase}} + \bar{X}_{\text{Replace}}}{2} \right) - \bar{X}_{\text{Control}} \right]$$

$$b_1 = \frac{1}{3} \left[\frac{4.75 + 2.67}{2} - 5 \right]$$

$$= -0.43$$

(16.19)

I studied the equations hard. I noticed that by dividing everything by 2 the right-hand side of the equation became the average of the experimental group means minus the mean of the control group. That seemed to make sense because in this first contrast we lumped those groups together and compared them to the control. It seemed like b_1 represented this contrast quite literally: it was the average score of the two memory groups (in other words, the average score if we treated them as a single group) compared to the average score in the control group. I put this idea to Alice and her face lit up.

'Yes! Yes! Yes! b_1 represents the difference between the average of the two memory groups and the control group, which is exactly what we set up contrast 1 to do! Notice, though, that rather than being the true value of the difference between experimental and control groups, b_1 is a third of this difference, which controls the familywise error.

'Now let's look at the erase group. Similar to before, if we know someone was in the erase group then the predicted value of the outcome is the mean of that group, and we also know that this group is represented by contrast codes of 1 for both dummy variables. If we place these values into the equation and rearrange it, you can see that b_2 is a function of the mean of the erase group and the other two bs.' **(EQUATION 16.20)**

$$\text{Recall}_i = b_0 + b_1 \text{Dummy} 1_i + b_2 \text{Dummy} 2_i$$

$$\bar{X}_{\text{Erase}} = b_0 + (b_1 \times 1) + (b_2 \times 1)$$

$$b_2 = \bar{X}_{\text{Erase}} - b_1 - b_0$$

(16.20)

I had a sinking feeling that told me that we were about to replace the bs with what they represented, and this meant that things were going to get hairy. Sure enough, Alice swiped her screen and showed me a gorilla of an equation.

'This looks bad ...' she began

'You aren't frippin' joking.'

Alice frowned at me and continued '... but it's not: we just need to clean it up a bit. First, we can multiply everything by 3 to get rid of some of the fractions.' **(EQUATION 16.21)**

$$b_2 = \bar{X}_{\text{Erase}} - b_1 - b_0$$

$$b_2 = \bar{X}_{\text{Erase}} - \frac{1}{3} \left[\left(\frac{\bar{X}_{\text{Erase}} + \bar{X}_{\text{Replace}}}{2} \right) - \bar{X}_{\text{Control}} \right] - \frac{\bar{X}_{\text{Erase}} + \bar{X}_{\text{Replace}} + \bar{X}_{\text{Control}}}{3}$$

$$3b_2 = 3\bar{X}_{\text{Erase}} - \left[\left(\frac{\bar{X}_{\text{Erase}} + \bar{X}_{\text{Replace}}}{2} \right) - \bar{X}_{\text{Control}} \right] - \bar{X}_{\text{Erase}} + \bar{X}_{\text{Replace}} + \bar{X}_{\text{Control}}$$

(16.21)

'Oh yeah, that helps a lot,' I said sarcastically.

Alice directed another of her finest scowls at me. 'Perhaps it will become clearer if we get rid of the remaining fractions by multiplying everything by 2. **(EQUATION 16.22)** Once we have done that we can simplify

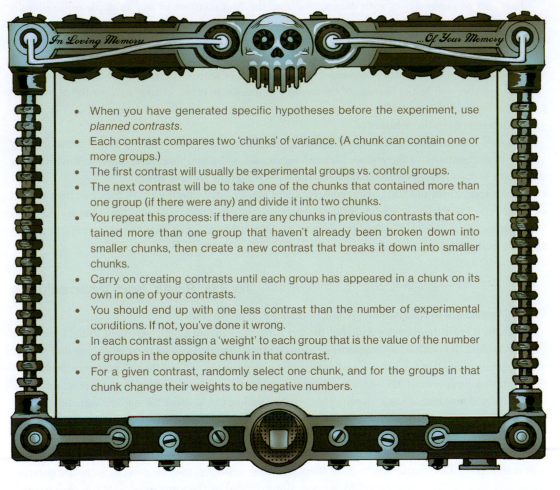

In Loving Memory ...Of Your Memory

- When you have generated specific hypotheses before the experiment, use *planned contrasts*.
- Each contrast compares two 'chunks' of variance. (A chunk can contain one or more groups.)
- The first contrast will usually be experimental groups vs. control groups.
- The next contrast will be to take one of the chunks that contained more than one group (if there were any) and divide it into two chunks.
- You repeat this process: if there are any chunks in previous contrasts that contained more than one group that haven't already been broken down into smaller chunks, then create a new contrast that breaks it down into smaller chunks.
- Carry on creating contrasts until each group has appeared in a chunk on its own in one of your contrasts.
- You should end up with one less contrast than the number of experimental conditions. If not, you've done it wrong.
- In each contrast assign a 'weight' to each group that is the value of the number of groups in the opposite chunk in that contrast.
- For a given contrast, randomly select one chunk, and for the groups in that chunk change their weights to be negative numbers.

Zach's Facts 16.2 *Planned contrasts*

things further by gathering up the terms. For example, we have 6 times the mean of the erase group, but also minus one times that mean and minus two times that mean, so what we actually have is $6-1-2 = 3$ times the erase mean. What you end up with is quite simple: that b_2 is a function of the difference between the erase and replace group means. What was contrast 2 set up to test?'

'The difference between the erase and replace group means.'

'Exactly, and that is what the b for contrast 2 represents. As with contrast 1, it does not represent the actual difference between means, but the difference between means divided by 2, and by b being smaller than the actual difference the Type I error rate is again controlled.'

$$6b_2 = 6\bar{X}_{\text{Erase}} - \left(\bar{X}_{\text{Erase}} + \bar{X}_{\text{Replace}} - 2\bar{X}_{\text{Control}}\right) - 2\left(\bar{X}_{\text{Erase}} + \bar{X}_{\text{Replace}} + \bar{X}_{\text{Control}}\right)$$

$$6b_2 = 6\bar{X}_{\text{Erase}} - \bar{X}_{\text{Erase}} - \bar{X}_{\text{Replace}} + 2\bar{X}_{\text{Control}} - 2\bar{X}_{\text{Erase}} - 2\bar{X}_{\text{Replace}} - 2\bar{X}_{\text{Control}}$$

$$6b_2 = 3\bar{X}_{\text{Erase}} - 3\bar{X}_{\text{Replace}}$$

$$b_2 = \frac{\bar{X}_{\text{Erase}} - \bar{X}_{\text{Replace}}}{2} \tag{16.22}$$

$$= \frac{4.75 - 2.67}{2}$$

$$= 1.04$$

This sort of made sense: with contrast coding, the first contrast in our example quite literally lumped the erase and replace memory groups together and treated them like a single group. I still wasn't entirely sure what was being compared here, so I asked Alice.

'You're right, the erase and replace groups are literally treated like a single entity. Their means are 4.75 and 2.67, and because they contained equal numbers of scores, the average of all of those scores lumped together will be the average of the two group means. In other words (4.75 + 2.67)/2, which is 3.71. The mean of the control group was 5, so this contrast asks whether the mean of 3.71 is significantly different from the mean of 5.'

I looked back at the original model. **(FIGURE 16.3)** 'Right, but the erase memory group mean is really similar to the control and the replace memory mean isn't, so by lumping them together it reduces the difference that you'd otherwise see between the replace and the control group.'

'That's true, Zach, but the second contrast helps you to infer whether that's the case, because if it is, you'd expect to find a significant difference between the erase and replace group. That would imply that the non-significant difference in contrast 1 might reflect the fact that the experimental groups produce quite different results.'

16.3.4 Post hoc procedures

'It seems weird not to compare everything to the control group,' I said.

'Perhaps it is for the memory data, but the fact is that those contrasts reflected our initial hypotheses even if the data did not end up supporting them. Another approach can be used when you do *not* have specific predictions. *Post hoc* tests consist of **pairwise comparisons** of all of the different combinations of the treatment group means. It's a bit like taking every pair of groups and performing a *t*-test on each pair.'

'If you're doing lots of tests, doesn't that create problems with error?' I vaguely remembered the Secret Philanthropic Society talking about that.

'Yes, it's the same problem that we have already discussed: it inflates the Type I error. The price you pay for doing lots of tests is that each test is corrected to make it stricter, so that across all tests the error rate is controlled. One example is to use a Bonferroni test where, instead of using alpha as the criterion for significance (which is usually 0.05), you use alpha divided by the number of tests you plan to use.'

This sounded familiar. I thought the Secret Philanthropic Society had told me about the Bonferroni correction. **(SECTION 10.1.7)**

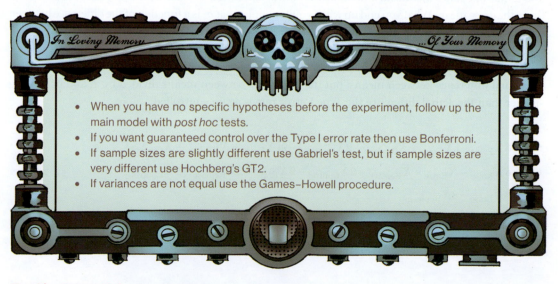

- When you have no specific hypotheses before the experiment, follow up the main model with *post hoc* tests.
- If you want guaranteed control over the Type I error rate then use Bonferroni.
- If sample sizes are slightly different use Gabriel's test, but if sample sizes are very different use Hochberg's GT2.
- If variances are not equal use the Games–Howell procedure.

Zach's Facts 16.3 *Post hoc tests*

'There are lots of other methods too,[119, 120] and many of them are designed for situations where the assumptions of the model are broken. For example, if the sample sizes are slightly different then use Gabriel's procedure because it has greater power, but if sample sizes are very different use Hochberg's GT2. If there is any doubt that the population variances are equal then use the Games–Howell procedure. There is an argument for using the Games–Howell procedure regardless, because it's never possible to know for certain that population variances are equivalent.'

I felt a sudden longing for the time – only a few moments ago – when the Bonferroni correction was the only method I knew about.

16.3.5 Contrasts and post hoc tests using a computer

'Of course you can ignore the equations and just let a computer do this for you,' Alice said as if sensing my brain fatigue. She gracefully moved her finger around the screen before showing it to me; it was populated with tables.

'Look, these two tables (OUTPUT 16.4) show the planned comparisons that we just designed. The first displays the weights that we devised; remember that groups with negative weights are compared to those with positive weights, so contrast 1 compares the control group against the two memory groups, and contrast 2 compares the erase group to the replace group. In the second table, if the homogeneity of variance assumption is met then read the rows labelled *Assume equal variance*; if not, use the rows labelled *Does not assume equal variances*. The value of the contrast is the weighted sum of the group means.'

I must have looked bemused because Alice explained, 'It's the sum of each group mean multiplied by the weight for the contrast of interest. For example, the first contrast yields a value of –2.58.' Alice scribbled out the calculation. (EQUATION 16.23)

$$\sum \bar{X}W = (5 \times -2) + (4.75 \times 1) + (2.67 \times 1) = -2.58 \tag{16.23}$$

Alice continued, 'The table also gives the standard error of each contrast and a *t*-statistic and its associated *p*-value. Contrast 1 shows that the memory erasing and replacing groups had mean recall scores that were not significantly different from controls ($p = 0.201$). Contrast 2 tells us that mean recall scores were not significantly different in the erasing and replacing groups ($p = 0.078$).'

'What about the *b*s?' I asked. After all, Alice had virtually liquidized my brain showing me what they represented.

'We can look at these. (OUTPUT 16.5) Notice that, as I mentioned before, b_0 is 4.139, which matches the mean of all scores. (TABLE 16.1) The *b* for contrast 1 is –0.43, which matches the value we calculated: it's one-third of the difference between the average of the memory groups and the control group mean. Finally, the *b* for contrast 2 is 1.04, which matches our calculated value: it is half of the difference

Contrast Coefficients

Contrast	Experimental Group		
	Control	Erase	Replace
1	-2	1	1
2	0	1	-1

Contrast Tests

		Contrast	Value of Contrast	Std. Error	t	df	Sig. (2-tailed)
Memory Recall (Out of 10)	Assume equal variances	1	-2.58	1.981	-1.304	33	.201
		2	2.08	1.144	1.822	33	.078
	Does not assume equal variances	1	-2.58	1.836	-1.407	25.980	.171
		2	2.08	1.221	1.706	19.121	.104

Output 16.4 *Planned contrasts using IBM SPSS Statistics*

between the memory groups. Note that the significance values for these bs are 0.201 and 0.078 respectively, which match the values in the previous table.'

Alice swiped to another table. **(OUTPUT 16.6)** 'Here I have used two *post hoc* methods: Bonferroni and the Games–Howell procedure. Look at the Bonferroni comparisons first. The control group is compared to the erase group and reveals a non-significant difference (because *Sig.* is greater than 0.05). It is then compared to the replace group, revealing another non-significant difference ($p = 0.148$). The final comparison is between the erase and replace groups, for which the difference is also not significant ($p = 0.233$). These comparisons are repeated in the bottom half of the table, but using the Games–Howell procedure, which is used when homogeneity of variance can't be assumed. Are the groups significantly different?'

Coefficients^a

Model		Unstandardized Coefficients B	Unstandardized Coefficients Std. Error	Standardized Coefficients Beta	t	Sig.	95.0% Confidence Interval for B Lower Bound	95.0% Confidence Interval for B Upper Bound
1	(Constant)	4.139	.467		8.866	.000	3.189	5.089
	Memory groups vs. Control	-.431	.330	-.212	-1.304	.201	-1.102	.241
	Erase vs. Replace	1.042	.572	.295	1.822	.078	-.122	2.205

a. Dependent Variable: Memory Recall (Out of 10)

Output 16.5 *Coefficients for the model of the memory data using IBM SPSS Statistics*

CHECK YOUR BRAIN: Look at Output 16.6. Are any of the groups significantly different when compared using the Games–Howell procedure?

'No,' I replied, 'the p-value when comparing the control with the erase group is 0.964, when comparing the control with the replace group it's 0.165, and when comparing the erase and replace groups it's 0.229. These values are all greater than 0.05, so none of the groups are significantly different.'

Multiple Comparisons

Dependent Variable: Memory Recall (Out of 10)

	(I) Experimental Group	(J) Experimental Group	Mean Difference (I–J)	Std. Error	Sig.	95% Confidence Interval Lower Bound	95% Confidence Interval Upper Bound
Bonferroni	Control	Erase	.250	1.144	1.000	-2.63	3.13
		Replace	2.333	1.144	.148	-.55	5.22
	Erase	Control	-.250	1.144	1.000	-3.13	2.63
		Replace	2.083	1.144	.233	-.80	4.97
	Replace	Control	-2.333	1.144	.148	-5.22	.55
		Erase	-2.083	1.144	.233	-4.97	.80
Games–Howell	Control	Erase	.250	.962	.964	-2.17	2.67
		Replace	2.333	1.227	.165	-.78	5.45
	Erase	Control	-.250	.962	.964	-2.67	2.17
		Replace	2.083	1.221	.229	-1.02	5.18
	Replace	Control	-2.333	1.227	.165	-5.45	.78
		Erase	-2.083	1.221	.229	-5.18	1.02

Output 16.6 *Post hoc tests using IBM SPSS Statistics*

16.4 STORM OF MEMORIES

It seemed, then, as though JIG:SAW's attempts to erase or replace people's memories had not been successful, which made me wonder why they'd bothered doing a second experiment. Alice shrugged her shoulders when I asked.

Roediger and Milton had been talking intensely. Periodically the dog lunged at Milton and ran off expecting the cat to chase him. I'd never seen Milton look so fed up. If Alice didn't know why the second experiment was done then I'd have to get it out of Roediger. Remembering his issue with obeying instructions, I crouched down, patted my knees excitedly to get his attention and said, 'It would make me so happy if you *don't* tell me why you pursued this research after the first study failed.'

'What? You want to know why we pursued this research? No problem. It was because of the case studies on the DRM process: the distal removal of memory,' he replied.

I heard Clint's pace quicken around the room. Alice looked shocked. 'Case *studies*? You mean *study*?' she said.

'No, *studies*. The first case study was Celia,' Roediger's breathy voice made her name sound like *wheelia*, 'then we did some more. It works: they collapse and don't remember anything. It's no problem.'

That's why Chippers have been collapsing and losing their memories, I thought. JIG:SAW have used their ID chips to erase their memories remotely.

'Why wasn't I told?' Alice demanded. She looked lost. Whatever she was doing here, this was new information. What did the dog mean by Celia being a case study? My mind conjured an image of Celia in trouble, being experimented on. I wished in that second that I could help everyone here: the code 1318s, Alice, Celia, the collapsing guy on the bench, and even the rude cat and exciteable dog.

'Celia was a case study?' I asked.

Roediger looked sheepish, his head dipped and his eyes raced around the room before settling on me.

'Mr Nutcot made Roediger wipe Celia's memory after she went to spy on Alice. It was no problem,' he slobbered.

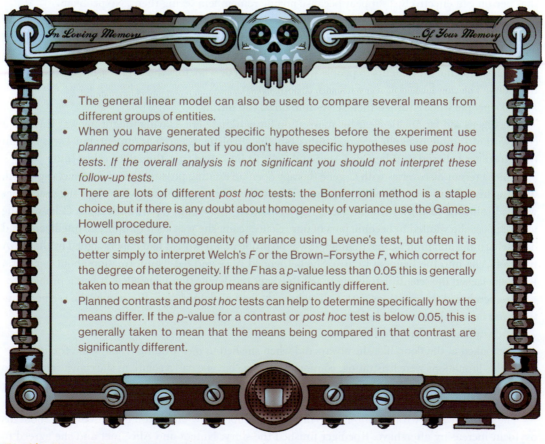

In Loving Memory ...Of Your Memory

- The general linear model can also be used to compare several means from different groups of entities.
- When you have generated specific hypotheses before the experiment use *planned comparisons*, but if you don't have specific hypotheses use *post hoc* tests. *If the overall analysis is not significant you should not interpret these follow-up tests.*
- There are lots of different *post hoc* tests: the Bonferroni method is a staple choice, but if there is any doubt about homogeneity of variance use the Games–Howell procedure.
- You can test for homogeneity of variance using Levene's test, but often it is better simply to interpret Welch's F or the Brown–Forsythe F, which correct for the degree of heterogeneity. If the F has a p-value less than 0.05 this is generally taken to mean that the group means are significantly different.
- Planned contrasts and *post hoc* tests can help to determine specifically how the means differ. If the p-value for a contrast or *post hoc* test is below 0.05, this is generally taken to mean that the means being compared in that contrast are significantly different.

Zach's Facts 16.4 *One-way ANOVA*

What? Celia spied on Alice? The colour had drained from Alice's face when the dog mentioned other case studies, but she hadn't flinched at the mention of Celia being one or at being spied on. Did Alice know about this already? If Celia had spied on Alice, had she been spying on me too? Had she been pretending to like my band and me? Suddenly I registered something more important in what Roediger had said: he'd wiped her memory. Was this what Celia had meant when she told me that she'd had to reinvent herself? Did she have to take on a new name and become a new person because her memories were erased? It made sense, but it didn't explain her gravestone. Had The Head made a mistake, or was the gravestone a metaphor for the death of her former self? Why would someone buy a tombstone as a metaphor, and if she had no memory, how would she remember that she had a former self to bury? The more I thought about it, the less sense I found. I felt sure that the key to finding out was Roediger: in one sentence he had already dropped two bombshells.

I tried to tempt the dog over with a friendly call, but he sneaked off looking guiltily over his shoulder, mumbling 'I think Roediger left a ball over here ...' I called him again, but assertively, and the spaniel instinctively waggle-danced towards me. He looked panicked. 'Roediger didn't mean anything ...' he squeaked, '... just followed Mr Nutcot's orders to discover ways to make someone disappear.'

There it was, bombshell number three: the research here was aimed at trying to make people disappear. I made a mental note never to trust a spaniel with important information. If the aim was to disappear, the invisibility work in the previous building made sense, but how did memory fit in? I gently patted the dog's head trying to forget he was once a physicist, and asked him not to tell me about his work.

'Roediger developed two parallel approaches to the problem of making someone disappear. The first you saw in the other laboratory: masks that obfuscated the face beneath. The second was to manipulate memory. If you replace the memory of someone's image with that of someone else, then that person can effectively disappear because no one remembers seeing them. No problem.'

That was some rad stuff, but from the first experiment it looked like it didn't work. I wondered why Nutcot would want to make someone disappear. I asked the dog.

'It is part of JIG:SAW's Less Ingrained Evil in Society programme. We pursue altruistic lines of research – imagine the benefits to people who are injured or who, for whatever reason, don't like how they look.' The dog looked at me with sad, droopy eyes.

'Like people who've turned themselves into dogs, you mean?'

Roediger's sad face made clear his motivation for working here. Having fought my way through a courtyard of zombie research rejects, I didn't buy the altruistic research argument, but I was certain that Roediger believed it. Where did Alice and Celia fit into all of this, though? I asked him.

'Alice's recent discoveries with C-gene therapy open up exciting possibilities,' the spaniel explained, wagging his tail furiously. 'Roediger wanted to know about her secret work. Mr Nutcot suggested that we send someone to work with Alice as a research intern who would report back to us. Celia was the ideal choice: she wanted to become part of our science team, she was keen to impress, intelligent, and had a charming and professional manner. It was no problem. Mr Nutcot had papers signed by the WGA that got Celia into the Beimeni Centre. She befriended Alice and fed us information about her work. But Celia lacked the scientific training to tell Roediger the details that he needed. It was a problem.'

I remembered the meetings with Celia where she had explained statistics to me; she seemed anything *but* lacking in scientific training.

'And you had no idea?' I asked Alice.

She looked at the floor, like she always did when she lied to me. 'I thought she was a friend'.

'Celia's limitations were frustrating,' continued the dog, 'but she had a solution: she convinced Alice to meet Mr Nutcot to discuss continuing her work for JIG:SAW. Celia was convinced that once Alice saw our facilities, and Mr Nutcot explained our altruistic plans, she would join us. Mr Nutcot can be persuasive.'

The spaniel wasn't wrong, I thought to myself, remembering what Milton had discovered about his oxytocin-increasing aftershave. Roediger finished the story: Nutcot and Alice met and she agreed to work here. I assumed that they also made her give up her life, give up me, to come and work here in secret. The final puzzle was why Celia became a case study. Roediger explained that once she had fulfilled her purpose as a spy, Nutcot ordered him to wipe her memory. She became the first test of their DRM process.

This final revelation made me really angry. I demanded to know *why* they would wipe Celia's memory.

'After working at the Beimeni Centre, Celia changed,' Roediger replied. 'She turned up for work erratically and she asked too many questions about our research. Once we had Alice, Mr Nutcot thought it best that she forget her mission … just to be safe.'

My rage escalated. 'And you just did it: you zapped her memory? Zapped her *life* from her?' I screamed at him.

The spaniel army-crawled backwards, whimpering 'Schrödinger's prison'. With his body still pressed to the floor and his apologetic eyes staring up at me, he mumbled again that Mr Nutcot could be very persuasive. Would Nutcot's oxytocin aftershave work on a dog, I wondered. I wasn't sure, but I believed that whatever Roediger had done, he'd done out of fear, and perhaps a need to be seen as a human again. Nutcot was the villain, not Roediger, except that he had turned out to be no more than a puppet. The question was who had pulled his strings.

Roediger seemed to sense my forgiving vibe, and offered his belly for a rub. I obliged, hoping it would get me more information. I asked him what happened to Celia.

'It was no problem,' he said spinning over onto his feet. 'Mr Nutcot messaged Celia and she remembered nothing. She found her ID card for JIG:SAW in her bag but could not remember Mr Nutcot, Alice, or anything about her job. Mr Nutcot invited her back and told her it was an opportunity to wipe the slate clean, to start afresh, a new name, none of the baggage of the past, she could be whatever she wanted to be. Unfortunately, what she wanted to be was someone who dressed less appropriately and listened to terrible music. Roediger thinks she is happier now.'

16.5   REPEATED-MEASURES DESIGNS

Alice interrupted. 'Regardless of Celia, once I started here and looked at the data from properly controlled experiments, I found that their memory erasing and replacing techniques did not work.' She looked shifty.

Clint had stopped pacing around the room and cast a foreboding shadow over me.

'How do you know?' he asked Alice.

Hearing his serpenty voice spooked me: since we'd met him he had silently kept his council like a really conspicuous fly on the wall. Why was he suddenly interested in the experiments?

Alice didn't share my concern and explained. 'The second experiment demonstrates perfectly,' she said. 'This experiment used a repeated-measures design. Five participants engaged in three different scripted encounters with an experimenter during which 10 unusual things happened. Participants were asked to recall what happened. After one encounter we left them alone (control), after another we implanted verbal descriptions of 10 different things into their ID chips while they were recalling, and after the third we implanted visual images of 10 different things using their ID chips while they recalled. We then asked them to recall the original encounter again and measured how many of the 10 unusual events that they recalled. Their data are here,' she said, showing us her Proteus screen. (TABLE 16.6)

I studied the table. 'The recall scores were lower for the encounters where visual interference was used afterwards.'

Table 16.6 *Data for the memory-implanting experiment*

Participant	No interference	Verbal interference	Visual interference	Mean	s^2
1	7	6	2	5.00	7.00
2	8	3	8	6.33	8.33
3	7	7	3	5.67	5.33
4	5	4	1	3.33	4.33
5	8	10	0	6.00	28.00
Mean (SD)	**7.00 (1.22)**	**6.00 (2.74)**	**2.80 (3.11)**		

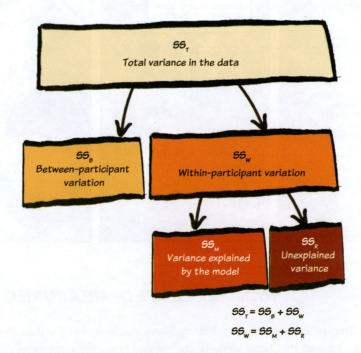

$$SS_T = SS_B + SS_W$$
$$SS_W = SS_M + SS_R$$

Figure 16.11 *Partitioning variance for repeated-measures designs*

'True,' Alice replied, with the look of a woman realizing that she was going to have to explain some more statistics to her annoying boyfriend who had turned up at her work uninvited. 'The fact it is a repeated-measures design slightly changes how we break down the variance in recall scores.'

Alice drew Clint and me a diagram. **(FIGURE 16.11)** 'Look. We end up with all of the same measures of variability as before: the total variability (SS_T), the variability due to the experimental manipulation (SS_M), and the variability created by factors we haven't measured (SS_R). However, how we get to them is slightly different because in a repeated-measures design the SS_M and SS_R are found *within* participants' scores. The variance within a participant's scores across different conditions will be made up of two things: the effect of the memory manipulation and individual differences in their performance at different points in time. There will also be individual differences *between* participants – for example, some people have better memories than others – and this is captured by SS_B.'

16.5.1 The total sum of squares, SS$_T$

'The fact that we have a repeated-measures design doesn't change a lot,' Alice continued; 'just that the model and residual sum of squares are now contained in the within-participant variation. Most of the calculations of sums of squares are the same as before. The exception is the residual sum of squares, because a repeated-measures design enables us to differentiate variance in recall due to individual differences, which is captured by SS_B, and variance in recall that is due to unmeasured variables that affected performance within an individual across the treatment conditions, which is captured by SS_R. The design is more sensitive because some of the error that is included in the residual sum of squares in an independent design can be removed, which makes SS_R smaller. Let's start, as we did before, by calculating the total sum of squares. You calculate this in exactly the same way as I explained before.'

CHECK YOUR BRAIN: Use what you have learnt in this chapter to help Zach to work out the total sum of squares. Some values that will help you are in Figure 16.12.

Clint watched with interest as I thought back to the previous experiment and worked through the current one. In the previous experiment, Alice had treated all of the data as a single group. I wrote this down **(FIGURE 16.12)** and calculated the overall mean for the scores, which was 5.267. I drew myself a table **(16.7)** and put the recall scores in a column, next to them I put the value of the grand mean (column 3). Then just as Alice had done, I calculated the error or difference between each score and this grand mean (column 4). I squared these differences and placed them in the final column. This final column now contained the values of the squared errors for each score; to get the total, I added the scores together. With the help of a calculator app I reached the conclusion that the total sum of squares was 122.93. **(TABLE 16.7)**

$$
\begin{array}{ccc}
7 & 6 & 2 \\
8 & 3 & 8 \\
7 & 7 & 3 \\
5 & 4 & 1 \\
8 & 10 & 0 \\
\end{array}
$$

Mean = 5.267
Variance = 8.781

Figure 16.12   *Treating the data as a single group*

16.5.2 The within-participant variance. SS_W

Alice squeezed my forearm. 'Well done,' she said, before placing her affection back under her emotional tombstone. 'The key thing to calculate in a repeated-measures design is the variance within participants, SS_W. When scores were independent, like they were in the previous experiment, we calculated individual differences within *groups*. The difference in a repeated-measures design is that this variance is now within *participants*, rather than within groups. However, we can use the same equation, the only difference is that we apply the equation to each *person* rather than each *group*.'

'You mean we look at the sum of squares within an individual's scores and then add these up for all of the people in the study?'

'Exactly.' Alice wrote an equation. **(16.24)** 'Look, this is the same as the equation we used before to work out the SS_R **(EQUATION 16.12)**, except that we're applying it to each person.' Alice activated a table **(TABLE 16.8)** and pointed at it. 'Look, I have rearranged the scores from the experiment from my original table **(TABLE 16.6)** so that each score is in its own row. The first three rows are the scores for the first participant in the different conditions. We can work out the sum of squared errors within this participant by using their mean score. The mean score for the first person was 5, which we can see because it is their three scores summed and divided by 3 $((7 + 6 + 2)/3 = 5)$. To calculate the sum of squared errors within this person we first calculate the difference between each of this person's scores and their mean score. For example, in the no-interference condition the first person had a recall score of 7, their mean score was 5 so the difference is 7 minus 5, which is 2. I have put this error value in column 5. If I do the same for their score in the verbal interference condition I get 6 minus 5, which is 1. Finally, for the visual interference condition I get 2 minus 5, which is −3. These are the raw errors and we square them – as we always do. I have placed these squared values in column 6. By squaring the values, 2 becomes 4, 1 remains the same and −3 becomes 9. To get the sum of squared errors within this person we add these squared errors, which gives us 4 + 1 + 9, which equals 14.'

'Presumably you repeat this for every person?'

Table 16.7 *Calculating the total sums of squares for the memory-implanting experiment*

	Recall	Grand Mean	$x_i - \bar{X}_{grand}$	$(x_i - \bar{X}_{grand})^2$
No interference	7	5.267	1.733	**3.003**
	8	5.267	2.733	**7.469**
	7	5.267	1.733	**3.003**
	5	5.267	−0.267	**0.071**
	8	5.267	2.733	**7.469**
Verbal interference	6	5.267	0.733	**0.537**
	3	5.267	−2.267	**5.139**
	7	5.267	1.733	**3.003**
	4	5.267	−1.267	**1.605**
	10	5.267	4.733	**22.401**
Visual interference	2	5.267	−3.267	**10.673**
	8	5.267	2.733	**7.469**
	3	5.267	−2.267	**5.139**
	1	5.267	−4.267	**18.207**
	0	5.267	−5.267	**27.741**
Σ				**122.933**

'Yes, we'd do the same for the next person and carry on until the final participant. Obviously a computer does this very quickly. When we have the sums of squared errors within each person we add them up.' Alice pointed at her equation (16.24), which showed that when we added up the sum of squared errors for each person the total was 106.

$$SS_W = SS_{Entity\,1} + SS_{Entity\,2} + \ldots + SS_{Entity\,n}$$
$$= 14 + 16.67 + 10.67 + 8.67 + 56 \tag{16.24}$$
$$= 106$$

'The degrees of freedom for each person,' Alice continued, 'are one less than the number of scores on which each sum of squares is based, $n - 1$. For each person we based their sums of squares on 3 values, so the degrees of freedom for each person would be 3 – 1, which is 2. The degrees of freedom overall, df_W, will be the sum of the degrees of freedom for each person.'

For each person there were 2 degrees of freedom, and there were five participants; so I calculated that the total degrees of freedom were 2×5, or 10.

I could hear Clint breathing behind me.

Table 16.8   *Calculating the within participant sums of squares for the memory-implanting experiment*

Person	Condition	Recall	Person's Mean	$x_i - \bar{x}_{Person}$	$(x_i - \bar{x}_{Person})^2$	SS_{Person}
1	No interference	7	5.00	2.00	4.00	
	Verbal interference	6	5.00	1.00	1.00	**14.00**
	Visual interference	2	5.00	–3.00	9.00	
2	No interference	8	6.33	1.67	2.79	
	Verbal interference	3	6.33	–3.33	11.09	**16.67**
	Visual interference	8	6.33	1.67	2.79	
3	No interference	7	5.67	1.33	1.77	
	Verbal interference	7	5.67	1.33	1.77	**10.67**
	Visual interference	3	5.67	–2.67	7.13	
4	No interference	5	3.33	1.67	2.79	
	Verbal interference	4	3.33	0.67	0.45	**8.67**
	Visual interference	1	3.33	–2.33	5.43	
5	No interference	8	6.00	2.00	4.00	
	Verbal interference	10	6.00	4.00	16.00	**56.00**
	Visual interference	0	6.00	–6.00	36.00	
Σ						**106.00**

16.5.3 The model sum of squares, SS_M

'This within-participant variance is made up of the variance created by individuals' memory performances in the three different conditions,' Alice continued. 'Some of this variation is the result of our experimental manipulation and some of it is random fluctuation in performance. The next step is to work out how much variance is attributable to each. To work out how much is due to the experimental manipulation – the different ways of interfering with memory – we can calculate the model sum of squares in exactly the same way as we did before.'

CHECK YOUR BRAIN: Use what you have learnt in this chapter to help Zach to work out the model sum of squares. Some values that will help you are in Table 16.6 and Figure 16.12.

I thought back to the previous experiment. We had looked at the means for each experimental condition and compared these to the overall mean. Basically, we measured the variance resulting from the differences between condition means and the overall mean. **(EQUATION 16.9)** If we applied the same equation here, then we'd take each condition mean from the data table **(TABLE 16.6)**, and subtract from it the mean of all 15 scores, which I calculated before. **(FIGURE 16.12)** I'd need to square these differences to get the difference for each person, and then multiply each difference by the number of people who took part in each condition, in this case 5. The result was 48.133. **(EQUATION 16.25)**

$$
\begin{aligned}
SS_M &= 5(7-5.271)^2 + 5(6-5.271)^2 + 5(2.8-5.271)^2 \\
&= 5(1.729)^2 + 5(0.729)^2 + 5(-2.471)^2 \\
&= 14.947 + 2.657 + 30.529 \\
&= 48.133
\end{aligned}
\tag{16.25}
$$

Alice explained how to work out the degrees of freedom associated with the value, df_M; it was the number of conditions minus 1 or $k - 1$, which in this case would be 2.

16.5.4 The residual sum of squares, SS_R

I was impressed with myself, but if Alice was too she didn't show it.

'Listen Zach, the final sum of squares is the residual sum of squares (SS_R), which tells us how much of the variation cannot be explained by the experimental manipulation. The simplest way to get this value is by knowing that SS_W is made up of SS_M and SS_R. **(FIGURE 16.11)** Therefore, we can calculate SS_R by subtracting SS_M from SS_W. If you do that you'll find that SS_R is 57.87.' **(EQUATION 16.11)**

$$
\begin{aligned}
SS_R &= SS_W - SS_M \\
SS_R &= 106 - 48.133 \\
SS_R &= 57.867
\end{aligned}
\tag{16.26}
$$

'And the degrees of freedom?'

'You use the same logic: the residual degrees of freedom are the model degrees of freedom subtracted from the within-participant degrees of freedom.' **(EQUATION 16.27)**

$$
\begin{aligned}
df_R &= df_W - df_M \\
&= 10 - 2 \\
&= 8
\end{aligned}
\tag{16.27}
$$

16.5.5 Mean squares and the F-ratio

Basically the process was very similar whether you had different groups of scores or scores within the same entities. I asked whether this meant that we'd have to convert the sums of squares to mean squares.

The lid of Alice's emotional coffin lifted a few millimetres, enough to catch a glimpse of tenderness. 'Well done. From now the process is identical: each sum of squares is divided by its degrees of freedom to calculate mean squares for the model and a residual mean squares, and then the model mean squares is divided by the residual to get a value of F. We then calculate the probability of getting an F at least that big, if the null hypothesis were true.'

 CHECK YOUR BRAIN: Help Zach to calculate the mean squares and F-ratio.

I thought back to the equations we used in the previous example. (EQUATION 16.13 & 16.14) I replaced the values Alice and I had just calculated to first work out the mean squares (EQUATION 16.28) and then the F-ratio itself. (EQUATION 16.29) Just as I'd learnt earlier, MS_M represented the average amount of variation explained by the experiment, the variance in recall created by the different memory interventions, whereas MS_R gauged the average variation explained by other variables that might affect memory performance at different points in time.

$$MS_M = \frac{SS_M}{df_M} = \frac{48.133}{2} = 24.067$$
$$MS_R = \frac{SS_R}{df_R} = \frac{57.867}{8} = 7.233$$

(16.28)

The F-ratio was again a signal-to-noise ratio: the ratio of the variation explained by the model to the variation explained by unsystematic factors. I compared the value of 3.327 against a critical value from the table Alice had shown me (SECTION A.4) based on df_M and df_R, which were 2 and 8. The critical value was 4.46, so our value was lower, which meant that the difference between recall in the three conditions was not significant.

$$F = \frac{MS_M}{MS_R} = \frac{24.067}{7.233} = 3.327$$

(16.29)

I told Alice my conclusions, as Clint's eyes reached over my shoulder on their stalks. 'Well done,' she said. 'See how the value of F and your conclusions match my conclusions in my report.' (LAB NOTES 16.1)

I studied her report and noticed that the degrees of freedom that she had reported were different than mine: she had reported 1.01 and 4.06 for df_M and df_R, whereas I worked them out to be 2 and 8. I asked why.

'Oh, I corrected them for **sphericity**.'

'For what?'

'You don't want to know,' Alice said impatiently. She suddenly became twitchy and keen to leave. 'Look, Zach, we need to go. Now! You've got the answers you came for, now let me get you somewhere safe, somewhere away from here. *Please.*' With that she gave me a look that suggested that she was a lot more stressed by this situation than she'd let on. I still sensed she knew more than she was letting on. Getting to know Celia over the past few weeks had highlighted just what a closed book Alice was. Celia wore her heart on her sleeve; I wasn't sure Alice even had a heart right now. 'I've got work to do to get you out of this mess,' she said and took herself off to a computer terminal across the room.

My diePad beeped with a message from Milton. **(MEOWSINGS 16.2)** It proved one thing: Alice was right, I didn't want to know about sphericity.

16.5.6 Repeated-measures designs using a computer

Alice cut a frustrated figure as she poked and swiped at the screen in front of her. Clint had followed her once we'd finished looking at the experimental data and was likewise engaged in some computer activity behind her. I guess he was trying to help us get out too. While Alice had explained the second experiment, Milton and Roediger had been arguing. It was strange to think that these two animals had

Dear Human,

Interesting thing, sphericity; it refers to the equality of variances of the *differences* between treatment levels. In the memory-implanting experiment there are three treatment conditions: no interference, verbal interference and visual interference. We can calculate the difference between scores for every pair of conditions. Table 16.9 shows this: the fourth column is the difference between the no-interference condition and the verbal interference condition (for the first participant, the result is $7 - 6 = 1$); the next column is the difference between the no-interference condition and the visual interference condition ($7 - 2 = 5$ for the first participant); the final column is the difference between the verbal interference condition and the visual interference condition. Having done this, we can calculate the variance of these differences. For example, the variance of the differences between no interference and verbal interference is 6.5. Sphericity is met when the variances of these differences are roughly equal. As such, the assumption is like homogeneity of variance *but applied to the differences between conditions*. In this example, the variances of differences seem quite unequal: they are 6.5, 8.2 and 28.7, which suggests that sphericity does not hold.

Mauchly's test examines the hypothesis that the variances of the differences between conditions are equal: if it is significant (i.e., the *p*-value is less than 0.05) sphericity cannot be assumed. Like any significance test, Mauchly's test depends upon sample size: in big samples small deviations from sphericity can be significant, and in small samples large violations can be non-significant (Milton's Meowsings 12.3).

There are two estimates of the degree to which sphericity is met that result in a value that is 1 when data are spherical and less than 1 when they are not: the **Greenhouse–Geisser estimate**[121] and the **Huynh–Feldt estimate**.[122] The Greenhouse–Geisser estimate is favoured except when estimates of sphericity are greater than 0.75, in which case the Huynh–Feldt estimate is preferred.[122–124] The degrees of freedom for the corresponding *F*-ratio are multiplied by these estimates to correct for the deviation from sphericity: when sphericity is met, the estimate is 1 and the degrees of freedom do not change, but deviations from sphericity will yield an estimate less than 1 and smaller degrees of freedom. The smaller degrees of freedom will make the *p*-value associated with the *F*-ratio larger (i.e., less significant). Because the estimates correct for the exact degree of sphericity in the data, there is an argument to always look at the corrected values and ignore Mauchly's test.

Best fishes,
Milton

Table 16.9   *Calculating the variance of the differences between conditions*

No interference	Verbal interference	Visual interference	No–Verbal	No–Visual	Verbal–Visual
7	6	2	1	5	4
8	3	8	5	0	–5
7	7	3	0	4	4
5	4	1	1	4	3
8	10	0	–2	8	10
		Variance:	6.5	8.2	28.7
		Mean	1.0	4.2	3.2
		SD	2.55	2.86	5.36

Milton's Meowsings 16.2   *Sphericity*

once sat together on the precipice of human discovery. If they could have seen the future – actually watched themselves in this lab padding about, play-fighting and sniffing each other inbetween scientific debates – what would they have thought of their futures? Milton was a victim of his own undoubted genius, whereas Roediger was a sobering reminder of how brilliant people, even scientists, could put their ego before what actually mattered: the science. I suspected Roediger's personality had benefited from having a spaniel's perspective; his spaniel had not been quite so lucky. I asked them why they were arguing; Milton told me that Roediger was puzzled by the discrepancy between the case study that they had done with Celia, and these experimental results. Roediger complained that Milton was less interested in play-fighting than he used to be.

Milton asked to see Alice's data. I still had her Proteus, so I went to give it to him but Roediger intercepted it.

'Only a masochist would do this by hand,' he said, as he swiped his tongue around the screen. 'Look, Roediger did the analysis in a second, it was no problem.' The dog beamed. He looked excited, 'Look! It's Mauchly's test. **(OUTPUT 16.7)** The significance value (0.005) is less than the critical value of 0.05, which means that the assumption of sphericity has been violated. I like a violation of sphericity. Walkies?'

I frowned at him, and he looked disappointed. 'No problem,' he said softly, before his excitement returned. 'The table tells us the estimates of sphericity: the Greenhouse–Geisser estimate, $\hat{\varepsilon}$ = 0.507, and the Huynh–Feldt estimate, $\hat{\varepsilon}$ = 0.514. These estimates are used to correct the degrees of freedom for the F-ratio in the main part of the output.'

'Milton told me to ignore Mauchly's test,' I said. Milton looked pleased with me.

'What?' replied the spaniel. 'But we had a tiny sample size, which means low power to detect departures from sphericity, so the significance *does* suggest a problem.' Milton grimaced.

The dog waved the output at me. 'In the main table **(OUTPUT 16.8)** the rows labelled *MemoryInterference* are the overall experimental effect: we are told the sums of squares for the model (SS_M = 48.13), the degrees of freedom, 2, and the mean squares for the model, which is 24.07. The rows labelled *Error*

tell us the residual sum of squares, SS_R, which is 57.87 units, the degrees of freedom, which are 8, and the mean squares (MS_R), which are 7.23.'

Mauchly's Test of Sphericity[a]

Measure: MEASURE_1

Within Subjects Effect	Mauchly's W	Approx. Chi-Square	df	Sig.	Epsilon[b]		
					Greenhouse-Geisser	Huynh-Feldt	Lower-bound
MemoryInterfere nce	.027	10.792	2	.005	.507	.514	.500

Tests the null hypothesis that the error covariance matrix of the orthonormalized transformed dependent variables is proportional to an identity matrix.

a. Design: Intercept
   Within Subjects Design: MemoryInterference

b. May be used to adjust the degrees of freedom for the averaged tests of significance. Corrected tests are displayed in the Tests of Within-Subjects Effects table.

Output 16.7   *Mauchly's test using IBM SPSS Statistics*

Tests of Within-Subjects Effects

Measure: MEASURE_1

Source		Type III Sum of Squares	df	Mean Square	F	Sig.
MemoryInterference	Sphericity Assumed	48.133	2	24.067	3.327	.089
	Greenhouse-Geisser	48.133	1.014	47.474	3.327	.141
	Huynh-Feldt	48.133	1.028	46.827	3.327	.140
	Lower-bound	48.133	1.000	48.133	3.327	.142
Error (MemoryInterference)	Sphericity Assumed	57.867	8	7.233		
	Greenhouse-Geisser	57.867	4.056	14.269		
	Huynh-Feldt	57.867	4.112	14.074		
	Lower-bound	57.867	4.000	14.467		

Output 16.8   *Fitting a repeated measures model using IBM SPSS Statistics*

'Those values match Alice's calculations. Why are there lots of rows with the same information?'

'Sphericity,' the dog replied, eyes bulging. 'It's no problem. The other rows show the adjustments to the degrees of freedom based on the estimates of sphericity. Changing the degrees of freedom changes the p-value for F because it changes the shape of the F-distribution that is used to obtain p. The sums of squares and F-ratio remain unchanged. The degrees of freedom are multiplied by the estimate of sphericity. Look, the Greenhouse–Geisser estimate of sphericity was 0.507, the original degrees of freedom for the model were 2, so the corrected degrees of freedom are 2×0.507, which equals 1.014. Similarly, the error df change from 8 to 8×0.507, which equals 4.056. The table also shows an exact p-value based on the Greenhouse–Geisser corrected degrees of freedom and it is 0.141, which is greater than 0.05 and, therefore, not significant.'

'Yeah, all of those values are the same as what Alice reported. **(LAB NOTES 16.1)** I guess she knows her stuff.'

16.6 ALTERNATIVE APPROACHES

16.6.1 EFFect sizes

'Oh yeah,' replied the hound, nodding enthusiastically. 'Alice is brilliant. I love Alice. One thing I'd love more than Alice is ...'

'Alice's dog, yeah, I get it,' I interrupted.

Milton looked serious. 'The results match the report, sure enough,' he said, 'so why did memory erasing work for Celia but not for people in general?'

'Maybe the model is wrong,' I suggested.

'Wrong?' Roediger exclaimed.

'Yeah, I've learnt all about fitting robust models, and Bayesian approaches, and even effect sizes. Maybe we need to Bayes these data up a bit?'

Milton rolled his eyes but stopped midway. 'Perhaps you have a point,' he said. 'Let us begin with effect sizes. Remember when we discussed the linear model, we talked about R^2?' **(SECTION 14.1.7)**

'Yes,' I lied.

'R^2 is an effect size measure. When the linear model involves group means it is called **eta squared, η^2**, but it is the same: it is the ratio of the model sum of squares to the total sum of squares, or the proportion of total variance accounted for by the model.'

'That looks small,' I said as Milton announced the value of 0.13. **(EQUATION 16.30)**

$$R^2 = \eta^2 = \frac{SS_M}{SS_T} = \frac{39.39}{298.31} = 0.13 \tag{16.30}$$

'It is, and it is also biased as an estimate of the population effect size because it is based purely on sample sums of squares without reference to their degrees of freedom. A less biased measure is **omega squared, ω^2**.' Milton drew a horrible equation. **(16.31)** 'Omega squared is slightly smaller than eta squared. It has been suggested that values of 0.01, 0.06 and 0.14 represent small, medium and large effects, respectively,[125] in which case the effect in experiment 1 is medium in size. However, the effect size should be interpreted within the context of the research literature.'

$$
\begin{aligned}
\omega^2 &= \frac{SS_M - df_M \times MS_R}{SS_T + MS_R} \\
&= \frac{39.39 - 2 \times 7.85}{298.31 + 7.85} \\
&= \frac{23.69}{306.16} \\
&= 0.08
\end{aligned}
\tag{16.31}
$$

'What's the point', interrupted Roediger, 'of quantifying the overall effect? Whether the means overall are different isn't as interesting as *which* means differ.' The spaniel waggled his hind excitedly.

'Indeed,' the cat agreed. 'We can use measures such as Cohen's d to quantify the more specific effects. Zach will do this for you.'

CHECK YOUR BRAIN: Help Zach to calculate Cohen's d (Section 11.2.1) for the effect of each group compared to the control group. Use the control group standard deviation in your calculations.

After my initial shock at the cat volunteering me, I remembered back to what I had been told **(SECTION 15.5.1)** about Cohen's d. For independent designs, it was the difference between means dividing by an estimate of the variance. In the first experiment there had been a control group so it made sense to quantify each experimental group against the control group, and to use the control group standard deviation as my measure of variance. I wrote out my calculations for the first memory experiment. **(EQUATION 16.32)** For repeated-measures designs, like in the second memory experiment, I could use the difference scores from Milton's message **(TABLE 16.9)** and compute d by dividing the mean difference score by its standard deviation and then multiplying the result by the square root of 2. **(EQUATION 16.33)**

Something was quite odd: despite the lack of significant effect, in the first experiment the 'replace' group had recall scores about 1 standard deviation below the control group, and in the second experiment the encounters where visual interference was used resulted in recall scores more than two standard deviations lower than when no interference was used. These effects seemed huge, but Alice had not reported them and had instead focused on the non-significant fit of the model. **(LAB NOTES 16.2)**

$$\hat{d}_{\text{Erase}-\text{Control}} = \frac{\bar{X}_{\text{Erase}} - \bar{X}_{\text{Control}}}{s_{\text{Control}}} = \frac{4.75 - 5}{2.37} = -0.11$$

$$\hat{d}_{\text{Replace}-\text{Control}} = \frac{\bar{X}_{\text{Replace}} - \bar{X}_{\text{Control}}}{s_{\text{Control}}} = \frac{2.67 - 5}{2.37} = -0.98$$

(16.32)

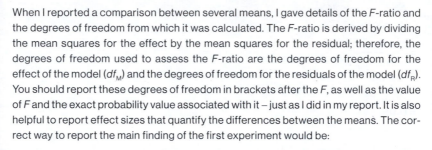

When I reported a comparison between several means, I gave details of the F-ratio and the degrees of freedom from which it was calculated. The F-ratio is derived by dividing the mean squares for the effect by the mean squares for the residual; therefore, the degrees of freedom used to assess the F-ratio are the degrees of freedom for the effect of the model (df_M) and the degrees of freedom for the residuals of the model (df_R). You should report these degrees of freedom in brackets after the F, as well as the value of F and the exact probability value associated with it – just as I did in my report. It is also helpful to report effect sizes that quantify the differences between the means. The correct way to report the main finding of the first experiment would be:

✓ Recall was slightly lower in the erase group compared to the control, $d = -0.11$, and was nearly a standard deviation lower in the replace group compared to the control, $d = -0.98$.

✓ Recall was not significantly different across the three groups, $F(2, 33) = 2.51$, $p = .097$. This finding suggests that there is not sufficient evidence that ID chips can be used to erase or replace memories.

In repeated-measures designs make sure you report the corrected degrees of freedom if a correction for sphericity has been applied. Otherwise, report the analysis in the same way. I could have reported the second memory experiment as follows:

✓ Recall was half a standard deviation lower when verbal interference was used compared to no interference, $d = 0.55$, and over 2 standard deviations lower when visual interference was used compared to no interference, $d = 2.08$.

✓ Recall was not significantly different after verbal, visual or no interference, $F(1.01, 4.06) = 3.33$, $p = .141$. This finding suggests that there is not sufficient evidence that ID chips can be used to implant new memories over old.

Alice's Lab Notes 16.2   *Reporting comparisons between means*

$$\hat{d}_{\text{No–Verbal}} = \frac{\overline{D}}{s_{\overline{D}}} \times \sqrt{2} = \frac{1}{2.55} \times \sqrt{2} = 0.55$$

$$\hat{d}_{\text{No–Visual}} = \frac{\overline{D}}{s_{\overline{D}}} \times \sqrt{2} = \frac{4.2}{2.86} \times \sqrt{2} = 2.08$$

(16.33)

I told Milton and Roediger my thoughts. Roediger sat on his haunches looking up at me with his tongue pulsing in and out between his front teeth. He looked like he was waiting for a command, or a treat. Milton paced between my legs in a figure of eight, his tail and head pointing up to my face. 'The studies will have low power,' he said. 'The sample sizes are very small. Perhaps too small to detect these large effects.'

'Or maybe the effect sizes or model are biased by outliers?' I offered.

16.6.2 Robust tests of several means

Milton took control of Alice's Proteus and frantically swiped the screen with his front paw as though shovelling dirt in his litter tray. He handed me the device.

'Like we did with Alice's previous report, we can reanalyse these data with techniques that use trimmed means (SECTION 9.3.2) and bootstrapping. (SECTION 9.3.5) I have used functions by Wilcox[34] in the R app[25] to do these robust tests. The first part of the screen (OUTPUT 16.9) shows the reanalysis of the first memory experiment, which is significant, $F_t = 4.13$, $p = 0.032$. The confidence intervals from the *post hoc* tests show that if these are from the 95% of confidence intervals that contain the population value, then (1) the real difference between the control group and erase means could be zero, [−1.92, 3.92]; (2) the difference between the control group and replace means is greater than zero, [0.24,

```
tlwaybt():

$test
[1]  4.127349

$p.value
[1]  0.03222558

$Var.Explained
[1]  0.2605768

$Effect.Size
[1]  0.5104672

lincon():

$test
      Group Group      test      crit       se        df
[1,]      1     2 0.9222976 2.691329 1.084249 13.94851
[2,]      1     3 2.8953224 2.697741 1.208846 13.70529
[3,]      2     3 2.1205631 2.705213 1.178932 13.43238

$psihat
      Group Group psihat   ci.lower ci.upper    p.value
[1,]      1     2    1.0 -1.9180700 3.918070 0.37205188
[2,]      1     3    3.5  0.2388454 6.761155 0.01196329
[3,]      2     3    2.5 -0.6892624 5.689262 0.05310528
```

Output 16.9 *Output from the tlwaybt() and lincon() functions using R*

6.76]; and (3) the difference between the erase and replace means could also be zero, [−0.69, 5.69]. In other words, the overall effect is likely to be driven by a difference in recall when attempts were made to replace memories compared to the control group.'

"What?' Roediger said excitedly, chasing his tail. 'Roediger's experiment worked?'

'Apparently so,' replied the cat. 'And look at the second experiment. *(OUTPUT 16.10)* The trimmed means were 7.33 (control), 5.67 (verbal interference) and 2.00 (visual interference), and these means are significantly different too, $F(2, 4) = 9.18$, $p = 0.032$. The confidence intervals from the *post hoc* tests suggest that if they are from the 95% of samples that contain the population value, then the difference between no interference and verbal interference could be zero, [−2.46, 3.79], and the difference between means is likely to be greater than zero when comparing no interference to visual interference, [1.21, 7.46], and verbal interference to visual interference, [0.54, 6.79]. To sum up, the overall effect is driven by a difference in recall when visual interference was used compared to both verbal and no interference.'

```
rmanova():

$test
[1] 9.178082

$df
[1] 2 4

$siglevel
[1] 0.03201293

$tmeans
[1]  7.333333 5.666667 2.000000

$ehat
[1]  0.8082815

$etil
[1] 1

rmmcp():

$test
     Group Group        test      p.value p.crit         se
[1,]     1     2  1.632993  0.244071054 0.0500  0.4082483
[2,]     1     3 10.614456  0.008759293 0.0169  0.4082483
[3,]     2     3  8.981462  0.012170839 0.0250  0.4082483

$psihat
     Group Group      psihat    ci.lower ci.upper
[1,]     1     2 0.6666667  -2.4559445 3.789278
[2,]     1     3 4.3333333   1.2107222 7.455944
[3,]     2     3 3.6666667   0.5440555 6.789278
```

Output 16.10 *Output from the rmanova() and rmmcp() functions using R*

16.6.3 Bayesian analysis of several means

Milton had also run some Bayesian analyses on the two experiments. He showed these to Roediger and me. 'I have computed Bayes factors based on some reasonable default prior beliefs. In the first memory experiment *(OUTPUT 16.11)* the Bayes factor is 433.95, which means that the data are 433.95 times more likely given the alternative hypothesis compared to the null hypothesis.'

'I should shift my belief in the alternative hypothesis relative to the null by a factor of 433.95?' I asked.

'Yes. For the second experiment **(OUTPUT 16.12)**, the Bayes factor is 116.64, which again strongly favours the alternative hypothesis.'

'That means that the data are 116.64 times more likely under the alternative hypothesis compared to the null. I should shift my belief in the alternative hypothesis relative to the null by a factor of 116.64.'

The cat nodded at me.

```
Bayes factor analysis
--------------
[1] Group : 433.9494 ±0%

Against denominator:
  Intercept only
---
Bayes factor type: BFlinearModel, JZS
```

Output 16.11   *Output from the anovaBF() function using R*

```
Bayes factor analysis
--------------
[1] Group + ID : 116.6446 ±1.05%

Against denominator:
  Recall ~ ID
---
Bayes factor type: BFlinearModel, JZS
```

Output 16.12   *Output from the anovaBF() function using R*

16.7   THE INVISIBLE MAN

Roediger was beside himself; he waggle-danced around the floor, whimpering with excitement. I felt less excited. Not for the first time, Alice had lied. I didn't believe for a second that someone of her scientific knowledge would make this kind of error: she had deliberately written reports that made it look as though memory recall could not be worsened by sending information to ID chips to rewrite those memories.

I looked over to her, poking and patting the touch screen in front of her. I rarely saw Alice in a flap, but she was trying desperately to haul herself back inside her comfort zone. Clint, on the other hand, was calmness personified. Every move Alice made he seemed to mirror with activity on his own screen. Alice slammed her fist on the desk and marched over to us. She had tears in her eyes. Her usual composure had vanished. Clint followed her. He looked pleased with himself. His gills undulated with red fire.

'I'm locked out of every system,' Alice said, 'my access is denied. I can't bypass the lockdown. This is not good, Zach. Why would my access be denied?'

'Perhaps because you've been lying in your reports?'

I knew it wasn't a helpful thing to say, but I was fed up with her lies. Alice looked shocked, and before she could speak, I explained.

'First, the invisibility studies. Your report says that they were successful, but if you look at the data with robust methods or you Bayes those data up, they *weren't*. You've tried to make it seem like calcite paste works, but it doesn't. Then, you do the opposite with the memory studies: you claim that the experiments failed in your report, but guess what? When you analyse the data properly, you *can* frip with people's memories.'

Alice looked mortified. I couldn't tell whether it was because I was exposing her or because I knew about Bayes' theorem. Clint looked intrigued; his fingers twitched with interest as I spoke.

'I came here to find you, Alice, to find the woman I love. The woman I've loved and admired since I was 16. I haven't found you though, Alice, I've lost you. I've lost the Alice who played my songs constantly on her Proteus, the Alice who came to every one of my gigs, the Alice who knew that I put her on such a frippin' pedestal that she needed oxygen to breathe up there. All I found here was a hole inside me where you used to be.'

A tear rolled down Alice's cheek. 'It's not like that,' she whispered, barely able to stop her voice cracking. I'd had a gutful of this insanity and it was time to take control. She'd run away from me, lied to me, and I'd taken it, but not any more. It was time to tell her what I thought of her obsession with science.

'You weren't even pleased to see me, Alice ... and ... ,' I stared at Milton and Roediger in disbelief, '... these animals are a walking metaphor for your future. You're so obsessed with science that you've forgotten what is important, what matters, and one day you'll probably turn yourself into a spaniel and you won't be horrified: you'll think that it's great because it's science, and who cares if you have to spend your life sniffing everyone you meet if you've made an amazing scientific discovery!'

My outburst seemed to pull her together. 'You're right. I *have* lost track of what's important. Zach, have I ever let you down? Have you ever had cause to doubt me or how much I love you?'

'Not until recently.'

'Then trust me.'

We stared intensely at each other. Roediger looked up at us expectantly, as though waiting for the resolution of a cliff-hanger in a soap opera. Despite everything, I trusted Alice. When things are out of control, have faith in others.

'You're right, I lied,' Alice said. 'I lied because I knew Rob Nutcot *wasn't* in charge here, and as Milton told you earlier, the activities here have all of the hallmarks of Vic Luten. He is an evil man, and the research here is *not* to help people. I couldn't find out who Vic Luten is, but I could at least stop his research. I had a plan, and it was working until you showed up and started thumping people. I don't have a plan B.' Alice looked on the verge of hysteria, Roediger whimpered and shook. Alice continued, 'I lied about the calcite mask research because it doesn't work: I made it look like it works to deflect resources into a fruitless line of research. I made the memory experiments look like they *didn't* work, because they do, and they're dangerous and Vic Luten must not know that they worked.'

'Why?'

'Think Zach, think. In a world where, for the first time in history, those in charge achieved a society in which everyone was happy, he's a man whose sole ambition was to undermine that ideal. Now think about the work going on here. If I could erase or replace your memory of meeting me, then my footprint on reality would be invisible: nobody would remember meeting me, or seeing me, or know what I looked like or what I had done. I could erase myself in history in real time. I could do anything I wanted, and nobody would remember that I had done it or know that I'd even existed. If you're a guy who got the WGA to set up a sub-agency to allow you to spread evil, then imagine what you would do if you could erase all knowledge of your deeds. That's why I came here, Zach, to stop Vic Luten and the research here and to make sure he didn't find out about mine. I couldn't leave my work on a constellation in case it was hacked; the safest thing was to have a single copy on a memory stone. I had to leave it with someone I could trust to look after it, but who wouldn't be able to decipher it and tell anyone what the results showed. That's why I left it with you, the person I trust most in the world.'

The contrast between Alice's words now and her behaviour to me since I arrived here was confusing. Was she trying to manipulate me? The phrase 'faith in others' came to mind again. The song, our song, the song that reminded us that, no matter what, we must believe in each other. I had to trust her, didn't I? I grabbed the memory stone from my pocket and said proudly, 'I *did* keep it safe for you.'

Alice went pale. 'You have got to be kidding!' She looked frantic, desperate. 'Why did you bring that? Whoever runs this place must never see that work: it will give them exactly what they want: anonymity, the ability to move through history without a footprint.'

'Who would want anonymity?' I asked.

'Perhaps someone like Vic Luten who is hell bent on spreading evil through society but cannot because he is so hideously deformed that he is somewhat overly conspicuous,' said Milton, looking up at Clint.

Clint grabbed the memory stone out of my outstretched hand and smiled. The smile didn't suit him. Holding his arms aloft, he puffed out his chest, and leaned back with a maniacal laugh. The technicians cowered, some screamed, and Alice sprinted across the laboratory towards the exit. As she did, Clint grabbed me in a headlock and squeezed hard. I couldn't breathe. He shouted at Alice, 'Come back, or he dies!' I heard more screams, people running up into the pews around us, things crashing to the floor, the sound of panic. I was drifting, floating away, my focus on Alice blurring more with each compression of my throat. She jumped on a steam elevator and as her legs disappeared below the floor she shouted, 'Zach! Faith in others!'

My lungs spluttered into life and my limp body fell hard to the floor. Clint was screaming and clutching his leg, which had Roediger attached to it. Milton was swatting a horizontal screen as though chasing a laser pen. I noticed the steam elevator hatches close and all of the doors shut. Milton was trapping us in the room with Clint. What was he up to? Then it hit me: he was buying Alice time to escape. Clint's Proteus fizzed into life: with a spray of steam a miniature figure of Celia appeared and Clint spoke to her. 'Get Alice!' he ordered. 'Put her in the Schrödinger prison.'

Roediger released his grip on Clint's leg. His back legs shook so much that he couldn't stand. He whined as his quivering head muttered 'Schrödinger prison' over and over. Clint went over to the steam elevator hatches and pulled at them. Given what he had done to a steel door earlier on, it was only a matter of time before he broke free of the room.

KEY TERMS

Analysis of variance (ANOVA)	Huynh–Feldt estimate	Planned contrasts
Brown–Forsythe F	Mauchly's test	Post hoc tests
Dummy coding	Omega squared, ω^2	Sphericity
Eta squared, η^2	Orthogonal	Weights
Greenhouse–Geisser estimate	Pairwise comparisons	Welch's F

JIG:SAW'S PUZZLES

1   When Zach entered the JIG:SAW complex he tried garlic, rTMS and Tasers to deter the zombie security. Afterwards, he decided to do a study to test which of these weapons was best. Based on his experiences, he predicted that Tasers and rTMS would be better deterrents than garlic, but that there would be no significant difference between Tasers and rTMS. He randomly assigned 5 people a Taser, 5 people an rTMS device, and 5 people a necklace of garlic. He then put them in a pit with 10 hungry zombies. He counted how many of the 10 zombies were incapacitated for each participant. The data are in Table 16.10. Compute the F-ratio. Were there significant differences between the mean number of zombies incapacitated by the different weapons?

Table 16.10   The number of zombies incapacitated by three different weapons for 15 different participants

	Taser	rTMS	Garlic
	5	6	2
	2	4	1
	5	7	1
	6	5	2
	3	5	1
$\bar{x}$	4.2	5.4	1.4
s^2	2.7	1.3	0.3

Grand Mean = **3.667**
Grand Variance = **4.238**

2   Based on Zach's predictions, construct some contrasts and weights for those contrasts to test his predictions.

3   Calculate omega squared for the zombie data, and also calculate Cohen's d for the difference between means of the three conditions (use the pooled estimate of the standard deviation).

4   Rob Nutcot used an oxytocin spray to try to make people trust him more. Zach set up an experiment to see whether oxytocin affected trust. He took 7 people who were delivered a speech about different products to keep you looking younger by three different people. Before each speech they were sprayed with either (1) a placebo that smelled like oxytocin spray but had no active ingredient, (2) a spray with a low dose of oxytocin in it, or (3) a spray with a high dose of oxytocin in it. Each participant was, therefore, exposed to each dose of oxytocin. The outcome was how much they believed the claims about the product (out of 10). The data are in Table 16.11. Calculate the F-ratio. Did oxytocin affect trust in the product?

Table 16.11   Trust scores in seven participants after three doses of oxytocin

ID	Placebo	Low Dose	High Dose	s^2
1	5	5	5	0.000
2	7	5	8	2.333
3	6	4	10	9.333
4	4	8	9	7.000
5	4	7	8	4.333

Table 16.11 *Continued*

ID	Placebo	Low Dose	High Dose	s^2
6	6	5	9	4.333
7	4	4	8	5.333
$\bar{x}$	5.143	5.429	8.143	
s^2	1.476	2.286	2.476	

Grand Mean = **6.238**
Grand Variance = **3.790**

5 Earlier in his journey, Zach looked at some data showing the strength, footspeed and vision of different groups of JIG:SAW employees (code 1318, scientists, security, professional services and technicians; see Figure 9.1). There were 240 employees in total. Milton forced him reluctantly to test whether the mean strength differed across the five groups. Then, because he is an evil cat, he erased some of the values from the summary (Table 16.12). Can you help Zach to fill in the blanks? (Hint: think about the degrees of freedom first.)

Table 16.12 *Summary table for an ANOVA on strength across different professions at JIG:SAW*

Source	SS	df	MS	F
Model	8490624			
Residual			89636	
Total				

6 That cat, Milton, is such a japester that he has done the same thing to the summary table (Table 16.13) for the comparison between means of footspeed across the five job types (see puzzle 5). Help Zach to fill in the blanks before he dies of tedium.

7 When Celia was trying to woo Zach, she looked at whether there was a significant association between how you rated the costs and rewards of your relationship and openness to alternative relationships (see Reality Check 13.2). She decided to see whether you could manipulate a person's openness to alternative relationships. She took five people and asked them to list all the costs and rewards of their current relationship, then asked them to rate their openness to alternative relationships. At another point in time she asked the same people to study a list of potential costs to being in a relationship and again got them to rate their openness to alternative relationships. At a final point in time she asked the same people to study a list of potential benefits or rewards to being in a relationship and again got them to rate their openness to alternative relationships. Each person completed these tasks a week apart and in random order. The data are in Table 16.14. Use these values to compute the *F*-ratio. Is openness to alternative relationships affected by focusing on lists of potential costs or rewards compared to generating your own costs and rewards?

8 Output 16.13 shows the results of an analysis on the data in Table 16.14 (see puzzle 7), to compute a Bayes factor based on a reasonable default prior. Interpret this output.

9 The second experiment in Alice's report (Alice's Lab Notes 16.1), when Zach reanalysed it, seemed to suggest that sending visual images to someone's ID chip while they recalled a memory would interfere with it (i.e., result in lower recall of the event). Roediger decided to do a follow-up study. He took 18 participants: 6 of them received no memory interference while they recalled an event, 6 received visual interference unrelated to the event they were recalling, and 6 received visual interference related to the event they were recalling. The data are in Table 16.15. Compute the *F*-ratio. Were there significant differences in recall between the three groups?

10 Output 16.14 shows the results of an analysis on the data in Table 16.15 (see puzzle 9), to compute a Bayes factor based on a reasonable default prior. Interpret this output.

Table 16.13 *Summary table for an ANOVA on footspeed across different professions at JIG:SAW*

Source	SS	df	MS	F
Model				
Residual	3256			
Total	3272			

Table 16.14 *Openness to alternative relationships ratings (out of 5) in five participants after three manipulations*

ID	Free List	Focus on Costs	Focus on Rewards	s^2
1	3	5	3	1.333
2	6	4	3	2.333
3	4	4	3	0.333
4	3	5	2	2.333
5	2	4	0	4.000
$\bar{x}$	**3.600**	**4.400**	**2.200**	
s^2	**2.300**	**0.300**	**1.700**	

Grand Mean = **3.400**
Grand Variance = **2.114**

Table 16.15 *Recall of 10 events for 18 participants who either had no interference, had related visual interference, or unrelated visual interference*

	No Interference	Unrelated Visual Interference	Related Visual Interference
	6	6	1
	8	4	0
	8	8	5
	10	6	2
	7	4	5
	8	3	3
$\bar{x}$	**7.833**	**5.167**	**2.667**
s^2	**1.767**	**3.367**	**4.267**

Grand Mean = **5.222**
Grand Variance = **7.477**

```
Bayes factor analysis
--------------
[1] Group + ID : 5.083384 ±0.57%

Against denominator:
  Alternatives ~ ID
---
Bayes factor type: BFlinearModel, JZS
```

Output 16.13 *Bayes factor for the data in Table 16.14*

```
Bayes factor analysis
--------------
[1] Group : 51.56887 ±0%

Against denominator:
  Intercept only
---
Bayes factor type: BFlinearModel, JZS
```

Output 16.14 *Bayes factor for the data in Table 16.15*

IN THE NEXT CHAPTER, ZACH DISCOVERS ...

What a superpositional state of living death might be like

Factorial designs

Interaction effects

Alternative approaches to factorial designs

What the hell has been going on for the last few weeks of his life

Alice had shouted 'Faith in others!' as she ran off. Perhaps it was coincidence, but the phrase had followed me around over the past few weeks: she had left that song on the memory stone, she had played it the evening before she left, I had played it in The Repository with Celia, and now Alice shouted its title at me. Of all the things she could have said as she abandoned me, she, quite deliberately, chose those three words that connected us to our inception. It was a thread that bound us together. Was she reminding me of our vow to trust each other and in doing so imploring me to rediscover my faith in her? Despite her ambivalence to seeing me, was she letting me know that our past still meant something to her? When I'd thought about the words of the song all those weeks ago, my mind had painted a bleak image of their meaning. Perhaps I'd missed her point?

All of this was going through my head as Clint, or Vic Luten as we now knew him to be, carried me effortlessly over his shoulder down the steam elevator and through the underground corridors that connected the pieces of the JIG:SAW complex. All the time he bellowed instructions at Celia through his Proteus. He was not happy. We'd all tried to stop him following Alice with enough success to delay him, but with a burst of fire from his gills he had ripped the elevator hatch apart, scooped me up, and swatted Milton and Roediger away. Over the past few weeks I had often been convinced of Milton's indifference to me, so it surprised me to see his ginger figure galloping after me with Roediger by his side. They made an unlikely pair of saviours, but they were all I had other than faith, and I wasn't sure that I had any of that left.

Several corridors and a steam elevator later, we emerged into what I assumed to be the centrepiece of JIG:SAW. It was a huge room, and in the middle was a huge box: a room within a room. The box had no doors or windows; just a large JIG:SAW corporation insignia that glowed a pleasant shade of green. As we came into the room I had caught a glimpse of Alice inside the box, and then Celia walking out looking pleased with herself. How had I been so stupid as to be taken in by her? It was obvious now that she had been using me: she had done her homework and she knew how to press my buttons to get me here with Alice's data.

Vic stomped over to the box and started talking to Celia. As he spoke, his arms reached out to various screens, and we found ourselves locked in the room. He hooked up the memory stone to another screen and stared at Alice's report. He looked confused. I'd figured out from Roediger's quivering body that the box must be the Schrödinger's prison that Vic had told Celia to lock Alice in. I still didn't know what such a thing was, so the dog filled me in, telling me that it was a prison based on Schrödinger's cat.

'A prison based on what?'

'Schrödinger's cat was a thought experiment devised by Erwin Schrödinger to highlight the ridiculousness of the Copenhagen Interpretation of quantum theory,' the dog continued, as though that would help. I reached for my reality checker and asked The Head about the Copenhagen Interpretation. (REALITY CHECK 17.1) I was barely the wiser when he had finished, although I did like the idea of a probability bus.

'Schrödinger imagined that a cat was placed in a steel chamber with a "diabolical device" that contains a radioactive substance that has a 50% probability of an atom decaying, and a 50% probability

The Head looked wide-eyed. 'Are you sure, Z?' he said. 'Quantum physics is over the wall. Here goes, then.

'If you were to fire an individual electron at a detector through two slits, you'd expect it to go through one slit or the other and be detected only behind the one through which it had passed. If you sent a stream of electrons through those same slits you'd expect about half of them to be detected behind one slit, and the other half to be detected behind the other. This would show up as a dark strip on the detector behind each slit (where the electrons ended up), with a white void in between (where few electrons were detected *between* the slits). That ain't what happens in experiments. Instead, you get a zebra: you get a row of stripes on the detector showing electrons detected in a regular pattern. This happens because individual electrons behave like a wave: they interfere, creatin' peaks and troughs in where the electrons end up. This finding implies that a single electron passes through both slits *simultaneously*. That's quantum mechanics right there – it'll fry your brain.

'The Copenhagen Interpretation goes something like this: electrons have mass and charge but also an associated probability wave that predicts the probability of where the particle will be in the universe at a given time. Until the particle is observed, it exists in several simultaneous *superpositions* determined by the probability wave. In other words, it exists in lots of different places at the same time, and the probability wave is made up of the probabilities of it being at all of those places. When a scientist measures the particle's location, the probability wave collapses: it becomes 1 at the place where the particle was measured and 0 everywhere else. This interpretation explains the quantum measurement puzzle: when scientists measure *where* particles are they find them in one place, but when they look at *how they got there* they seem to have existed at different places at the same time. Particles don't travel on the train along a straight track like we do, they've got a pass on the probability bus.'

Reality Check 17.1   *Quantum theory and the Copenhagen Interpretation*

that it does not,' Roediger said. 'The device can detect if an atom decays, and if it does hydrochloric acid is released, which kills the cat. It's no problem.'

Milton winced. Roediger ignored him. 'Before the chamber is opened, the probability wave of the atom says that there is a 50% chance of it decaying. Because this quantum event has consequences for the cat, it also means that there is a 50% chance that the cat is dead.'

Milton gulped.

'The Copenhagen Interpretation implies that before the chamber is opened, the cat exists in a superposition,' Roediger explained.

The Head had used that term too; I didn't understand it. 'What the frip is a superposition?'

'It means that the cat is simultaneously alive and dead,' Roediger said excitedly. 'Only when someone opens the chamber and observes the cat does the probability wave collapse to a single outcome: the cat is observed to be either alive or dead.'

'That's stupid,' I said. 'A cat can't be alive and dead at the same time.'

Roediger smiled and span in a circle. 'Exactly! That was Schrödinger's point: when you take the explanation of the experimental data from microscopic objects such as particles and scale it up to macroscopic objects such as cats, it becomes counterintuitive. Nevertheless, the data tell us that particles *do* behave in this way.'

I was still confused. 'What's a Schrödinger's prison, then?'

The cat had decided to stop cowering and join in. 'Do we really have to explain everything?' he grumbled. 'It is quite simple. The box in front of you is the steel chamber and Alice is the cat.'

I started to panic. 'What? There's a radioactive thingy decaying in there and Alice is both alive and dead?'

'Not quite, she is currently quite alive: the prison is not yet active,' Milton said. 'However, if the prison is activated by pressing that rather fetching green insignia, then any unauthorized attempt to deactivate it triggers a process similar to the chamber in Schrödinger's imaginary experiment: it sets off a quantum event, an event that has a 50% chance of happening. If it happens then cyanide is released into the chamber.'

That seemed like a really over-elaborate way to imprison someone. 'Let me check this. You're saying that any unauthorized attempt to deactivate the box will result in Alice being in a superposition of being both alive and dead?'

'*Purr*cisely, until you actually succeed in opening the box, at which point she will be either alive or dead.'

'What's the point of that?'

'Let us imagine that you were trying to free someone from a prison. Would you want to subject them to a superpositional state of being both alive and dead for only a 50% chance that they would survive?'

'I guess not.'

'No, and you especially would not if you had ever met someone who had been in a superpositional state,' Milton said with a sombre tone. 'According to the limited number of first-hand accounts that exist, it is not pleasant. It feels like being stuck at the point of death: you have the overwhelming panic that you are about to die but the feeling never subsides because you remain alive. You try to move and breathe because you are alive, but you feel like you cannot because you are dead. You are stuck motionless, gasping for air, contemplating the eternity of nothingness. Even if it takes your saviours a few minutes to release you, it feels like years to you.'

It sounded like a statistics lecture. I felt claustrophobic thinking about it. I wondered why humanity was capable of such evil. It saddened me that we had learnt nothing from the Reality Revolution.

My thoughts were interrupted by Vic screaming at the prison wall; he was pressed against it, demanding that Alice tell him what her research report meant. Alice was silent. He made a second demand, his rage fuelled by her silence. Nothing. Alice was playing a dangerous game by ignoring Vic. Was she banking on him not activating the prison? I started to well up, thinking about her stuck in a state of perpetual dying. Vic's third and final demand for answers was met again with silence. He screamed and his hand quivered over the insignia. I *had* to do something.

'Maybe I can help,' I said, my voice cracking with nerves. A blur replaced Vic by the prison and, before my eyes could follow it, I felt his arm around my neck.

'How can *you* help?' he asked in a measured tone.

'You've been with us all day; you've seen what I can do. I was the one who showed that Alice had misled you. I can interpret Alice's research for you.'

Milton jabbed a claw in my leg, and I kicked him away.

'Why would you do that?' asked Vic.

'A simple deal: I tell you what you want to know and you set Alice free and let all of us leave safely.'

The giant lizard thought about it. 'Very well, but any sign of treachery and I activate the prison.' With that he zipped back to the prison where he stood next to Celia, his hand hovering above the activation insignia. 'Be quick about it' he said. Celia – the apostate – winked at me, I turned away in disgust.

17.1 FACTORIAL DESIGNS

I turned to Milton, who glared at me. 'Have you lost your senses? You're going to betray Alice, betray the world? Do you realize what Vic Luten will do with this information? You can't trust him, he'll never let Alice go free.' He spoke quietly so Vic wouldn't hear, but his anger was evident.

I remembered Vic's ears twitching throughout our time at JIG:SAW – who knew what he could and couldn't hear – so I turned to face Milton and, with my back to Vic, I mouthed, 'I'm buying us time.' Then for Vic's benefit I declared that we should get to work. Milton eyed me suspiciously and Roediger looked a little in awe of my bravado.

They wandered to one of the many transparent sheets of glass in the room, the one that Vic had connected to the memory crystal. Milton dragged up Alice's report and summarized the procedure that she had used. She had tested a group of patients with facial injuries. All of them were given the chameleon gene, C-gene therapy, which had been shown to help people to rehabilitate wounds, but half were also given a genetic toggle switch which was hypothesized to help them to control the chameleon gene. Half of the participants were asked to look at a photograph of themselves from before their injury and to imagine the cells in their faces changing to become like the photo. The remainder acted as a control and were asked to look at a picture of a same-sex stranger and to try to

Table 17.1 Alice's top-secret research data

Gene Condition	C-Gene		C-Gene + Toggle Switch	
Picture Type	Self	Other	Self	Other
	43	9	75	80
	72	6	79	87
	44	6	87	88
	37	12	99	85
	61	9	85	93
	42	7	92	85
	59	12	87	86
	54	8	85	78
Total	**412**	**69**	**689**	**682**
Mean	**51.50**	**8.63**	**86.13**	**85.25**
SD	**11.964**	**2.387**	**7.357**	**4.652**
Variance	**143.143**	**5.696**	**54.125**	**21.643**

change their face to become the person in the picture. The outcome was how much their face resembled the picture that they studied, as a percentage.

CHECK YOUR BRAIN: Reread Alice's research report (Alice's Lab Notes 2.1).

Milton explained that when scientists conduct experiments they sometimes manipulate more than one independent variable. This is known as a **factorial design** (because independent variables are sometimes referred to as *factors*). Alice's experiment was a factorial design because she had manipulated two independent variables: the type of gene therapy (C-gene or C-gene with a toggle switch) and also the type of picture that participants tried to emulate (a picture of themselves or of a same-sex stranger). This design is a **two-way design** because there were two independent variables, but you could have more complex designs such as a **three-way design** (three independent variables), a **four-way design** (four independent variables), and so on. Finally, Milton pulled up the raw data on the screen. **(TABLE 17.1)**

17.2 GENERAL PROCEDURE AND ASSUMPTIONS

I guessed that we'd start off like we always did, by looking at the data, screening for outliers and unusual cases, and generally getting a feel for what was happening in each of the four groups. Milton confirmed my beliefs, and added that to explore whether the resemblance scores could be predicted from the two variables, we would fit a linear model, just like we had in every other analysis he'd shown me; because of this, he said that in general we'd follow the same procedure **(SECTION 16.1)** and test the same assumptions **(CHAPTER 12)** as for any linear model.

17.3 ANALYSING FACTORIAL DESIGNS

17.3.1 Factorial designs and the linear model

'Very well,' Milton began. 'Alice's experiment had two variables that she manipulated: the type of C-gene therapy, I will refer to this variable as *Gene*, and the type of picture the participant tried to resemble, which I will refer to as *Picture*. We will fit a linear model.'

I thought back to the many times we'd looked at the linear model **(EQUATION 4.2)** and I wrote out outcome$_i$ = (model) + error$_i$ on the screen for Milton.

'Good,' the cat said. 'The specific linear model that we will fit is made up of several predictors (X) and the parameters associated with them (b), just as we have seen before.' **(EQUATION 14.28)** The cat wrote out the equation for the model to remind me. **(EQUATION 17.1)** 'Remember that when we wanted to compare group means, we adapted the model to conceptualize the groups in terms of two dummy variables, variables that can take only values of 0 or 1.' **(EQUATION 16.2)** The cat repeated the equation on the screen. **(EQUATION 17.1)** 'In our current example, we have two variables: *Gene* (C-gene vs. C-gene and toggle switch) and *Picture* (self vs. other). We can code each of these variables with zeros and ones; for example, we could code *Gene* as C-gene = 0, C-gene and toggle switch = 1, and we could code *Picture* as 0 = self, 1 = other. We could then directly copy the model we had when we compared means before.' **(EQUATION 17.1)**

$$Y_i = b_0 + b_1X_{1i} + b_2X_{2i} + \cdots + b_nX_{ni} + \text{error}_i$$
$$Y_i = b_0 + b_1\,\text{Dummy}\,1_i + b_2\,\text{Dummy}\,2_i + \varepsilon_i$$
$$\text{Resemblance}_i = \left(b_0 + b_1\text{Gene}_i + b_2\text{Picture}_i\right) + \varepsilon_i \tag{17.1}$$

I looked at the equations the cat had drawn. We were just taking the same model that we used before to compare means, but this time the dummy variables were representing the two independent variables. So, we simply predict the degree of resemblance from the type of gene therapy (coded with 0s and 1s) and the type of picture (also coded using 0s and 1s). Milton smiled. It was the kind of smile that someone gives you just before you sit on the whoopee cushion that they have planted on your seat while you weren't looking.

'Of course, this model does not consider the **interaction effect** between *Gene* and *Picture*. The interaction effect is the combined effect of two variables; it tells us whether the effect of one predictor is different at different levels of another, which is a form of **moderation**. For example, we could look at the difference in resemblance scores when people looked at a picture of themselves compared to a picture of a stranger. We could then ask whether this difference is the same in the C-gene group compared to the toggle switch group. Moderation would occur if, for example, the difference between the picture and self conditions was much larger in the C-gene group than in the toggle switch group, or vice versa.'

None of what Milton had just said made an awful lot of sense to me. He raised an eyebrow as he stared at my blank expression.

'You have the face of a man who has painted eyes on his eyelids so as to convince the world that, while asleep, he is actually awake. It is of no consequence; I will get into what an interaction is in due course. For now, just understand that this interaction term can be added to the model just like any predictor, by adding it and assigning it a parameter (*b*).' Milton swiped his paw over the screen to produce an extension of our previous model. **(EQUATION 17.2)** 'In general terms, we are predicting an outcome from the first independent variable (*A*), the second one (*B*) and their interaction (*A* × *B*). In specific terms, we predict resemblance scores from the gene condition, the picture condition and their interaction. I have written the interaction term as *Gene* × *Picture* quite deliberately because this term is literally the gene and picture predictor variables multiplied together.'

$$\text{Outcome}_i = \left(b_0 + b_1 A_i + b_2 B_i + b_3 A \times B_i\right) + \varepsilon_i$$
$$\text{Resemblance}_i = \left(b_0 + b_1 \text{Gene}_i + b_2 \text{Picture}_i + b_3 \text{Gene} \times \text{Picture}_i\right) + \varepsilon_i \tag{17.2}$$

Milton scuttled sideways in a crab-like motion to a blank part of the screen and drew a table on it. **(TABLE 17.2)** 'Look, this table shows how all of the predictors in the model are coded. People in the C-gene condition are assigned 0 for the gene variable, and people in the toggle switch condition are assigned 1; people who tried to emulate a picture of themselves are given a 0 for the picture variable and those trying to emulate a stranger are assigned a 1. The interaction variable is the value of the gene dummy variable multiplied by the value of the picture dummy variable. For example, someone in the C-gene only condition who looked at a picture of a stranger would have a value of 0 for the gene variable, 1 for the picture variable and 0 for the interaction variable.

Table 17.2 *Coding scheme for factorial ANOVA*

Gene Condition	Picture Type	Dummy (*Gene*)	Dummy (*Picture*)	Interaction (*Gene* × *Picture*)	Mean
C-Gene	Self	0	0	0	51.50
C-Gene	Other	0	1	0	8.63
C-Gene + Toggle	Self	1	0	0	86.13
C-Gene + Toggle	Other	1	1	1	85.25

'To see what the *b*-values represent in this model, we can insert the values of our predictors (*Gene* and *Picture*). Remember that the model is trying to predict group means, so we can also use these means **(TABLE 17.2)** as our predicted values for specific groups. To begin with, let us look at people in the C-gene condition who looked at a picture of their own face. For these people, the value of *Gene* is 0, the value of *Picture* is 0 and the value of the interaction is also 0. The predicted value of resemblance is the mean of this group (51.50).' Milton wrote the equation of the model on the screen, replaced the outcome and predictor variables with their values and reduced everything down. **(EQUATION 17.3)**

$$\text{Resemblance}_i = \left(b_0 + b_1 \text{Gene}_i + b_2 \text{Picture}_i + b_3 \text{Gene} \times \text{Picture}_i\right) + \varepsilon_i$$

$$\bar{X}_{\text{C-Gene,Self}} = b_0 + \left(b_1 \times 0\right) + \left(b_2 \times 0\right) + \left(b_3 \times 0\right)$$

$$b_0 = \bar{X}_{\text{C-Gene,Self}}$$

$$b_0 = 51.50$$

(17.3)

'So, the constant, b_0, is the mean of the group for which all predictor variables are coded as 0.'

'*Furball*ous! It is the mean value of the base category (in this case, people who had only the C-gene and studied a picture of their own face). We can do the same thing with the model to look at the group who received the toggle switch and studied a picture of their own face. The predicted value of *Resemblance* is the mean of this group. *Gene* will be 1, and *Picture* and *Gene* × *Picture* will be 0. **(TABLE 17.2)** We have just discovered that b_0 is the mean of people in the C-gene group who looked at a picture of their own face.' Milton wrote out the model again and replaced the variables with their values. **(EQUATION 17.4)** It seemed to me that b_1 represented the difference between people who had only the C-gene and those that also had the toggle switch when they studied a picture of their own face. I confirmed this with the cat.

$$\bar{X}_{\text{Toggle,Self}} = b_0 + \left(b_1 \times 1\right) + \left(b_2 \times 0\right) + \left(b_3 \times 0\right)$$

$$\bar{X}_{\text{Toggle,Self}} = b_0 + b_1$$

$$\bar{X}_{\text{Toggle,Self}} = \bar{X}_{\text{C-Gene,Self}} + b_1$$

(17.4)

$$b_1 = \bar{X}_{\text{Toggle,Self}} - \bar{X}_{\text{C-Gene,Self}}$$

$$b_1 = 86.13 - 51.50$$

$$b_1 = 34.63$$

'*Claw*rect. More generally, b_1 is the effect of *Gene* for the base category of *Picture* (the base category being the one coded with 0).

'Let us move on to a different group and again replace the predictor and outcome variables with their values. For people who received only the C-gene therapy and studied a picture of someone else's face, the predicted value of the outcome will be the mean of this group. For the predictors, *Gene* is 0, *Picture* is 1, and *Gene* × *Picture* is 0. We know that b_0 is the mean of the people in the C-gene condition who looked at a picture of their own face, so we can insert this value too.' As with the other groups, Milton wrote out the model, replaced the values for the predictors and outcome, and tidied everything up. **(EQUATION 17.5)**

$$\bar{X}_{\text{C-Gene,Other}} = b_0 + \left(b_1 \times 0\right) + \left(b_2 \times 1\right) + \left(b_3 \times 0\right)$$

$$\bar{X}_{\text{C-Gene,Other}} = b_0 + b_2$$

$$\bar{X}_{\text{C-Gene,Other}} = \bar{X}_{\text{C-Gene,Self}} + b_2$$

(17.5)

$$b_2 = \bar{X}_{\text{C-Gene,Other}} - \bar{X}_{\text{C-Gene,Self}}$$

$$b_2 = 8.63 - 51.50$$

$$b_2 = -42.87$$

I asked whether b_2 represented the difference between participants studying their own face and participants studying someone else's face in the group who were exposed only to the C-gene.

'Yes,' Milton replied. 'It is the effect of the *Picture* variable in the base category of *Gene*: the category of *Gene* that was coded with a 0, in this case C-gene. This leaves us with one final group, which contains people who had the C-gene and toggle switch who studied a picture of someone else's face. The predicted resemblance score is again the mean of this group, and values of *Gene*, *Picture*, and *Gene* × *Picture* are all 1. We can also replace b_0, b_1, and b_2 with what we know they represent.'

$$\bar{X}_{\text{Toggle, Other}} = b_0 + (b_1 \times 1) + (b_2 \times 1) + (b_3 \times 1)$$

$$\bar{X}_{\text{Toggle, Other}} = b_0 + b_1 + b_2 + b_3$$

$$\bar{X}_{\text{Toggle, Other}} = \bar{X}_{\text{C-Gene, Self}} + \left(\bar{X}_{\text{Toggle, Self}} - \bar{X}_{\text{C-Gene, Self}} \right) +$$

$$\left(\bar{X}_{\text{C-Gene, Other}} - \bar{X}_{\text{C-Gene, Self}} \right) + b_3 \tag{17.6}$$

$$\bar{X}_{\text{Toggle, Other}} = \bar{X}_{\text{Toggle, Self}} + \bar{X}_{\text{C-Gene, Other}} - \bar{X}_{\text{C-Gene, Self}} + b_3$$

$$b_3 = \left(\bar{X}_{\text{Toggle, Other}} - \bar{X}_{\text{C-Gene, Other}} \right) -$$

$$\left(\bar{X}_{\text{Toggle, Self}} - \bar{X}_{\text{C-Gene, Self}} \right)$$

$$b_3 = (85.25 - 8.63) - (86.13 - 51.50)$$

$$b_3 = 42$$

Milton gave a little wiggle of his buttocks and moved his paws frenetically across the screen, creating a terrifying set of equations **(17.6)**. It was a lot to take in, especially given my heightened state of anxiety due to the massive lizard man threatening to trap Alice in some weird alive–dead superposition. Sensing my panic, Roediger threw me a lifeline.

'It's no problem,' he said, wagging his tail. 'The equation shows that b_3 takes the difference between the C-gene and the C-gene + toggle switch conditions when participants study their own face and compares it to the same difference when participants studied someone else's face. It compares the effect of the gene manipulation after studying their own face to the effect of the gene manipulation after looking at a stranger's face. The cat has inserted parentheses in the equation **(17.6)** to highlight these two differences between means.' The spaniel looked up with droopy, reassuring eyes and a panting tongue. It was what I needed to see. Just as my tension was easing, my diePad beeped as a message arrived. As I went to read it, I noticed Milton smiling mischievously to himself. **(MEOWSINGS 17.1)** It was the first time he'd ever addressed me as Zach rather than 'human'.

Milton looked bored; he tip-toed around in circles as though looking for food. Roediger continued his explanation. 'Maybe it will help if we look at the interaction effect visually,' the dog said; he drew me a diagram on the screen. **(FIGURE 17.2)** 'The top left part of the diagram is what is called the **interaction graph** because it shows the means of all combinations of the predictor variables. The effect of therapy type (the difference between having C-gene alone and also receiving the toggle switch) is the distance between the two lines. It's easy to see, no problem. Look at this distance for people who looked at photos of themselves; it is 34.63.'

'The value of b_1?'

'Yeah! Now, is the distance between the lines greater when we look at participants who looked at a photo of another person's face?'

I looked at the graph before replying that I thought the distance *was* greater.

'Yes! It is nearly twice as big: it is 76.63. This is one of the things that the interaction effect represents: the effect of gene therapy, the distance between the lines, is greater for participants who studied a photo of a stranger's face than those who studied a photo of their own face. I have plotted these distances between the lines in the graph underneath – the bottom left. This line is sloped, showing that the effect of therapy is greater in the other-face group compared to the own-face group. In other words, the interaction effect is not zero. In fact, the slope of this line is b_3 in our model, it is $76.63 - 34.63 = 42$.'

'What does the right-hand side show?'

'It shows when an interaction effect is zero. The top right-hand side **(FIGURE 17.2)** shows the same data except that I changed one of the four means: those who received a toggle switch and looked at a picture of a stranger now have a mean of 43.25. The other three means are the same as for Alice's actual data. The lines are now parallel, showing that the effect of the type of picture in the C-gene group (red line) is the same as in the toggle switch group (blue line). Let's look at the difference between the lines again. The difference between having C-gene alone and receiving the toggle switch, for people who looked at photos of themselves, is 34.63, the same as before. This same difference for people who studied a photo of a stranger has changed (because we changed one of the means): it is now also 34.63. I plotted these differences on a new graph underneath (bottom right) and connected them with a line. Unlike the real data, this line is flat, telling us that the effect of therapy in the C-gene group is the same as in the toggle switch group. The gradient of this flat line would be 0, meaning that b_3 in our model, which quantifies the interaction effect, would also be 0. It's no problem.'

Dear Zach,

Despite being an inferior species, the spaniel is correct. However, you can also phrase the interaction the opposite way around: it is equally valid to say that it represents the effect of studying pictures of your own face compared to a stranger's face in people who had the C-gene therapy compared to those who received the C-gene and toggle switch. We can see this by rearranging the equation:

$$\bar{X}_{\text{Toggle, Other}} = \bar{X}_{\text{Toggle, Self}} + \bar{X}_{\text{C–Gene, Other}} - \bar{X}_{\text{C–Gene, Self}} + b_3$$

$$b_3 = \left(\bar{X}_{\text{C–Gene, Self}} - \bar{X}_{\text{C–Gene, Other}}\right) - \left(\bar{X}_{\text{Toggle, Self}} - \bar{X}_{\text{Toggle, Other}}\right)$$

$$b_3 = (51.50 - 8.63) - (86.13 - 85.25)$$

$$b_3 = 42$$

By expressing b_3 in this way compared to Eq. 17.6, you can see how the same equation expresses two different things, depending on how you arrange it. In both cases, though, it shows that the interaction term represents the effect of one predictor variable at different levels of another (Figure 17.1).

Best fishes,
Milton

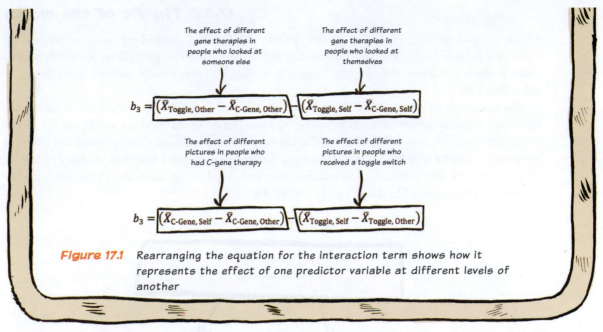

Figure 17.1 Rearranging the equation for the interaction term shows how it represents the effect of one predictor variable at different levels of another

Milton's Meowsings 17.1 Interaction terms

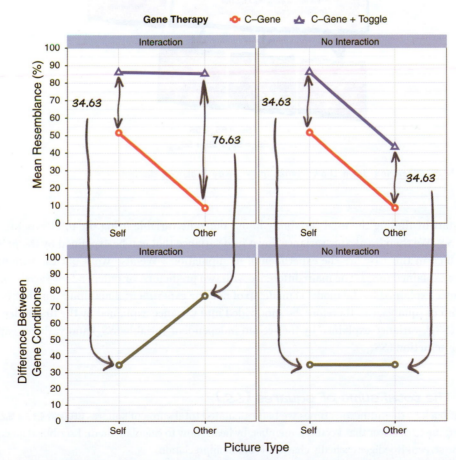

Figure 17.2 Breaking down what an interaction represents

17.3.2 The fit of the model

Milton stopped circling. He looked vaguely irritated by the dog's helpful explanation; perhaps he didn't like the dog having explained interaction effects better than he had. Given Alice's life was at stake, it seemed inappropriate for him to be side-tracked by interpersonal politics. Nevertheless, it galvanized him.

'Pay attention!' he said urgently. 'What matters here is how we actually get at whether these predictors make a significant contribution to predicting resemblance scores. In other words, are the group means different enough to be significant? Whether we are comparing means across groups that make up one predictor **(CHAPTER 16)** or two, or indeed looking at a continuous predictor **(CHAPTER 14)**, the basic principles are the same. The fit of the model is ascertained using the same sums of squares that I have explained to you before.' Milton paused to sketch a picture. **(FIGURE 17.3)**

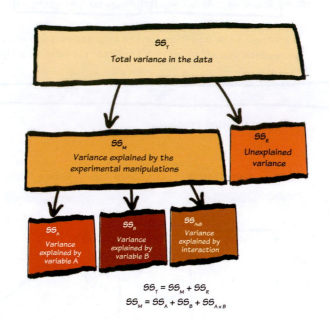

Figure 17.3   *Breaking down the variance in two-way factorial design*

'We start by finding the total variability in our outcome variable using the total sum of squared errors (SS_T). We then break this variance down into variance that can be explained by the predictors (SS_M), which in this case are the experimental manipulations. We also work out the variance that cannot be explained (SS_R). The main difference with two predictors, or independent variables, is that the variance explained by the model is made up of not one experimental manipulation, but two. The model sum of squares, can therefore, be subdivided into variance explained by the first independent variable (SS_A), variance explained by the second independent variable (SS_B) and variance explained by their interaction ($SS_{A\times B}$).'

17.3.2.1 The total sums of squares (SS_T)

I thought back to the numerous times we had calculated total sums of squares **(SECTIONS 4.3.2 & 16.2.3)**, and it horrified me to discover that I could remember, by heart, how to calculate them. I scribbled an equation **(17.7)** on the screen. Roediger excitedly chased his tail in appreciation.

$$SS_{\mathrm{T}} = \sum_{i=1}^{N} \left(x_i - \bar{x}_{\mathrm{grand}} \right)^2 = 33681.5 \qquad (17.7)$$

'To calculate how much variability there is in resemblance scores when we ignore the experimental group from which they came, we would use this equation (17.7), which is the same one that you showed me before when we compared means,' (EQUATION 16.8) I said. 'Basically, we just work out the difference between each score and the mean of all scores, square these differences and add them up.'

I noticed Milton nodding in appreciation.

CHECK YOUR BRAIN: Help Zach to calculate the grand mean and grand variance of the data in Table 17.1.

Roediger batted Milton's collar, which transformed into a screen protruding out of the cat's neck. It was his Proteus. After a frenzied tongue assault on the screen, Roediger showed me a diagram and some numbers. (FIGURE 17.4) 'If you lump all of the scores into a single group, then the mean is 57.875. It's no problem.'

All data			
43	9	75	80
72	6	79	87
44	6	87	88
37	12	99	85
61	9	85	93
42	7	92	85
59	12	87	86
54	8	85	78

Grand mean = 57.875

Grand variance = 1086.5

Figure 17.4 Collecting the scores into a single group

I thanked Roediger, and he drew up a spreadsheet to help me to do the calculation. (TABLE 17.3) He placed the resemblance scores into different rows in the second column. In the third column he placed the value of the mean of all scores (57.875). This value was the same for every participant. He then calculated the error between each score and the overall mean by subtracting the overall mean from each score (column 4). He squared these scores to get rid of any negative values (column 5). This column of squared errors contained the squared error for each score in the data, so to get the total sum of squared errors we simply added everything in that column, which gave us a total sum of squared error of 33,681.5. I remembered that the degrees of freedom should be $N-1$, and that we had 32 scores in total. I asked Roediger whether the degrees of freedom would, therefore, be 31 and he nodded.

17.3.2.2 The model sum of squares, SS_M

'That is merely the beginning ...', Milton said ominously.

'Sure, model sum of squares,' I interrupted. 'Easy enough, we've done it before. **(SECTION 16.2.4)** We looked at the difference between each group mean and the overall mean. I assume that we do the same here. If we combine the two independent variables, we end up with four means: C-gene with self, C-gene with other, toggle switch with self, toggle switch with other.'

I wrote out the equation that Milton had shown me when we had looked at comparing means before. **(EQUATION 16.9 & 17.8)** Roediger had calculated the grand mean for us (57.875), so all we had to do was subtract this value from each group mean, square each difference and multiply it by the number of people in each group, which was 8.

$$SS_M = \sum_{k=1}^{k} n_k \left(\bar{x}_k - \bar{x}_{grand} \right)^2 \qquad (17.8)$$

Table 17.3 Calculating the total and residual sums of squares for the C-gene experiment

	Resemblance	Grand Mean	$x_i - \bar{x}_{grand}$	$(x_i - \bar{x}_{grand})^2$	Group Mean	$x_i - \bar{x}_{group}$	$(x_i - \bar{x}_{group})^2$
C-Gene, Self	43	57.875	−14.875	221.266	51.50	−8.50	72.250
	72	57.875	14.125	199.516	51.50	20.50	420.250
	44	57.875	−13.875	192.516	51.50	−7.50	56.250
	37	57.875	−20.875	435.766	51.50	−14.50	210.250
	61	57.875	3.125	9.766	51.50	9.50	90.250
	42	57.875	−15.875	252.016	51.50	−9.50	90.250
	59	57.875	1.125	1.266	51.50	7.50	56.250
	54	57.875	−3.875	15.016	51.50	2.50	6.250
							$SS_{C\text{-}Gene,\,Self} = 1002$
C-Gene, Other	9	57.875	−48.875	2388.766	8.63	0.37	0.137
	6	57.875	−51.875	2691.016	8.63	−2.63	6.917
	6	57.875	−51.875	2691.016	8.63	−2.63	6.917
	12	57.875	−45.875	2104.516	8.63	3.37	11.357
	9	57.875	−48.875	2388.766	8.63	0.37	0.137
	7	57.875	−50.875	2588.266	8.63	−1.63	2.657
	12	57.875	−45.875	2104.516	8.63	3.37	11.357
	8	57.875	−49.875	2487.516	8.63	−0.63	0.397
							$SS_{C\text{-}Gene,\,Other} = 39.875$
C-Gene and Toggle, Self	75	57.875	17.125	293.266	86.13	−11.13	123.877
	79	57.875	21.125	446.266	86.13	−7.13	50.837
	87	57.875	29.125	848.266	86.13	0.87	0.757
	99	57.875	41.125	1691.266	86.13	12.87	165.637
	85	57.875	27.125	735.766	86.13	−1.13	1.277
	92	57.875	34.125	1164.516	86.13	5.87	34.457
	87	57.875	29.125	848.266	86.13	0.87	0.757
	85	57.875	27.125	735.766	86.13	−1.13	1.277
							$SS_{Toggle,\,Self} = 378.875$

C-Gene and Toggle, Other	80	57.875	22.125	489.516	85.25	−5.25	27.563
	87	57.875	29.125	848.266	85.25	1.75	3.063
	88	57.875	30.125	907.516	85.25	2.75	7.563
	85	57.875	27.125	735.766	85.25	−0.25	0.063
	93	57.875	35.125	1233.766	85.25	7.75	60.063
	85	57.875	27.125	735.766	85.25	−0.25	0.063
	86	57.875	28.125	791.016	85.25	0.75	0.563
	78	57.875	20.125	405.016	85.25	−7.25	52.563

$$SS_{\text{Toggle, Other}} = 151.50$$

Σ		33681.50	1572.25

I continued writing on the screen, and using my diePad I calculated the difference between each mean and the grand mean, and followed the calculation through. To ice the cake that I had very proudly produced, I added, 'Of course, the degrees of freedom will be 3 because we used four group means in the calculation and the degrees of freedom are the number of groups, k, minus 1.'

$$
\begin{aligned}
SS_{\text{M}} &= 8(51.5 - 57.875)^2 + 8(8.625 - 57.875)^2 + 8(86.125 - 57.875)^2 \\
&\quad + 8(85.25 - 57.875)^2 \\
&= 8(-6.375)^2 + 8(-49.25)^2 + 8(28.25)^2 + 8(27.375)^2 \\
&= 325.13 + 19404.5 + 6384.5 + 5995.13 \\
&= 32109.26
\end{aligned}
\tag{17.9}
$$

17.3.2.3 The main effect of gene therapy, SS_A

Milton raised his eyebrow. 'Not bad,' he said. 'We know that the model (our experimental manipulations) explains 32,109.26 units of variance out of the total of 33,681.5 units. The question is exactly how the predictors and interaction contribute to those 32,109.26. In other words, we must break down this model sum of squares to see how much variance is explained by our independent variables separately. How do you do that?'

Of course, I didn't know the answer and Milton knew that I didn't know; he was putting me in my place. As I shook my head to indicate my cluelessness, he paused and frowned, allowing a little guilt about his behaviour to seep in. His tone softened.

'Actually, you *do* know how to do it. You apply the same principle that you did to calculate the model sum of squares, but group the scores according to each predictor, one at a time. For example, to work out the variance accounted for by the first independent variable (in this case, gene therapy) we group the scores according to which therapy the person received.' Milton quite pointedly erased Roediger's interaction figure from the screen and replaced it with his own illustration. **(FIGURE 17.5)** 'Look here,' he said. 'I have grouped all of the scores from the C-gene condition together, and all of the scores from the toggle switch condition are grouped separately. I have completely ignored whether a person studied a picture of their own face or a stranger's. It is as though that variable does not exist. I then calculate the mean and standard deviation for these two groups. It is the means of the two groups that will be compared in the main effect of *Gene*.'

Milton wrote out an equation **(17.10)**.

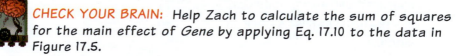

A1: C-Gene		A2: C-Gene + Toggle	
43	9	75	80
72	6	79	87
44	6	87	88
37	12	99	85
61	9	85	93
42	7	92	85
59	12	87	86
54	8	85	78

$$\text{Mean}_{C\text{-}Gene} = 30.063$$
$$SD_{C\text{-}Gene} = 23.657$$

$$\text{Mean}_{Toggle} = 85.688$$
$$SD_{Toggle} = 5.963$$

Figure 17.5 *The main effect of gene condition*

'That's exactly the same equation that I wrote out,' **(EQUATION 17.8)** I said, disgruntled.

CHECK YOUR BRAIN: Help Zach to calculate the sum of squares for the main effect of *Gene* by applying Eq. 17.10 to the data in Figure 17.5.

'Indeed it is,' replied Milton. 'You can take the means for the two groups from my diagram. **(FIGURE 17.5)** Each group contains 16 scores (*n*), and the grand mean is the same value as before, 57.875.'

$$SS_{A} = \sum_{n=1}^{k} n_{k} \left(\bar{x}_{k} - \bar{x}_{grand} \right)^{2} \tag{17.10}$$

I replaced these values into Milton's equation and calculated the total as 24,753.13. **(EQUATION 17.11)** 'So, the model sum of squares is made up of 32,109.26 units, and of those, 24753.13 can be attributed to which gene therapy a person received?'

'*Fur*fectly true, and the degrees of freedom are again the number of groups used, *k*, minus 1. Because we used two groups (C-gene and C-gene + toggle switch) the *df* will be 1.'

'Just to be clear about this, the main effect of *Gene* compares the mean of all scores in the C-gene group to the mean of all scores in the C-gene and toggle switch group, ignoring the type of picture they studied.'

'*Purr*fect,' the cat smiled.

$$\begin{aligned} SS_{Gene} &= 16(30.063 - 57.875)^{2} + 16(85.688 - 57.875)^{2} \\ &= 16(-27.813)^{2} + 16(27.813)^{2} \\ &= 12376.12 + 12377.01 \\ &= 24753.13 \end{aligned} \tag{17.11}$$

17.3.2.4 The main effect of picture type, SS_B

'Presumably,' I said, 'you could calculate the main effect of picture type in the same way: just ignore which type of gene therapy a person had?'

Milton nodded respectfully. He drew a diagram, which split the data into the type of picture that participants tried to resemble and showed the means for the resulting groups. (FIGURE 17.6)

 CHECK YOUR BRAIN: Help Zach to calculate the sum of squares for the main effect of picture type by applying Eq. 17.10 to the data in Figure 17.6.

I did what I had done a minute ago: I applied the same equation as before. (EQUATION 17.8 & 17.12) I took the means for the two groups from Milton's diagram (FIGURE 17.6), which also showed that each group contained 16 scores (n), and the grand mean hadn't changed, so I knew that value too. I replaced these values into the equation and calculated the total as 3828.13. (EQUATION 17.13) The degrees of freedom I assumed were again 1 because the number of groups used was 2, so k minus 1 would be 1.

B1: Self		B2: Other	
43	75	9	80
72	79	6	87
44	87	6	88
37	99	12	85
61	85	9	93
42	92	7	85
59	87	12	86
54	85	8	78

$$\text{Mean}_{Self} = 68.813 \qquad \text{Mean}_{Other} = 46.938$$
$$SD_{Self} = 20.292 \qquad SD_{Other} = 39.730$$

Figure 17.6 The main effect of picture type

$$SS_B = \sum_{n=1}^{k} n_k \left(\bar{x}_k - \bar{x}_{grand} \right)^2 \tag{17.12}$$

Milton clapped his hands together, 'what you have shown is that the model sum of squares is made up of 32109.26 units, 24753.13 of these units can be attributed to which gene therapy a person received, and 3828.13 can be attributed to the type of picture that the participant was trying to resemble.'

$$SS_{\text{Picture}} = 16(68.813 - 57.875)^2 + 16(46.938 - 57.875)^2$$
$$= 16(10.938)^2 + 16(-10.937)^2 \tag{17.13}$$
$$= 1914.24 + 1913.89$$
$$= 3828.13$$

17.3.2.5 The interaction effect, $SS_{A \times B}$

'The final piece of the jigsaw, if you will excuse the pun, is to work out how much variance is explained by the interaction of the two variables.' The cat grinned. 'This is very simple given that we know that the SS_{M} is comprised of the SS_{A}, SS_{B}, and $SS_{\text{A} \times \text{B}}$.' Milton pointed to his earlier diagram. **(FIGURE 17.3)** 'Look here, I even wrote out that you can get SS_{M} by adding the other three sums of squares together. All we have to do is to rearrange this equation to put the interaction term on the left-hand side.'

Milton wrote out an equation **(17.14)**. 'The interaction term is calculated by taking the model sum of squares and subtracting from it the sums of squares for the two main effects.'

$$SS_{A \times B} = SS_M - SS_A - SS_B \tag{17.14}$$

I replaced the values that we had just calculated into Milton's equation **(EQUATION 17.15)**, and with some electronic help found out that the interaction effect explained 3528 units of variation.

$$SS_{A \times B} = SS_M - SS_A - SS_B$$
$$= 32109.26 - 24753.13 - 3828.13 \tag{17.15}$$
$$= 3528$$

'How do we know the degrees of freedom?' I asked.

Milton wrote out a similar equation **(17.16)**. 'In the same way: we know the model degrees of freedom so we subtract from it the degrees of freedom for both main effects. It is also the case that the degrees of freedom for the interaction effect are equal to the degrees of freedom for the main effects multiplied together. Whichever method you use, you will find in this case that they are 1.'

$$df_{A \times B} = df_M - df_A - df_B \qquad df_{A \times B} = df_A \times df_B$$
$$= 3 - 1 - 1 \qquad\qquad\quad = 1 \times 1 \tag{17.16}$$
$$= 1 \qquad\qquad\qquad\quad = 1$$

17.3.2.6 The residual sum of squares, SS_R

'These sums of squares for the main effects and interactions tell us the variance in resemblance scores accounted for by these variables,' I said, 'and every time we have looked at the linear model before we've had an error term: a residual sum of squares that tells us how much variance is not accounted for by the model.'

'The same applies here,' Milton replied. 'It is calculated in exactly the same way as with a model with a single predictor: by looking at the error in prediction. When we are using group means as our predicted values, that means looking at the difference between individual scores and the mean of the group to which the score belongs.' **(SECTION 16.2.5)**

I thought back to the equation that Milton had showed me when we looked at the memory data. **(EQUATION 16.11)** The idea was that we should calculate the sum of squares *within* each group and add them up. To do this we calculate the difference between each score and the mean of the group to which the score belonged; then we square this difference. We do this for each score and then add up these squared errors within each group. To get the residual sum of squares we add together the sums of squares within each group. I wrote what I had remembered on the screen. **(EQUATION 17.17)**

$$SS_R = \sum \left(Y_{ik} - \bar{Y}_k \right)^2$$
$$= SS_{C-Gene,\,Self} + SS_{C-Gene,\,Other} + SS_{Toggle,\,Self} + SS_{Toggle,\,Other} \tag{17.17}$$

'You do exactly the same thing here,' Milton replied as he added some columns to Roediger's table. **(TABLE 17.3)** He placed the value of the mean for each group into the table (column 6), then used the app to calculate the difference between each resemblance score and the mean of the group to which the score belonged (column 7). As expected, some of the values were positive and others negative, so he squared the errors to make them all positive and these values appeared in the final column.

'Sweet, so to get the sum of squared errors within each group, we add up the values in the final column for each of the four groups?'

Milton nodded as he wrote out the values and added them together. **(EQUATION 17.18)** 'You see, we add the sum of squared errors for the four different groups, which gives us a total of 1572.25, which is the residual sum of squares.'

$$SS_R = SS_{C-Gene,\,Self} + SS_{C-Gene,\,Other} + SS_{Toggle,\,Self}$$
$$+ SS_{Toggle,\,Other}$$
$$= 1002 + 39.875 + 378.875 + 151.5 \tag{17.18}$$
$$= 1572.25$$

'Remember that each group's sum of squared error has an associated degrees of freedom that is $n-1$,' the cat continued. 'For each group there were 8 scores, and therefore the degrees of freedom are 7. To get the residual degrees of freedom we add the degrees of freedom for each group, which gives us a value of 28.' **(EQUATION 17.19)**

$$df_R = df_{C-Gene,\,Self} + df_{C-Gene,\,Other} + df_{Toggle,\,Self} + df_{Toggle,\,Other}$$
$$= 7 + 7 + 7 + 7 \tag{17.19}$$
$$= 28$$

17.3.2.7 The F-ratios

When we looked at comparing means from a single independent variable, Milton had explained that this variable was assessed using an *F*-ratio, which told us whether using the group means significantly improved the model's ability to predict outcome scores. In other words, it told us whether the means were significantly different. To get these *F*-ratios we converted the sum of squared errors into a mean squared error by dividing by the degrees of freedom. **(SECTION 16.2.6)** I asked Milton whether we did the same here.

He nodded. 'We calculate the mean squared error for each effect by taking its sum of squares and dividing by the respective degrees of freedom. This should be done for the residual term, too.' The cat wrote out the equations for the mean squares for the main effects of *Gene*, *Picture*, their interaction and the residual term. **(EQUATION 17.20)**

Something looked odd to me. 'All of the mean squares for the effects are the same as the sums of squares. Is that right?'

'Yes, remember that for all of these effects the degrees of freedom were 1, so to make the conversion from a total sum of squares to an average, we divide by 1, which of course results in the value with which we started. It is perfectly claw-rect.'

$$MS_A = \frac{SS_A}{df_A} = \frac{24753.13}{1} = 24753.13$$

$$MS_B = \frac{SS_B}{df_B} = \frac{3828.13}{1} = 3828.13$$

$$MS_{A \times B} = \frac{SS_{A \times B}}{df_{A \times B}} = \frac{3528}{1} = 3528$$ \hfill (17.20)

$$MS_R = \frac{SS_R}{df_R} = \frac{1572.25}{28} = 56.152$$

'And, the F-ratios, are these calculated in the same way as when we just had one independent variable?'

'Yes, each effect has an F-ratio, which is the signal-to-noise ratio for that variable. It is the mean squared error for the effect (the signal) divided by the mean squared error for the residual (the noise).' Milton wrote out the calculation for each of the three effects **(EQUATION 17.21)**, and then drew up a table summarizing all of our calculations. **(TABLE 17.4)** 'It can be helpful to place these values in a table, so that for each effect you can see the sums of squares, the degrees of freedom, the mean squares and the resulting F-ratio.'

$$F_A = \frac{MS_A}{MS_R} = \frac{24753.13}{56.152} = 440.82$$

$$F_B = \frac{MS_B}{MS_R} = \frac{3828.13}{56.152} = 68.17$$ \hfill (17.21)

$$F_{A \times B} = \frac{MS_{A \times B}}{MS_R} = \frac{3528}{56.152} = 62.83$$

'Presumably, we compare these values of F against the critical values for a 0.05 probability in that table that you showed me last time.' **(SECTION A.4; FIGURE 16.6)**

'Yes. For each effect you look up the value for the degrees of freedom for the effect, which in each case in these data is 1, and the residual degrees of freedom, which is 28 in all cases.'

'So, the value that is in the column labelled 1, and the row labelled 28.'

'*Purr*cisely,' replied the cat, bringing up the table of critical values on the screen. 'The critical value for 1 and 28 degrees of freedom is 4.20.'

'All our F-ratios exceed this value, so they are all significant, right?'

'Yes, and of course we can get a computer to calculate exact probabilities.'

Table 17.4 *Summary table for a factorial linear model*

Source	SS	df	MS	F
Model	32109.26	3		
Gene Therapy	24753.13	1	24753.13	440.82
Picture Type	3828.13	1	3828.13	68.17
Gene Therapy × Picture Type	3528.00	1	3528.00	62.83
Residual	1572.25	28	56.152	
Total	33681.50	31		

17.3.3 Factorial designs on a computer

'ENOUGH!' bellowed an irate Vic from behind us. His hand quivered in rage over the insignia on the front of the prison, 'Stop your drivelling and start telling me what the research means, or I activate the prison.' His snake-like tongue hovered over every *s*.

I was surprised that Milton leapt to my defence, quite literally: Vic's shouting frightened him into a 180-degree jump. He landed crouched, with his fur standing to attention; with his portly shape he looked like a hairy blowfish.

'Look, lizard,' he spat. 'Three weeks ago this ape thought that kurtosis was a dental hygiene problem; all things considered, we are moving swiftly. Go and lick your eyeballs, or whatever you lizards do, for five minutes and we will have you an answer.'

Vic seethed, flames bellowing from his neck. 'Five minutes,' he said in a measured tone, 'then she dies.'

My panic came surging back. I couldn't contemplate a world without Alice. I felt sick. I had bought us time by looking at the report, but that time was running out and I still had no idea how I would get Alice out of the prison unless by some miracle Vic was true to his word. I knew only too well that it was unlikely.

Milton beckoned me to kneel down and whispered in my ear, 'Worry not, she will not die, she will merely enter a superpositional state of being both alive and dead.'

Eisel.

Roediger was scared. He wiggled flat on the floor like his stomach was stuck to it. In an attempt to distract himself from his fear, he reared up on his hind legs and started scratching at a screen in front of us. It was as though the screen were a locked door that he wanted to open. 'Five minutes, no problem,' he said nervously.

The screen lit up with tables of numbers, and the spaniel explained, 'The first table (OUTPUT 17.1) shows Levene's test. (SECTION 12.2.3) The significant result, $F(3, 28)$, $p = 0.002$, implies that the variance in resemblance scores is different across the four combinations of gene therapy and type of picture.'

'Stupid canines!' tutted Milton. 'I have told you before to ignore that test,' (MEOWSINGS 16.1) he said as he padded around thinking.

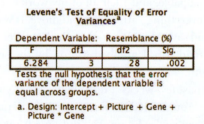

Levene's Test of Equality of Error Variances[a]

Dependent Variable: Resemblance (%)

F	df1	df2	Sig.
6.284	3	28	.002

Tests the null hypothesis that the error variance of the dependent variable is equal across groups.

a. Design: Intercept + Picture + Gene + Picture * Gene

Output 17.1 Levene's test for the gene data using IBM SPSS Statistics

Roediger used his sad dog eye expression to show that he was offended. I patted his head and he wagged his tail. 'You want a summary table of the main results like Milton drew? It's no problem,' he said pointing to the screen. (OUTPUT 17.2)

The sums of squares, mean squares, degrees of freedom and F-ratios all matched the values that we had calculated closely enough. (TABLE 17.4) but the output also showed the exact p-value associated with each F-ratio in the column labelled *Sig*.

'They're all zero,' I noted. I remembered Celia telling me when we were talking about finding relationships in categorical data (SECTION 13.1.8) that when p-values are below 0.001 we see only the zeros. I asked if that was the case here and Milton said that it was.

Tests of Between-Subjects Effects

Dependent Variable: Resemblance (%)

Source	Type III Sum of Squares	df	Mean Square	F	Sig.
Corrected Model	32109.250ᵃ	3	10703.083	190.610	.000
Intercept	107184.500	1	107184.500	1908.835	.000
Picture	3828.125	1	3828.125	68.175	.000
Gene	24753.125	1	24753.125	440.825	.000
Picture * Gene	3528.000	1	3528.000	62.830	.000
Error	1572.250	28	56.152		
Total	140866.000	32			
Corrected Total	33681.500	31			

a. R Squared = .953 (Adjusted R Squared = .948)

Output 17.2   *ANOVA table for the gene data using IBM SPSS Statistics*

The effects of *Gene*, *Picture* and their interaction were all significant because their *p*-values are less than 0.05, but what did the effects actually mean, I wondered out loud.

Vic thumped the side of the prison. My heart raced until I noticed that he hadn't thumped the insignia.

'I do not care that the effects are significant. What do these effects mean, and how do I know Alice hasn't tried to fool me like in every other report?' he raged.

17.4   FROM THE PINNACLE TO THE PIT

Celia was still standing guard by the prison. I caught her gaze and she tried to reassure me with a smile. I felt betrayed by her, but was I being a hypocrite: I had led her on to get information; I hadn't been entirely honest with her. Had she really behaved any worse than I had? Perhaps not, but somehow my deceit didn't seem as bad as imprisoning the woman who I love. That was an act of true cruelty; I'd misjudged her badly. I couldn't really understand why she'd willingly lock Alice up: she surely didn't think it cleared the way to be with me? Demonstrating sociopathic tendencies is never a winner in the dating game. Perhaps it was simple retribution: an eye for an eye, a tooth for a tooth, and perhaps a broken heart for a broken heart?'

The tension in the room was palpable, and I felt all of my work over the past few weeks slipping away: I realized that I could blow everything with one stupid move. It was time to focus, time to think, time to give Vic what he wanted and save Alice. If not, then the last three weeks would become nothing more than a perverse statistical road trip. I grabbed Milton by the scruff, leaned into his ear and addressed him through gritted teeth.

'You've been my guide for the past few weeks. I don't believe that you simply want your freedom: there is stuff you're not telling me. You warned me not to trust chimeras, and here we are locked in a room with one. You know more than you've let on. You put on a front of wanting to stay away from here, and yet at every hurdle you have helped me to get here. You've brought me here for a reason and – despite your constant belittling of me – I believe that you might be on my side. Well, this is it: we're at the apex, so now's the time to drop the pompous cat thing that you have going on, front up and let me in on whatever it is that's going on. So, is there anything you want to tell me?'

'How to get effect sizes for Alice's study?' he asked, with his sarcastic little cat face.

17.5   ALTERNATIVE APPROACHES

17.5.1 Calculating effect sizes

Milton paused briefly to enjoy my frustrated expression before continuing.

'We can use omega squared (ω^2) as we did before **(SECTION 16.9.1)**, but this is quite complicated to calculate and we do not have enough time,' he explained. 'There are plenty of good sources[11, 51] for you to learn about this later when your girlfriend is not about to enter a quantum-physical state of superpositions.'

'Great. What can we use instead?'

'Of course, for the main effects of *Gene* and *Picture* we compared two sets of scores, so we could compute Cohen's d in the usual way. You could also compute Cohen's d for one independent variable at each level of the other.'

'What, like compute Cohen's d for the difference between self and other pictures in the C-gene condition, and then another Cohen's d for the toggle switch condition?'

CHECK YOUR BRAIN: Use the means and standard deviations in Figures 17.5 and 17.6 to compute Cohen's d for the main effects of gene therapy and picture type.

'*Purr*cisely. You can also convert an F-ratio into the effect size r **(SECTION 11.2.2)** when it has only 1 degree of freedom for the effect.' Milton wrote out the equation for me. **(EQUATION 17.22)**

'Why does the F have to have 1 degree of freedom?'

'Because that means it has compared a specific effect. For example, our picture type effect had 1 degree of freedom because it compared two things: pictures of the self and others. Likewise, the effect of gene condition had 1 degree of freedom because it compared two things: C-gene therapy with and without a toggle switch. The interaction, too, had 1 degree of freedom because it compared the difference between means in two conditions: for example, the difference in resemblance scores after studying a picture of the self or a stranger, in the C-gene group compared to the toggle switch condition. The equation itself is simple: you take an F-ratio with 1 degree of freedom for the effect and whatever the residual degrees of freedom (df_R) are and divide it by itself plus the residual degrees of freedom. You then square root the result.'

CHECK YOUR BRAIN: Use the F-ratios in Table 17.4 and Eq. 17.22 to compute the effect sizes for the main effects of gene therapy, picture type and their interaction.

$$r = \sqrt{\frac{F(1, df_R)}{F(1, df_R) + df_R}}$$

(17.22)

I quickly gathered the F-ratios for each effect, and the residual degrees of freedom for each, which were 28 for all three. I plugged these values into the equation and calculated r for each effect. From what I remembered, r could lie between 0, which was no effect at all, and ± 1, which was the strongest effect possible. The main effect of gene therapy had an effect size of 0.97, which is a near perfect effect, the main effect of picture type was 0.84, also extremely strong, and for the interaction effect it was 0.83, again very strong. **(EQUATION 17.23)** It didn't look as though Alice was trying to conceal her findings, but we needed to do robust analyses to be sure.

$$r_{Gene} = \sqrt{\frac{440.83}{440.83 + 28}} = 0.97$$

$$r_{Picture} = \sqrt{\frac{68.18}{68.18 + 28}} = 0.84$$

(17.23)

$$r_{Gene \times Picture} = \sqrt{\frac{62.83}{62.83 + 28}} = 0.83$$

17.5.2 Robust analysis of factorial designs

Milton quickly produced a robust test of the effects for me. (OUTPUT 17.3)

'This analysis has been performed on 20% trimmed means using a function called *t2way()*[34] in the R[25] app. The trimmed means appear at the bottom, so for the C-gene group, the mean resemblance scores when studying the picture of themselves was 50.5% but when studying a stranger was 8.5%; whereas in the toggle switch group these means were 85.83% and 85.17%, respectively. Compare these values with the untrimmed means we saw earlier,' he said, pointing to the original table of data. (TABLE 17.1) 'They're pretty similar.' He continued to explain that *$Qa* and *$A.p.value* were the test statistic and its *p*-value for the main effect of gene therapy, *$Qb* and *$B.p.value* were the same values for the main effect of picture type, and *$Qab* and *$AB.p.value* were the values for the interaction effect.

I noted that, even when a robust analysis was done, all three *p*-values were still significant: they were all 0.001.

'Yes, the robust analysis confirms Alice's findings,' Milton agreed.

```
$Qa
 Milton confirmed[1]  451.3583

$A.p.value
[1]  0.001

$Qb
[1]  65.50325

$B.p.value
[1]  0.001

$Qab
[1]  61.47326

$AB.p.value
[1]  0.001

$means
          [,1]       [,2]
[1,]  50.50000   8.50000
[2,]  85.83333  85.16667
```

Output 17.3 *Output from the t2way() function using R*

17.5.3 Bayes factors for factorial designs

With a sense of urgency I had, until now, not seen in Milton, he produced some more analysis. (OUTPUT 17.4–17.6) 'These are Bayes factors for the three effects, based on some reasonable default prior beliefs.[126, 127] First, we put the main effect of gene therapy into the model (OUTPUT 17.4) and see that the Bayes factor is 16,929,560.'

That was huge. 'I should shift my belief in the alternative hypothesis relative to the null by a factor of 16,929,560?' I asked. 'This means my belief in gene therapy predicting resemblance scores should shift a lot.'

'*Purr*cisely. We then add the main effect of picture type and see how this improves the model, compared to when we only include gene therapy as a predictor. (OUTPUT 17.5) The Bayes factor for this main effect is 244.14.'

I pointed out that the value was much smaller.

'True, but remember that a value of 1 means that your belief in the alternative hypothesis relative to the null should not change, so a value of 244 still suggests that your beliefs should move a lot in favour of the type of picture predicting resemblance scores. Finally, we include the interaction effect and compare this to the model that included only the main effects. (OUTPUT 17.6) The Bayes factor for the interaction term is 187,385.6.'

Another huge number. 'Sick, so the data are 187,385.6 times more likely under the alternative hypothesis for the interaction term compared to the null. I should shift my belief in the alternative hypothesis relative to the null by a factor of 187,385.6.'

Milton nodded.

```
Bayes factor analysis
--------------
[1] Genes : 16929560 ±0%

Against denominator:
  Intercept only
---
Bayes factor type: BFlinearModel, JZS
```

Output 17.4   *Testing the main effect of genes with a Bayes factor using lmBF() in R*

```
Bayes factor analysis
--------------
[1] Genes + Picture : 244.1401 ±3.49%

Against denominator:
  Resemblance ~ Genes
---
Bayes factor type: BFlinearModel, JZS
```

Output 17.5   *Testing the main effect of picture type with a Bayes factor using lmBF() in R*

```
Bayes factor analysis
--------------
[1] Genes + Picture + Genes:Picture : 187385.6 ±11.1%

Against denominator:
  Resemblance ~ Genes + Picture
---
Bayes factor type: BFlinearModel, JZS
```

Output 17.6   *Testing the interaction effect with a Bayes factor using lmBF() in R*

17.6   INTERPRETING INTERACTION EFFECTS

I turned to Vic.

'I have the information you want,' I declared. I told him how the effect sizes, robust analyses and Bayesian analysis all confirmed what Alice had written in her report. When it came to predicting resemblance scores, the type of picture had an effect, the type of gene therapy had an effect, but these variables also combined to have an effect.

Vic's eyes popped out on their sinew-like stalks and danced around while never losing their fix on me. He let out a laugh that escalated into a bellow that continued as he slowly paced the room. Then he stopped abruptly, clenched his fists and scowled at me. He disappeared, leaving a vapour trail in his wake that led back to the prison where his body emerged. Holding his quivering hand by the insignia, he screamed 'Do you take me for a fool? You have told me nothing! *Nothing*!'

I was confused by his rage: I thought I'd been helpful. What did he want from me?

'I've shown you that you can trust Alice's analysis,' I offered hoping to pacify him.

He calmed a little. 'But you have not told me what the results mean, or how I can use them to ... to ... help my situation.'

What did he mean by his situation? Anonymity? Invisibility? People forgetting him? I asked him.

'We discovered that Alice was working on ways to help people to heal their physical wounds,' he said. He looked down at his body. 'Look at me ... I wanted perfection: the best hearing, vision, smell ... to be the strongest, fastest – the greatest being who ever lived. I took the best that the animal kingdom has to offer, and I merged it with my own DNA. But it turned me into – this.' He gestured at his body in disgust. 'I have improved everything about myself, but at what price? I am a monster, a walking wound. I need to be healed.'

I understood. Vic's appearance made it impossible for him to interact with the world; he was a prisoner of his own ambition. Nobody would knowingly work for or do business with something that looked as terrifying as Vic. It explained Rob Nutcot: Vic had created him to be the acceptable face of JIG:SAW; a smiling, mimicking robot with trust-inducing aftershave. It was a shame he hadn't worked harder on Nutcot's speech circuits.

Milton raised his eyes to the heavens and shook his head, but I felt sorry for Vic. He looked a mess, for real. Perhaps he did just want to look normal again, perhaps Milton was wrong, maybe he wasn't this evil guy – even Milton had admitted that he hadn't found evidence of Vic's evil, it was all hearsay.

I turned my back on Vic and knelt by the cat. 'Maybe Vic is just desperate to fit in,' I whispered. 'You and he are not so different, you've become a cat and he's become ... well, a sort of zoo. Surely you can relate to him wanting to look human again?'

Milton scowled at me. 'During our short association you have proved that you are not stupid. Please do not undo your good work now. I do not relate to anything to do with Vic Luten because I am not the sort of person who wipes the memories of innocent people, or who uses an innocent girl to get information for me before I kill her, or who lures people with the promise of jobs and then zombifies them, I have never tried to asphyxiate you, and I would not place a brilliant and innocent scientist in a Schrödinger prison and threaten to inflict a living death upon her; I do not build robots to do my dirty work ...'

He'd made his point. I stood, desperately trying to think of my next move. Before I could, Milton paced confidently towards Vic and said, 'For an evil genius, you are very stupid.'

What the frip was he playing at? I'd done well to pacify Vic, so why on earth was Milton winding him up again? Why was he goading him?

'WHAT?' screamed Vic as jets of fire shot from his gills. Celia ducked.

'You are missing the obvious,' Milton replied.

Vic shook with rage, his hand tensed above the insignia. 'I *will* activate the prison!' he assured us.

'That would only compound your mistake,' Milton replied calmly. 'Let me explain. We have verified the analysis in Alice's report, confirmed her conclusions, all you need is an interpretation of those results. Ask yourself who in this room is best equipped to provide such an explanation. I am a humble physicist, I can verify the analysis but I do not possess the knowledge of genetics to know what Alice's results mean. Zach is a humble imbecile, a simple creature who has done well to understand some of the more rudimentary aspects of data analysis, but is ultimately battling against unmitigated intellectual deficiencies. You could ask Roediger, but he has had the wool pulled over his eyes all too easily by Alice before. Celia? Well, she is, or was, merely Rob's personal assistant, hardly versed in the ways of science. Even if you did want us to help, why would we? Apart from Zach, none of us have any reason to care whether Alice lives or dies. Negotiating with Alice is your optimal strategy.'

'She seems unwilling to talk,' Vic Luten said pointedly.

'True,' the cat replied. 'She'd probably be more willing if it were Zach in the prison instead of her, don't you think?'

What the frip? Did Milton really just tell the lizard psycho to put *me* in the prison? My legs buckled beneath me. I thought I'd been brave over the past few weeks, but my bravery deserted me now as I thought of a living death. What was wrong with the cat? No matter how hard I had tried to impress him, he still thought of me as an idiot. I had given him everything: a home, affection, food, and as much enthusiasm as I could muster for his lessons. In return, he would happily see me dead if it got him out of trouble – a typical cat!

Then it hit me like a brick: he'd chosen his words more carefully than I first realized. For a start, he was lying: he worked with Alice, he knew about genetics, yet he presented himself to Vic as ignorant. He also knew that Celia had a lot more knowledge about statistics than she let on, and his insults about me deflected Vic's attention from what I *did* know. Roediger was perfectly capable of giving Vic what he wanted. Milton's whole speech was carefully designed to make Vic think that none of us were useful to him. What I didn't understand was why he wanted me inside the prison instead of Alice. What did he know that I didn't?

Vic's hand hovered over the insignia periodically twitching. He seemed hesitant to trust the cat but also unable to counter his logic. I prayed for Alice to capitulate now, to save me, but her silence lingered over me like a final nail in my heart. With a puff of air Vic appeared beside me and grabbed me by the neck. He compressed my throat so I couldn't breathe. The room blurred and we appeared at the prison door. Fire bellowed from his neck as he growled, 'Let's see how much your boyfriend really means to you?' I feared the answer almost as much as the prison.

I grabbed Celia by the shoulders. 'What the frip have you done? Alice is in there!' It was only then I noticed my tears. Celia put her hands gently on my cheeks, and traced her fingers down the tracks of my tears. She kissed my forehead and the softness of her touch broke the levee. I felt mentally and physically exhausted, and I gave myself up completely to my emotions, sobbing uncontrollably into her shoulder. She cradled my head in her arms, stroking my hair while I regained some composure. She fixed my pathetic gaze with soft eyes and said, 'You heard what Vic said, the room was empty.'

I didn't understand.

Milton tugged my trousers and led me away from Celia, who started checking the prison. He took me to the screen we'd been working on. 'Let us finish what we started,' he said. His voice was soft and compassionate.

'I can't,' I said pathetically. 'I'm done, I've got nothing more. I came here to find Alice, but she's gone. She wouldn't even save me when she thought Vic would put me in the prison. I've got nothing left. Please, just take me home.'

The cat nuzzled into my leg. 'You are the best student I've ever had,' he said. 'I have taught many brilliant scientists, but they are naturals – it is pushing at an open door. You are different: you find this hard, people have told you that you can't do it, but you've been determined, you've stuck with me, you've never given up and, looking at Alice's report ... you were brilliant, quite brilliant.' He paused and looked up at me. 'What do you say, young man? One more lesson, just for old times?'

I didn't answer, but the cat knew he had convinced me.

'Sometimes, you must trust that you have the ability to find the answers yourself. Now use all that you have learned, and think,' he said reassuringly.

I looked again at the results. The main effect of gene therapy was significant. For this effect we had collected all of the scores for the C-gene group together, and likewise the scores for those that had the toggle switch as well. We had used the means of these groups of scores when calculating the sums of squares for this effect, so the effect must compare these means. I looked at the earlier diagram where we'd grouped these scores **(FIGURE 17.5)**, and drew myself a graph. **(FIGURE 17.7)**

'Presumably, the main effect of gene therapy tells us that scores were significantly higher for participants who received C-gene therapy and a toggle switch than for those who received C-gene therapy alone,' I said to Milton.

'*Fur*fectly true, but what do the scores represent?'

'They were how closely the person's face matched the picture that they looked at; so people with the toggle switch resembled the pictures significantly more than those without.'

'*Claw*rect. What about the main effect of picture type?'

That effect had been significant too. To calculate this effect we had collected all of the scores for the group that studied and tried to resemble pictures of themselves and compared them to all of the scores from people who studied pictures of strangers. As before, I used the earlier diagram where we'd grouped these scores **(FIGURE 17.6)** to help me draw a graph of the means. **(FIGURE 17.8)**

'Does the significant main effect of picture type mean that resemblance scores were significantly higher for participants who studied photos of themselves compared to those who studied a photo of a stranger? That makes sense because Alice's report **(LAB NOTES 2.1)** said that the people who studied photos of a stranger were a control group, right? I mean, this therapy is to help people with facial injuries to heal themselves, to look like they did before their injuries. So, this effect is consistent with that – you wouldn't expect resemblance scores to be high when they study a photo of a stranger because they shouldn't be able to make themselves look like the stranger.'

'Indeed they should not,' Milton replied. 'You have grasped the theory of the study extremely well. What about the interaction effect?'

I plotted the means of the four groups on a graph. **(FIGURE 17.9)** This effect had been significant too. I remembered Roediger telling me that an interaction looked at the effect of one predictor at each level of the other. I looked at Milton.

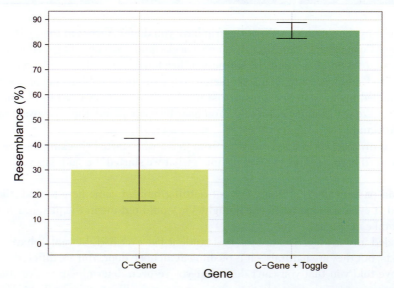

Figure 17.7 *Graph showing the main effect of gene therapy on resemblance scores*

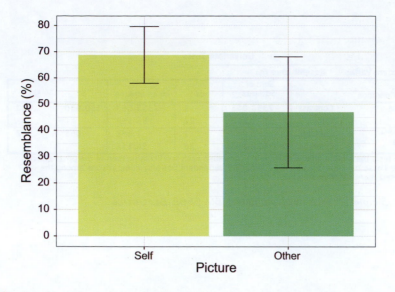

Figure 17.8   *Graph to show the main effect of picture type on resemblance scores*

'To break this effect down we need to look at the effect of one predictor within each level of the other, don't we? So, I could look at the effect of studying a picture of your own face compared to a stranger's face (the control) in the C-gene group and then see how that differs compared to what happens in the group that also received the toggle switch.'

The cat nodded and smiled. 'Yes, you could do this formally with something known as **simple effects analysis**. This analysis looks at the effect of one independent variable at individual levels of the other independent variable.' Milton swished his paws on the screen and produced a table. **(OUTPUT 17.7)** 'This is a simple effects analysis, it does a significance test on the effect of picture type, but separately

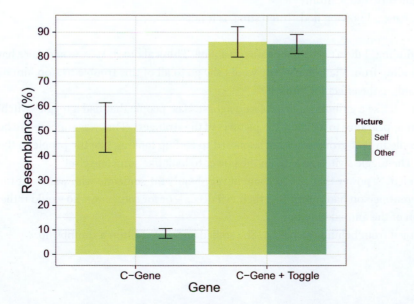

Figure 17.9   *Graph of the interaction of gene therapy and picture type on resemblance scores*

Univariate Tests

Dependent Variable: Resemblance (%)

Gene Condition		Sum of Squares	df	Mean Square	F	Sig.
C–Gene	Contrast	7353.063	1	7353.063	130.950	.000
	Error	1572.250	28	56.152		
C–Gene + Toggle	Contrast	3.063	1	3.063	.055	.817
	Error	1572.250	28	56.152		

Each F tests the simple effects of Picture Type within each level combination of the other effects shown. These tests are based on the linearly independent pairwise comparisons among the estimated marginal means.

Output 17.7 Simple effects analysis using IBM SPSS Statistics

within each of the therapy groups. Each effect has an *F*-ratio with an associated *p*-value, which tells us whether the effect of picture type is significant.'

I studied the table. It looked like in the C-gene group there was a highly significant effect of the type of picture because the *p*-value was given as 0.000, which is less than 0.05. This mirrored what my graph showed (**FIGURE 17.9**), because in the C-gene group the bars are different heights: the mean for those studying photos of themselves was much higher than for those studying photos of other people. People with C-gene therapy resembled the picture more when they tried to look like themselves than when they tried to look like a stranger. However, when people received a toggle switch as well as the C-gene therapy, there was no significant effect of picture type, because the *p*-value was 0.817, which is much larger than 0.05. This also matched what the graph showed because in the toggle switch condition the bars for the picture groups were the same height. This would mean that for people receiving C-gene therapy with a toggle switch it didn't matter if they studied a picture of themselves or someone else – their resemblance scores were very high in both cases. I explained this to Milton.

Milton gave me a knowing nod. 'Interesting, is it not?'

'What?'

'That last finding.' I didn't get what he was on about. 'Think about it. Why would Alice have wanted to hide that finding from Vic Luten? Why would she go to all of this trouble to stop him discovering her work or finding the effect for himself?'

The penny fell like a guillotine. 'Frip!' I said aghast. 'The people that had a toggle switch managed to change their appearance to look like the pictures of the strangers. That was supposed to be a control group: the people in that group were not supposed to end up looking like the people in the pictures, but they did! The toggle switch gave them the power to look like someone else!'

Milton smiled. 'A power that would come in very handy for someone who wanted it to appear as though a different person had committed their evil deeds – or for someone who would rather not look like a car crash of the animal kingdom.'

Celia emerged from behind the prison. She smiled and gave Milton a thumbs up.

574

'And Alice discovered this genetic therapy?' I asked.

'Indeed,' Milton replied.

I was dumbstruck. I always knew Alice was brilliant, but this was over the wall, she truly was a genius – the most magnificent, astonishing, amazing person. I suddenly realized I was speaking out loud.

'Thank you,' Celia said. 'You're pretty amazing yourself, rockstar.'

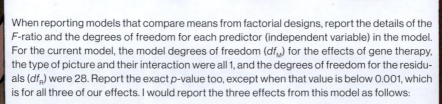

When reporting models that compare means from factorial designs, report the details of the F-ratio and the degrees of freedom for each predictor (independent variable) in the model. For the current model, the model degrees of freedom (df_M) for the effects of gene therapy, the type of picture and their interaction were all 1, and the degrees of freedom for the residuals (df_R) were 28. Report the exact p-value too, except when that value is below 0.001, which is for all three of our effects. I would report the three effects from this model as follows:

✓ There was a significant main effect of whether the participant had the chameleon gene alone or in combination with the genetic toggle switch, $F(1, 28) = 440.83$, $p < .001$, $r = .97$. Resemblance to the picture was significantly higher in participants receiving the C-gene and toggle switch ($M = 85.69$, $SD = 5.96$) than in those receiving only the C-gene ($M = 30.06$, $SD = 23.66$).

✓ There was a significant main effect of whether the participant tried to resemble a photo of themselves pre-injury or a photo of a same-sex stranger, $F(1, 28) = 68.17$, $p < .001$, $r = .84$. Resemblance to the picture was significantly higher in participants who tried to look like themselves ($M = 68.81$, $SD = 20.29$) than a stranger ($M = 46.94$, $SD = 39.73$).

✓ There was a significant interaction between the gene therapy combination and the type of picture that the participants tried to emulate, $F(1, 28) = 62.83$, $p < .001$, $r = .83$. In participants receiving the C-gene and toggle switch, resemblance scores were very high regardless of whether they tried to resemble themselves ($M = 86.13$, $SD = 7.36$) or a stranger ($M = 85.25$, $SD = 4.65$). However, for participants receiving only the C-gene, resemblance scores were much higher when they tried to resemble themselves ($M = 51.50$, $SD = 11.96$) compared to when they tried to emulate a stranger ($M = 8.63$, $SD = 2.39$).

Alice's Lab Notes 17.1   *Reporting factorial ANOVA*

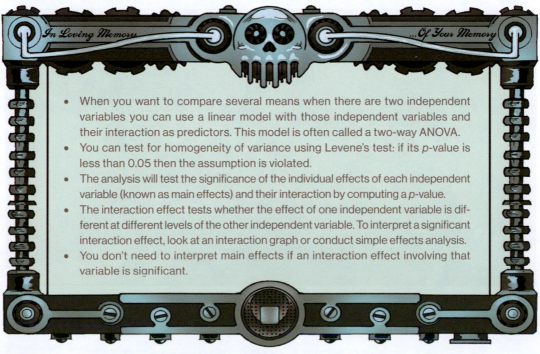

- When you want to compare several means when there are two independent variables you can use a linear model with those independent variables and their interaction as predictors. This model is often called a two-way ANOVA.
- You can test for homogeneity of variance using Levene's test: if its p-value is less than 0.05 then the assumption is violated.
- The analysis will test the significance of the individual effects of each independent variable (known as main effects) and their interaction by computing a p-value.
- The interaction effect tests whether the effect of one independent variable is different at different levels of the other independent variable. To interpret a significant interaction effect, look at an interaction graph or conduct simple effects analysis.
- You don't need to interpret main effects if an interaction effect involving that variable is significant.

Zach's Facts 17.1   *Analysing factorial designs*

KEY TERMS

Factorial design

Four-way design

Interaction effect

Interaction graph

Moderation

Simple effects analysis

Three-way design

Two-way design

JIG:SAW'S PUZZLES

1   Using Alice's gene study data, compute Cohen's d for the difference between self and other pictures in the C-gene condition, and then another Cohen's d for the toggle switch condition. Use the pooled estimate for the standard deviation.

2   On Zach's journey he discovered that people can perform better on a statistics test if they take the test under a fake name (Reality Check 8.1). He found some data in which men and women took a statistics test. They were assigned to one of three groups in which they took the test using their own name, a fake female name, or a fake male name. The outcome was the percentage on the test, with Zach finding 10 test scores per group for men and women. Zach ran a factorial linear model (ANOVA) to see whether participant gender, the type of name they used, or the interaction between these variables affected test results. However, when the summary of results appeared on his diePad (Table 17.5), Milton used the magic eraser tool to delete some of the numbers. He's an eisel like that. Help Zach to fill in the blanks and to determine whether each F is significant at $p = 0.05$. [Hint: think about the degrees of freedom for each predictor variable.]

3   Figure 17.10 shows the means for the interaction effect in Table 17.5. Interpret this effect.

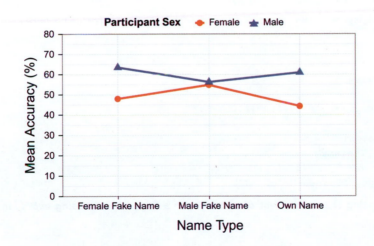

Figure 17.10   *Interaction graph for the Name Type × Sex interaction*

4   Alice tried to see whether she could use her toggle switch therapy to rehabilitate the zombie code 1318 workers. She took 14 zombies, and 14 humans with facial injuries as controls. Half of each group received her original C-gene therapy, whereas the other half received a toggle switch as well. All participants were asked to study a picture of themselves before their injury/zombification. The outcome was how closely (as a percentage) they resembled the photo. The data are in Table 17.6. Fit a two-way linear model to these data to test the main effects of therapy (C-gene vs. C-gene plus toggle switch), species (human vs. zombie) and their interaction. Is each F-ratio significant?

Table 17.5 Summary table for an analysis of accuracy scores for men and women taking a stats test under their own name, a fake male name, or a fake female name

Source	SS	df	MS	F
Model	7854.25			
Sex				
Name Type	351.50			
Sex × Name Type			1023.50	
Residual	69226.70	176		
Total				

5 Draw the interaction graph for Alice's zombie rehabilitation data (Table 17.5) and interpret the interaction effect.

6 Outputs 17.8–17.10 show the Bayes factors for each effect in Alice's zombie rehabilitation data. Interpret each Bayes factor. Do they support or contradict the findings from the linear model?

```
Bayes factor analysis
--------------
[1] Therapy : 647.7348 ±0%

Against denominator:
  Intercept only
---
Bayes factor type: BFlinearModel, JZS
```
Output 17.8 Testing the main effect of therapy with a Bayes factor using *lmBF()* in R

```
Bayes factor analysis
--------------
[1] Therapy + Species : 0.376888 ±1.22%

Against denominator:
  Resemblance ~ Therapy
---
Bayes factor type: BFlinearModel, JZS
```
Output 17.9 Testing the main effect of species with a Bayes factor using *lmBF()* in R

```
Bayes factor analysis
--------------
[1] Therapy + Species + Therapy:Species : 0.858355 ±2.83%

Against denominator:
  Resemblance ~ Therapy + Species
---
Bayes factor type: BFlinearModel, JZS
```
Output 17.10 Testing the interaction effect with a Bayes factor using *lmBF()* in R

7   Milton and Roediger were having an argument about whether cats or dogs were the most gullible. Milton cited a study in which dogs were given the choice of either a large or small quantity of food on 12 occasions.[128] On 6 of these, the dog chose one or other quantity without interference. On the other 6 occasions, their owner used ostensive cues to mislead the dog into choosing the smaller portion: the owner picked up the bowl, put it to their mouth, looked at the food, then the dog and then said 'Ow wow, this is good, this is so good.' Without influence the dogs chose the larger portion more than when the owner used ostensive cues to make the smaller portion seem better. Milton argued that this proved that dogs were stupid. To counter this, Roediger organized a replication study in which cats were tested too. Table 17.7 shows the number of trials (out of 6) that 12 dogs and 12 cats chose the larger portion of food when left to their own devices (no influence) and when their owner tried to mislead them using ostensive cues. Compute the two-way linear model for these data to test the main effects of influence (none vs. misleading), species (cat vs. dog) and their interaction. Is each F-ratio significant?

Table 17.6   Alice's zombie rehabilitation data: resemblance scores (%) for humans and zombies undergoing two types of therapy

Gene Condition	C-Gene		C-Gene + Toggle Switch	
Species	Human	Zombie	Human	Zombie
	75	48	89	53
	62	62	79	100
	56	63	75	60
	43	57	96	100
	34	48	85	63
	41	60	85	70
	55	59	78	74
Mean	52.29	56.71	83.86	74.29
SD	14.020	6.264	7.221	18.821
Variance	196.571	39.238	52.143	354.238

8   Draw and interpret the interaction graph for Roediger's food choice data (Table 17.7) and interpret the interaction effect.

9   Outputs 17.11–17.13 show the Bayes factors for each effect in Roediger's animal influence data. Interpret each Bayes factor. Do they support or contradict the findings from the linear model?

10 Output 17.14 shows a robust analysis of Roediger's animal influence data (Table 17.7). Interpret the output. Do any of your conclusions change from when you fitted the normal linear model?

Table 17.7   Data on animal food choices after human influence (or not)

Influence Condition	No Influence		Counterproductive Influence	
Species	Dog	Cat	Dog	Cat
	4	6	4	4
	5	4	3	4
	5	5	2	5
	5	4	2	4
	5	5	2	4
	5	4	3	5
Mean	4.833	4.667	2.667	4.333
SD	0.408	0.816	0.816	0.516
Variance	0.167	0.667	0.667	0.267

```
Bayes factor analysis
--------------
[1] Influence : 16.0891 ±0%

Against denominator:
  Intercept only
---
Bayes factor type: BFlinearModel, JZS
```

Output 17.11 *Testing the main effect of influence with a Bayes factor using lmBF() in R*

```
Bayes factor analysis
--------------
[1] Influence + Species : 1.99659 ±1.63%

Against denominator:
  FoodChoice ~ Influence
---
Bayes factor type: BFlinearModel, JZS
```

Output 17.12 *Testing the main effect of species with a Bayes factor using lmBF() in R*

```
Bayes factor analysis
--------------
[1] Influence + Species + Influence:Species : 9.584772 ±2.71%

Against denominator:
  FoodChoice ~ Influence + Species
---
Bayes factor type: BFlinearModel, JZS
```

Output 17.13 *Testing the interaction effect with a Bayes factor using lmBF() in R*

```
$Qa (Species)
[1] 4.326923

$A.p.value
[1] 0.063

$Qb (Influence)
[1] 20.94231

$B.p.value
[1] 0.001

$Qab (Interaction)
[1] 14.01923

$AB.p.value
[1] 0.003

$means
      [,1]  [,2]
[1,] 4.25  4.5
[2,] 2.50  5.0
```

Output 17.14 *Robust analysis of Roediger's animal influence data*

Epilogue:
The Genial Night
Si Momentum Requiris, Circumspice

The reality prism made my head buzz. It wasn't unpleasant; it felt like my brain was gently vibrating as it tried to process the two different versions of reality. At first I thought Alice had stepped out from behind Celia and I felt a rush at knowing she was alive, but then my brain began to piece everything together. Alice had discovered a way for people to change their appearance, and the prism showed me two different versions of the same reality ... Alice hadn't stepped from behind Celia, Alice *was* Celia. I started to cry again. When I removed the prism it was Alice stood in front of me, but wearing Celia's clothes. She bit her lip, just like she used to do back in college. She looked as though she wished she had a prism that would show her my thoughts.

'I'm so sorry!' she blurted.

'Wait.' I interrupted. It was too soon for apologies, there was still so much that I didn't understand and I needed someone to explain what the last three weeks had been about. I felt torn between anger and relief. 'Are you Alice or Celia?' I asked.

Alice looked at me as though wondering which person I'd prefer her to be. 'I'm Alice ... *your* Alice,' she replied hesitantly.

'How can you be Celia as well? I've visited her grave, and Roediger said that Celia was spying on you. Were you spying on yourself?'

I noticed tears in her eyes. She was shaking. She looked like she needed a hug. I couldn't go there just yet. She took a deep breath. 'There was a Celia,' she began, 'the person whose appearance I stole when she died. You visited her grave and she's the one who spied on me. Like Roediger told you, she was the first of JIG:SAW's attempts to delete memories using ID chips, but it killed her. I thought she was the only one.'

'Is that why you were so angry when Roediger told you that there had been other case studies?'

'Roediger thought Celia was alive,' the dog whimpered as though soliciting forgiveness.

'Yes, because unlike him, I knew what happened to Celia; I knew he'd risked more innocent lives.'

'Did I meet *that* Celia?' I asked.

'No,' Alice replied. 'Weeks before I disappeared, a young, intelligent intern turned up at the Beimeni Centre. Professor Pincus would never usually have let her near our highly sensitive work, but when someone arrives with papers signed by the WGA there is no choice. Whatever concerns we had were short-lived because Celia worked hard and did everything we asked of her. She was charismatic, eager to learn, smart, helpful and kind. Professor Pincus and I were completely taken in by her. Milton was suspicious: he was convinced that Celia had been sent by the WGA to find him, so he started to follow her outside of work.'

'I am a fantastic spy,' Milton said proudly. 'No one thinks anything of a cat following them down the street.'

'Milton discovered that Celia was meeting Rob Nutcot, and passing on information about our work at the Centre – especially mine. I was angry and hurt by Celia's deceit, but Catherine remained calm. We confronted Celia with what we knew, and she confessed. She told us that she had worked at JIG:SAW for two years. It had been an exciting place to be: they were doing work using genetics to cure terminal disease and repair organs, and she aspired to join the scientific team. Her manager promised that she could train there and, in time, work her way into the research labs. After a year, everything changed. Her manager didn't turn up for work one day, and Rob Nutcot arrived in his place. Then the research focus shifted. Rumours circulated about genetic experiments, rumours that appeared to be confirmed by the appearance of the code 1318 security team. Worse still, Celia began to notice that members of the security team resembled people she had recently recruited to work at JIG:SAW. More frightening were the rumours that Nutcot was Vic Luten.'

'Nutcot did seem to have persuasive powers, just like the stories about Vic Luten,' interrupted Milton, in a serious tone, 'and of course this was very interesting to me because if Vic Luten was involved, then whatever was going on at JIG:SAW, and whatever their interest in Alice's work, it was not for the benefit of humanity.'

'Celia wasn't a bad person,' Alice continued. 'Nutcot used his aftershave to persuade her to spy on us. Every time she met him he'd mesmerize her, but when he was gone and the influence wore off, she didn't know why she had agreed to his demands. It was too late, though, she was in too deep. She was scared of us finding out, but *terrified* of what Nutcot would do to her if she betrayed him: she'd seen what they were capable of with the code 1318s.'

'What happened?'

'We protected her at the Beimeni Centre. I used what I'd found in my own research to take on her appearance and met Nutcot in her place. He was getting frustrated that I couldn't tell him what Alice's secret research was, and we were getting frustrated that we couldn't find out what was going on at JIG:SAW without arousing his suspicions. The only way to access their research and unravel their interest in mine was to get inside JIG:SAW as a scientist rather than as Nutcot's PA. As Celia, I convinced Nutcot that I could persuade Alice to discuss working there. Catherine and Milton disapproved, but what else could I do?'

'Go to the WGA and let them deal with it?' I suggested.

'Celia's papers were signed by the WGA, Zach. Who could we trust there?'

I shrugged.

'Exactly. Nutcot took the bait: arrangements were made and a few days later I met him at JIG:SAW, as Alice. We toured their facilities and it was easy to be enthusiastic and impressed by their ground-breaking work and state-of-the-art facilities. Nutcot kept probing about my work, and I hooked him in by telling him that the crucial experiments hadn't been finished. I told him that I was lacking the facilities to do what I needed to, but that JIG:SAW had them. If he would let me come there I could complete my work. He was delighted. I set two conditions: I wanted to oversee *all* of their research programmes, and I wanted Celia to work in my team.'

I wondered why would she set conditions. As if reading my thoughts, Alice continued.

'From Nutcot's point of view, Celia had been successful in getting me to him, and he would expect her to return to JIG:SAW as his assistant. By becoming Celia I could use that to find out information from him; after all, he trusted her. The problem was that I couldn't be in two places at once, so I needed a reason for Celia to be away from Nutcot. If Nutcot thought she was on my team, it became easy to switch between Celia and myself as I needed to. The real Celia would be safe with Professor Pincus at the Beimeni Centre, or so we thought, but shortly after I started working at JIG:SAW she started feeling pains in her head. One evening she collapsed and woke

up not knowing who she was; the following day she lost consciousness, and that evening she died. That was the day before I left you.'

'It was devastating, Zach: a young, intelligent, woman with her life ahead of her *murdered* by the people controlling JIG:SAW,' Alice said, a lump gathering in her throat. 'It showed us what Nutcot, or Vic Luten, was capable of. Professor Pincus insisted that I get out, but if I did then JIG:SAW would carry on their work, they'd continue trying to find out about my research. Someone had to stop them. I had no choice.' Alice bowed her head in shame. 'We concealed her death and carried on as though nothing had happened.'

That was cold. I wondered, not for the first time, whether I really knew Alice. She'd become friends with Celia, and yet her death didn't derail her plans. Then I remembered how strangely Alice had acted the day before she vanished – the day that the real Celia died. She'd been playing the album we used to listen to, she was tetchy, stressed, she wasn't herself at all. Perhaps she'd been seeking the comfort of familiar music because she was upset, because she faced a decision that she didn't want to make. It would have been easier to walk away, but she fronted up when the world needed a saviour. The more I thought about it, the more that *was* the Alice I knew: she *always* took responsibility, *always* cared about making the world a better place. It was the act of an incredibly brave woman, not a cold one.

I'd been lost in thought, and my silence worried Alice. She looked incredibly exposed, desperate to find the social cues that would tell her that everything was fine. My silence was destroying her, so she filled the space with words.

'Pincus acted quickly. She answered Nutcot's messages on Celia's Proteus, and the following day I arrived at his office, as Celia, pretending I remembered nothing. He told me that they had given me a reboot, an opportunity to start again. His words stuck in my mind: I kept asking who I would most like to be and what would make me happiest. I realized that the time I was happiest was when we met: before work, responsibility, age and the expectations that come with it eroded a space between us. What would make me happy was being Alice Nightingale aged 16. That's what Celia, the Celia you met, became.'

That sounded ridiculous. 'How is that possible?' I asked. 'I understand how you could look like her, because of your research, but your personalities are so different. After 10 years, Alice, I *know* you and you weren't in The Repository with me a few weeks ago. That was someone else, someone spontaneous, passionate, emotional and so ... so, in the moment.' My words hung in the air like a judgement. A tear slid down Alice's cheek.

'With time' she said, 'we habituate to everything: age doesn't only kill our cells, it conceals the moment until eventually it becomes lost, and with it us too. At 16 I didn't know *what* I was, but I knew how I *felt*. Happiness was being with Zach Slade; I didn't need proof and I didn't require evidence. Everywhere I looked I found the moment. But I have grown up, and I have become a scientist and faith without evidence is anathema to me, and what is love without faith? Nutcot was right, being able to re-create myself was a great gift: everyone should have the chance to see the world through new eyes, because only then can you realize that to find the moment you need only look around you. Being Celia transported me to a time when no one had decided who Alice Nightingale was, and how she could behave. Celia freed me.'

Was this for real? I couldn't understand *how* simply looking like someone else could unlock feelings and characteristics that had gone. If it could then I was envious of Alice, because sometimes being an adult felt like a prison.

As I watched Alice's discomfort at not knowing what I thought, I felt angry with myself for not doing something to reassure her. I wondered if I'd behave differently if she looked like Celia right now. Maybe appearances really could change how you feel. For now, though, I could see Alice's face, not Celia's, and I felt hurt that she'd deserted me and hadn't trusted me to help her. I asked her why she hadn't told me, why she had just vanished.

'I had to protect you, Zach. They killed an innocent woman, they turn people into zombies, what do you think they'd do to you if they thought it would get them closer to understanding my work? I *had* to keep you away; I *had* to keep you safe. Regardless of how this ended, I needed to know that you would be fine. I put our song on to let you know that I still love you, and I left.'

I thought back to the lyrics of the song, words that I'd dissected for clues when Alice vanished.

The grave of our youth is up ahead
And life has become a burden
We move in circles of suppressed despair
Waiting for the sun
And turning stones to find evidence
But it hides in the recesses of our hearts[19]

'How did that song tell me that you loved me?' I asked. 'The lyrics go on about letting go of the past, and stopping trying to find reasons to stay together. It told me it was over.'

Alice looked desolate; her eyes were streaming. 'No, Zach, no,' she said, pleading for me to believe her. 'It told you that as we leave our youth behind it's easy to get caught up in everyday life, for it to become a burden. We forget what really matters, and the reminders of what is important are hidden in our hearts if only we make the effort to look for them. We used to say that this song meant that we should always trust each other. I was asking you to trust me, to look deep in your heart and know that I would never betray or hurt you; that you should trust that I was disappearing for a reason. I was asking you to trust me, to leave me alone until I'd done what I had to do, but of course you wouldn't leave it, would you, Zach? You wouldn't give up on me.'

'Didn't you know I wouldn't?'

'The way things have been, I wasn't sure, but just in case, I asked Milton to keep you out of harm's way ...'

'... because no one notices a cat on the street?' I interrupted, mocking Milton. Alice laughed nervously, hoping that this was a sign that I was lightening up.

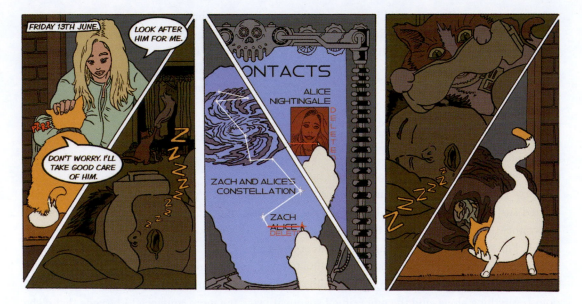

'Milton helped me to vanish. He removed all signs of my existence. I had to keep everyone I knew safe, and the best way to do that was to remove all connections to me. That way, if Nutcot or Vic Luten found out the truth I would be the only one to suffer: they would have no way of hurting the people I love. Since this whole thing started, I believed that I had no choice but to leave you, and that when you knew *why* I had gone you would forgive me. Nothing would change, I told myself, but standing here in front of you, searching for the right words, my faith is deserting me.'

Brave *and* selfless, I thought to myself. Everything she had done was so like Alice, she had prioritized the world before herself, and top of that list had been me. How had I not realized? How had I ever doubted her? How could I have thought she'd ever work for an organization like JIG:SAW? If anyone had lost faith, it was me.

'Milton told me you had visited Dr Genari,' she continued, 'so I asked him to deter you from trying to find me. He decided that the best deterrent was to teach you statistics.'

'That *should* have been enough to deter any right-minded person,' the cat joked.

'He tried,' Alice said, looking affectionately at the cat, 'but when you persisted in your ludicrous mission to find me I had no choice but to get involved. I made sure that you found out about the JIG:SAW recruitment event so that you could meet me, as Celia. She was the perfect solution: a distraction to keep you away from JIG:SAW. I knew it would destroy me if you took the bait, but I could live with that if it kept you safe.'

'So when I arrived at the event you pretended to like me ...'

'There was no pretending,' Alice interrupted, 'but I hadn't anticipated how much I'd love seeing you, and seeing you through Celia's eyes was so new: you acted differently to me, Zach, like you used to be, all nervous and awkward and not knowing what to say. Your eyes glistened with anticipation when our gaze met. I felt wanted again, and wanted by this amazing, creative guy, who I'd admired for 10 years, admired more than anyone else in the universe. I tried to stick to the task of keeping you away from JIG:SAW, I lied to you to convince you not to take a job there, but you kept coming back, and I loved the fact that you wanted to see me. I was enjoying seeing you so much that I started to take stupid risks.'

'Like letting me meet Nutcot?' I wondered.

'I knew he was harmless.'

'His aftershave wasn't ...'

'A party trick. We knew he'd been using a chemical agent to brainwash Celia. One of the first things I did at JIG:SAW was to find the research files. It was a simple matter to devise a compound that would counteract his aftershave. I mixed the compound with my lipstick, so I was always protected. Every time you met Nutcot I kissed you, passing on the protective agent.'

She is brilliant, I thought to myself, before remembering that I *had* been affected. 'It didn't always work,' I said. 'What about at Hermes?'

'I didn't kiss you that day,' she replied looking guilty. 'I'd briefed Nutcot that you were a trouble-maker, that he should put you off JIG:SAW. I *wanted* his aftershave to work to convince you to stop investigating.'

'So why come to our gig and ask to meet me?'

'How could I not, Zach? I've never missed one. I wanted to see you so badly. I knew Nutcot had started suspecting something and following me, but I still came to your gig and I met you in The Repository. I feel awful, I wasn't thinking. When I was with you I could forget this madness and be myself. I'm sorry, I put you in danger.' She was crying again.

'I was convinced that Alice had underestimated you,' Milton said. 'I kept telling her how determined you were, how quickly you were learning and how brave you were. I was worried about Alice doing everything alone, and the more time I spent with you, the more convinced I became that if she needed help then she could not get better help than you. I stopped discouraging you and started to help you instead.'

I looked down at the cat with a beaming smile. 'You actually said that about me? You said I was a quick learner?'

'Quick – for an imbecile!' the cat joked, rubbing his cheek on my leg.

The room fell silent. There was one last thing I needed to know, but it was the question I feared most. Where did this leave us? Alice, too, looked like a heavy question weighed upon her. We both gazed awkwardly at the floor.

'I guess we're done, then,' I said. Alice gagged as though her throat had constricted.

'I don't expect you to forgive me,' she said. 'I lied to you, I left you, with no explanation, I erased myself from your life, and worse than all of that, I lost faith in you.'

'*You* forgive *me*?' I replied. 'I'm the one who needs forgiving. Every time I met Celia, I was meeting you, so you know that at a time when I should have been fighting for our relationship, she tempted me. I took her to The Repository and relived our memories with her, I flirted with her, I let her kiss me, and you saw and heard everything. You looked in my eyes and saw in them feelings for someone completely different from you.'

'Was she really so different, Zach?'

'Yes.' I gave the vexed sigh of a man resigned to telling a painful truth. 'She was spontaneous, in the moment, had a zest for life and wore her heart on her sleeve. She didn't question everything; she didn't need evidence for what she believed. She had faith – she had faith *in me*. She was everything I loved about you when we first met.' I paused while my words sank in.

Alice took my hands and spoke through her tears. 'Whatever temptation I threw at you, you were faithful. I kissed you, but you never kissed me back. You *always* told me you needed to find out where you stood with Alice. You risked your life, you crossed probability bridges and fought zombies just to find out if there was even a chance of a future with me. When I looked into your eyes I didn't see you falling in love with another woman, I watched you rediscover your love for me.'

As our lips met it was as though they never wanted to be parted again.

Alice had built up enough evidence over three weeks for Professor Pincus to convince the WGA to hand over the facilities at JIG:SAW to the Beimeni Centre. Alice set to work to restore the code 1318 workers using her C-gene therapy. She said this solution was smoke and mirrors that required a lot of mental energy to sustain the transformation. It wasn't a permanent solution, but she built a team at JIG:SAW to work on one.

Milton was given his own building to pursue his research with Roediger. Seeing them working gave me a window into what their former partnership was like: Milton came up with grand schemes and Roediger would bounce off excitedly to try to make them a reality. You soon realized that despite his constant shows of annoyance with the dog, Milton was at his best having such an enthusiastic and loyal peer. They complemented each other: Milton the eccentric genius and Roediger the hard-working pragmatist. They dismantled the probability bridge and set to work on a project to use reality prisms to help people to find the moment by showing them the here and now and shielding them from the past or future.

In the middle of this hub of research was a box with a glowing green insignia. It stood in the centre of the control room as a reminder of what this complex had once been. Inside, suspended in a state of living death, was a thing, a collection of the best parts of the animal kingdom put together for the worst purpose. The prison couldn't be moved, and so it stood there as a reminder to everyone that the new purpose of JIG:SAW was to further humanity, not to destroy it. As the months passed people paid less and less attention to the box.

I carried on with music. Our latest collection of songs formed an interconnected story – like the concept albums in the old days. The response to it was over the wall, especially the songs 'Bridge of Death', 'The Secret Philanthropic Society' and 'Zombie Army'. We were planning a handful of concerts in different cities and maybe even a few in different countries. We were going to be the first band to play live outside of our home city in over 50 years: the buzz was sick and tickets sold out in minutes. Alice was going to come along: she never misses a gig, although she once came in someone else's body.

I liked hanging out at JIG:SAW; sometimes I even helped out with the stats. Our journey had given Milton, Roediger, Alice and me a special bond, and we'd meet to reminisce. One lunch, Alice arrived bursting with excitement. Roediger bounded up to her and Milton, as ever, retained an indifferent distance. Alice approached him. She was carrying a syringe, two towels and a piece of paper. She squatted down in front of the cat.

'Milton, my dear, dear friend,' she said, kissing his head, 'I can finally thank you for everything you have done for me.' She showed him the paper.

As Milton read it his eyes filled with water. It was spooks seeing such an emotionless creature as a cat in tears. The paper, stamped by the WGA, was an official pardon. It relieved Milton of all responsibility for the Reality Revolution, citing evidence, collected by Alice, that the revolution could be traced back to the sudden mass production of prisms, which had been started by Vic Luten.

'Thank you,' Milton said.

'You're very welcome,' Alice said, as she wrapped a towel around him and stabbed him with the syringe. He yowled, but the yowl became a scream as his body changed. Under a towel where once a cat had been there was now an old man. He didn't look as I expected. He had a kind face, etched with wrinkles from years of smiling. The professor patted his new human form. He felt his cheeks as though looking for whiskers, and rubbed the top of his head as though expecting ears. Roediger span with excitement and ran over to lick the Professor's face. Milton smiled an enormous smile and patted the dog as he laughed, incredulous at what Alice had done.

'You are ... *unbelievable*, Alice Nightingale,' he said.

'Only because I had a good teacher,' she replied, as she placed a towel on Roediger and plunged the needle into him.

Moments later a second man, slightly younger than Milton, lay next to him with a face consumed with joy.

Alice turned to me. 'I think we should give them some time,' she said, winking at me. She led me out of the room towards the canteen. As we headed towards the main control room a young man came at us from the opposite direction. I hadn't seen him before. He had a strange, deliberate gait, like a puppet or something. It seemed familiar. He stopped at the control centre door and went to buzz himself in. As he entered the room he turned back to us and said, 'Good to interface'.

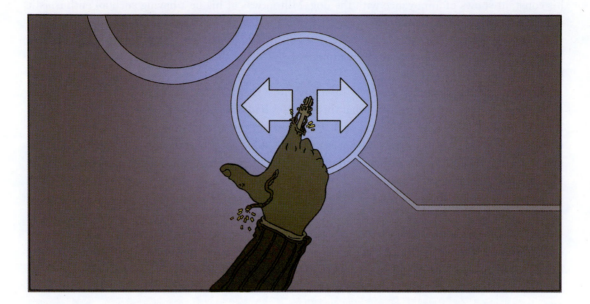

Appendix

A.1 THE STANDARD NORMAL DISTRIBUTION

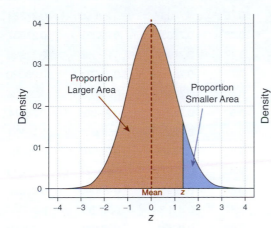

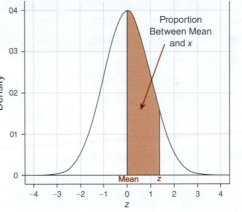

z	Larger Proportion	Smaller Proportion	Mean to z	z	Larger Proportion	Smaller Proportion	Mean to z
0.00	0.50000	0.50000	0.00000	0.12	0.54776	0.45224	0.04776
0.01	0.50399	0.49601	0.00399	0.13	0.55172	0.44828	0.05172
0.02	0.50798	0.49202	0.00798	0.14	0.55567	0.44433	0.05567
0.03	0.51197	0.48803	0.01197	0.15	0.55962	0.44038	0.05962
0.04	0.51595	0.48405	0.01595	0.16	0.56356	0.43644	0.06356
0.05	0.51994	0.48006	0.01994	0.17	0.56749	0.43251	0.06749
0.06	0.52392	0.47608	0.02392	0.18	0.57142	0.42858	0.07142
0.07	0.52790	0.47210	0.02790	0.19	0.57535	0.42465	0.07535
0.08	0.53188	0.46812	0.03188	0.20	0.57926	0.42074	0.07926
0.09	0.53586	0.46414	0.03586	0.21	0.58317	0.41683	0.08317
0.10	0.53983	0.46017	0.03983	0.22	0.58706	0.41294	0.08706
0.11	0.54380	0.45620	0.04380	0.23	0.59095	0.40905	0.09095
				0.24	0.59483	0.40517	0.09483

z	Larger Proportion	Smaller Proportion	Mean to z	z	Larger Proportion	Smaller Proportion	Mean to z
0.25	0.59871	0.40129	0.09871	0.62	0.73237	0.26763	0.23237
0.26	0.60257	0.39743	0.10257	0.63	0.73565	0.26435	0.23565
0.27	0.60642	0.39358	0.10642	0.64	0.73891	0.26109	0.23891
0.28	0.61026	0.38974	0.11026	0.65	0.74215	0.25785	0.24215
0.29	0.61409	0.38591	0.11409	0.66	0.74537	0.25463	0.24537
0.30	0.61791	0.38209	0.11791	0.67	0.74857	0.25143	0.24857
0.31	0.62172	0.37828	0.12172	0.68	0.75175	0.24825	0.25175
0.32	0.62552	0.37448	0.12552	0.69	0.75490	0.24510	0.25490
0.33	0.62930	0.37070	0.12930	0.70	0.75804	0.24196	0.25804
0.34	0.63307	0.36693	0.13307	0.71	0.76115	0.23885	0.26115
0.35	0.63683	0.36317	0.13683	0.72	0.76424	0.23576	0.26424
0.36	0.64058	0.35942	0.14058	0.73	0.76730	0.23270	0.26730
0.37	0.64431	0.35569	0.14431	0.74	0.77035	0.22965	0.27035
0.38	0.64803	0.35197	0.14803	0.75	0.77337	0.22663	0.27337
0.39	0.65173	0.34827	0.15173	0.76	0.77637	0.22363	0.27637
0.40	0.65542	0.34458	0.15542	0.77	0.77935	0.22065	0.27935
0.41	0.65910	0.34090	0.15910	0.78	0.78230	0.21770	0.28230
0.42	0.66276	0.33724	0.16276	0.79	0.78524	0.21476	0.28524
0.43	0.66640	0.33360	0.16640	0.80	0.78814	0.21186	0.28814
0.44	0.67003	0.32997	0.17003	0.81	0.79103	0.20897	0.29103
0.45	0.67364	0.32636	0.17364	0.82	0.79389	0.20611	0.29389
0.46	0.67724	0.32276	0.17724	0.83	0.79673	0.20327	0.29673
0.47	0.68082	0.31918	0.18082	0.84	0.79955	0.20045	0.29955
0.48	0.68439	0.31561	0.18439	0.85	0.80234	0.19766	0.30234
0.49	0.68793	0.31207	0.18793	0.86	0.80511	0.19489	0.30511
0.50	0.69146	0.30854	0.19146	0.87	0.80785	0.19215	0.30785
0.51	0.69497	0.30503	0.19497	0.88	0.81057	0.18943	0.31057
0.52	0.69847	0.30153	0.19847	0.89	0.81327	0.18673	0.31327
0.53	0.70194	0.29806	0.20194	0.90	0.81594	0.18406	0.31594
0.54	0.70540	0.29460	0.20540	0.91	0.81859	0.18141	0.31859
0.55	0.70884	0.29116	0.20884	0.92	0.82121	0.17879	0.32121
0.56	0.71226	0.28774	0.21226	0.93	0.82381	0.17619	0.32381
0.57	0.71566	0.28434	0.21566	0.94	0.82639	0.17361	0.32639
0.58	0.71904	0.28096	0.21904	0.95	0.82894	0.17106	0.32894
0.59	0.72240	0.27760	0.22240	0.96	0.83147	0.16853	0.33147
0.60	0.72575	0.27425	0.22575	0.97	0.83398	0.16602	0.33398
0.61	0.72907	0.27093	0.22907	0.98	0.83646	0.16354	0.33646

z	Larger Proportion	Smaller Proportion	Mean to z	z	Larger Proportion	Smaller Proportion	Mean to z
0.99	0.83891	0.16109	0.33891	1.36	0.91309	0.08691	0.41309
1.00	0.84134	0.15866	0.34134	1.37	0.91466	0.08534	0.41466
1.01	0.84375	0.15625	0.34375	1.38	0.91621	0.08379	0.41621
1.02	0.84614	0.15386	0.34614	1.39	0.91774	0.08226	0.41774
1.03	0.84849	0.15151	0.34849	1.40	0.91924	0.08076	0.41924
1.04	0.85083	0.14917	0.35083	1.41	0.92073	0.07927	0.42073
1.05	0.85314	0.14686	0.35314	1.42	0.92220	0.07780	0.42220
1.06	0.85543	0.14457	0.35543	1.43	0.92364	0.07636	0.42364
1.07	0.85769	0.14231	0.35769	1.44	0.92507	0.07493	0.42507
1.08	0.85993	0.14007	0.35993	1.45	0.92647	0.07353	0.42647
1.09	0.86214	0.13786	0.36214	1.46	0.92785	0.07215	0.42785
1.10	0.86433	0.13567	0.36433	1.47	0.92922	0.07078	0.42922
1.11	0.86650	0.13350	0.36650	1.48	0.93056	0.06944	0.43056
1.12	0.86864	0.13136	0.36864	1.49	0.93189	0.06811	0.43189
1.13	0.87076	0.12924	0.37076	1.50	0.93319	0.06681	0.43319
1.14	0.87286	0.12714	0.37286	1.51	0.93448	0.06552	0.43448
1.15	0.87493	0.12507	0.37493	1.52	0.93574	0.06426	0.43574
1.16	0.87698	0.12302	0.37698	1.53	0.93699	0.06301	0.43699
1.17	0.87900	0.12100	0.37900	1.54	0.93822	0.06178	0.43822
1.18	0.88100	0.11900	0.38100	1.55	0.93943	0.06057	0.43943
1.19	0.88298	0.11702	0.38298	1.56	0.94062	0.05938	0.44062
1.20	0.88493	0.11507	0.38493	1.57	0.94179	0.05821	0.44179
1.21	0.88686	0.11314	0.38686	1.58	0.94295	0.05705	0.44295
1.22	0.88877	0.11123	0.38877	1.59	0.94408	0.05592	0.44408
1.23	0.89065	0.10935	0.39065	1.60	0.94520	0.05480	0.44520
1.24	0.89251	0.10749	0.39251	1.61	0.94630	0.05370	0.44630
1.25	0.89435	0.10565	0.39435	1.62	0.94738	0.05262	0.44738
1.26	0.89617	0.10383	0.39617	1.63	0.94845	0.05155	0.44845
1.27	0.89796	0.10204	0.39796	1.64	0.94950	0.05050	0.44950
1.28	0.89973	0.10027	0.39973	1.65	0.95053	0.04947	0.45053
1.29	0.90147	0.09853	0.40147	1.66	0.95154	0.04846	0.45154
1.30	0.90320	0.09680	0.40320	1.67	0.95254	0.04746	0.45254
1.31	0.90490	0.09510	0.40490	1.68	0.95352	0.04648	0.45352
1.32	0.90658	0.09342	0.40658	1.69	0.95449	0.04551	0.45449
1.33	0.90824	0.09176	0.40824	1.70	0.95543	0.04457	0.45543
1.34	0.90988	0.09012	0.40988	1.71	0.95637	0.04363	0.45637
1.35	0.91149	0.08851	0.41149	1.72	0.95728	0.04272	0.45728

z	Larger Proportion	Smaller Proportion	Mean to z	z	Larger Proportion	Smaller Proportion	Mean to z
1.73	0.95818	0.04182	0.45818	2.10	0.98214	0.01786	0.48214
1.74	0.95907	0.04093	0.45907	2.11	0.98257	0.01743	0.48257
1.75	0.95994	0.04006	0.45994	2.12	0.98300	0.01700	0.48300
1.76	0.96080	0.03920	0.46080	2.13	0.98341	0.01659	0.48341
1.77	0.96164	0.03836	0.46164	2.14	0.98382	0.01618	0.48382
1.78	0.96246	0.03754	0.46246	2.15	0.98422	0.01578	0.48422
1.79	0.96327	0.03673	0.46327	2.16	0.98461	0.01539	0.48461
1.80	0.96407	0.03593	0.46407	2.17	0.98500	0.01500	0.48500
1.81	0.96485	0.03515	0.46485	2.18	0.98537	0.01463	0.48537
1.82	0.96562	0.03438	0.46562	2.19	0.98574	0.01426	0.48574
1.83	0.96638	0.03362	0.46638	2.20	0.98610	0.01390	0.48610
1.84	0.96712	0.03288	0.46712	2.21	0.98645	0.01355	0.48645
1.85	0.96784	0.03216	0.46784	2.22	0.98679	0.01321	0.48679
1.86	0.96856	0.03144	0.46856	2.23	0.98713	0.01287	0.48713
1.87	0.96926	0.03074	0.46926	2.24	0.98745	0.01255	0.48745
1.88	0.96995	0.03005	0.46995	2.25	0.98778	0.01222	0.48778
1.89	0.97062	0.02938	0.47062	2.26	0.98809	0.01191	0.48809
1.90	0.97128	0.02872	0.47128	2.27	0.98840	0.01160	0.48840
1.91	0.97193	0.02807	0.47193	2.28	0.98870	0.01130	0.48870
1.92	0.97257	0.02743	0.47257	2.29	0.98899	0.01101	0.48899
1.93	0.97320	0.02680	0.47320	2.30	0.98928	0.01072	0.48928
1.94	0.97381	0.02619	0.47381	2.31	0.98956	0.01044	0.48956
1.95	0.97441	0.02559	0.47441	2.32	0.98983	0.01017	0.48983
1.96	0.97500	0.02500	0.47500	2.33	0.99010	0.00990	0.49010
1.97	0.97558	0.02442	0.47558	2.34	0.99036	0.00964	0.49036
1.98	0.97615	0.02385	0.47615	2.35	0.99061	0.00939	0.49061
1.99	0.97670	0.02330	0.47670	2.36	0.99086	0.00914	0.49086
2.00	0.97725	0.02275	0.47725	2.37	0.99111	0.00889	0.49111
2.01	0.97778	0.02222	0.47778	2.38	0.99134	0.00866	0.49134
2.02	0.97831	0.02169	0.47831	2.39	0.99158	0.00842	0.49158
2.03	0.97882	0.02118	0.47882	2.40	0.99180	0.00820	0.49180
2.04	0.97932	0.02068	0.47932	2.41	0.99202	0.00798	0.49202
2.05	0.97982	0.02018	0.47982	2.42	0.99224	0.00776	0.49224
2.06	0.98030	0.01970	0.48030	2.43	0.99245	0.00755	0.49245
2.07	0.98077	0.01923	0.48077	2.44	0.99266	0.00734	0.49266
2.08	0.98124	0.01876	0.48124	2.45	0.99286	0.00714	0.49286
2.09	0.98169	0.01831	0.48169	2.46	0.99305	0.00695	0.49305

z	Larger Proportion	Smaller Proportion	Mean to z	z	Larger Proportion	Smaller Proportion	Mean to z
2.47	0.99324	0.00676	0.49324	2.84	0.99774	0.00226	0.49774
2.48	0.99343	0.00657	0.49343	2.85	0.99781	0.00219	0.49781
2.49	0.99361	0.00639	0.49361	2.86	0.99788	0.00212	0.49788
2.50	0.99379	0.00621	0.49379	2.87	0.99795	0.00205	0.49795
2.51	0.99396	0.00604	0.49396	2.88	0.99801	0.00199	0.49801
2.52	0.99413	0.00587	0.49413	2.89	0.99807	0.00193	0.49807
2.53	0.99430	0.00570	0.49430	2.90	0.99813	0.00187	0.49813
2.54	0.99446	0.00554	0.49446	2.91	0.99819	0.00181	0.49819
2.55	0.99461	0.00539	0.49461	2.92	0.99825	0.00175	0.49825
2.56	0.99477	0.00523	0.49477	2.93	0.99831	0.00169	0.49831
2.57	0.99492	0.00508	0.49492	2.94	0.99836	0.00164	0.49836
2.58	0.99506	0.00494	0.49506	2.95	0.99841	0.00159	0.49841
2.59	0.99520	0.00480	0.49520	2.96	0.99846	0.00154	0.49846
2.60	0.99534	0.00466	0.49534	2.97	0.99851	0.00149	0.49851
2.61	0.99547	0.00453	0.49547	2.98	0.99856	0.00144	0.49856
2.62	0.99560	0.00440	0.49560	2.99	0.99861	0.00139	0.49861
2.63	0.99573	0.00427	0.49573	3.00	0.99865	0.00135	0.49865
2.64	0.99585	0.00415	0.49585	3.01	0.99869	0.00131	0.49869
2.65	0.99598	0.00402	0.49598	3.02	0.99874	0.00126	0.49874
2.66	0.99609	0.00391	0.49609	3.03	0.99878	0.00122	0.49878
2.67	0.99621	0.00379	0.49621	3.04	0.99882	0.00118	0.49882
2.68	0.99632	0.00368	0.49632	3.05	0.99886	0.00114	0.49886
2.69	0.99643	0.00357	0.49643	3.06	0.99889	0.00111	0.49889
2.70	0.99653	0.00347	0.49653	3.07	0.99893	0.00107	0.49893
2.71	0.99664	0.00336	0.49664	3.08	0.99896	0.00104	0.49896
2.72	0.99674	0.00326	0.49674	3.09	0.99900	0.00100	0.49900
2.73	0.99683	0.00317	0.49683	3.10	0.99903	0.00097	0.49903
2.74	0.99693	0.00307	0.49693	3.11	0.99906	0.00094	0.49906
2.75	0.99702	0.00298	0.49702	3.12	0.99910	0.00090	0.49910
2.76	0.99711	0.00289	0.49711	3.13	0.99913	0.00087	0.49913
2.77	0.99720	0.00280	0.49720	3.14	0.99916	0.00084	0.49916
2.78	0.99728	0.00272	0.49728	3.15	0.99918	0.00082	0.49918
2.79	0.99736	0.00264	0.49736	3.16	0.99921	0.00079	0.49921
2.80	0.99744	0.00256	0.49744	3.17	0.99924	0.00076	0.49924
2.81	0.99752	0.00248	0.49752	3.18	0.99926	0.00074	0.49926
2.82	0.99760	0.00240	0.49760	3.19	0.99929	0.00071	0.49929
2.83	0.99767	0.00233	0.49767	3.20	0.99931	0.00069	0.49931

z	Larger Proportion	Smaller Proportion	Mean to z	z	Larger Proportion	Smaller Proportion	Mean to z
3.21	0.99934	0.00066	0.49934	3.49	0.99976	0.00024	0.49976
3.22	0.99936	0.00064	0.49936	3.50	0.99977	0.00023	0.49977
3.23	0.99938	0.00062	0.49938	3.51	0.99978	0.00022	0.49978
3.24	0.99940	0.00060	0.49940	3.53	0.99979	0.00021	0.49979
3.25	0.99942	0.00058	0.49942	3.54	0.99980	0.00020	0.49980
3.26	0.99944	0.00056	0.49944	3.55	0.99981	0.00019	0.49981
3.27	0.99946	0.00054	0.49946	3.57	0.99982	0.00018	0.49982
3.28	0.99948	0.00052	0.49948	3.58	0.99983	0.00017	0.49983
3.29	0.99950	0.00050	0.49950	3.60	0.99984	0.00016	0.49984
3.30	0.99952	0.00048	0.49952	3.61	0.99985	0.00015	0.49985
3.31	0.99953	0.00047	0.49953	3.63	0.99986	0.00014	0.49986
3.32	0.99955	0.00045	0.49955	3.65	0.99987	0.00013	0.49987
3.33	0.99957	0.00043	0.49957	3.67	0.99988	0.00012	0.49988
3.34	0.99958	0.00042	0.49958	3.69	0.99989	0.00011	0.49989
3.35	0.99960	0.00040	0.49960	3.71	0.99990	0.00010	0.49990
3.36	0.99961	0.00039	0.49961	3.74	0.99991	0.00009	0.49991
3.37	0.99962	0.00038	0.49962	3.75	0.99991	0.00009	0.49991
3.38	0.99964	0.00036	0.49964	...	...	...	...
3.39	0.99965	0.00035	0.49965	3.80	0.99993	0.00007	0.49993
3.40	0.99966	0.00034	0.49966	...	...	...	...
3.41	0.99968	0.00032	0.49968	3.85	0.99994	0.00006	0.49994
3.42	0.99969	0.00031	0.49969	...	...	...	...
3.43	0.99970	0.00030	0.49970	3.90	0.99995	0.00005	0.49995
3.44	0.99971	0.00029	0.49971	...	...	...	...
3.45	0.99972	0.00028	0.49972	3.95	0.99996	0.00004	0.49996
3.46	0.99973	0.00027	0.49973	...	...	...	...
3.47	0.99974	0.00026	0.49974	4.00	0.99997	0.00003	0.49997
3.48	0.99975	0.00025	0.49975	...	...	...	...

Values computed by the author using R

A.2 THE t-DISTRIBUTION

Proportion in One Tail
(right or left)

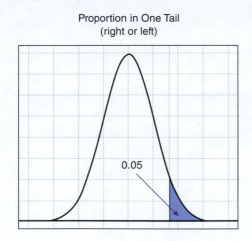

0.05

Proportion across Two Tails
(total)

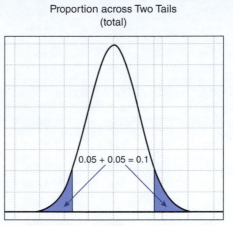

0.05 + 0.05 = 0.1

	Proportion in One Tail				
	0.10	0.05	0.025	0.01	0.005
	Proportion across Two Tails				
df	0.20	0.10	0.05	0.02	0.01
1	3.078	6.314	12.706	31.821	63.657
2	1.886	2.920	4.303	6.965	9.925
3	1.638	2.353	3.182	4.541	5.841
4	1.533	2.132	2.776	3.747	4.604
5	1.476	2.015	2.571	3.365	4.032
6	1.440	1.943	2.447	3.143	3.707
7	1.415	1.895	2.365	2.998	3.499
8	1.397	1.860	2.306	2.896	3.355
9	1.383	1.833	2.262	2.821	3.250
10	1.372	1.812	2.228	2.764	3.169
11	1.363	1.796	2.201	2.718	3.106
12	1.356	1.782	2.179	2.681	3.055
13	1.350	1.771	2.160	2.650	3.012
14	1.345	1.761	2.145	2.624	2.977
15	1.341	1.753	2.131	2.602	2.947
16	1.337	1.746	2.120	2.583	2.921
17	1.333	1.740	2.110	2.567	2.898
18	1.330	1.734	2.101	2.552	2.878
19	1.328	1.729	2.093	2.539	2.861

Proportion across Two Tails

df	0.20	0.10	0.05	0.02	0.01
20	1.325	1.725	2.086	2.528	2.845
21	1.323	1.721	2.080	2.518	2.831
22	1.321	1.717	2.074	2.508	2.819
23	1.319	1.714	2.069	2.500	2.807
24	1.318	1.711	2.064	2.492	2.797
25	1.316	1.708	2.060	2.485	2.787
26	1.315	1.706	2.056	2.479	2.779
27	1.314	1.703	2.052	2.473	2.771
28	1.313	1.701	2.048	2.467	2.763
29	1.311	1.699	2.045	2.462	2.756
30	1.310	1.697	2.042	2.457	2.750
35	1.306	1.690	2.030	2.438	2.724
40	1.303	1.684	2.021	2.423	2.704
45	1.301	1.679	2.014	2.412	2.690
50	1.299	1.676	2.009	2.403	2.678
55	1.297	1.673	2.004	2.396	2.668
60	1.296	1.671	2.000	2.390	2.660
70	1.294	1.667	1.994	2.381	2.648
80	1.292	1.664	1.990	2.374	2.639
90	1.291	1.662	1.987	2.368	2.632
100	1.290	1.660	1.984	2.364	2.626
∞	1.282	1.645	1.960	2.326	2.576

Values computed by the author using R

A.3 CRITICAL VALUES OF THE CHI-SQUARE DISTRIBUTION

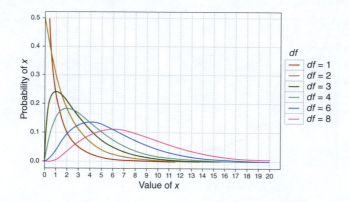

df	p 0.05	0.01		df	p 0.05	0.01
1	3.84	6.63		26	38.89	45.64
2	5.99	9.21		27	40.11	46.96
3	7.81	11.34		28	41.34	48.28
4	9.49	13.28		29	42.56	49.59
5	11.07	15.09		30	43.77	50.89
6	12.59	16.81		35	49.80	57.34
7	14.07	18.48		40	55.76	63.69
8	15.51	20.09		45	61.66	69.96
9	16.92	21.67		50	67.50	76.15
10	18.31	23.21		60	79.08	88.38
11	19.68	24.72		70	90.53	100.43
12	21.03	26.22		80	101.88	112.33
13	22.36	27.69		90	113.15	124.12
14	23.68	29.14		100	124.34	135.81
15	25.00	30.58		200	233.99	249.45
16	26.30	32.00		300	341.40	359.91
17	27.59	33.41		400	447.63	468.72
18	28.87	34.81		500	553.13	576.49
19	30.14	36.19		600	658.09	683.52
20	31.41	37.57		700	762.66	789.97
21	32.67	38.93		800	866.91	895.98
22	33.92	40.29		900	970.90	1001.63
23	35.17	41.64		1000	1074.68	1106.97
24	36.42	42.98				
25	37.65	44.31				

Values computed by the author using R.

A.4 CRITICAL VALUES OF THE F-DISTRIBUTION

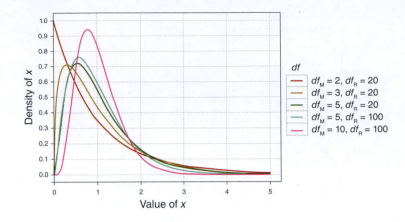

P = 0.05

df_R	df_M													
	1	2	3	4	5	6	7	8	9	10	15	25	50	100
1	161.45	199.50	215.71	224.58	230.16	233.99	236.77	238.88	240.54	241.88	245.95	249.26	251.77	253.04
2	18.51	19.00	19.16	19.25	19.30	19.33	19.35	19.37	19.38	19.40	19.43	19.46	19.48	19.49
3	10.13	9.55	9.28	9.12	9.01	8.94	8.89	8.85	8.81	8.79	8.70	8.63	8.58	8.55
4	7.71	6.94	6.59	6.39	6.26	6.16	6.09	6.04	6.00	5.96	5.86	5.77	5.70	5.66
5	6.61	5.79	5.41	5.19	5.05	4.95	4.88	4.82	4.77	4.74	4.62	4.52	4.44	4.41
6	5.99	5.14	4.76	4.53	4.39	4.28	4.21	4.15	4.10	4.06	3.94	3.83	3.75	3.71
7	5.59	4.74	4.35	4.12	3.97	3.87	3.79	3.73	3.68	3.64	3.51	3.40	3.32	3.27
8	5.32	4.46	4.07	3.84	3.69	3.58	3.50	3.44	3.39	3.35	3.22	3.11	3.02	2.97
9	5.12	4.26	3.86	3.63	3.48	3.37	3.29	3.23	3.18	3.14	3.01	2.89	2.80	2.76
10	4.96	4.10	3.71	3.48	3.33	3.22	3.14	3.07	3.02	2.98	2.85	2.73	2.64	2.59
12	4.75	3.89	3.49	3.26	3.11	3.00	2.91	2.85	2.80	2.75	2.62	2.50	2.40	2.35
14	4.60	3.74	3.34	3.11	2.96	2.85	2.76	2.70	2.65	2.60	2.46	2.34	2.24	2.19
16	4.49	3.63	3.24	3.01	2.85	2.74	2.66	2.59	2.54	2.49	2.35	2.23	2.12	2.07
18	4.41	3.55	3.16	2.93	2.77	2.66	2.58	2.51	2.46	2.41	2.27	2.14	2.04	1.98
20	4.35	3.49	3.10	2.87	2.71	2.60	2.51	2.45	2.39	2.35	2.20	2.07	1.97	1.91
22	4.30	3.44	3.05	2.82	2.66	2.55	2.46	2.40	2.34	2.30	2.15	2.02	1.91	1.85
24	4.26	3.40	3.01	2.78	2.62	2.51	2.42	2.36	2.30	2.25	2.11	1.97	1.86	1.80
26	4.23	3.37	2.98	2.74	2.59	2.47	2.39	2.32	2.27	2.22	2.07	1.94	1.82	1.76
28	4.20	3.34	2.95	2.71	2.56	2.45	2.36	2.29	2.24	2.19	2.04	1.91	1.79	1.73
30	4.17	3.32	2.92	2.69	2.53	2.42	2.33	2.27	2.21	2.16	2.01	1.88	1.76	1.70
33	4.14	3.28	2.89	2.66	2.50	2.39	2.30	2.23	2.18	2.13	1.98	1.84	1.72	1.66

df_R							df_M							
	1	2	3	4	5	6	7	8	9	10	15	25	50	100
35	4.12	3.27	2.87	2.64	2.49	2.37	2.29	2.22	2.16	2.11	1.96	1.82	1.70	1.63
40	4.08	3.23	2.84	2.61	2.45	2.34	2.25	2.18	2.12	2.08	1.92	1.78	1.66	1.59
45	4.06	3.20	2.81	2.58	2.42	2.31	2.22	2.15	2.10	2.05	1.89	1.75	1.63	1.55
50	4.03	3.18	2.79	2.56	2.40	2.29	2.20	2.13	2.07	2.03	1.87	1.73	1.60	1.52
55	4.02	3.16	2.77	2.54	2.38	2.27	2.18	2.11	2.06	2.01	1.85	1.71	1.58	1.50
60	4.00	3.15	2.76	2.53	2.37	2.25	2.17	2.10	2.04	1.99	1.84	1.69	1.56	1.48
65	3.99	3.14	2.75	2.51	2.36	2.24	2.15	2.08	2.03	1.98	1.82	1.68	1.54	1.46
70	3.98	3.13	2.74	2.50	2.35	2.23	2.14	2.07	2.02	1.97	1.81	1.66	1.53	1.45
75	3.97	3.12	2.73	2.49	2.34	2.22	2.13	2.06	2.01	1.96	1.80	1.65	1.52	1.44
80	3.96	3.11	2.72	2.49	2.33	2.21	2.13	2.06	2.00	1.95	1.79	1.64	1.51	1.43
85	3.95	3.10	2.71	2.48	2.32	2.21	2.12	2.05	1.99	1.94	1.79	1.64	1.50	1.42
90	3.95	3.10	2.71	2.47	2.32	2.20	2.11	2.04	1.99	1.94	1.78	1.63	1.49	1.41
95	3.94	3.09	2.70	2.47	2.31	2.20	2.11	2.04	1.98	1.93	1.77	1.62	1.48	1.40
100	3.94	3.09	2.70	2.46	2.31	2.19	2.10	2.03	1.97	1.93	1.77	1.62	1.48	1.39

$P = 0.01$

df_M

df_R	1	2	3	4	5	6	7	8	9	10	15	25	50	100
1	4052.18	4999.50	5403.35	5624.58	5763.65	5858.99	5928.36	5981.07	6022.47	6055.85	6157.28	6239.83	6302.52	6334.11
2	98.50	99.00	99.17	99.25	99.30	99.33	99.36	99.37	99.39	99.40	99.43	99.46	99.48	99.49
3	34.12	30.82	29.46	28.71	28.24	27.91	27.67	27.49	27.35	27.23	26.87	26.58	26.35	26.24
4	21.20	18.00	16.69	15.98	15.52	15.21	14.98	14.80	14.66	14.55	14.20	13.91	13.69	13.58
5	16.26	13.27	12.06	11.39	10.97	10.67	10.46	10.29	10.16	10.05	9.72	9.45	9.24	9.13
6	13.75	10.92	9.78	9.15	8.75	8.47	8.26	8.10	7.98	7.87	7.56	7.30	7.09	6.99
7	12.25	9.55	8.45	7.85	7.46	7.19	6.99	6.84	6.72	6.62	6.31	6.06	5.86	5.75
8	11.26	8.65	7.59	7.01	6.63	6.37	6.18	6.03	5.91	5.81	5.52	5.26	5.07	4.96
9	10.56	8.02	6.99	6.42	6.06	5.80	5.61	5.47	5.35	5.26	4.96	4.71	4.52	4.41
10	10.04	7.56	6.55	5.99	5.64	5.39	5.20	5.06	4.94	4.85	4.56	4.31	4.12	4.01
12	9.33	6.93	5.95	5.41	5.06	4.82	4.64	4.50	4.39	4.30	4.01	3.76	3.57	3.47
14	8.86	6.51	5.56	5.04	4.69	4.46	4.28	4.14	4.03	3.94	3.66	3.41	3.22	3.11
16	8.53	6.23	5.29	4.77	4.44	4.20	4.03	3.89	3.78	3.69	3.41	3.16	2.97	2.86
18	8.29	6.01	5.09	4.58	4.25	4.01	3.84	3.71	3.60	3.51	3.23	2.98	2.78	2.68
20	8.10	5.85	4.94	4.43	4.10	3.87	3.70	3.56	3.46	3.37	3.09	2.84	2.64	2.54
22	7.95	5.72	4.82	4.31	3.99	3.76	3.59	3.45	3.35	3.26	2.98	2.73	2.53	2.42
24	7.82	5.61	4.72	4.22	3.90	3.67	3.50	3.36	3.26	3.17	2.89	2.64	2.44	2.33
26	7.72	5.53	4.64	4.14	3.82	3.59	3.42	3.29	3.18	3.09	2.81	2.57	2.36	2.25
28	7.64	5.45	4.57	4.07	3.75	3.53	3.36	3.23	3.12	3.03	2.75	2.51	2.30	2.19
30	7.56	5.39	4.51	4.02	3.70	3.47	3.30	3.17	3.07	2.98	2.70	2.45	2.25	2.13
33	7.47	5.31	4.44	3.95	3.63	3.41	3.24	3.11	3.00	2.91	2.63	2.39	2.18	2.06
35	7.42	5.27	4.40	3.91	3.59	3.37	3.20	3.07	2.96	2.88	2.60	2.35	2.14	2.02
40	7.31	5.18	4.31	3.83	3.51	3.29	3.12	2.99	2.89	2.80	2.52	2.27	2.06	1.94

df_M

df_R	1	2	3	4	5	6	7	8	9	10	15	25	50	100
45	7.23	5.11	4.25	3.77	3.45	3.23	3.07	2.94	2.83	2.74	2.46	2.21	2.00	1.88
50	7.17	5.06	4.20	3.72	3.41	3.19	3.02	2.89	2.78	2.70	2.42	2.17	1.95	1.82
55	7.12	5.01	4.16	3.68	3.37	3.15	2.98	2.85	2.75	2.66	2.38	2.13	1.91	1.78
60	7.08	4.98	4.13	3.65	3.34	3.12	2.95	2.82	2.72	2.63	2.35	2.10	1.88	1.75
65	7.04	4.95	4.10	3.62	3.31	3.09	2.93	2.80	2.69	2.61	2.33	2.07	1.85	1.72
70	7.01	4.92	4.07	3.60	3.29	3.07	2.91	2.78	2.67	2.59	2.31	2.05	1.83	1.70
75	6.99	4.90	4.05	3.58	3.27	3.05	2.89	2.76	2.65	2.57	2.29	2.03	1.81	1.67
80	6.96	4.88	4.04	3.56	3.26	3.04	2.87	2.74	2.64	2.55	2.27	2.01	1.79	1.65
85	6.94	4.86	4.02	3.55	3.24	3.02	2.86	2.73	2.62	2.54	2.26	2.00	1.77	1.64
90	6.93	4.85	4.01	3.53	3.23	3.01	2.84	2.72	2.61	2.52	2.24	1.99	1.76	1.62
95	6.91	4.84	3.99	3.52	3.22	3.00	2.83	2.70	2.60	2.51	2.23	1.98	1.75	1.61
100	6.90	4.82	3.98	3.51	3.21	2.99	2.82	2.69	2.59	2.50	2.22	1.97	1.74	1.60

Values computed by the author using R

α-level: the probability of making a *Type I error* (usually this value is 0.05).

Abscissa: the horizontal axis of a *graph*. Also known as the *x*-axis.

Additive law: in probability theory, the probability of the *union* of *mutually exclusive* outcomes can be ascertained by adding the probability of the individual outcomes. For example, if two outcomes *A* and *B* are mutually exclusive, then the probability of *A or B* occurring is the sum of their individual probabilities: $p(A \cup B) = p(A) + p(B)$.

Alternative hypothesis: the prediction that there will be an effect (i.e., that your experimental manipulation will have some effect or that certain variables will relate to each other).

Arithmetic mean: an alternative name for the *mean*.

Average: an alternative name for the *mean*.

b_i: unstandardized regression coefficient. Indicates the strength of relationship between a given predictor, X_i, and an outcome in the units of measurement of the predictor. It is the change in the outcome associated with a unit change in the predictor.

b_n: unstandardized regression coefficient for the *n*th variable.

β_i: see *standardized regression coefficient*.

β-level: the probability of making a *Type II error* (Cohen[50] suggests a maximum value of 0.2).

Bar graph: a graph in which a summary statistic (usually the mean) is plotted on the *y*-axis against a categorical variable on the *x*-axis (this categorical variable could represent, for example, groups of people, different times or different experimental conditions). The value of the mean for each category is shown by a bar. Different-coloured bars may be used to represent levels of a second categorical variable.

Batticks: a word I invented as an, at best, thinly veiled device to avoid using a rude word. It's the sort of thing men might exclaim if someone kicked them in the batticks.

Bayes factor: the ratio of the probability of the observed data given the *alternative hypothesis* to the probability of the observed data given the *null hypothesis*. Put another way, it is the *likelihood* of the alternative hypothesis relative to the null. A Bayes factor of 3, for example, means that the observed data are 3 times more likely under the alternative hypothesis than the null hypothesis. A Bayes factor less than 1 supports the null hypothesis by suggesting that the probability of the data given the null is higher than the probability of the data given the alternative hypothesis. Conversely, a Bayes factor greater than 1 suggests that the observed data are more likely given the alternative hypothesis than the null. Values between 1 and 3 are considered evidence for the alternative hypothesis that is 'barely worth mentioning', values between 3 and 10 are considered 'substantial evidence' ('having substance' rather than 'very strong') for the alternative hypothesis, and values greater than 10 are strong evidence for the alternative hypothesis.

Bayes' theorem: a mathematical description of the relationship between the *conditional probability* of events A and B, $p(A|B)$, their reverse conditional probability, $p(B|A)$, and individual probabilities of the events, $p(A)$ and $p(B)$. The theorem states that

$$p(A \mid B) = \frac{p(B \mid A)p(A)}{p(B)}$$

Bernoulli trial: in probability, a Bernoulli trial is a random *experiment* that has two possible outcomes. Tossing a (fair) coin is a Bernoulli trial: it will land either heads up or tails up.

Between-groups design: another name for *independent design*.

Between-subjects design: another name for *independent design*.

Bias corrected and accelerated (BCa) confidence interval: a variant of the *percentile bootstrap confidence interval* that is adjusted for *skewness* and to be *median* unbiased. In general, it has better coverage (i.e., more often contains the true value being estimated) than the percentile confidence interval.

Biased estimator: a statistic taken from a random sample that does not equal its corresponding population parameter; for example, a sample mean that is not equal to the population mean. See also *unbiased estimator*.

Bimodal: a description of a distribution of observations that has two *modes*.

Binary variable: a *categorical variable* that has exactly two mutually exclusive categories (e.g., being dead or alive) – see also *dichotomous variable*.

Biserial correlation: a standardized measure of the strength of relationship between two variables when one of the two variables is *dichotomous*. The biserial correlation coefficient is used when one variable is a continuous dichotomy (e.g., has an underlying continuum between the categories).

Bivariate correlation: a correlation between two variables.

Bonferroni correction: a correction applied to the α-*level* to control the overall *Type I error rate* when multiple significance tests are carried out. Each test conducted should use a criterion of significance of the α-level (normally 0.05) divided by the number of tests conducted. This is a simple but effective correction, but tends to be too strict when lots of tests are performed.

Bootstrap: a technique for estimating the sampling distribution of a statistic of interest (e.g., the *mean* or the b coefficient) by taking repeated samples (with replacement) from the data set (so, in effect, treating the data as a population from which smaller samples are taken). The standard error of the statistic is estimated as the standard deviation of the sampling distribution created from the bootstrap samples. From this, confidence intervals and significance tests can be computed.

Bootstrap samples: a bootstrap sample is constructed by randomly selecting scores from an observed sample of scores and replacing them (so that the score is available for selection again) until the bootstrap sample contains as many scores as the original sample.

Boredom effect: refers to the possibility that performance in tasks may be influenced (the assumption is a negative influence) by boredom/lack of concentration if there are many tasks, or the task goes on for a long period of time. In short, what you are experiencing reading this glossary is a boredom effect.

Boxplot (or *box–whisker diagram*): a graphical representation of some important characteristics of a set of observations. At the centre of the plot is the *median*, which is surrounded by a box the top and bottom of which are the limits within which the middle 50% of observations fall (the *interquartile range*). Sticking out of the top and bottom of the box are two whiskers, which extend to the smallest and largest extreme scores, excluding scores considered to be outliers.

Box–whisker diagram: see *Boxplot*.

Brown–Forsythe *F*: a version of the *F-ratio* designed to be accurate when the assumption of *homogeneity of variance* has been violated (see also *Welch's F*). The Brown–Forsythe *F* uses an adjusted residual sum of squares in which the group variances are weighted not by their sample size, but by n/N, the sample size as a proportion of the total sample size. This reduces the impact on the resulting *F* of large sample sizes with large variances:

$$F_{\text{BF}} = \frac{SS_{\text{M}}}{SS_{R_{\text{BF}}}} = \frac{SS_{\text{M}}}{\sum s_k^2 \left(1 - \frac{n_k}{N}\right)}$$

Categorical variable: any variable made up of categories of objects/entities. The major of the degree you are studying is a categorical variable: you can major in psychology, biology, medicine, or maths, but you can't major in more than one of them. We can compare people who major in maths with those who major in psychology, for example.

Central limit theorem: this theorem states that when samples are large (above about 30) the *sampling distribution* will take the shape of a *normal distribution* regardless of the shape of the population from which the sample was drawn. For small samples the *t*-distribution better approximates the shape of the sampling distribution. We also know from this theorem that the *standard deviation* of the sampling distribution (i.e., the *standard error* of the sample *mean*) will be equal to the standard deviation of the sample (*s*) divided by the square root of the sample size (*N*). The *central* in the name refers to the theorem being important and far-reaching and has nothing to do with centres of distributions.

Central tendency: a generic term describing a *parameter* or *statistic* that represents the centre of a *frequency distribution* of observations as measured by the *mean*, *mode*, and *median*.

Chart: information displayed as a diagram, *graph*, or table. The word is often used synonymously with 'graph', although the term 'chart' encompasses a wider range of information displays than just graphs.

Chartjunk: superfluous material that distracts from the data being displayed on a graph.

Chi-square distribution: a *probability distribution* of the sum of squares of several normally distributed variables. It tends to be used to test hypotheses about categorical data, and the fit of models to the observed data.

Chi-square test: although this term can apply to any *test statistic* having a *chi-square distribution*, it generally refers to Pearson's chi-square test of the independence of two categorical variables. Essentially, it tests whether two categorical variables forming a *contingency table* are associated.

Class interval: when data along an interval or ratio scale of measurement are grouped by dividing the scale into equal portions, these portions are known as 'classes'. For example, a scale ranging from 0 to 10 might be divided into five equal classes of 0–2, 2–4, 4–6, 6–8, and 8–10, or two equal class intervals of 0–5 and 5–10.

Class interval width: when data along an interval or ratio scale of measurement are grouped into equal class intervals, the class interval width is the distance from the smallest to the largest value within the interval. For example, a scale ranging from 0 to 10 might be divided into five equal classes of 0–2, 2–4, 4–6, 6–8, and 8–10, the class interval width would be 2 because the distance between the smallest and largest value within each interval is 2. Similarly, the same scale could be divided into two classes of 0–4, 5–10 resulting in a class interval width of 5.

Classical probability: is the theoretical *probability* of an *event*. For a given *trial* or set of trials, the classical probability of an event, assuming that all *outcomes* are equally likely, is the *frequency* of an event divided by the *sample space*, or total number of possible outcomes. For example, when Zach contemplated crossing the bridge of death, there were two possible outcomes: he lives or dies. Therefore, the sample space for a single trial contains two events (alive or dead). Assuming these outcomes occur with equal frequency, then the classical probability of living is the frequency of living in the sample space (which is 1) divided by the total number of events in the sample space, 2. In other words, it is 0.5 or 50%. Compare with *Empirical probability*.

Coding: converting a variable measured on a *nominal scale* (e.g., a *categorical variable*) to a numerical variable. This conversion is achieved by assigning numbers to each category; for example, instead of using 'Male' and 'Female' as response outcomes for the sex of a person, you could use 0 and 1 (e.g., 0 = Male, 1 = Female).

Coefficient of determination: the proportion of variance in one variable explained by a second variable. It is the *Pearson correlation coefficient* squared.

Cohen's *d*: The standardized difference between two means. When there is a control group, it is usually calculated as:

$$\hat{d} = \frac{\bar{X}_{\text{Experimental}} - \bar{X}_{\text{Control}}}{s_{\text{Control}}}$$

When there isn't an obvious control (and sometimes when there is) a pooled standard deviation is used instead of the control group standard deviation:

$$\hat{d} = \frac{\bar{X}_1 - \bar{X}_2}{s_p}$$

$$s_p = \sqrt{\frac{(N_1 - 1)s_1^2 + (N_2 - 1)s_2^2}{N_1 + N_2 - 2}}$$

Complementary: in probability theory the probabilities for outcomes are complementary if they sum to 1. For example, the probability that you are bored reading this glossary and the probability that you are not bored reading this glossary are complementary, because if you are bored then, by definition, you can't also be not bored, so the probabilities of these outcomes will sum to 1.

Concurrent validity: a form of *criterion validity* where there is evidence that scores from an instrument correspond to concurrently recorded external measures conceptually related to the measured construct.

Conditional probability: the probability of an outcome given that some other outcome has already happened. For example, the probability that you are bored given that you have read this glossary entry is a conditional probability, p(boredom|read glossary).

Confidence interval: for a given statistic calculated for a sample of observations (e.g., the mean), the confidence interval is a range of values around that statistic that are believed to contain, in a certain proportion of samples (e.g., 95%), the true value of that statistic (i.e., the population parameter). What that also means is that for the other proportion of samples, the confidence interval won't contain that true value. The trouble is, you don't know which category your particular sample falls into.

Confounding variable: a variable (that we may or may not have measured) other than the *predictor variables* in which we're interested that potentially affects an *outcome variable*.

Construct: something that cannot be measured directly but is indicated by things that can be measured directly. For example, intelligence is a construct; although we cannot measure it directly, intelligent people tend to do well on IQ tests and don't generally drink their own urine or fall into holes in the road.

Contaminated normal distribution: see *mixed normal distribution*.

Content validity: evidence that the content of a test corresponds to the content of the construct it was designed to cover.

Contingency table: a table representing the cross-classification of two or more *categorical variables*. The levels of each variable are arranged in a grid, and the number of observations falling into each category is noted in the cells of the table. For example, if we took the categorical variables *superhero party costume* (with three categories: Supergirl, Wonder Woman, Catwoman), and *injured* (with two categories: yes or no), we could construct a table as below.

		Injured at party		
		Yes	No	Total
Party costume	Supergirl	20	5	**25**
	Wonder Woman	23	45	**68**
	Catwoman	32	50	**82**
	Total	**75**	**100**	**175**

Continuous variable: a variable that can be measured to any level of precision. (*Time* is a continuous variable, because there is in principle no limit on how finely it could be measured.)

Correlation coefficient: a measure of the strength of association or relationship between two variables. See *Pearson's correlation coefficient*, *Spearman's rho*, *Kendall's tau*.

Correlational research: a form of research in which you observe what naturally goes on in the world without directly interfering with it. This term implies that data will be analysed so as to look at relationships between naturally occurring variables rather than making statements about cause and effect. Compare with *cross-sectional research*, *longitudinal research* and *experimental research*.

Counterbalancing: a process of systematically varying the order in which experimental conditions are conducted. In the simplest case of there being two conditions (*A* and *B*), counterbalancing simply implies that half of the participants complete condition *A* followed by condition *B*, while the remainder do condition *B* followed by condition *A*. The aim is to remove systematic bias caused by *practice effects* or *boredom effects*. See *Latin square design*.

Covariance: a measure of the 'average' relationship between two variables. It is the average *cross-product deviation* (i.e., the cross-product divided by one less than the number of observations).

Credible interval: in Bayesian statistics a credible interval is an interval within which a certain percentage of the posterior distribution falls (usually 95%). It can be used to express the limits within which a parameter falls with a fixed probability. For example, if we estimated the average length of a romantic relationship to be 6 years with a 95% credibility interval of 1 to 11 years, then this would mean that 95% of the posterior distribution for the length of romantic relationships falls between 1 and 11 years. A plausible estimate of the length of romantic relationships would, therefore, be 1 to 11 years.

Criterion validity: evidence that scores from an instrument correspond with (*concurrent validity*) or predict (*predictive validity*) external measures conceptually related to the measured construct.

Cross-product deviation: a measure of the 'total' relationship between two variables. It is the deviation of one variable from its mean multiplied by the other variable's deviation from its mean.

Cross-sectional research: a form of research in which you observe what naturally goes on in the world without directly interfering with it by measuring several variables at a single time point. In psychology, this term usually implies that data come from people at different age points with different people representing each age point. See also *correlational research*, *longitudinal research*.

Cumulative frequency: the *frequency* of a category in a series of ordered categories along a *scale of measurement* expressed as the total of the current category and all those preceding it. The categories can be in either descending or ascending order (depending on which is most appropriate for the scale of measurement that you are trying to summarize).

Cumulative percentage: the *frequency* of a category in a series of ordered categories along a *scale of measurement* in the current category and all those preceding it expressed as the percentage of the total number of scores. The categories can be in either descending or ascending order (depending on which is most appropriate for the scale of measurement that you are trying to summarize).

Degrees of freedom: an impossible thing to define in a few pages, let alone a few lines. Essentially, it is the number of 'scores' that are free to vary when estimating some kind of statistical parameter. In a more practical sense, it has a bearing on significance tests for many commonly used *test statistics* (such as the *F-ratio*, *t-test*, *chi-square statistic*) and determines the exact form of the *probability distribution* for these *test statistics*.

Density: the relative likelihood (or probability) of a given score on a scale of measurement occurring.

Dependent *t*-test: another name for the *paired-samples t-test* (and also the *matched-pairs t-test*).

Dependent variable: another name for *outcome variable*. This name is usually associated with experimental methodology (which is the only time it really makes sense), and it is so called because it is the variable that is not manipulated by the experimenter and so its value depends on the variables that have been manipulated. I prefer the term *outcome variable* because it makes sense across different methodologies.

Descriptive statistics: procedures for summarizing or organizing data collected from a *sample*.

Deviance: the difference between the observed value of a variable and the value of that variable predicted by a statistical model.

Dichotomous variable: description of a variable that consists of only two categories (e.g., gender is dichotomous because it consists of only two categories: male and female) – see *binary variable*.

Discourse analysis: a *qualitative method* that operates on the assumption that by studying what we say (and how we interact) we can gain access to real-life processes. The starting point for a discourse analysis could be a transcribed individual interview (which has the advantage of control) or a group discussion (which has the advantage that you can look at natural interactions).

Discrete variable: a variable that can only take on certain values (usually whole numbers) on the scale. For example, the number of boyfriends you have had ought to be discrete (unless you're a psychopath, you should not have had 3.7 boyfriends).

Disjoint: see *mutually exclusive*.

Dummy coding: a way of recoding a categorical variable with two or more categories into one or more variables that are *dichotomous* with values of only 0 or 1. There are seven steps in creating such variables. (1) Count the number of groups you want to recode and subtract 1. (2) Create as many new variables as the value you calculated in step 1 (these are called dummy variables). (3) Choose one of your groups as a baseline (i.e., a group against which all other groups should be compared, such as a control group). (4) Assign that baseline group values of 0 for every dummy variable. (5) For the first dummy variable, assign the value 1 to the first group that you want to compare against the baseline group (if relevant, assign all other groups 0 for this variable). (6) If you have a second dummy variable assign the value 1 to the second group that you want to compare against the baseline group (assign all other groups 0 for this variable). (7) Repeat step 6 until you run out of dummy variables.

Durbin–Watson test: tests for serial correlations between errors in *regression models*. Specifically, it tests whether adjacent residuals are correlated, which is useful in assessing the assumption of *independent errors*. The test statistic can vary between 0 and 4, with a value of 2 meaning that the residuals are uncorrelated. A value greater than 2 indicates a negative correlation between adjacent residuals, whereas a value below 2 indicates a positive correlation. The size of the Durbin–Watson statistic depends upon the number of predictors in the model and the number of observations. For accuracy, look up the exact acceptable values in Durbin and Watson's original paper.[130] As a very conservative rule of thumb, values less than 1 or greater than 3 are definitely cause for concern; however, values closer to 2 may still be problematic, depending on the sample and model.

Ecological validity: evidence that the results of a study, experiment or test can be applied, and allow inferences, to real-world conditions.

Effect size: an objective and (usually) standardized measure of the magnitude of an observed effect. Measures include Cohen's *d*, the *odds ratio*, and *Pearson's correlation coefficient*, *r*.

Eisel: Pronounced ay-sel. A made-up insult. It is my confabulation of the Dutch insults 'eikel' (ask your reality checker), 'ezel' (donkey), which a Dutch colleague told me about, and the English insult 'arsehole'. My incompetent memory birthed the word 'eisel' and since it did it has enjoyed a place in my wife's and my lexicons as an affectionate way of saying 'arsehole' when we actually really like the thing to which we're referring. For example, I might say to her 'Was the dog being an eisel on his walk today?' By which I mean was he being loveably naughty. If you ever meet me and I say 'don't be an eisel' rest assured that I am fond of you, but if I say 'don't be an arsehole' I am not. If you reply 'You're the one being an eisel' I will laugh, if you say 'you're the one being an arsehole' I will cry. I hope that's cleared things up for you.

Elpis: The city in which the story is based.

Empirical probability: Another term for *relative frequency*. The empirical probability is the *probability* of an *event* based on the observation of many trials. Like *classical probability*, it is the *frequency* of an event divided by the *sample space*, but the frequency and sample space are determined by actual observations. For example, when Zach contemplates crossing the bridge of death, there were two possible outcomes: he lives or dies. If he watched 10 people cross the bridge, noted the outcome and 7 people died, then the empirical probability of living is the frequency of living (the number of people he observed who survived, 3) divided by the sample space, which is the total number of observations, 10. In other words, it is 0.3 or 30%. Compare *classical probability*.

Empirical question: A question that can be answered through collecting data such as by observation and/or experimentation.

Error bar: a vertical line protruding from the end of a bar (or line) on a *bar graph* (or *line graph*) that represents the precision of the value being displayed by the bar (or line). Typically they are used when the bar (or line) represents the mean, and the error bar will represent the precision of the mean in one of three ways: (1) the length from the mean to the end of the error bar will represent one *standard deviation* from that mean; (2) the length from the mean to the end of the error bar will represent one *standard error* from that mean; or (3) the length from the mean to the end of the error bar will represent 1.96 *standard errors* from that mean, in other words the full length of the error bar represents the 95% confidence interval of the mean.

Eta squared (η^2): an *effect size* measure that is the ratio of the *model sum of squares* to the *total sum of squares*. In essence, *the coefficient of determination* by another name. It doesn't have an awful lot going for it: not only is it biased, but also it typically measures the overall effect of an ANOVA, and effect sizes are more easily interpreted when they reflect specific comparisons (e.g., the difference between two means).

Event: in *probability* theory, an event is a subset of the *sample space* to which you can assign a probability. It consists of one or more outcomes of a *trial*. For example, imagine you had 100 friends' phone numbers stored in your mobile phone, and the *experiment* is to randomly select a friend. You might be interested in the probability of selecting someone called Andy, or the probability of selecting a female friend, or the probability of selecting someone whose name begins with an F. All of these would be 'events' in probability terms.

Evidence: in *Bayes' theorem*, evidence is another name for the *marginal likelihood*.

Experiment (probability): in *probability* theory, an experiment is a procedure that has a well-defined set of outcomes and can be repeated over several *trials*. For example, imagine you had 100 friend's phone numbers stored in your mobile phone. Selecting a friend at random from your contacts would be, in probability terms, an experiment because there is a well-defined set of outcomes: there are exactly 100 names that could be chosen.

Experiment (research): a procedure to test a *hypothesis*. Ideally, an experiment should provide a comparison of conditions in which a proposed cause is present with a comparable condition in which the cause is absent, while controlling for all other variables that might influence the effect of interest.

Experimental hypothesis: synonym for *alternative hypothesis*.

Experimental methods: a research method in which one or more variables is systematically manipulated to see their effect (alone or in combination) on an *outcome variable*. This term implies that data will be able to be used to make statements about cause and effect. Compare with *cross-sectional research* and *correlational research*.

Experimentwise error rate: the probability of making a *Type I error* in an experiment involving one or more statistical comparisons when the null hypothesis is true in each case.

F_{max}: see *Hartley's F_{max}*.

F-ratio: a test statistic with a known *probability distribution* (the *F*-distribution). It is the ratio of the average variability in the data that a given model can explain to the average variability unexplained by that same model. It is used to test the overall fit of *a linear model*.

Factorial design: an experimental design incorporating two or more categorical *predictors* (or *independent variables*).

Familywise error rate: the probability of making a *Type I error* in any family of tests when the null hypothesis is true in each case. The 'family of tests' can be loosely defined as a set of tests conducted on the same data set and addressing the same empirical question.

Fisher's exact test: Fisher's exact test[93] is not so much a test as a way of computing the exact probability of a statistic. It was designed originally to overcome the problem that with small samples the sampling distribution of the chi-square statistic deviates substantially from a chi-square distribution. It should be used with small samples.

Fit: how sexually attractive you find a statistical test. Alternatively, it's the degree to which a statistical model is an accurate representation of some observed data. (Incidentally, it's *wrong* on every level to find statistical tests sexually attractive.)

Forced entry regression: a method of *multiple regression* in which *predictor variables* are entered into the model, and their *regression coefficients* estimated, simultaneously.

Four-way design: an experimental design incorporating four categorical *predictors* (or *independent variables*).

Frequency: the number of times that a score, range of scores or category occurs.

Frequency distribution: a graph or table showing the categories along a *scale of measurement* alongside how many scores within a data set fall into each category. See also *histogram*.

Frequency polygon: a graph with ascending values of observations on the horizontal axis, and points displaying the frequency (on the vertical axis) with which each value occurs in the data set. The dots are connected with straight lines to form a polygon. See also *histogram*.

Frippin': another desperately transparent expression to circumvent offending people who don't like my unfortunate habit of using bad language. I was going to use frimmin', which I thought

I had invented until I looked it up online and found a definition in the urban dictionary that I wish with all of my heart I could unread. Frippin' also appeared there but has an altogether more pleasant meaning of losing control of one's faculties and having a bit of a rant, which seemed to fit the contexts in which I wanted to use it.

G-test: see *Likelihood ratio test*.

Generalization: the ability of a statistical model to say something beyond the set of observations that spawned it. If a model generalizes it is assumed that predictions from that model can be applied not just to the sample on which it is based, but also to a wider population from which the sample came.

Girifinsect: A mythical creature that is a little bit giraffe and a little bit stick insect. I invented it to keep my 2-month-old son amused. A girifinsect can turn into a starfish by sticking its arms and legs out, but a starfish cannot turn into a girifinsect. That distinction is important, lest you be fooled into thinking a girifinsect is a starfish in disguise. The girifinsect has its own song, but I'll probably keep that safely within the confines of our home.

Graph: a visual display of data depicting the values or a summary of one or more variables. Typically, two axes at right angles to each other are used to quantify values of the variables.

Greenhouse–Geisser estimate: an estimate of the departure from *sphericity*. The maximum value is 1 (the data completely meet the assumption of sphericity). Values below 1 indicate departures from sphericity and are used to correct the *degrees of freedom* associated with the corresponding *F-ratios* by multiplying them by the value of the estimate. Some say the Greenhouse–Geisser correction is too conservative (strict) and recommend the *Huynh–Feldt correction* instead.

Grounded theory: a *qualitative method* in which the analysis of qualitative data informs the development of a theory rather than vice versa.

Grouped frequency distribution: a *frequency distribution* in which categories on the scale of measurement are grouped using *class intervals*.

Hartley's F_{max}: also known as the *variance ratio*, this is the ratio of the variances between the group with the biggest variance and the group with the smallest variance. This ratio is compared to critical values in a table published by Hartley as a test of *homogeneity of variance*. Some general rules are that with sample sizes (n) of 10 per group, an F_{max} less than 10 is more or less always going to be non-significant, with 15–20 per group the ratio needs to be less than about 5, and with samples of 30–60 the ratio should be below about 2 or 3.

Heterogeneity of variance: the opposite of *homogeneity of variance*. This term means that the variance of one variable varies (i.e., is different) across levels of another variable.

Heteroscedasticity: the opposite of *homoscedasticity*. This occurs when the residuals at each level of the predictor variables(s) have unequal variances. Put another way, at each point along any predictor variable, the spread of residuals is different.

Hierarchical regression: a method of *multiple regression* where the order in which predictors are entered into the regression model is determined by the researcher based on previous research: variables already known to be predictors are entered first, new variables are entered subsequently.

Histogram: a graph with ascending values of observations on the horizontal axis, and vertical bars rising up to the frequency (on the vertical axis) with which each value occurs in the data set. See also *frequency polygon*.

Homogeneity of variance: the assumption that the variance of one variable is stable (i.e., relatively similar) at all levels of another variable.

Homoscedasticity: an assumption in regression analysis that the residuals at each level of the predictor variables(s) have similar variances. Put another way, at each point along any predictor variable, the spread of residuals should be fairly constant.

Huynh–Feldt estimate: an estimate of the departure from *sphericity*. The maximum value is 1 (the data completely meet the assumption of sphericity). Values below this indicate departures from sphericity and are used to correct the *degrees of freedom* associated with the corresponding *F-ratios* by multiplying them by the value of the estimate. It is less conservative than the *Greenhouse–Geisser estimate*, but some say it is too liberal.

Hypothesis: a proposed explanation for a fairly narrow phenomenon or set of observations. It is not a guess, but an informed, theory-driven attempt to explain what has been observed. A hypothesis cannot be tested directly but must first be operationalized as predictions about variables that can be measured. See *experimental hypothesis, null hypothesis*.

Independent design: an experimental design in which different treatment conditions utilize different entities (in psychology, this would mean using different people in different treatment conditions) and so the resulting data are independent. Also known as *between-groups* or *between-subjects* design.

Independent errors: an assumption in ordinary least squares regression that says that for any two observations the *residuals* should be uncorrelated (or independent).

Independent t-test: a test using the *t-statistic* that establishes whether two means collected from independent samples differ significantly.

Independent variable: another name for a *predictor variable*. This name is usually associated with experimental methodology (which is the only time it makes sense), and it is so called because it is the variable that is manipulated by the experimenter and so its value does not depend on any other variables (just on the experimenter). I prefer the term *predictor variable* because the meaning of the term is not constrained to a particular methodology.

Inferential statistics: statistical procedures for generalizing findings based on data from a *sample* to the *population* from which that sample came.

Interaction effect: the combined effect of two or more *predictor variables* on an *outcome variable*.

Interaction graph: a graph showing the means of two or more *independent variables* in which means of one variable are shown at different levels of the other variable. Usually the means are connected with lines, or are displayed as bars. These graphs are used to help understand *interaction effects*.

Interquartile range: the limits within which the middle 50% of an ordered set of observations falls. It is the difference between the values of the *upper quartile* and *lower quartile*.

Intersection: The probability of two or more outcomes occurring simultaneously is the probability of the intersection. The probability of the intersection of two outcomes A and B would be denoted as $p(A \cap B)$, meaning the probability of A *and* B occurring. Compare with *union*.

Interval estimate: using a range of values to estimate the likely value of an unknown quantity. See *confidence interval*.

Interval scale: a scale of ordered categories along the whole of which intervals are equal. For example, people's ratings of this book on Amazon.com can range from 1 to 5. For these data to be interval it should be true that the increase in appreciation for this book represented by a change from 3 to 4 along the scale should be the same as the change in appreciation represented by a change from 1 to 2, or 4 to 5.

Kendall's tau: a correlation coefficient similar to *Spearman's rho*, but preferred for small data sets with a large number of tied ranks.

Kolmogorov–Smirnov test: a test of whether a distribution of scores is significantly different from a *normal distribution*. A significant value indicates a deviation from normality, but this test is notoriously affected by large samples in which small deviations from normality yield significant results.

Kurtosis: this measures the degree to which scores cluster in the tails of a frequency distribution. There are different ways to estimate kurtosis and in SPSS no kurtosis is expressed as 0 (but be careful because outside of SPSS no kurtosis is sometimes a value of 3). A distribution with positive kurtosis (*leptokurtic*, kurtosis > 0) has too many scores in the tails and is too peaked, whereas a distribution with negative kurtosis (*platykurtic*, kurtosis < 0) has too few scores in the tails and is quite flat.

Latin square design: a method for *counterbalancing* tasks using a Latin square, which is an *n* by *n* grid of symbols where every symbol appears exactly once in every row and column location. Imagine you have three tasks, *A*, *B*, and *C*. The number of tasks is *n* so this leaves you with a 3 × 3 grid (3 rows by 3 columns). The rows represent different counterbalancing orders, and the columns represent the tasks to be performed. The first group performs the task in the order *ABC*. The order for the second group is determined by placing the last task of the previous order at the beginning and moving the other tasks to the right. Therefore, the second group performs the tasks in the order *CAB*. The final group's order is again determined by placing the last task of the previous order at the beginning and moving the other tasks to the right. Therefore, they perform the tasks in order *BCA*. Note that each task appears once as the first task, once as the middle task and once as the final task. As such, the order of tasks is counterbalanced. More complex grids can be used for four or more tasks.

$$
\begin{array}{ccc}
A & B & C \\
C & A & B \\
B & C & A
\end{array}
$$

Leptokurtic: see *Kurtosis*.

Levels of measurement: the relationship between what is being measured and the numbers obtained on a scale.

Levene's test: tests the hypothesis that the variances in different groups are equal (i.e., the difference between the variances is zero). It basically does a one-way ANOVA on the *deviations* (i.e., the absolute value of the difference between each score and the mean of its group). A significant result indicates that the variances are significantly different – therefore, the assumption of *homogeneity of variances* has been violated. When samples sizes are large, small differences in group variances can produce a significant Levene's test.

Likelihood: When using *Bayes' theorem* to test a hypothesis, the likelihood is the probability that the observed data could be produced given the hypothesis or model being considered,

p(data|model). It is the inverse conditional probability of the *posterior probability*. See also *marginal likelihood*.

Likelihood ratio test: in a general sense likelihood ratio tests are used to compare models using maximum-likelihood estimation. A special case is when the test is used in place of the *chi-square test* to evaluate the hypothesis that two categorical variables are related.

Linear model: a model that is based upon a straight line. It can be described by the equation

$$_i = b_0 + b_1 X_{1i} + b_2 X_{2i} + \ldots + b_n X_{ni} + \text{error}_i$$

Line graph: a graph in which a summary statistic (usually the mean) is plotted on the y-axis against a categorical variable on the x-axis (this categorical variable could represent, for example, groups of people, different times or different experimental conditions). The value of the mean for each category is shown by a symbol, and means across categories are connected by a line. Different-coloured lines may be used to represent levels of a second categorical variable.

Longitudinal research: a form of research in which you observe what naturally goes on in the world without directly interfering with it, by measuring several variables at multiple time points. See also *correlational research*, *cross-sectional research*.

Lower quartile: the value that cuts off the lowest 25% of the data. If the data are ordered and then divided into two halves at the median, then the lower quartile is the median of the lower half of the scores. It is also known as the first quartile.

M-estimator: a robust measure of location. One example is the median. In some cases it is a measure of location computed after outliers have been removed; unlike a *trimmed mean*, the amount of trimming used to remove outliers is determined empirically.

Marginal likelihood (evidence): When using *Bayes' theorem* to test a hypothesis, the marginal likelihood (sometimes called evidence) is the probability of the observed data, p(data). See also *likelihood*.

Matched-pairs t-test: another name for the *paired-samples t-test* (and also the *dependent t-test*).

Mauchly's test: a test of the assumption of *sphericity*. If this test is significant then the assumption of *sphericity* has not been met and an appropriate correction should be applied to the *degrees of freedom* of the *F-ratio* in *repeated-measures ANOVA*. The test works by comparing the *variance–covariance matrix* of the data to an *identity matrix*; if the variance–covariance matrix is a scalar multiple of an *identity matrix* then sphericity is met.

Mean: a simple statistical model of the centre of a distribution of scores. A hypothetical estimate of the 'typical' score. It is the sum of observed scores divided by the number of observed scores.

Mean squares: a measure of average variability. For every *sum of squares* (which measure the total variability) it is possible to create mean squares by dividing by the number of things used to calculate the sum of squares (or some function of it).

Measurement error: the discrepancy between the numbers used to represent the thing that we're measuring and the actual value of the thing we're measuring (i.e., the value we would get if we could measure it directly).

Median: the middle score of a set of ordered observations. When there is an even number of observations the median is the average of the two scores that fall either side of what would be the middle value.

Meta-analysis: this is a statistical procedure for assimilating research findings. It is based on the simple idea that we can take *effect sizes* from individual studies that research the same question, quantify the observed effect in a standard way (using effect sizes) and then combine these effects to get a more accurate idea of the true effect in the population.

Method of least squares: a method of estimating parameters (such as the *mean*, or a regression coefficient) that is based on minimizing the *sum of squared errors*. The parameter estimate will be the value, out of all of those possible, which has the smallest *sum of squared errors*.

Mixed normal distribution: a normal-looking distribution that is contaminated by a small proportion of scores from a different distribution. These distributions are not normal and have too many scores in the tails (i.e., at the extremes). The effect of these heavy tails is to inflate the estimate of the population variance. This, in turn, makes significance tests lack power.

Mode: the most frequently occurring score in a set of observations.

Model sum of squares, SS_M: a measure of the total amount of variability for which a model can account. It is the difference between the *total sum of squares* and the *residual sum of squares*.

Moderation: Moderation occurs when the relationship between two variables changes as a function of a third variable. For example, the relationship between watching horror films (predictor) and feeling scared at bedtime (outcome) might increase as a function of how vivid an imagination a person has (moderator).

Multicollinearity: a situation in which two or more variables are very closely linearly related.

Multilevel linear model: a linear model (just like regression, ANOVA, etc.) in which the hierarchical structure of the data is explicitly considered. In this analysis regression parameters can be fixed (as in regression and ANOVA) but also random (i.e., free to vary across different contexts at a higher level of the hierarchy). This means that for each regression parameter there is a fixed component but also an estimate of how much the parameter varies across contexts.

Multimodal: description of a distribution of observations that has more than two *modes*.

Multiple regression: a *linear model* in which an outcome is predicted by a linear combination of two or more predictor variables. The form of the model is:

$$_i = b_0 + b_1 X_{1i} + b_2 X_{2i} + \cdots + b_n X_{ni} + \varepsilon_i$$

in which the outcome is denoted as Y, and each predictor is denoted as X. Each predictor has a *regression coefficient*, or *parameter*, b, associated with it, and b_0 is the value of the outcome when all predictors are zero.

Mutually exclusive: in probability, outcomes are mutually exclusive or disjoint if they cannot co-occur. In other words, if the probability of their *intersection* is zero, $p(A \cap B) = 0$.

Negative kurtosis: see *Kurtosis*.

Negative skew: see *Skew*.

NHST: common abbreviation for *null hypothesis significance testing*.

Nominal scale: a scale on which numbers represent names. For example, the numbers on sports players shirts: a player with the number 1 on her back is not necessarily worse than a player with a 2 on her back. The numbers have no meaning other than denoting the type of player (full back, centre forward, etc.).

Noniles: a type of *quantile*; they are values that split the data into nine equal parts. They are commonly used in educational research.

Normal distribution: a *probability distribution* of a random variable that is known to have certain properties. It is perfectly symmetrical (has a *skew* of 0), and has a *kurtosis* of 3 (although some computer packages subtract 3 so that the value is 0 in a normal distribution). Technically, the distribution is described for any variable, v, with a mean of μ and a standard deviation of σ as:

$$f(v, \mu, \sigma) = \frac{1}{\sigma\sqrt{2\pi}} e^{-\frac{(v-\mu)^2}{2\sigma^2}}$$

But seriously, don't bother memorizing that, it won't impress anyone.

Null hypothesis: the reverse of the *experimental hypothesis* that your prediction is wrong and the predicted effect doesn't exist (i.e., it is zero). Essentially, this hypothesis is never true, but that doesn't stop lots of people from pretending that it might be.

Null hypothesis significance testing (NHST): a framework for establishing whether a hypothesis is true by working out the probability of observing a statistic at least as large as the one observed if the *null hypothesis* were true. If this probability is below 0.05, then the *null hypothesis* is rejected and the *alternative hypothesis* (i.e., that there is a significant effect) is accepted. Despite widespread use within science, this framework is so flawed that it led one eminent scientist to claim that calling it 'statistical hypothesis inference testing' would yield a more appropriate acronym.[59]

Odds: the probability of an event occurring divided by the probability of that event not occurring.

Odds ratio: the ratio of the *odds* of an event occurring in one group compared to another. So, for example, if the odds of understanding odds ratios after reading this glossary entry are 4, and the *odds* of understanding odds ratios if you don't read it are 0.25, then the odds ratio is 4/0.25 = 16. This means that the odds of understanding odds ratios after reading this glossary entry are 16 times higher than if you don't. Obviously they're not, I made the numbers up. An odds ratio of 1 would indicate that the *odds* of a particular outcome are equal in both groups.

Omega squared: an *effect size* measure associated with comparing several means. It is a (sometimes hideous) function of the *model sum of squares* and the *residual sum of squares* and isn't a lot of use because it quantifies the overall difference between lots of means and so can't be interpreted in a meaningful way. In all other respects it's great, though.

One-tailed test: a test of a directional hypothesis. For example, the hypothesis 'taking a stats test while pretending to be Florence Nightingale will lead to higher marks than taking the test as yourself' requires a one-tailed test because I've stated the direction of the relationship (see also *two-tailed test*). In general, don't do one-tailed tests.

Operational definition: a procedure (or set of procedures) for determining and quantifying the existence of something. In research, we usually want to quantify the existence of a *construct*. For example, the operational definition of the construct of anxiety in a study could be 'heart rate in response to an unpleasant picture', but in another study might be 'pressing a button to avoid an unpleasant picture'. As such, these operational definitions describe how the researcher has operationalized the measurement of the construct of anxiety.

Ordinal scale: a scale that tells us not only that things have occurred, but also the order in which they occurred. These data tell us nothing about the differences between values. For example, gold, silver and bronze medals are ordinal: they tell us that the gold medallist was better than the silver medallist, but they don't tell us how much better (was gold a lot better than silver, or were gold and silver very closely competed?).

Ordinate: the vertical axis of a *graph*. Also known as the *y*-axis.

Orthogonal: means perpendicular (at right angles) to something. It tends to be equated to *independence* in statistics because of the connotation that perpendicular *linear models* in geometric space are completely independent (one is not influenced by the other).

Outcome: a measurable result of some process. For example, if you toss a coin the outcome will be that it lands face up or face down, and if you take an exam the outcome might be your mark.

Outcome variable: a variable whose values we are trying to predict from one or more *predictor variables*.

Outlier: an observation or observations very different from most others. Outliers bias statistics (e.g., the mean) and their standard errors and confidence intervals.

***p*-value:** the name often used for the probability of observing a *test statistic* at least as big as the one observed if the *null hypothesis* were true. It is used in *null hypothesis significance testing*.

Paired-samples *t*-test: a test using the *t-statistic* that establishes whether two means collected from the same sample (or related observations) differ significantly. Also known as the *dependent t-test* or *matched-pairs t-test*.

Pairwise comparisons: comparisons of pairs of means.

Parameter: a very difficult thing to describe. A parameter is something that summarizes a *population*. Statistical models have *variables* and parameters: variables are measured constructs that vary across entities in the sample, whereas parameters are estimated from the data and are (usually) constants believed to represent some fundamental truth about the relations between variables. Of course it's not quite as simple as that. The word also works as a good replacement for 'Mah Nà Mah Nà' in the 'Mah Nà Mah Nà' song made famous by The Muppets: 1, 2, 3 … 'Para-meter … doo, do, be-do-do … Para-meter .. do do do do …' OK, enough of that.

Partial correlation: a measure of the relationship between two variables while adjusting for the effect of one or more additional variables on both.

Pearson's correlation coefficient: or Pearson's product-moment correlation coefficient, to give it its full name, is a *standardized* measure of the strength of linear relationship between two variables. It can take any value from −1 (as one variable changes, the other changes in the opposite direction by the same amount), through 0 (as one variable changes the other doesn't change at all), to +1 (as one variable changes, the other changes in the same direction by the same amount).

Percentage bend correlation: a *robust statistic* to measure the linear relationship between two variables (in place of the *Pearson correlation coefficient*).

Percentile bootstrap confidence interval: a *confidence interval* constructed empirically by taking several (e.g., 1000) bootstrap samples, estimating the parameter of interest in each one, and noting the limits within which a certain percentage (usually 95%) of estimates fall. See also *Bias corrected and accelerated (BCa) confidence interval*.

Percentiles: are a type of *quantile*; they are values that split the data into 100 equal parts.

Perfect collinearity: exists when at least one predictor in a *regression model* is a perfect linear combination of the others (the simplest example being two predictors that are perfectly correlated – they have a *correlation coefficient* of 1).

Planned comparisons: another name for *planned contrasts*.

Planned contrasts: a set of comparisons between group means that are constructed before any data are collected. These are theory-led comparisons and are based on the idea of partitioning the variance created by the overall effect of group differences into gradually smaller portions of variance. These tests have more power than *post hoc tests*.

Platykurtic: see *Kurtosis*.

Point-biserial correlation: a standardized measure of the strength of relationship between two variables when one of the two variables is *dichotomous*. The point-biserial correlation coefficient is used when the dichotomy is discrete, or true, dichotomy (i.e., one for which there is no underlying continuum between the categories). An example of this is pregnancy: you can be either pregnant or not, there is no in between.

Point estimate: using a single value, or point, to estimate the likely value of an unknown quantity. Compare with *interval estimate*.

Population: in statistical terms, this usually refers to the collection of units (be they people, plankton, plants, cities, suicidal authors, etc.) to which we want to generalize a set of findings or a statistical model.

Population mean: the *mean* of an entire *population* of scores.

Positive kurtosis: see *Kurtosis*.

Positive skew: see *Skew*.

Posterior odds: the ratio of *posterior probability* for one hypothesis to another. In Bayesian hypothesis testing the posterior odds are the ratio of the probability of the alternative hypothesis given the data, $p(\text{alternative}|\text{data})$, divided by the probability of the null hypothesis given the data, $p(\text{null}|\text{data})$.

Posterior probability: When using *Bayes' theorem* to test a hypothesis, the posterior probability, is our belief in a hypothesis or model *after* we have considered the data, $p(\text{model}|\text{data})$. This is the value that we are usually interested in knowing. It is the inverse conditional probability of the *likelihood*.

***Post hoc* tests:** a set of comparisons between group means that were not thought of before data were collected. Typically these tests involve comparing the means of all combinations of pairs of groups. To compensate for the number of tests conducted, each test uses a strict criterion for significance. As such, they tend to have less power than *planned contrasts*. They are usually used for exploratory work for which no firm hypotheses were available on which to base planned contrasts.

Power: the ability of a test to detect an effect of a particular size (a value of 0.8 is a good level to aim for).

Practice effect: refers to the possibility that participants' performance in a task may be influenced (positively or negatively) if they repeat the task because of familiarity with the experimental situation and/or the measures being used.

Precision: in science generally, precision is the degree to which you get the same results when you measure something under the same conditions. In statistics, precision has a specific definition of 1/*variance*, which quantifies the error around a *statistic* (remember that the variance is a gauge of how representative a statistic is of the data it represents, so large variance means more error and less precision). The term is used generally to refer to the extent to which a statistic represents what it is supposed to represent. For example, a precise statistic is one with low variance and, therefore, a narrow confidence interval, suggesting that it is relatively representative of the sample data and is close to the parameter it estimates; conversely, an imprecise statistic is one with high variance and a wide confidence interval, suggesting that it is unrepresentative of the sample data and could be quite different than the parameter it estimates.

Predicted value: the value of an outcome variable based on specific values of the predictor variable or variables being placed into a statistical model.

Predictive validity: a form of *criterion validity* where there is evidence that scores from an instrument predict external measures (recorded at a different point in time) conceptually related to the measured construct.

Predictor variable: a variable that is used to try to predict values of another variable known as an *outcome variable*.

Prior odds: the ratio of the probability of one hypothesis/model compared to a second. In Bayesian hypothesis testing, the prior odds are the probability of the *alternative hypothesis*, p(alternative), divided by the probability of the *null hypothesis*, p(null). The prior odds should reflect your belief in the alternative hypothesis relative to the null *before* you look at the data.

Prior probability: When using *Bayes' theorem* to test a hypothesis, the prior probability is our belief in a hypothesis or model before, or prior to, considering the data, p(model). See also *posterior probability, likelihood, marginal likelihood.*

Probability (p): the probability of an event, p(event), is the number of times the event occurs divided by the total number of possible events (i.e., the *sample space*).

Probability density function: the function that describes the probability of a random variable taking a certain value. It is the mathematical function that describes the *probability distribution.*

Probability distribution: a curve describing an idealized *frequency distribution* of a particular variable from which it is possible to ascertain the probability with which specific values of that variable will occur. For categorical variables it is simply a formula yielding the probability with which each category occurs.

Programmable matter: matter that can change from one physical form to another; so, a bit like the liquid metal T-1000 in *Terminator 2* that can change shape. It's more of a reality than you might think.

Proportion: although this is not the formal mathematical definition, a proportion in statistics usually quantifies the portion of all measured data in a particular category in a *scale of measurement*. In other words, it is the frequency of a particular score/category relative to the total number of scores:

$$\frac{\text{frequency of score}/\text{category}}{\text{total number of observations}} = \frac{f}{N}$$

Qualitative methods: extrapolating evidence for a theory from what people say or write. Contrast with *quantitative methods*.

Quantiles: values that split a data set into equal portions. *Quartiles*, for example, are a special case of quantiles that split the data into four equal parts. Similarly, *percentiles* are points that split the data into 100 equal parts and *noniles* are points that split the data into 9 equal parts (you get the general idea).

Quantitative methods: inferring evidence for a theory through measurement of variables that produce numeric outcomes. Contrast with *qualitative methods*.

Quartiles: a generic term for the three values that cut an ordered data set into four equal parts. The three quartiles are known as the *lower* (or first) *quartile*, the second quartile (or *median*) and the *upper* (or third) *quartile*.

Quasi-experimental design: A research design in which the experimenter has no control over either the allocation of participants to conditions, or the timing of the experimental manipulations.

Random sample: if the entities in a *population* or *sample space* have an equal chance of being selected then a *sample* resulting from this selection process is a random sample.

Range: the range of scores is value of the smallest score subtracted from the highest score. It is a measure of the dispersion of a set of scores. See also *variance*, *standard deviation*, and *interquartile range*.

Ranking: the process of transforming raw scores into numbers that represent their position in an ordered list of those scores. The raw scores are ordered from lowest to highest and the lowest score is assigned a rank of 1, the next highest score is assigned a rank of 2, and so on.

Ratio scale: an *interval scale*, but with the additional property that 0 is a meaningful value and, therefore, ratios on the scale are also meaningful. Imagine that we measure knowledge of statistics after reading this book on a scale from 0 to 10. To treat this scale as ratio it would need to be the case that a difference in statistical knowledge between people scoring 1 and 2, for example, was equivalent to the difference between two people scoring 7 and 8. In addition, a score of 0 would have to plausibly equate to a complete absence of statistical knowledge and, therefore, someone scoring 10 would know twice as much as someone scoring 4 (as indeed would someone scoring 6 compared to someone scoring 3). You get the gist.

Raw score: another name for a *score*, used to indicate that the score is expressed in its original units of measurement (i.e., has not undergone a *transformation*).

Regression coefficient: see b_i and β_i.

Regression line: a line on a scatterplot representing the *regression model* of the relationship between the two variables plotted.

Regression model: see *multiple regression*, *simple regression*.

Related design: another name for a *repeated-measures design*.

Relative frequency: the frequency of a score, range of scores or category expressed relative to the total number of observations:

$$\frac{\text{frequency of response}}{\text{total number of responses}} = \frac{f}{N}$$

Reliability: the ability of a measure to produce consistent results when the same entities are measured under different conditions.

Repeated-measures design: an experimental design in which different treatment conditions utilize the same entities (in psychology, this would mean the same people take part in all experimental conditions) and so the resulting data are related. Also known as *related design* or *within-subject design*.

Residual: The difference between the value a model predicts and the value observed in the data on which the model is based. Basically, an error. When the residual is calculated for each observation in a data set the resulting collection is referred to as the *residuals*. See also *deviance*.

Residual sum of squares, SS_R: a measure of the variability that cannot be explained by the model fitted to the data. It is the total squared *deviance* between the observations, and the value of those observations predicted by whatever model is fitted to the data.

Response bias: a general term for participants giving responses that do not necessarily reflect their true beliefs. This can take the form of giving responses that they think the researcher wants, giving socially acceptable responses rather than their less socially acceptable beliefs, or response acquiescence where the participant agrees with survey questions without really thinking.

Reverse phrasing: normally questions on a survey are phrased so that a large response represents more of the construct being measured. For example, a questionnaire measuring boredom might include an item 'Writing glossary entries is indescribably tedious'. Reverse phrasing is where a question is phrased oppositely such that a low score would represent more of the construct being measured. For example, one reverse-phrased variant of the previous example might be 'Writing glossary entries is indescribably stimulating'. The more someone endorses that item, the *less* bored they are (and the more mentally ill).

Reverse scoring: when *reverse phrasing* is used, responses on those items need to be 'flipped' so that high scores on the same questionnaire items consistently represent more of the construct being measured. This is done by subtracting the score on a reverse-phrased item from the maximum score for that item plus the minimum score. Imagine an item where five responses are possible (0, 1, 2, 3, 4). The maximum plus minimum score is 4 + 0 = 4. Reversing the scores is therefore achieved by subtracting each score from 4, so 0 becomes 4 (4 − 0 = 4), 1 becomes 3 (4 − 1 = 3), 2 stays as 2 (4 − 2 = 2), 3 becomes 1 (4 − 3 = 1), and 4 becomes 0 (4 − 4 = 0). If the scale had ranged from 1 to 5 (instead of 0 to 4), then the maximum plus minimum score is 5 + 1 = 6. Reversing the scores is therefore achieved by subtracting each score from 6, so 1 becomes 5 (6 − 1 = 5), 2 becomes 4 (6 − 2 = 4), 3 stays as 3 (6 − 3 = 3), 4 becomes 2 (6 − 4 = 2), and 5 becomes 1 (6 − 5 = 1).

Robust estimation: A term applied to procedures to estimate *statistics* or the *standard errors* and *confidence intervals* of statistics that are not unduly biased by the shape of the *probability distribution* or *outliers* and extreme scores.

Sample: a smaller (but hopefully representative) collection of units from a *population* used to determine truths about that population (e.g., how a given population behaves in certain conditions).

Sample mean: the *mean* of a *sample* of scores.

Sample space: in *classical probability* theory, the sample space is the set of possible outcomes that can occur for a given *trial* of an *experiment*. In *empirical probability* theory, the sample space is the set of observed outcomes of several trials of an *experiment*.

Sampling distribution: the *probability distribution* of a statistic. We can think of this as follows: if we take a *sample* from a *population* and calculate some statistic (e.g., the *mean*), the value of this statistic will depend somewhat on the sample we took. As such the statistic will vary slightly from sample to sample. If, hypothetically, we took lots and lots of samples from the population and calculated the statistic of interest, we could create a frequency distribution of the values we got. The resulting distribution is what the sampling distribution represents: the distribution of possible values of a given statistic that we could expect to get from a given population.

Sampling error: the difference between the value of a population *parameter*, and the value estimated from the *sample*.

Sampling variation: the extent to which a statistic (the mean, median, *t*, *F*, etc.) varies in samples taken from the same population.

Sampling with replacement: when a *sample* is constructed from a *population* or *sample space* such that after an entity is selected to be in the *sample*, it is put back into the *population* or *sample space* so that it can be selected to be in the sample on a subsequent occasion.

Sampling without replacement: when a *sample* is constructed from a *population* or *sample space* such that after an entity is selected to be in the *sample*, it is taken out of the *population* or *sample space* so that it cannot be selected to be in the sample on a subsequent occasion.

Scales of measurement: see *levels of measurement*.

Scatterplot: a graph that plots values of one variable against the corresponding value of another variable.

Scores: a score is a measurement or observation of a single instance of a *variable*. Scores are a collection of measurements or observations of many instances of a *variable*. See also *raw score*.

Shapiro–Wilk test: a test of whether a distribution of scores is significantly different from a *normal distribution*. A significant value indicates a deviation from normality, but this test is notoriously affected by large samples in which small deviations from normality yield significant results.

Simple effects analysis: this analysis looks at the effect of one *independent variable* (categorical *predictor variable*) at individual levels of another *independent variable*.

Simple regression: a *linear model* in which one variable or outcome is predicted from a single predictor variable. The model takes the form:

$$Y_i = b_0 + b_1 X_{1i} + \varepsilon_i$$

in which Y is the outcome variable, X is the predictor, b_1 is the regression coefficient associated with the predictor and b_0 is the value of the outcome when the predictor is zero.

Simultaneous entry regression: see *forced entry regression*.

Skew: a measure of the symmetry of a *frequency distribution*. Symmetrical distributions have a skew of 0. When the frequent scores are clustered at the lower end of the distribution and the tail points towards the higher or more positive scores, the value of skew is positive. Conversely, when the frequent scores are clustered at the higher end of the distribution and the tail points towards the lower more negative scores, the value of skew is negative.

Spazcore: A genre of music typified by frequent rhythm and tempo changes that make the songs sound unstructured and chaotic (and very difficult to play!). Examples would be The Dillinger Escape Plan and The Locust.

Spearman's rho: a standardized measure of the strength of relationship between two variables that does not rely on the assumptions of the *linear model*. It is *Pearson's correlation coefficient* calculated on data that have been converted into ranked scores.

Sphericity: the assumption that the variances of the differences between scores from the same entity across different treatments are equal. This assumption is most commonly found in *repeated-measures ANOVA*, but applies only where there are more than two points of data from the same participant. See also *Greenhouse–Geisser estimate, Huynh–Feldt estimate*.

Standard deviation: an estimate of the average variability (spread) of a set of scores around the mean expressed in the same units of measurement as the raw scores. It is the square root of the *variance*.

Standard error: the standard deviation of the *sampling distribution* of a statistic. For a given statistic (e.g., the *mean*), it tells us how much variability there is in this statistic across *samples* from the same *population*. Large values, therefore, indicate that a statistic from a given sample may not be an accurate reflection of the population from which the sample came.

Standard error of differences: if we were to take several pairs of samples from a population and calculate their means, then we could also calculate the difference between their means. If we plotted these differences between sample means as a *frequency distribution*, we would have the *sampling distribution* of differences. The standard deviation of this sampling distribution is the *standard error of differences*. As such it is a measure of the variability of differences between sample means.

Standard error of the mean: the *standard error* associated with the *mean*. Did you really need a glossary entry to work that out?

Standard normal distribution: a normal distribution of a standardized variable (i.e., z-scores); it has a mean (μ) of 0, and a standard deviation (σ) of 1.

Standardization: the process of converting a variable into a standard unit of measurement. The unit of measurement typically used is *standard deviation* units (see also *z-scores*). Standardization allows us to compare data when different units of measurement have been used (we could compare weight measured in kilograms to height measured in inches).

Standardized distribution: a standardized distribution is a version of a distribution of *raw scores* where the scores have been transformed to yield specific values of the *mean* (μ) and *standard deviation* (σ). Standardized distributions are usually used to make incomparable distributions comparable.

Standardized regression coefficient: indicates the strength of relationship between a given predictor, X_i, and an outcome in a *standardized* form. It is the change in the outcome (in standard deviations) associated with a one standard deviation change in the predictor.

Statistics: a statistic is something that summarizes a *sample* of scores. It is usually computed from the sample data and is sometimes used to estimate the corresponding *parameter* in the population.

Stepwise regression: a method of *multiple regression* in which *predictor variables* are entered into the model based on a statistical criterion (the semi-partial correlation with the outcome variable). Once a new predictor is entered into the model, all predictors in the model are assessed to see whether they should be removed.

Sum of squared errors: another name for the *sum of squares*.

Sum of squares (SS): an estimate of total variability (spread) of a set of observations around a parameter (such as the *mean*). First the *deviance* for each score is calculated, and then this value is squared. The SS is the sum of these squared deviances.

Systematic variation: variation due to some genuine effect (be that the effect of an experimenter doing something to all of the participants in one sample but not in other samples, or natural variation between sets of variables). We can think of this as variation that can be explained by the model that we have fitted to the data.

***t*-distribution:** a family of *probability distributions* describing samples taken from a population that is normally distributed. The shapes of the distributions are similar to normal in that they are symmetrical and bell-shaped. However, the exact shape of the distribution is determined by the *degrees of freedom*, which are the sample size minus 1 ($n - 1$). As the degrees of freedom increase, the distribution gets closer to a normal distribution until it approximates it at about 30 degrees of freedom.

Tedium: what you experience when trying to write a chapter on *z*-scores – actually that might be utter tedium or possibly super-tedium, but it certainly involves some level of tedium that no one should have to endure.

Tertium quid: the possibility that an apparent relationship between two variables is actually caused by the effect of a third variable on them both (often called *the third-variable problem*).

Test–retest reliability: the ability of a measure to produce consistent results when the same entities are tested at two different points in time.

Test statistic: a statistic for which we know how frequently different values occur. The observed value of such a statistic is typically used to test *hypotheses*.

Theory: although it can be defined more formally, a theory is a hypothesized general principle or set of principles that explain known findings about a topic and from which new hypotheses can be generated. Theories have typically been well-substantiated by repeated testing.

Three-way design: an experimental design incorporating three categorical *predictors* (or *independent variables*).

Tolerance: tolerance statistics measure *multicollinearity* and are simply the reciprocal of the *variance inflation factor* (1/VIF). Values below 0.1 indicate serious problems, although Menard[91] suggests that values below 0.2 are worthy of concern.

Total sum of squares, SS_T: a measure of the total variability within a set of observations. It is the total squared *deviance* between each observation and the overall mean of all observations.

Transformation: the process of applying a mathematical function to all observations in a data set; for example, to correct some distributional abnormality such as *skew* or *kurtosis*, or converting to a *z*-score.

Trial: in probability theory, a trial is a repetition of an *experiment*.

Trimmed data: Data after a certain percentage of the distribution has been removed at the extremes. For example, 20% trimmed data would remove the top and bottom 20% of ordered scores. Imagine we had 20 scores representing the annual income of students (in thousands), rounded to the nearest thousand: 0, 1, 2, 2, 3, 3, 3, 3, 3, 4, 4, 4, 4, 4, 4, 4, 4, 4, 40. A 10% trim removes 10% of scores from the top and bottom. With 20 scores, removing 10% of scores involves removing the top and bottom 2 scores. This gives us: 2, 2, 3, 3, 3, 3, 3, 4, 4, 4, 4, 4, 4, 4, 4, 4.

Trimmed mean: a statistic used in many *robust tests*. It is a mean calculated using *trimmed data*. For example, a 20% trimmed mean is a mean calculated after the top and bottom 20% of ordered scores have been removed. Imagine we had 20 scores representing the annual income of students (in thousands), rounded to the nearest thousand: 0, 1, 2, 2, 3, 3, 3, 3, 3, 4, 4, 4, 4, 4, 4, 4, 4, 4, 40. The mean income is 5 (£5000), which is biased by an outlier. A 10% trimmed mean will remove 10% of scores from the top and bottom of ordered scores before the mean is calculated. With 20 scores, removing 10% of scores involves removing the top and bottom 2 scores. This gives us: 2, 2, 3, 3, 3, 3, 3, 4, 4, 4, 4, 4, 4, 4, 4, 4, the mean of which is 3.44. The mean depends on a symmetrical distribution to be accurate, but a trimmed mean produces accurate results even when the distribution is not symmetrical. There are more complex examples of robust methods such as the *bootstrap*.

Two-tailed test: a test of a non-directional hypothesis. For example, the hypothesis 'taking a stats test while pretending to be Florence Nightingale will lead to different marks than taking the test as yourself' requires a two-tailed test because it does not suggest the direction of the relationship, i.e., whether marks will be higher or lower when the test is taken as Florence. See also *one-tailed test*.

Two-way design: an experimental design incorporating two categorical *predictors* (or *independent variables*).

Type I error: occurs when we believe that there is a genuine effect in our population, when in fact there isn't.

Type II error: occurs when we believe that there is no effect in the population when, in reality, there is.

Unbiased estimator: a statistic from a sample that equals the corresponding population parameter. For example, a sample mean that is equal to the population mean.

Union: The probability of one outcome or another occurring is the probability of the union. The probability of the union of two outcomes A and B would be denoted as $p(A \cup B)$, meaning the probability of A or B occurring, but not both. Compare with *intersection*.

Unsystematic variation: this is variation that is not due to the effect in which we are interested (so could be due to natural differences between people in different samples, such as differences in intelligence or motivation). We can think of this as variation that cannot be explained by whatever model we have fitted to the data.

Upper quartile: the value that cuts off the highest 25% of ordered scores. If the scores are ordered and then divided into two halves at the median, then the upper quartile is the median of the top half of the scores. It is also known as the third quartile.

Validity: evidence that a study allows correct inferences about the question it was aimed to answer or that a test measures what it set out to measure conceptually. See also *concurrent validity, content validity, criterion validity, face validity, predictive validity*.

Variables: anything that can be measured and can differ across entities or across time.

Variance: an estimate of average variability (spread) of a set of scores. In a *sample*, it is the *sum of squares* divided by the number of values on which the sum of squares is based, or, if trying to estimate the value in the population, the sum of squares is divided by the number of values on which the sum of squares is based minus 1.

Variance inflation factor (VIF): a measure of *multicollinearity*. The VIF indicates whether a predictor has a strong linear relationship with the other predictor(s). Myers[90] suggests that a value of 10 is a good value at which to worry. Bowerman and O'Connell[89] suggest that if the average VIF is greater than 1, then multicollinearity may be biasing the regression model.

Variance ratio: see *Hartley's F_{max}*.

Weight: a number by which something (usually a variable in statistics) is multiplied. The weight assigned to a variable determines the influence that variable has within a mathematical equation: large weights give the variable a lot of influence.

Welch's F: a version of the F-ratio designed to be accurate when the assumption of *homogeneity of variance* has been violated. See also *Brown–Forsythe F*.

WGA: acronym for the World Governance Agency, which at the time of the story is a single government body that regulates the planet.

Winsorizing: a method for reducing the impact of extreme scores and *outliers*. Although there are different ways to implement winsorizing, the basic idea is to replace the most extreme scores with the next highest score in the data set. The most common implementations are to replace a fixed percentage of scores at the extreme (e.g., 10%) or to identify scores that are extreme and replace only those. Compare this approach with *trimmed data*; using the same data (0, 1, 2, 2, 3, 3, 3, 3, 3, 4, 4, 4, 4, 4, 4, 4, 4, 4, 4, 40), a 10% winsorization entails replacing the bottom 10% (the 2 scores of 0 and 1) with the next lowest score in the data (2), and the top 10% (the 2 scores of 4 and 40) with the next highest (4). This would give us 2, 2, 2, 2, 3, 3, 3, 3, 3, 4, 4, 4, 4, 4, 4, 4, 4, 4, 4. A different approach would be to identify the score of 40 as the only extreme and replace this score with the next lowest in the data set, giving us 0, 1, 2, 2, 3, 3, 3, 3, 3, 4, 4, 4, 4, 4, 4, 4, 4, 4, 4.

Within-subject design: another name for a *repeated-measures design*.

x-axis: the horizontal axis of a *graph*. Also known as the *abscissa*.

y-axis: the vertical axis of a *graph*. Also known as the *ordinate*.

Yates's continuity correction: an adjustment made to the *chi-square test* when the *contingency table* is 2 rows by 2 columns (i.e., there are two categorical variables both of which consist of only two categories). In large samples the adjustment makes little difference and is slightly dubious anyway.

z-score: the value of an observation expressed in standard deviation units. The sign of the score indicates whether it is above (positive) or below (negative) the mean, and the value quantifies how many standard deviations the score is from the mean. A z-score is calculated by taking the observation, subtracting from it the mean of all observations, and dividing the result by the standard deviation of all observations. By converting a distribution of observations into z-scores a new distribution is created that has a mean of 0 and a standard deviation of 1.

References

1. Knaian, A. N. (2013). Programmable matter. *Physics Today*, *66*, 64–65.
2. Wiley, J. (2013). Just a few minutes a day on a mobile phone 'raises cancer risk'. *Daily Express*, 31 July.
3. Macrea, F. (2011). Mobile phones may cause cancer, warn world health chiefs: After years of contradictory claims, an authoritative verdict. *Daily Mail*, 1 June.
4. Berl, R. P. (2013). Cellphone use and cancer: New study suggests a link. *US News and World Report*, 5 August.
5. Freeman, D. W. (2011). Mobile phones may cause cancer, experts say. CBS News, 31 May.
6. Gallagher, J. (2011). Mobiles 'may cause brain cancer'. BBC News, 31 May.
7. Feingold, A. (1992). Good-looking people are not what we think. *Psychological Bulletin*, *111*, 304–341.
8. Hume, D. (1965) [1739–1740]. *A treatise of human nature* (ed. L. A. Selby-Bigge). Oxford: Clarendon Press.
9. Hume, D. (1927) [1748]. *An enquiry concerning human understanding*. Chicago: Open Court.
10. Mill, J. S. (1865). *A system of logic: ratiocinative and inductive*. London: Longmans, Green.
11. Field, A. P. (2013). *Discovering statistics using IBM SPSS Statistics: And sex and drugs and rock 'n' roll* (4th ed.). London: Sage.
12. Zhang, S., Schmader, T., & Hall, W. M. (2013). L'eggo my ego: Reducing the gender gap in math by unlinking the self from performance. *Self and Identity*, *12*, 400–412.
13. Myung, S.-K., Ju, W., McDonnell, D. D., et al. (2009). Mobile phone use and risk of tumors: A meta-analysis. *Journal of Clinical Oncology*, *27*, 5565–5572.
14. Goldacre, B. (2008). *Bad Science*. London: HarperPerennial.
15. Galton, F. (1869). *Hereditary genius: An inquiry into its laws and consequences*. London: Macmillan.
16. Bandura, A., Ross, D., & Ross, S. A. (1961). Transmission of aggression through the imitation of aggressive models. *Journal of Abnormal and Social Psychology*, *63*, 575–582.
17. Paivio, A. (1971). *Imagery and verbal processes*. New York: Holt, Rinehart, and Winston.
18. Piaget, J. (1953) [1936]. *The origin of intelligence in the child*. London: Routledge & Kegan Paul.
19. Opeth (2014). Faith in others. On *Pale Communion* [CD]. New York: Roadrunner Records.
20. Hendrick, S. S., Dicke, A., & Hendrick, C. (1998). The Relationship Assessment Scale. *Journal of Social and Personal Relationships*, *15*, 137–142.
21. Billig, M. (1997). Rhetorical and discursive analysis: How families talk about the royal family. In N. Hayes (Ed.), *Doing qualitative analysis in psychology* (pp. 39–54). Hove: Psychology Press.
22. Laeng, B., & Falkenberg, L. (2007). Women's pupillary responses to sexually significant others during the hormonal cycle. *Hormones and Behavior*, *52*, 520–530.
23. Ha, T., Overbeek, G., & Engels, R. C. M. E. (2010). Effects of attractiveness and social status on dating desire in heterosexual adolescents: An experimental study. *Archives of Sexual Behavior*, *39*, 1063–1071.

24. DeCarlo, L. T. (1997). On the meaning and use of kurtosis. *Psychological Methods*, 2, 292–307.

25. Field, A. P., Miles J. N. V., & Field, Z. C. (2012). *Discovering statistics using R: And sex and drugs and rock 'n' roll*. London: Sage.

26. Tufte, E. R. (2001). *The visual display of quantitative information* (2nd ed.). Cheshire, CT: Graphics Press.

27. Raven, J., Raven, J. C., & Court, J. H. (1998). *Manual for Raven's Progressive Matrices and Vocabulary Scales. Section 1: General overview*. San Antonio, TX: Harcourt Assessment.

28. Carson, S., Peterson, J. B., & Higgins, D. M. (2005). Reliability, validity, and factor structure of the Creative Achievement Questionnaire. *Creativity Research Journal*, 17, 37–50.

29. Petrides, K. V., & Furnham, A. (2006). The role of trait emotional intelligence in a gender-specific model of organizational variables. *Journal of Applied Social Psychology*, 36, 552–569.

30. Smith, L., Ciarrochi, J., & Heaven, P. C. L. (2008). The stability and change of trait emotional intelligence, conflict communication patterns, and relationship satisfaction: A one-year longitudinal study. *Personality and Individual Differences*, 45, 738–743.

31. Field, A. P. (2010). Teaching statistics. In D. Upton & A. Trapp (Eds.), *Teaching psychology in higher education* (pp. 134–163). Chichester: Wiley-Blackwell.

32. Wilcox, R. R. (2010). *Fundamentals of modern statistical methods: Substantially improving power and accuracy*. New York: Springer.

33. Tukey, J. W. (1960). A survey of sampling from contaminated normal distributions. In I. Olkin, S. G. Ghurye, W. Hoeffding, W. G. Madow, & H. B. Mann (Eds.), *Contributions to probability and statistics: Essays in honor of Harold Hotelling, Issue 2* (pp. 448–485). Stanford, CA: Stanford University Press.

34. Wilcox, R. R. (2012). *Introduction to robust estimation and hypothesis testing* (3rd ed.). Burlington, MA: Elsevier.

35. Grayson, D. (2004). Some myths and legends in quantitative psychology. *Understanding Statistics*, 3, 101–134.

36. Efron, B., & Tibshirani, R. (1993). *An introduction to the bootstrap*. New York: Chapman & Hall.

37. Wright, D. B., London, K., & Field, A. P. (2011). Using bootstrap estimation and the plug-in principle for clinical psychology data. *Journal of Experimental Psychopathology*, 2, 252–270.

38. Neyman, J., & Pearson, E. S. (1933). On the problem of the most efficient tests of statistical hypotheses. *Philosophical Transactions of the Royal Society of London, Series A*, 231, 289–337.

39. Fisher, R. A. (1991) [1925]. *Statistical methods, experimental design, and scientific inference*. Oxford: Oxford University Press.

40. Salsburg, D. (2002). *The lady tasting tea: How statistics revolutionized science in the twentieth century*. New York: Owl Books.

41. Fisher, R. A. (1925). *Statistical methods for research workers*. Edinburgh: Oliver & Boyd.

42. Mather, K. R. A. (1951). Fisher's *Statistical Methods for Research Workers*: An appreciation. *Journal of the American Statistical Association*, 46, 51–54.

43. Yates, F. (1951). The influence of *Statistical Methods for Research Workers* on the development of the science of statistics. *Journal of the American Statistical Association*, 46, 19–34.

44. Lehmann, E. L. (1993). The Fisher, Neyman–Pearson theories of testing hypotheses: One theory or two? *Journal of the American Statistical Association*, 88, 1242–1249.

45. Karageorghis, C. I., & Priest, D.-L. (2012). Music in the exercise domain: A review and synthesis (Part I). *International Review of Sport and Exercise Psychology*, 5, 44–66.

46. Karageorghis, C. I., & Priest, D.-L. (2012). Music in the exercise domain: A review and synthesis (Part II). *International Review of Sport and Exercise Psychology*, 5, 67–84.

47. Lombardi, C. M., & Hurlbert, S. H. (2009). Misprescription and misuse of one-tailed tests. *Austral Ecology*, 34, 447–468.

48. Ruxton, G. D., & Neuhaeuser, M. (2010). When should we use one-tailed hypothesis testing? *Methods in Ecology and Evolution*, 1, 114–117.

49. Kimmel, H. D. (1957). Three criteria for the use of one-tailed tests. *Psychological Bulletin*, 54, 351–353.

50. Cohen, J. (1992). A power primer. *Psychological Bulletin*, 112, 155–159.

51. Howell, D. C. (2012). *Statistical methods for psychology*. (8th ed.). Belmont, CA: Wadsworth.

52. Cumming, G., & Finch, S. (2005). Inference by eye – Confidence intervals and how to read pictures of data. *American Psychologist, 60*, 170–180.

53. Cumming, G. (2012). *Understanding the new statistics: Effect sizes, confidence intervals, and meta-analysis.* New York: Routledge.

54. Tai, K., Zheng, X., & Narayanan, J. (2011). Touching a teddy bear mitigates negative effects of social exclusion to increase prosocial behavior. *Social Psychological and Personality Science, 2*, 618–626.

55. Koole, S. L., Sin, M. T. A., & Schneider, I. K. (2014). Embodied terror management: Interpersonal touch alleviates existential concerns among individuals with low self-esteem. *Psychological Science, 25*, 30–37.

56. Rosenberg, M. (1965). *Society and the adolescent self-image.* Princeton, NJ: Princeton University Press.

57. Kosfeld, M., Heinrichs, M., Zak, P. J., Fischbacher, U., & Fehr, E. (2005). Oxytocin increases trust in humans. *Nature, 435*, 673–676.

58. Ziliak, S. T., & McCloskey, D. N. (2008). *The cult of statistical significance: How the standard error costs us jobs, justice and lives.* Ann Arbor: University of Michigan Press.

59. Cohen, J. (1994). The earth is round ($p < .05$). *American Psychologist, 49*, 997–1003.

60. Cohen, J. (1990). Things I have learned (so far). *American Psychologist, 45*, 1304–1312.

61. Dienes, Z. (2011). Bayesian versus orthodox statistics: Which side are you on? *Perspectives on Psychological Science, 6*, 274–290.

62. Kruschke, J. K. (2013). Bayesian estimation supersedes the t test. *Journal of Experimental Psychology: General, 142*, 573–603.

63. Kruschke, J. K. (2010). Bayesian data analysis. *Wiley Interdisciplinary Reviews – Cognitive Science, 1*, 658–676.

64. Kruschke, J. K. (2010). What to believe: Bayesian methods for data analysis. *Trends in Cognitive Sciences, 14*, 293–300.

65. Cohen, J. (1988). *Statistical power analysis for the behavioural sciences* (2nd ed.). New York: Academic Press.

66. Baguley, T. (2004). Understanding statistical power in the context of applied research. *Applied Ergonomics, 35*, 73–80.

67. Lenth, R. V. (2001). Some practical guidelines for effective sample size determination. *American Statistician, 55*, 187–193.

68. McGrath, R. E., & Meyer, G. J. (2006). When effect sizes disagree: The case of r and d. *Psychological Methods, 11*, 386–401.

69. Cooper, H. M. (2010). *Research synthesis and meta-analysis: A step-by-step approach* (4th ed.). Thousand Oaks, CA: Sage.

70. Field, A. P. (2003). Can meta-analysis be trusted? *Psychologist, 16*, 642–645.

71. Field, A. P. (2005). Is the meta-analysis of correlation coefficients accurate when population correlations vary? *Psychological Methods, 10*, 444–467.

72. Field, A. P. (2012). Meta-analysis in clinical psychology research. In J. S. Comer & P. C. Kendall (Eds.), *The Oxford Handbook of Research Strategies for Clinical Psychology.* Oxford: Oxford University Press.

73. Field, A. P., & Gillett, R. (2010). How to do a meta-analysis. *British Journal of Mathematical and Statistical Psychology, 63*, 665–694.

74. Hedges, L. V., & Olkin, I. (1985). *Statistical methods for meta-analysis.* Orlando, FL: Academic Press.

75. Hunter, J. E., & Schmidt, F. L. (2004). *Methods of meta-analysis: Correcting error and bias in research findings* (2nd ed.). Newbury Park, CA: Sage.

76. Andrews, M., & Baguley, T. (2013). Prior approval: The growth of Bayesian methods in psychology. *British Journal of Mathematical and Statistical Psychology, 66*, 1–7.

77. Kruschke, J. K. (2011). *Doing Bayesian data analysis: A tutorial with R and BUGS.* Burlington, MA: Academic Press.

78. Stone, J. V. (2013). *Bayes' rule: A tutorial introduction to Bayesian analysis.* Sheffield: Sebtel Press.

79. Jeffreys, H. (1961). *Theory of probability* (3rd ed.). Oxford: Oxford University Press.

80. Zak, P. J. (2012). *The moral molecule: The source of love and prosperity*. New York: Dutton.

81. Berry, W. D. (1993). *Understanding regression assumptions*. Sage University Paper Series on Quantitative Applications in the Social Sciences, 07–092. Newbury Park, CA: Sage.

82. Gelman, A., & Hill, J. (2007). *Data analysis using regression and multilevel/hierarchical models*. Cambridge: Cambridge University Press.

83. Hayes, A. F., & Cai, L. (2007). Using heteroskedasticity-consistent standard error estimators in OLS regression: An introduction and software implementation. *Behavior Research Methods, 39,* 709–722.

84. Levene, H. (1960). Robust tests for equality of variances. In I. Olkin, S. G. Ghurye, W. Hoeffding, W. G. Madow, & H. B. Mann (Eds.), *Contributions to probability and statistics: Essays in honor of Harold Hotelling* (pp. 278–292). Stanford, CA: Stanford University Press.

85. Pearson, E. S., & Hartley, H. O. (1954). *Biometrika tables for statisticians, Volume I*. Cambridge: Cambridge University Press.

86. Lumley, T., Diehr, P., Emerson, S., & Chen, L. (2002). The importance of the normality assumption in large public health data sets. *Annual Review of Public Health, 23,* 151–169.

87. Nagasawa, M., Kikusui, T., Onaka, T., & Ohta, M. (2009). Dog's gaze at its owner increases owner's urinary oxytocin during social interaction. *Hormones and Behavior, 55,* 434–441.

88. McCullough, M. E., Churchland, P. S., & Mendez, A. J. (2013). Problems with measuring peripheral oxytocin: Can the data on oxytocin and human behavior be trusted? *Neuroscience and Biobehavioral Reviews, 37,* 1485–1492.

89. Bowerman, B. L., & O'Connell, R. T. (1990). *Linear statistical models: An applied approach* (2nd ed.). Belmont, CA: Duxbury.

90. Myers, R. (1990). *Classical and modern regression with applications* (2nd ed.). Boston: Duxbury.

91. Menard, S. (1995). *Applied logistic regression analysis*. Sage University Paper Series on Quantitative Applications in the Social Sciences, 07-106. Thousand Oaks, CA: Sage.

92. Mark, K. P., Janssen, E., & Milhausen, R. R. (2011). Infidelity in heterosexual couples: Demographic, interpersonal, and personality-related predictors of extradyadic sex. *Archives of Sexual Behavior, 40,* 971–982.

93. Fisher, R. A. (1922). On the interpretation of chi square from contingency tables, and the calculation of P. *Journal of the Royal Statistical Society, 85,* 87–94.

94. Pearson, K. (1900). On the criterion that a given system of deviations from the probable in the case of a correlated system of variables is such that it can be reasonably supposed to have arisen from random sampling. *Philosophical Magazine, 50,* 157–175.

95. R Core Team (2015). *R: A language and environment for statistical computing*. Vienna: R Foundation for Statistical Computing.

96. Love, J., Selker, R., Verhagen, A. J., et al. (2014). JASP (Version 0.4).

97. Kurdek, L. A. (1997). Relation between neuroticism and dimensions of relationship commitment: Evidence from gay, lesbian, and heterosexual couples. *Journal of Family Psychology,* 109–124.

98. Fisher, R. A. (1921). On the probable error of a coefficient of correlation deduced from a small sample. *Metron, 1,* 3–32.

99. Cook, R. D., & Weisberg, S. (1982). *Residuals and influence in regression*. New York: Chapman & Hall.

100. Sandvik, H., & Baerheim, A. (1994). Does garlic protect against vampires? An experimental study. *Tidsskrift for den Norske lægeforening: Tidsskrift for praktisk medicin, ny række, 114,* 3583–3586.

101. Kobayashi, M., & Pascual-Leone, A. (2003). Transcranial magnetic stimulation in neurology. *Lancet Neurology, 2,* 145–156.

102. Di Lorenzo, C., Tavernese, E., Lepre, C., et al. (2013). Influence of rTMS over the left primary motor cortex on initiation and performance of a simple movement executed with the contralateral arm in healthy volunteers. *Experimental Brain Research, 224,* 383–392.

103. Leitgeb, N. (2014). Cardiac fibrillation risk of Taser weapons. *Health Physics, 106,* 652–659.

104. Zipes, D. P. (2014). TASER electronic control devices can cause cardiac arrest in humans. *Circulation, 129,* 101–111.

105. Ho, J. D., Dawes, D. M., Chang, R. J., Nelson, R. S., & Miner, J. R. (2014). Physiologic effects of a new-generation conducted electrical weapon on human volunteers. *Journal of Emergency Medicine, 46,* 428–434.

106. Studenmund, A. H., & Cassidy, H. J. (1987). *Using econometrics: a practical guide*. Boston: Little, Brown.

107. Miles, J. N. V., & Shevlin, M. (2001). *Applying regression and correlation: A guide for students and researchers*. London: Sage.

108. Liang, F., Paulo, R., Molina, G., Clyde, M. A., & Berger, J. O. (2008). Mixtures of *g* priors for Bayesian variable selection. *Journal of the American Statistical Association*, *103*, 410–423.

109. Rouder, J. N., & Morey, R. D. (2012). Default Bayes factors for model selection in regression. *Multivariate Behavioral Research*, *47*, 877–903.

110. MacCallum, R. C., Zhang, S., Preacher, K. J., & Rucker, D. D. (2002). On the practice of dichotomization of quantitative variables. *Psychological Methods*, *7*, 19–40.

111. DeCoster, J., Gallucci, M., & Iselin, A.-M. R. (2011). Best practices for using median splits, artificial categorization, and their continuous alternatives. *Journal of Experimental Psychopathology*, *2*, 197–209.

112. DeCoster, J., Iselin, A.-M. R., & Gallucci, M. (2009). A conceptual and empirical examination of justifications for dichotomization. *Psychological Methods*, *14*, 349–366.

113. Morey, R. D., & Rouder, J. N. (2014). BayesFactor: Computation of Bayes factors for common designs. R package version 0.9.9.

114. Nader, K. (2003). Neuroscience – Re-recording human memories. *Nature*, *425*, 571–572.

115. Nader, K. (2003). Memory traces unbound. *Trends in Neurosciences*, *26*, 65–72.

116. Nader, K., & Einarsson, E. O. (2010). Memory reconsolidation: an update. In A. Kingstone & M. B. Miller (Eds.), *The Year in Cognitive Neuroscience 2010* (pp. 27–41). Boston: Blackwell. (*Annals of the New York Academy of Sciences*, *1191*, 27–41.)

117. Nader, K., Schafe, G. E., & Le Doux, J. E. (2000). Fear memories require protein synthesis in the amygdala for reconsolidation after retrieval. *Nature*, *406*, 722–726.

118. Zimmerman, D. W. (2004). A note on preliminary tests of equality of variances. *British Journal of Mathematical and Statistical Psychology*, *57*, 173–181.

119. Klockars, A. J., & Sax, G. (1986). *Multiple comparisons*. Sage University Paper Series on Quantitative Applications in the Social Sciences, 07-061. Newbury Park, CA: Sage.

120. Toothaker, L. E. (1993). *Multiple comparison procedures*. Sage University Paper Series on Quantitative Applications in the Social Sciences, 07-089. Newbury Park, CA: Sage.

121. Greenhouse, S. W., & Geisser, S. (1959). On methods in the analysis of profile data. *Psychometrika*, *24*, 95–112.

122. Huynh, H., & Feldt, L. S. (1976). Estimation of the Box correction for degrees of freedom from sample data in randomised block and split-plot designs. *Journal of Educational Statistics*, *1*, 69–82.

123. Barcikowski, R. S., & Robey, R. R. (1984). Decisions in single group repeated measures analysis: Statistical tests and three computer packages. *American Statistician*, *38*, 148–150.

124. Girden, E. R. (1992). *ANOVA: Repeated measures*. Sage University Paper Series on Quantitative Applications in the Social Sciences, 07-084. Newbury Park, CA: Sage.

125. Kirk, R. E. (1996). Practical significance: A concept whose time has come. *Educational and Psychological Measurement*, *56*, 746–759.

126. Rouder, J. N., Morey, R. D., Speckman, P. L., & Province, J. M. (2012). Default Bayes factors for ANOVA designs. *Journal of Mathematical Psychology*, *56*, 356–374.

127. Marshall-Pescini, S., Passalacqua, C., Petrazzini, M. E. M., Valsecchi, P., & Prato-Previde, E. (2012). Do dogs (*Canis lupus familiaris*) make counterproductive choices because they are sensitive to human ostensive cues? *PLoS One*, *7*(4), e35437.

128. Durbin, J., & Watson, G. S. (1951). Testing for serial correlation in least squares regression, II. *Biometrika*, *30*, 159–178.

Index

Tables and Figures are indicated by page numbers in bold print. Statistical terms and procedures from boxes – Milton's Meowsings, Zach's Facts, Alice's Lab Notes and Reality Check – are marked by page numbers in italics.

Acknowledgements

In about 2010 a rival publisher contacted me about writing an introductory statistics textbook for a high-profile range that they produce aimed at dummies. I never liked the use of the word 'dummies' in the title, but despite that I was taken with the idea. It would have to be written to the series template, but being part of a brand that everyone knows was appealing. I contacted SAGE, who publish my other statistics books, to see whether they were OK with my doing it. Ziyad (the big cheese at SAGE London who in a younger incarnation commissioned my first SAGE book – the SPSS one) phoned me. The conversation was a little longer than this, but here's the gist:

Ziyad: 'Of course you can write a book for someone else, but why not write it for us?'
Me: 'Well, I like the idea of linking up with a well-known brand ...'
Ziyad: 'But you'd have to follow their template. With us, you'd have complete control. You could do whatever you like – express yourself fully.'
Me: 'Seriously? You'd give me complete control, even after "the incident"?'
Ziyad: 'Yes, you can do *whatever you want*.'

The phrase 'whatever you want' stuck in my head, and not just because of hearing that Status Quo song too many times. It stuck because 'whatever I wanted', statistics book-wise, was to try to embed a statistics book in a fictional story with some graphic novel artwork. An idea from which, I'm fairly sure, all other publishers would have run screaming. Not SAGE, though. True to their word, they have rolled with every ill-conceived plan related to this book that I have thrown at them. They have nurtured and supported throughout. I owe Ziyad a huge debt of gratitude for giving me the opportunity to write this book, and for empowering his colleagues at SAGE to give me the freedom to write 'whatever I want'.

In the planning stage and the first half (or so) of writing, Michael Carmichael was instrumental in making things happen. I especially appreciate him enabling some of my more bizarre ideas to become a reality. For the second half of the writing, Robin Lupton and Mark Kavanagh took over Mike's reins and, along with Ben Sherwood, Izzi Drury, and Ian Antcliff, have been a fantastic team with whom to work. Robin especially provided me with extremely helpful page notes on the fictional story, and has been a very sympathetic and supportive colleague. I must also thank Karen and her husband Kevin, who don't work directly on my books, but do provide excellent company at football matches!

I'm really grateful to Shen Zhang and Thao Ha for sending me their data to use within the book. I really appreciate their generosity and trust in me to represent their work. Zoltan Dienes and, especially, Richard Morey had many educational exchanges with me about Bayesian methods while writing. I learnt an enormous amount from both their papers and their emails. Unfortunately, they can't be blamed if I have completely bolloxed up the sections on Bayes, but it would have been a lot worse were it not for them generously spending their time answering my idiotic questions.

I rarely write in silence, and I thank the following artists for providing the soundtrack to the creation of this book and for the protective effect they have had on my stress levels: 1349, Absu, AC/DC, Acid Reign, Akercocke, Alice Cooper, Amiensus, Anthrax, Ash Borer, Behemoth, Black Crown Initiate, Blind Guardian, Kate Bush, Camel, Cardiacs, COB, Colosseum, Cradle of Filth, The Darkness, Deafheaven, Emperor, Enslaved, Exodus, Eye of Solitude, Faith No More, Fairport Convention, Falloch, Fen, Fish, A Forest of Stars, Fvnerals, Genesis (early), Gentle Giant, Ghost, Goblin, Hell, Hexvessel, Ian Anderson, Ihsahn, IQ, Iron Maiden, Jethro Tull, Judas Priest, Kiss, Lamb of God, Led Zeppelin, Marillion, Mastodon, Melechesh, Metallica, Mike Oldfield, Monuments, Motörhead, Opeth (a lot), Ozzy Osbourne, Protest the Hero, Queen (pre 1980), Rainbow, Rush, Russian Circles, Sabbat, Satyricon, Skyclad, Slayer, Slipknot, Solstafir, Status Quo, Steven Wilson, Taake, Tesseract, Tool, Voices, The Who, Winterfylleth, Wodensthrone, Wolves in the Throne Room.

I've never attempted to write fiction before, and there might be a good argument to be made for my never attempting to again. However bad my fiction is, rest assured that it was a lot worse before Gillian Stern cast her eyes over my draft manuscript. In only two meetings and many pages of notes she taught me an enormous amount that I wish I had known before I started. I want to thank her especially for her light (and kind) touch when providing feedback and for giving me the opportunity to benefit from her impressive insights into writing and storytelling.

Special thanks to James Iles for his absolutely brilliant artwork, which I think is the best part of the book. I looked at over 80 illustrators to work on this book; from the off I had a good feeling about James, but I never imagined just what a fantastic find he would be. I literally can't imagine how difficult it must be to take some of my garbled descriptions, poorly drawn stick people/animals and (on a good day) out-of-proportion digital mock-ups, and transform them into exactly what I had in my head, only much better. The book has benefited enormously from his vision in how to frame scenes and his incredible imagination. As with many textbooks, timelines have been ripped up and thrown away, deadlines have passed, and he's had to tolerate my inventing large portions of story on the hoof because I didn't plan as well as I might have. He's rolled with it all with good humour. He has also been incredibly positive, enthusiastic and supportive throughout. I am extremely lucky to have had the opportunity to work with him.

Finally, I want to thank my friends and family and also share a story. Let's do the family thing first. Thanks to my parents, Paul, Julie, my niece Melody and my nephew Oscar for being a lovely family who always support me. My wife, Zoë, not only provided endless love and support but gave me invaluable feedback on the entire book. You know you've struck marital gold when the love of your life voluntarily reads your stats book. My friends tolerate my going incommunicado on them while I write; a few particularly lovely ones are: Mark and Hanna, Ben and Peggy, Rob and Bri, Pad, Graham, Kate and Matt, and Jeremy and Becky. I hope that I might finally have written a book interesting enough for them to want to read. (To be fair, Paul has read some of the others.) Is it weird to thank a dog? I'm not sure, but thanks to Ramsey, our cocker spaniel. He made more of a contribution to this book than you might expect from a spaniel: his early morning walks very frequently gave me the mental space to think through parts of the story with which I was struggling. He also reminded me, every day, to try to be more in the moment. (If we were all a bit more like spaniels the world would be a nicer place, although that would be offset somewhat by having to sniff each other's anuses all the time.) He was taken from us too soon, and I miss him dearly. RIP buddy.

Now here's the story. I became a dad in the middle of writing the first edition of this book (and wrote a lot of it during the night while on extended parental leave). Anyone stalking me on social media will discover that our son is called Zach, and so is the main character in this book. During the planning stage of the book, my wife was pregnant and we were discussing potential names; 'I really like the name Zach,' she said. I wasn't keen and made a mental note to add it to my 'veto list'. At about that time, I was looking for a name for the main character of this book. It had been Alex during the first few years of planning, but as the writing loomed, I decided that I wanted something a bit more rockstar. 'How about Zach?' my wife said. 'Hmm,' I thought, 'that *does* sound like a rockstar name.' It was perfect – for a character in my book, but not for our son. Every day for the last 6 months of her pregnancy I wrote about a guy called 'Zach', a guy who in my head was sweet, honest, talented and super-cool. The more time I spent with the Zach in my head, the more I liked him. During those lonely nights of writing he became like an imaginary friend: I loved everything about him, especially his name, which triggered lots of positive associations with the character. When our son was born, we still hadn't decided on a name. 'How about Zach?' my wife said, triggering 6 months of positive associations in my brain. 'I love that name!' I said and our son became Zach. My wife works in mysterious and extremely clever ways to get what she wants.

JAMES ILES

In February 2014, I found myself sitting in a London juice bar, waiting to meet Professor Andy Field: master of statistics, heavy metal fan, successful writer, cat lover. He was something of an enigma to *me*, having only communicated via email and a single, semi awkward Skype meeting, at the end of which I think we both felt too uncomfortable to press the 'end call' button. Now I was about to meet the man. In ... a juice bar? Well now, this just wasn't very rock and roll.

Despite the inappropriate venue, however, that meeting went well enough for Andy to entrust me with the task of bringing his beloved characters, Zach, Alice, Milton and company to life in graphic novel form.

First and foremost, my enormous thanks and respect must go to Andy, firstly for somehow completing this monumental achievement of a book, while juggling his professional commitments and major life events, including the birth of his son Zach. I really don't know how he pulled it off. He's been nothing but a pleasure to work with, providing me with rich descriptions of environments and characters, and always eager to discuss exciting new ideas. I'm hugely grateful to him for his faith in my ability to turn his unique, incredibly well written fictional story into illustrated artwork, which I really hope enriches your journey through the book.

Huge thanks also to Robin Lupton, Mark Kavanagh, Michael Carmichael and Ian Antcliff at SAGE, who have been nothing but supportive and encouraging throughout the entire process of illustrating the book, allowing us a tremendous amount of creative freedom, and being exceptionally flexible as I jumped between *The Reality Enigma* and various other projects.

Every hour I spend at the drawing board is accompanied by a stack of graphic novels at my side, ever ready for inspiration. My influences are varied, and mercilessly highlight every aspect in which my own work falls short, but I am forever grateful to artists including David Mazzucchelli, Erik Larsen, Dave Gibbons, Jack Kirby and Moebius, aka, Jean Giraud for continuing to inspire newcomers like myself with their beautiful artwork.

Special thanks to my family, for supporting my dream to work in this field. From the moment I could draw, I was subjecting my poor parents to drawings of monsters and superheroes. I'd cover their living room floor with my comic collection, drag my dad in, make him choose his favourite cover, and tell me why. It must've been a weird ritual for him, but he feigned enthusiasm with the best of them, and always encouraged my interest in art. My mum was the creative one in the family, and did everything to help me on my way, including defending my right to draw beasts and aliens at age 6, when school teachers wondered if I was 'all right'.

I'm also incredibly grateful to my beautiful wife Maija, who has been amazingly understanding and patient as I've worked on this project. At the end of a long day at the drawing board, let's just say that my social skills can get a little ... slow. Maija, thanks for always bringing me back to the land of the living!

And finally, I'd like to give huge thanks to you, the reader, for giving our, somewhat different, statistics textbook a chance. It's been a huge undertaking for all involved, but I'm sure you'll get a feeling of just how much we've all enjoyed working on the book. I really hope to see Zach again. But if Andy's son grows up to look like my drawings, that will just be weird.

http://www.jamesilesstudio.com/